Praise for
COLONIZING SOUTHAMPTON

"In this history, Mr. Goddard has reached beyond the local to produce an analytic study of business interests and conflict. He has deciphered the multiple strands of activity at play and provided judicious explanations of behavior ... this detailed book makes significant contributions to our historical understanding ... Goddard has forged the often disparate pieces of Southampton history into an interpretive whole, and he has made sense out of the dramas in the town's legal, business, and social history."

— *East Hampton Star*

"*Colonizing Southampton* ... takes a real look at the historical and economic legacy of the Hamptons, even when it has reared its ugly head."

— *Southampton Press*

"Goddard's treatment of local history is sophisticated, well informed, and analytically sound. He handles complex concepts adroitly and has made an important contribution to the literature on local history, which has too often been burdened with parochial perceptions and, occasionally, by outright boosterism."

— John A. Strong, author of *The Montaukett Indians of Eastern Long Island*

"What I find extraordinary is the author's ability to combine depth and breadth in this book. As a person who was born and raised in Southampton and a student of its social dynamics, I particularly admire Goddard's grasp of the often fraught relations between the area's wealthy resort population and its year-round residents. His insights into the economic and social ramifications of their symbiotic but wary relationship are truly impressive, as are his lively portraits of the major figures in that drama. He has treated local history with a rare seriousness and makes an important contribution to social history in America at the end of the nineteenth century."

— Mary Cummings, author of *Southampton*

COLONIZING SOUTHAMPTON

COLONIZING SOUTHAMPTON

*The Transformation of a
Long Island Community, 1870–1900*

DAVID GODDARD

excelsior editions
State University of New York Press
Albany, New York

Cover photo, Collection of the Southampton Historical Museum.

Published by State University of New York Press, Albany

© 2011 State University of New York

All rights reserved

No part of this book may be used or reproduced in any manner whatsoever without written permission. No part of this book may be stored in a retrieval system or transmitted in any form or by any means including electronic, electrostatic, magnetic tape, mechanical, photocopying, recording, or otherwise without the prior permission in writing of the publisher.

For information, contact State University of New York Press, Albany, NY
www.sunypress.edu

Excelsior Editions is an imprint of State University of New York Press

Production by Kelli W. LeRoux
Marketing by Fran Keneston

Library of Congress Cataloging-in-Publication Data

Goddard, David.
  Colonizing Southampton : the transformation of a Long Island community, 1870–1900 / David Goddard.

      p. cm.
  "Excelsior editions."
  Includes bibliographical references and index.
  ISBN 978-1-4384-3797-2 (hc : alk. paper)—978-1-4384-3796-5 (pb : alk. paper)
  1. Southampton (N.Y.)—History—19th century.   I. Title.

F129.S7G65 2011
974.7'25—dc23   2011022518

10 9 8 7 6 5 4 3 2 1

CONTENTS

Preface		vii
Introduction		1
Chapter 1	Southampton	13
Chapter 2	The Beach, the Lake, the Church and the Improvement Association	51
Chapter 3	The Association and the Village Community	79
Chapter 4	The Mecox Bay Affair	111
Chapter 5	Mecox Redux	143
Chapter 6	Early History of the Shinnecock Hills	175
Chapter 7	Partition and Sale of the Hills	213
Chapter 8	The Summer Colony Consolidated 1888–1900	255
Chapter 9	The Betts Case	289
Epilogue		311
Maps		319
Notes		327
References		355
Index		359

PREFACE

The idea for this book came to me one hot August afternoon in 1998. Adele Kramer, then the director of the Southampton Historical Museum, took me upstairs in the museum on Meeting House Lane to poke around in its somewhat neglected library and archive; in search of what I was not at the time precisely sure. A year or two later, I should add, a generous grant to the museum allowed its board to invest in a considerable upgrading of its library facilities. Ultimately, I was to become a part of this process of expansion.

Meanwhile, in the still, dry atmosphere upstairs I found what I had vaguely been looking for. It was the transcription of a trial, a nineteenth-century court case concerning beach rights in Southampton. It pitted an early summer resident, Frederic H. Betts, against the Trustees of the Freeholders and Commonalty of the Town of Southampton, a venerable body dating back to Southampton's second colonial patent in 1686. Betts had claimed for his own, the beach below his dune property as far as the low water mark. He had even gone so far as to threaten to fence his property off to that farthest point. The gist of the trial concerned who owned the beach and, if anyone did, how far toward the water did that ownership extend. Did it go beyond the line of the dunes as far as low water or only as far as mean high tide? And was ownership a private or public matter? Was the beach town land or was it in private hands and available for sale like any other piece of privately owned real estate? And if it was private, was there a right-of-way on it accessible to the public? These were not settled matters in 1892 when the trial took place before the Supreme Court of the State of New York, but the trial did go a considerable way toward resolving them. But what interested me much more about the case was its exposure of the tensions between an old and traditional community, with a history dating back to the early seventeenth century, and a summer colony of upper-class wealth and privilege that had descended on Southampton from New York as recently as the late 1870s. This new colony was, in numerous ways since then, engaged in a concerted attempt to impose its tastes, interests, and prejudices on what euphemistically might be described as the host community. The trial, in particularly dramatic fashion, shone a powerful light on some of the events of this latter-day process of colonization and on the divisions it created in the community.

I had in fact thought to begin the book with an examination of the issues that were exposed in the Betts trial, particularly because many of the protagonists in the two communities were participants in the proceedings, but in the event left it until the last chapter. The suddenness of the summer invasion and its consolidation as a settled and influential colony in the village of Southampton by 1882, and then its increasing hold over the village after that, seemed to require a good deal of prior explanation. Additionally, I wanted to look at the impact of development projects in the town as a whole in the 1880s that were financed with liberal amounts of external capital originating with New York investors.

These two separate but related processes of social change, neither of them free of conflict—the colonization of the village and efforts at outside economic development—marked Southampton's uneasy and sometimes reluctant progress into the modern age at the turn of the nineteenth century. How the town reacted to such rapid change and to the sudden influx of upper-class newcomers, with whom they had little if any previous experience, is the subject of what follows in the chapters in this volume.

There are inevitably many people to thank for their support and assistance in the preparation of this book. In particular, I am extremely grateful for the help extended me by two directors of the Southampton Historical Museum, Richard Barons and Tom Edmonds. I worked under both of them as the museum's archivist and learned much as a result. I am especially grateful to the museum for permission to reproduce a number of photographs from its collection. Emily Oster, the town archivist, extended me every courtesy and full access to the Town of Southampton Archives over a lengthy period of research beginning in 2001. I am similarly grateful to the reference staff of the Rogers Memorial Library for their patience and assistance. Jim Van Nostrand, the village administrator, also was extremely helpful in locating early village records and those of the Village Improvement Association. John Strong, professor emeritus of history at Southampton College (LIU), and Mary Cummings of the *Southampton Press* and now at the Historical Museum both read the manuscript at various stages. Their comments and suggestions were invaluable in helping me improve it. I also thank Kelli Williams-LeRoux, senior production editor and her staff at SUNY Press for guiding me through the publication process.

Finally, I am as always grateful for my wife Monica's solicitude, forbearance, and advice in the several years it has taken me to write this book.

INTRODUCTION

In September 1863 at the height of the Civil War a young doctor, Theodore Gaillard Thomas together with his wife Mary, took a leisurely trip from New York along the south shore of Long Island. Thomas is generally thought to be the founder of Southampton's summer colony a dozen years later, as well as its spiritual leader. But at that time thoughts of a summer residence in a quiet village by the sea were far from his mind. He was a rising star in the medical profession at the outset of a distinguished career and had no other purpose than to restore his health and seek some relaxation after a long summer in a large and busy practice.

They had taken a light wagon and a good pair of horses, crossed the 34th Street ferry with the intention of heading for Montauk, and set out along the sandy but well-traversed South Country Road through the villages strung out on the shores of the Great South Bay. They stopped at a hostelry at Babylon for two nights and then went on to Quogue, already in the 1860s a small watering spot with several boarding houses that had long attracted hunters and fishermen. Besides sportsmen, Quogue was host to a growing number of summer boarders who stayed either with local farmers or at one or other of the boarding houses. These had sprung up for the most part after 1844 when the Long Island Railroad's (LIRR) single trunk line reached out the length of the island, bisecting it, from Long Island City to Riverhead at the head of Peconic Bay and then to Greenport, a farming and fishing community on the North Fork. Riverhead in eastern Suffolk County was in the nineteenth century a small port and market town with some light manufactures and was also the county seat. A town in itself only since 1792, when it was created by an act of the state legislature, it stood at the boundary of the Town of Southold to the north and Southampton to the south on the South Fork of the island. It had formerly been a village at the western edge of Southold.

Quogue was less than ten miles south of Riverhead and thus within easy striking distance of rail service from New York. Among its many charms to visitors, the village was separated from the ocean beach by only the narrowest of channels. It was situated on several necks of land that lay between Quantuck Bay to the west and Shinnecock Bay and was in consequence the first village east of the Rockaways where it was possible to walk to the beach. It was to this that William Pelletreau, writing in 1882, attributed Quogue's prosperity. The place, he said, "is now almost wholly composed of large boarding-houses, which are very liberally patronized."[1] "Thrifty and intelligent" farmers also did well with the summer trade by renting out accommodations to well-to-do city people for as much as four months of the year. Per capita, Pelletreau regarded Quogue (twenty years after the Thomases brief visit) as "the wealthiest town on Long Island." The ocean beach was its chief attraction. It afforded the opportunity of sea bathing, walking, beach combing, and a quiet atmosphere for rest and contemplation away from the pressures of city life whether of a business or social nature.

The couple pressed on to Southampton where they stopped at either the Post House or John Howell's Ocean House, the latter a small commercial hotel in the middle of the village catering largely to traveling salesmen and others with business in the area. But Gaillard Thomas was impressed with the local community. Almost forty years later and shortly before his death in 1903, he recounted in a letter to William Pelletreau that he had remarked to his wife at the time that he had been "charmed with this quiet old village; most agreeably impressed by its great advantages and by the respectability and apparent worth of the good people who inhabit it, and I am fully determined that should I ever build a summer home it shall be located here."[2] Perhaps Quogue, filled with duck hunters and fishermen from Brooklyn, appeared a little overcrowded.

The letter, which recounted the transformation of a rustic village into a thriving resort in little more than a quarter of a century, represents a sort of genesis myth of the founding of the summer colony in what he referred to as "the ancient village of Southampton." Its seventeenth-century lineage, as much as its bucolic charm and healthful airs (he was a doctor) as well as its apparent isolation from city influences, constituted its appeal. That there were no signs of tourism such as already existed further west, and even in Easthampton a few miles to the east, made Southampton even more attractive as a pristine site for potential summer settlement. The letter was modest in tone, but it was clear that Thomas took the credit for initiating the transformation of this hitherto underappreciated coastal village into a successful summer community. Alice Garner, in her recent study of a comparable nineteenth-century metamorphosis of a remote fishing village in southwestern France, Arcachon, found that there as elsewhere in other French resorts there was always some "far-sighted individual, a hero-founder" to conceive the image and orchestrate the transition.[3]

Southampton, at that time, had few accoutrements of modern living and no tourist trade; its apparent simplicity of life, its harmonious rusticity and location so close to the ocean beach with its splendid dunes, may thus have combined to persuade him that here was a neglected little Shangri-la that one day might beckon him back. Whether he met William Pelletreau or others in the village hierarchy during his visit is unknown, but he would certainly have brought with him letters of introduction to smooth his passage through the villages along the way and what contacts he made would have confirmed his initial positive impressions. Pelletreau was then Southampton's youthful town clerk, a man of intellectual distinction and a descendant of an old eighteenth-century Huguenot family, who was shortly to embark on an extraordinary project to transcribe Southampton's town records from the old rolls going back to the seventeenth century and have them printed. It is inconceivable that Thomas did not have a quiet conversation with him. Or with George Rogers Howell, Southampton's other great litterateur, who was in the midst of writing his own history of the town predating Pelletreau's by more than ten years and later was to become assistant state librarian in Albany.[4] Both would have had much to tell him of old Southampton and of its present condition, as would many others among Southampton's leading citizens, for example, Jonathan Fithian or Squire Fithian as he was known, a former town clerk and former resident of Easthampton, justice of the peace, and now in 1863 town supervisor, who once professed that he could not read the old town records and that only the devil could decipher their crabbed and faded lettering. There were others besides, Posts and Fosters particularly who had always been at the center of Southampton affairs, who Thomas may also have met.

The Thomases went on to Easthampton, an easy ride of fifteen miles that passed through the little parish of Bridgehampton and then crossed Southampton's town line in the Wainscott plains, a stretch of rolling upland that had first been cultivated in the 1640s.[5] Some of Southampton's first settlers who had farmed at this eastern edge of the town moved even farther east after 1648 and established Easthampton. There is much evidence to suggest that Easthampton became a summer resort well before Southampton. After the railroad reached Greenport in the mid-1840s, the village became much more accessible. An easy sailboat ride to Sag Harbor brought visitors to within a few miles of Easthampton and the toll road to the village was both shorter and better maintained than the circuitous route to Southampton. As in Quogue, and for similar reasons, a boarding house trade developed and began to flourish in the 1850s and 1860s. Even before the railroad, modest summer invasions from the city were becoming quite common. Regular sailing service down Long Island Sound to Sag Harbor had made this possible.

It is not an uncommon experience that when the inhabitants of a closed and relatively isolated community, quite far removed from urban civilization, begin to notice strangers in their midst feelings of ambivalence begin to surface. This happened in Easthampton as early as the 1830s when the influx of summer visitors first became evident. Later it happened in Southampton. One of the town's famous sons, John Howard Payne, noted it in an article published in 1838. Seagoing passenger service to Sag Harbor had brought with it "city rovers in quest of sea air and rurality" but this "irruption of barbarians of aristocracy and fashion" had created much apprehension among the local citizenry. When a marine accident temporarily suspended ferry operations all exulted: "There would be no more arrivals of the unknown from vicious large cities to stir up extravagant ideas and unsettle the husbandman from his dependence on his plough by dreams of speculation." And yet, Payne mournfully concluded, "the sweet solitude of East Hampton is inevitably destined to interruption from the city" transforming "this quiet, simple, and primitive little community" into an annex of the metropolis.[6] Payne was writing in part with tongue in cheek but he was sharply criticized by the community for subjecting Easthampton to "undeserved ridicule if not derision" as its noted historian Judge Henry P. Hedges was later to put it.[7] It was too close to the descriptions of provincial social life that were floated out by cosmopolitan magazines such as *Harper's* weekly. Nobody wants to be defined as a country bumpkin or yokel from "Lonelyville" in that common appellation so smugly or even gleefully utilized by writers whose own boots quite often still bore traces of the farmyard. Still, James Fenimore Cooper reflected the same romantic nostalgia for the passing of a seeming rural simplicity when he wrote that the arrival of the railroad in Greenport in 1844 had put an end to the innocence of Orient, a tiny hamlet a few miles to the east. Once, Orient had possessed "an air of rural and moral beauty" but now "its seclusion, its simplicities, its peculiarities, and, we had almost said, its happiness" were gone and gone perhaps for good.[8] Cooper had begun his career as a writer in Sag Harbor.

But Payne was quite prophetic. He could not, however, have predicted the invasion of the artists in the 1870s and 1880s who descended on Easthampton almost en masse to render its weathered charms, bucolic vistas, and local characters on sketch pad, tile, and canvas, to put its antiquity in aesthetic perspective while ignoring the sea changes it was undergoing; much as anthropologists—in search of the uncorrupted and pristine nature of primitive custom—once neglected to mention that the peoples they are in the process of studying have long been subject to colonial rule and altered by it. Regional lives were frequently celebrated for their marginality and isolation in sketches of provincial social worlds and their pure and simple values provided by and for urban cosmopolitans. Eventually, Easthamptoners came round to adopting the ancient and unsullied image of it that others had first proposed—or painted—and ignored or repudiated for the sake of their self-esteem and the apparent continuity of their history the changes going on around them. Unfriendly wags in Southampton later put it about that Easthampton had become so enamored of the image of itself propagated by others that "its isolation has made it famous. It is old-fashioned or nothing. It prides itself on antiquity . . . paint is considered extravagant. To see East Hampton in its primitive purity one should visit in the dead of winter."[9] It was unworthy and probably unfair and reflected, if anything, the usual jealousies prevailing between long-standing neighboring communities. The same issue of the Southampton newspaper referred to an eye disease apparently prevalent in its sister town to the east as "the East Hampton twitch," an affliction said to be caused by an excess of intermarrying among the town's founding families.

The Thomases then arrived in an environment that had already begun to experience change but a change that would not yet be obvious to outsiders and was only recently understood (and partly rejected) by the town's increasingly perceptive residents. But this would hardly have been a matter of interest to Thomas. In looking over Easthampton in 1863 he could have seen no obvious differences between it and Southampton. The same typically New England main street, home lots and farms, blacksmith shops and Presbyterian churches, the same prudent distance of the village from the ocean, the same landscape of woodlands to the north and fertile plain to the south, the same sand dunes. Thomas might have just as easily chosen Easthampton over Southampton for his eventual summer residence but ultimately did not. One explanation for this, easy but insufficient although it is, is the introduction of railroad service to Southampton, Bridgehampton, and Sag Harbor—but not to Easthampton—in 1870. Yet after all, whatever Thomas may have written to Pelletreau in 1901, a letter commemorating the twenty-fifth anniversary of his summer residence in

Southampton, he would not have been particularly likely to recall that he might just as well have settled in Easthampton. But in 1876, when he finally returned, an important consideration for him may have been that no one else—apart from a friend of his, Leon de Bost—had yet "discovered" Southampton. It had hardly changed since 1863 whereas Easthampton by now was increasingly overrun by city people. Thomas was like Robinson Crusoe. He had found a deserted paradise—deserted at least if one overlooked the presence of its native inhabitants or regarded them as part of the landscape—as fortuitously as Crusoe had even if in rather more fortunate circumstances. Not unlike the first English settlers who arrived in Southampton in 1640 and found themselves in a virgin land occupied only by what almost certainly was the remnant of a once large tribe of Indians, the Shinnecock, Thomas resolved to make it his own and those who would later follow him.[10] As for the native inhabitants, Thomas, in a fashion similar to the English settlers preceding him, would essentially have only to deal with the local sachems, that is, with the village hierarchy. The parallels between the two colonizations, 240 years apart, are unmistakable. It was as unforeseen to the inhabitants as was their ancestors' arrival to the Shinnecock. It was a second visitation, a second coming, as profound in its consequences as was the first. One can hardly say that the colonists of the 1640s and those of the late 1870s descended like a plague of locusts, their early numbers being no more than a trickle, but descend, nonetheless, they did.

The doctor and his wife took their leave of Easthampton and set off for Montauk, the road winding partly but gently uphill through Amagansett, then a farming village that was also a staging area for the annual cattle drive to Montauk. Cattle, sheep, and horses had been driven to pasture on Montauk since the middle of the seventeenth century, and the twelve thousand acres of the peninsula itself had remained in the hands of a hundred or so Easthampton men and their descendants—the Montauk Proprietors—in the intervening two hundred years. East of Amagansett the road, such as it was at that time, drops to sea level and crosses the sandy wastes and marshes of Napeague, a five-mile inhospitable expanse empty of habitation and subject to heavy flooding by occasional ocean storms. It also was famous for its mosquitoes. Thomas reported that they were nearly devoured by "phenomenal hordes" of the insects as they struggled across what had become little more than a cattle track. It must undoubtedly have been the worst part of their trip thus far, although the remaining ten miles to Montauk Point—their destination being the lighthouse—were equally arduous.

Montauk was a world far different than anything they had encountered since leaving New York. It was a place of wild beauty and often fierce weather. The terrain was rugged and not for the uninitiated. It was easy to get lost and in some parts today it still is. One might imagine that Dr. Thomas and his wife, bone-weary from a jarring and interminable ride across an execrable highway, were relieved at finally sighting the lighthouse. There were then only four Easthampton families living on Montauk and only four permanent structures to house them. One was that of the lighthouse keeper, whereas the other three were those of the stock keepers responsible for the several thousand heads of livestock. But the land was also home to the Montaukett Indians and had been since antiquity. Once numerous and powerful and inhabiting the whole of the peninsula, the Montauketts were much reduced by the 1860s. The loss of their land by sale to Easthampton proprietors in the seventeenth century coupled with subsequent restrictive covenants imposed on them by the town had combined to disperse them. Some few had remained and lived on what de facto was a reservation in an area a mile or two from the lighthouse known as the Indian Field.[11] It is probably unlikely that the Thomases met or encountered any of them in their brief sojourn at the Point, although there is no reason to think that they would not have welcomed the opportunity to gain first-hand knowledge of Indian life and its conditions. Gaillard Thomas, as it later was to transpire during his years in Southampton, was or had become a man with pronounced community interests and social convictions although, it is true, they may not always have extended to those in less fortunate circumstances than his.

Thomas wrote that he and his wife found pleasant accommodations at the lighthouse. It may be, however, that memory failed him after so long an interval (there being no guest rooms at the lighthouse) and that they in fact stayed at Third House, the easternmost of the keepers' houses that had also been used as an inn since the 1840s and catered to visiting sportsmen. Montauk was already well known as a paradise for hunters. Having now reached the very end of the island, the two returned by the same route to Easthampton and turned north for Sag Harbor where they spent the night before embarking for Greenport on the North Fork and a short sail across Gardiner's Bay. From there they made their way back to New York through the villages of the North Shore.

Staying only a short while in Sag Harbor, Thomas would have had little opportunity to savor the atmosphere of this once bustling little port. The Harbor, peculiarly located on both sides of the town line dividing Southampton from Easthampton, had for a century been the commercial hub of the East End of Long Island. It also was the largest village in Suffolk County. It had been incorporated as a village by the state legislature in 1818 primarily to designate it as an independent fire district after a fire the previous year had destroyed part of the business district. As early as the 1760s it was considered by the colonial government of New York as the province's second port, the only other being New York itself, and was designated a port of entry by the federal government in 1798. Its fortunes had risen sharply in the eighteenth century through shipbuilding and trade with New England, the West Indies, and England itself and through a certain adroitness of its merchants in evading or challenging onerous customs provisions imposed by the colonial authority in New York who were anxious to undercut duty-free trade with New England and ultimately European ports.

But it was the whale fishery that made Sag Harbor what became, but was no longer, the wealthiest village on eastern Long Island. Beginning in the 1780s, it ushered in many decades of prosperity before beginning to decline in the 1850s largely as a result of intense over-fishing but also because of the discovery of oil in Pennsylvania and gold in California. Lamp oil, hitherto supplied by the whaling industry, was rapidly in the process of being replaced by a superior product refined within easy reach of New York; while the gold rush attracted many who saw their fortunes in whaling beginning to decline. When Gaillard Thomas came to Sag Harbor, the village was in a steep depression and struggling not very successfully to reinvent itself as a manufacturing center. Whaling had collapsed and the last whaling ship sold in 1862. Thomas would have observed lingering signs of decay in the warehouses lining the waterfront. In addition, Sag Harbor's fortunes had not been helped by a second disastrous fire in 1845 that swept through the western part of the village. Rebuilding was not yet fully complete. Only the proud houses of merchants and whaling captains, the long wharf for which Sag Harbor was famous, and several fine churches stood as reminders of the village's past glories.

So this had been Gaillard Thomas's introduction to the East End. Whether Southampton remained much in his mind after he and his wife returned to New York is not known but the likelihood is that it did not. He had an extensive practice to attend to and his career was about to take off. Thomas was born on Edisto Island near Charleston, South Carolina in 1831, the son of an Episcopal minister, and attended the College of Charleston before entering medical school. After his general training, he specialized in obstetrics and gynecology. He then spent a year in Paris where he underwent further training in his specialty before coming to New York in 1855. He was immediately taken into a remunerative partnership, probably arranged by his medical college in South Carolina, and at the same time joined the faculty of the medical department of City College. In 1863, not yet thirty-two, he was thought of highly enough to be appointed to the prestigious College of Physicians and Surgeons. Two years later he succeeded to the chair of obstetrics there and later became professor of gynecology.

His contributions to the profession were many, notably in diagnosis, surgical techniques, and the invention and development of surgical instruments. After 1872, he divided his time between his teaching responsibilities at the college and at Woman's Hospital where he was appointed attending surgeon. In this latter capacity he established a small recuperative home for women patients on the Hampton Road in Southampton sometime after he took up residence in the village. He wrote extensively and his 1868 *Practical Treatise on the Diseases of Women* became the standard work in the field. He retired from the college as professor emeritus in 1890, a distinguished and apparently beloved figure, but continued in private practice until 1900. He died in 1903 a wealthy man as might be expected given his professional success. So successful was he that he was able to build a large house at 600 Madison Avenue for $50,000 in 1886. It featured "tier upon tier of windows" and a small hospital for family members on the top floor.[12] As is seen later, his ventures in Southampton reflected a man of substantial means and authority. He was possessed of a fundamentally benevolent temperament although he was inclined to be imperious with those not of his class. His obituary described him as being kind, generous, and hospitable and one who always brought confidence and cheer into the sick room. He also was once described by a journalist who perhaps knew him only slightly as being as "modest as a maiden," whereas William Pelletreau, who knew him better, noted that he was generous to a fault in supporting any worthwhile public enterprise but was given to haggling with local farmers over the price of eggs.

But Thomas, for all his wealth and success, never ascended to the rarefied heights of New York society. He was not to become a member of Caroline Astor's semi-mythical Four Hundred, the social elite of the Gilded Age, whose names were first breathlessly released to the press in 1892 by Mrs. Astor's gatekeeper and publicist, Ward McAllister, who had oiled his way via Newport to New York from Charleston, South Carolina, the seat of Southern society.[13] Those on the list were the people who "counted" in New York. They came from diverse walks of life but were united, it was said, by money, status, and lineage. "The three Bs," as McAllister was to put it—birth, background, and breeding—determined membership of this select status group. Carolyn Astor, the "Mystic Rose" McAllister adoringly called her, had them all.

Writing in the early 1920s, May King Van Rensselaer, the elderly and entirely disapproving dowager of a founding Dutch family of the Hudson Valley aristocracy, dismissed the notion that birth and breeding had any longer much to do with social standing. By the late 1870s, she said, it was all about money and social climbing. Mrs. Astor's fancy balls, like those of the Vanderbilt's or of Mrs. Theodore Havemeyer and—most egregiously—the Bradley Martins in 1897, had become supremely costly pageants attended by those "hysterically anxious for social recognition."[14] Mrs. Van Rensselaer's opinion was understandable. The old order of New York Society, once dominated by the Hudson Valley Dutch, had collapsed, overtaken by waves of new wealth amassed on Wall Street, in railroads, coal, iron and steel, mines, wheat, or worse, Civil War contracts. Carolyn Astor's claim to the leadership of this new elite world was, however, only one of many in this hothouse atmosphere of status competition. In New York and Newport, where she reigned, she had been preceded by Mrs. Van Rensselaer as the leading hostess of the day, a fact that may have influenced her acid view of those who came after.

There were doctors on Mrs. Astor's list but Thomas was not one of them. Strangely or not, none of those who followed him to Southampton were to become members of this charmed and almost mystical circle, although some could claim connections to it. A Schermerhorn, for instance, did eventually appear in Southampton (Mrs. Astor was a Schermerhorn), as did members of some of New York's old respected merchant families—Howlands, Schieffelins, Duers, Ruggles, Kilbreths—but the majority represented new money. Although it was sometimes the sort of money vastly disapproved of by Mrs. Van Rensselaer it was not on the scale of the unheard of fortunes that were being amassed in New York at the time during a prolonged period of frenzied economic growth and periodic financial catastrophes. As is seen here, she had kind words for Southampton's early summer colony and did not associate its members with the financial and social extravagances of New York's hyperventilated elites. The real money went to Newport and failed to make an appearance in Southampton.

Southampton's summer colony might usefully be described as belonging to a second tier of affluence in New York, upwardly mobile, successful, and reputable men and women of undoubtedly good, if frequently provincial, background yet who were less socially visible. They belonged to the same clubs as the elites, lived in the same neighborhoods, attended the same churches, pursued similar professional and business careers in finance, medicine, trade, real estate, insurance, and law—there were many lawyers among them and several judges—but they were of a less exalted social position even though many were recognized and occasionally honored for their contributions to civic life. Yet in the 1870s, post-Civil War, New York was becoming a quite open society, its elites overlapping, differentiated, mobile, and certainly not cohesive; everything that Mrs. Van Rensselaer complained about.

The lawyers were particularly successful in clambering into the upper classes. As businesses consolidated and incorporated in the 1870s and 1880s, in an effort to avoid the disastrous effects of excessive competition, the demand for corporate lawyers shot up exponentially. This was the beginning of the era of trusts, holding companies, and ingenious compacts to control production and markets. It gave birth to a new breed of trained lawyers skilled in creating necessary instruments of agreement between one company and another or, for that matter, water-tight provisions of control over one company by another. A number of these white-shoe lawyers found their way to Southampton. Some of them even defended their co-residents in suits brought against them (see below). By the mid-1880s then, New York's upper classes had become much more differentiated and heterogeneous than they had been in the years following the Civil War. The rapid growth of the legal profession was one of several indications of this.

The upper-class system in New York as it had developed was quite unlike Boston with its fixed, caste-like Brahmin upper class that firmly shut the door on newcomers however impeccable otherwise were their social credentials. Birth was the key in Boston, the ironic apotheosis, if nothing else, of the great Puritan migration of the 1630s that brought to the Massachusetts shores an unpretentious and "middling" sort of people. But godliness often has strange consequences. Birth also was once a key in New York, although unlike New England, religious enthusiasm had little to do with it. Ultimately, money and success, the great equalizer as the upwardly mobile deluded themselves into thinking, had come to determine status. Yet whether this was enough to guarantee admission to the higher circles was another matter. In the Gilded Age, the Caroline Astor's and Ward McAllister's appeared to dispose over such things, for a time anyway. The new bourgeoisie, awash with cash and living in sumptuous circumstances at posh new addresses, anxiously—abjectly even—awaited the call.

But not everybody was happy with Caroline Astor's domination of New York society. New York's upper class had become just too large and too wealthy to admit this kind of exclusivist hegemony. She held court at her Fifth Avenue and 34th Street mansion well into the 1890s, giving her annual Patriarch's Ball for those within her narrow field of social vision, but already in 1883 found herself seriously challenged from farther up the avenue. William K. Vanderbilt's Alabaman wife, Alva, sank $3 million into an opulent chateau at Fifth and Fifty Second, possibly better suited to the Loire Valley than Fifth Avenue (it was modeled on the Chateau de Blois), and promptly announced a ball to which she had invited twelve hundred of New York's prominent citizens (Mrs. Astor was not initially on the guest list but, craving an invitation, was tardily issued one by Mrs. Vanderbilt). This ultimately precipitated a sea change in the definition of what constituted society and opened the doors wide to newcomers of all sorts. The Four Hundred was now under direct fire as a "Social Trust"; a "body corporate" as someone sniffed. Four years later, the Social Register was launched listing two thousand names of wealthy and successful New Yorkers. Many members of Southampton's new summer colony, including Gaillard Thomas, were to be found among them. Perhaps then it would be more true to say that they represented less a second tier of New York wealth than a rapidly expanding sphere of new wealth. Money, especially Wall Street money, had come to mean everything. The small bourgeois world of the 1860s had given way to a much larger and more anonymous upper class. As Sven Beckert put it, New York's upper class was constantly being reconfigured but simultaneously stabilized by its ability to absorb newcomers.[15] Writing in 1925 at a safe distance from the 1880s, May King Van Rensselaer differently claimed that "all at once society was assailed from every side by persons who sought to climb boldly over the walls of social exclusiveness" shattering the traditional social structure.[16]

Thirteen years after his first visit, Thomas returned to Southampton to buy property. It is very possible, in fact very likely, that he visited the area several times before deciding to purchase. In New York he had formed a friendship with a man who had long-standing ties to the village and visited it frequently. This was Leon dePeyre de Bost. Like Thomas, he had French Huguenot roots (there were Huguenot ancestors on Thomas's mother's side) and this shared heritage may have partly accounted for a relationship developing between them. They were also virtually the same age. De Bost's connection to Southampton was through his maternal grandfather, the Reverend David Schuyler Bogart whose own father had had the good fortune to marry into the Schuyler family, members of the original Dutch elite in New York. De Bost's father, a New York merchant of substantial means had married the reverend's daughter. The couple had died young and several of the children, among them Leon dePeyre, were sent to live with Bogart in Southampton, now in retirement from his pastoral duties. Bogart had been called to the Presbyterian ministry in Southampton three times between 1796 and 1813 but on each occasion had remained only a few years. He returned in failing health in the late 1820s and died in 1839 when de Bost was seven. The boy and one of his several brothers were then put up with a widow on South Main Street just south of Toylsome Lane—a Mrs. Brown—and remained there for ten years, attending Southampton Academy just up the street at the corner of Job's Lane or what was then Academy Lane, until leaving for the promise of business opportunities in dry goods in New York.

De Bost did not lose contact with the area, however, and apparently returned annually with his brothers on hunting and fishing expeditions. According to Edward Moeran, the son of an early summer colonist in the mid-1880s, de Bost eventually bought the Brown homestead and land from the heirs of Mrs. Brown in the early 1870s.[17] One of the owners of the land was apparently William Pelletreau who also owned property a little to the north on South Main Street. Pelletreau, another fellow Huguenot descendant, also was a friend of Leon de Bost and possibly edged him into buying the Brown property. This was a substantial piece of land extending on both sides of South Main to Town Pond. There is, however, some confusion in respect to the chronology of de Bost's purchase (or possibly purchases) and no trace of Mrs. Brown in the records.[18] On the east side of the street de Bost erected a house in 1875 having apparently demolished the existing homestead. Thomas built a year later on land he had bought farther south at the beach. Moeran's contention was that de Bost, not Thomas, was Southampton's first vacationer. The business of firsts frequently is an obsession of local historians claiming to be in the know for reasons not difficult to discern. Still, it is fairly obvious that de Bost was instrumental in bringing Thomas back to Southampton and that he probably advised him on the purchase of the land at the beach. Pelletreau concurs with this story as does another noted Southampton historian, Lizbeth

Halsey White.[19] Thomas himself was rather cautious in the matter and confined himself to denying that de Bost had introduced him to Southampton. To the contrary, he said, he had introduced himself perhaps not wishing to cast doubt so late in the game (his letter was written in 1902) on his status as the "founder-hero" of the summer colony.

The property Thomas subsequently bought consisted of fifteen acres at the foot of Main Street and hard by the ocean to the south of Gin Lane. It had once belonged to an elderly farmer, Sylvanus Howell, who, having no nearby living relations, put it in the hands of an attorney and went to live with his brother in the western part of the state. It eventually was put up for auction, but there were few bids. The land had little to recommend it for it was at the beach and it was universally thought that "the ocean is a bad neighbor." Additionally, it was partly "outside the fence," that is, south of the fencing that ran the length of Gin Lane parallel to the beach banks to prevent cattle straying near the water. It was knocked down for $25 an acre and then sold privately the following day for $27.50. This had been sometime in the late 1860s. The buyer was, according to Pelletreau, a thoroughly practical farmer who easily made his money back within a few years. He then sold it to Thomas for the unprecedented sum of $200 an acre. This naturally sent shock waves through the village. First, no one in their senses would dream of buying land in the teeth of the ocean with a view to building. The property ran along a beach that was constantly shifting and at the mercy of winter Northeasters, tropical storms, and occasional hurricanes. Second, land at that time typically fetched anywhere between $1 or $2 and $50 an acre depending on its location and what, if any, valued resources it contained. For the most part, $25 to $30 an acre was an average price. There may have been not a few guffaws among village regulars at the outlandish offer Thomas had made. The lucky seller was Captain Charles Goodale, another descendant of a seventeenth century family. It was the beginning of a sea change in village real estate and of a boom that no one, not even William Pelletreau, could have possibly anticipated.

Thomas put up his house on Gin Lane the following year. He called it "The Dunes" but locals nicknamed it "The Birdcage." Nothing like it had been seen in Southampton. It was three stories tall, built just inside the line of the beach banks, and its first two floors featured ornate verandas wrapped around the entire edifice. The house was perfectly square. For the first year of their tenancy the Thomases were quite alone at the beach, the South Beach as it was then called. Their nearest neighbors were the Sayres, also descendants of one of Southampton's first settlers. Henry Sayre's farm was a quarter mile to the north at a safe distance from the ocean and inside the fence. The Dunes looked over Town Pond immediately to its west, a long body of water running from the village toward the ocean and quite typical of the geography of the south shore of Long Island. In the 1880s, it was renamed Lake Agawam by new summer inhabitants under the unconfirmed and in fact erroneous assumption that the area of Southampton was once called Agawam by the local Shinnecock Indians. It also was briefly named Silver Lake by a romantic summer artist who had built on its western shore not long after Thomas and perhaps spent her evenings admiring the light of the moon on its surface. The renaming of streets, localities, bodies of water, and so on, later became a small cottage industry for the summer colony as it settled in and put down roots.

Town Pond stretched northward to Job's Lane (named for Job Sayre in the late 1640s) and the village and disappeared into a marsh that was later to cause much concern to Dr. Thomas and others in the summer colony concerned with the purity of the lake's waters. Almost beneath his veranda, or at least directly in view, was an abandoned lifesaving station on the shore of the pond. Within two years of moving in, Thomas bought it and had it removed to a location at the foot of Town Pond and barely inside the line of the dunes. It was transformed into an Episcopal church to serve the needs of the growing body of summer residents who otherwise might have remained destitute of spiritual nourishment in what essentially had always been a Presbyterian and, latterly, a Methodist community. Also within sight of his verandas was a small bathing station at the beach operated by John Howell, yet another descendant of a seventeenth-century family. It was located on a small section of the common lands of the town that were annually leased out to him and had long been enjoyed by local residents. It was quintessentially a public space where Thomas might have observed local men, women, and children in various states of undress frolicking in the surf. Whether the proximity of such signs of native pleasure disturbed him is unknown; but within a few short years of the founding of the summer colony, its governing body, the Southampton Village Improvement Association (SVIA), took over the management of the pavilion, financing it, and regulating its activities. A dress code governing what areas of the body could be exposed would quite probably have been drawn up.[20]

This part of the beach had always been—and perhaps Thomas had not been aware of this—a central location for inshore whaling and fishing activities. He would have seen fishing boats drawn up on the seaward side of the dunes and fishing nets drying on the landward side, but he would not have known that whales harpooned offshore had been pulled in to the beach and cut up, preparatory to their consignment to the try-pots (fortunately located elsewhere), since time immemorial and right beneath what were to become his windows. It was a local work space and its uses were later to be contested between Southampton and summer residents who had settled at the beach. Inshore whaling had languished and all but disappeared in the nineteenth century, the right whale having been virtually fished out, but an occasional whale was spotted and out went one or two aging and retired whaling captains to try their hands for one last time. There were several such instances in the 1870s but they generally occurred in the winter when the Thomas cottage was shut tight against the elements.

This, then, was Gaillard's summer environment. He was to be joined by others within a year or so but for the moment he could, we must suppose, enjoy his seaside solitude in true Crusoean fashion. As he himself put it, he was entirely without neighbors. There was not another cottage existing, he told Pelletreau, "between Mecox Bay on the east, the Atlantic Ocean on the south, the gate of the Shinnecock reservation on the west, and Long Springs on the north" rather overlooking the fact that a densely populated village existed a little less than a mile to the north of him interposed between the ocean and Long Springs.[21] These isolated circumstances, as he remembered them, were to change very dramatically over the next several years.

CHAPTER 1

SOUTHAMPTON

I: EARLY HISTORY

The early beginnings of Southampton, and the sort of community it was in the last part of the nineteenth century before the summer invasion, are important to describe here as they form the essential and irreducible backdrop to this story. It also is the historical context that the members of the new colony unavoidably encountered. They were to find Southampton both charming for its air of village antiquity with which they wished to identify and at the same time exasperating for its obduracy, its stubborn inability or refusal (as it seemed to them) to come to terms with the modern world, their world and its particular expectations. But nonetheless, the charms of its history, its extreme antiquity in American terms, certainly outweighed any obstacles to progress that might be misguidedly thrown up in their way.

In 1870, Richard Bayles, a writer and native of Suffolk County, had taken it on himself to bring up to date two earlier histories of Long Island.[1] By his own admission he found the project rather too daunting and scaled back his effort to cover only two-thirds of the Island, that is, only Suffolk County. The result was less the history claimed in the title than a lively contemporaneous account of the life of towns and villages that he encountered in his travels.[2] In three or four pages he gave us a description of Southampton as a small farming community with perhaps not very much to distinguish itself apart from its slightly greater age than other communities in the area. It was settled in 1640, beating Southold to the punch, its neighbor to the north, by a few months although Southold at the time of Bayles's writing still vigorously protested Southampton's claimed historical precedence and still does.[3] Southampton antedated the five other Suffolk towns by no more than ten or fifteen years. It was a small farming village situated in a fertile plain stretching south to the Atlantic beach a mile from its center and in 1870 contained slightly fewer than one thousand inhabitants and less than one hundred dwellings. It was, Bayles thought, "a village of sober, industrious, well-to-do farmers."[4] Earlier writers in Long Island history, Nathaniel Prime and Benjamin F. Thompson notably, had similarly observed that the lives of its residents were cautious, thrifty, and hardworking and attributed this to an abiding attachment to the discipline of Presbyterian religion.

The large majority lived along South and North Main streets, which ran from the ocean to beyond the new railroad that had come through in 1870 and ended in Long Springs, as well as on the east to west streets of the Shinnecock Road (now Hill Street) and the Bridgehampton Road (now simply the Hampton Road), which extended east toward Water Mill and Bridgehampton. The commercial center of the village was on Main Street between Job's Lane (a continuation of the Shinnecock Road) and the Bridgehampton Road. There were to be found several stores, three hotels or boarding houses, two churches (Presbyterian and Methodist Episcopal), a post office, and one of three schools (the Southampton Academy). Two district schools were located a short distance away and served the children of what were known as the North and South Ends of the village. Elsewhere, there were two or three blacksmith shops, a grist mill (on Windmill Lane), a machine shop, a railroad depot on North Main Street, and a hall for public gatherings on Job's Lane or Academy Lane, as it was called in the nineteenth century. There were two cemeteries; one off South Main Street dating from the mid-seventeenth century that had been used only sporadically since the 1720s and a larger cemetery in the North End of the village. According to Bayles, there were no saloons. He noted approvingly that the descendants of the Puritan or, more generally, Presbyterian settlers had continued to guard carefully "the moral purity of their society" but failed to remark that there was a little bar on Job's Lane owned by one of the Hildreths and known as John Hen's. There were also two pharmacies that dispensed alcohol and alcohol-based prescriptions, long objected to by a vociferous temperance movement led by the Methodist Church that finally managed to have a "no license" town excise board voted through in the 1880s.

The village, then, was strung out along two axes in a rough grid pattern, other streets within the interstices of the grid more or less conforming to this model. It was not something that had been deliberately planned but had emerged spontaneously and quite logically from an early decision to locate the village along the length of Main Street between the ocean beach and Long Springs. This decision had been made in the mid-1640s at several meetings of the general or town court. The first settlers had built a cluster of dwellings and a meetinghouse a mile to the east of what was in 1648 to become the Town Street (as Main Street was first called and sometimes still was by older residents). This location had been on high ground and near a spring or stream that intermittently fed into a long pond running down toward the ocean. It was named Farrington's Pond, after an early arrival who left within a few years, but later came to be known as Old Town Pond. The first inhabitants, having grown in number through increase and in-migration, evidently found these first quarters cramped and inconvenient and agreed that it was in their interest to establish new home or house lots on the eastern shore of the next pond over or at what shortly came to be known as Town Pond. In 1652, a new meetinghouse was erected a short distance down the new street leading to the ocean and a cemetery next to it.

The settlement arrangement reflected what geographers and human ecologists were later to call a dispersed or string village.[5] This was quite common in early New England. Settlers often dwelled at a distance from each other and had only one focal point of communal gathering in the meetinghouse that served as church, town court, school, and hostelry (or ordinary, as inns were then usually called). In such villages, cottages were not intimately clustered around a village green or common, mill pond, church, and burying ground as we are accustomed to expect them to be but dispersed in relatively large home lots of three or four and sometimes as many as six acres. The arrangement was functional inasmuch as almost all the planting fields in 1648 were to the east and south of the town street and thus within easy reach of the home lots of the freeholders. It clearly did not reflect any fear of Indian attack despite the fact that relations with the local Shinnecocks often were tense and mutually uncomprehending. But homesteads still were situated fairly close to one another and not scattered through the fields in isolated farms.

This arrangement also seems to have reflected the pronounced individualism of the settlers, a characteristic they shared in common with all other Puritan migrants in New England. While of necessity they began forming cooperative relations among themselves immediately on arrival in Southampton in order to survive in what must have seemed a strange and occasionally hostile environment—and before setting out on what was understood to be a collective enterprise had drawn up several documents outlining the rights and obligations of the members of the group—Southampton was by no means a fully solidary or cohesive community in its first few years. The settlers formed a church, built a small meetinghouse, hired a minister, and established minimal but effective civil government; but the main purpose of the enterprise was to allocate land to its subscribers for their productive use in an economically rational manner. Within a year or so of settlement land was thus divided in the immediate vicinity of Old Town, just to its east and south, and allotted to the first inhabitants. There was little that could be described as a communitarian impulse in this settlement pattern. Timothy Breen outlines a similar experience in Easthampton—initially an offshoot of Southampton—in the 1650s. There was, he argued, no "dense collective existence."[6] The town records in both cases show that social relations were often fragile and that problems of social control over individual behavior were encountered early. From the very first, individual economic motivations were paramount even if they did not override the need for collective security in dealing with the local Indians or, more tellingly, were subsumed under cooperative (and lucrative) arrangements once offshore and drift or beached whales had been spotted and their profitability recognized, a fortunate accident as Breen points out. This unexpected winter harvest gave the settlers early access to large markets. But even here communal arrangements to establish whale watches and a division of labor for processing whale carcasses quickly gave way to the development of small companies formed exclusively to hunt whales offshore for private profit.

But in 1648, despite the collective agreement to relocate to a new town street, Southampton had few of the qualities of an integrated or solidary community. It had no collective past, a basic ingredient of any enduring social formation. That was to change in the 1660s and 1670s when it came under the jurisdiction of the new English colonial authorities in New York, but the original individualist and acquisitive impulse of the first settlers not only remained but also was considerably enlarged in consequence of this new political arrangement. This was very much the result of the town's successful integration into the emerging market economy of New England and New York—the new Atlantic world—that in great part had been made possible by the expansion of inshore whaling after 1660 and the growing demand for whale products. At the same time, Southampton emerged as a political community with a distinct political identity. Between 1664 and 1686, the town's leaders fought a steadily losing battle with successive colonial governors for its political independence. This, more than any other single collective experience, forged the sense of community that had previously remained relatively undeveloped.

We have used the term *village* to refer to Southampton, but the community was not a village in the 1870s in any official sense and had not been thought of or referred to by its inhabitants as a village since its seventeenth-century founding. The references to a town street or a town pond and the early town records that are replete with references to the business of the town should make this clear. The "village" was no more than the small initial settlement located in the much broader bounds of the town covering a wide area. This conformed to a pattern typical of New England town formation in the seventeenth century. Moreover, most New England emigrants lived in the town and were not village dwellers and thought of themselves as such, holding land of their own, as freeholders. Many also, as Virginia Anderson notes, were familiar with an urban market economy either as artisans (tailors, weavers, carpenters, shoemakers, etc.) or as yeomen or husbandmen with surplus produce to sell in local markets.[7]

Those from small manorial villages did, it is true, experience the dying impact of feudal restrictions on tenure but ancient feudal tenures were in the last stages of dissolution in seventeenth-century England and were abolished entirely by Charles II in 1660. Almost all tenures were reduced to money rents in free and common socage. Yet a relatively small minority of New England migrants did originate in open field villages that in the 1630s were still prevalent in the central and southern sections of England and in part remained feudally organized. In such villages, tenant farmers continued to owe service to the manorial lord and participated in manorial courts while tilling their strips or lots in the open or common fields. Some of Southampton's settlers may have come from such villages—the land system they established suggests this—but to have done so they would have needed sufficient capital to finance the trip and establish themselves and their families overseas. Some open field villages were, however, quite prosperous and located near thriving markets. This was particularly true of southern England. Researching the origins of migrants to New England, Sumner Chilton Powell examined the conditions of village life and the fortunes of tenant farmers in a small open field village in Hampshire and found that the most enterprising among them were well able to accumulate the funds necessary to underwrite such an expensive and adventurous voyage into what must have seemed an uncertain and unpredictable future. As might be expected they brought with them the patterns of life they were familiar with, patterns that included the organization of land tenures that had prevailed in the communities they had left.[8] There is no reason to think that Southampton's settlers were different.

The small community of Southampton then was simply the administrative center, and the first area to be settled, of an extensive tract of land that circumscribed the area of the town and had always been known—or almost always known—as the Town of Southampton. Only after 1894 when the settlement was incorporated as a village under the laws of New

York State did it come to be called the Village of Southampton with some self-governing powers. Other places in the nineteenth century were called villages—Bridgehampton, Good Ground, Quogue, Speonk, even the largest village of all in 1870, Sag Harbor—but all these other settlements that had emerged slowly and for the most part well after 1700 had always been villages within the bounds of the town. None of them, except Sag Harbor, were incorporated until much later—and most remained hamlets as they are today—although by the late nineteenth century, all had churches and post offices.

But initially in the 1640s, the Southampton settlement was simply "the house-covered space" of the town situated in the wider context of the town's land. Nineteenth-century historian Frederic W. Maitland described the legal geography of early English towns and their lands in this fashion, a fashion that would have been thoroughly familiar to New England inhabitants. The town, being house covered, was surrounded by broad lands that included arable and common pastureland, water meadows, woodland, and waste. The totality comprised "an agrarian commonwealth" of township and borough.[9] Similarly, in seventeenth-century New England usage, settlements generally were referred to as the town plot (sometimes plat) or the town spot with the understanding that they also were surrounded by large and varied hinterlands that were under the settlement's jurisdiction and could be divided into lots to be allocated to individual town proprietors.

When Southampton was settled in 1640 it was under the terms of a patent or grant from the Scottish Earl of Stirling who in turn had received a grant of lands from the Council for New England, a private land company chartered by James I in 1621. The Council disbanded in 1635 and distributed its New England lands among its members, one of whom was the earl. Stirling received Long Island, offshore islands along the coast of Massachusetts (Nantucket, Martha's Vineyard, the Elizabeth Islands), and northern Maine or "the County of Canada." His agent in New England responsible for disposing of these lands was James Farrett, a young Scotsman, who had arrived earlier in 1637 or 1638. Maine was all but ignored and later entirely forgotten by the Stirling heirs (the earl died in 1640), but Farrett set about selling rights to settle large tracts in the remaining lands covered by the Stirling grant and in particular on Long Island. He was only partially successful; but in the two years he spent here he managed to find patentees, or grantees, for part of the land that is now Southold, part of what was to become Oyster Bay, Gardiner's Island (already purchased of the Montaukett Indians by Lyon Gardiner in 1639 but without the benefit of a patent), the offshore islands (later disputed by the Massachusetts Bay Colony) and part of Southampton east of Canoe Place. After Stirling died, Farrett, apparently short of cash, transferred the patent rights to the remaining lands of Long Island to a consortium of Connecticut speculators, led by the governors of Hartford and New Haven, in exchange for a three- or five-year loan of one hundred pounds sterling. He left for Scotland, never to repay the loan, and in due course the governors foreclosed and exercised their right to purchase the Stirling lands from different groups of Indians. Among those purchased were 30,000 acres acquired from the Montauketts that were later in 1651 to become Easthampton.

Farrett had been fortunate in 1639 in making contact with a group of settlers in Lynn, Massachusetts who were dissatisfied with the land allocated to them and were actively searching for somewhere else to settle. Very probably John Winthrop, several times governor of the Massachusetts Bay Colony, had arranged for Farrett to meet with them. Before meeting Farrett, some twenty men had drawn up two documents outlining their plans to settle a new plantation, the means by which they determined to do it, and how they expected to organize themselves once there. These were the Disposall of the Vessell and A Declaration of the Company.[10] There was nothing unusual about this in the Bay Colony in the late 1630s. The first Massachusetts settlements were filling up through heavy migration and new immigrants, anxious to acquire land but finding most of it already taken up, had few options but to form themselves into ad hoc companies, apply to the general court in Boston for a grant of land if they were to move within the jurisdiction of the Bay, and strike out to establish a new settlement where they could negotiate a land purchase with whatever Indians happened to live there. This "hiving out," as it often is referred to, was an integral part of the process of "peopling and planting" whereby new groups were continually moving out into the wilderness from crowded centers of population to establish their land claims and improve the land they had been granted. Improvement signified possession and was essential to the Puritan conception of ownership.[11]

The Lynn men followed this pattern. That they moved out of the Bay was not unusual either. Many before them had already moved to Connecticut and Rhode Island, frequently because of religious tension and disagreement, and some had even departed to establish towns in New Netherland in the western part of Long Island to place themselves under the relatively benign authority of the Dutch who professed none of the theocratic pretensions of many in the Bay Colony. There may have been such overriding religious motivations in some cases, but for the most part the reasons for searching out a new plantation were economic. There also were political motives in settling Long Island and Connecticut. Dutch territorial claims extended far to the east of New Amsterdam, and Bay authorities were anxious to counter that in the 1630s.

A further key to understanding this process of out-migration is that in all cases the men involved formed companies to finance the venture and bought shares in them. As John Frederick Martin put it, they were plantation companies formed for the purpose of land development in the expectation of gaining a return on their investment; land being the principal capital of early New England and the point of acquiring it being to convert it to private ownership.[12] How much capital a man put in would ultimately determine how much land he would be allocated, an allocation that was moreover always in fee simple and thus heritable and transferable. Land was the pay-off for the initial investment.

Few writers on early New England today cite Max Weber and his analysis of Puritan asceticism and its connection to the ethical basis of capitalist activity—the spirit of capitalism as he called it—but it remains highly relevant. It was precisely the settlers' desire for land and its possession and improvement that reflected those disciplined motivations that Weber thought were essential in accounting for the rise in the seventeenth century of what he called rational bourgeois capitalism. The small plantation companies springing up in the Bay Colony, of which the Lynn company (with its own charter or articles) was simply one of many, exemplified the early capitalist development that Weber sought to understand and explain.[13] It was a rational economic enterprise in pursuit of profit and the accumulation of capital in the form of improvement to the land and its productive use. In the sixteenth and early seventeenth centuries men who subscribed stock in companies in pursuit of commercial profit in some enterprise abroad, for example cod-fishing off Newfoundland, were called adventurers, venturing, that is, their capital. The members of the Lynn company described themselves as undertakers, that is, they agreed to undertake and finance the establishment of a new plantation in return for which they would each receive freehold rights to land covered by the terms of the grant or patent according to the value of their shares or rights to the plantation's common land yet to be taken up and divided among them. It was a prescription for individualism. The members of all such companies were always defined as tenants in common of the land for which they held a patent, but this did not mean that they would pursue the development of the land's resources as a communal enterprise. Only in specific instances would they do so when collective labor became a necessity. This was the case in early whaling in Southampton. The entire company was divided into squadrons in the mid-1640s to watch for beached or close inshore whales and was organized to pursue them, cut them up, and render the oil. This arrangement, however, quickly gave way to private enterprise and the formation of small, chartered companies, a change Weber would have just as quickly appreciated and predicted.

Thoughts of establishing a town, a corporate political entity, were not in those formative years considered a priority or even a necessity. A town would have meant to most—coming from England as they did—a relatively large and diverse borough, perhaps possessed of a royal charter, a market and perhaps a manufacturing economy, a main center of commerce. Small early New England communities, such as Southampton with no more than twenty founding families, met none of these conditions of township. If there was such a thing as a town, it was simply understood to be in the form of a joint stock company, a business enterprise. The Farrett grant to the Lynn men contained only the barest reference to the establishment of civil government or a church. It would not, however, be true to say that the communal, legal, religious, and other "nonbusiness aspects" of town life were ignored. To the contrary, the earliest town records of Southampton show a lively involvement of the stockholders in the varied fortunes and problems of what was clearly understood to be a civic as well as an economic enterprise even if it was not yet quite a civil and political community. Yet in this connection, the early inhabitants did form some minimal administration of the town's affairs: They elected officials, kept records, insisted on attendance at town meetings, adjudicated disputes, clarified the responsibilities of stockholders in respect to land, livestock, the control of wild animals (wolves especially), formed train bands for military protection and, when new problems surfaced, elaborated collective responses to them—an instance of which was the discovery of the potential that whaling represented. As early as December 1641, the town court "ordered" that there should be four quarter courts and "one generall meeting" each year to be called into session by "the Magistrates," an indication from the beginning that an administration of the town's affairs was thought to be an absolute necessity.[14]

Similarly, in regard to religion, there was never any question that the establishment of a church and the retention of a minister would not be a priority. Prior to setting out for Southampton, the leaders of the company arranged for a well-regarded Boston minister to follow them. Abraham Pierson was a young Yorkshireman who had arrived in Boston with his parents in 1638. He had been educated at Cambridge, the holder of a master's degree, and ordained in Boston after which he appears to have settled in Lynn, the embarkation point for Southampton's settlers. That he was a fashionably orthodox Puritan, even something of a firebrand and theocratically inclined, must have seemed initially attractive to the little congregation that hired him. He joined the settlers in December 1640, six months after their own arrival and after they had already constructed a small meetinghouse in readiness. Yet it must be stressed that, pious though they no doubt were, this small band did not leave Lynn or the Bay in general for religious reasons as perhaps they had left England. They left for land. Pierson lasted a few years only, a division within the church over the question of whether church membership was to be a prerequisite for the election of town officials having led to his departure. The town was firmly against it but a small number of his parishioners departed with him. There was a second reason connected with his leaving. In 1644, the General Court decided to join with the Connecticut Colony in Hartford for reasons largely having to do with security. Pierson, however, favored an alignment with New Haven, a radically sectarian colony whose views on theocratic government accorded fully with his. But more moderate opinion prevailed and he left for a succession of ministries in Connecticut and New Jersey. His son, also Abraham Pierson, later became the first president of Yale College.

The projected group of settlers met with James Farrett, probably at first in Boston and then later in New Haven, and agreed that they should plant themselves somewhere on Long Island. Between 1639 and 1640, Farrett gave them two and possibly three deeds, each of them slightly different, the last of which provided for an extremely generous sixty-four square miles of land ("eight miles square") between Canoe Place on the west and a line to the east extending south from "Mr. ffarret's Island" (Shelter Island) to the ocean. (Farrett had mistakenly thought that he had purchased the island for himself from its inhabitants, the Manhansett Indians. They later denied it claiming that they had merely let him live there.) This was a much larger tract than the Bay Colony was accustomed to granting, usually only six miles square or thirty-six square miles. The fortunate colonists then set sail from New Haven to North Sea Harbor in Peconic Bay with their families, belongings, probably a few servants, some essential livestock, building materials, and their copy of the Stirling patent. They arrived in June 1640. This story has been many times told and does not need repeating here,[15] but there is sufficient complexity in the events prior to the settlers' arrival in Southampton, as well as some problems with the dating of them, to suggest that there were at least two if not three failed attempts at settlement in various Long Island locations before arriving in North Sea Harbor.[16]

The patent had given the settlers only the right to purchase the land from the Indians who occupied it, and whose right of possession was recognized by the crown under English common law, but not the purchase of the land itself. A sale was negotiated with the Shinnecock Indians, the inhabitants, and a deed drawn up and signed in December. It is highly unlikely that the Shinnecock, knowing nothing of the English law of property and having their own distinct ideas of land ownership, realized that they were transferring their land to the new arrivals. They had no sense of land as a commodity capable of being exchanged. Much more probable is that they thought they were providing usufruct rights to the settlers in exchange for what must have been understood by them as gift goods as well as assurances that the English would provide them with security from potential attack by other Indian groups.[17] This was not how the settlers saw it, of course, and it set the tone for what was to become an enduring pattern of continual misunderstandings and disagreements between the two groups that ultimately became increasingly embittered. That pattern has continued into the present.

The first purchase from the Indians, corresponding to the area outlined in the Farrett grant as running from Canoe Place to a somewhat indeterminate eastern boundary in the Wainscott plains, was always known as the Town Purchase. There were further purchases beginning in the late 1650s. Hog Neck or Hoggenock (now North Haven) was acquired from the Manhansett Indians of Shelter Island, and several individual purchases were made by Southampton men between 1659 and 1662 of the lands west of Canoe Place in what is broadly Quogue. Wyandanch, the sachem of the Montaukett, sold Shinnecock land to John Ogden in 1659 while in 1662 Thomas Topping purchased land farther to the west from the Shinnecock, but overlapping with Ogden's purchase. The area in question was much larger than the Town Purchase and ran as far west as the yet to be determined eastern boundary of Brookhaven, a town that had been settled in 1655 on land sold by different groups of Indians and apparently approved by the Connecticut holders of the residue of the Stirling patent or by a later group known as the Committee for Connecticut.[18]

The story of the Quogue purchases has been explored in detail by a recent historian, John Strong, and often is referred to as the Great Quogue Land Grab.[19] These private and obviously speculative purchases caused great consternation in Southampton and led ultimately to the intervention of the colonial governor. New Netherland had fallen to the English in 1664 and Richard Nicolls, who had orchestrated the Dutch defeat, became the first English governor of what was now named New York. It had been so named for James Duke of York and Albany, the younger brother of Charles II, and the holder of a crown charter to all the Dutch lands. The patent lands of New York, which included the Long Island lands under the Stirling patent, were now virtually a royal colony and later would become one when James ascended the throne in 1685. Nicolls, anxious to deal with the English towns on eastern Long Island in order to bring them under colonial governance and seeing the necessity of putting some order into a turbulent Indian real estate market, ruled that Ogden and Topping must deliver their titles to the Quogue lands to Southampton in return for adequate compensation by the town. Thus, in 1666, Southampton more than doubled the size of its land base through this acquisition of what were respectively called the Quogue and Topping's Purchases. They were still called that at the end of the nineteenth century but this later fell into disuse.

The Town of Southampton then occupied approximately 170 square miles or more than 100,000 acres, an extraordinary amount of land for the time. It was far larger than Easthampton or its neighbor to the north, Southold, although nowhere near the size of Brookhaven, which was already through successive purchases 250 square miles by 1660. The small settlement, the "house-covered space" less than one mile from the ocean, perhaps occupied less than one percent of Southampton's area. By the late nineteenth century, the village had expanded sufficiently to include almost four thousand acres. The town as a whole, however, extended thirty miles along the south shore of Long Island where the majority of its villages were located. These communities generally were situated on necks of land extending into a series of large land-locked, but interconnected, bays that were to be found to the east of the Great South Bay and also connected to it. The bays were to some extent protected from the ocean by a narrow ribbon of barrier beach that extended eastward from the Rockaways to a point just short of the village of Southampton. The beach was vulnerable to storms, particularly winter storms from the northeast, and was periodically breached by the action of the waves forming temporary inlets. Beyond Southampton the shoreline was unprotected except in a small way at Mecox Bay and farther east at Georgica Pond.

The town was geographically divided into two parts separated by hills and the narrow isthmus of Canoe Place. Here, the Shinnecock had once drawn their canoes across the half mile of low-lying land separating Peconic and Shinnecock bays. In 1882, the state legislature approved the financing of a canal connecting the two bays. It was opened a decade later. The Shinnecock Hills, the old lands of the Indians where village sites and burial grounds dating back several millennia were later found, constituted in the early years of settlement a true barrier to communication between the eastern and western sections of the town. The Hills, as they were always simply called, were a product of glacial action pushing debris before the ice sheet almost as far as the sea. They were once densely wooded but by the end of the eighteenth century had been virtually denuded of trees following a typical pattern of deforestation both to meet the demand for wood products and increase the area of grazing land. They had been used for pasture since early settlement times which suggested that there was always much grassland. Sheep, cattle, and horses were pastured on the Hills through the 1880s but then the practice abruptly ended when the land was sold to outside development interests. The road through them was always rough and winding, often impassable in winter, and possibly this contributed to a sense of social distance between the two halves of the town and the semi-isolation of the less developed western part from the older and wealthier east. Political power had always been concentrated in the east—Southampton was the seat of town government—and most of the inhabitants of the town lived there. It was not until 1882 that the political monopoly of the east was effectively challenged.[20]

The northern boundary of the town was described by the Peconic River and estuary and by Peconic Bay. Beyond the river and the bay lay Southold and Riverhead. A low ridge of wooded hills, primarily of oak, ran along Southampton's northern perimeter, a residue of the retreat of the ice sheet twelve thousand years earlier. This was the Ronkonkoma Moraine that ran along the north shore of Long Island, beginning in Brooklyn, and falling into the sea at Montauk and its few outcrops in Block Island Sound. To the east was Easthampton beginning in Wainscott on a line between the two towns that was the subject of dispute between them until 1695 when it was resolved in committee.

There is a question, not a trivial one, about the naming of Southampton. A considerable body of opinion, represented by many generations of local historians, believed that Southampton was named either for the Earl of Southampton, a significant if not perhaps crucial figure in very early seventeenth-century efforts at American colonization, or for the port in England from where it is assumed that the Southampton settlers, bound for New

England, might have embarked. Neither seems particularly compelling. To take the second issue first: It would have been a remarkable coincidence if all Southampton's settlers, having arrived individually in Massachusetts Bay at different times between 1630 and 1637 and being unknown to one another, had set sail from the same port and that that port had been Southampton. There were any number of ports they might have embarked from—Plymouth, Falmouth, Bristol, Weymouth, Barnstaple, Sandwich, Great Yarmouth, Ipswich, Gravesend, and London—depending on their points of origin, usually no more than forty miles from the port of embarkation.[21] That in 1640 (the first reference to Southampton in the town records is in 1641) a number of them who, let us assume, did embark from Southampton and approached the town court with the suggestion that what more appropriate a name for the town could there be other than this, even if none had any connection to Southampton except as a possible point of departure, is equally unconvincing.

Similarly far-fetched is the idea favored by those with apparent royalist or aristocrat inclinations that, even while professing Puritan sympathies, it was in deference to the memory of the Earl of Southampton that the town was so named by the little company that planted itself there. Henry Wriothesly, third Earl of Southampton1573–1624), was certainly a formidable and memorable figure in the Jacobean age.[22] He was born into one of the great Catholic families of England but converted to Protestantism about the time of the accession of James I in 1603. He became an Anglican and was little touched by Puritan ideas (apart from some youthful instruction apparently in Paris), maintaining instead a moderate and circumspect stance on religious matters as well as considerable sympathy for the plight of Catholics, most of whom among the well-born he had known since childhood. He also was a strong royalist under both Elizabeth and James and had campaigned in Ireland in 1599, sent there by Elizabeth, in one of many attempts to subdue the Irish. In late 1601, the queen was thought to be not far from death and rumors were circulating through London that a cabal that included Sir Walter Raleigh was intent on installing the Spanish Infanta on the throne. Southampton joined with the Earl of Essex, a strong Protestant, and others to oust the Spanish faction from the Court and force Elizabeth to recognize James VI of Scotland as her heir.[23] This was the famous but abortive Essex Rebellion. Elizabeth moved fast and had Essex, Southampton, and the other conspirators imprisoned in the Tower. Southampton was lucky to escape with his head (Essex was not) but languished in confinement until after Elizabeth's death.

One of James I's first acts was to order his release. The new king then thought highly of Southampton (he was to revise his opinion), but they were never close and the latter spent little time at Court preferring a life of ease on his various estates (particularly the Isle of Wight in the English Channel where he had been appointed captain by James I in 1603 and spent many rewarding years there improving its defenses), the luxury of travel abroad, and an indulgence in the arts. In respect to this last pursuit, he became William Shakespeare's sole patron and perhaps is best of all remembered for this. He did, however, become involved with American colonization.

As early as 1602, he was much interested in the fortunes of the Catholic colony in Virginia. When that failed and the London and Plymouth Companies were folded into one Virginia Company in 1609, the Earl of Southampton was one of its many incorporators.

How deeply involved he was in the affairs of the company in the following years is not known, but in 1620 he was elected treasurer with James's approval. James I had never liked the Virginia Company and found its single-minded devotion to the production of tobacco—this "filthie noveltie" he had called it—unacceptable. He must have hoped that the earl would effectively diversify the colony's commercial activities. Southampton was by now a member of the Privy Council (having been passed over for many years), and James probably thought that the company would be in good hands. Yet he was apparently mistaken, for within a year, unhappy with the fortunes of the colony under the earl's stewardship, he had him arrested. In 1622, after his release, Southampton was again elected treasurer beating out the king's candidates by a hefty margin. James struck back. He cancelled the earl's substantial state pensions on which he had been heavily dependent. It was a vindictive blow from which there was little chance of financial recovery. Two years later he died of complications of a fever contracted in Holland. James had reluctantly—never fully trusting him—sent him there in command of a regiment to support the Dutch in the ongoing war with Spain in what was to become the Thirty Years War (1618–1648).

Shortly before his death, the Privy Council had instituted quo warranto proceedings against the Virginia Company's charter and revoked it thus ending any further contribution to the colonization of America that the Earl of Southampton might have made. Henry Wriothesly's legacy in America was scant. The Virginia town of Hampton was named for him—as was the harbor of Hampton Roads—but he did nonetheless lead a very remarkable and varied life, colonization activities perhaps representing only a smaller part of his accomplishments. Still, it was not the kind of life that, on the face of it, would lead a small group of Puritan settlers to exclaim that here was precisely the kind of man for whom they should name their new town.[24]

The same could easily be said, if not with more emphasis, of the town of Northampton, Massachusetts. Perhaps the settlers there in 1656 never intended in their choice of a name any allegiance to the Earl of Northampton, a contemporary but possibly no friend of the Earl of Southampton. For a Puritan community to have done so would have been quite incomprehensible. In 1604, with James not a year on the throne, Southampton was summarily arrested amid wild rumors of plots against the king or plans to massacre the Scots who had trooped south with him (the Earl of Stirling, incidentally, among them) but then just as quickly released. No charges ever surfaced and the whole matter may have been hushed up, but it appears that the man who accused Southampton was probably Lord Henry Howard, Earl of Northampton. Here was a wily old conspirator well-schooled in the jungle politics of the Elizabethan court, a zealous Catholic, and possibly a Spanish spy. It does not seem possible that the godly citizens of Northampton would have chosen to name their little settlement in the wilderness in honor of a man (or any of his heirs) of so questionable a reputation.

Joseph Wood suggests in his analysis of New England villages that before 1675 settlers planted a considerable number of towns with the suffix "-field" (or "ham," "hamp," or "hamm") in place-names. "Ham" refers to "a flat, low-lying pasture near a river."[25] Springfield and Deerfield are Wood's examples, as is Northampton. In regard to the last, George Stewart notes that the town "was at the time the most northerly settlement in that area, so that the name must have been considered partially descriptive" and discounts any connection to the earl, "a prominent Royalist."[26] The term *ham* itself contains several references and suggests many examples. It can refer to a pasture or meadow enclosed with a ditch; a small plot of ground growing by the rivers or "Thames-side" (a 1617 definition); enclosed land; or as "home" shortened to "ham" where there are "several hams or home closes of meadows"; or, "the forests would be converted by degrees into common pastures or hams" (1796). The *Oxford English Dictionary* tells us that "ham" was sometimes meant in the sense of "town, village, or manor" and cites, with Hampstead, Hampton, Oakham, Lewisham, and also Hamm, a town in Westphalia, as examples. Examples of the same usage abound in New England and, it seems obvious, on Long Island. "Hams," then, can refer to settled areas, communities, in the first instance. *Hamlet*, obviously, is a term still in use.

When in 1640, the small band of settlers disembarked in North Sea Harbor and made their way south through the woods to the plains bordering the ocean they found themselves in land capable of cultivation or utilization in some fashion as fields. They established their first small settlement there at Old Town Pond near these potential fields, in fact near one referred to early in the town records as "the old ground" or "the Indian field." It became in time the Little Plain. In naming the town Southampton or "South Field Town," it may have occurred to them that there could not be any more practical or appropriate name for their new home than this, a name not burdened with the memory of a past they had definitively left or, if it were, only very faintly. Then later, of course, there were the east fields of Easthampton and the fields between the towns in Bridgehampton (but it was to the bridge over Sagg Pond that we owe the name of that early village).

II: THE NINETEENTH CENTURY

The population of the Town of Southampton in 1860 had almost exactly doubled since the first federal census in 1790. It stood at 6,803, up from 3,408 in 1790, and had steadily increased in the intervening seventy years. By comparison, the first detailed census of inhabitants in 1698 gave a population figure of 973, including 83 slaves and 152 Shinnecock Indians, indicating that the increase in population more than tripled in the eighteenth century and then somewhat slowed after the Revolution.[27] The reasons for this may in part be attributed to the town's decreasing capacity to absorb immigrants after the eighteenth century, its internal needs for labor and skills having stabilized at a more or less optimal level. Nonetheless, it was a period of steady if unspectacular demographic growth from the beginning of the nineteenth century until 1860. The next big increase occurred between 1880 and 1910 when the population again almost doubled, this time to more than eleven thousand from an 1880 figure of 6,352. This coincided with a period of heavy ethnic immigration from New York and New Jersey beginning in the late 1890s—Polish, Ukrainian, Italian, Irish, particularly—attracted by the possibilities of farm work and eventual farm ownership. It also partly reflected the rapid growth of the summer colony after the mid-1880s. Summer residents obviously were not included in the decennial census, but the demand for labor that the colony represented in the shape of construction trades, service, and retail clearly was.

Earlier however, between 1860 and 1870, the number of inhabitants declined considerably. The 1870 census showed a net loss of nearly seven hundred in the decade after the previous count and only a slight gain between 1870 and 1880. Still, the 1880 census showed a net loss of 450 in the twenty years after the 1860 count. In the 1870s, the town's population had in effect sunk to a level not seen since 1840. The figure is striking inasmuch as the population of all other Suffolk County towns suffered no such decline or showed a slight increase over the same decade. The much smaller town of Easthampton, for example, experienced a net gain of one hundred for the period.

Some of this sharp decrease might be accounted for by losses incurred in the upheaval of the Civil War. According to the town records, upwards of five hundred men from Southampton served in the war (this figure included large numbers of substitutes from elsewhere—perhaps as many as half) and at least fifty-five were either killed or died of war-related causes.[28] Yet, other towns would have experienced similar losses. A more significant factor, however, was unquestionably the decline or near collapse of the whale fishery, already well underway before the Civil War. Many young men previously engaged in whaling left for the California gold fields after 1848—there appeared to be a general exodus of 250 in 1849 and more left through the 1850s—not all of whom returned to Southampton. Of all the villages in Southampton, Sag Harbor was the most affected by the virtual end of the whaling industry and by the exodus to California. It was a community of merchants, shipbuilders, and seafarers whose livelihood was severely affected by what was to many an economic catastrophe.[29] By the 1860s, Sag Harbor had become what one writer described as "a ship-less bay with an abandoned wharf."[30] It also was by far the largest village in the town with more than two thousand inhabitants and accounted for nearly one-third of the total population. Any substantial reduction through out-migration from Sag Harbor would be bound to have an impact on the overall census figures.

But by far the most significant element accounting for population decline, and this was generally true of rural communities throughout the northeast, was the general fall in agricultural prices beginning after the Civil War and accentuated by the long depression of the 1870s. Since the opening up of eastern markets to western farmers through the development of new transportation routes in the 1830s and 1840s, Long Island farm production, which on a limited land-base had always been small scale, had become much less competitive. The Erie Canal, completed in 1827, and the complex of associated waterways connecting with Great Lakes shipping dramatically reduced freight rates for western produce well before the Civil War. Railroads, introduced in the 1840s, had a similar effect and produced an important added advantage: a reduction in transportation time. The beneficiaries ultimately were farmers in western New York, Ohio, Pennsylvania, and as far west as Michigan, Indiana, Illinois, Iowa, and Wisconsin where crop yields and farm sizes by the 1870s were higher and larger than in New York and New England. Eastern farmers came increasingly under pressure from the combined effects of falling prices, improved productivity from larger and more efficient farms in the west and their better access to the major eastern markets.

Falling prices and competition, however, were not the sole or immediate causes of a marked fall in the farming population of rural towns like Southampton. The Homestead Act, passed by a Republican Congress in 1863, was a major catalyst triggering western migration from New York and New England to the Ohio valley and to states like Illinois and Iowa; both of which advertised extensively in the east for new settlers. Homesteading was specifically geared to attract eastern settlers to establish farms on relatively large tracts in the underpopulated western states. A secondary, but clearly important, reason for the legislation was to reduce the impact in eastern cities like New York of an emerging industrial working class in a period of rapid industrialization and European immigration. The Republican party of the 1860s and later emphasized the importance of individual upward mobility and economic independence and feared the development of a permanent European-style proletariat, a class of wage laborers endemically hostile to capitalism. Republicans were committed to policies of free soil, free labor, and free men epitomized by homesteading legislation, but it also was reflective of their earlier embrace of Emancipation. Southern slavery, as a condition of radically unfree labor, was not equivalent to formally free industrial labor in the north but there were sufficient similarities, enough for Republicans to fear their consequences. Homesteading was meant to avoid or at least ameliorate the effects of institutionally segregated labor in the cities by promoting opportunities for independent farm ownership and artisanship in the west. It was to be the path to democratic citizenship and an open and prosperous society. It had, however, little impact on New York and other industrializing and immigrant cities. Those who struck out for new opportunities in the west were those who left their farms or left farm labor, forced out by economic conditions. Not many were from the urban working classes.

Between 1870 and 1890, two-thirds of New York towns lost population as, similarly, did three-fifths of New England villages. In Massachusetts alone in the same period fifteen hundred farms were abandoned and overall in the northeast 300,000 people were estimated to have migrated in search of better opportunities in the west.[31] Overwhelmingly, these were poor farmers with small holdings unable to compete with larger and more productive farms in western states. Estimates indicate that western farms of five hundred acres or more increased by 40 percent between 1880 and 1890 suggesting a growing demand for farm labor with much of it coming from the east. How seriously this affected Southampton and other Long Island towns beginning in the 1870s depression cannot be established easily, but small farmers in the East End must certainly have felt the pressure to move away. In Southampton, and particularly in the traditionally poorer western section of the town in the Quogue and Topping's Purchases, times must have been especially hard for the baymen and farmers eking out a living on small lots along the shores of the bays and relying on those bays to supplement their incomes. As seen later, this specific social group became politically active in the early 1880s as outside economic interests began to exert pressure on their limited resources. However, by the 1890s, Long Island farmers with substantial holdings in land fared better. Unable to compete with large-scale corn, wheat, and beef production in the West, they diversified their own production specializing in varied seasonal crops for sale in New York markets. This prefigured a later pattern of truck farming that, in the twentieth century, came to define much of the agricultural production of eastern Long Island.

Nonetheless, conditions in Southampton were aggravated by the specific pattern of landownership that had developed in the town since the seventeenth century. Essentially, the major and best part of the town's land was in the hands of approximately no more than 250 individuals. Briefly considered here (and discussed later), these were the descendants of the original settlers and others who had later bought shares in the purchase of the town. This small minority, 5 percent of the town's inhabitants in 1880, owned about 80 percent of the land in sizable although often scattered parcels through the town. Ownership of shares in successive purchases of the town's lands—the Town Purchase in 1640 and the Quogue and Topping's Purchases in 1666—effectively conferred rights on shareholders to participate in drawing lots as land was progressively divided in the seventeenth and eighteenth centuries. In consequence, land was accumulated in the hands of a small number, passed on from one generation to the next and rarely sold to outsiders. This proprietary system had caused much dissension in the early years of the nineteenth century and continued to fuel political tensions in the community into the 1880s. Its effect had been to confine small farmers to largely marginal land. Combined with the long-term downward pressure on farm prices, this historical and apparently permanent inequity in land distribution may have driven many to leave. Just how many is uncertain but there are scattered indications in local newspaper reports that some did leave the area. But those fortunate enough to control prime farm land in the town managed to weather the worst effects of agricultural depression between the 1870s and the 1890s and felt no particular pressure to look for new opportunities elsewhere.

A last but not major factor contributing to the population exodus in the 1860s and 1870s was the opening up of the national economy after the Civil War, in particular in New York City. Economic growth was extremely rapid despite financial panics and severe recessions (the first of which began in 1873) and the opportunities in what was essentially an emerging new economy were a powerful attraction to young men in the provinces. The old New York mercantile economy based on the profits of financing Southern cotton production and the demand for European imports was in steep decline after the defeat of the Confederacy and was partially in process of being replaced by the developing manufacturing sector. New York was a good place for young men to be, particularly if they were educated as many were in Southampton. A few from the town would seek their fortunes in the city or in other urban locations in a gradual process of rural-urban migration.

Geographically, the surface area of the town, and its consequent resource base, consisted of level lands of light sandy loam interspersed with what the 1860 *Gazetteer* of the State of New York described as "sterile plains or barren sandhills" or sometimes as brushy plains. There was no native rock except that left by glacial action, but woodland was abundant south of the Peconic estuary and river and along the narrow escarpment in the northern part of the town fronting Peconic Bay. The most noticeable feature of the town's lands was the extent to which they were covered by water. The inland bays east of the Great South Bay in Brookhaven covered almost 20 percent of the town's total area of just over 109,000 acres. Besides the bays, the many fresh water ponds and other bays on both the north and south shores of the town (Mecox Bay, Cold Spring Pond, Bullhead Bay, and North Sea

Harbor particularly) increased the amount of land under water to 22 percent or 19,968 acres.[32] The waters of the town and the Atlantic Ocean were and always had been a major source of the town's wealth and profitability.

In fact, the products of these waters became an indispensable and central part of the town's economy from the earliest years of settlement and remained so into the twentieth century. A flourishing shellfish industry, locally financed by small private companies, grew up in the middle of the eighteenth century and provided for both domestic and external consumption needs. Clams, mussels, scallops, eels, and especially oysters were a lucrative business. After the Civil War, the market for oysters in New York increased exponentially with the city's growth and led city investors in 1882 to buy up the most productive of the bays. The hundred-plus acres of Mecox Bay had traditionally contained the richest of the oyster beds as its fresh waters were periodically nourished by the ocean through opening the beach to form a temporary inlet. But outside investment on such a large scale was unheard of in Southampton at that time and the sale of Mecox, as well as of the other major bays, provoked a predictable backlash in the town and eventually led to a classic court battle between the town trustees and the oyster company.[33] There was, besides shellfish, an immense floating fishery in the waters surrounding the town in both the ocean and Peconic bays. This also obtained for Shinnecock Bay, the largest body of water in the town, insofar as an adequate outlet to the sea could be maintained. This was not always possible, however. Occasionally, as was the case in the 1880s, tens of thousands of fish died in waters that had become stagnant.

Yet there was no organized fishing industry in the town to take advantage of the inshore abundance and variety of the fishery, particularly striped bass, fluke, and bluefish. Until the 1850s, fishing had been almost exclusively understood as confined to the whale fishery. Cod fishing, like whaling also out of Sag Harbor, began to develop after the beginning of the nineteenth century but then sharply declined in the 1850s. In 1860, less than two hundred tons of cod were taken in inshore fishing, but a decade later that figure had increased to more than fifteen hundred tons indicating a revival. Evidently, much of the fishing fleet had stayed in port in the 1850s while the crews went off to California in search of easier and less dangerous ways—as they must probably have thought—of making a living.

Fishing for menhaden or moss bunkers, a branch of the herring family and essentially a waste fish, was another matter entirely. It was a migratory fish that moved in vast schools northward from southern waters in the spring and returned in the fall. Most of this summer fishery was taken between Cape May and Narragansett Bay. By the early 1870s, it was the most important fishing interest in eastern Long Island. Menhaden had been taken for fertilizer and spread over farm fields since at least the middle of the eighteenth century. Reports from the 1790s indicate that large quantities of menhaden were taken with seines in the waters of the Peconics as well as inshore off the ocean beaches. As many as 250,000 fish in one haul was not uncommon. Other uses for menhaden were discovered later. By the late 1840s, it was found that the oil from this fish could be used for tanning and dressing leather, for rope making, and for paint as well as for various other products. It became a major if relatively short-lived industry. The oil was extracted by boiling the fish in large iron pots and skimming the oil from the surface of the water. The first pot-works—as they came to be called—was set up in Jessup's Neck in 1847 or 1848.

Over the next two decades, fish factories were established along the shores of the Peconic Bays and Gardiner's Bay—in Southampton, Riverhead, Southold, Shelter Island, Greenport, East Marion, Amagansett, and Napeague. By 1874, there were sixty-four such factories employing almost one thousand men and more than fifteen hundred fishermen in 283 sailing vessels or steamers. The catch that year was an astonishing half billion fish (492,878,000) and the amount of oil rendered almost 2.5 million gallons; enough, one might have thought, to ensure the extinction of this lowly but highly valuable fish. That was not to be the case, but the catch was slightly lower seven years later in 1881 and the quality of the fish taken was said to be "unusually poor."[34] Thereafter, the menhaden fishery declined. This probable result of overfishing had not, however, deterred investors in the late 1870s, almost all of them local and all of the investment in fairly small pot-works. In 1881, the numbers of factories had increased from sixty-four to ninety-seven, the number of men employed to more than five thousand throughout the East End, and the capital invested from $2,500,000 in 1874 to $4,750,000 in 1881 (if these last figures are to be believed given the inflated valuation of companies in this overextended business era). But the oil rendered from the fish taken was only half that extracted in 1874. By 1884, the catch was estimated as down to 176,500,000 (this was still a prolific fish) and the quantity of oil retrieved under 1 million gallons. Still, the value of the product processed in pot-works on Gardiner's and Peconic Bays was thought to be slightly more than $600,000. Employment in this large-scale industry may have alleviated the plight of many a small farmer and bayman reduced in circumstances by the fall in farm prices.

One unavoidable by-product of the menhaden fishery was that it was an extremely malodorous business, so much so that all the towns involved eventually demanded that pot-works be established only at a safe remove from centers of population. In Easthampton, for example, the factories were confined to the dismal and unpopulated stretch of land along Gardiner's Bay in Napeague. Apart from Jessup's Neck, the only other Southampton fish factories were on the north shore of Shinnecock Bay in the Shinnecock Hills, where almost no one lived, and east of Canoe Place on Peconic Bay. Shelter Island was another matter. Its two great hotels—the Manhanset House and the Prospect House—had gone up at the beginning of the 1870s catering to tourists and Methodist revivalists from New York and Massachusetts, but Shelter Island was a focal point of the menhaden industry. There were no fewer than a dozen fish factories on this small island. There were inevitable complaints and resulting town ordinances. In Southampton in 1874, the town's board of health ordered that "the proprietors of Fish Oil works desist from the manufacture of Fish Oil, Guano, and Scraps within one hundred rods of any village," a distance equal to three-quarters of a mile.[35]

These various fisheries as a large-scale industry were a relatively late development in the economic history of Southampton. All of the original Suffolk County towns—Brookhaven, Easthampton, Huntington, Southold, and Southampton—had always been cattle towns. As late as 1860, and including the later and smaller towns of Islip, Riverhead, Smithtown, and

Shelter Island, Suffolk County was home to more than 7,000 horses, 13,000 working oxen, almost 11,000 cows, and 28,000 sheep, not to mention 20,000 swine. Southampton's share of the total livestock of approximately eighty thousand in the county was close to thirteen thousand or about 16 percent. As celebrated by Jeannette Edwards Rattray, Easthampton was always romantically projected as the great cattle town of the East End because of its famed cattle drives to the pasturelands of Montauk.[36] Legend has it that cattle were driven east from as far away as Patchogue, but there is little reliable evidence that this was the case. There was excellent pasture in Brookhaven and in the nearby Hempstead Plains in Huntington and no reason to drive cattle fifty miles (and back) that they might graze in Montauk's fatting fields. Yet Easthampton, with a smaller land area and population than Southampton, possessed large herds of livestock and played host to farmers in Bridgehampton desiring summer pasture. Bridgehampton seemed to be the westerly limit of the cattle drive.

Raising horses, sheep, and beef cattle had been a profitable business in Southampton since the late seventeenth century. Horses, beef, hides, and pork were staple exports to the West Indies, especially to Barbados, along with sheep, corn, and wood products (staves, shingles, planking, hoops). Other export products were furs, skins, feathers, tallow, and candles. Ships returned with their holds filled with molasses, sugar, and rum. There was a similar trade with the wine islands of Madeira and the Canary's as well as an active coastal trade with New England and the Middle Colonies. The export of horses to the Caribbean was particularly prized as their mortality in tropical climates was unreliable and necessitated a constant replenishment of the stock.[37] One medical report claimed that horses lost their hair on arrival, and an 1842 government inquiry in Barbados reported that mortality rates were as high as 25 percent, noting that the island's entire stock needed to be replaced every four years. Stockbreeders in Suffolk County were surely aware of this unfortunate circumstance. In 1860, more than seven thousand horses were raised in the county with Southampton the third largest producer after Brookhaven and Huntington.

In crop production, corn, potatoes, and wheat were the most widely cultivated, as were barley, rye, oats, and hay. Orchard products—particularly strawberries, peaches, and apples—were an important part of the local economy, as were poultry and dairy products. Commercial duck farms were beginning to make an appearance in the middle of the nineteenth century, and there were few farmers who did not raise at least some ducks for market. It was, despite falling prices, a well-rounded and stable agricultural economy, fortunate in its proximity to the New York market, and employing in the 1870s approximately 70 percent of the town's labor force. Twenty years later, William Pelletreau bemoaned the fact that the introduction of summer wealth from New York into Southampton had seduced its young people from the farms and into domestic service (they may have had few other options given the severe depression of the 1890s) but the fact remained that the town remained essentially a farming and fishing community well into the twentieth century.[38]

Other significant products of Southampton in the nineteenth century were cordwood, fired bricks, and cloth. The great expanse of pine plains in the northern sections of Brookhaven and Southampton west of Canoe Place provided much of the fuel needs of New York after the 1780s. Brookhaven particularly was able to export 100,000 cords annually for this purpose but Southampton was not far behind. The extensive woodland between the Quogue Plains and the Peconic River was divided into large wood lots in 1782 (the so-called Last Divisions in Quogue and Topping's Purchases) and much of the timber there cut over the next fifty years. This profitable business, however, ended suddenly. Forest fires in 1844 and 1845 consumed thousands of acres of the remaining woodland. The fires were a probable result of lightning strikes on land and vegetation dried out by decades of systematic deforestation.

Cloth weaving also had always been a central part of the Southampton economy whether for immediate consumption or export. The production of wool and flax was a side business for most farmers, and it was rare that a family farm did not possess a loom for manufacturing cloth. In 1778, half of Southampton men out of a total of 544 who signed a loyalty oath to the crown authorities in New York (possibly exacted under duress) described themselves as farmers. But among those who signed, fully one hundred of them reported that they were weavers. This is a surprisingly large number—20 percent—but the sample may not be representative of the general population that then numbered 3,408. Nineteenth-century censuses did not break down town populations by occupation, nor did they go further than list the numbers of those engaged in various broad economic pursuits such as agriculture, mining, commerce, manufactures, navigation and trades. In 1840 for instance, the male working population aged twelve to sixty-five was approximately 1,900 (of a total population of 6,205) of whom 1,233 were farmers, 294 engaged in manufactures and trades, and 436 in navigation either on the ocean or in the bays. The 1870 census is no more revealing. It is impossible to tell from these figures how many of both categories were engaged in the production of wool or cloth whether part time or full time. Nonetheless, there is no question that it was an important cottage industry well into the nineteenth century.

But that Southampton—even in depression years and given the existence of sizable numbers of small farmers—was a relatively wealthy agricultural town in the 1870s there can be no doubt. This had in fact been the case since at least the late eighteenth century when the fortunes of the town took off with the second whaling boom. The first offshore whaling enterprise beginning in the 1660s had gone into a sharp decline by 1730, as Atlantic right whales were becoming increasingly scarce, whereas deep-water whaling did not begin in earnest until fifty years later when larger and sturdier vessels capable of lengthy voyages over great distances were designed. They were constructed in shipyards up and down the New England coast including facilities in Sag Harbor and Greenport on the North Fork.

However, Southampton's prosperity was only partly dependent on the profits of the whale fishery. Individual wealth always had been measured in terms of land ownership, the productivity of land, and the livestock and buildings in the possession of the owner. Between the late 1640s and 1782, almost all of Southampton's common lands, that is, the lands of the town belonging to the first purchasers and their heirs and assigns, had been divided and allotted among them. There were forty such divisions made over this period covering most of the town's quite vast area. As each new division was laid out, only those with rights or shares in the purchase of the town (rights that were both heritable and transferable to others) were eligible to receive lots. The lots were drawn in a town meeting and those eligible would receive land "according to their right" or share in the original purchase. Lists of rights or shares by individual names were meticulously kept and periodically updated. No others could receive land unless it was specifically ordered by the town court. Usually this occurred only when the town was attempting to attract skilled labor of one sort or another. A blacksmith or miller, for instance, might be offered a three-acre home lot with an amount of upland and woodland, perhaps twenty acres, that he might raise a few livestock or grow corn or cut wood for fuel and fencing. This practice died out in the eighteenth century as the town filled up and could provide for its own skills.

The only other way to acquire land was to buy a share or right in the purchase of the town. These came to be known as commonage rights or rights in the common and undivided lands. Any owner of such a right, however small, entitled the holder to some degree of access to the remaining common lands, such as grazing rights for his cattle or sheep, and to at least some part of a lot in any new division of land that the town decided to lay out. Those who came to own commonage rights, either through inheritance or outright purchase from someone who did own them, were called *proprietors*. This term came into use in the 1680s and referred to any descendant of the first settlers, who had originally purchased the town's lands, and those who came later and purchased for themselves and their heirs such rights as they could. It made for a very lively trade. The early eighteenth-century town records are filled with references to the purchase of such rights.

There was an equally vigorous trade, again especially in the eighteenth century, among those who already possessed land in the form of lots in the divisions and were anxious to concentrate their holdings in, for example, a particular division by buying or exchanging lots or parts of lots with others. The key to understanding this process was the obvious desire of every generation after settlement to acquire as much land as possible and in a form as convenient as could be obtained. The volume of land sales and exchanges in the 1700s was thus extremely high and only began to level off in the period about twenty years after the last divisions were laid out in 1782. By then, presumably, most families had accumulated as much land as they could profitably absorb and consolidated it in ways that best suited their needs or economic interests. The number of proprietors stabilized around 250 by the end of the eighteenth century and remained at that level.

Laying out land in a divisional pattern was common to all Long Island towns and to New England in general. It partly, but by no means entirely, reflected the open field system in England that had existed since the early Middle Ages. Typically, the tenants of medieval villages divided only a small portion of the lands surrounding the lord's demesne and that for purposes of tillage. The rest was common pasture, meadow, woodland, and waste. The tillable land was laid out in quite narrow unfenced strips (although the field would be enclosed) that had the effect of forcing tenants to cooperate in planting the same crop in a given field. The advantage of this strip system was that it equalized the quality of the land allocated. Its disadvantage was that tenants had no choice but to plow, seed, hoe, and harvest strips that were often inconveniently far apart. Some of New England's settlers had experience of the open field system, but many had migrated from southeastern England where wood and pasture areas that were more suitable for raising livestock were predominant. Pastures were separated from each other by patches of woodland or hedgerows. This particular geography also fostered the enclosure of lands and the dispersion of family farms across the countryside, a fact that encouraged individualism in ways that the medieval nucleated or compact village could not.[39] But features of the open field system were reinvented in New England, albeit on a much larger scale, in fact on a scale that would have been unimaginable to the typical English villager of that or any previous time. In Southampton, wood and pasture coexisted with open fields providing a significant mixed husbandry.

Laying out the land in strips was the most obvious, effective, and equitable means of distributing land among eligible proprietors. The strips or lots, however, often were extremely large, sometimes as much as 120 acres, and could also be of considerable length. Those in the two Last Divisions in Quogue divided in 1782, consisting primarily of timber, were at least three miles in extremity. The same was true of the Great North and Great South Divisions north and east of Southampton village stretching as far as Sag Harbor where the lots ran north to south for well over one mile and averaged seventy acres. The purpose of this pattern of land distribution was, as in early England, to equalize the quality of the land drawn by proprietors. Where inequities appeared, adjustments were made and what were called "amendments." Amendments were allocated to those who had drawn unusable land or land that was otherwise waste such as swampland. In the earliest years, when tillable land was laid out, the common field as a whole was enclosed, as in early England, and the settlers planted a common crop in their various unfenced strips. Fencing of arable land was essential in view of the prevalence of free-range livestock in early Southampton and most other towns in Long Island and elsewhere. Swine were an especial nuisance. They multiplied fast, ate anything, and penetrated all but the densest of fences. Fencing was the responsibility of the owners in fee of the lots drawn by them while fence-viewers were employed to make sure the job was properly done.

By the late eighteenth and early nineteenth centuries the most significant consequence of the divisional system and the way it had been set up since the 1640s was the gradual consolidation of holdings by a relatively few number of landowners, that is, by the proprietors, the descendants of the first town purchasers, and men who had later purchased rights in the town and had themselves become proprietors. This process of land consolidation over a period of more than one hundred years was recorded in the town records and collected together by William Pelletreau in two volumes of deeds known as the Red and Yellow Books.[40] Together they provide an extraordinary picture of the extent of land transactions, who were most involved in them, and the concentration of land holdings among Southampton's leading families. But for a more systematic picture of who owned the land and its value the best source is the tax records.

Almost none of the eighteenth-century tax assessment rolls have survived, but several have been preserved dating to the early nineteenth century. The earliest to be found in Southampton's town archives is from 1818. It lists the real and personal estate of the freeholders and inhabitants of the town. In general, it shows that the assessed worth of the town's taxpayers, numbering 630 residents of an 1814 census population of 3,527 (4,229 in 1820), was $1.3 million.[41] This figure is not easily commensurable with modern-day values, but it is substantial and suggests that there had been an explosion of wealth throughout the eighteenth century; excluding the Revolutionary period when the town was occupied by British forces for several years inducing many to evacuate to Connecticut. Economic growth resumed at the beginning of the nineteenth century.

Of these 630 heads of households, the real and personal estate of 76 residents of the town was assessed at an average value of $5,000 or more. To get a sense of the magnitude of this figure in current values a multiplier of twenty would not be an overestimation. There is much that can be said about the membership of this list. All of Southampton's leading families were represented on it: Cooks, Coopers, Corwiths, Fosters, Halseys, Hedges, Herricks, Howells, Jessups, Piersons, Posts, Rogers's, Roses, Sandfords, Sayres, Toppings, Whites, Woodruffs—family names that extended back to the founding of the town or to later in the seventeenth century. All were proprietors, and eight of them were members of a corporate body newly created by the state legislature in 1818 known as the Trustees of the Proprietors of the Common and Undivided Lands, Marshes and Mill Streams of Southampton, hereafter referred to as the proprietor trustees or trustees of the proprietors.[42] They are to be distinguished from the town trustees, one of two governing bodies of the town since the last years of the seventeenth century. The town trustees were created by the English colonial authority together with the beginnings of an administrative town board in 1686. The 1818 legislation allowed for twelve such proprietor trustees, the same number as made up the committee of town trustees. More of the proprietors' organization and the circumstances that led up to its formation are discussed later, but for the moment it is enough to say that it represented the established land-owning interests in the town. In 1818, the leading taxpayers then were all substantial proprietors.

Just how substantial this was is indicated by the extensiveness of family networks. Of those 630 taxpayers, 395 as family heads were connected to thirty-four families in the town. These thirty-four families might be considered as influential clans although, in the absence of primogeniture, this did not translate into the development of great, consolidated estates or necessarily into a commonality of family interest. For instance, the Halsey clan, which four decades later in 1862 numbered forty-two farm families spread throughout the town, collectively owned nearly 3,300 acres but not one of those nuclear families owned more than 250 acres and most owned less than 100 acres. But out of Southampton's almost four hundred leading families, it is not surprising that fully half of them were proprietors who owned both land in the divisions and commonage rights that the general run of inhabitants lacked.

In 1819, according to the proprietor trustee land records, there were 238 proprietors with rights in one or more of the three different town purchases of land—that of the town itself in 1640 and the Quogue and Topping's purchases in 1666—whereas 179 of these proprietors were numbered among the town's four hundred families.[43] To put it another way, thirty-four clans among their individual member household heads collectively owned two-thirds of the town's tax-assessable land and controlled 80 percent of the proprietor votes. Seventeen family networks of ten or more households totaling 287 households, listed between them 122 of the total number of 238 proprietors or almost exactly half of them.

These numbers suggest a heavy and long-standing concentration of land in the hands of an extremely small number of inhabitants most if not all of whom had roots in the town's seventeenth-century beginnings.

Of course, this did not mean that the general run of inhabitants owned no land. Of those 630 household heads assessed taxes in 1818, approximately 550 possessed some real estate. The land system had become sufficiently flexible by the beginning of the nineteenth century to ensure that most men and their spouses owned some land, however small the parcel and most often to be found in a fraction of a lot, even if they owned no shares in the three original town purchases. As noted earlier, almost all the common land in the three purchases had been divided by 1782. This fact alone inevitably diminished the value of commonage rights as there was little common land remaining for traditional uses (pasturing, etc.) and which, by the same token, rendered those rights superfluous in obtaining any newly divided land since, obviously, there was none to be had. The one remaining tract of undivided land in the town was the Shinnecock Hills. However, this had been under lease to the Shinnecock Indians since 1703 and technically could not be divided. That lease was abrogated in 1859—in, it must be said, dubious circumstances as are discussed in a later chapter—and the Hills, although never laid out as a division, were sold at auction in 1861 to a small but important group of proprietors.

In practice, the essential collapse of the commonage system in the nineteenth century—which really meant the demise of the seventeenth- and eighteenth-century land system—meant that anyone, whether a proprietor or not, could buy land from those who owned lots in the existing divisions. All that mattered was the price. The requirement that anyone showing an interest in purchasing real estate in the town must show some proof of connection to the original purchase of the town by ownership of some part or fraction of a share was tacitly dropped in the late eighteenth century. It was effectively an anachronism. Even so, this barely affected the distribution of land in the town. Additionally, the trustees of the proprietors routinely sold temporary or seasonal rights in commonage each year at public auction throughout the nineteenth century. Anyone could lease such rights. For example, rights to cut the common grasses in the proprietors' undivided sedge meadows, or rights to collect seaweed or other drift material on the town's beaches that were long claimed to be proprietor land or—prior to the 1818 legislation incorporating the proprietors—rights to harvest oysters or other shellfish in the town's bays all were regularly advertised and sold at the post office. All profits from the sales of these rights accrued to the accounts of the proprietors and not to the town.

The only other residue of common land belonging to the proprietors consisted of highways that over time had been cut through the divisions as they were laid out and reserved to the proprietors, that is, both to the owners of lots within those divisions and to the proprietors in general. They were not then town or public roads although the general public was not excluded from traveling on them, in fact had the right to do so. The remnant of that proprietor ownership today is to be found in the few remaining town trustee roads on the South Beach and in the northeast section of the town near Sag Harbor.

The town trustees were a corporate body established by the colonial authority in

New York in the late seventeenth century under a patent from the governor, then Thomas Dongan. They were annually elected by the town's freeholders and had full jurisdiction over the town's internal affairs as these related to the administration of the lands and the waters within its territory. After the patent, and as the town grew in size and complexity in the eighteenth century, a separate administrative system emerged overseen by an elected town supervisor, town clerk, justices, and a variety of municipal committees and officials responsible for such matters as taxes, roads, schools, the poor of the town, and the general maintenance of order. The patent had provided for this system of government and made officials directly responsible to the colony. It should be emphasized that although this administrative apparatus developed quite slowly, and did not supplant the town trustees as a powerful body disposing over the town's resource base, eventually in the nineteenth century it became the primary focus of political power and electoral competition within the town.

The town trustees then confined their attention to the management of the lands and the waters. They had their own clerk, formerly the town clerk, but now simply clerk to the trustees. The town clerk had become a separate elected office with new and different duties. This political shift did not mean that the town trustees lost any of their formidable patent powers as they continued to manage the town's physical resources through a system of licenses, fees, leases, fines, and sales of what was left of the town's common lands. But well before 1800 they no longer influenced the general affairs of the town. These were squarely in the hands of the supervisor, his second-in-command, the clerk, and what was effectively becoming a town board. One might say that the patent had in effect erected a two-tier governmental structure: magistrates, constables, supervisors, clerks, and assessors on the one hand and town trustees on the other.

A further change in the fortunes of the town trustees occurred in the first two decades of the nineteenth century. Since the beginning of the town, political activity—whether in relation to the trustees or administrative officials—had been monopolized by the founding families (the original purchasers), their descendants, and others who had bought into the town in the early years after settlement. This arrangement had been effectively institutionalized by the two successive colonial patents issued to the town, the first by Governor Edmund Andros in 1676 and the second by Governor Dongan a decade later. The operative patent was in fact Dongan's since it subsumed and enlarged on the Andros patent. It was Dongan who set up the town trusteeship system of twelve annually elected trustees.

It is of no surprise to learn that the first town trustees in 1686 were composed of men recognized and named by Thomas Dongan as the principal representatives of the town he had dealings with in respect to the delivery of the patent. They were all signatories to the patent and were all, obviously enough, proprietors. Although nothing in the patent prevented other inhabitants who were not proprietors from being elected to the trustees, for more than a century afterward none were. Thus, throughout the eighteenth century, the administration of the town's land and water resources and any profits to be gained from them was in the hands of a committee made up exclusively of proprietors. They also were elected by proprietors or, to put it another way, by the body of freeholders that in 1686 and through the first part of the eighteenth century comprised the majority of the town's inhabitants. The town trustees, legally charged with managing proprietor-owned resources—the common lands and all the products of the town's waters except the surface fishery—then worked solely for the benefit of the owners of these resources. All the profits went into the proprietors' treasury, dividends from which were distributed from time to time. For its administrative expenses and any tribute demanded by the colonial government in New York the town relied on local taxation or rates.

To be fair, the proprietors had substantial expenses of their own in respect to the management, division, surveillance, and upkeep of the lands and waters under their control, expenses that contributed to the overall well-being of the town as a whole. Chief among them were the regulation of livestock. There were, for example, pounders, fence viewers, shepherds, and herdsmen to pay. Surveyors charged with laying out the divisions of land were required to be reimbursed for their labors. The waters had to be watched to keep out poachers whether they were local or, worse, from out of town. Ponds, creeks, bridges, and millstreams required maintenance, while the ocean beach posed its own special problems. Opening and closing breaches or inlets, or seapooses as they were called referring to the swift currents between bay and ocean, had to be controlled and needed heavy labor. The responsibilities of the proprietors were manifold and were mostly beneficial for the town. They also as individuals contributed disproportionately to the town's taxation needs as they owned in varying individual amounts the land that had been divided among them for their benefit, land being the primary source of taxation.

Still, it was no wonder that in the early years of the nineteenth century some questions began to arise among the general inhabitants about this extraordinary monopoly and, expenses aside, the role of the trustees in extracting as much profit from it as they could. There were then, as said, no more than 250 proprietors owning rights in common in all three town purchases. In contrast, the population of the town in 1810 when these issues began to be aired was slightly under four thousand. Matters came to a head in 1815 when several inhabitants who were not proprietors managed to get themselves elected to the town trustees, the managing body of the proprietors since 1686. Two years later, committees representing the interests of the town on the one hand and the proprietors on the other came to an agreement that the interests of the proprietors would in future be met solely through their continued management of the common lands, while the waters of the town and their products would come strictly under the jurisdiction of the town and be managed by the town trustees on behalf of all the town's inhabitants. It was a simple, logical, and lucrative solution (since the waters were more productive of revenue—although not of taxes—than the diminishing common lands) to the dilemma of a town that had grown in size for more than a century without any corresponding adjustment of the social and economic structure to reflect the large growth in population of inhabitants who were not proprietors.

A petition went to the state legislature in Albany in 1818 requesting this separation of the lands and waters and their administration with the result that appropriate legislation was quickly enacted. The legislation also contained a provision for the incorporation of proprietor trustees to be charged with managing the common and undivided lands as well as the marshes and mill streams in the town.[44] The effect of this legislation was to break the proprietors' century-long domination of the town trustees and sharply reduce their control over the town's resources. It was an important victory for the town, although it did not prevent the trustees of the proprietors from attempting to reassert their rights in the waters on several later occasions. In 1882, as briefly mentioned earlier, the proprietors—in what was really a rather dazzling move—sold off the lands under the waters of the town to various outside parties. These submerged lands, their lawyers assumed, were common and undivided land. The courts, however, after several years of litigation, did not think so.

Yet this political victory for the town at large in 1818, while redistributing resources in its favor, did not and could not affect the pattern of land ownership that had developed over two centuries. The proprietors were still proprietors and controlled the lion's share of the real estate. There was little public land (including the beaches and shorefronts claimed by the proprietors) and few public spaces dedicated by long usage to particular purposes such as cemeteries, schools, or parade grounds. The public could go on the town waters without hindrance but were barred from taking most of their products without a license from the town trustees. To some degree, the proprietors were put on the defensive by the 1818 legislation, and the town's inhabitants generally emboldened by it, but it did not materially affect power relationships in the town except briefly in the 1820s and early 1830s. In the first flush of victory, the new town trustees, now free of proprietor control, acted vigorously in defending the town's rights to the products of the waters, effectively managed access to the bays and ponds, regulated what could be taken from them and when, and added to the town's accounts through an effective system of fees, fines, and leases.

Thereafter, the trustees fell into a slumberous routine, awakened only once in the 1860s when the proprietor trustees laid claim to the seaweed washed up on the shores of the bays surrounding the Shinnecock Hills. In the ensuing court action the defendants, two local men who the proprietors alleged had illegally removed seaweed from the beach on Shinnecock Bay and demanded recompense from them, lost the case despite the assistance of the town trustees and some not inconsiderable financial support provided them by the town. It was not a reprise of 1818 but it was widely felt that it was yet again a matter of town versus proprietors. All of this may seem extraneous to the main story, even archaic, from the standpoint of a new community erupting almost full-blown into existence—and with alien suddenness—within the time-honored interstices of Southampton life. But this was not to be the case. Whether the dealings of the summer colony concerned land purchases, the beaches, the bays, or a variety of other seemingly innocuous questions, its members found themselves enmeshed in the consequences of matters done or left undone between town and proprietors over not merely decades but centuries.

III: SOCIAL CLASS AND POLITICS IN THE 1870S

In the 1870s, the town several times elected men to the town trustees board who had close ties to the proprietors. Among them was William Pelletreau who served on both the town trustees and the proprietor trustees from 1872 to 1882. This suggests perhaps no immediate conflict of interest but does indicate that the town trustees had lost some of their radical political luster in the intervening years since 1818. Pelletreau himself was a staunch supporter of proprietor rights and forthrightly said so. It was not until 1882, however, when the proprietor trustees endeavored to sell off the lands under the waters of the bays and ponds of the town, that the town woke up to the fact that the proprietors were still a vigorously active and acquisitive body and threw out the town trustees at the next annual election for failing to prevent the sale. Pelletreau, as a proprietor trustee, had supported the proprietors' claim to own the bay bottoms and perhaps more than most deserved to lose his seat on the town trustees for failing in his responsibilities (as was thought by many at the time) to the commonalty of the town, the general run of inhabitants. Later, Pelletreau also resigned his proprietor trusteeship and expressed reservations—although historical and not contemporaneous reservations—about some of the past activities of the proprietors. Still, when what came to be called the Mecox Bay case came to trial—a trial in which the town trustees with wide support from the town had taken on an outside oyster company (the brainchild of a New York lawyer) in a suit of ejectment for its purchase from the proprietors of the Mecox Bay bottom—he apparently was not constrained from testifying for the defense. Ipso facto his testimony could be nothing but faithful to the interests of the proprietors.

As for the proprietors, although they had drawn in their horns in the aftermath of 1818, they continued to exert major political influence in the town's general affairs. Throughout the nineteenth century, they were dominated by four families: the Roses of North Sea and Bridgehampton, the Fosters, the Posts, and (after 1860) the Scotts, or, more precisely, Lewis Scott, again of North Sea and the wealthiest landowner and the largest tax payer in Southampton. All four had their roots in the 1650s or earlier. Roses, Fosters, and Posts had early established themselves as important families whose members were constantly in one public office or another, whereas Lewis Scott was a descendant of one of the most intriguing and disreputable figures in early colonial history, Colonel John Scott, a speculator and shape shifter of almost heroic proportions.[45] Lewis Scott never held public office, never mind his extraordinary ancestor who was much too busy making deals for such mundane duties, but he was a dominating figure on the proprietor trustees from 1860 to 1888 when he passed the torch to his son. Between them by 1870, the Roses, Fosters, Posts, and Scotts controlled about six thousand acres of the tax-assessable lands of the town or not quite 15 percent.

The Roses had been the key to the effectiveness and continuity of the proprietors since the beginning of the 1800s. Abraham Rose, a Revolutionary War general, had negotiated the separation of the interests of the proprietors from those of the town (the lands and the waters) in 1818 and became the first president of the newly created proprietor trustees. Other Roses followed him in that office and there were never less than three Roses on the trustee committee for the remainder of the century. But the Roses were also, like the Fosters and the Posts, routinely elected to town offices throughout the same period, whether as supervisor, town clerk, or justice of the peace. It attested to the continued power and prestige of these families at a time when the proprietors in general were increasingly held in low repute, and the activities of their trustees viewed with suspicion. When the seaweed controversy erupted in the 1860s, for example—a struggle between the town and the proprietors for control of this valuable by-product of the seas—Edwin Rose was both town supervisor and president of the proprietor trustees. It was perhaps a personal victory for him that he managed to remain above the fray and emerged with his reputation intact.

Among the social groups in Southampton in the nineteenth century there was first and foremost, as we have seen, an elite of landed proprietors and farmers, long dominated by a few families who possessed substantial political influence. But land was not the only source of wealth and influence. There were merchants, lawyers, real estate and insurance agents, brokers, retailers—a post-Civil War middle class—who did well in the rising economy of the 1860s and survived the depression of the 1870s without much difficulty. Most were scions of the old families of Southampton (e.g., the Hildreths who began their department store on Main Street as early as 1843 or the Corwiths who built a pharmacy business), but there were also newcomers settling in the town in the mid-nineteenth century and drawn to the area by its commercial opportunities. Sag Harbor was a magnet for some. The French brothers, Huguenots from New England, invested in whaling in the 1850s, made money in California and Hawaii, and established themselves as merchants and proprietors of a flour mill after the Civil War. Lawyers were attracted by Sag Harbor. Henry Hedges of an old Bridgehampton family and its Easthampton branch set up a practice there as did out-of-town lawyers like Everett Carpenter from Rhode Island, Thomas Bisgood of England, and George Whitaker. All four were to be central figures in events described in this book. Other newcomers included Joseph Fahys, born in France in 1832, emigrating with his mother in 1848, and eventually apprenticing himself to a watch case manufacturer in New Jersey. In 1881, with two successful businesses behind him, one in New Jersey and one in Brooklyn, he established his own factory in the Harbor. He had married a local girl, one of the Hommedieus, an old Sag Harbor family with Huguenot roots. Fahys was emblematic of a small but influential manufacturing class that had begun to provide factory jobs.

Another such Sag Harbor family was the Sleights, a seventeenth-century family with roots in the Dutch aristocracy of the Hudson Valley that was distantly connected by marriage with the Derings and Sylvesters of Shelter Island, the two earliest and largest landowners on the island. Brinley Dering Sleight was born in Sag Harbor, his grandfather having brought the family there in the early 1800s. In 1859, freshly graduated from Yale College, he purchased the Sag Harbor *Corrector*, then Southampton's only newspaper. The *Corrector* had been established in 1822 by Howard W. Hunt, an out-of-towner from Boston. When Hunt died in 1857, Sleight bought out his son, John Howard Hunt, and turned it into an organ of the Democratic Party. Meanwhile Hunt, a Republican, established a rival paper in the same year, the Sag Harbor Express. Until his death in the early 1900s, Hunt was a staunch defender of the Republican Party, the party of economic growth, and continued, as the Patchogue Argus remarked in an admiring profile in 1898, the "unshaken line of Hunt editorial thought."

These were the only two newspapers in the town until the *Seaside Times* was established in Southampton village in 1881. This paper was also Republican and seems to have emerged as a response to the growing appetite for local news and news of itself by the fledgling summer colony. Its proprietor was Walter R. Burling, who produced more than a dozen newspapers on Long Island in the mid-nineteenth century, all of which were Republican and all of which were profitable. In 1880, he moved from Flushing to Southampton and ran the *Times* until his son, George H. Burling, took it over in 1890. George Burling had edited the *East Hampton Star* after his father had founded it in 1885. In 1896, the *Seaside Times* was sold to Charles A. Jaggar, a Princeton PhD and former college professor born in Southampton. Walter Burling promptly established the *Southampton Press* a year later, much to Jaggar's mortification, and established his son as editor and proprietor. Both papers survived the competition and both broadly espoused the modernizing and progressive impulses of Republicanism. The *Seaside Times* was heavily supported in the mid-1880s by the SVIA, the organization formed in 1881 by the leaders of the summer colony for the purpose of preserving and enhancing the rural charm of the village and improving both its appearance and sanitary condition.[46] Its views were always sympathetically presented in the *Times*, but in the late 1890s the association began to shift its support to the larger and possibly better managed Southampton Press.

Virtually all members of Southampton's post-war middle class were Republican and favored local economic development as, indeed, did the principal members of the old landowning elite among whose sons were to be found many of this new economic class. It is difficult to sort out local party affiliations during this period of approximately 1870 to 1890 and why in particular a minority of the established propertied classes continued to vote Democrat after the Civil War. The northern Democrats had been wracked by the war and their general ambivalence toward the plantation South, emancipation, Reconstruction, and lingering Southern sectionalism and then later tainted by their association with corrupt big-city political machines that assiduously courted the immigrant (and largely Catholic) vote. New York City Democrats, overwhelmingly identified with Tammany Hall and the rise of William Tweed and his successor, John Kelly and his "Tammany braves," were described by a contemporary observer as "a lying, perjured, rum-soaked and libidinous lot."[47] This did little to improve the reputation of the party in the provinces. The national party did revive in the early 1870s, led by Samuel Tilden, a New York railroad attorney, but in comparison to the Republican Party its appeal to small town businessmen and prosperous farmers seemed limited.

Its policies were vigorously laissez-faire and opposed to government intervention in the economy and regulation of any sort. In particular, the Democrats were against protective tariffs for infant industries—a centerpiece of Republican politics—and any government subsidies or privileges for particular interests, especially to railroads and corporations connected with them. It was in favor of expanding the money supply with silver coinage (opposed by Wall Street) that would help small farmers by raising depressed prices and reducing farm debt, but this played better in the west than in the east. The party was generally for economic justice and vigorously anti-tax but a continued, although electorally necessary, entanglement with Southern elites and its equivocal attitude toward emancipation hampered its renewal. The best that could be said about the appeal of the Democrats in small towns in the northeast like Southampton is that it stood for self-help, localism, or "home rule" in the Jeffersonian sense and small government. It opposed federalism and the development of a strong, centralized national government and called for the reduction of federal revenues and functions. It favored resisting all efforts to integrate or subordinate small communities to larger structures and was in this sense for state's rights. And it particularly and strenuously opposed the expansionist plans of the Republican Party for national economic development with all that implied for the concentration of capital in monopolistic hands.

With the exception of a brief period in the 1870s when the party captured the House of Representatives and the two Cleveland administrations in 1884–1888 and 1892–1896, the Democrats were in the political wilderness for most of the post-Civil War period. Grover Cleveland's second term was a disaster for the party and sealed its reputation as backward looking and out of touch with modern realities. It remained trapped in the myth of agrarianism, localism, and the independent American farmer while refusing to come to terms with the obvious maturation and growing consolidation of industrial capitalism. William Jennings Bryan, a Nebraska populist appearing seemingly from nowhere in 1895 and the surprise presidential nominee at the party convention, ran on this myth. He also hammered away at a favorite Democratic theme, especially appealing to southern and western farmers, of free silver coinage—a device to increase the money supply and relieve farm indebtedness as well as ameliorate the effects of falling commodity prices. But for all his charisma and his justly famous "cross of gold" speech, Bryan could do little to derail the Republican juggernaut and its formidable eastern support. Despite his attacks on the injustice of the "money power" in New York and his populist appeal in the depressed farm belt, he lost the election to William McKinley and a well-organized Republican campaign that attracted the labor vote as much as it did better-off farmers. The loss ensured that the Democrats would continue to wander in the wilderness for years to come.

The Democrats were the true conservatives of the era, unable to embrace capitalism or federalism, unable to accept the fact of rising new corporate elites and the shift in economic and political power that this implied. At the same time, as the election made clear, they were poorly united in comparison to the Republicans. Their structure was vague and consisted of unlike elements: urban ethnic classes, rural poor in the North, western individualism smarting at the moneyed East, and a South clinging to its old sectionalist politics. Disunity was the "old party curse" but its general negativism toward change spelled its inevitable demise as a viable national entity in the 1890s.

If the Democrats appealed to small-town inhabitants at all in this period—and in Southampton they were considered to be a "hopeless minority"—it was to those who thought their small-scale and traditional way of life was potentially threatened by outside interests, whether government or corporate, or disliked the pace of change advocated by the modernizing and dominant Republican Party. In the 1880s in Southampton, the Democrats were to find substantial support in local politics among the poorer social classes living primarily in the western part of the town, that is, with small farmers and baymen. It was, as it always proclaimed itself to be, the party of justice, the party of the little man. The issues before them, as is discussed in a later chapter, were tailor-made for Democrats. They concerned the threatened invasion of their lands and waters by external corporate and monopolistic interests symbolized by the already much-disliked Long Island Railroad (LIRR) and its high-handed president, Austin Corbin, about whom more is discussed later.

A decade earlier in 1872, a number of like-minded citizens had joined together to form the First Democratic Association of Southampton. Its membership was noteworthy for the fact that it contained almost no well-known names from Southampton's elite. Lawyers were well represented—George Whitaker, Doyle Sweeney, and Thomas Bisgood constituted the association's leadership—but the majority of the membership was drawn from less centrally connected families from especially west of Canoe Place (e.g., the Squires, Pennys, Carters, and Quinns). They had little success in annual local elections in the 1870s but were galvanized into action by the Mecox Bay scandal beginning in 1881. One man, George Gilbert White, a founding member of the association and a retired whaling captain deeply respected by all, led the charge against the town trustees—who had sat on their hands while the trustees of the proprietors sold the bay bottoms out from under the town—and orchestrated an attack on Republican interests that were in favor of developing the bays and supported townwide economic modernization in general. For much of the next two decades the town trustees under White's leadership were controlled by the local Democratic Party organization. At the same time, the town's administrative offices remained safely in the hands of the Republicans where they had reposed since shortly before the Civil War.

The Republicans had organized in Southampton immediately after the national party was formed from the exhausted and embattled remnants of the Whigs in 1855, a casualty of the growing furor over slavery and Southern sectionalism and the increasingly beleaguered situation of New York merchants whose wealth was dependent on plantation production—cotton predominantly but also sugar and rice—in the South. The new party represented a fresh start in American politics and was well received throughout the northern and midwestern states. It had particular appeal among small-town farming and business interests for its emphasis on prosperity—its slogan was free land, free soil, free labor—and the projected role of government in promoting economic growth, the expansion of trade through tariff protection and the underwriting or support of infrastructure projects such as canals and railroads.[48] In towns like Southampton after the Civil War it was widely perceived as the party of progress, patriotism, and also, not unimportantly, of morality. The Democrats often were effectively portrayed as the party of the saloonkeeper, ballot-box stuffer, and ethnic immigrants. This may have played well in Southampton where temperance was a perennial issue and the local laboring classes were seen as too often frequenting taverns in Sag Harbor. This issue was to divide the town along party lines in the 1886 local government elections when what the Republicans described as "the rum element" (i.e., the Democrats) won a significant vote to continue the licensed sale of alcohol and at the same time succeeded in dislodging the long-serving Republican town clerk, Edward H. Foster, who had sided with the temperance forces.

Overall, the Republican Party was able to dominate town government in the last third of the nineteenth century. Judge Henry Hedges, the Sag Harbor lawyer and historian of Easthampton, as well as a descendant of the first settlers, was the principal figure in organizing the party at the county level in 1856. He also helped found Southampton's first bank—the Sag Harbor Savings Bank—and was elected its first president in 1869. The party had immediate and strong appeal among progressive forces in Southampton anxious to see that this large township would participate in post-Civil War economic development. These forces included most elements of the old landed oligarchy but most particularly the professional and business class symbolized by men like William Pelletreau who, at the same time, came from old stock in the town. Others with deep roots in the old town elite and embraced modernization were Edward Foster, the town clerk since Pelletreau had relinquished that position in 1870, and James Pierson, the modest and judicious town supervisor from 1881 to 1902. Pelletreau was involved in real estate and an acknowledged expert in title searches while Foster, a former school teacher, had gone into insurance and brokerage, ideal professions to meet the requirements of economic development projects. They were part of the Republican wave that, as H. Wayne Morgan put it, "bore up so many young men in the 1850s."[49]

The party also was supported by relative newcomers such as Everett Carpenter, again a Sag Harbor lawyer and the attorney who defended the oyster company in its claims to the bottom of Mecox Bay; Steven B. French, the Sag Harbor merchant, also with interests in the oyster company and a powerful figure in the party; and Joseph Fahys who ushered Sag Harbor into the industrial age in 1881 with his watch case company. Besides these influential figures, the owners of all the newspapers on the East End with the exception of Brinley Sleight and his Democrat Sag Harbor Corrector, espoused the progressive Republican cause. All, and this included Sleight, got behind the lobbying effort in 1868 to bring in the Sag Harbor branch railroad from Manorville through Southampton and Bridgehampton to the Harbor, and all wanted the Shinnecock Canal in the 1880s. Similarly, all of them treated the development of the summer colony in Southampton as an economic boon to the area—particularly, although not exclusively, in land values. It represented progress of the sort that the Republican Party everywhere supported.

Finally, the Republican appeal after 1865 reflected its victory in the war. It was the party of the Union and the party of patriotism. Small towns such as Southampton had made their particular sacrifices in men, treasure, and economic difficulty and now anticipated that they would go forward on a new path of economic growth and prosperity. The Republicans seemed to be saying that they would take the country in a new direction, away from factionalism and the vicissitudes of laissez-faire, and toward a new and apparently well-structured future benefiting industry, transportation, and agriculture. Southampton's citizens voted overwhelmingly in favor of Republicans in local, state, and national elections for the next thirty years.

There were in Southampton as there were everywhere else in small towns excluded groups. Small farmers had never had much of a say in town affairs before the 1880s and, if they shared collective interests at all in the early part of the century, were never able to articulate them effectively. In 1818, they had watched the struggle over the lands and the waters between proprietors and town from the sidelines, perceiving it as an intramural struggle within the elite, and while benefiting from the outcome had little or no influence over it. It was not until 1882 that they found a political voice after they realized that the proprietor trustees had sold off a significant part of their livelihood—the bays. The Mecox Bay affair was the catalyst for this new political consciousness. It was remarkable that between 1882 and 1890 the numbers of those voting in annual town elections steadily climbed swelled by the political engagement of this marginal class. The farmers and baymen coalesced around the one issue that threatened their economic position and became instrumental in forcing the town, even if only indirectly, to confront the proprietors. In winning the Mecox Bay case against the oyster company, the town trustees, now dominated by Democrats and put into office by an emergent small farming constituency, ushered in a period of populist politics in Southampton. It was a considerable shock to the Republicans who had enjoyed a long and profitable dominance in town government and were not used to large voter turnouts. It by no means ended that domination, but the Democrats had served notice that they were still the party of the small man as well as against monopoly and that Mecox, the issue of the day, had captured everyone's attention. It was a watershed period for local democracy in the town, the beginning of wider electoral representation. It was also, but just barely, marked by the beginning of a new wave of European immigration into the area. Poles, Ukrainians, Italians, and Irish moved into the North and South Forks in search of farm work and eventually farm property. But it was some years before they would become a factor in local politics, in fact not until the twentieth century.

There were two other groups in Southampton that were socially and economically marginalized and ignored politically: the Shinnecock Indians and African Americans. The Shinnecock had lost what title they could claim to their ancestral lands in the Shinnecock Hills as a result of state legislation two decades earlier in 1859 and had since resided exclusively in approximately eight hundred acres in Shinnecock Neck. Estimates of the land area in the Neck vary between seven and eight hundred acres but what eventually came to be known as the Shinnecock Reservation—never a federal reservation and only recognized by the state as a reservation by default as a result of its own legislation—had never been accurately surveyed. The Shinnecocks now owned the Neck in fee in exchange for giving up the 3,500 acres of the Hills proper. This decisive segregation of Shinnecock lands had been obtained by the proprietors from the state legislature. The subsequent legislation in its effect awarded the Hills to the proprietors, perhaps in the mistaken belief that the proprietor trustees represented the town, to do with them as they wished.[50] A suit in protest of this legislation was initiated by three members of the tribe later in 1859. The suit, which began as an attempt to overturn the legislation and reclaim the whole of the Hills, changed direction and argued rather more pragmatically for a more equitable distribution of the lands as between the proprietors and the Shinnecock Indians. Nothing, however, became of it and the case never came to trial.

In the 1870s, there were perhaps no more than 150 to 170 men, women, and children calling themselves Shinnecock and living in Shinnecock Neck or nearby. This was a figure little different from the census of 1698 nearly two centuries earlier when 152 Shinnecock Indians were listed. Before English settlement in 1640, there may have been as many as five times that number living in scattered villages between Quogue on the west and Wainscott at the town line with Easthampton but any figure is inevitably speculative.[51] This was the rough extent of Shinnecock lands. It corresponded with the territory they agreed to give up to the settlers, or agreed that the settlers might inhabit and cultivate, in several deeds beginning in December 1640 and culminating in confirmation agreements in 1687 and 1703 attesting to all previous real estate transactions. After 1703 and until 1859, the Shinnecock lived in villages at Canoe Place, Sebonac, Cold Spring, and Shinnecock Neck and leased the Shinnecock Hills (including the Neck) from the town at a nominal rent of one ear of corn a year for a period of one thousand years. The 1859 legislation had agreed to the abrogation of this lease, on petition from the trustees of the proprietors (not the trustees of the town) and from several members of the Shinnecock that, later, other tribal members disavowed.

The Shinnecock were a forgotten group in the last years of the nineteenth century more or less pushed aside by the town and the proprietors (who had effectively confined them in Shinnecock Neck), and in the context of the changing economic circumstances of the village as the summer invasion began. They survived as subsistence farmers, in service positions in the village and on the developing estates of the new summer visitors, or in leasing their land to local farmers (a practice institutionalized as far back as the 1790s). They also were further struck by an unanticipated and dreadful blow of fate. A dozen of their young men perished in a shipwreck while attempting a rescue of the crew and the ship's cargo off Southampton's beach. The ship was the Circassian that had foundered a few hundred yards offshore in the winter of 1876.[52] Few realized at the time what a colossal blow this would mean for the immediate future of the tribe. The loss of twelve men, however tragic the circumstances, should not have had such an adverse and disproportionate impact. But it did. If the Shinnecock population as a whole was no more than 150 to 170, the able-bodied adult male population would have numbered somewhere between thirty-five and fifty, women, children, and the elderly accounting for the remainder with a demographic emphasis on relatively young children given the typically large families of the time. The loss of twelve young men—possibly as many as 25 percent of active adult males in the tribe—would be bound to have an immediate and profound psychological impact on the circumstances of what was already a demoralized group.

It is sometimes suggested that the Circassian disaster contributed to, or accelerated, the intermarriage between the Shinnecock and African Americans who had resided in Southampton either as slaves or free men since the end of the seventeenth century. There is no evidence that this was the case, but it certainly is true that a pattern of intermarriage between the two groups began to emerge in the early years of the eighteenth century. As generally excluded or marginal groups, Indians and African Americans shared a good deal in common. There is some evidence to suggest that there were free blacks in seventeenth century Southampton (the most usually cited case is that of Pieter Negro who was granted three acres by the town court in 1659), but the overwhelming experience of most until the early 1800s was as slaves or indentured servants. In like fashion, Shinnecocks were often bound out to the households of wealthy farmers in the eighteenth century, although the numbers were comparatively small and their servitude generally, if not always, short. There were reported instances where it was for life.[53]

Second, after the 1780s free blacks and Indians were heavily represented in the whale fishery, then and well into the nineteenth century about the only form of non-farm and nonhousehold employment locally available to males. Linda Day estimates that after New York's gradual emancipation legislation of 1799 as many as three thousand African Americans on Long Island signed articles with whaling vessels, whereas Shinnecock, Montaukett, and other Indian groups continued to participate regularly in the industry as they had since the late seventeenth century.[54] Most of them shipped out of Sag Harbor. It is not unreasonable to think that a common seagoing heritage would have developed among them and their families, and that this would create and cement bonds between them.

A third and perhaps more significant factor in cementing ties between the two groups was the emergence of the underground railroad from the South. A branch or spur of it in the Northeast in the 1840s extended from Brooklyn to Sag Harbor. Two free black communities already existed in the area by that date: Freetown in the Springs section of Easthampton and the Eastville section of Sag Harbor. Freetown was established earlier in the 1800s by freed slaves from Gardiner's Island. They were later joined by remnants of the Montaukett Indians who were reluctantly leaving their Montauk lands out of economic necessity. The Montaukett had been confined by Easthampton proprietors to a small area of land near Montauk Point known as the Indian Field after successive Easthampton purchases covering the whole of Montauk between 1661 and 1687. What few of them remained were forced out by development interests in the 1880s and, under duress, retreated to Freetown.

Some of the Montaukett had previously left earlier in the century for Eastville and other parts of Long Island, as well as to upstate New York and Connecticut. In Eastville, St. David's African Methodist Episcopal Church, established in 1840, provided a haven for many escaped slaves before the Civil War. Just as significantly, Indian communities sheltered many from recapture after the 1850 passing of the Fugitive Slave Act. The Poospatuck reservation of the Unkechaug Indians in Mastic was said to have received many such escapees. Whether the Shinnecock took in escaped slaves at this time is not known. But in Eastville and Freetown particularly, both black and Montaukett lived side by side in reciprocal relations.

These several factors and shared experiences of both groups over a long period combined to create a strong sense of kinship between Indians and African Americans. It is important to recall, however, that the pattern of intermarriage between the two began well before the onset of emancipation in New York beginning in 1799. It had its roots in the colonial period. In 1800, 18 percent of Suffolk County households kept slaves or manumitted workers. Approximately the same percentage probably held true for Southampton. In respect to this, the town records show increasing numbers of manumissions in the following twenty years prior to the state's final abolition of slavery in 1827. The 1840 federal census gives a total of 529 "free colored persons" in Southampton, a surprisingly large number but it probably included the Shinnecock. Prior to this, between 1809 and 1824 there were upwards of fifty reported manumissions of slaves in Southampton households.[55] As African Americans gained their freedom during this period it is fairly certain that the incidence of intermarriage also increased. The common historical experience of both groups, coupled with their low social status in the white community and their comparatively small size, would have encouraged or even necessitated it. Other less tangible factors in traditional culture and religion where syncretism and polytheism played a central role in belief also may have contributed to a sense of commonality. Day thinks that the general recognition of shared experience and the growing prevalence of intermarriage created a genuine conception of "dual identity" for members of both communities as the boundaries between them partially dissolved.[56] How true this may have been is not easy to determine.

By the 1870s, the Civil War done with and Indians everywhere confronting the loss of tribal lands to white encroachment, little was to be heard in Southampton from either Indian or African American. The Shinnecock attempted to revive their suit for the return of the Hills in 1885 but, for want of funds, the effort failed. Apart from mounting a separate action in 1890 in reference to an alleged trespass on their Westwoods lands on Peconic Bay (a suit they won), the Shinnecock as a community receded from public view and they or their interests were seldom cited in the local newspapers. Historians of Southampton such as Howell and Pelletreau referred to them with what can at best be described as condescension unmixed with affection, albeit with a peon to the redoubtable antiquity of "the redman" and his perspicacity and farsightedness in bowing to fate and giving up his lands to the English. Both writers, in the face of persistent and considerable evidence to the contrary, emphasized the historically amiable and accommodating relations between the two communities as did other later local historians, notably the sisters Abigail Fithian Halsey and Lizbeth Halsey White in the 1920s and 1930s. This interpretation of the past persists into the present. All communities have myths of their beginnings, their relations with others who they may have displaced, and their subsequent history. This, the English version, is one of them. The Shinnecock Indians have another.

Even further removed from the public eye were those few African Americans who had not intermarried with the Shinnecock and had come from the South, particularly the Carolinas and Virginia. However, with some exceptions this migration had largely taken place during and after World War II. All had come as farm laborers and were housed in migrant labor camps in generally appalling conditions. They had begun to gather in small neighborhoods within the town such as Hillcrest on the outskirts of Southampton village or in Flanders, Bridgehampton, and Sag Harbor but were little noticed. But in the nineteenth century there were few such free blacks in Southampton who had not already intermarried with the Shinnecock.[57] Neither Indian nor black—unlike the other marginal class discussed previously, the baymen—could be said to be a significant factor in political or economic life in Southampton in the waning years of the nineteenth century.

These two struggling communities aside, neither of which was admitted into the political life of the town or could affect it in any way, Southampton in the late nineteenth century was quite clearly a society marked by a high degree of inequality. Early Puritan towns two hundred years before had accepted with equanimity the reality of economic and social differentiation in their midst and understood it as simply a providential ordering of individuals and social relations. That God had never intended that men should all occupy the same social and economic status and that some should achieve material advantage or "competency," as it was then called, and others not was interpreted as a sign either of spiritual grace or regeneracy or its lack. Those who were perceived as not having toiled or not having toiled enough, and thus not the recipients of just economic rewards, were easily seen as unregenerate and as least likely to enter into or be capable of entering into a church covenant of grace or a political covenant offering them equal standing in the community. Their low status in fact precluded most of them from doing so. Puritans from the beginning were comfortable with the facts of economic stratification and were able to provide a religious explanation and justification of them, in effect a theodicy of poverty and riches. At the same time, towns in the seventeenth century were generally peopled by "middling" social classes (precisely the sort of people who had left England in the Great Migration in the 1630s) with no great extremes of wealth or poverty. There was assumed a rough equality where all men, excluding servants (at least for the duration of their service), possessed some land—the principal capital of the period and for most towns for the next two centuries—and sought to make it productive. If some men gained more than others without any inordinate display of their newly acquired wealth, it was usually perceived to be the result of the godly virtues of intelligence, thrift, and industry at work in the fields of the Lord.

No one in the late seventeenth century could have foreseen that in less than two hundred years Southampton would have become a society with marked class and status divisions that manifested themselves in periods of dissension and sharp political disagreement. The first sign of this was the conflict between the town's inhabitants and the proprietors between 1815 and 1818. The second coincided with the arrival of the first summer colonists and principally involved the sale of the bay bottoms and the beginnings of political action by Southampton's economically weakest social classes. It also involved a sale of the Shinnecock Hills to agents of a resort development company in 1881 but this, perhaps not so surprisingly, had less of an impact on the community as a whole than the issue of the lands under water. The Hills were understood by most people in Southampton to be private lands, once the undivided lands belonging to the proprietors and, after 1703, under lease to the Shinnecock Indians, but lands that could be disposed of by whoever were the current owners now they were free of Indian encumbrance.

It was into this generally mixed social and economic environment marked by much dissatisfaction that Southampton's newest settlers inserted themselves at the end of the 1870s; or, more accurately, situated themselves in but not quite of the confines of the village at a remove from its residential core and at the edge of the beach and the uninhabited southern extremity of Town Pond. They were, as it quickly became clear, full of plans—for the village if not for the town as a whole—but they were plans that bore no relation to the interests and difficulties of many of the inhabitants. Oblivious to these, and there is no reason why they should have been aware of them, the advance guard of what was to become within five years a major force in the affairs of the village decided that the essential issues confronting Southampton were its hygiene, the purity of its waters, and the refinement and development of its more attractive rural features in combination with the elimination of those that were not.

It seemed, on the face of it, a modest agenda but it was to have vast consequences for the habitual life of the village. Moreover, the suppositions underlying it bespoke an act of possession, a sense even of rightful ownership, a desire bred of responsible upper-class citizenship to impose on Southampton an image of itself—cleaned up, sanitized, beautified, civilized—that was eventually to surprise its inhabitants and confront them with a new reality that nothing in their collective experience could have anticipated for them.

CHAPTER 2

THE BEACH, THE LAKE, THE CHURCH AND THE IMPROVEMENT ASSOCIATION

I: SETTLING IN

Considering Southampton and the South Beach where T. Gaillard Thomas established himself in splendid isolation from the village—his house in 1877 now built—alone with the surf and an endless expanse of dunes stretching in both directions, ponds interspersed with flat meadows, occasional fences, barely a tree in sight, a muddy track around the foot of Town Pond and an insalubrious marsh at its head, here and there a few head of lowing cattle and other signs of cultivation; fishing boats pulled up on the dunes and nets spread out to dry, and his nearest neighbor an unpretentious, weather-beaten, and simply appointed bathing pavilion shut up for three-fourths of the year—one wonders why he chose such an apparently bleak and unprepossessing spot.

Perhaps it was the beach itself that attracted Thomas, a zone of seemingly unsullied, virgin foreshore entirely separate from the village one mile inland and devoid of other private dwellings. It was deserted except for a few fishing smacks and bathing huts to provide some native color and to remind him that this also was a domestic and domesticated scene, although it was otherwise essentially empty. It also might have brought to mind childhood memories of growing up on Edisto Island a few miles south of Charleston with its wild beach and sweeping vistas of the Atlantic. Perhaps he relished the memory of that solitude. Unfortunately, he left no record of such sentiments, but it is not implausible to suggest that he might have been affected by them and found on Southampton's beach a reality he had been familiar with thirty years before. Whether or not he was led to think of it, there was an imagined or apparent Crusoean aspect to Thomas's chosen situation. He was alone with the dunes and the sea, cut off from his normal experience of civilization, and removed from the hinterland of the village and its yet-to-be-understood social and political life. It was, as Jean-Didier Urbain observed in his analysis of the primordial culture of the beach, the "virginity of the site" that might have constituted its appeal, a place of discovery and possession almost free of a native presence, essentially uninhabited.[1] For a man like Thomas, wealthy, a powerful figure in his forties, used to the conveniences of modern life in New York, it must have represented a refreshing experience, whether new or reappropriated. To some degree, the relative simplicity of his initial circumstances (not, however, to last very long as shorefront real estate was quickly acquired) presaged those of other summer residents who trickled in after him between 1877 and 1880. The extent of their activities in those first few years was to build capacious summer cottages in ample and attractive surroundings, some on the shore and others (most) at a safe remove from the ocean on the banks of the lake. There was, in this early period, no thought given to create a resort and construct a social life on the model, for example, of Newport where New York's socially visible elites had begun to congregate at approximately the same time. Southampton, self-consciously or not, was to become an anti-Newport. Thomas later went on record that he had always been quite against any such development.

Not so many years before Thomas's arrival in Southampton, Newport on the cold New England coast appeared to have little to recommend it to New York's wealthy classes. Before the Civil War it had been a modest little resort on Aquidneck Island, frequented by Southerners, adjacent to a once great but now impoverished port. It sustained, May King Van Rensselaer wrote, "a feeble commerce in coals and fish" and the locals got by with gardening jobs. It was windswept, chilly, and damp and the ocean temperature seldom rose much above 60 degrees. Nor, with its dank and stony beaches, did it have much in the way of natural charm. Its summer season lasted a bare six weeks from July to September. Yet none of these drawbacks presented any deterrent to the millionaires who at the beginning of the 1880s transformed this unlikely spot into the summer center of New York's social universe and in the process created, in a status display of baroque residential construction, a series of massive monuments to the architectural excesses of the Gilded Age, enormous stone palaces, "smothered," as Henry James put it in a late novel, "in senseless architectural ornament" suggesting to him a degree of "witlessness" that he thought should have been prohibited. As the summer camp of the rich, Newport replaced Saratoga, fast becoming a gambling haunt for celebrities and politicians, and for the remainder of the century was never rivaled by other arguably more attractive venues in Bar Harbor on the Maine coast, Lenox the social capital of the Berkshires, the various Springs of Virginia thronged with Southern belles, or even the emergent Hamptons that by the 1890s had settled into a pattern of more or less rustic elegance, cottage-style, and had unobtrusively begun to mimic the manners of Newport. Of the latter resort, Mrs. Van Rensselaer remarked that the chief business was the investigation of social credentials and the "granting, or withholding, (of) social recognition."[2] Very much later this was to become true of Southampton, although with less of the cloying bad taste, so richly larded, that permeated the cultural atmosphere of Newport in the 1890s as the Gilded Age at last began to expire. Van Rensselaer sniffed that there had been "few contributions to human culture by the wealthy thousands who gather there yearly."[3]

In contrast, she thought that Southampton had been "founded during a reaction to the spendthrift atmosphere of Newport" as it began "its rapid slide down a gilded chute into crassness and vulgarity."[4] Her collaborator in *The Social Ladder*, Frederic Van de

Water, contributed a chapter on Long Island resorts in which he advanced the same view. Southampton's colonists, having little concern for wealth and waging social campaigns and having "never found it necessary to fight or buy their way into Society," Van de Water concurred that "the founders of the summer colony, repelled by the spectacular extravagances of Newport, sought a haven in (this) ancient village," finding in it a peaceful little rural retreat to repair the mind and body.[5] Gaillard Thomas would have heartily endorsed such an opinion; and had he been around in 1924, when the book was published, he might have informed Van de Water that it had from the beginning been his intention to create just such a haven from the busy world of social competition. This was an image that generations of summer cottagers sought to perfect. The sister-in-law of Henry Ford II said very much later that "we spend all day just sitting around in old shirts and wet bathing suits." The Southampton of the 1920s, however, with its ever larger estates and mansions bearing little resemblance to the airy (and probably drafty) shingled cottages of the 1880s, might have suggested to Thomas that some of the excesses of Newport had managed after all to surface in the intervening decades.

But in 1877, all such changes were in the future and could not possibly be anticipated. Dr. Thomas and his wife were alone to contemplate their almost empty beach landscape and the flat and generally unbroken vistas around them, their thirteen acres of privacy apparently assured. The lack of available amenities in what must have seemed to them the rather humdrum farming village to the north—a village sorely, as it transpired, in need of modernization and improvement—appeared to be of no immediate concern. Accordingly, the Thomases set about attracting other like-minded New Yorkers to follow them. They came fairly quickly, those either excluded from Newport or appalled by it.

The tax-assessment records are as good a guide as any to whom came first and bought a plot of land with the idea in mind of building a summer cottage, but this tells us nothing of the numbers of those who first came to board in one of the several hostelries available and others created in their own homes by local residents in the expectation of a healthy summer trade. In regard to this, 1882 is the first year in which information about those who came to board and rent was published.[6] For that season there were some thirty boarders scattered in several boarding houses located in the village, fifteen homes of Southampton residents rented out including those of families such as the Posts, Sayres, Fithians, and Halseys, and ten of the thirty summer cottages owned by those of the nascent summer colony who chose not to occupy their homes that season or who had built additional housing in order to capitalize on the demand for summer rental accommodations. Very early in the history of the summer colony this became quite a business.

Thomas had built the Dunes in 1877. He was then the only nonresident taxpayer who could be described as a summer resident. His thirteen acres were assessed at $3,500 in 1878, soon to be increased to sixty acres (much of it to the east at Old Town and Wickapogue) at a modest evaluation of $11,000 in 1882 or under $200 an acre, a little less than he had paid for it. All of it was along the beachfront. In 1878, only two other families had put down summer roots in Southampton. These were the Kilbreths and the Hoyts. James T. Kilbreth, a noted jurist and later collector of the Port of New York, purchased fourteen acres just to the north of Leon de Bost's property on South Main Street fronting Town Pond. According to Pelletreau, Kilbreth constructed a little village of his own suggesting either that he had a very large family or that he intended to rent out to friends and associates several small cottages distributed here and there on the property. Not long after, he purchased land across the lake at First Neck south of Pond Lane. His brother, John W. Kilbreth, also picked up several plots of land east of Town Pond including a large tract south of Toylesome Lane. It was very much a family affair.

The Hoyts established themselves on the opposite shore buying five acres (later increased to nine) on First Neck Lane. The land and the house they constructed on it was assessed in 1878 at $3,000, a significantly higher figure than Thomas's and a sign that prices were already beginning to rise in locations preferred by summer residents. The southwestern shore of the lake—and very soon afterward all of the western shore—quickly became the most sought after area for real estate purchases. For one thing, it was almost completely undeveloped land. It marked the beginning of the Great Plain, a division of lands dating from the late 1640s, and was largely free of buildings except for the occasional farmhouse or barn close. It had been generally used for pasture, although there were scattered planting fields. It had been lotted out to private owners from almost the beginning of settlement but it quickly became clear that farmers were more than willing to sell. In this instance, the Hoyts picked up part of two lots belonging to Henry Reeves and Augustus Halsey.[7]

For another, the east shore of the lake—South Main Street—was land that had always been used for home lots since 1648 when the town decided to relocate. It was thus fully developed with farmyards, barns, equipment, geese, swine, cattle, and all the other usual accoutrements of agricultural living. Initially, it was not perhaps to everyone's taste, but within a few years (following the leads of Kilbreth and Leon de Bost) newcomers bought many of the farmers out on both sides of South Main, tore down not a few ancient structures and built new ones. Some they did leave intact. A. J. Peabody, for example, bought the 1660 homestead of Thomas Halsey in 1886 that very much later, after a succession of summer owners that included the Dupont family, came into the possession of the Southampton Colonial Society in 1961. Another factor in those first years of summer settlement was probably some deep reluctance to sell on the part of local home owners. All around them evidence of the steady alienation of old properties to summer buyers was on the increase. Edward Foster, the former town clerk, hung on to his family's house and extensive home lot until the early 1920s when it was sold, after his death, to the newly formed Southampton chapter of the Daughters of the American Revolution, an organization whose membership however, like that of the Colonial Society, was purely local.

The Hoyts were the first to buy and build in First Neck. The house and its location, like the Thomases, was an object of local bemusement as Pelletreau wryly reported:

> Now, the bane and blessing of this world have been people who were not like other folks and the village people, with commendable but misplaced charity, supposed she [Mrs. Hoyt] was like themselves, and of course would do as they would under similar circumstances. It was generally agreed that the new house

would be placed next the lane, not wasting too much ground on a dooryard, and on the rest of the land they probably supposed that Mr. H. would engage in the laudable business of raising corn and potatoes, a vision that failed to be realized. But when they saw a pile of brick and preparations made to build at the opposite end, and overlooking the pond, they awoke from their dream. There have been many such awakenings. To people who are "like other folks" it is difficult to understand why anyone should wish, in erecting a modern house, to imitate the inconveniences that plagued our ancestors, and which they endured because they could not avoid them. The result of this effort was complete success in creating a building which some call quaintly artistic, and others a monstrosity, but it is an object of interest as the first mansion erected in that locality.[8]

In a few words Pelletreau managed to convey the extent of the cultural misunderstandings between the village and the summer residents that was already evident at the beginning of settlement. The idea of a country cottage devoted to rest and relaxation and the pursuit of leisured activities in pleasant surroundings was simply too much for the imaginings of most inhabitants. Not only was the house poorly situated, it was altogether too large and undeniably ostentatious. Farmers passing by the scene of construction on their way into the Great Plain scratched their heads and muttered something about the strange ways of the Yorkers before continuing about their business. For some reason—Pelletreau never explained it—the Hoyts were not popular among local residents.

William Hoyt was from Dutch merchant stock in Pelham, New York but never managed to make much of himself. Either bad business decisions, a declining trust fund from a merchant house facing bankruptcy, or a serious drinking problem led to financial difficulties in the 1880s. In 1885, the Hoyt's sold their Agawam estate (how else to call nine acres and this very substantial cottage known as "Windybarn") for twice what they had paid for it and removed to the Shinnecock Hills where land was extremely cheap. There, the couple built a Pasadena style arts-and-crafts house of great charm, bought the village's only and now disused gristmill on Windmill Lane, and moved it to their new property. For a while, Hoyt managed the Shinnecock Hills lands for the company that had bought them in 1881—the Long Island Improvement Company (LIIC)—and all seemed to be well. But the marriage collapsed, the money ran out, and by 1900 William Hoyt was in Puerto Rico where he eventually died in 1905 of unspecified causes.

Mrs. Hoyt was another matter. Born Janet Ralston Chase in 1847, she was the daughter of former Secretary of the Treasury and U.S. Supreme Court Justice Salmon Chase, a man who was a major power in Washington after the Civil War. It seems to be the case that she, rather than her husband, discovered Southampton in the 1870s. A brother, William Chase, had bought eighty acres in Southampton in 1876—where is uncertain but it was not on the Shinnecock Hills and it was for no more than $50 an acre—and Janet Hoyt (she married in 1871) spent one or two summers there. She was an amateur landscape painter and probably was responsible for the short-lived and much-ridiculed appellation "Silver

Lake" (a romantic rendition of the prosaic and workaday Town Pond) that momentarily upstaged "Agawam" as the preferred choice of other summer residents. Pelletreau remarks that she rather, not her husband, purchased the land at the lake, less perhaps to suggest Hoyt's declining fortunes than in deference to Mrs. Hoyt's considerable character. George Rogers Howell, the author and state librarian, was not particularly averse to some of the efforts at renaming streets and locations, but Silver Lake was too much for him. In one of his many missives to the *Seaside Times*, he thought that it should have been "choked to death at the very start."

Once on the Shinnecock Hills in 1886, Mrs. Hoyt fully came into her own if, indeed, she had not already done so. The windmill was one thing, trucked up from the village in 1888 at great expense, but when a golf club opened on the Hills in summer 1891—what became the storied Shinnecock Hills Golf Club—she made certain that the women of the colony would have their own golf course to play on. Achieving this, she successfully tutored her fifteen-year-old daughter, Beatrix, into winning three successive women's national golf championships. At the same time, she orchestrated the establishment of a summer school of art at the edge of the Hills at what came to be known as the Art Village and brought in the well-known and increasingly impressionist painter William Merritt Chase (no relation) as its director. Janet Hoyt left Southampton shortly after 1900 but later returned and built a small cottage on Peconic Bay where she occasionally summered until her death in 1925.

Summer pioneers though the Hoyts were, they had much less of an impact on the growth of the summer colony than a number of others. Among these were particularly the brothers Betts, Frederic and C. Wyllys. Between the two of them they cornered much of the real estate between the ocean, First Neck Lane, and Town Pond. Both were originally from upstate New York, graduated from Yale, and were already successful lawyers in their mid-thirties when they first came out to Southampton. Frederic Betts had the more notable career of the two. He was an authority on patent law and had spent several years as a legal advisor with Drexel, Morgan, which later became J. P. Morgan & Co in 1895, and was one of the new breed of corporate lawyers. He also was much involved with New York City Republican politics in the 1880s serving on several citizens' reform committees. Wyllys Betts—the younger of the two—died of pneumonia at age forty-two in 1887. Pelletreau remembered him as "a learned and polished gentleman," a sentiment that, as seen later, was not shared by all in the village.

Lawyers had become an important professional status group in New York by the 1870s where previously they had gained little serious attention. Now they were closely linked to the ascendant classes that controlled industrial, merchant, and finance capital and had become indispensable in facilitating the legal complexities and dealings of increasingly large corporations. Young men like the Betts brothers made their fortunes in the interstices of a modern corporate capitalism that was fast developing in the 1870s and 1880s. The late nineteenth century was, as a direct consequence, in process of becoming the age of corporate lawyers, not a few of whom found their way to Southampton. Lawyers, as Sven Beckert points out, were quickly becoming part of a new business and professional class in New York. While lacking capital of their own, they increasingly participated in the social and cultural world of the bourgeoisie, lived in the same neighborhoods and worked downtown. Half of all lawyers were listed in the Social Register, although not all members of this professional class that included physicians, professors and managers could "get in," that is, enter the social ranks of the upper bourgeoisie controlled by the Astors, Vanderbilts, and others who were the arbiters of social taste and acceptability.[9]

Another such rising star in the legal and corporate firmament was Charles L. Atterbury. For a time the Betts's had been in partnership with Atterbury, a railroad lawyer originally from Detroit and also a Yale graduate, who followed the brothers to Southampton in 1880. Atterbury was a contemporary of both brothers and probably formed an association with them at Yale. He eventually left Betts, Atterbury, and Betts to join the legal department of the Erie Railway and was subsequently appointed their legal counsel. Once in Southampton he was, with the Hoyts, among the first to buy land on the Shinnecock Hills in 1886 where he established a compound of almost thirty acres at Sugar Loaf, the highest point on the Hills, overlooking Shinnecock Bay. His son was Grosvenor Atterbury, an architect of great distinction, who was responsible for the design of the Parrish Art Museum in 1898 and several fine commercial buildings at the corner of Job's Lane and Main Street that were constructed in the mid-1920s to house the summer colony's favorite New York department stores such as Bonwit Teller, Best and Co., and Saks Fifth Avenue. He is perhaps most famously remembered for the remarkable mock-Tudor apartment house designs that still grace what was then the garden suburb of Forest Hills. Unfortunately for him, and for reasons that remain obscure, Charles Atterbury disinherited him. The Atterbury estate remains nonetheless, even if somewhat dismembered and in name only, at its original Sugar Loaf location.

Of the two brothers, Wyllys Betts perhaps left the greater mark on Southampton. To begin, with he clearly sized up the potential real estate market very astutely. By 1881 he was in possession of twenty-eight acres between the ocean and Lake Agawam east of First Neck Lane thus sitting on what was to become the most desirable and expensive property in the village. Not that he planned to sell any of it. Instead he built seven houses in various pleasant dune or lakeside locations and rented out most of them to summer visitors. One cottage was attached to a windmill imported from Good Ground (renamed Hampton Bays in the 1920s) and survives into the present. Frederic Betts, by contrast, settled for five acres (later eight) on the southwest corner of the lake and built what was arguably the most attractive and certainly the largest of the early summer cottages. It still stands today, one of the few to do so from that period. Betts bought the land from George O. Post. It was a lot that had been in the Post family since 1795. It fetched $450 an acre, a price that in 1880 was still low.

The provenance of Wyllys Betts's land is less obvious. Most of it lay immediately to the south and west of his brother's land on the lake. Twenty-three acres in the Great Plain bordering the lake and including a barn close belonged to Isaac Halsey in 1665 and had been bought from John Woodruff in the same year. It apparently remained in the Halsey family until Betts arrived on the scene and managed to purchase all of it. Additionally, he leased then subsequently bought beach land from the proprietor trustees. This was land on part of which he built one seaside house and eventually donated the other part, after buying it outright, for the establishment of an Episcopal chapel for summer residents. It initially had been leased by a small summer group, which included Betts, for this purpose. The chapel was first called Saint Andrews-by-the-Sea but its governing body changed it to Saint Andrew's Dune Church in 1884. Both brothers were among the church's first founders together with Thomas, William Hoyt, and Dr. Albert Buck, an associate of Thomas, who came to Southampton in 1878 a year before the Betts brothers and purchased four acres of land to the north of Wyllys Betts on the lake. More is to be said of the founding of this church and its significance for the summer colony later in the chapter.

The purchase of dune land by Wyllys Betts from the proprietor trustees, and particularly his subsequent decision to claim ownership of the beach down to low water mark, raised many questions in Southampton both at the time and later. It was very shortly to become a contested space. The purchase was coupled with the threat, possibly never carried out, to fence in both sides of his property far below the line of the dunes in an act of possession. If this meant anything, it signaled a desire to expel the locals and as far as possible remove all trace of them and their rustic pursuits. In late 1881, the *Seaside Times* reported that several "staid old residents" were incensed enough to threaten to tear down any fences and "burn every inch" of them.[10] Several years later, the town trustees brought suit against him, or rather against his brother since Wyllys Betts was dead before the complaint was filed—an action of ejectment—on the grounds that the beach had been used as a public highway since time long ago or "time immemorial," as the suit claimed, to indicate a civic relation to the foreshore long predating any titles or deeds. Originally included in the suit was Saint Andrew's Dune Church but the court permitted the church to withdraw leaving the matter in the hands of Frederic Betts who, with other family members, had inherited his brother's land including the land of the church. Wyllys Betts had requested in his will that the church land be conveyed to the church if his brother saw fit. This Frederic Betts did. The case, when it came to court in 1892, led to an important ruling in regard to beach lands. The court affirmed Betts's private ownership of the beach, but only as far as mean high water, while at the same time it recognized that the beach was a highway—it was referred to as the Old Beach Road—and that the public had the right at all times to pass over it. It was a victory for the town but a small one because the town trustees had hoped to have the original lease and sale by the proprietor trustees in 1879 thrown out on the grounds that the beach was not common and undivided land for the proprietors to dispose of. The question of who owned the shores, and hence who could sell them, had become a long-running battle between town and proprietors in Southampton (as it did in Easthampton at the same time) and the court's finding only went part of the way toward satisfying the interests of the town.

The case, however, inadvertently raised significant questions about the town's (and the summer colony's) relationship to the foreshore. Sea bathing, for both medicinal and recreational purposes, had become popular among summer visitors to the shore after the middle of the nineteenth century. This was true also of natives of the seashore whose little huts beneath Thomas's verandas attested to a similar taste and one possibly less restricted by bourgeois conventions of decorum in respect to dress (total coverage in the case of women) and other rituals of immersion and beach activity. But beyond the shared enjoyment of sea bathing lay a more deep-seated question regarding the conception and use of the beach. For Thomas, Betts, and others who chose to live close to it (and bought most of the dune land between First Neck Lane and Old Town by the early 1880s), the beach represented a restful zone of contemplation, leisurely walks up and down the strand, beachcombing, occasional immersions, and an area of peace daily purified and cleansed by the tides.

For the local townspeople, in contrast, it had always been a work space, a place to beach fishing boats and whales (the beach sometimes and since "time immemorial" running thick with their blood and blubber), a place to dry and mend nets and repair boats, and a necessary public highway connecting small hamlets to east and west—along which carts could be driven freely at low tide—with Southampton. The area of the beach in question, at the foot of Town Pond, was particularly important to the town. It contained several "sluiceways" or openings in the line of the dunes that happened to be located between new properties owned by Thomas and Wyllys Betts. These sluiceways, convenient to the village, were extremely valuable for drawing up boats for repair, carting fish, and transporting whale blubber and baleen to locations within the village for trying and cleaning. Tellingly, the dunes through which these sluiceways ran were referred to locally as "beach banks," a line of sand hillocks separating upland from beach and providing partial protection from the sea to the fields and habitations beyond. But "dunes," a different and romantic nomenclature calling up soothing and feminine images of a bosom-like seaside world, was the preferred usage of the new summer visitors. It differentiated their conception of the beach symbolically from the workaday and practical definitions of the natives who harbored no such illusions. These were the issues that were to come up in the Betts trial. The beach had always been a central public venue but Wyllys Betts and others (among them Thomas) claimed it as private property and had raised their expensive villas on or near to it with the hope and expectation that they would be adjudicated the rightful owners down to the water's edge—at, naturally, low tide. There was, unmistakably, a deepening view that local inhabitants were interlopers in their own lands.[11]

The beach controversy, which had smoldered on through the 1880s, did little to endear the town to the Betts brothers and must have raised questions in the minds of many about the sorts of actions the new summer residents might potentially involve themselves in. The new president of the town trustees, George White, was particularly incensed by the issue and had no liking for Wyllys Betts. He had not approved of the way in which this polished young lawyer, nearly half his age, had taken it on himself to explore ways in which a town hall might finally be provided for the village when the Methodists decided in 1882 to vacate their church on Main Street and build a new one farther to the north. The church was originally built in 1707 by the Presbyterians and had been occupied by the Methodists since 1843 when the Presbyterians constructed a new church (their third) to its south. Betts had no doubt acted with the best of intentions and with no more than civic improvement in mind (the existing facility for town meetings, Agawam Hall on Job's Lane while commodious was in poor repair) but White would have none of it. He informed the readers of the local paper that Betts's interest in the village was "first-class humbug," a rather stinging public rebuke that did not endear him either to Betts or the summer colony's other leaders.[12]

White was never at a loss for an opinion, yet his sincerity was evident in all matters whether it concerned the rights of the freeholders and commonalty, that is, the public at large or, for that matter and as we shall see, those of the Shinnecock Indians, but in this case—the proposed village hall—he may have overreached himself. On the question of the ownership of the beach, however, White was on strong legal grounds and the outcome of the case significantly protected the rights of the public. But it is noteworthy how quickly fault-lines opened between the town and the embryonic summer colony. Barely had the first summer residents settled in when tensions began to surface. Neither side betrayed much understanding of the other from the outset. Many townspeople, particularly those with little to gain, early came to resent this influx of rich newcomers and came to refer to them with some derision as *Yorkers*, a term that had a long history in a community that still retained a cultural affinity with New England and its Yankee past. Others were not so sure. Farmers with land to sell were willing to sell it while members of the middle class with political and economic interests in the future of the village and the town at large were happy to broker relations with the new residents.

Men like William Pelletreau, Edward Foster (the town clerk), James Pierson (the supervisor), and a number of other key figures in the village, were astute enough to realize by 1880 that this developing summer presence was bound to bring with it major economic benefits to the area as a whole. Thomas understood this as well as did the Betts brothers. Summer resident real estate taxes alone would provide a not unwelcome contribution to the town's treasury in the 1880s. By 1885, for example, nonresident property in the village totaled almost 350 acres and was assessed for taxation at $130,000, far more per acre than the average village inhabitant was assessed.[13] Wyllys Betts may have been an unusual case, but as early as 1881 he was one of the three largest taxpayers in the town as a whole with property assessed at $14,500. There were other obvious benefits besides tax revenues. The market in real estate, associated building trades, retail services, and employment on the new cottage estates all began to experience rapid growth after 1880. This had, as might be expected, predictable and positive consequences for the local economy. It was a boom in the making. However, it did entail unanticipated social consequences that within a few years began to trouble men like Pelletreau who came to see the local community increasingly as "an appendage to the city colony." Pelletreau was caught between his progressivist interest in the economic advancement of Southampton and a concern that such development might alter the old community's character beyond recognition.[14]

II: REAL ESTATE

It was not until 1879 that summer residents began to establish a noticeable presence in Southampton village. Their numbers were still small but enough property changed hands to suggest that they were beginning to make an impact in the community. Including the land previously purchased by Thomas, the Hoyts, and Dr. Buck, about ninety acres had been sold to New Yorkers by the end of that year. Almost all of it was located on what quickly came to be seen as prime land on the west bank of the lake and between Gin Lane and the ocean. The average assessed value of this land was $225 an acre, a figure that contrasted sharply with all other town lands subject to property taxes and owned by local residents. According to the 1880 assessment rolls, the average valuation was $37 an acre. Five years later an acre was still assessed at an average of no more than $40 while summer property had climbed to an unprecedented $370 an acre.[15]

This was, if anything, an indication of an early and intense competition for land and the recognition of real estate brokers and farmers that there was no discernible upper limit on prices. Moreover, the figure of $370 an acre by 1885 conceals the fact that new residents had begun to buy up cheap farmland in the Great Plain and the Ox Pasture (another mid-seventeenth-century division of land) from Cooper's Neck to Heady Creek. Property in the vicinity of Cooper's Neck not far from Lake Agawam remained at between $200 and $250 an acre for much of the decade and was lower, with one or two exceptions, farther to the west. But typical tax assessments at First Neck Lane and Gin Lane began to average $500 an acre by 1885 or more than double what they had been in 1880.

This early boom in real estate did not go unnoticed. It produced quite widespread complaints in the local press both from residents and the occasional New Yorker. One of the latter wrote that a village real estate agent had told him that anywhere between $500 and $1,000 an acre was "rock-bottom." He warned that "the rapacity of the landowners of your village" can only induce "irretrievable ruin" if they persist in such "absurd pretensions." The *Times*, which had a few months earlier declared that "Southampton is booming up quite finely now," responded with an unconvincing plea for restraint: "Let us not be extravagant in our demands" it weakly admonished.[16] A few weeks later, a local citizen took a different view and blamed the rise in prices on the newcomers, arguing that farmers had no wish to sell but that their land was "wrested from them" almost forcibly. Exorbitant prices were thus to be expected and fully justified. Another observed that the price of land was "not unreasonable to the man who can afford to build a six or ten thousand dollar cottage on a five acre lot to occupy two or three months of the year" but was wholly beyond the reach of the average mechanic who merely wanted to make a living off it. With a heavy irony that was quite prescient he urged "capitalists" to "buy us all out. Let us share in a small percent of the profits."[17] One might conclude from this that he had a fairly accurate view of what the future was to bring and what farmers would do, reluctantly or not, with their lands.

The town clerk, Edward Foster, weighed in on the issue by suggesting that local residents should form a company and buy ocean front land for the purpose of leasing it for a hotel or cottages capable of accommodating up to one hundred guests. There was plenty of unoccupied land available, he said, but unfortunately its owners "have Southampton by the throat." Presumably he was referring to local landowners or to the proprietors of the common lands but he might equally have meant summer owners who were snapping up land as fast as it came on the market. Gaillard Thomas, for instance, increased his beach front holdings to sixty acres in 1881 and, as Foster would have known, was preoccupied with formulating plans for the erection of a large hotel and casino somewhere along the beach in the area of Old Town all of which he now effectively owned. Thomas was no promoter of "an architecture of pleasure"—there would be no piers, promenades (both popular in European seaside resorts) or ornate resort hotels on the model of Coney Island and Babylon that were already under construction—but it was evident from the outset that he sensed that limited and tasteful commercial opportunities could be successfully pursued in Southampton.[18] Foster himself was in favor of progress, but his letter suggests that he would like to see the village and its leading property owners take a more active role in promoting it. Others condemned what was early becoming a speculative boom in property. It was clear to many by the beginning of 1882 that real estate prices were rising because, as one correspondent to the newspaper put it, "much land has been purchased by monied men in New York and elsewhere who refuse to sell for a reasonable price and are holding it with the expectation of a still further advance."[19]

However, there was another more general factor involved here that related to economic conditions in New York. In 1873, the first major financial crisis occurred since the Civil War, in fact the first since the panic of 1857. The immediate cause of it lay in the collapse of the banking concern of Jay Cooke & Co. brought on by its inability to sell millions of Northern Pacific Railroad bonds that had flooded an already saturated securities market. In the wake of this, other banks failed and the New York Stock Exchange suspended trading for the first time in its history. It was, one hysterical investor said without any apparent irony, "the worst disaster since the Black Death." People took their money very seriously in those days. The underlying cause of the crisis was the extraordinary overexpansion of railroads since the mid-1860s and the speculative fever that had accompanied it. When railroads began to fail, the banks that had provided the capital for their expansion went down with them. But not only the banks. The industries that had depended on railroad development—coal mining and iron manufactures particularly—went into an immediate decline. The impact on the economy was far-reaching and it plunged the country into a six-year depression from which recovery was slow.[20] More than that, it ushered in a prolonged period lasting until the end of the century of slow growth, periodic crises and depressions (1884 and 1893), excess competition, and falling prices. It led directly to a major concentration of industrial corporations, limiting competition and controlling prices and, *ipso facto*, it led to the rise of a new class of corporate lawyers to provide the necessary legal scaffolding in this effort at stabilizing capital.

The effect of the financial crisis on real estate in New York also was felt immediately. The pace of real estate development in the city since the war ended had been frenzied. Residential construction up the East Side to north of 59th Street and the beginnings of property development on the Upper West Side had combined to inflate property values to an unprecedented extent. When the banks began to fail, the real estate boom, as David Scobey noted, was "pricked in an instant" and it set off a cascade of failures across the industry.[21] However, in the ensuing depression real estate came to be seen by investors as a comparatively safe haven relative to railroad and other industrial securities. As Scobey put it, it became a sort of "high-interest savings bank" and property increasingly became a financial asset to be bought and sold. The relative security of real estate investment fueled a new construction boom in the city in the late 1870s, and it also had an impact elsewhere especially in the expanding suburbs of Westchester, New Jersey, and Long Island. That this in turn should have an effect on the attitudes of wealthy New Yorkers toward investment in land, beyond its simple enjoyment, in fledgling resort communities in areas like the Hamptons seems then beyond doubt. After the beginning of the 1880s, summer residents began to gobble up farmland between the village and the Shinnecock Hills in what were once known as the Great Plains and Ox Pasture divisions—in anticipation, it might well be assumed, of "a still further advance."

But in 1879, such developments in Southampton were still a year or so in the future. Land purchases were for the moment prized for their use value. Exchange value came a little later. Among those who bought in Southampton that year were George R. Schieffelin and his brother William (in two separate purchases), Salem Wales, Susanna Steers, Sidney Harris, and Rufus Sanger. Between them they took much of the remaining land south of Hill Street between First Neck Lane and Lake Agawam that had not been purchased earlier by the Betts brothers, the Hoyts, or Albert Buck. One or two bought east of Thomas on Gin Lane (Harris was one), but it was clear that the early, preferred location was the shore of the lake rather than the dunes. Wyllys Betts, on the other hand, displayed like his neighbor, Thomas, a preference for the beach but a beach purified, cleansed of its connection to rustic labor and emptied of its local inhabitants.

The Schieffelins became and remained long-time presences in Southampton. They were descendants of a German merchant family that had settled in Pennsylvania in the eighteenth century. George Schieffelin was an attorney like the Betts brothers and about their age. He was to become in particular a power in the new church on the dunes, in the Improvement Association formed in 1881, and in the several summer clubs that were established after 1883. He joined Thomas as one of the key leaders of the summer colony and was widely respected for his legal knowledge and sophisticated classical learning. The same can be said of Salem H. Wales, once the managing editor of the *Scientific American* since its infancy in the late 1840s and also a part owner. Later in the 1870s he had been appointed a commissioner of Public Parks in New York and its president. He ran for mayor of the city on the Republican ticket in 1874 as a previous supporter of Mayor William Havemeyer, and the anti-Tweed forces that had put Havemeyer in office, but was defeated. He was again appointed parks commissioner in 1879, the year he came to Southampton, and was involved in a large number of civic enterprises and philanthropies. He was connected to Thomas through his involvement with two hospitals in the city, both of which he was president. There is little doubt that it was Thomas who persuaded him to come to Southampton. Pelletreau thought that Wales did more to make himself a part of the village than any other summer resident except perhaps Thomas himself. He plays a large role in this story.

Salem Wales bought land at Pond Lane (briefly renamed Park Avenue in the 1880s), eventually totaling thirty acres, which possessed a long historical pedigree. It extended south of Hill Street almost to the Point, a small headland jutting into Lake Agawam, much of which was once parsonage land. It was located in the Ox Pasture, the narrow strip of grazing land between Hill Street and Ox Pasture Road, and had been allocated in 1675 to John Harriman, briefly Southampton's third minister, for his sustenance and perhaps to limit his expense to the community. This special acreage continued to be dedicated to the Presbyterian ministry well into the eighteenth century before it was divided and sold. The town's original pledge that the land was "to remain forever to the use of the ministry" was destined to remain unfulfilled. Wales began with ten acres in 1879 for a trifling $1,500 and added more in the early 1880s. He acquired the Point in 1884 in a separate purchase of $200 from the proprietor trustees who claimed this small gore of land as proprietor or common land. This sale immediately became controversial for some in the village, among them George White and George Rogers Howell, who regarded the Point as public rather than common land where whale blubber had once been carted from the beach or floated up the town pond and tried out on the hill above it. Salem Wales however—though after a good deal of local grumbling—held on to the Point. In 1907, after his death, this small piece of land was condemned and removed by the village as part of a plan to bulkhead the shores of the lake. The earth removed was used as landfill to reclaim the marsh at the head of the pond in 1914, long a bone of contention with the summer colony for its unhealthy condition, and a park eventually created on it. In 1923, a memorial to those who died in World War I was erected within its bounds and overlooking the lake.

On parsonage land, Wales built two houses, one for himself and his family (appropriately named "The Ox-pasture") and one for his son-in-law, Elihu Root, a young corporate lawyer who had made a considerable name for himself in New York legal and political circles in the 1870s and was associated with Theodore Roosevelt in his unsuccessful bid for the mayoralty in 1886, the year Root came to Southampton. He became Secretary of War in the McKinley administration during the Spanish-American War and then Secretary of State under Roosevelt. But he had largely come to prominence as a result of his role in creating Henry O. Havemeyer's Sugar Trust in 1887, a move designed to drive out competition from independent sugar refineries in New York by control of production and pricing "to advance the common good" as it was later deftly put.[22] When this failed as a result of the Sherman anti-trust legislation in 1890, Root simple advised Havemeyer to consolidate his various trust holdings in other companies by incorporating as the American Sugar Refining Corporation, thereby ensuring an almost complete monopoly of national output. He did for sugar what Morgan did for railroads or Rockefeller for oil, propping up unviable entities and housing them in holding companies. He was a consummate and effective corporation lawyer, one of the first of the white-shoe breed. At the same time, he was not above taking on clients with smaller stakes at risk. He was, for instance, the lead attorney for the defense in the Betts case in 1892.

After 1880, the rush for property was on and the real estate market moved into high gear. The 1882 tax rolls show a total of thirty summer owners and a dozen cottages built by this date with more scheduled for construction. "Cottage" is something of a misnomer, calling up quaint rural images of quiet little retreats from the hurly-burly of city life. To the contrary, these were quite extravagant affairs built to contain numerous family members, servants, and guests with large acreages surrounding them. Most were designed in what was widely, and perhaps rather loosely, thought to be Queen Anne style with broad verandas and charmingly gabled roofs. None, however, approached the opulence of Newport mansions, or at least until the 1890s when stone began to compete with wood as the principal material of construction.[23] The shingle-style architecture made fashionable by McKim, Mead, and White, architects to a more muted facet of the Gilded Age than they or their clients favored in New York or Newport, continued the Queen Anne look and became immensely popular in Southampton in the 1880s and 1890s. It was combined with Beaux-Arts flourishes McKim had picked up in Paris and a sense for vernacular New England architecture of the eighteenth century. It was a sure-fire winner with New York social classes desperate for a leisured country life and desirous of well-appointed dwellings sufficiently rural in appearance but capable of housing large numbers of persons—metaphorically above and below stairs. McKim, Mead, and White delivered.

Stanford White and Charles McKim were probably responsible for upwards of a dozen private houses in the village and a club house and a church on the Shinnecock Hills during this period. For those who could not afford to build or, more likely, were contemplating building, there were always the boarding houses and private homes for summer rental. The newspaper noted that for this purpose "the natives have turned their humble homes into hostelries for summer boarders." A nice sentiment, if perhaps a little forelock tugging, but Southampton also contained many fine houses of substantial vernacular design and appearance—most dating from the eighteenth century but a few from as far back as the first fifty years of settlement—as one might expect in an old and comparatively wealthy community.

Among those who settled around the lake and on Gin Lane were Charles Atterbury, the Duers, Blaize Harsell, Judge Henry E. Howland (whose family left a remarkable photographic record of summer life in Southampton),[24] McKeevers, James Ruggles, the Sieberts, and a Mrs. Schermerhorn (presumably Mrs. William C. Schermerhorn), all well-known New York names, the last a relative by marriage to Caroline Astor. James Ruggles, for example, was the secretary of the West Side Association formed by landowners in 1866 intent on developing their property west and north of Central Park. Ruggles, a developer himself and a lawyer and apparently the very picture of primness and precision, was in the thick of this. His father, Samuel B. Ruggles, a mid-century lawyer with ties to the merchant elite, had much earlier, even larger development interests. In 1832, having amassed an extraordinary number of building lots in the East Twenties, he laid out Gramercy Park and prevailed on the state legislature to insert Lexington Avenue between Third and Fourth Avenues to provide an access road to it.[25] His son began modestly in Southampton and bought four acres for $500 west of First Neck Lane. Five years later, he had added a further ten acres extending west to Cooper's Neck Pond. In 1887, the property as a whole was worth close to $6,000. The Duers had their roots in an eighteenth-century banking family one member of which—William Duer—had married a descendant of the Earl of Stirling. "Lady Kitty," as she was fondly known, was the daughter of William Alexander who had claimed title (unsuccessfully) to the Scottish earldom and compensation for the Long Island patent lands of the original earl, also William Alexander (see Chapter 1), which had been expropriated by James, Duke of York in 1664 when the province of New York was established. The Duers had then, although in a rather attenuated sense, "come home" to their ancestral lands even if only putatively. They also were connected by marriage earlier in the nineteenth century to the Hoyts. Howlands were old Knickerbocker families, as of course were the Schermerhorns, and had established large shipping interests in New York at mid-century. There was a good leavening of the old merchant class among the first summer settlers.

East of First Neck Lane and fronting the lake, Louis Siebert and Charles Atterbury took much of the limited remaining property south of Wales, Kilbreth, and Schieffelin and north of the Hoyts and Frederic Betts. Each of them purchased six acres. The last tract available, ten acres, was purchased by Uriel A. Murdock, a New York businessman with a Wall Street address. He clearly was unusual in comparison with other summer residents insofar as he had first leased and then purchased land in Little Neck at Fort Pond south of the Shinnecock Hills in 1875. The Proprietors of the Shinnecock Hills and Sebonack Sedges, a group that had purchased the Hills in 1861 from the proprietor trustees, had sold Murdock what appears to have been five acres for $60, a respectable price for the time and location. Murdock added more land to this tract a few years later in 1880. Whether he farmed it as did another New Yorker, Naturin Delafield, who bought land close to Murdock on Shinnecock Bay, is not known. Delafield also had his roots like Ruggles, Duers and others in the old merchant class of New York.

One other who appeared to eschew living in the village entirely, which Uriel Murdock did not, was A. H. Barney, a Wall Street banker. Barney established a stock farm on three hundred acres in Cow Neck near North Sea Harbor in 1881. He made separate purchases from Samuel Scott (descendant of the disreputable but incandescent John Scott who blazed through Long Island in the late 1650s on a speculative real estate binge), including Scott's farmhouse, and from Austin Rose of the powerful North Sea Rose family for about $15 an acre. When Barney died, the land descended to his son, Charles T. Barney, but the latter sold it and moved to the shores of Agawam evidently preferring the cosseted surrounds of the summer colony. He purchased the Hoyt cottage when they decamped to the Shinnecock Hills in 1886. Somewhat later, he sold the North Sea farm to Henry Huddleston Rogers, the son of Henry Huttleston Rogers (there has always been confusion about the various spellings), the Standard Oil tycoon. The estate continues to this day, although no longer as a stock farm or (under Rogers) a shooting preserve, in the hands of the widow of Peter Salm who had earlier inherited it from H. H. Rogers, his uncle. Rogers himself had bought land at Mecox earlier in 1881 and later purchased a large tract from Gaillard Thomas on the dunes at Old Town. There he erected an imposing Mediterranean-style mansion with gaily tiled roofs. His beach parties in the 1920s were said to be of legendary proportions.

As for Charles Barney, he had many a happy summer in Southampton until business caught up with him in 1907. As president of the Knickerbocker Bank, he was trapped by a scheme of his own and others' making to corner the market in copper shares. A resulting overextension of the bank's assets led to a panic on Wall Street, a run on the Knickerbocker, and a J. P. Morgan-enforced bailout of the bank to relieve the crisis. Barney's suicide a short while later—he died in his wife's arms of a gunshot wound—added a gothic note to what had been an unfortunate, scandalous, and—as financial panics usually go—destabilizing affair.

One of the most noticeable things about real estate transactions in the 1880s is the slow drift to the west. Both sides of First Neck Lane were almost completely sold by 1882 and a good deal of property had changed hands on the other side of the lake on South Main Street. There was vacant land on Gin Lane between First Neck and Old Town but not much. To the east there was land at Wickapogue but no road into it except via the beach. Gaillard Thomas had added to his holdings in that area awaiting developments in the empty lands toward Flying Point and Mecox Bay and possibly contemplating a hotel in that part of the beach. To the west, Gin Lane ended not far past First Neck Lane, almost but not quite as far as Cooper's Neck Pond; and there were no takers for ocean-front property much west of Wyllys Betts at First Neck. Road or not, land adjoining the beach at first held out little attraction for the summer colony except for the hardy few like Thomas, the Mitchells, or Harris. Yet by the end of the decade, all of the beach land to the east was taken up, whereas to the west the beach remained empty. Henry Howland for many years owned the last house on what came to be called Dune Road (the continuation of Gin Lane and confusingly sometimes known as Meadow Lane after it was named for the Meadow Club when it removed to that location in 1887) that was well short of Cooper's Neck Pond. It was not until the beginning of the 1920s that serious building began on this western section of the South Beach, but even then it went no farther than Halsey's Neck at the beginning of Shinnecock Bay.

To the north of the ocean beach in the 1880s was another matter. Much of the land in the Great Plain and the Ox Pasture was sold off to summer interests during the decade. The most favored locations west of Cooper's Neck Pond were in Captain's Neck and the Ox Pasture. George Schieffelin and his son-in-law, Henry Trevor, acquired four separate parcels in the mid-1880s amounting to about fifty acres that covered the southern part of Captain's Neck fronting Shinnecock Bay, Heady Creek, and Taylor's Creek. A little farther north in the Ox Pasture Schieffelin bought a large tract of thirty acres. Others who found this part of Southampton desirable were Frederic Betts (two parcels of about fifteen acres each on Great Plains Road and Ox Pasture Road), James Kilbreth (thirty acres on Halsey's Neck Lane and fifteen acres adjoining it south of Great Plains Road), Susanna Steers, Edward Moeran, General Thomas H. Barber, the publisher Edward Mead of Dodd, Mead and Co., and Professor H. H. Boyeson of Columbia University (the colony's sole academic in those years), all of whom bought smaller but apparently quite satisfying lots of land in this emergent summer area.

One other who purchased land in the Ox Pasture—two lots at the farthest western extremity of the village totaling almost seventy acres—was J. Bowers Lee, a banker originally from Cooperstown, New York. Lee, who brought a wide-ranging selection of family members to Southampton and was distantly related to Robert E. Lee, had first bought land between First Neck Lane and Cooper's Neck Pond. He had built a house on it, and then sold the property—house and all—to the recently formed Meadow Club in 1887 for an extraordinary $30,000. It was little more than ten acres. Southampton was very evidently preparing to enter, if it had not already, the era of serious money. With the proceeds of this noteworthy sale, Bowers Lee moved west to the low end of the market and established a family colony just south of Hill Street. He built a capacious house to accommodate his large family network, named it of all things "Holme Lea" (he was obviously a man of humor), and had a road built off Hill Street along the boundary of his property that was aptly named Lee Avenue. The name survives to this day, a curious anomaly of the 1880s when roads, places, and ponds were constantly in process of being rechristened by the summer leadership to reflect a satisfyingly imagined past. There is, perhaps surprisingly, no other street in Southampton that is named for a former summer resident (although, as one might expect, there are many honoring local families). There is, of course, Squabble Lane, named for two of the feuding New York Irish families who settled in Wickapogue in the 1900s and were held somewhat at arm's length by the waspish summer colony. They were admitted to the colony's clubs graciously enough but socialized with only infrequently.[26]

Not surprisingly, very little of this land purchased between Cooper's Neck and Captain's Neck was graced with new summer cottages in the 1880s. Most of it appears to have been acquired for investment purposes. The 1894 map of Southampton village, produced by F. W. Beers and based on surveys probably made a year or two earlier, shows that almost no houses had been constructed west of Cooper's Neck Lane, none on Captain's Neck and, apart from Bowers Lee's compound south of Hill Street, no more than half a dozen others in the long swathe of the Great Plain. This changed later in the 1890s when the land south of Hill Street to Ox Pasture and Great Plains roads became prime residential locations for those fortunate enough to have bought property when it was still cheap and when all of it was farmland.

It also looked like farmland, but then so did locations on First Neck Lane where prices were by 1882 already going through the roof. What we see today of lushly landscaped estates with privacy ensured by manicured privet hedges of immense height (quite unknown in the 1880s and 1890s) and streets deeply shaded by trees took half a century to create. There are still patches of farmland left in the Great Plain, mostly devoted to the cultivation of corn, but these are our only inadequate reminders of what the land might have looked like more than a century ago. In 1885, most of the land continued to be farmed including the land purchased by members of the summer colony who leased it back to the owners they had bought it from. Other than those who had sold out early and cheaply, and perhaps lived to regret it, there were Fosters, Whites, Havens', Hildreths, Enstines, Sanfords, Howells, and Hunttings who still owned land there and held on to it for a few more years, probably in the expectation that prices could do no other than rise. Walter Havens, for instance, parted with four acres on the south side of Ox Pasture Road in 1888 for $16,000, an indication that prices were escalating at an extremely rapid rate. The new owner was Susanna Steers who eventually moved there from First Neck Lane. There is no record of local complaint at this rapid selling off of historic farmlands in two of the oldest divisions in the town, the Ox Pasture and Great Plains divisions, but it should have given pause to some. All of this land had been in local hands since it was originally divided and lotted out in the 1650s. Yet in little more than a decade, it was gone and given over to new uses—luxury estates in the making—that could not have been imagined in 1875 as neither could the distortion of its traditional economic value as farmland.

Real estate values in these first few years of summer settlement were then in constant flux. Their impact on the lives of the majority of village inhabitants, however, was fairly limited and limited generally to those who were the fortunate possessors of land desired by the new residents or to the realtors who arranged the deals. This had no impact on land prices elsewhere in the village or in the town at large. But by 1882, the summer colony was already a distinct presence along the ocean beach and especially around the shores of what used to be known as Town Pond. Village residents slowly adjusted to this change and to the presence in their midst, bemusing in many ways though it was, of a quite foreign community with its own customs and demands, a willingness to spend what must have seemed exorbitant amounts of money, and its desire to transform a very old settlement into something it very evidently was not—a summer resort.

III: THE CHURCH IN THE DUNES AND THE IMPROVEMENT ASSOCIATION

The embryonic summer colony, led by Gaillard Thomas—as indeed it was destined to be for many years to come—was not satisfied simply with the ownership of property and a few well-located cottages to occupy for two or three months of the year or with the speculative opportunities in real estate that began to present themselves. It wanted to transport or create institutions and associations it was familiar with in the metropolis, and, in so doing, exert some influence on the activities and social organization of what might be described, with some inevitable qualification, as the "host" community. Its first effort in this direction was the establishment of a church.

Well in advance of this small flood of new inhabitants, but evidently in anticipation of it, Thomas decided in early 1879 that the new community would need its own place of worship. It must be assumed that these early summer residents were without exception all Episcopalians (the Schieffelins, for example, were old members of the elite Grace Episcopal Church at Eleventh Street in the city), and that for doctrinal reasons, and certainly for social ones, they would find membership of a Presbyterian or Methodist congregation inappropriate if not altogether déclassé. At any event, the first collective action of Thomas, the Betts brothers, and others was to establish a modest Episcopal chapel. As fortune would have it, the federally mandated lifesaving station at the foot of Lake Agawam, built in 1851, had been abandoned and replaced with a new one at a location a short distance away. Thomas purchased this large and solidly built structure from the government and had it removed in September 1879 to its present location on beach land leased from the proprietor trustees by Wyllys Betts in 1878, closer, that is, to the surf than its previous governmental owner had deemed prudent. Betts subsequently bought the land and, upon his death, left it to his brother who in turn, as earlier noted, donated it to what shortly became a church. There were five founders: Thomas, Dr. Albert Buck, the Betts brothers, and William Hoyt. Frederic Betts became the first president. It was originally named St. Andrew's-by-the-Sea, but it was then changed to Saint Andrew's Dune Church in 1884 by resolution of its trustees. In 1887, it was incorporated as a free church, rather than a chapel, under the laws of the state. In a free church, pews may not be rented, although it was as unlikely then as it is today that anyone unconnected with this exclusive congregation would come in off the street for Sunday devotions any more than they would walk into the Bathing Corporation next door for lunch.

In retrospect, the insistence on the necessity of a house of worship may seem at first sight extraordinary and not only because in 1879 there was barely a congregation to fill its pews. On the other hand, consciously or not, it was meant to symbolize the distinctiveness of the emerging community and its separateness from the village. Through the performance of a particularly ornate form of liturgy, an interpretation of the sacraments that had hitherto appealed to few in the Protestant middle classes but which had its special attractions for upper class churchgoers in the city, it would set them apart and establish an identity. It thus served as much as a barrier to social as it did to spiritual intercourse. In this sense it was, besides its manifest religious function, a totemic sign of the unity of a new tribe. Underlying it, of course, was the related and perennially difficult question of social class that was to show itself in a myriad different ways in relations between the colony and Southampton. Episcopalianism, with its deep roots in the English church had long been the religion of the rich in America and had always been saturated with money, bloated with it, some would say. This was to be the case in Southampton. The new church was to become the summer colony's symbolic meetinghouse and spiritual center much as the rude little shelter at Old Town had served that collective purpose for the first settlers at the beginning of the 1640s. It might only be open three months of the year but it would have its governors, its president, and its summer ministers—clergymen of their own sort—and it would be well endowed. It was probably not anticipated nor hoped for that there would be any local converts from the local Presbyterian bourgeoisie, not to mention the Methodists who had their own persistent differences with their Presbyterian brethren. Neither would have been comfortable with the mustiness of its Episcopalian ritual and its incomplete internalization of the Reformation in its Puritan phase. Yet ultimately, the new church symbolized the stratification of the two communities. It was marked from the beginning by its location far removed from the village center, and its houses of worship, but most of all by its upper-class exclusivity.

Thinking about the meaning of this very early move, it is hard not to conclude that this little church, in process of becoming represented a statement, a claim on the part of a new and ambitious community, had arrived and was here to stay, whether Southampton wanted it or not. It was an act or ceremony of possession, a claim on the beach and to the south end of the village and a consecration of a new fact on the ground, a legitimation of it. There is no record of reaction in the village but two things might have struck local residents: the church's perilous location at the beach between sluiceways with only a dune to protect it and the questionable status of the real estate it stood on. As it happened, the church was fortunate to remain out of the struggle over the beach lands and their use that was to develop between Frederic Betts and the town trustees. As far as the ocean was a factor, the church sustained many blows from storms in subsequent years but rode them out until almost sixty years after its founding. It met its match, however, in the catastrophic hurricane of 1938. Loosed from its foundations, it was partially destroyed in an afternoon of wind and shattering sea. It was resurrected of course and continues to this day, Canute-like facing the waves and unprotected by bulkheads, but for all that spiritually braced for an inevitable rematch.[27]

The simple barnlike structure Thomas had purchased for the church underwent many transformations in the following few years to the point where it ceased to resemble a lifesaving station and became more like a house of worship. The growing summer colony in the 1880s lavished care, attention, and money on it and took a prideful interest in it as it slowly shed its chrysalis. The nave, as it became, had been the lifesaving station. The side aisles to it and the north and south transepts were added in 1883 and enlarged further in 1887. The choir and chancel extensions were also constructed in 1887 and then again enlarged in 1893. A belfry tower came later in 1903 when a north entrance to the nave was built. It thus gradually took on the appearance of a church, a homely but well-endowed church, a church fattened on sacks of gold buried in the sands beneath it. It benefited from the advice of leading architects who were members of the summer colony, among them Robert H. Robertson who was known for his ecclesiastical designs. Its interior furnishings, decorations, pipe organ (purchased in 1897), stained-glass windows, and early English ecclesiastical ornamentation contrived to create in less than twenty years after its beginnings a little architectural jewel in the dunes. Pelletreau remarked as early as 1893 that "under its present form" none would recognize the original building.[28] Edward Moeran, in his later reminiscences of the formation of the summer colony in which he grew up, gushed over it. "This gem-like sea-sprayed house of worship," he noted with proprietary affection, lay comfortably in "its sandy sanctuarial cradle," immune, one might conclude, or protected by a benign Episcopalian God, from the indifferent pounding of the waves behind the sole dune standing between it and the broad wastes of the Atlantic.[29]

Saint Andrew's was the summer colony's first institution and its statement of the colony's incontrovertible establishment at the far south end of the village. Its second institution came two years later in December 1881 and was secular in intent, nature, and organization. This was the Southampton Village Improvement Association, an organization that still exists though entirely lacking in the formidable political clout that it exercised in its formative years. The choice of the term *improvement association* is interesting but typical of the period. There were improvement or development companies everywhere where improvement was envisaged and whatever it was devoted to: land, profit, real estate development (the Long Island Improvement Company or the Monterey Development Corporation in northern California are good examples of the latter); the upgrading of local communities into wholesome resorts (as in the case of Southampton and also Easthampton); or the economic development of whole countries such as, for example, the Santo Domingo Improvement Company. Whatever its focus or purpose, "improvement" was a guiding principle of the times, a Republican ideology of necessary or even inevitable progress that should be helped along its way toward some profitable or desirable outcome.

The village of Southampton lacked any such organization oriented to some scheme of improvement and; indeed, at this time was without any mechanism of self-government of its own being reliant on town authorities for its administrative needs. It was incorporated a few years later in 1894 under state legislation and provided limited powers of self-rule within the general jurisdiction of the town. Interestingly, the Improvement Association supported this move to village government and appears to have suggested it. Its motives for doing so were not entirely pure however; its interest in the spread of democracy being somewhat less than its desire for village taxation to fund the improvements it sought but could no longer afford or was unwilling to assume. But in 1880 this was far in the future. Perhaps to its relief the fledgling summer colony found that there were no burdensome ranks of local officialdom to deal with apart from what appeared to be a pliant town administration. And there was little in the way of local democracy to contend with, the electorate having been for many years routinely controlled by the Republicans. Democracy, anyway, was not a means favored by upper class New Yorkers for transacting political business. Two commissions in the 1870s, reacting to the populist appeals of Tammany Hall and Tweed's redistributive policies, had favored elite control of municipal affairs in the interest of social and economic stability. The second commission, chaired by former governor Samuel Tilden, recommended that the "excess of democracy be corrected" and that appointed commissioners, not elected officials, be responsible for city administration. It represented ambivalence by the upper class toward democracy and popular suffrage (limited though that was) and reflected a widely held view that the city ought, as Beckert noted, to be no more than a "corporative administration of property interests."[30] Seen in this light, Southampton's summer colony, thoroughly accepting of New York's political culture and its central premise, might have been relieved to find in its first years that the local political system, absent in the village if not in the town, was unlikely to challenge it. And it was in the village where its interests, property, and priorities were located and focused.

The Improvement Association then, in an important sense, had stepped into a political vacuum but did so with an agenda that would not have been familiar to local residents and town officials even though the progressive-minded among them already harbored hopes for some measure of economic change. The association was clearly the brainchild of Gaillard Thomas. Its organization meeting was held at his house on lower Fifth Avenue in late October 1881. It was attended by twelve of the leading citizens of the summer colony including the Schieffelin and the Betts brothers, Judges Henry Howland and James Kilbreth, Dr. Buck, and Leon de Bost. They represented with Thomas the inner circle of the colony, its first leadership. The meeting clearly went well. The group adopted what might be described as a mild statement of its purposes: the association "shall have for its principal objects the beautifying of the principal streets and open places of the village, and the removal of all such nuisances as tend to make the place unpleasant or unhealthy."[31] Beautification perhaps but what were these "nuisances"? It seems obvious that Thomas and the others had much in mind based on two or so years of experience of summer life in the village. The meeting was adjourned to November 10 and a committee appointed to draw up a constitution and bylaws and duly report.

In summer 1880 there had been an outbreak of dysentery in the village of Southampton; seventeen cases had been reported; four had proved fatal, including one child. Two of the cases were in boarding houses catering to summer residents. This might not have been a particularly unusual occurrence in small towns such as Southampton, even if it was, as the subsequent report was to put it, "renowned for healthfulness," but it created great alarm in the little summer colony. In August, sixteen members of the colony, among them four doctors including Thomas, signed a letter to the State Board of Health requesting an investigation into the causes of the outbreak. However, not content with bringing it to the attention of the proper authorities, perhaps fearing that the state would not respond in a timely fashion to what to them was a serious health matter, the group took it on itself to mount its own investigation. An additional factor in all likelihood was that two summer boarding houses were implicated. One of the four physicians, Dr. P. Brynberg Porter of West 33rd Street in New York, undertook the task. He completed it in the heat of late summer and issued his report to the state authorities in November. The report was later published. It contained a map of the location of cases and diagrams of the position of outdoor privies and wells at the affected residences. Most cases were to be found on both sides of Main Street from north of the railroad to just south of the Presbyterian parsonage. Dr. Porter had advanced his enquiry on the supposition that privies and wells were situated too close together such that the contents of the first leached into the soil and contaminated the wells, or that the privies were dug on a higher elevation than the wells. Either case, he thought, would lead to contamination. Aggravating factors were that the soil was extremely porous and that the water-table in many areas was very close to the surface.

Dr. Porter could not probably have conducted his research unaided for his report contained detailed measurements of the distances between residences, wells, and privies and the relative depths of the latter, a task undertaken in scorching heat and only with the permission of affected residents. He would have needed local help. Southampton at this time had its own board of health as mandated by New York state law in 1850, and twice amended since in 1854 and 1867, in an act for the preservation of the public health.[32] The board's minutes after 1874 (the earliest to survive) indicate several regulations concerning the spreading of dead fish on fields, the location of fish factories in relation to population centers, the disposal of dead beasts (livestock), and the proper disinfection of "privy-vaults."[33] Dr. David H. Hallock, a local physician, was appointed health officer and continued in that position through the 1880s until Dr. John Nugent, also local, replaced him. The town supervisor was always chosen as president of the board and other board members included justices of the peace. The health regulations, which did not directly address questions of disease, were substantially elaborated after the 1880 dysentery episode in regard to sanitary measures and the prevention of diseases such as typhoid, diphtheria, and cholera. Dr. Porter undoubtedly consulted with Dr. Hallock in detail before proceeding with his investigation, probably not wishing to offend the local medical establishment and the board of which he was a member. The outcome was that James H. Pierson (who was about to become town supervisor and president of the board) and George White agreed to assist in the investigation. It could not have been a pleasant task. Pierson and White took the measurements and Porter, we assume, jotted them down.

Fear obviously had spread through the summer colony in summer 1880. It appeared to the colony with unpleasant abruptness that their newly acquired summer paradise was vulnerable to exactly the kinds of diseases they sought to distance themselves from in the city. It was no wonder that they alerted the state health authorities and then rushed to investigate the matter themselves and publicize their own findings. It is easy to dismiss this reaction as hysteria but for upper-class New Yorkers who sought healthful surroundings in the countryside, or what they took to be healthful surroundings, the discovery that the diseases they were familiar with in the city were to be found by the seaside with its cleansing ocean breezes was especially unnerving. Cholera, typhus, smallpox, tuberculosis, diphtheria and other major diseases made routine appearances in many if not most neighborhoods in New York and effective medical treatments were frequently inadequate or unavailable. Public health authorities could limit the spread of diseases by imposing quarantines on local areas in tenement neighborhoods or, more easily, on immigrants and immigrant ships. For instance, effective public health measures in 1892 contained—in fact defeated—a cholera epidemic that had killed thousands in Russia and Germany and threatened to establish itself in New York. Only nine people died as a result.

For the most part, infectious diseases and those occurring from poor sanitation, overcrowding, and poverty were confined to the tenement slums that had sprung up with the full industrialization of New York beginning in the 1870s. In Manhattan, these were to be found in the lower East and West Side wards, formerly the province of the rich, where factories had been established and tenement housing built for the working class. The bourgeoisie had slowly streamed north—less from the fear of disease than from the loss of their old neighborhoods to an emergent proletariat—first to Union Square, then to Murray Hill, and then even farther north to the empty lands of the Upper East Side adjacent to the raw expanse of Olmsted and Vaux's newly created Central Park. Above 59th Street the security of these new environs had been anchored by the construction of the armory on Lexington Avenue and 66th Street in 1880.

The upper classes then were not only escaping the diseases of the poor, which spread rapidly in the overcrowded and fetid slums that had overrun much of lower Manhattan where tenements, factories, sweatshops, foundries, gasworks, and wharves competed for space, but also the threat of class hostility and the appalling conditions under which laboring people and the poor lived. The rich, of course, were not immune to disease, but its incidence in uptown wards was relatively low compared with that found in tenement districts. The death rate from a cholera epidemic in 1866 reached 195 per one thousand in the worst affected areas but remained under 20 in the well-cared-for upper class regions farther uptown.[34] This disparity in the incidence and impact of potentially fatal diseases continued for the remainder of the century even with improvements in public health and medical care.

Seen in this light, the reaction of Southampton summer residents to a number of cases of dysentery is more easily understood. Disease was an ever-present reality in the lives of New Yorkers, rich and poor alike, and most diseases were resistant to treatment. Without the benefit of later medical techniques, the best that physicians and health officials could do was to focus on the conditions that produced diseases such as dysentery, typhoid, or cholera. The control, where possible, of overcrowding, poor sanitation, and water supply were considered as key factors limiting the spread of contagious disease. Containment and prevention were the focus.

This was precisely the thrust of Dr. Porter's extremely thorough investigation and report.[35] He concluded that "there has been contamination of wells by human excrement, which has given rise to the existence of serious disease in a locality which is naturally one of the most healthful in the world." He urged the state's health authorities to adopt effective measures to prevent any future occurrence. Evidently the state did, for a year later in 1881 the town's own board of health adopted stringent regulations covering the reporting of cases of typhoid, cholera, smallpox, and diphtheria in Southampton households and what must be done to isolate them and limit any spread of disease. There were no other major health problems in Southampton until 1884 when several cases of dysentery or possibly cholera in Atlanticville (East Quogue) were reported in the New York papers. The *Seaside Times*, not wishing to have any taint attached to Southampton's reputation for healthfulness, was outraged by what it claimed were exaggerated and sensationalized reports and was equally unhappy with the publication of a pamphlet by a summer resident, Dr. Beckwith, outlining the spread of the disease. In a surprising criticism of Thomas and other doctors, the paper alluded to "the unnecessary visit" of the State Board of Health in 1880 to review Dr. Porter's findings. It was not, said the editor, good publicity.[36]

It is an interesting question how the village community reacted to outsiders poking around their households, peering into their privies, and generally exerting inquisitorial powers. Although Pierson and White lent a definite sense of local legitimacy to the investigation, it was obvious that the inspections had not been carried out under the authority of the town's board of health even if, as is very probable, it acquiesced in them. Neither of the village's two doctors had been involved nor asked to contribute to the subsequent report. However, it was, as is seen later, only the first of many intrusions into the public and private lives of Southampton's citizens. Most, like this, were well intentioned, but as the summer colony strengthened its powers many subsequent acts were interpreted as gratuitous or even needlessly high-handed and abrasive and as ultimately trespassing on the good will of the host community.

There is every reason to think that the impetus behind the formation of the Southampton Village Improvement Association in fall 1881 resulted from the fears generated the previous year by the outbreak of dysentery. The beautification of the village was certainly a priority but if Southampton was to retain its reputation for hygiene and its healthful, disease-free airs—and continue to attract new residents—it was imperative that some organization be established to monitor the area. It must have been clear to Thomas and the other doctors on his committee that matters could not be left to the town's health board whose interests appeared to go no further than the disinfecting of privies, the spreading of fish on fields, the location of fish factories, and the interment of dead animals. This was, no doubt, unfair to the board of health but Thomas and his colleagues brought with them superior medical knowledge, forged in the best medical schools and in the furnaces of city epidemics, and were unprepared to deliver the health of their families into the hands of simple country doctors whose medical training, they very likely and probably wrongly thought, was inferior to theirs and far from up to date. In thus fashion the SVIA was formed.

An organization meeting for what was to become the association met in November 1881 at Dr. Thomas's Fifth Avenue residence. A full year had passed since Dr. Porter had delivered his report to the state. The probable explanation of the delay in forming the organization was that the colony's leaders had spent some considerable time over the year examining how viable or effective it might be, what level of support they could count on among summer residents, and what would be the response of the village and its leading citizens. To this last question they may have found that the reception to the proposal to form such an organization was fairly positive among the local elite. These were men who identified with the future of Southampton, were not afraid of change or progress, and were already committed to the success and development of the summer colony. Some of them—real estate brokers, lawyers, boarding house owners, tradesmen, builders—had begun to do very well for themselves in the few years since Thomas had settled on the dunes. They saw the potential for future growth and prosperity.

William Pelletreau was among this group in 1881, and made money for himself in title searches that also fitted very nicely into his historical interests in the town and its lands, but ten years later he was not so sure of the benefits that the summer colony brought to Southampton. He acknowledged that "the new population . . . seem willing and anxious to identify themselves with everything that concerns the welfare and advancement of the village" and that there had been "an advance in the wealth of the community" but it had come at a considerable economic and social cost. By the early 1890s he noted that the best farming land had been bought up and that agriculture had declined. Yet he reserved his most serious criticism for the state of relations between the summer and local community remarking that "(t)he points of contact between city and country are few in number, and the line between them is strongly defined."[37] For a man who moved easily between the two, unlike most others, this was an unexpectedly sharp observation.

However, in 1881 such misgivings were all in the future. Pelletreau and others had no reason to doubt the good intentions of the summer colony in forming a village improvement association and realized that its objectives would be limited. It was not, obviously, a part of any governing authority in the town and would be a voluntary organization without jurisdictional powers. It could not usurp the town board or the town trustees in any matter concerning the village or the town as a whole. The best it could do was to act as a pressure group in pursuit of its own goals. These goals were, as Article II of the association's constitution stated, to "encourage, promote and carry on projects for the beautifying and sanitary improvement of the village of Southampton." It would be difficult for local residents to object to the formation of such a useful enterprise, which seemed to trespass on no village or town prerogative, and none at the time were reported as doing so. It had also been judicious and diplomatic of Thomas and others to inquire as to the likely reaction of the village and, as seen here, include with considerable foresight representatives of the village in the membership of the new organization.

The committee entrusted with drawing up the association's constitution and bylaws presented a draft to the seventeen members present at the November meeting. There were sixteen articles to the constitution and all but two were accepted without reservation. The first concerned the number of vice presidents, increased from four to five, and the second a definition of who may become a member of the association. Most articles were of a strictly routine nature and could be found in the bylaws of any private club or voluntary organization. The annual dues, for instance, were set at $3 with $25 life memberships also available for those in for the long haul. Article VII gave some sense of how the association might function. An executive committee would "direct and superintend all improvements of the Association at their discretion" meeting monthly or more often as necessary. It also would—in a clause replete with possibility—"institute a system of premiums" or incentives for those who took it on themselves to make improvements on their own. Planting ornamental trees was one desired option. Later, beautifying the grounds or yards of residents, summer or otherwise, was included under this rubric, and SVIA judges offered prizes.

It was a thorough and workman-like document. Attached to it was a projected membership list. It included all current members of the summer colony who by this time numbered more than thirty families. Sixty-five names were recommended for election (wives were listed separately) and all were accepted unanimously. Local residents were listed at the end but their election was included in the unanimous vote. Initially, the bylaws had been written without explicit reference to summer colony members, their eligibility for membership in the association being assumed, but Article IX had contained a provision that "only freeholders or householders in the township of Southampton and their wives shall be eligible for membership." This was stricken out and replaced with "(a)ny person may become a member . . . by election by the Executive Committee—three negative votes shall exclude a candidate." This gracious bow in the direction of democratic universalism yielded a further forty-one names. It later led the *Seaside Times*, in its report on the meeting, to recommend that "our people should at once take a leading part in the association."[38]

"Our people" were mostly drawn from the business and political classes of Southampton though few were from the old guard of proprietors except Edwin Post, the redoubtable secretary to the proprietor trustees, and two of the Fosters, one of whom, James Foster, was a justice of the peace. But the Roses, Scotts, Jennings's, Harris's—the old North Sea mafia that had ruled the proprietors through much of the century—were noticeably absent. The town's political class was represented by James Pierson, the newly elected town supervisor; Edward Foster, the town clerk since 1870; George White who had recently become president of the town trustees; and William J. Post, a member of the important Post family—he was the son of Edwin Post—who later became town clerk in 1888 following the death of Lewis Bowden who had replaced Edward Foster in an upset election the previous year. A cousin of Post's later became mayor of the newly incorporated Village of Southampton in 1894. Local business was well represented by members of the Herrick, Hildreth, and Corwith clans, William Van Brunt (another future mayor of the village), Lewis Bowden, a successful real estate agent, and Mrs. Atkinson, the proprietor of a boarding house popular with the summer colony. The ecclesiastical and medical professions were not neglected: the Rev. Dr. Andrew Shiland, the Presbyterian minister, and Dr. Hallock were among those elected.

Finally, the name of Pyrrhus Concer appeared in this roll of local names. His was the only African American name to do so, indeed, according to the tax rolls, the only African American eligible to pay taxes in Southampton. Concer plied a daily ferry in the summer season between the head of Lake Agawam, where he lived, and the beach and must have come to the attention of summer folk for that reason. He had had, in addition, a remarkable career in the whale fishery and, in advancing age, had settled into a comfortable and respected life in the village and was known and, it was said, loved by all. The summer colony leadership may not have had its liberal values on display here, indeed what if any liberal values it may have had, but at least its recognition of the virtues and significance of local citizenship the possession of which few in Southampton would deny to Pyrrhus Concer. He was always referred to as "Old Pyrrhus," betokening a superficial love of the native as was the case in many resorts where "Old Foley," a Bar Harbor cab driver, or "Old Eddy" the bartender at the Lenox Club were fondly remembered by old guard resorters as representing the true stuff of local life. Such individuals were always satisfyingly seen as belonging to the deferential classes but, at the same time, never entirely trusted, the suspicion being that given a chance they would "do," as the expression went, the very people they owed a living to.[39]

The meeting then proceeded to the election of officers. Frederic Betts was named the association's president and Henry Howland the secretary. But of most interest was the election of several Southampton residents to positions within the new organization. That they were not present at the meeting seems not to have mattered particularly; that they were included, even if only later notified of their inclusion, appears to have been the main point. James H. Foster and William R. Post were elected vice presidents and James Pierson named the treasurer. None made it, however, to the all-important executive committee that had been charged in the bylaws with the day-to-day operations of the association. Gaillard Thomas, Wyllys Betts, and George Schieffelin here put themselves firmly at the helm. A committee of four, including Schieffelin and Frederic Betts, were appointed to take steps to incorporate the association. Nothing was left to chance and it all went very smoothly. The meeting adjourned and repaired to "a generous collation" prepared by their host, Dr. Thomas. Here then, on lower Fifth Avenue, was born the Southampton Village Improvement Association.

CHAPTER 3

THE ASSOCIATION AND THE VILLAGE COMMUNITY

I: EARLY TRIALS AND SUCCESSES

The first few years of the Southampton Village Improvement Association are instructive in showing its priorities and its planning for the development of the village. In March 1882, the *Seaside Times* reported that the SVIA was organized and "ready for business." The executive committee had already met and drafted plans for planting shade trees along Main Street and Job's Lane, formed a committee to approach the Long Island Railroad to do something about the unsightly conditions surrounding the depot on North Main Street, requested that Gaillard Thomas draw up regulations covering the construction of cesspools, and appropriated $50 for dredging the upper reaches of Town Pond under the supervision of Salem Wales, all this being duly reported in the paper.

The paper did not mention, however, that the committee had elected its publisher, Walter R. Burling, an honorary member of the association. In electing him, sympathetic coverage of the activities of the association and of the doings of the summer colony in general could be expected to be guaranteed. In this the committee proved not mistaken as the *Times* was to be a loyal camp follower in the years to come, faithfully publishing the association's minutes and reports, reporting on the comings and goings and altruistic activities of summer residents, and generally representing the views of the summer leadership. In fairness, it did provide lively and significant coverage of local events and issues and always threw its pages open to the opinions of the local citizenry, opinions that were legion, superlatively literate, and addressed to a variety of problems both historical and contemporaneous. Its journalistic integrity then remained more or less unsullied. In any event, small-town newspapers at this time were invariably the house organs of political parties or organizations formed for particular special-interest purposes. The *Seaside Times* was no exception to this. One of the first acts of the association was to inform Mr. Burling of his election and request that his paper publish its constitution and list of officers and print up 250 copies of its founding document.

In July, the SVIA held its first annual meeting and weighed in on the village issues that had come to preoccupy it. These were several and were to have an immediate impact on the look of the village and its environs. By order of the executive committee, 190 shade trees had already been planted and appeared to be in thriving condition. "Sign boards" had been erected on principal streets—the names of which had previously been taken for granted by local inhabitants—in order "to perpetuate the ancient names which by their quaintness recall the antiquity of the settlement." Thus Gin Lane (a year or two later renamed East Riding Lane—only one meaning of "gin" being known—in commemoration of Governor Nicolls' 1665 reorganization of the Duke of York's Long Island domains into "ridings" or districts of the county of Yorkshire, but then just as quickly forgotten as few could understand this historical reference either), Job's Lane, Toylesome Lane, First Neck Lane (shortly to become, if only briefly, Atlantic Avenue), or Meeting House Lane (designating the location of the first church at Old Town) appeared in suitably antiqued scripts to remind people of where they were. The hope was expressed at a later meeting that the signs were sufficiently legible "for all ordinary purposes" and that they possessed a suitable flavor of "antiquity about their spelling and design to satisfy the antiquarians of the community." Vines were planted at the foot of each sign to impart an air of rural harmony and tranquility.

Activities relating to the condition of the waters in the lake and the surrounds of the railroad station—committees had been appointed and were active—were reported. In regard to the railroad, whose depot was well to the north of the village and was only accessible by one road—Main Street—running through the business district, it was the sense of the association that a new road should be constructed to the east of the depot and run southward to the ocean beach. This eventually became, after consultation with local property owners respecting rights-of-way (one of whom was William Pelletreau), Elm Street. Probably some summer residents, among them Thomas, found access to their cottages at the beach and the lake, impeded by traffic conditions on Main Street and were simply looking for a convenient bypass. If so, the origin of Elm Street may be found in one of the first efforts in Southampton—perhaps the very first—to address the question of traffic circulation in the village. That it was horse-drawn is hardly the point. Unsurprisingly, Dr. Thomas was appointed to head a committee with power to act. Once off the New York train, with a little jog to the east he could trot home at a brisk pace and avoid Main Street entirely. Well not quite. Elm Street went only as far as the Bridgehampton Road as the Hampton Road was then called. A year later, the association petitioned the town highway commissioners for a road extending north from Gin Lane to meet up with Elm Street calling it "a great public necessity." It did not quite meet up for it involved a little jog to the west at the Bridgehampton Road but it was good enough. It was first named the East Road but quickly became Little Plains Road, a finely antiqued reference to the first division of land in the 1640s in what was called the Little Plain, a small area of planting field that was now partly owned by Thomas. It originally contained Frog Pond, but that had long since been swallowed up by the encroaching sea.

These were and were not major issues that the association addressed, but where it showed its true colors was in its approach to how the village should present itself in its streets and business premises. In a word, how it should look. The question came down, as the meeting was to put it, to one of "neatness." It was thought that perhaps "the greatest benefit of the Association" was the influence it could exert on the inhabitants to avoid "the exhibition of anything unsightly along the roadside, and (to enlist) the individual cooperation of the owners of premises on the streets and lanes of the village to do all in their power to increase their neatness and attractiveness." In a reference to what were obviously thought of as the slovenly habits of local businesses it was earnestly hoped that "especial care will be taken to keep rubbish, paper, straw, old cans and all kinds of litter out of the road." Grass and weeds were also to be kept under control by the owners of businesses; and perhaps also by householders though this was not specified. They were to be "cut and neatly trimmed." Furthermore, a letter was to be sent by the secretary to the "market" store, probably a grocery, of H. O. Vail requesting that he clean up his front yard on Main Street, that is, in the central district where summer residents would be most apt to pass by. Possibly to everyone's relief Vail sold his store the following winter to W. G. Corwith who promptly opened a watch and jewelry shop. It is still in business today. Similarly, negotiations were to be entered into with one of the Rogers family for the removal of his blacksmith shop. Its presence on Windmill Lane had evidently offended the sensibilities of some in the summer colony for the association was willing to spend up to $25 to have it moved to a new and less visible site. The duty of informing Rogers of the decision to relocate his shop, depending on the expense, was delegated to Lewis Bowden, the association's secretary and well-known local realtor and broker. The transmission of unpleasant news was invariably assigned to a local official of the association to render it more palatable and limit damage.

Given that half of those attending the meeting were local (only twelve members showed up), there may have been some awkwardness while this discussion was taking place, some uncomfortable shifting in the seats as two of their fellow citizens were singled out for special consideration, and the gaze of the association directed critically at the general lack of attention paid by others to maintaining clean and neat establishments. But it was all, the minutes of the meeting concluded, in a good cause for "our beautiful village may be a model to all others." Whose village was it now becoming? The use of the possessive pronoun, indirect though it was, might have led some local members of the audience to wonder whether a campaign of annexation was underway and that "our" village was in danger of becoming "their" village." At the very least, as was pointed out at the 1883 annual meeting of the SVIA, it was thought that the operations of the association "have already made a permanent impression on the village."[1] This impression was only to deepen in the future.

Activities proceeded apace in the following years. Membership was increased in 1883 with the election of sixty new summer members and almost thirty local. Correspondingly, membership subscriptions doubled from the previous year yielding receipts of $501 as compared to $244 in 1882. In 1884, $700 was collected. Well in funds by its third year of operations, the SVIA was in a good position to expand its activities. Still, in 1883, it moved slowly. Money was again appropriated for improving the condition of the northern part of the lake. A plank walk from the South Beach extending up First Neck Lane and designed eventually to reach the village by traversing both sides of the lake was begun.

A decaying guard rail running up Job's Lane was replaced, the new posts being made of locust and "neatly painted."

Where the association ran into its first real difficulty was in its dealings with the Long Island Railroad. What Thomas and others wanted was an entirely new and larger station building and greatly enlarged grounds around it. Additionally, Thomas wanted North Main Street, on grounds of safety, carried under the tracks. Railroad officials had, however, never been an easy group of men to deal with as communities along the line of the road from Long Island City east could well attest. Whether under the reign of Oliver Charlick, president of the LIRR in the late 1860s when the Sag Harbor branch was pushed through Southampton to that village, or that of Austin Corbin, receiver of the railroad and then its president in 1880, cries of lamentation about fares, freight rates, and service in general had been heard from far and wide but always to no avail. Not so many years before, railroad workers had been ordered to remove the Quogue depot from its convenient location in that hamlet to a remote spot far into the woods, the citizens of Quogue having offended Oliver Charlick in some fashion. This vindictive move was accomplished in the silence of the night while Quogue slept. The same had happened in 1869 in Riverhead when its citizens showed insufficient enthusiasm for a planned junction in their community for the projected branch line to Sag Harbor. Charlick retaliated by removing it miles to the west, bypassing Riverhead altogether, and locating it in the unpopulated wilderness of Manorville. In the early 1880s, the *Seaside Times* printed complaints from outraged citizens on an almost monthly basis concerning service, rates, and the failure of obsequious town officials to assess the railroad sufficient taxes. The company was impervious to all such protestations and treated its ungrateful customers with the disdain it thought they rightly deserved.[2]

But a well-heeled group of Southampton summer residents, who after all would be constrained to believe that Austin Corbin was one of their class and thus amenable to reasonable requests for the consideration of what were to them desirable projects, convinced themselves that only sweetness and light would pour forth from the railroad. They were mistaken. After years of intermittent negotiations an under-grade crossing at North Main was constructed but a new and much larger station appeared to be out of the question. In spring 1883, Frederic Betts and Judge Howland met with Ralph Barton, the manager of the railroad, and presented him with plans drawn by none other that Charles McKim for a better and "more tasteful" depot than the shed then in existence. Barton accepted the plans but it is not clear that he did anything with them. There is some suggestion in the paper that a few renovations were undertaken in 1884 and that the depot now looked quite presentable, but it is doubtful that McKim's plans for a little architectural jewel to welcome new visitors to the village were implemented. Of special concern to the SVIA was that visitors not receive a poor impression of the community the moment they stepped off the train. The grounds and roadway around the station were in similarly deplorable condition, the roadway a threat to life and limb. Southampton's handsome brick and stucco station was not built until 1902, in fact not until several years after Austin Corbin's death. In 1895, the SVIA had at last persuaded railroad officials to rectify matters at the depot and make a substantial investment in a new station. Land was bought in 1897 to expand the adjacent grounds; the association—to the tune of $1,000—underwrote extensive ornamental plantings to beautify them, and the roadway was improved beyond recognition from its rutted past state. It was several more years before the station was built, but that it was built at all was testimony to the persistence of the association in fighting for it. Thomas, who had started that fight twenty years earlier, died the winter after the station opened and probably did not live to see the charming results of his labors, a country station decorated with seashells.

If the association could not claim an immediate success with the railroad in 1883, although remaining hopeful of one in the near future, its beautification project for cleaning up the village was evidently not proceeding at a fast enough pace. Not all village businesses, and perhaps some residents too, appeared to be on board. It issued a second appeal. "Again your committee," the minutes read, "would call attention to the importance of keeping the streets free from rubbish and it is earnestly hoped that all will cooperate to that end. A little care and a little thoughtfulness on the part of each individual will result in a very large aggregate of improvement. Neatness and order about our dwellings and streets not only give an air of thrift and beauty to the place and are pleasing to the eye, but beyond this unquestionably have a favorable effect upon our own characters and upon those of our growing children so susceptible to impressions from objects around them."[3] These were the words of George Schieffelin, secretary to the meeting and one of only two summer members of the association present. Perhaps too little time had elapsed since the inception of the association and the insertion of its ideas, plans, and hopes into the minds and habits of its intended audience for these to have fully taken root and become habits themselves. It was to be an ongoing project tackled year by year, season by season.

Did the village collectively sigh with relief in October when the last of the summer inspectors had left, the weeds now allowed to grow to their heart's content, the trash to accumulate at the shopkeeper's door, the inevitable complaints at season's end now given voice? Unfortunately we can never know. Those responses—if there were responses and surely there would have been—are buried in the past and were unrecorded. Similarly, the reaction of Schieffelin's audience to his remarks at the annual meeting—held, incidentally, at the hall on Job's Lane and attended by eight of Southampton's citizens but only two of the summer colony's—are also unknown. Possibly some irritation at Schieffelin's apparent presumption replaced the previous year's probable discomfort but that too cannot be known. Nevertheless, these few assembled townsmen learned that one of their own, James H. Foster the well-regarded justice of the peace, had been elected to the executive committee. He continued as vice president while James Pierson remained treasurer and Lewis Bowden secretary. But it was becoming clear, if it had not been earlier, that the use of local dignitaries in SVIA offices was good cover for the association and quite useful for propaganda reasons. Foster and Pierson were particularly employed when it came to matters that might cause concern in the village. They were, for instance, made a committee "with power" (as the expression then went) to oversee the ticklish process of getting Elm Street through the road commissioners and past potential hold-outs (there were a few) owning property along the line of the projected route to the ocean. Besides these two, George White, ordinarily no great friend to some of the designs of the summer colony, Lewis Bowden, and Edward

Foster the town clerk were willing to cooperate with some of the aims of the SVIA if they thought they were in the general interests of the village. White agreed to supervise the development and maintenance of sidewalks on village streets, an issue that had captured the attention of the association when it was realized that the simple act of walking around was not without risk—if not to life and limb but at least to the well-shod feet of the lady members of the colony. White, a pragmatist as well as a local booster, would have seen the advantages to shopkeepers of better access to their establishments.

In July 1884, Schieffelin reported for the executive committee at the annual meeting of the association that "the Society continues in a flourishing condition" and that "its work can be seen in every part of the village adding to the attractions with which nature has so richly endowed the place." He then turned the meeting over to Thomas who was to present a scientific analysis of the condition and future prospects of Lake Agawam. Thomas had long thought that the lake was the focal point of the summer colony—"the very center," as he put it—and the key to the growth of Southampton as a summer resort. The cottages of summer residents were uniformly clustered around it and Lewis Bowden, "our enterprising" real estate agent, had informed him that the ability to rent cottages to city dwellers was measured by "the distance which separates them from this beautiful sheet of water whose waves are constantly cloven by a swan-like fleet of pleasure boats" (Thomas's words not Bowden's).[4] Salem Wales, who was a committee of one charged with improving its upper portion and had already had it dredged and deepened in front of his parsonage lot, fully agreed with Thomas's view of the importance of the lake. Three years later, as president of the association, Wales noted that every square foot of its surface had been at all times subjected to constant scrutiny. "Not a weed or leaf that floats on its surface escapes our notice," he told the annual meeting in 1887. "We should," he concluded, "watch it as we would a precious jewel."

The lake faced two sets of problems. The first, which preoccupied Wales, was the purity of its waters. As cottage construction proceeded rapidly along both its shores, the issue of waste disposal became a matter of real concern. Wales recommended building cement-lined cesspools to limit leaching of human waste and strict controls over the use of laundry soap. For obvious reasons large households generate large amounts of laundry and frequently employed a full-time washerwoman. He also urged cleaning out cesspools on a regular basis. Wales, who seemed to live in terror of both air and water-born diseases (he strenuously argued for cremation and the removal of cemeteries from residential areas because of the exhalations of "noxious gases" from the remains of the interred), had the lake water frequently tested by experts to check for impurities.[5] After one such analysis he announced that there was scarcely a trace of sewage to be found in the lake and that "the water compared favorably with those of the best lakes in this country and Europe." It was, he had been told by the expert in charge, quite drinkable although he had to admit it was slightly brackish.

It was precisely this brackishness, according to Dr. Thomas, that was the cause of the second problem facing the lake and which required the attention of the Improvement Association. Town Pond, like most other ponds near the beach, owed its fresh water to springs that fed into its northern extremity. That it also contained some salt water at any given time was a result of storm surges occasionally overwhelming the protecting dunes, and particularly the sluiceways, and pouring over its southern shore less than one hundred yards from mean-high tide. The presence of salt water had, Thomas contended, led to an explosive growth of sea grass that threatened to choke the lake entirely and render boating, fishing, and swimming virtually impossible. This species of grasses (he did not identify it) flourished in neither fresh nor salt water but only in waters that consisted of a mixture of the two. He cited research he had conducted at Wickapogue Pond, adjacent to land he had recently purchased, where there was no sea grass and in fact no sea water as the previous owner had sealed it off from the ocean a quarter of a century ago. Thomas also owned land across from Old Town Pond, a quarter mile west of Wickapogue, where he found a luxurious growth of sea grass. Over the course of three seasons he had blocked sea water from entering the pond and completely eliminated the offending grass. Thus, the solution to eliminating weed from Agawam was not to remove it physically, as was currently the practice and with the good-hearted assistance of George White (whose responsibility, as a town trustee, it was), but to attack the problem at its roots by excluding the ocean. A related problem had emerged from not protecting the southern shore of the lake. Storms had washed vast amounts of sand into it and its southern end had become almost too shallow for boating.

To deal with both problems Thomas proposed building a large embankment of sand, earth, and brush—a levee on the south bank of the lake—to hold back the sea. This proved to be an expensive undertaking for the association, but Thomas persisted in it and his efforts did yield results. Chemical analysis of the water a year later indicated that less than 2 percent was sea water and the growth of sea grass also appeared to be markedly lower. Still, the effort to clean up the lake was costly. In 1884 alone, it consumed half of the association's budget or $295. But the weed problem persisted for several years to come. In 1887, Salem Wales, that year's president, reported that some progress had been made, but he remained doubtful that shutting out seawater represented the true solution and observed that just the opposite was the case at Sagg Pond. There, with apparent success, the inlet to the sea had been kept running to kill off the weed. Resignedly, he concluded: "Our duty is plain. We must fight this weed" but did not recommend any further allocation of funds to achieve it.

However, the problem might never have arisen had Thomas and other summer residents not objected several years earlier to the efforts of the proprietor trustees to close the sluiceways or openings in the line of the dunes directly south of the lake. This was, the trustees claimed, common land owned by the proprietors and theirs the responsibility to maintain. In 1879, Isaac P. Foster, a proprietor trustee, had been instructed to "put brush in the sluices" to raise the beach bank between pond and ocean. In the light of this claim to ownership, as we saw earlier, they had also sold some of this dune land to Wyllys Betts including the land of the Episcopal Church and a small parcel immediately to its east. In closing the dunes the trustees hoped to protect not just the lake but the southern end of the village from storm surges that could travel well inland. High tides and high winds during tropical or winter storms could drive water up the lake and into the low-lying areas of Job's Lane and Windmill Lane and in extreme conditions even farther north. Windmill Lane is a valley. It served then, as it does today, as a drainage basin for storm run-off but was, and still is, vulnerable to wind-driven water surging in from the ocean and up the lake. But Thomas and Betts, finding the eminently sensible protective barriers of brush and piled up sand in the sluiceways an unsightly addition to their view of the pristine beach beneath their verandas, had them removed on the grounds that they had been constructed on land they now owned. It was rather remarkable, in fact rather obtuse, that having pulled down one barrier to the encroaching ocean they should build another even larger one a few years later only fifty yards farther inland and at far greater expense.

It is an interesting question whether Thomas, Betts, and the SVIA had any legal right to construct an embankment at the foot of the lake and if in doubt (since the foot of the lake was also a passing road) whether they sought permission to do so and if they did, from whom. Maps of the immediate area prepared for the Betts trial of 1892, in which the town trustees contested Frederic Betts's claim to the beach and the dunes, indicate that the Betts property as well as that of the church and an undeveloped Betts parcel to its east extended north to the southern shore of the lake. Farther east alongside the road that led to Main Street and clear of the lake was Thomas's land. Between the road and the church were two small plots, both purchased from the proprietors in 1881 at the same time Wyllys Betts purchased his land from them, respectively owned by Pelletreau and John Howell (or so Howell's widow claimed though there is no evidence that Howell had anything more than a twelve-year lease beginning in 1878). The map also shows a passing road on the south bank connecting Main Street with First Neck Lane. This road, which White in 1885 claimed was constructed long ago by "the village people" or probably by the eighteenth-century town trustees acting for the proprietors and to which White had recently made some improvements that spring, then appeared to run through the property owned by Betts and the church.[6] Given that neither the proprietor trustees nor the town trustees objected, at least publicly, to the dismantling of the proprietors' barriers in the sluices—now, it was thought by many, definitively on private property because it had been sold to Betts by the proprietor trustees—or the construction of a new embankment at the lake, suggests that at that time (1884) no one seemed prepared to argue that Betts was not perfectly within his rights to allow Thomas and the SVIA to go ahead with their project since it appeared be on Betts's own land. Perhaps also both bodies of trustees came to the conclusion that any barrier to the ocean was better than none. White, now president of the town trustees since 1882, said nothing. Probably tired of organizing weed-clearing crews in what was obviously a futile effort to rid the lake of unwanted sea grass, he might have been thankful that Thomas had come up with another solution especially as it replaced the damage already done by removing the proprietors' work on the dunes. Yet at the same, a few months later in spring 1885, Betts's title to his lands at the beach came under fire from none other than White himself and the town trustees.

Yet the Improvement Association's proprietary approach to the lake, its contents, its use, its protection, and its surroundings raises other and deeper questions about the new colony's attitude toward the village and its natural attributes. There is no question that

Lake Agawam was a central attraction of the village for the summer colony, perhaps at this early date *the* central attraction, and one that far outweighed the beach as a desirable place to live. It could have escaped no one's attention, however, that within five years of the construction of the Hoyts cottage in 1879 both sides of the lake were now privately owned and built up by new summer residents. Only the swamp at the bottom of Windmill Lane, a short stretch of Pond Lane in Salem Wales's parsonage lot, and the southern end were available as public access points. Public access may have been even more limited than this. Wales had bought the Point from the proprietors (an illegal sale of public land according to White), which then extended a third of the way across the lake, just south of the parsonage lot, and had taken steps to improve the lake frontage across Pond Lane. His land, assuming the lot ran to the water as the parsonage lot did originally, included Pond Lane just as Wyllys Betts's land included the passing road at the south end of the lake. Public access to the lake, while it certainly still existed in these two vicinities, was nevertheless moot despite the probable noblesse oblige of the two owners who endlessly protested their fidelity to the rural and time-honored traditions of their adopted village. Could, for example, local townsmen and their children fish and swim, skate or launch boats at these locations? There is no evidence at all that they could not, but at the same time it is quite clear that almost all of the shore of Lake Agawam had been largely closed off to Southampton inhabitants by as early as 1884.

All the waters of Southampton—ponds, bays, streams—had been declared beyond the reach of private ownership since the beginning of the settlement in 1640. The Disposall of the Vessell, the founding document of the community was unambiguous:

> (F)furthermore noe person nor persons whasoeur shall challenge or claime any proper Interest in seas, rivers, creeks, or brooks howsoeuer bounding or passing through his grounds but ffreedom of fishing, fowling and nauigation shall be common to all within the bankes of the said waters whatsoeur.[7]

In addition to this, both the Andros and Dongan patents, in confirming the original purchase of the lands of the town from the Indians, granted and released those lands to the freeholders and inhabitants and in doing so saw fit to include the waters—"(r)ivers Rivolets waters lakes ponds Brookes streames."[8] Neither patent addressed the issue of private ownership of the waters, but the town records thereafter made it abundantly clear that riparian owners could not own any part of the waters their properties abutted and were required to furnish public rights-of-way for freedom of access to them. There seems to be no question that cottage owners at any time sought to include in their property the waters of the lake fronting them but it had already become perfectly clear by 1884 that collectively they, and especially the SVIA representing them, had come to view Lake Agawam as their private lake and as theirs to do with as they deemed useful or necessary.

With perhaps the exception of Salem Wales, whose thiry-acre parsonage lot on Pond Lane extended almost a quarter of a mile down the west bank, cottage owners were less than diligent in assuring public access to the lake by providing rights-of-way through or even between their properties. Writing more than half a century later, Frank W. Burnett, then in his late seventies and a boy at the time the cottages were built, observed that "no trespassing" signs were not slow to go up. Previously, he said, anyone could fish, swim, boat, or skate in it or on it from any point on the shores of what was still fondly called by the old guard of the village Town Pond, among them White who never lost an opportunity to refer to it by its original name.[9] In the space of a few short years, however, that had changed and, as far as it is possible to see today, had changed forever. Yet the village did not entirely lose its pond. After village incorporation in 1894 and after the eventual decline in the power of the SVIA in village affairs by the 1920s, the new village board began to assert its interest in all matters within its jurisdiction. These included issues concerning the lake, now for all time Lake Agawam, but that did not in any way mean that public access was one of those issues. That had been settled in 1884.

II: BEACH RIGHTS, THE BETTS BROTHERS, AND THE VILLAGE HALL

The Dongan patent of 1686 had included in its grant of the lands of the town to the freeholders and inhabitants of Southampton, or freeholders and commonalty as it is more accurate to say, a reference to the beaches as among those "all and singular" premises granted to them within the bounds of the town. The patent said nothing, however, about the potential for private ownership of any lands including those of the beaches on the ocean or the shores of the bays. In its discretion, it had left this question to the decision of the town trustees, a corporate body erected by the patent for the management of the town's lands, waters, and general economic resources. The town trustees, who henceforth in fact managed the town's lands and waters exclusively on behalf of the proprietors; that is, those who were the heirs and assigns of the original purchasers of the town, were authorized at the direction of the proprietors in a town meeting to divide and allot meadowlands along both the northern shores of the bays and their south shores running up to the ocean dunes or beach banks, on the narrow ribbon of barrier beach, as well as on the shores of Peconic Bay. These divisions of meadows or sedges were seen as highly valuable from the earliest years of settlement, predating the Andros and Dongan patents, inasmuch as they were sources of a variety of products such as winter fodder for cattle, roofing or insulation for housing.

Between Speonk at the western extremity of the town and Sagaponack at the border with Easthampton, at least five divisions of meadowlands along the ocean beach covering nearly thirty miles were made between 1653 and 1737 and lotted out to private owners by the town trustees acting for the proprietors. In the nineteenth century, three miles of undivided beach land in Quogue were sold by the proprietors to a company organized by George O. Post in 1846. In the same year, the proprietors sold similarly undivided meadowlands at the beach at Mecox. In 1882, representatives of the Long Island Improvement Company bought out the owners of most of the beach lots in the Pine Division of Meadows that extended from Tiana to Cooper's Neck. Beach land purchased by Thomas and other summer residents between Agawam and Old Town Pond originally consisted of parts of lots in the

Little Plain that had been divided in 1654. In 1882, the proprietor trustees quitclaimed undivided land at Old Town to Thomas. It ran to the southern boundary of Old Town Pond and included the beach banks and beach. Next east were lands at Wickapogue that were similarly divided early and later sold (some eventually to Thomas). The picture that emerges here is that beach land down to and including the beach banks was always recognized as common land belonging to the proprietors that could be divided, allocated to those in possession of proprietary rights in the common lands, or sold.

C. Wyllys Betts had come by his land at the foot of Lake Agawam in this fashion. He had bought it directly from the proprietors in 1881 just as George Post had bought his land in Quogue from the proprietors in 1846. However, Betts's title to his land was challenged by White and the town trustees on the grounds that that particular stretch of beach amounting to no more than one-tenth of a mile was in reality public land, long used by the general run of inhabitants for a variety of purposes from whaling and fishing to sea-bathing, and had never been considered proprietor or common land. This charge turned out to be an unexpected blow for Betts and the summer colony in general.

This unfortunate situation might never have developed and inflamed opinion in both the summer colony and the local community had Betts, and probably Thomas as well, proceeded with a little more tact. As we have already seen, the beach was a flashpoint of early contention not long after Betts purchased his land. He had threatened to fence his section of beach down to the low water mark. This had infuriated many in the village and Betts had wisely refrained from proceeding with his plan. Then in 1884, he, Frederic Betts, Thomas, Judge Kilbreth, J. Lawrence McKeever, and Schieffelin had come up with plans to build a beach house or casino on the land Betts owned east of the church in the dunes and adjacent to the small bathing station run by John Howell. This is the land now occupied by the Bathing Corporation that was formed very much later in 1923. The casino was to be a quite extravagant affair, one hundred feet long with wide porches or piazzas, and would cost about $8,000, a very considerable sum. Betts and his partners formed a small company and were, it seems, poised to issue shares of stock in the venture when something happened. In mid-April 1885, the *Seaside Times* reported that work on the building was to start "in a few days." But then on May 7, Wyllys Betts wrote to the paper announcing "the probable abandonment" of the casino project.[10]

It is not clear what precisely had happened but some of it can be pieced together from the ensuing exchange of heated correspondence in the pages of the *Times*. Strictly, the Village Improvement Association was not involved in the controversy, although all of its leaders were, and it studiously avoided alluding to it in its minutes. But it did strike at one of its dearest objectives, sanitizing the beach in order to maintain it in its pristine state. In 1882, the association had announced that it was "assuming the duties" of the Southampton Beach Association, that is, John Howell's small operation on land under lease from the proprietor trustees. This was a local organization predating the summer colony by many years although it may not have gone under that name. It consisted of small bathing huts—bowers—that were rebuilt annually of sturdy branches covered with leaves to provide shade. They were sometimes referred to locally as "wigwams" and had in different forms enjoyed a long existence before the habit of sea bathing took hold. Earlier versions of them had been used as shelters in the winter months, often with fires lighted within them (like wigwams they were at that time open at the top), for spotting whales off the beach. There had been, according to White, a wigwam on the seaward side of the dune next to the cottage of Wyllys Betts. He introduced this as evidence that this was "the people's beach." But people's beach or not, some members of the summer colony did not like wigwams. Wales and Schieffelin, on a tour of inspection, thought they were a "disgrace" and had them removed at their own expense. The beach, they were reported as saying, must be kept "clean and neat."[11] The following year, some of these beach houses were renovated and removed farther east, that is, away from Wyllys Betts's dune where their presence was considered particularly offensive. Meanwhile, the SVIA had invested substantially more than $200 in its plank walk to facilitate access to the beach and in a "pavilion of rest" at the beach itself. This sounds to have been a fairly makeshift affair that would have to do while more elaborate plans were drawn up. But this was the extent of the association's involvement in the development of beach facilities.

Why White took it on himself—and induced his fellow trustees to take it on themselves—to address the casino issue (he claimed to be in favor of a new beach house) is not obvious, but he pursued it with a vengeance and forced Wyllys Betts and his associates to withdraw. The town trustees claimed that all the land between the pond and the ocean was public land and had been so "since time immemorial" as White was again to put it. The beach was "a free beach" and the road beneath the dunes was "an open road." In summary, the trustees claimed all of Betts's land as belonging to the town and as having been illegally sold by the proprietor trustees four years previously. It was a bold claim, one that eventually led White and the town trustees to sue for the ejection of Frederic Betts (Wyllys' heir) from his beach lands in late 1891, a suit that ultimately failed after several appeals.

But in 1885, White dangled a possible solution in front of Wyllys Betts and his casino company that could have kept the casino project alive. He offered a twenty-one-year town trustee lease for a nominal rent of $1 a year. This was obviously unacceptable to Betts and his associates. If he accepted such a lease, it amounted to admitting that the proprietor deed to his lands was invalid. He countered by requesting that the town trustees quitclaim the land to him, an action that would remove any possible cloud on his title and effectively state that the town had no legal or equitable interest in his beach or, for that matter, probably any other beach. Only this, he wrote in a letter to the paper, could convince him and the casino company to proceed with the project because it would give him a clear title. If he were to sign a lease, he said, it would virtually eliminate any possible future law suit he might bring for the return of his lands as it would amount to a formal renunciation of title. He noted that he had bought the land in the first place "solely for the advantage of the public" and had planned to make a "present" of the eastern parcel for the erection of a beach house. He thought White had embarked on "a most unwise and short-sighted policy" that could have no other result than to "estrange" summer residents in general. Self-righteously he declared that he found "the inability of our townspeople to recognize their own best interests" quite beyond him.[12]

The two town historians weighed in on the issue. William Pelletreau rehearsed the history of the division of beach lands and meadows from the earliest days of settlement to the proprietors' sale to Betts. How, he asked, can it be said that if the proprietors originally owned thirty miles of common land at the beach, which in the course of two centuries they had divided, allotted, and sold, that they did not then own the beach at Town Pond? He found White's claims "utterly preposterous" and without foundation.[13] The latter's reply to this reasonable statement of the historical record was in the same issue of the *Seaside Times* and White went after Pelletreau on what he knew was a sensitive question. Pelletreau, as a proprietor holding some small rights in commonage, had been a member of the proprietor trustees since 1871, although he had taken himself off the board the previous year in 1884. As White knew, he had benefited from proprietor sales of land on at least two recent occasions. He had bought a small piece of beach land at Town Pond in 1877 and then in 1882 a considerable acreage at and including Red Creek Pond, a salt-water pond on Peconic Bay in the Canoe Place Division. White's response was blunt—neither had much love for each other (they were often at odds on town issues and their backgrounds were quite dissimilar)—and not particularly pleasant: "WSP, being a proprietor, having a lot staked out on this beach marked WSP, will write and manufacture plenty of evidence to make his claim good" and avoided addressing the historical facts as Pelletreau had laid them out.[14]

George Rogers Howell, on the other hand, temporized—as he often did—and looked for a middle road to solve the developing stand-off between White's trustees and Wyllys Betts. He based the town's claim on the beach's use as a highway "as a road in continual use when necessary . . . between the edge of the cliff on the beach banks and the fence that formed the southern boundary of arable lots bordering on the beach." (Surprisingly, Howell was mistaken here. The highway ran beneath the seaward side of the dunes. Fenced land ran only up to the dune.) At the same time, he concurred with Pelletreau that "the title to every inch of land in the town goes back to the Proprietors."[15] So where precisely did this leave Betts? Howell thought that it was imprudent of the town trustees to quitclaim or sell beach land, but that it was equally imprudent of Betts, described as "an able lawyer," to buy from the proprietors when the beach "in law" is a highway. The "proper and graceful thing" to do, Howell thought, was for the town trustees to offer a fifty-year lease to Betts and, it has to be supposed, push the problem to some far distant date in the future when most if not all of the current protagonists were gone from the scene. According to Howell then, Betts had legally bought from the proprietor trustees but should lease his land from the town trustees, both a curious and illogical recommendation.

George White would have none of this. But as he must have realized, his town trustees were on ambiguous legal ground if they gave Betts a quitclaim deed. It could conceivably entangle them in a lawsuit with the proprietor trustees over ownership of the beaches that would be both embarrassing and expensive and which the town trustees would probably lose. Moreover, it was possible that Betts himself might sue the town trustees for wrongfully claiming ownership of the beach and harassing its legal owner. In this connection, White had threatened to drag Thomas into the dispute by claiming town ownership of his land at Old Town Pond that Thomas had purchased from the proprietor trustees in 1882. The thought that the two of them might wheel out some heavy legal artillery from New York aimed at the town trustees may have been too much for White to contemplate. In 1885, he was preoccupied with the upcoming Mecox Bay trial, a costly and involved town trustee suit against Richard Esterbrook's Mecox Bay Oyster Company that had taken title to the bottom of Mecox Bay—all twelve hundred acres of it—from the proprietor trustees in 1882. Enough perhaps was enough.

White fell back on the beach highway question—that the town had always had such a highway—and threw in the passing road through Betts's property at the lake for good measure but essentially dropped the main issue. Probably Betts bowed to the inevitable and allowed the public to pass both in front of his house at the dunes—he had named it "Sandymount" appropriately enough—and along the passing road by the lake behind. He would have been a fool not to if, indeed, after the brouhaha of 1882, when the town feared he would fence in his section of the beach, he had not already done so. The upshot of this little storm between the two communities was predictable. The twenty-one-year lease to Betts with what White had called "liberal provisions" was quietly forgotten, and the possibility of a quitclaim deed allegedly to protect Betts's title never once mentioned again. But Wyllis Betts unknowingly, in buying from the proprietors, had inherited two roads through his property: one to the south by the dunes claimed by White as a public highway and one to the north bounded by the lake through what was originally common land laid out by the proprietors and, as a passing road, similarly available to the public. Realizing this must have been galling to him to say the least.

Yet the lull in hostilities did not last for very long. Victory in the Mecox Bay case in 1888 found White once again with his eye on Betts, this time Frederic Betts since his brother had died the previous year, and White charged into the lists anxious to prove he was right in the first place.[16] Still, it is not quite clear why he had taken on Wyllys Betts to begin with. The question of Betts fencing the beach had apparently been satisfactorily resolved three years before. It seems to have been a combination of things. Who controlled the beach, and in particular a crucial and historically freighted section of it, very evidently was for White—an old whaling captain it should be remembered—an issue loaded with emotion. White, no friend to the proprietors and their land claims, saw the beach as public property defined by long historical usage, but now here was Wyllys Betts and his brother with their extravagant cottages—interlopers—lording it, as he must have thought, over the town's strand as if the beach had no history at all. But there was even more to the story of his relations with the Betts's.

There had been bad blood between White and the Betts brothers for several years before 1885. Its origin had much to do with the assumptions of class and status as well as an underlying anti-urban sentiment generating resentment in old timers like White. In general he and others perceived that this wave of new arrivals was attempting to dictate the future of the village to its inhabitants. Philosophically, old New York bourgeois elites and those who identified with them devoutly believed in their civilizing mission, their responsibility as citizens to pursue civic and charitable works of community improvement. That they were willing to undertake a variety of altruistic projects for the common welfare, as they invariably understood it, also was a satisfying mark of status and status superiority. It was this, particularly, that rankled White. It was not that he refused to recognize the value to Southampton of several of the summer colony's initiatives—sidewalks, concern for the town pond (in which he continued to toil at Thomas's request), street watering to reduce dust in summer (another contentious project to be reviewed here)—but it was the self-satisfied air of noblesse oblige, the sheer self-regarding righteousness of it all with which such projects were promoted that galled him. He was certainly not alone in this visceral reaction.

Such was the case with the proposed new village or town hall that was ardently pursued by the Betts brothers in 1883. Agawam Hall at the foot of Job's Lane, even if a somewhat worn and shabby barnlike structure, had served adequately as a meetinghouse and community center for several decades and, as it transpired, would continue to do so for several more to come. Town meetings were held there as were pageants, theatricals, anniversaries of the founding of the town, and other celebratory festivities. However, there were some in the village besides the Betts brothers, or were persuaded by the brothers, who thought that a handsomer and better-equipped building might be more appropriate for village functions.

In 1882, as briefly discussed earlier, the Methodist Episcopal Church decided to vacate its building on Main Street and erect a new church on a lot a little farther to the north across the Bridgehampton Road. The original church had formerly belonged to the Presbyterians and had been built in 1707 as their third church. The first, of which no trace remained, had been at Old Town on what the town records called "the old meeting-house lot" and lasted only a few years until a more permanent edifice was constructed on the east side of South Main Street in 1651. The second church was occupied for little more than half a century before a new one was built on the same side of the street farther to the north, this being the 1707 church. It was located on part of a northeast corner lot at the intersection with Meeting House Lane that belonged to Obadiah Rogers. But in 1842, requiring a larger and more up-to-date space the church elders decided to sell the building and raise a new one across Meeting House Lane immediately to its south on land purchased from the Mackie family. In the meantime, the emerging Methodist congregation in Southampton, a religious minority that was not much esteemed in the village at that time and had no choice but to worship in private homes, was looking for a church building of its own and rather naturally cast its eyes on the about-to-be-vacated 1707 church. Unfortunately, the Presbyterians somewhat churlishly refused to do business with the Methodists and, according to Pelletreau, sold it to an unnamed farmer who moved it a few yards north to a lot adjacent to Rogers that the farmer had purchased from Charles Howell. The original lot on which it had stood for more than a century was then sold back to the heirs of Obadiah Rogers by the Presbyterian Church. It is now part of the grounds of the Southampton Historical Museum. The Methodists were not, however, left out in the cold. The farmer, according to legend or to Pelletreau, took pity on the Methodists and quickly sold them the building and the land. Yet the newspaper account of the sale indicates that Charles Howell was the seller.[17] What was the precise sequence of events and whether Howell profited from the transaction is not known, but when the Methodists left in 1882 it was not certain whether they or Howell (or the unnamed farmer) held title to the property and thus whether they were in a position to sell it. In question was whether the church was incorporated in 1843 when the property came into the congregation's hands. It turned out that it was, and that the church corporation possessed a valid title.

It was this building that the Betts brothers decided would be perfectly suited for a village hall. It would need some architectural modification even though it had lost its steeple many years before. In early 1882, Frederic Betts wrote to Lewis Bowden suggesting that if the town were interested and willing to share in the costs, the building and land could be had for $3,500 and remodeled for a further $3,000. He thought it should eventually contain an archive, library, and a museum besides space for meetings and told Bowden he was willing to pay for an architect to assess its condition and plan for its reconstruction. Charles McKim, who had recently sketched plans for a new railroad station, was to be the architect and had already produced a preliminary plan for alterations. It was evident at the outset that Betts was not particularly enamored of the church's appearance and, for all the summer colony's infatuation with all things old, was unimpressed by the fact that at 175 years it was one of the oldest and better-preserved buildings still standing in the village. It was said to have been beautifully and austerely built with singularly massive interior timbers but Betts, notwithstanding, advocated the addition of an entirely new façade. "A few hundred dollars," he was later to say, would make it presentable.[18]

Betts's idea caught on well with several in the local business community. Bowden almost immediately began soliciting subscriptions and raised $2,300 by mid-March. Among those who were willing to play a role in the venture besides Bowden were James Pierson, Edgar A. Hildreth of E. A. and H. Hildreth's department store, David Hallock, also a store owner, Edward Foster, and none other than George White. Within one month, Frederic Betts moved to incorporate what had already become informally known as the Village Hall Company. It was to be the Southampton Company with a capital stock of $6,000 divided into 240 shares of $25 apiece. But Betts recommended that voting rights in the corporation be confined to those holding a minimum of five shares. He knew that he and his brother had put in a substantial amount of the purchase price and, having a majority interest in the company's stock, could easily determine the shape and trajectory of the development of the new village hall. White, as might easily have been predicted, strenuously objected to this virtual monopoly of the project and informed the readers of the *Seaside Times* that the Betts's interest in the village—past, present, and future—was spurious, humbug.

The Village Hall did, nonetheless, open for business the following year, the sale by the Methodists having been finalized in July 1884. How far Betts's architectural plans for its renovation went is unclear, but it was reported that two hundred chairs were purchased to replace the ancient pews that had been sat on by almost two centuries of Presbyterians and Methodists, respectively, and were now to be ripped out. In a gesture of support for the Betts's project the SVIA held its 1884 annual meeting in the new hall and continued to do so in subsequent years. It was fated, still, to be sparingly used by the community—town meetings continued to be scheduled at Agawam Hall—a result perhaps of the high-handed tactics employed by the Betts brothers in bringing it into being. In the late 1890s, it was bought by Samuel L. Parrish, a city lawyer and summer resident who had arrived in Southampton in 1887 and about whom we shall have much to say later in regard to his substantial and much-remembered impact on the village. Parrish had bought the Rogers house and lot at the corner of Meeting House Lane for his residence. Finding the underused new village hall next door to him, he purchased it and, in a magnanimous gesture, transformed it into a gymnasium for the youth of the village. For a while it was a success but not long afterward it was destroyed by fire.

So, what had begun with Frederic and Wyllys Betts in 1883 as a philanthropic contribution to the development of the village, and one that was supported by at least a number of leading local citizens, ended not much more than a decade later in failure. The reason for this was not only a matter of tactics—the brothers had made sure that carrying through the project would remain essentially in their hands—but in a failure to consider whether the village really wanted a new hall. Instead, they had simply presented it to the village as a fait accompli and perhaps also expected a grateful citizenry to thank them for their generosity. They might, for instance, have arranged to have the idea unveiled at the annual town meeting in April 1883 when the project was in its formative stage and have it put to a vote. Any one of their supporters—Pierson or Foster particularly—could have proposed it. But for whatever reason they did not. As much as anything it was a political failure and one that emphasized the widening gulf between the two communities.

III: THE SVIA, THE CEMETERY, AND THE SWAMP

Another vexatious issue emerged at about the same time that exercised the patience of both the village and the Improvement Association and affected relations between them. Although it did not directly involve Frederic Betts and his brother, it did involve White in his capacity as president of the town trustees and also Wales on behalf of the association. What was in question was the condition of the South End Burying Ground lying between South Main Street and the new East or Little Plains Road leading to the beach. This small one-acre cemetery had been dedicated by the town sometime in the early 1650s though no record of it appears until 1665. It was situated next door to the second church. It was effectively given up in 1721 after it was almost filled even though there were occasional burials well into the nineteenth century. The new cemetery—the North End Burying Ground—was opened that year at the junction of North Sea Road and North Main Street. Parenthetically, this cemetery was almost full in the 1880s and plans were already afoot to establish a new and much larger one of seven acres to the north of the village. Edward Foster, the town clerk, formed a committee of townspeople in 1884 to investigate potential sites and to form a company to finance a new cemetery.

The earliest graves in the South End cemetery dated from the beginning of the 1680s (of those gravestones that had survived or could be identified) but very probably there were many much earlier burials. By the late nineteenth century, this old ground containing the remains of some of Southampton's first settlers appeared to have been largely forgotten and was evidently in a state of advanced neglect. It might well have remained so had not SVIA officials in August 1883, on one of their periodic tours of inspection in the village, entered it via an ancient right-of-way off South Main Street and were appalled by the condition they found it to be in. The reason for the visit was historical and was to establish the feasibility of providing some enduring mark of recognition of the first settlers and where it might be placed. It was an exploratory mission. The association had not at this point arrived at a consensus regarding how it proposed to honor the founders of the town and did not do so for more than a year after its discovery of the situation at the burying ground. Its plan, as it transpired in 1885 at the annual meeting, was to erect a monument to their memory within the cemetery's precincts as a joint venture with the town. The resolution to this effect read in part (it was presented by James Pierson and seconded by Frederic Betts) that "a suitable monument to the memory of the founders of Southampton whose remains rest in unmarked graves" be established. The costs, it appeared, were to be shared between the association and the town. The resolution was a fine gesture of respect but, more than that, it represented a further step in the summer colony's continuing efforts to memorialize the venerable antiquity of their adopted village. It was as if to say to any unsuspecting visitor from the outside that their village was older than theirs (wherever "theirs" was) which, of course, was generally true except for a fair sprinkling of nearby communities in Massachusetts, Rhode Island, and Connecticut.

All might have been well and the resolution put through sooner had the inspection committee found nothing more untoward in the old cemetery than its long neglect and a few unmarked graves. The real shock was that they had found, witnessed no less, that it was overrun with cattle and other livestock including horses and pigs trampling through an estimated forty or fifty graves and thirty or so gravestones, many of which latter had been used as scratching posts and toppled over. These livestock belonged to Edwin Post whose farm lay immediately to the east of the cemetery and who was long accustomed to driving his cattle over the old right-of-way and through the semi-abandoned cemetery. If some of his charges lingered en route to enjoying these inviting pastures, it was no particular concern of his. In fact it later emerged that he and his father had long considered the cemetery as their own and were accustomed to using it as both a private pasture and an occasional last resting place.

Edwin Post, then in his early seventies, was a significant landowner at this time and a man to be reckoned with. He had been a proprietor trustee since the 1850s and had served as clerk and treasurer to that body since the death of Jonathan Fithian in 1864, the former town clerk and supervisor as well as clerk to the proprietor trustees. Fithian had been preceded by James Post, Edwin Post's father and another former supervisor, in that same capacity. Like the North Sea Roses and Scotts, or the Fosters, the Posts were key members of Southampton's proprietary elite. For this reason, and because Edwin Post had a reputation as a difficult man to deal with, the town's inhabitants and officials had generally turned a blind eye to the goings-on at the burying ground and had no wish to engage him in a dispute that would inevitably become an unpleasant confrontation. After all, many may have satisfied themselves, hardly anyone had been buried there for 150 years—and those that had had been connected to the Post family—and few if any townsmen had ever raised any question about the cemetery's upkeep. The one person who had occasionally referred to the cemetery was Pelletreau but then only to remind his readers in the paper of who among the early settlers lay there.

The SVIA, however, chose to bring what it began to refer to as "the desecration" of this "hallowed ground" to the attention of the public. No sooner had its committee completed its investigation than the *Seaside Times* reported that Wales and Edward Foster were to call on Post to review the situation. (It is worth noting again that in all potentially sensitive issues concerning the village the association always preferred to involve a prominent local citizen—in this case the clerk—to assist in case there was trouble). The two found Post obdurate when it came to the question of whether he or the town had title to the right-of-way into the graveyard or, for the matter, to the graveyard itself. Post claimed both and that the footpath in fact ran through his land.[19] On receiving this report, the association then wondered whether it should "redeem" the land by, presumably, buying out or otherwise satisfying Post, but then a week later withdrew on the grounds that it was "particularly anxious not to appear meddlers in so delicate a matter." These words, authored in a letter to the paper by Old Mortality Secundus, who was most likely Wales, nonetheless included a challenge to the village that it reluctantly and slowly but ultimately took up. "Does the community," asked Wales, "regard the matter of sufficient importance to cast off its apathy and (make) an effort to reclaim this hallowed ground?"[20] George Rogers Howell offered his support and said he was "glad to learn that a movement is on foot to rescue from the cows the graves of our ancestors."

It was an embarrassing moment for the village. An esteemed and to many an intimidating citizen stood accused of desecrating the graves of the ancestors of many of the inhabitants (including his own), and here was a key figure in the summer colony, representing the views of its constituent members, demanding that something be done about it. But three years passed and nothing was. Entreaties to Edwin Post were made from time to time, always with the same result, but no other action was taken and perhaps the village concluded that tempers had cooled and the issue had blown over. But it had not for Salem Wales. When he became president of the SVIA in 1886 it was still on his agenda and he spoke to it in blunt terms quite disregarding his previous tactful concern for village sensibilities by meddling in village affairs.

"(N)othing can be done (short of legal action)," he said at the annual meeting the following year, "to remove the reproach that justly attaches to all who are in any way guilty of this almost criminal neglect and desecration of this ancient burial-place. It is not creditable I say to the authorities of the Town of Southampton that for a century of years no effort appears to have been made by them, until lately, to protect and keep in order [this] hallowed spot." It was histrionic but it had its effect. That nearly four years had elapsed since Wales's initial attempt at interceding with Post suggests that the townspeople had little interest in (or stomach for) a battle over the cemetery, a battle that would be symbolic at best from their point of view and satisfy no pressing local interest. Besides, many had long since accepted Post's claim to ownership of the cemetery land and what he did with it was his business. But the issues were confused and possibly conflicting.

Wales and the SVIA had set their hearts on building a memorial to the founders but realized they were blocked at every turn by the unresolved question of title to the land and the footpath leading into it by Post's farm. A second issue, one hinging on a satisfactory solution to the first, was whether the grounds would be cleaned up, the gravestones righted, and the cattle once and for all ejected. Yet few, apart from White, expressed much concern about the condition of the cemetery or with the behavior of Post's cattle. And White's motivations, after Wales drew him into the dispute with Post, were open to question. Nor did White display any particular interest in a memorial. Instead, he seemed to be driven as much by personal animosity toward Post as by concern for the graveyard.

White, as we have had occasion to note, had always been antagonistic to the proprietors and to the trustees of the proprietors—the North Sea oligarchy—in particular. He saw them, so he frequently told the readers of the paper, as having "robbed us of all our rights" and privileges in the common lands, waters, and their products (before 1818) and, in general, monopolizing the town's resources to the disadvantage of the general run of inhabitants, the commonalty of whose trustees he was president. And now here was Post, the redoubtable clerk to the proprietor trustees, quite emphatically rejecting the town's claim to its own ancient burying ground and the equally ancient right-of-way leading into it. White was affronted by Post's position and made no secret of it. At the same time, his occasional penchant for fevered speculation got the better of him. Somehow he had got it into his head that Post and his fellow proprietors wanted to divide the cemetery into planting lots for their own use, a new "last" division of land, the first since 1782. "Are you willing," he demanded in the paper, "that this burying ground should be divided and (your ancestors) bodies used as fertilizers"?[21] He repeated the charge a year later in no less incendiary terms just before he persuaded the town trustees to frame a resolution threatening Post with a suit. He had already retained legal counsel in the person of Judge Thomas Young, who was handling the Mecox Bay case for the trustees at the time. Young had affirmed that there was "an open undefined right-of-way to (the cemetery) which the town bought of James Herrick," the first owner of Edwin Post's land in 1650 and running through lots owned by Herrick and now Post. In 1665, in an entry in the town records, the overseers of the town had agreed to give Herrick an acre of land behind his home lot "in consideration of a foot way for people upon his lott to the burying place where the towne have one acre for that use."[22] Evidently, this entry would play a crucial role in any suit against Post. The only and rather minor point Young raised concerned the location of the footway. It was undefined whether on the north or south side of the lot. The trustees published two resolutions in the local paper:

> Resolved, that the President of the Board, with the Clerk, order to remove or fill up the well in the old burying ground, to abstain from pasturing it or making a thoroughfare over it to cart farm produce and fertilizers, and to remove certain fences which he has laid out in it, and if he refuses to do this to take legal measures to compel him to do so.

> Resolved, that the President and the Clerk have full power to make an exchange with Mr. Post of the Town's open right of way to and from the burying ground for a highway.[23]

What was new in the first resolution was the reference to a well Post had apparently dug in one part of the cemetery. White pounced on this as a powerful public issue, not as simply secondary to the legal question of the right-of-way, but (with its lurid implications) calculated to inflame collective opinion.

White was a happy man in summer 1886. The town trustees had won their suit against the Mecox Bay Oyster Company earlier in the year, effectively ending all existing and any future claims to the ownership of the bottoms of the town's bays. The suit would be appealed, but White was confident that no court would uphold it. The *Brooklyn Daily Eagle* saw the outcome of the trial as a victory for "the free American people" over "the old feudal lords," a sentiment profoundly shared by White.[24] It was a vindication of his leadership of the town trustees in the 1880s, as well as an immensely popular result in the village, and may well have encouraged him to come down heavily on Post, possibly an even more hostile opponent than the oyster company. This victory, amid the hubris that inevitably follows, perhaps also led him to renew his attack on Wyllys Betts and other summer residents who claimed the beach as private land. He had arranged to have printed in the same issue of the *Seaside Times* a third trustee resolution that gave Betts and Thomas fair notice that he had not forgotten the town's claim to the use of beach land as a public highway. It read as follows:

> Resolved that this President and the Clerk confer with Mr. Betts and others who have located on land belonging to the Town south of the Town pond and Captain's pond that is the beach lying between the ponds and the ocean, from First Neck road to the Town road, where the Town had had an open road and undisputed right of way all over it for two hundred and forty five years.

Negotiations between White and Post, however, did not go well. Edwin Post obstinately refused to acknowledge any town claim to a right-of-way leading through his land to the burying ground and did nothing to improve conditions in the cemetery itself. Regarding the offending well, he ignored the request to fill it in and half humorously questioned whether a well was capable of being physically "removed" as the resolution had requested. The SVIA remained a curious onlooker at these events and developments and Wales held his tongue while White attempted to resolve the situation. But by spring 1887, it was clear to all that he had failed for at that point he brought Wales in to make one last effort to avert a suit against Post. As Wales later put it at the annual meeting of the SVIA in August, he had been asked to undertake "an honorable and speedy adjustment of (this) vexatious dispute" but his effort at conciliation he regretted to say "was not a success."

The matter thus went to court, whether at the urging of Wales, White, or both is unknown. It was no longer, however, a town trustee suit; now it was to be undertaken by the town. The reasons for this, although they had apparently not occurred to White, the trustees, and Judge Young their counsel until almost the last moment, are not hard to find. Since the separation of the interests and responsibilities of the town trustees and the proprietors in respect to the lands and the waters in 1818, the town trustees no longer possessed a jurisdiction over the town's lands except possibly—but unclearly—the foreshore (the beaches and shores of the bays). Young must have realized that cemeteries, although certainly not proprietor land (despite White's fevered speculations about their imminent division into planting lots), were public lands dedicated to a singular purpose that fell within the exclusive authority of the town and its own administrative offices. The three issues involved—the condition of the burying ground, the ownership of the footpath into it, and the ownership of the burying ground itself—were then town rather than town trustee issues.

By the same token, incidentally, White could not have failed to notice that the passing road through Wyllys Betts's property at the foot of the town pond was a town road passing through what had once been proprietor land and could not then be of legal interest to the town trustees. At one time, before the town's creation of a system of highway commissioners in the late eighteenth century charged with the responsibility of laying out and maintaining the town's roads, the proprietors could have laid claim to overseeing such a road since it passed through land they had divided or sold and that they and not the town had caused to be laid out. On the other hand, the town trustees did have legal power over the beach highway passing through Betts's property to the south at the dunes as it lay—as it was later and successfully established at the Betts trial in 1892—on the foreshore or on what was accepted at the trial as in some sense town trustee land or, which comes to the same thing, public land.

On Young's advice, the town trustees quitclaimed the burying ground to the town (in case there was any doubt as to ownership) in October 1887 and the Town of Southampton filed the trustee's suit against Post. The complaint raised both the question of the town's right-of-way into the cemetery and the ownership of the cemetery itself and stated that in July 1886 Post had wrongfully entered the area with horses, cattle, and hogs and "depastured the same, and trod and trampled down the graves therein and disturbed and injured the fences around the same, and broke down the tombstones therein and dug up and carried away the soil therefrom."[25] The case was heard in State Supreme Court in Riverhead in December. The town was represented by Thomas Young and Post by James Griffing. Post denied any wrongdoing and claimed title to the burying ground by adverse possession. It had come down to him through his father, James Post, who had died in 1855, and Post in turn traced the title to Obadiah Rogers, James Post's father-in-law, who possibly believed that his possession derived originally from the Herrick family. James Herrick had been allotted his land in 1650, shortly before the burying ground was opened, and it had remained in his family until 1777 when Obadiah Rogers bought it. These three families had also always been intricately connected through intermarriage.

Young countered by quoting the specific entry in the town records from 1665 that effectively rebutted this title claim. In full it read "(t)he overseers have agreed with James Herrick that hee shall have one acre of land at the reere of his home lot in consideration of a foot way for people up his lott to the burying place where the towne have one acre for that use, & James Herrick is to have the hearbridge (herbage) of it." The judgment, which inevitably went against Post given this incontrovertible evidence of town possession, also noted that title claims on the basis of adverse possession "cannot be construed as embracing a public burying ground because such a parcel of land from its very nature can form no part of a messuage (dwelling house)"[26] Post was ordered to pay $446 in costs and damages. Perhaps the most surprising detail that emerged from the trial was that several witnesses clearly thought that the cemetery was private, belonging to the Post family, and that only Posts and those related to them could be buried there. George Herrick, for instance, had been interred there as recently as 1873. Harriet Rogers, a granddaughter of Obadiah Rogers and thus a cousin to Post, testified that she had been under the impression that "when people were buried there permission was asked of Mr. Post, it was considered his burial ground" but acknowledged that close family members of hers had been occasionally buried there without permission.[27] Post appealed in late 1888 but to no avail.

Salem Wales and the Improvement Association had no choice but to shelve any plans they had developed for erecting a monument to the first settlers until the final appellate decision was handed down in 1889. But ultimately the association deferred proceeding indefinitely. In the first place, Wales perhaps recognized that the issues had become far too contentious, and that he and others had had much to do with bringing them about and had precipitated a court action that the town had every reason to avoid. Second, they also were sensible enough to see that any move toward building such a monument would inevitably be interpreted in a negative fashion. They would be accused of hounding Post into court, of manipulating the cemetery situation for their own ends, of forcing the town trustees and the town into a court fight nobody wanted, of humiliating the village by publicizing the condition of the cemetery, of appropriating to themselves the right to construct a sacred monument to commemorate Southampton's own ancestors in the village's own burying ground. And surely more; it did not bear contemplating. It was best by far for the association to withdraw. Moreover, besides the drumbeat of their own substantial agenda, they had yet another crisis on their hands in 1886 that was unfortunately also of their own making.

This crisis concerned a local family in Southampton, the head of which was a bootlegger and sometime distiller and, since 1884, a resident of the low-lying area at the foot of Windmill Lane bordering the town pond that was then, before later reclamation in the 1900s, largely a marsh. These were the Moores. All small towns have men like George Moore who live on the far fringes of respectability but who may nonetheless perform some needed function in the community and into whose activities in pursuit of it most respectable citizens choose not to enquire too deeply. Such, one assumes to have been the case, with Moore. He had plied his trade peacefully enough out of his home in North Sea, arrested once in a while for selling liquor without a license and then just as quickly released, and might well have continued this marginal existence largely out of sight of the local authorities had he not decided to remove to Windmill Lane and therefore closer to market. It was this decision that led, if not quite to his downfall, at least to a further change in his fortunes. Let us not forget that at this time and for many years to come this portion of Windmill

Lane lay in a basin that in the wet winter months was a quagmire that disappeared into a swamp fed by springs that drained into Lake Agawam. The boundary of the lake shifted with the weather, and it was not uncommon for the women of the village to be rowed across the bottom of Job's Lane when the area flooded. The condition of this part of the village had long been of concern to the SVIA so close was it to the banks of the lake where summer cottages were already lined up or in process of being built.

A year or so after the Moores relocated, a letter to the paper complained that "a filthy and dangerous hot-bed of pestilence, and a depot of supply of putrid materials has been allowed to establish itself at (the lake's) upper portion just where the springs which supply it exist and at its very fountain head."[28] In the interests of keeping the lake "pure and undefiled," the letter went on to outline what needed to be done and what had at least been the immediate cause of the problem. The Moores, of course, were singled out, their makeshift living quarters, their sanitary habits, their laundry, their numerous children, their dubious economic activities, all at little more than a stone's throw from the parsonage lot where Salem Wales had built and now lived in "The Ox-Pasture" and whose sensitivity to the condition of the lake was well known. The author, under a pseudonym (perhaps it was Wales himself), described the piteous situation of this family as fighting "a losing battle with life" and was now "stranded in this community, poor and friendless" sinking inexorably into "a physical and moral mire." The *Seaside Times* in 1884 had warned Moore, who it described as "in the whisky business," against leaving the relative anonymity of North Sea for the village and proclaimed it "a bad move," a prediction that turned out to be altogether too true.[29] It did not help Moore's situation or reduce his visibility that he had set up his house and business next door to Rogers' blacksmith shop, an eyesore to Gaillard Thomas and to the association, which Thomas was in the middle of arranging to have removed to a location where summer sensibilities would not be offended. Rogers had been bought out—for $25—and went quietly and without complaint and also without much objection in the village.

The letter went on to recommend that the town board of health should condemn the marsh as unfit for habitation and that "the shanty" and its owner removed elsewhere "blotting out" once and for all "this pest-hole." This is exactly what was done. In fact, a campaign was already in motion, orchestrated by Thomas, Wales, and the doctors of the summer colony to achieve precisely the end the writer, who was evidently privy to what was intended for the Moores, had advocated. George Moore was persuaded to leave, offered $500 in compensation for the land (which he apparently held title to), and resettled in Sebonac on four acres acquired by Thomas from an opportunistic farmer who charged him $100 an acre. Sebonac Road was two miles from the village, safely out of sight. The house was trucked up, slightly damaged in transit (more compensation), and Moore, with his family, and his meager belongings unceremoniously abandoned to reorganize their lives, no longer quite so poor but undeniably still friendless. As for where the house had previously stood, "the unsightly spot has been leveled, cleaned, and covered with lime."

It was all accomplished a few days before the SVIA's annual meeting in August 1886 but was mentioned only indirectly in the report of the executive committee. George Schieffelin briefly noted that "(t)he most important subject of the health of the neighborhood has received due attention." Because the Moores had been evacuated only earlier in the week, and because the topic under discussion was drainage and public health, it is fair to assume that it was to the Moores that Schieffelin was referring. But there was more to the story than these few facts convey. It unfolded in the newspaper in the following weeks.

The removal of the Moores had been effected by the SVIA's health committee, which had been set up by Thomas in 1882 to monitor public health issues following the dysentery outbreak in 1880. Its membership consisted of the summer colony's several doctors. But the committee did not act alone in the Moore case. Thomas and Wales had established a fund for the Moore's removal, both as compensation to Moore for his inconvenience and his plot at Windmill Lane and for the land at Sebonac to which he, his house, and his family were to be dispatched. Thomas, more aware than he usually was of the need for community support and equally concerned not to generate sympathy for the Moores, enlisted the support of the business community in subscribing to the fund. He and Wales also might have chosen a more propitious moment to address the Moore matter as the controversy over the state of the cemetery and how to deal with Post was fast heating up. This was in no small part due to Wales who had found it increasingly difficult to hold his tongue while White was endeavoring to find a solution to the cemetery problem short of legal action.

But it had been a wet summer and the condition of the swamp at the lake was worse than in normal years. Summer residents living nearby complained that it was particularly malodorous, and Wales was predictably alarmed at what was insidiously draining into the lake if, indeed, there was anything genuinely harmful draining into it. In the event, there was little choice but to act and get rid of the Moores as the symbol of effluence, disease, and dissolute morality that everyone, at least in the summer colony, thought them to be. The general consensus was aptly summed up by a summer resident who wrote after the Moore's were resettled that "property owners along the lake have a proprietary right in the purity of their own waters, and could and would restrain by summary injunction any subsequent settler."[30] In a few short years, the summer colony had come a long way in laying down its proprietary claims.

It was fortunate for Thomas and Wales that the business community was willing to contribute a large part of the costs, more than $600, to cover both the land and Moore's putative needs. The *Seaside Times* listed a large number of local contributors, all of them with downtown business interests—Hildreths, Howells, Herricks, Culvers, Corwiths, Bishops, Havens, Burnetts, Bowdens, Fosters, Terrys—a who's who of most of the economic movers and shakers in the village. In total, there were more than forty subscribers, a slight majority of whom were townspeople. The SVIA and its health committee had obviously prepared the ground well for what they proposed to do. Whatever the general public might think of what many would interpret as a typically high-handed action of the association, it could not be accused of failing to enlist the support of at least one sector of the community, in fact the most influential sector. It was hoped by this that any charge of acting unilaterally could be avoided.

Thomas's committee also had taken the precaution of petitioning the town's board of health. The petition, short and to the point, noted that "the premises of George Moore and family are prejudicial to the progress of the town, an eye-sore to the neatness of the place, and a menace to the health of the community." "Public safety," it concluded, demanded the removal of the Moores. The committee also invited two experts to render opinions. The president of the New York City Board of Health, Charles F. Chandler who happened to be summering in Westhampton, paid a visit and endorsed the health committee's position while a sanitary engineer from New York State's health board was persuaded to declare that the marsh was unfit for habitation and should be drained and filled. Given this marshalling of expert opinion and the pressure brought to bear on the town's own board of health, as well as the existence of a subscription fund, it might reasonably be assumed that this was a planned operation dating back a number of weeks or even months.

Moreover, the *Seaside Times* had given no hint of what was about to befall the Moores until two days before the association's annual meeting. Walter Burling, editor and publisher of the *Times*, must have known of it, because he subscribed to the fund to remove the Moores along with other local businessmen, but kept it out of the paper until the last minute. In fact, the land at Sebonac had been bought and Moore's house was already on its way before Wales's outraged letter (assuming he wrote it) was published. At the end of the annual meeting, and as if to acknowledge Burling's loyalty in not publicizing the disposition of the Moore situation, the SVIA publicly thanked him in a resolution "for the uniform alacrity with which he has given to (the association) the valuable aid of his journal and the active interest which he has manifested in furthering all its efforts for the good of the town."[31]

But for all this business support and the cooperation of the newspaper, the "Moore Matter," as it quickly became known, consumed the interest of a bemused public. Walter Burling had no choice, if he was to maintain the impartial reputation of the paper and its interest in the community as a whole, than to report on all subsequent developments. This he did. A few more details began to emerge that had the effect of casting the actions of Thomas and his committee in a less heartless or damaging light. It was, in point of fact, an effort at damage control. "B" (possibly one of the Betts's?), for instance, wrote admiringly of Thomas's energy and persistence in bringing about a satisfactory resolution of the situation. As soon as the Moore fund was fully subscribed, the writer said, "the Moore family were called upon . . . it was represented to them firmly, but in a kindly spirit, that the coercive machinery of the health authorities would be put in motion against them" if they proved to be uncooperative.[32] It was as though it was obvious that it was in the Moore's best interest to move. Perhaps it was. It would cost them nothing and Moore would gain in addition four acres of apparently arable land and keep the house. The land was to be put in trust for the children, a rather intelligent move given Moore's reputation, and the trust administered by Henry Herrick a subscriber to the fund to have the family moved. It began to look like humanitarian aid, which in a sense it was, but nobody probed the wisdom of the action or inquired into the single-minded motivations of the summer colony in pursuing it in order to protect what they without question thought was rightfully their lake.

Walter Burling published no negative commentary, if in fact there was any, but did report at length on a meeting between the SVIA's health committee and Southampton's board of health in early September.[33] What emerged was interesting especially for the light it shed on the views of the health board. Thomas brought with him to the meeting Wales and another doctor. From the outset he was defensive in regard to the manner in which the Moores had been removed—"it was not a good one"—acknowledging that "it might seem rather a stretch of liberty on the part of the gentlemen from the city, a kind of interference with the rights of the townspeople." But what choice, he asked, had there been? A legal struggle to evict the Moores would have been lengthy and in doubt as to whether "this intolerable nuisance" could be eliminated. He may, he said, have been "over-zealous," but lives and property were at stake. At this point Thomas went on the offensive and reminded the board of health that summer residents had invested $500,000 in real estate over the previous ten years, and that it was perfectly natural that they should wish to preserve the health of their families. That figure of $500,000 may have sounded to some members of the board as rather like a threat, a small warning that the real estate boom might come to a halt unless the views of the summer colony were respected. But if they reacted to it, it was not reported. Thomas, however, not averse to an opportunity to drive a point home, said that in his experience newcomers to a community were frequently susceptible to sicknesses to which local inhabitants had built up some immunity. This was undoubtedly the case with the "insalubrious marsh" that was in such unfortunate proximity to many new residents now spending their summers around the lake. It was not just the Moores, it was the swamp itself. It had to be drained and cleaned out as an urgent matter of public safety. Its general "unsightliness," he also informed the meeting, was always remarked on by visitors and left them with an unnecessarily negative impression of the village.

Salem Wales heartily agreed and referred to the importance of state public health laws, the role of town health boards in enforcing them, and pointed to the fact that the state's board had condemned—or was about to condemn—the marsh for human habitation. The marsh, he continued, was a receptacle, "an open cesspool" for surrounding businesses. Twenty of them had opened since 1880, including a blacksmith's shop and a livery stable, and all of them were creating sewage that was "polluting the springs, defiling the lake, and infecting the water." He remembered the dysentery outbreak in 1880, his first season in Southampton, which caused him acute unease about settling in the village. Were not the circumstances precisely the same now where human and animal wastes were discharging into the lake? Then it had been wells located too close to privies, now it was a shining body of water that summer residents saw as their very own, the exact center of their summer universe. Wales did not say this, but may well have thought it, for it was to him his lake that was under attack. He who had had it tested, who scrutinized its surface, who had as it happened stocked it with his favorite fish. He did not nonetheless, and for all his genuine concerns for the health of the lake, raise the question of how much lake pollution could be attributed to discharges from the increasing numbers of cesspools on its shores as the number of summer cottages grew and how much from what he and Thomas claimed was the open sewer of the swamp.

The town's board of health did not, as they might justifiably have done, take them up on this issue. But they were unmoved both by the explanation of the necessity for removing the Moores and the characterization of the marsh as festering in pollution and disease. James Pierson, the town supervisor and president of the board of health, presided over this discussion. Others present at the meeting were Lewis Bowden, James H. Foster, and the health officer, Dr. David Hallock. Pierson turned the meeting over to Hallock. Dr. Hallock wasted little time getting to the point. In twenty-five years as a physician in Southampton, he said, he had never seen a single case of sickness attributable to the condition of the marsh. Although acknowledging that the marsh did contain pollutants, he strongly opposed building any direct drainage system at its head because that would have no other result than to deliver contaminants immediately into the lake. He favored limiting building around the marsh—he dismissed filling it in as too expensive—and leaving it to natural processes of drainage to flush it out over time. What would aid this process was the presence of forty rods of "clean white sand" between the marsh and the lake that would act as a natural filter. With that unequivocal statement, and basing its action on Hallock's recommendations, the board of health passed a simple resolution opposing the erection of any new buildings at the marsh "as dangerous to the public health." In furtherance of this, the board noted, it would use the courts if it became necessary.

This outcome, possibly unforeseen, represented a substantial defeat for Thomas and Wales and the SVIA in general. Worse, a full report of the proceedings was spread throughout the newspaper. Burling devoted four columns of small print to it. That nothing was done, however, nor would be done, to improve conditions at the head of the lake was evident from remarks made by Wales at the association's annual meeting the following year. There still existed, he felt bound to say, "two or three instances of the most shameful disregard of ordinary decency, one of which exists on Lake Agawam and well deserves the attention of the health board." But he left it there. Everyone present knew to what he was referring and the presence in their lives of the malodorous swamp, its exhalations and slow drainings into their beloved lake, was something the summer colony needed little reminding of and all knew, of course, that the town's board of health had made up its mind a year ago that nothing needed to be done. But he brightened up and finished on a happier note. The lake, he was pleased to say, was infinitely attractive to real estate investment while its shores had markedly appreciated in value since 1880 and were projected to do so even more in the future. In 1880, land along its perimeter was a modest $300 an acre. Now, in 1887, it had climbed to $4,000 an acre and showed no sign of stopping its dizzying ascent.

Two or three years later, Edward Foster, now a private citizen after losing the town clerkship to Lewis Bowden in a hotly contested election in 1886, reminisced with the local literary society about Southampton and how it was changing. Between stories of adolescent japes and Captain Ike's pigpen, where the captain heaved up onto an ever-growing hill of excrement the evacuations of his charges in order later to spread them liberally on his corn fields, Foster turned his attention to the summer colony's obsession with the purity of the waters, any waters, the waters of Lake Agawam, or any others apart from those of the ocean which were deemed, if a little salty, sufficiently pure. "If there is anything absurd and ridiculous," he told his audience, "it is for city people, who don't know what it is to have a breath of pure air, or a drink of pure water, from one month's end to another, to come to Southampton, where air and water are both as pure as God ever made them, and then keep up a constant harping about contaminations and dangers to health."[34] It was a salutary comment. Yet it symbolized the growing gap between local and summer cultures just as did Dr. Hallock's blunt disclaimer of any connection between the marsh and disease. The summer colony and its attendant doctors were never able to reconcile their interpretations of public health risks with those of local inhabitants, professional or otherwise, who drew on long experience of sickness and what did and what did not cause it. Local physicians were certainly capable of being wrong, and in the 1880 cases of dysentery they probably were, but in general their assumptions about what was likely to cause disease were considerably more down to earth than the hyperventilated anxieties of summer colony leaders who appeared to find the threat of disease wherever they looked. Still, they had got the Moores out and that, after all, had been the point.

In 1884, the association reported that Gaillard Thomas had generously donated an "ornamental well" to cover the antiquated and rusty village pump at the corner of Main Street and the Bridgehampton Road that had served the community for decades and perhaps for very much longer. This seemed to have been well received in the village, but a year later ambitious plans were developed to water the village's principal streets in an effort to hold down the dust in summer. A key question was water supply and how to deliver it. Not everybody was in favor of street watering, among them Thomas and Wales, both because of the considerable expense involved in purchasing equipment and supplying labor and because they thought the effort would be steeped in futility. But Frederic Betts pressed the matter on the grounds that many summer boarders often cut short their visits—a potential loss of new residents—owing to the Sahara-like conditions that frequently obtained in July and August. The women of the colony also complained of their dusty feet and dust-streaked frocks.

Nothing happened for another year, but Thomas eventually relented, importuned particularly by the wives, and the executive committee of the association decided that street watering would be undertaken by subscription. All might have been well, but the committee faced the problem of transferring water from the village pump to the one watering cart purchased for the job. Thomas's solution was to place a large water tank over the pump and let gravity fill the cart. The ornamental well was thus to be discarded and replaced with a looming wooden receptacle, an enormous barrel, at a main intersection of the village. This was not a success, in fact in the eyes of the village it was an aesthetic disaster and Thomas found himself suggesting that it be removed and the experiment abandoned. James Foster, now on the executive committee, demurred, however. He suggested leaving it in place for a year and then gauging village reaction. This sensible advice was accepted, since in time people will get used to anything, but not before Thomas had weighed in on one of his favorite themes of relations with the local inhabitants. He wanted it on record that it was "the fixed policy of the executive committee of this association to do nothing which would prove distasteful to the people of the village and to direct all its efforts toward the maintenance of harmony and good feeling between the permanent residents and those who passed their summers here only."[35] It was a fine sentiment and its sincerity could not be questioned, but given that but a few days previously Thomas had presided over the uncertmonious—some would say, forced—removal of George Moore and his family to the outer reaches of Southampton, a removal he had spent weeks or longer engineering, it might well be wondered if he ever questioned the propriety of some of his own actions and the reasons lying behind them. But Thomas did not seem to be the sort of man given much to that kind of introspection.

Whether the tank remained more than the year Foster suggested is unknown. It may have not, for according to an elderly village resident in the 1950s, who had been around at the time, a quite ingenious solution was adopted for supplying water to the cart. Frank Burnett, a boy in 1886, recollected that the watering carts were boxes on low wheels that were backed into the lake at Pond Lane and filled from the bottom through a trap door that closed automatically with the weight of the water. The water was then sprayed on the streets from pipes. It was called by some local village wag "Pond's Extract."[36] Wales, ever the booster of summer residence, and obviously pleased with the efforts to calm the dust that was "the only serious drawback to our blissful summer life" remarked that "if we can put down the dust on our numerous fine roads, no one doubts that another property boom will at once set in. All therefore who are in favor of another boom should contribute at once to the street watering fund."[37] The ayes would appear to have had it and the fund in consequence prospered.

A decade had passed since Thomas had erected his cottage on the dunes in 1877 and now there were fifty such cottages with the prospect for this booming summer community for another fifty or even a hundred more, who could tell. The Village Improvement Association, like the real estate market, had moved from strength to strength recording several notable victories and only a few defeats. Yet as an informal government of the village, a role it would always deny, it had not always endeared itself to local citizens and had managed to alienate or antagonize many of them. Where it had been successful was in enlisting the support of key members of the village community, both officials in town government and businessmen. The latter especially stood to gain from the free-spending habits of the summer colonists who patronized the stores, real estate and insurance agencies, livery stables, construction companies, and the like. Early account books from the period indicate a high volume of trade among such businesses. The day books for Hildreth's dry goods store, for example, reveal that a large number of summer residents maintained accounts there.[38] The same was true of most other business firms throughout the village. Some even had been established with the summer community with at least partly in mind such as a milliner and a jewelry shop. Most business owners had been elected to membership of the SVIA, were aware of its activities, and for the most part approved of its projects or at least found that none threatened their interests. Even demands that they clean up around their establishments or refrain from vulgar advertising, sometimes coupled with the threat of reprisals in the shape of withdrawal of custom, proved in time to be accepted. It was seen less as a burden and a cost of doing business than an opportunity to acquire more trade.

Similarly, the prominent role given local officials in the association—as secretary, treasurer, vice president, or member of the executive committee—was extremely useful in rendering more palatable some of the more intrusive projects that leaders of the association were apt to come up with. James Pierson, James Foster, and Lewis Bowden were particularly instrumental in lending it credibility and some degree of local legitimacy that otherwise it probably would not have been able to achieve. Foster, in a shrewdly designed move, was elected president of the association for the 1887–1888 year, the practice then being that presidents should serve one-year terms. Even White, president of the town trustees throughout the decade and always vigilant in the face of potential threats to the rights and privileges of the inhabitants, found he could cooperate with much that the association undertook. His issues with summer residents—the beaches, town rights, the sale or use of public land—were issues with individuals not with the association and reflected his role as a town trustee. He never served in any capacity on the SVIA and seldom attended meetings—his temperament was possibly unsuited to sitting on his hands and enduring the exhortatory perorations of men like Wales—but his willingness to assist in projects that seemed sensible to him was probably also a factor in enhancing its reputation. When he died several years later, Thomas wrote a moving tribute to his memory and observed that he was a man "(q)uick of temper, obstinate and outspoken in the expression of opinion, often uncompromising, he made enemies as well as friends in the discharge of what he deemed to be his duty. Yet no one ever charged him with a mean or unworthy action." His character, Thomas said, was incorruptible and his word final in questions of truth.[39] There were, and there were of course bound to be, points of contact and mutual respect between representatives of the two communities. Perhaps as well there were similarities between these two men.

Nonetheless, as everyone was aware, the Improvement Association was slated to remain a foreign body in the affairs of Southampton. Its sole object was to transform the village into an environment, both pleasing and safe, that suited the convenience and met the needs of the new summer colony. It had no other purpose. In pursuit of this end, its methods were essentially autocratic. Despite the integration of representatives of the local community into its ranks, its affairs were dominated and directed by no more than a half dozen men through its first five years of existence to 1887. Thomas, Wales, Schieffelin, the Betts brothers and, to a lesser extent, Howland and Kilbreth established the priorities and policies and also took the trouble to justify them in writing. These were then transmitted to the membership through the pages of the *Seaside Times*, which the association had some control over through its publisher, Walter Burling (through various subsidies), and to those local residents who took a lively interest in town and village affairs and also used its pages to great effect to debate other important issues. The paper routinely published the minutes and reports of the executive committee, which met monthly during the summer, as well as the year-end proceedings of the annual meeting in August. No one could complain that they were not adequately informed.

Yet it could not have been less than clear to all who read the paper that a cohesive leadership group monopolized decision making and carried out the policies it had formulated. Moreover, annual meetings were poorly attended. The dues-paying membership stood at about seventy between 1882 and 1887, perhaps one-third of whom were local, but never more than a dozen or so came to the annual meeting when the leadership summarized its actions and elections of officers were held. It may not suggest apathy or disinterest—there are other things to do on an August Saturday afternoon—but it does indicate an almost complete lack of democratic participation. This should come as no surprise. The association was not set up to be democratic in the first place but to provide leadership and focus to the interests of the summer community it more or less legitimately claimed to represent. The founding group, the dozen or so men who had met at Thomas's Fifth Avenue apartment in 1881, was and remained the core of the association through the 1880s. The only constraint on their power, paradoxically, came from the private advice given them by leading local citizens even if few of whom gave unequivocal support to their more extreme actions. Such counseling was not, as we have had occasion to see, always effective. The majority of summer members of the SVIA on the other hand, whose advice does not seem to have been much sought, appeared to have been content with whatever decisions the leaders would make on their behalf. There is no reason why it should have been otherwise. Few came to Southampton for the politics. It was for the sea air, the relaxing escape from the city. It was, in the priceless words of a later member of the colony, "the suction, you know" that brought them out, a beguiling and airy reference to the peculiarity, real or imagined, of the East End climate.[40]

The next two chapters discuss events and developments outside the village itself, particularly as they relate to the infusion of external capital and its investment in ambitious and quite large-scale projects. This was something that was also new to Southampton.

CHAPTER 4

THE MECOX BAY AFFAIR

I: LANDS UNDER WATER

Strictly speaking, the Mecox Bay affair, which began in 1882 and preoccupied Southampton for several years thereafter, had little to do with the emerging summer colony. Yet it hinged on the appearance of New York money in the town, money looking for investment opportunities as much as for the healthful and restorative powers of country living. It involved the seemingly innocuous and useful establishment of an oyster company on a body of water in Water Mill—Mecox Bay—known for more than two hundred years for its plentiful oyster harvests, which were only occasionally interrupted by over-fishing or some natural occurrence. But it tore the town apart, pitting town trustees and their vociferous supporters against both the proprietors of the common and undivided lands of Southampton and in particular against outside capitalist interests. In doing so, it raised deep legal and historical questions about the ownership of the waters and their products that went far back into the interpretation of the town's original patents and the land and water rights of key parties in the community. It affected everyone to a greater or lesser degree, but perhaps most of all the relatively poor baymen and farmers whose livelihood depended on the bays and whose political opinions began to count for the first time. Yet all the town's leading citizens also were drawn into the fray in one way or another and left for posterity a trail of conflicting and sometimes refreshingly eloquent opinion spread across the pages of the local newspaper. The affair opened up divisions and antagonisms in the town that had for the most part slumbered undisturbed through much of the century but now came glaringly to light. And it caused the town to examine its own past, and the evolution of those conflicts, in ways that would have been unimaginable a few years previously. It also led to a major lawsuit, the largest and certainly the most serious to that date in Southampton's history.

If the proprietors' sale of the Shinnecock Hills in 1861 had provoked some considerable controversy in the town, it was as nothing to the furor that erupted in 1881 and 1882 when first the trustees of the Shinnecock Hills sold out their entire interest in the 3,200-acre tract to representatives of Austin Corbin and his Long Island Railroad Company.[1] Then next, and within a year of that sale, the trustees of the proprietors disposed of all the remaining undivided common land in the town in which they possessed a valid right and could legally sell. At the same time, they sold an interest in other lands that happened to lie under water where their general legal claim to ownership as tenants in common was potentially suspect. Much of the town objected to this second and questionable part of the sale and resolved to challenge it through the town trustees who, it was rightly argued, had sole jurisdiction over the town's waters and possibly also the land that lay beneath them. Under the authority of the Dongan patent of 1686, the trustees, as incorporated by the patent, held the waters of the town (and before the state legislation in 1818 the town's unappropriated common lands) as a public trust for the beneficial enjoyment of the inhabitants. The trustees were therefore the appropriate legal body to take up the matter of the proprietors' sales and pursue it through the courts should they so decide or should the assembled inhabitants at town meeting enjoin them to do so. The situation quickly became so explosive that a long-standing board of town trustees was thrown out and a new one with a new president elected in its place. This was George Gilbert White, a farmer and retired whaling captain in his sixties and long the moral conscience of the community, a man we have already had ample occasion to meet.[2] The Mecox affair, and its outcome, largely came to define White's place in Southampton's history.

The lands in dispute lay under water. In the act of selling them, the trustees of the proprietors had essentially defined them as common lands under their sole ownership and management. They were the bay bottoms, lands under water in Mecox Bay, Shinnecock Bay, the West or Quantuck Bay, and Moriches Bay, which ran as far west as the Brookhaven town line. They also included smaller bays—Bull Head Bay, Cold Spring Bay—and a number of ponds, for example, Canoe Place Pond, Red Creek Pond, Fresh Pond.[3] Mecox covered twelve hundred acres and until the mid-1800s had traditionally been an immensely productive source of oysters, an oyster fishery regulated by the town trustees both before and after the historic compromise of 1818 effected with the proprietors over who was to control the lands and the waters.[4] The bay was open to all townsmen. Shinnecock Bay, known less for its oysters than for its scallops, clams, mussels, eels, and its rich floating fishery, contained sixteen thousand acres of land under water. In bays, ponds, and creeks Southampton possessed almost twenty thousand acres, or a little more than one-fifth of the total area of the town. But in one afternoon at a private sale in November 1882, the proprietors conveyed away virtually all of it in blanket quitclaim deeds for far less than their conceivable value.

Perhaps the storm that broke over the town in 1882 over the proprietors' sale of all the lands under water without exception would not have been quite so severe had not the purchasers represented outside interests from New York. Southampton at this time was, as we have seen, undergoing a fairly painful period of adjustment as substantial wealth was flowing into the community at an increasing rate and altering the economic landscape. The quitclaiming of the bays to outsiders was bound to provoke anxiety and suspicion. In the case of Mecox Bay, an oyster company was in the process of formation with its headquarters at the offices of Richard Esterbrook Jr. in downtown Manhattan. Esterbrook had been a Bridgehampton summer resident since 1879 and practiced law in New York on John Street. He was the son of a wealthy entrepreneur in Camden, New Jersey who had built a small empire manufacturing steel nib pens in the 1870s. This was to become the initial investment source for the oyster company.

Shell fishing in eastern Long Island, especially oysters, had become a major commercial activity for New York markets after the 1840s, very much facilitated by new rail routes providing rapid freight service to the city. Huntington, Islip, and Brookhaven, all with rich oyster fisheries in the Great South Bay, had seized on the economic possibilities of these markets even earlier and frequently leased out water lots in their bays and harbors to local residents and occasional outside investors for this purpose.[5] Once the Sag Harbor branch railroad had been completed in 1870, and particularly after its tracks had been linked to the South Shore line with the completion of the section between Eastport and Patchogue in 1881, the East End's access to New York markets for its produce was also immeasurably improved. For the first time, iced perishable goods could be moved into the city in a matter of hours without danger of spoilage.[6] In addition to this, the state had begun to take an active interest in Suffolk County's oyster fishery as a part of its general economic development policy of promoting commerce throughout the state, a policy it had been active in pursuing in many areas through much of the nineteenth century. In 1879, the legislature had authorized the formation of corporations in Suffolk County for the purpose of encouraging the development of the industry. An act was passed to promote "the planting, cultivation, taking up and protection of oysters, upon said several lots leased, occupied, or held by said persons"[7] This opened the way for outside corporate investment in a commercial area where it had previously been virtually absent. In fact, it is hardly unlikely that such interests, scenting major profits, prodded the legislature into action in the first place.

New York City's enthusiasm and apparently insatiable appetite for oysters, which ultimately had led to this legislation, began with the Dutch in the 1620s and peaked in the last half of the nineteenth century, by which time dozens of recipes, if not scores, had been committed to memory or the pages of cookbooks and hundreds of millions of oysters consumed. As Mark Kurlansky points out in his informative account of this culinary phenomenon, New York's surrounding waters contained some of the richest natural oyster beds to be found anywhere.[8] Wherever fresh water met salt water—in New York Bay, Princess Bay on Staten Island, the mouths of the Raritan and Navesink rivers in New Jersey, Jamaica Bay and the Rockaways, Great South Bay on Long Island, both shores of Long Island Sound beginning at the East River and City Island and extending as far east as Port Jefferson and Norwalk, Connecticut—large beds producing a seemingly inexhaustible supply of oysters were to be found. They were New York's cheapest food and a staple of the diet of working people who, it was said, lived all year "on nothing but oysters and bread." As a 1753 newspaper article put it, oysters were "the daily food of our poor" and the beds themselves "within view of the town."[9] In 1763, the first oyster bar opened in a cellar on Broad Street, an insalubrious part of downtown where oysters had been sold since the beginning of the century or even earlier.

The oyster boom continued until the late nineteenth century. At its peak, around 1870, the trade as a whole was estimated at $25 million annually, one-third of which was in New York.[10] After 1865, New York's central oyster market was moved for lack of wharf space from the East Side to Christopher Street on what was still known as the North River. At any given time, six million oysters were in barges tied up to Christopher Street wharves. By 1883, two hundred sloops a day were unloading on these oyster barges. None of this growth in the industry, however, necessarily implied prosperity. Oysters were cheap and had always been cheap. A report on the industry in 1881 said that oysters were sold at under $1.50 a basket or at a price that had not much changed in fifty years.[11] The key to success lay in bulk sales, but large-scale production had led to the predictable depletion of all natural oyster beds around New York by the early years of the century forcing buyers to look farther a-field for reliable sources of supply.

In part, this problem of large-scale production and resulting over-harvesting was addressed by cultivating oysters from seed. This was in fact Richard Esterbrook's intention in buying up the bottom of Mecox Bay as the natural beds had already been fished out years before. But cultivation was an expensive proposition. It was not new and, in the middle of the eighteenth century, had been introduced gradually to replace the exploitation of natural beds as these became unproductive. Experiments with the introduction of oyster seeds in parts of Great South Bay and off City Island had proved to be very successful and had effectively saved large-scale local oystering. However, it took three to four years, depending on conditions such as in particular water temperature, to produce marketable oysters of sufficient size. It also was expensive to maintain beds after harvesting to provide conditions suitable for raising future generations of oysters. Turning oysters into a renewable resource was an effective if costly way to prolong the life of the oyster industry more or less indefinitely, but it did not fully confront the necessity of harvesting in bulk to combat perennially low prices. To achieve this, more efficient means of harvesting had to be devised than the traditional method of employing oystermen in small boats using tongs to bring up the oysters, a method that did minimal damage to the beds.

Dredging had been introduced at the beginning of the century but it had opened to mixed reviews. First used by sailing vessels it involved dragging the sea floor with a heavy bar to which was attached a netting basket. It was certainly efficient, but at the same time highly destructive of the beds, roiling the bottom to such an extent that the material young oysters liked to attach themselves to was lost in the general slime of decaying organic matter. Dredging in the Navesink was banned as early as 1820 but later planted or renewable beds developed by private companies were exempted.[12] The same happened for the waters off City Island and in the Great South Bay. In 1870, the towns of Islip and Brookhaven banned dredging in the Bay but largely in response to the introduction of even more efficient (and destructive) methods of harvesting. Steam had replaced sail power with devastating results. Steam-powered vessels were estimated in 1880 to be capable of bringing to market twelve times the quantity of oysters typically expected from oyster fleets under sail.[13] The ban on dredging, nonetheless, was eventually lifted in the Great South Bay on the grounds that cultivated oyster beds were privately owned and the water lots in the bay containing them privately leased. With an eye to success at developing Mecox, Richard Esterbrook early purchased a small steamship for dredging his twelve hundred acres of bay bottom. He might reasonably have thought that Southampton's town trustees were unlikely to prohibit its use since he intended to seed the bay with his own oysters purchased elsewhere.

A further consideration that may have influenced Esterbrook's scheme to purchase Mecox Bay and capture some part of the New York market was the general pollution increasingly contaminating waters closer in to New York with catastrophic effects on the oyster population. Raw effluent flowed into these waters from rivers and streams while untreated sewage was dumped offshore in New York Bay—much of it fetched back by incoming tides—and the oyster beds suffered grievously. In the Rockaways, for instance, beds were closed because local towns had no means to dispose of waste other than to allow it to flow out into the bays. But Mecox Bay, for all Esterbrook may have known, was relatively pure and regularly opened to tidal action through cuts made in the narrow strand of beach by the town trustees that insured a steady, and, for the most part, annual circulation of fresh and salt water and the reduction of pollutants. With such a relatively pristine bay potentially available, he must have concluded that he could easily provide a decisive new source of supply to feed New York's unfailing appetite for fresh oysters. In an industry that had become heavily dependent on brand names he may have dreamt, who knows, of the Esterbrook Oyster, a worthy competitor to the Bluepoint, long the darling of connoisseurs. But, dreams aside, the key to his decision to go after Mecox Bay was unquestionably the open-door policy to oyster farming encouraging outside investment that was enshrined in the 1879 legislation.

Understandably, the towns affected were ambivalent about this legislation. Historically, the trustees of these towns, including Southampton, had managed and regulated shell fishing just as they controlled the use of all products of the waters from seaweed to gravel. And generally they had administered them for the public benefit of their own inhabitants while excluding nonresidents. Now, under a liberalizing state law, they could anticipate pressure from external business interests to lease or even sell water lots for cultivating and harvesting oysters. Town trustees, of course, still retained ultimate authority over town waters under their original patents (as these were recognized by the state) but now, as happened in some cases, they could face a flood of applications. Richard Esterbrook, obviously aware of this new legislation when he took up residence in Bridgehampton, must have considered it a key factor in his decision to form an oyster company and go after Mecox Bay. But equally persuasive would have been his erroneous conviction that he had only to deal with the trustees of the proprietors, a corporation with a specific interest in selling off all the lands under water that they now claimed as common and undivided land, a claim they had never previously made prior to 1881. Esterbrook would not have to deal with the town trustees at all and could, it appeared, afford to bypass them completely. Purchasing an interest in an entire bay, a twelve hundred-acre water lot, must have seemed to Esterbrook an extraordinary coup. Nothing like it had been seen in any other town in Suffolk County and nor was it likely to be.

Esterbrook's local involvement in Bridgehampton, and his subsequent success in purchasing the proprietors' interest in Mecox Bay, also was signally affected by his marriage to Antoinette Rose, the daughter of Judge Abraham T. Rose. Judge Rose had been a lifelong resident of Bridgehampton, born there in 1792, and an attorney in the village from 1820 until his death in 1857. At the time of his death, he had completed eight years as county judge. He was an important member of the powerful Rose family in North Sea, the same family that had dominated the proprietors and their board since early in the nineteenth century and in particular by General Abraham Rose who had organized the division of interests in the lands and waters between the town and the proprietors in 1818. The judge's younger cousin, Colonel David Rogers Rose, became president of the proprietor trustees in 1862, dying in office in 1889, and was influential in orchestrating the sales of the common lands above and under water in 1882. Abraham Rose, although never a trustee himself, acted on the proprietors' behalf on several occasions in the 1840s and 1850s in defending proprietor rights in court, principally in respect to their interests in the Shinnecock Hills. Richard Esterbrook thus was fortunate in choosing Antoinette Rose for a spouse, and indeed it proved decisive when he sought to purchase the bottom of Mecox Bay. He was especially well-placed to acquire advance knowledge of the proprietors' plans. The couple also accumulated considerable property along Ocean Road in Bridgehampton and built a handsome summer cottage there at the corner of Sagaponack Road.[14]

Meanwhile, Shinnecock Bay, the western bays, and other lands besides had been acquired from the proprietors in separate deeds by Henry W. Maxwell of Brooklyn, a young investment banker and broker and later a multimillionaire who at the time was a vice president and director of the Long Island Railroad and a trusted associate of Austin Corbin. In February 1883, Maxwell turned over his new properties to John A. Bowman, a banker and land speculator from St. Paul, Minnesota who was Corbin's agent for the purchase of the Shinnecock Hills in 1881. Bowman later conveyed all of this property—the Hills, the lands under water, and all other lands Maxwell had picked up—to the Long Island Improvement Company, a company that had been formed by Austin Corbin and others, also in 1881.[15]

None of these transactions and networks was lost on the inhabitants of Southampton. Early in 1883, Benjamin F. Squires of Atlanticville in the western part of the town at what was formerly known as Fourth Neck and is now East Quogue organized a campaign on what had quickly come to be called the Bay Question. However, the Bay Question for many, Squires included and certainly all of the baymen, meant Shinnecock Bay rather than Mecox Bay. The threat to the subsistence living of small farmers augmenting their incomes from the products of the bays was seen as primarily affecting those living along the shores of the western bays. The response in Bridgehampton and Water Mill to the takeover of Mecox Bay was, by contrast, much more muted. At Mecox there was only a seasonal oyster harvest to consider, and local dependence on the bay was correspondingly limited. The selling of Mecox became an issue of principle, whereas that of the western bays was understood as one of survival. Benjamin Squires owned thirteen acres, a half mile of bay front, and a hotel or boarding house for visiting sportsman on Tiana Bay, an arm of Shinnecock Bay, and was quick to see the threat to the bay and his business as well as to the livelihood of his neighbors. The new owners could easily and possibly legally close off the bays to duck hunters and sports fishermen as well as to the large numbers of baymen dependent on its rich resources. But not only the baymen. Some years later Squires noted that between 1882 and 1887 nearly $300,000 had been invested by summer homeowners in land, buildings, housing, and improvements along the shores of Shinnecock Bay from

Quogue to Ponquogue Light. If, he was later to say, those who had invested heavily in bayfront property had known that "when they stepped off their estates below low water mark they were trespassing on the lands under water of a greedy and unscrupulous corporation not a dollar of this money would be invested."[16]

At the first meeting of the campaign in early 1883, Squires told a packed crowd that their bay privileges were being eliminated "by the iron hand of monopoly." The bay bottoms, he went on, were economically the most valuable part of the town and water rights therein had been "enjoyed in peace for 243 years." Cries of "look out for our liberty" and "the bay must be free" were heard from the assembled baymen.[17] The Dongan patent, which for many seemed to protect those rights, was not yet waved aloft but it was about to be. It was printed in its entirety in the *Seaside Times* a short while later (probably for the first time since 1830 when the town trustees had it printed in pamphlet form to reinforce their legitimacy before the state legislature as Dongan trustees). A few weeks before, Squires had written to the paper that the town, not the proprietors, owned the lands under water and that "in common honesty" the proprietors should "refund the money" to those deceived into thinking that they were now the new owners.[18] But in a subsequent letter, John Bowman sought to assuage local opinion. The new company he represented—the LIIC—while claiming the bottom of Shinnecock Bay, would in no way interfere with surface fishing except in small areas where it might erect fish pens "under deed from the company."[19] William Pelletreau, a key member of the proprietor trustees and their most frequent and articulate spokesman, reacted favorably to this and observed in the same issue of the paper that this new ownership of the bay, giving it exclusive rights to plant oysters, might well turn the bay bottom "from its present unprofitable condition to one of usefulness and advantage." This was all very well, but it could have hardly been clear to Pelletreau at that moment, or indeed at any later time, that the purpose underlying the acquisition of Shinnecock Bay by Austin Corbin's associates was solely (or, indeed, at all) for the cultivation of oysters.

Nor would it have been clear to White who was now leading the charge against the sale of the bay bottoms, both in the pages of the local paper and through efforts to mount a town trustee suit of ejectment against the new owners of Mecox Bay, the Mecox Bay Oyster Company. The trustees, after much effort and preparation, eventually took the company to court in 1885 and won. They also won again after two unsuccessful appeals by the company in 1887 and 1889. The town, like the village could not have been more fortunate in the decade of the 1880s in having a man like White as president of the trustees. From 1883, when he was first elected, until his death in late 1893 he fought with consuming energy and determination for what he understood to be the rights of the common run of inhabitants. In this case, it was the right to the unobstructed use of the bays. Later he took on the question of the ownership of the beaches. He was new to political office in 1883, never having held a town post before but was no less effective for this lack of experience. He was cantankerous, truculent, no friend to the proprietors who he thought were simply in the business of lining their own pockets, and just as suspicious of the motives of the developing summer colony.[20] As an old-time whaling captain, White also enjoyed high prestige in the community, belonging to a small elite much admired for their courage and leadership abilities. Whaling had all but disappeared in Sag Harbor twenty years previously, but there were still a number of hardy old captains alive who, like White, commanded respect and occasionally went out in small boats after a stray right whale that had ventured too far inshore.

In the other celebrated lawsuit of that era—the Betts case, also an action of ejectment—White opposed the summer colony. In this instance, Wyllys Betts, a young lawyer and summer resident, had first leased in 1879 and then purchased a considerable acreage on the south west side of Lake Agawam from the proprietors. It included a section of the beach south of the dunes to the surf. Betts had constructed a small colony of his own on this property, in all erecting six cottages. Part of it he leased to Saint Andrew's Dune Church in 1881. As briefly noted when he died in 1887, he left the small dune parcel to the church while the rest of the property passed to his younger brother, Frederic. White led the town trustees into battle over the question of the ownership of this beach. Frederic Betts—the suit was brought after his brother's death—was cited for "unlawfully withholding" the land in dispute from the town. In testimony at the 1892 trial, White claimed that the beach was public land and its use "from time immemorial . . . exercised and enjoyed by the people of the town as a matter of common right." Notwithstanding, the town trustees lost the case in State Supreme Court. Betts successfully defended his title to the beach to high water mark, but in a later appeal the town trustees were able to claim the beach as a public highway.[21] The issues it raised, however, are important for they involved the increasingly widespread sale of beach lands and shorefront in general, sales taking place not only throughout Southampton but in Easthampton also. In 1882, the Easthampton town trustees quitclaimed all the beaches and adjacent common or unallotted lands in the town from Wainscott to Napeague and along much of Gardiner's Bay, that is, virtually all of Easthampton's shorefront. The principal buyer was Bowman, Corbin's agent. It raised a public outcry in Easthampton. Some of the sales were retracted and the town trustees were forced to give an account of their actions after being thrown out of office a year later. Southampton's town trustees experienced a similar fate in the same year over the question of the lands under water. An angry town accused them of paying insufficient attention to the proprietors' sales of the bay bottoms and voted in an entirely new board. It was this board—White's board—that took the oyster company to court and later sued Frederic Betts.

Captain White, then, was very much the man to take the measure of the trustees of the proprietors. He was never a proprietor himself though his roots lay in the seventeenth century among the early settlers of Southampton, and in the eighteenth century his family was certainly in possession of commonage rights. The earliest White on record—John White—came to Southampton in 1644. By the nineteenth century, the Whites were an extensive clan, its members found all over Southampton but particularly associated with the area of Sebonac adjacent to North Sea. But White, like several of his relatives, spent much of his life at sea. He went whaling as early as 1834 at the age of fifteen (he was a cabin boy), a career he pursued for much of the following thirty years. In 1844, he became master of the Tuscany, although it was unfortunately wrecked a year later in the Indian Ocean. His last voyage was in command of the Timor, a vessel of 280 tons, which embarked for the Pacific in 1856 and returned to Sag Harbor fully laden in 1859. Thereafter he described his occupation as farming and fishing even if his whaling days were never entirely over.

As late as winter 1882, he and his cousin, Captain Jetur R. Rose fastened to a right whale off the South Beach. Rose, as the *Seaside Times* put it, gave it "the finishing touch" and reported that thirty barrels of oil were to be expected from Burnett's try-works. This was the same Jetur Rose who became president of the proprietor trustees in 1889, succeeding his father Colonel David R. Rose. And the same Jetur Rose who, in 1881, as president of the trustees of the Shinnecock Hills, sold the Hills to John Bowman and relinquished his presidency to him. It rather suggests that however inflamed the politics of land sales might become, family ties as well as old bonds forged in the hazardous whale fishery could still assert themselves. Rose and White were further linked by the marriage of David R. Rose to a cousin of White's, Mary White. Jetur Rose was a few years younger than White and began his seafaring life a little later. It followed the same pattern as his cousin's of many years at sea until he retired in 1869 to "a quiet and useful life." But then suddenly in 1888 he left for a year's voyage to the Pacific unable to resist the call of the sea.

Possibly George White was better suited to the task of fighting outside interests and defending the rights of Southampton's freeholders than was the town supervisor, James H. Pierson. This was less a matter of ability than of temperament, but also of the nature and responsibilities of the office. Pierson had been elected on the Republican ticket in 1881 and served continuously throughout a very contentious time until 1902 when a relative unknown from Sag Harbor ousted him in a shockingly close vote. He was a descendant of Henry Pierson, one of the earliest of Southampton's town clerks, yet, in something of a paradox, was little suited for public life. Pelletreau, who knew him well, once observed that he distrusted his own ability, which all men knew he possessed in abundance, and that this prevented him from attaining the political prominence in the state that many thought he deserved. He was three times elected to the New York Assembly. But as Southampton's supervisor, an office he occupied longer than any incumbent since 1693 when it was created, he served the town well, was always held in the highest esteem, and preserved a firm Republican control over the town's politics.

This was still the party of progress, good government, and business growth. It represented the main land-owning and business interests of the community and during Pierson's tenure it had little difficulty turning aside Democratic challengers. Pierson was a conciliatory man, skilled in the art of compromise and, the evidence suggests, with little taste for or faith in strategies of confrontation. In a twenty-year period of quite dramatic social and economic transformation in Southampton, he proved to be both astute and patient. In particular, he reacted to the burgeoning demands of the summer colony and its increasingly powerful policy apparatus, the SVIA, with the tact of a diplomat, something that White would have found quite impossible to sustain. There is little in the record to show that the two worked especially closely together in the decade or so in which their tenures overlapped. Their respective functions were, anyway, quite different. The supervisor's role was largely administrative—schools, taxes, roads, policing, health, poverty, and so on—where the trustees' duties lay in regulating the use of the waters and their products and more generally in protecting the historical interests and rights—the Dongan rights—of the town. White took to this latter role with relish, and very likely James Pierson was relieved to have a man of such conviction running matters at the trustees. His Republican predilections might have led him to counsel moderation, but the developing Bay Question left him free to pursue town business and, fortuitously, kept the Democrats—of whom White was one—from his door. With the Mecox affair looming, the Democrats now had something to do and White, one is almost tempted to say out of historical necessity, was the man to do it.

Whereas James Pierson chose not to express himself publicly on the bay issue—he never wrote to the *Seaside Times* on any matter—Edward H. Foster, the town clerk since 1870, sided with White and questioned the right of the proprietors to sell the bays. In two letters to the paper in 1883, he reviewed the uneasy relations between the town and the proprietors that had persisted through much of the nineteenth century since 1818. The town, he said, had "chafed" under proprietor restraints throughout the period, monies from the sale of lands, leases, and privileges had disappeared into their pockets, and there had been occasional legal confrontations. One of these was the seaweed trial of 1866, a suit for which the town trustees had appropriated funds but ultimately lost. Any examination of the town records, he added, "speak for the town and oppose Proprietor interest."[22]

Foster was the son of a prosperous landowner and farmer in Southampton, Isaac Post Foster; and, like White, of an old respected seventeenth-century family. An earlier Foster also had served as clerk and scrupulously kept the eighteenth-century records of the town. Isaac Foster was one of the original twenty-two purchasers of the Shinnecock Hills in 1861, buying one of the fifty shares subscribed. He was also a proprietor trustee. Edward Foster taught school for a while and then went into business in insurance and real estate, accumulating in the process some independent wealth and property. He entered Republican politics as a young man, becoming town clerk in his twenties, and later served as commissioner of highways. He also was something of a scholar and assisted Pelletreau in preparing the first three volumes of the town records for publication. He was nearly as well versed as the latter in the town's history and wrote occasional pieces for the paper on historical issues. But he was an interesting example of how even members of leading families could turn against the old order of land and privilege in the developing crisis of the 1880s. However, like Pierson he was a man of compromise, a conciliator, and remained in the background. He did appear at the Mecox Bay trial in 1885 but only in his capacity as clerk and keeper of the town records. He was called on to recite some parts of those records but testified to nothing else. Nor did he deliver himself publicly of any further opinion in the matter. Ultimately perhaps, Edward Foster was his father's son. When Isaac Post Foster died in 1885, he replaced him on the proprietors' board of trustees.

Pelletreau, Foster's immediate predecessor as town clerk in the 1860s, was, unsurprisingly, not a member of White's new body of town trustees in 1883. After having served continuously on the board since 1870 he was not re-elected. He had been the main supporter of the proprietors and a most eloquent one at that—he was himself a proprietor trustee as well as a town trustee up to this point—but it was clear after the bay controversy erupted in 1882, that he could serve no further useful purpose on it. He was too closely identified with the proprietors for an angry town to countenance his re-election. And one senses anyway that Pelletreau had little sympathy for the concerns of the poorer inhabitants of the town who stood to be most hard hit by the developing crisis. Still, the presence of both he and White on the same board might have made for some lively exchanges. Although it was not to be, their opposing views of the Mecox Bay question were spread almost weekly on the pages of the paper for all to read: Pelletreau, ever the urbane, persuasive defender of proprietor rights, and White—intemperate as always—on the attack.

In one letter among several Pelletreau wrote, he maintained that the trustees of the proprietors were entirely within their rights in selling lands under water, that there was nothing in the 1818 compromise legislation to suggest that such lands were anything but common lands, and invoked the so-called "saving clause" at the end of the act. This clause allegedly left open for future discussion or litigation the legal ownership of the lands and the waters. George Rogers Howell, writing from Albany where he was now the assistant librarian in the State Library, also weighed in on this issue but from an opposite perspective.[23] He wrote in defense of the common law rights of the public to the waters, and claimed that he had been told that in 1818 an unnamed proprietor had "with remarkable shrewdness and foresight" inserted this clause "in order to nullify the whole compromise." This clause had stated that "the right to the fee of the lands and the waters shall not be affected by the act." Howell thought this was absurd and that the town was "not so stupid as (not) to detect such a trap."[24] As for the proprietors, he said, having bargained away the waters, they could not cancel the agreement in the next breath. A week later, he added that the proprietors have "no show of title to the water privileges they have gone through the forms of selling." Howell was, of course, a member of one of Southampton's old elite families tracing its history in the town back to 1640, in fact to one of its key leaders Edward Howell. He was a distinguished man of letters besides with several academic degrees to his name. Given his status in the community, it is perhaps surprising that he was so quick to side with White. Among that upper social class he was in fact virtually alone in doing so and committed himself at an early stage of the fight. Interestingly, at the town election held a month after he had written these letters, the same election at which Pelletreau's town trustees were swept from office, Howell ran for town clerk on the Democratic ticket against the incumbent, Edward Foster. But he lost.

II: THE FREE BAY BOARD

White was little interested in such niceties of legal argument, leaving them to the scholars, although he had in fact written to Howell for his opinion in the matter. With his usual bluntness, he wanted to know "if there is not a set of men preying on this town, selling our roads and highways to the new comers, the city people, for fabulous prices . . . It is the same on our waters."[25] And in another letter he raised the temperature even higher. Referring to the Maxwell purchase of Shinnecock Bay, he wrote "one thing is certain:

Mr. Wm. S. Pelletreau and the proprietors have sold every man who goes on the bay or water of this town to the Long Island Railroad."[26] Nor could he resist throwing back in Pelletreau's face something the latter had written in an article on Southampton the previous year. In 1818, Pelletreau had said, "the word proprietor was another name for grasping, unscrupulous avarice." But now, Pelletreau thought, the proprietors had always been "the bone and sinew of the settlement" and had laid the foundations for its successful growth. He was, of course, a proprietor trustee himself and had supported the blanket sales of common land in November 1882. Indeed, he had directly benefited from them in acquiring a sizable property at Red Creek Pond, in fact the pond itself and the land under it.

Immediately after this lively correspondence matters came to a head. At the annual town meeting at the beginning of April 1883, the existing board of town trustees was voted out almost to a man. Albert J. Post, clerk to the town trustees since before the Civil War and town clerk from 1858 to 1862, and two others were the sole holdovers. Pelletreau was gone after twenty years in town government, first as town clerk after Post and then on the trustees' board. It was a watershed election and a rude awakening for the political forces that had largely cooperated with the proprietors since the trustees' last attempt to rein them in over the seaweed question after 1862. In reality, it was the most serious crisis in town politics since the contentious years that led up to the compromise of 1818. Attesting to its importance to the town's electorate, a single issue had turned out of office a trustee's board that had been routinely reelected as a body by voice vote each year since at least 1872.

Underlying the Mecox Bay question was, however, a general dissatisfaction with the proprietors. Their actions had long been seen as self-serving, secretive, and conducted with little regard for the welfare of the community. The blanket conveyances of bay bottoms and all undivided common lands throughout the limits of the town, the location of much of which in the Quogue and Topping's purchases west of the Shinnecock Hills remained unknown—hurriedly and privately disposed of to outsiders or their own intimates—sent shock waves through the community. Added to this was the loss of the Shinnecock Hills to development interests in 1881, a sale engineered by men with close ties to the trustees of the proprietors. If White saw all of this as the not so gradual loss of the town's assumed birthright, he probably articulated the sentiments of a majority of the inhabitants.

The 1882 sales had been predicted well in advance. At the 1880 town meeting, a committee consisting of Edwin Hedges, William Pelletreau, and Doyle Sweeney, a local lawyer, had been appointed to search title to the lands under water and appropriated $50 for its expenses. Remarkably, Everett A. Carpenter, one of the best-known and successful attorneys on the East End and soon to be a principal stockholder in the Mecox Bay Oyster Company, was added to the committee as legal counsel. However, the committee could not agree on a final report, and each filed separate opinions. Predictably, Pelletreau wrote that the bay bottoms were undivided land and belonged to the proprietors; Sweeney concluded that they were washed by tidal waters frequently nourished by the ocean through breaches in the barrier beach and were thus in some sense public; while Hedges thought the question of ownership could only be settled through the courts. This weak and inconclusive result of the committee's work (it had taken most of a year) satisfied no one and the three reports were tabled in 1882. The failure to develop a clear and united position probably contributed to the collapse of the trustees' legitimacy a year later. Pierson and Foster avoided the general bloodletting that ensued, a result of the immunity of town government from trustee issues. Government and trustee jurisdictions had been sharply differentiated since the beginning of the nineteenth century as the administrative role of town government progressively expanded in scope. This reflected both the demographic growth of the town and its tax base, and its steady economic diversification after the Civil War.

The new town trustees under the populist leadership of White represented a shift to greater democracy in the town. For the first time, they had the active support of sections of the electorate whose voice in town affairs had generally been muted in the past and usually ignored. For all their differences with the proprietors, the trustees in the nineteenth century were part of the local establishment and elected from it. The split between town and proprietors in 1818, despite the support it gained from the inhabitants in general, had been a split within the elite. The post-1818 trustees, in taking over from the old board, simply continued the regulatory practices of the latter in respect to the waters and left the proprietors to their own devices. For the following sixty years the two groups had, with some exceptions, little to disagree about and coexisted quite amicably. Members of the trustees of the proprietors routinely served in administrative capacities in the town—supervisor, town justice, clerk, and so on—just as did many town trustees. By and large, it was a lengthy period of mutual accommodation between powerful sectors of the community.

But now the situation had changed radically with the Bay Question. Not only had the reputation of the proprietors suffered, so had that of the town trustees, now seen as unwilling or unable to challenge them. The bays had become a townwide issue and drew into it constituencies that were seldom heard from. These were the small farmers and baymen, perhaps some of the smaller shopkeepers and tradesmen, working people in general who supplemented their incomes from the bays or simply brought food to the table. The sale of the remaining undivided lands by the proprietors had much less of an impact on this largely rural working class. Proprietor restraints and regulation on access to common land had certainly been a source of discontent in the nineteenth century, but as more and more of it was sold off there was correspondingly less of it to raise an outcry about. In any case, it was the poorer class that had suffered most from regulation; those who could not afford to turn their geese and few livestock into the roads and common fields or who lacked rights to do so.

The most vocal support for the new trustees' board came from the small farmers and baymen who made a subsistence living on the periphery of the bays in the Quogue and Topping's purchases from Canoe Place to Speonk. There were estimated to be about five hundred of them. Their living was fairly marginal: small farm plots, some livestock, and a minimal income augmented by clamming, eeling, fishing, or oystering. Until the 1860s, that income had been reasonably sufficient as long as the bays remained productive. A new member of the town trustees from this western part of the town, Tuthill Carter, estimated that income from Shinnecock Bay had been about $125,000 in 1858 and increased to $150,000 in 1863. Every bayman could count on $2 to $5 a day in season from clamming alone. But with the subsequent decline of Shinnecock Bay, resulting from the inability to maintain a regular outlet to the ocean over the narrow barrier of the South Beach, income had fallen to $30,000 a year. The health of the bay, and with it that of the fishery, the scallop, clam, and mussel beds, was essentially a function of the periodic circulation of the waters in and out of the ocean. In addition to the uncertainty of the inlet and the cost of opening and maintaining it—reckoned at three thousand man-hours in the 1880s—Shinnecock Bay had badly silted up on its south side. A series of winter storms in the 1870s had washed great quantities of sand over the beaches and into the bay rendering it shallow and all but unnavigable except by small boats. It was for the most part land-locked and tideless. The lack of circulation had killed the clam beds and severely depleted the fish stocks.

It was principally for this reason that a campaign began in the 1870s to persuade the state legislature to approve construction of a canal connecting Peconic and Shinnecock bays at Canoe Place Pond (now part of the Shinnecock Canal). The science behind this was that the slightly higher elevation of Peconic Bay (almost a foot), coupled with strong tidal action from Gardiner's Bay and the Atlantic beyond, should combine to force heavy volumes of water into Shinnecock Bay. This in turn should open an inlet on the South Beach and also prevent it from closing. In northeast storms, when water is pushed by wind and tide against the western shore of Peconic Bay and some of that water is released through a canal, the effect of forcing the opening of an inlet was thought to be the likely result. A canal could then maintain a half-tide, keep the inlet running, and over time carry the sand flats out to sea. Moreover, the water in the Peconics was salt water and that was exactly what Shinnecock Bay and its fishery needed. Such was the theory. In practice, after the canal was built, these effects were less reliable than initially anticipated. Efforts were made through the 1920s to maintain tidal action in the bay, but it was not until the great hurricane of 1938 that the problem was finally solved. The hurricane opened a wide inlet from the ocean that was eventually stabilized and made permanent.

There were other reasons besides for the construction of a canal, among them the desire for an inland waterway—"a good inside passage"—connecting Greenport, Riverhead, and Sag Harbor to the Great South Bay, the Rockaways, and the Lower Bay in New York. These were new reasons, new in the 1880s, and reflected increasing concern over high and monopolistic freight rates imposed on merchants and farmers by the LIRR. A further and not insignificant reason for purifying the waters of Shinnecock Bay by improving circulation was to increase the attractiveness of its shores for summer residents and resort construction. In 1884, Austin Corbin and the Long Island Improvement Company, the new owners of the Shinnecock Hills, brought some pressure to bear in Albany for a new appropriations bill for the canal. From their point of view a land-locked Shinnecock Bay could become a stagnant pond. In summer 1881, the inlet had been closed and the heads of the creeks on the bay became unpleasantly malodorous. Several years later conditions had still not improved. In 1887, the shore of the bay was "white with dead fish" and the bay itself stagnant with muddy water. Did the town want to drive summer visitors away, someone asked in the newspaper, for if it did, "New Jersey stands ready to receive all such"?

But from the vantage point of the baymen a tide-less bay was more than just stagnant, it was dead. Its declining productivity threatened to undercut a good part of their livelihood if the canal was not built. Worse, canal or no canal, access to the bay was in doubt now that Henry Maxwell had gained control of the bottom of it and was about to deliver it into the hands of the LIIC. The canal was eventually built but only after an uphill struggle with a parsimonious legislature. It was finally completed in 1892. Besides this, there was opposition in both the town and the county from many who feared that the state would impose the cost of maintaining the canal on local authorities. And there were others besides who cared little for the plight of the baymen.

It was a difficult few years. Without the canal, the chances of maintaining an inlet for any length of time were small with predictable consequences for the health of Shinnecock Bay. The committee of the trustees did succeed in opening the beach in March 1888 but it closed within a month. Opened again in April, it ran wide and deep until late October, so much so that a schooner was reported as passing through it. But it was all too unpredictable, dependent on month-to-month and year-to-year weather conditions. Meanwhile, the construction of the canal (which was intended to solve the problem) proceeded at a glacial pace, hampered by winter storms that frequently undid a previous year's work and an inattentive legislature that doled out petty amounts for its continuation. It amounted to stop and start progress as each small appropriation was exhausted. Despite constant pleading from the state engineer and Edward Whitaker in the attorney general's office, between 1885 and 1891 never more than $15,000 was allocated in any one year. Storms washed out the canal's banks and, in one instance, destroyed the retaining dam constructed at the Peconic end. It took an extraordinary eight years to dredge a channel four thousand feet long and one hundred feet wide with a depth generally regarded as too shallow for the purpose. And ultimately it did not work.

After the canal's completion, it was beset with problems with its lock gates and bridge abutments through the 1890s. Adequate gates were not installed until 1919. But it was never able to fulfill its intended function of raising the water level in Shinnecock Bay so that a semipermanent inlet could be maintained or at least reopened when necessary. Had it not been for the devastating hurricane of 1938, it might have been judged a white elephant; good for connecting the bays for recreational boaters but not much more. The hurricane created a permanent inlet that was eventually stabilized, first with wooden pilings in 1939 and then, beginning in 1952, hardened with the construction of stone jetties. Regardless of the fact that the state had not done much of a good job in the 1880s—although its engineers can hardly be faulted in the absence of adequate resources—it eventually became obvious to everyone that controlling and directing tidal forces was far more complicated than had been imagined. But at least the town had its canal. In particular, it raised the hopes of the baymen whose livelihood was at stake and further fueled their demands for a Free Bay.[27]

Those, like Pelletreau, who thought that private development was essential if the bays in general were to become productive, took the position that the bays in their present condition would drive families into the poor house. White thought this was a complete fallacy. "Thrifty farmers," he said, "dwell around the bays. Their prosperity lies in the bays—that is where they get their fertilizer and loose change." For every dollar they gain from farming, he went on to say, they make ten from fishing, clamming, and eeling. Were the bays to be privatized, eliminating all uses of the bay bottoms, all privileges and old rights would be swept away. Others said the same thing. Even the right to drive an eel stake, set nets, or stake fish ponds would disappear. It would be nothing but a "monopoly of our water privileges by a few men, to the exclusion of the poor man from his natural and just rights."[28] Benjamin Squires had called it "the iron hand of monopoly" and thought that this, much more than the quality of the waters, could put a man and his family in the poor house. It was not surprising that the baymen were incensed and that they became the key factor in sweeping a new board of town trustees into power.

But more representative government after 1883 did not at all mean that the new town trustees would prove to be a modernizing and progressive force. In fact it was in many respects the opposite. The new board was much less able to deal with the changing realities of Southampton than the old and was deeply suspicious of change of any sort. Not surprisingly, it was anticapitalist and nativist, reflecting a small-town localism typical of the time that was mistrustful of large-scale capitalism and the impersonal urban values of money and success that it represented. The trustees went after the Mecox Bay Oyster Company and Richard Esterbrook rather than the proprietors who had quitclaimed the bay to them in the first place. The latter might surely have presented a more inviting target. Yet, at the same time, to have confronted the proprietors in court over such a contentious issue risked exposing the fractures within the community too openly and with potentially lasting damage. In the event the trustees did not, although it had been the proprietors who had initiated what they viewed as an illegal sale. The trustees' suspicion of the outside world was also reflected in their dealings with the fast-growing summer colony and the inroads it was making in the village. They did little to negotiate with the colony's leadership and took limited interest in the development of the village. Of course, given the jurisdiction of the trustees—responsibility for the waters of the town—they were under no obligation to concern themselves with conditions in the village except its two large ponds, other conditions being a matter for negotiation between the town's other elected officials and the Village Improvement Association.[29] In effect, it was a quite conservative board, even reactionary, devoted in the beginning to the one issue it had been elected to pursue and operating in what it and its supporters perceived as a hostile environment. Nonetheless, the town meeting of April 1883, and the clamor leading up to it resulting in the election of a brand new board, was a watershed in Southampton politics. The annual ritual, more or less moribund since the 1860s, now had new life breathed into it by a single crucial issue, and decisively put in office a group of men with few ties to the establishment. Most were Democrats or independents.

This was the Free Bay Board as it was called at the time and for years to come. The slate of twelve candidates rode into office on a "vote taken by uplifted hands (which) was large and unanimous." The new board, apart from two members of the vast Halsey clan and the much-respected Albert Post who altogether served thirty years as town trustee, consisted of a number of political unknowns, most from Atlanticville and Good Ground in the western part of the town. White himself was a neophyte in town politics, never having served in any previous capacity. Besides White, Post, and the two Halseys, none owned land to any extent. In contrast, the old board members owned substantial amounts of valuable farmland and other real estate. Only three members of the new board possessed commonage rights in proprietary lands, all of them minor, and none at all in the Town Purchase or eastern sector of the town.

Nonetheless, it was an effective board, proceeding with alacrity on the issue for which it had been elected. Benjamin Squires, two other members of the Squires family, and Tuthill Carter and John Quinn, led the western representatives. As noted, the western part of the town was much more alarmed at the loss of the bays than the east. Clearly, they saw the threat to the fisheries in Shinnecock Bay—a far larger and diversely productive body of water than Mecox—in much starker terms (Bowman's assurances to the contrary). Squires had led the mass meeting in Atlanticville in March when "monopoly forces" had been ringingly denounced. This new board of trustees was re-elected just as routinely as the previous one into the 1890s and, in its own way, became just as conservative. Although having decisively won the Mecox Bay case by 1889, it became much more disposed to leasing parts of the bays for oyster planting, in doing so resuming the practice of old boards going back as far as the eighteenth century. This precipitated a new fight between "Free Bay" and "Leased Bay" partisans that continued into the 1900s. Still, these trustees, with some inevitable changes of personnel, remained substantially popular throughout their period of dominance and even after White's death in 1893. Until 1891, they were returned by voice vote or a show of hands. In 1890, a resolution in town meeting to elect trustees and other officers by ballot failed, if not by much. The following year, the board as a whole was re-elected on ballot—votes had seldom been counted in the past and then only as they related to specific issues before the town—but the margin of victory was quite slim: 123 to 106. It suggested that the trustees' new policy of leasing the bays did not sit well with "Free Bay" sentiment.

Tighter voter controls over elections to the board were introduced in 1892 when all of the candidates, of whom by now there were many more than the twelve required by the Dongan patent, were subjected to a competitive election. The votes, along with the candidates' names, were published. Shortly before this, the two political parties had begun to publish their slates of candidates for all town offices in the newspaper. These developments in procedure were an indication that the old way of doing town business by a self-selected political class was on the way out.[30] What had been shaping up, and had been precipitated by the controversy over the bays, was a struggle with the town's elite. Whether it was an elite dominated by proprietors or one simply by wealth and status in the community, which may or may not have included ownership of proprietor rights, seemed less and less the point. White's trustees symbolized a shift in power in Southampton that was unprecedented and unanticipated even if it proved to be temporary.

In the first flush of victory in 1883, the town trustees secured an appropriation of $500 from the freeholders to retain counsel for an opinion on Mecox Bay. The vote was 178 to 8.[31] They engaged the services of two well-known East End judges, James C. Carter and Thomas Young. Carter had been the president of the New York City Bar Association and came to represent the trustees in their suit against the Mecox Bay Oyster Company in 1885. Young was a county judge of considerable repute. They filed their opinion with the trustees in March 1884. In substance it said that title to the bottom of all the bays, as well as all ponds, creeks, inlets, and coves, lay with the town and was vested exclusively in the town trustees "for the use and benefit of the inhabitants at large." The grounds for arguing this, although not spelled out in much detail, were that when the original settlers purchased the town in 1640 one of the main provisions of their corporate agreement was that there should be no private property in the waters.

This agreement was the Disposall of the Vessell, the earliest extant document to be found in the town records.[32] It stated simply that the waters were open to all for the freedom of fishing, fowling, and navigation and that no one may claim a private interest in them. This document set out in some detail the terms and regulations under which Southampton was to be settled. It was dated March 10, 1639, although as we saw many historians have claimed, including Pelletreau and Howell, that it was drawn up the following year. The justices inferred from this "original valid consecration," as they termed it, that the waters included the land under them. Second, they invoked the legislation of 1818. That act, they argued, clearly settled all doubts regarding title in the waters and authority to regulate their use. It lay with the town trustees. They concluded that the trustees of the proprietors were therefore "wholly ineffectual" in giving title or rights. "Such persons," they declared, "have none to convey."[33]

Armed with this seemingly irrefutable report, the town trustees had little difficulty in persuading the freeholders to appropriate $5,000, a large sum indeed, to go after the oyster company in court. The vote in the town meeting in April 1884 was 510 to 194 in favor.[34] The "no" vote evidently included a sizable majority of proprietors whose interests and strategies were obviously under attack. At that time there were approximately 190 individuals with commonage rights in the three purchases—Town, Topping's, and Quogue. Edwin Post, the clerk to the trustees of the proprietors, testified in the Mecox Bay case that there were as many as three hundred in all three purchases. However, in two dividends paid out in fall 1882 to holders of commonage rights in the Town Purchase alone, only one hundred names are listed. When the final dividend was paid in 1890, shortly before the proprietor trustees resigned and closed their accounts, there were 190 proprietors in all.[35]

Those who disagreed with the course the board was set on pursuing made no secret of their objections. Noting that the trustees were dominated by the western section and were unrepresentative of the town at large, one "Townsman," preferring to remain anonymous, wrote that the town meeting was "little less than sullen acquiescence in a cut and dried plan, which savored more of a packed Democratic caucus at Tammany Hall." He complained that the board was running the bay question unilaterally and using the town's finances to pay for a projected litigation about which there was no full agreement. "Townsman" added that the western and poorest part of the town contributed only one-fourth of all taxes. This drew an immediate response from a "Genuine Townsman" who asked if the first correspondent was "simply a disappointed member of the proprietors." Attesting to the heated nature of community sentiment over the issue, this townsman thought the letter of the first "an incoherent mass of rambling nonsense."

Even Pelletreau was unable to restrain himself. Responding to an inflammatory letter from White, in which White had claimed that the Maxwell purchase of Shinnecock Bay was fraudulent, he referred to his "personal peculiarities and extremely vigorous imagination." White had said quite logically that the bay would not have been sold so cheaply if the proprietors had any clear title to it. Otherwise it was worth at least $50,000. He also said that the LIIC, to whom Henry Maxwell had transferred title to the bay, had no other object in mind than to "fight" the town for its land. To this, Pelletreau replied that the company "has done more to benefit the Island than any other corporation" and will do more "if not prevented by a few short-sighted persons calling themselves the Town." In a swift rejoinder White shot back "I should like to see the first improvement this company has made except buying up the privileges of the laboring classes," adding that those "few short-sighted" made up nine-tenths of the town.[36] And so it went, the town now embroiled in an internally divisive conflict over fears of outside takeover and control and the threatened loss of its lands and freehold privileges. It had become abundantly clear that the town's sense of its own autonomy and independence, its control over its own destiny, was thought by many to be under attack.

III: THE BAYS AND THE INTERESTS OF THE PROPRIETORS

Well before this, the Mecox Bay Oyster Company, although not yet legally incorporated, had begun operations. In 1882, it had planted several hundred bushels of oyster seed over six acres and was considering several thousand more. The company also had purchased a steamboat and was reported to have ordered as many as a hundred boats to be used for harvesting. By the following year, the steamboat had been overhauled and was ready for launching. It was to be used for dredging the bay bottom, a practice widely thought to be injurious to the oyster beds and banned in some towns. It was evident that the company had large plans for the long-term exploitation of the bay bottom, among them plans for a canning factory. It had not, however, had an easy time gaining possession of Mecox Bay. This had not resulted from any effort made by the town to prevent its sale, for the old trustee board of 1881 had made only a feeble effort to investigate the town's rights to the ownership of lands under waters. Rather, other outside interests, in competition with both the oyster company and Henry Maxwell, had eyes on both bays and had successfully if briefly held up the proprietors' projected sale of all lands by court injunction in late 1882.

Representing these interests was Edward G. Whitaker, like Richard Esterbrook Jr. a New York lawyer and Esterbrook's immediate competitor for the development of a new enterprise. But Esterbrook had significant local support and a crucial marriage to his advantage. He was also to enlist major local involvement in his company. Yet Whitaker had much deeper family ties in Southampton that included ties to the proprietors. Ultimately, this was to do him little good though it made for interesting copy at the time. Like Esterbrook, he had offices in downtown Manhattan—on Nassau Street. In 1883, he was appointed clerk to the state attorney general, later becoming a deputy attorney general, and moved to Albany. Much later in life he was appointed a justice of the State Supreme Court.[37] In Albany he was instrumental in obtaining legislative approval for the proposed Shinnecock Canal; he helped draft the bill for an initial appropriation of $30,000. Like the LIIC, which also supported the canal scheme, Whitaker had his own interests in improving the quality of the bays. Work began on the canal in late 1884.

Mecox Bay itself, lying two miles east of Southampton village on flat outwash plain and due south of Water Mill, had always been an important body of water for the town. Its characteristics were unusual in that it was extremely large, fed by several streams or creeks, principally on its eastern and northern shore, and lay in much closer proximity to the ocean than other ponds in the vicinity—notably Old Town Pond and Lake Agawam in Southampton and Georgica Pond in Wainscott. It was the most southerly of the several glacial ponds or kettles in Scuttlehole below the Ronkonkoma moraine. Separated from the ocean by only a narrow strand of beach where dunes had little opportunity to form, it was subject to repeated and regular inundations from winter storms though an inlet between it and the ocean seldom formed on its own. It was never a bay properly speaking, not being an open roadstead, but its waters were subject to varying degrees of salinity depending on the frequency with which the ribbon of foreshore was breached or artificially opened. In much earlier times, the beach or sand bar may have been very much wider because of lower sea levels. If that was the case, Mecox Bay would once have been a fresh water pond.

Some of the earliest divisions of land were made out toward Mecox, and beyond its eastern shore, within a few years of Southampton's settlement. It was quickly seen as rich farmland and suitable for pasture. The first of these was the Ten Acre Division in 1651, so called because each proprietor could take up his ten acres as was convenient to him. Most chose to add their allotment on the rear of their Main Street home lots, that is, east toward Wickapogue and Mecox. The next division of land to the east was laid out in 1653 and was known as the Sagaponack Division. It consisted of several lands, some out toward the boundary with Easthampton bordering Sagg Pond and some on both shores of Mecox Bay. But the first interest in Mecox Bay was in its usefulness as a site for a watermill. Not on the bay itself precisely but at the narrow junction where Mill Pond to the north drains into Mill Creek and then into the bay itself, the pond lying at a slightly higher elevation than the bay.

It was here in 1644 that the town decided to erect a grist mill on what was essentially a natural millstream. The general court awarded the contract to Edward Howell, a principal leader of the company and previously the developer of a mill in Lynn, Massachusetts in 1638. Howell agreed "to build for himselfe to supply the necessities of the Towne a sufficient mill at Meacoxe."[38] He was also allocated forty acres of land adjacent to the mill site. For its part, the town agreed to build a dam, provide the necessary millstones and sufficient labor to open a gut at the beach on a regular basis. This was undertaken to ensure an adequate flow of water for the operation of the mill and was usually carried out in the fall of the year. The gut or cut in the beach was known then as a seapoose, an Algonquian word meaning "little river" for the swift outflow of water from the bay to the ocean.

The first recorded opening of the beach was made in October 1645. In consideration of the arduous labor involved, as well as its importance, every male in the town between the ages of sixteen and sixty was required to help under threat of fine for failing to do so.

The beach was then left to close naturally, usually some months later when winter storms subsided and easterly winds, drifting sand up in front of the cut, would close it. Occasionally, this natural replenishment failed to take place and the seapoose might remain open for as much as a year. This lowered the water level and increased the salinity of the bay. Not only did this adversely affect the operation of the grist mill, it also had serious effects on the shell fish population and in particular the oyster beds that relied on some fresh water content for their health. Conversely, if the inlet was closed early by late fall storms there was always the risk of riparian flooding of the surrounding pastureland. In either case the salinity would vary, either too little or too much, but in both cases impacting the fishery. It was a delicate balance.

The bay could also go out on its own, breaking through the narrow strand of beach if the water was high enough, but this was rare. Similarly, ocean storms might infrequently form a channel if a large enough volume of water broke over the beach that, in the action of going back out with the tide, it cut a natural inlet. In later years in the eighteenth century, the town trustees came to exert rigid controls over when and exactly where the Mecox gut should be dug out and by whom. By this time, the annual oyster crop, rather than grinding corn (there were now other grist mills and millstreams), had become the primary concern of the town. In 1772, for instance, there was some dispute over the location of the seapoose. Two parties began digging independently of each other at the eastern and western ends of the beach. The town trustees stopped both excavations for their "greate damage to the Community" and ordered that the bay could only be let out at the "Middle Place." The clear danger here—with two cuts in the beach in the making—was that the water level might drop so far that the bay could empty out entirely.[39] The economic importance of Mecox Bay had then been important from the beginning, but by the late eighteenth century it had become even more important as the profit potential of the oyster crop became apparent.

As the early settlers knew, Mecox Bay was rich in oysters but it was a century or more before the primary purpose of opening the beach was to regulate the saline content of the water and encourage the oyster crop. There is some suggestion that the Shinnecocks opened an inlet for this purpose long before the English settlement was established. Given the importance of shellfish in their diet, there is no reason to think otherwise. The abundance of ancient shell heaps in the town fully attests to it. Like the settlers, they would have made the cut in the late fall when the beach was usually at its weakest and with a full bay. As noted, after English settlement there was a secondary purpose in opening a channel between the bay and the ocean. That was to reduce or prevent flooding of the surrounding farmland when the bay became too full.

The systematic exploitation of the oyster beds, their close regulation and husbanding by the town, appears not to have begun until well into the eighteenth century. The earliest reference to oystering in the town trustee records appears in 1761 and it shows how valuable the town thought this resource to be:

> No oysters that are cetched or taken out of any part of the water called Mecoks bay may or shall be caryed or sold out of the bounds & limits of this Town by

any person or persons whatsoeuer on penalty of 3s. per bushel foe euery bushel that shall be caryed out or sold to strangers within the bounds and limits a-fore sd/ contrary to the true intent & meaning of this Act.[40]

And then again in 1785 where the fine for violations has been increased:

Oysters Not to be Caught.—Also it is voted and Ordered by said Trustees that Whereas it is said that Greate quantityes of Oysters hav bin taken out of Mecoks Bay & have bin sold to Strangers or Transported out of the Township to the Great hurt and damage of the inhabitants to Prevent which for the future It is Ordered and Enacted by the Trustees that Capt. William Rogers, Jonathan Rogers, Ananias Cooper, David Lupton, Capt. John Sandford, Phillup Howell, David Halsey, Joel Sandford, Zebulon Halsey & Silas Halsey are appointed to have the whol disposal of the Oysters in Mecoks Bay so that no person or persons on any pretence whatsovere shall take or or cetch any oysters out of said Bay without first Obtaining Leve of one or more of the above sd. Persons on penalty of Four Shillings pr. Bushel so taken or Cetcht conteary to the true intent and meaning of this Act and that any or more of the above named persons are Authorized and impourd to prosecute any person offending against this Act and that at the Towns Cost.[41]

Such was the threat of outside exploitation and depletion of the oyster beds—poaching must already have become a problem—that the town trustees obviously felt it necessary to award a monopoly to a local company and effectively provide it with police powers to fend off intruders.

Down to the end of the century and into the 1800s, the trustees routinely renewed the oyster act each year. By 1802, the act had been extended to cover precisely when in the year oysters might or might not be harvested. On penalty of eight shillings a bushel for every bushel caught, no oysters were to be taken from Mecox Bay during the spawning season between May 20 and September 1. This was a clear indication that not only had oysters become an important cash crop, but that efforts had to be made to conserve and protect them for the future. In 1816, regulations to prevent over-fishing were made even more stringent. Oystering was now permitted only on one day a week between sunrise and sunset. The penalties were severe: $10 for every offense, $1 for each bushel taken, and loss of oyster privileges for the rest of the year. The ban on selling oysters out of town remained in force, although how successful this was is open to question. Later, nonresident poaching of not just oysters but the bay fisheries as a whole became a problematic issue for the town trustees. At the beginning of the 1890s, George White was much exercised by the activities of Riverhead men in Shinnecock Bay. He eventually faced them down but not without a court fight in which the town records and the Dongan patent were brandished in defense of the town's exclusive rights to the products of its own waters.

When, in 1818, the proprietors relinquished their claim to the governance of the waters and their products under the legislation of that year, the responsibility for managing them passed to the town. This included the right of the town to collect fines and fees that had previously been deposited in the proprietors' treasury. Both had always been "applied to the Benefit of the proprietors" although collected by town officers who up to that time were themselves always proprietors. The new board of town trustees after 1818, now fully independent of the proprietors, made it clear in one of its first acts that oysters in Mecox Bay and adjoining creeks were now to be considered the public property of the town. Permission to harvest them was to come from the town, and the trustees would issue all regulations covering them. The oyster acts of the old board were continued and enforced with some amendments by the new board in a fairly seamless fashion. It has to be presumed that they were regularly renewed through the 1870s, but no record of them appears in either the town records of the period or in those of the trustees. The minutes of the trustees' meetings after the 1840s are sporadic and incomplete. None exist for the years 1847–1860 or for 1869–1882. The last reference to the oyster acts is in the early 1830s. But then they resurface at the end of the century. A significant feature of the town's case in the Mecox trial turned on the issue of the extent to which the trustees had exercised continuous control over the use of Mecox Bay since 1818 and whether the proprietors disputed this power of regulation. This was less in reference to the strict interpretation of the statute separating jurisdictions than to generally accepted usage and custom. Who was the accepted regulatory authority and, equally important, whether the inhabitants had free use of the bay subject to this regulation. It was fully clear from the ample testimony that the inhabitants did.

With the 1882 sale of the bay bottoms in mind, it is useful to remember that parts of Mecox Bay had been leased from time to time to small private companies of inhabitants as far back as 1767. In that year, one acre had been leased for oyster planting for a term of four years to Lieutenant David Halsey and Co. "for their peculiar use." In the lease the trustees stipulated that Halsey and his associates might prosecute trespassers as long as it was "at their own cost."[42] Two years later, the trustees leased another acre for the same purpose to Jedediah Howell and a company, this time for five years. When the lease was up, the water lot was "then to return to the Town," an interesting clause in the later circumstances of 1882 for it suggests that "the Town" rather than the proprietors assumed legal title to the land under the bay. In the same year, 1769, and under the same terms, a half acre was leased to Joel Sandford and others adjoining his lot.

This appears to have been a common practice in the late eighteenth century for it is even referred to in the oyster acts. Recipients of what were called "grants" from the trustees were specifically excluded from the restrictions on out-of-town sales of oysters, a recognition of the lucrative nature of the business and the reason why companies were formed to go into it in the first pace. Moonlighters might have operated to "the great hurt and damage to the Community" but companies under town lease were free to do business with the outside world as they chose. However, the multiplication of these companies in subsequent years may have seriously impacted the oyster fishery and depleted the oyster beds. It appeared to fall into a steep decline in the late 1830s or 1840s. Testifying at the Mecox trial in 1885, Thomas Sayre, living on an arm of the bay much of his life and then in his seventies, said that this was very likely due to over-fishing. As late as 1825, as many as 150 boats could be seen on the water on any given day in season, but ten years later the oysters were gone. David Burnett, in his testimony, attributed the failure of the oyster crop to problems with the inlet rather than with over-fishing. About 1850, he said, the inlet had been running for a year and all efforts to close it had failed. The increased salinity of the water resulting from this had killed off the eel grass, a vegetation characteristic of all the bays. When the eel grass decayed, the oyster beds were irreparably damaged. Burnett had long experience of oystering when he was younger—he was seventy-seven at the time of the trial—and his father had leased water lots for the purpose early in the century. But the oyster beds had partially revived by the 1870s and it was this, along with the renewed health of the bay, that encouraged Richard Esterbrook and his associates to pursue an old and profitable practice, but this time on a far larger scale.

The first reference in the proprietor trustee records to the possible sale of Mecox Bay is dated April 11, 1882. The trustees were to discuss the proprietor's right "to the bottom of Mecox Bay and to advise and decide as far as possible what is best to be done in relation thereto." At the beginning of June, they authorized the committee "to offer and sell the bottom of Mecox Bay, and adjoining creeks, to the adjoining landowners, in whole or in sections as they may think best . . . for a sum not less than $2,000."[43] The committee reported back later in the month that the owners on the shores of the bay were not interested. The group then decided to sell Mecox to "any other parties" but felt it prudent to retain counsel, this being J. Lawrence Smith, a local lawyer. It was a wise move, for trouble was in the offing. On August 29, they agreed among themselves to sell Mecox at public auction and immediately advertised it in the county newspapers as well as in the local *Seaside Times*. The sale was set for October 17 at the post office. Besides Mecox a large number of other tracts were to be sold. The auction notice was brief. It simply said that Mecox Bay and Long and Short Beaches at Hog Neck and all other undivided lands "described or not described" would go on the auctioneer's block. The proprietor trustees instructed their committee to sell "at their discretion such other lands belonging to the proprietors as they may think proper."

The reaction to the announcement was not long in coming but was focused exclusively on the Mecox Bay question, it not yet being fully apparent to all who might be interested that the trustees intended to sell all the bays to the west as well. It was known to some however. Richard Esterbrook Jr. and his partners in the yet-to-be-formed Mecox Bay Oyster Company found themselves under the threat of competition for the bay bottom from Edward G. Whitaker. Whitaker had similar plans to those of Esterbrook and associates but more ambitiously wanted all the bays for a company (the purposes of which were never fully clarified) he himself was setting up. To achieve this he adopted an ingenious strategy, one that had been successfully attempted at Montauk in 1875 and led to the sale at public auction of all the lands on that twelve thousand-acre peninsula belonging to the Proprietors of Montauk to one man, Arthur W. Benson of Brooklyn.

A New Yorker and just possibly an associate of Benson's, Robert H. Grinnell, purchased an eighth of a share in Montauk (voting stock was reckoned in eighths) and, armed with this, brought a partition suit against the Montauk proprietors for the bulk sale of all their stock.

In practice this meant the sale of all their lands. It is of interest here because a partition suit recognizes that when land is held by tenants in common and is thus undivided, and where the interest of each is measured by their proportionate rights or shares individually owned (ranging from very small to very large), then the land itself cannot be equitably divided and sold off piece by piece. In the case of the Southampton proprietors, if they owned the lands under water, then they owned them as tenants in common "according to each man's right" just as they owned the undivided lands above water in common. Of course, the proprietor trustees might attempt to sell off the bays piece by piece if they so wished, but a partition suit would prevent that and force a sale in bulk. This was precisely Whitaker's intention just as it had been Grinnell's. The Montauk partition suit had been a friendly suit, a formality in fact, for an overwhelming majority of the Montauk proprietors wanted to sell and sell at as high a price as possible. The proprietors believed that Montauk in 1879—the date of the auction—might be worth as much as $200,000. It went to Benson for $151,000 but no one, especially the larger stockholders, among them Henry P. Hedges of Bridgehampton, seemed to go home all that unhappy.

Edward Whitaker's partition suit was not, however, welcomed by Southampton's proprietor trustees. They saw it as hostile or, at any rate, eleven of the twelve board members did. From their perspective, it could undermine what was in process of development well before the scheduled auction, namely the sale of Mecox Bay to Esterbrook and his local supporters. Among these were particularly Everett Carpenter, the respected Sag Harbor lawyer, and Stephen B. French, a Sag Harbor merchant and part owner of the *Sag Harbor Express*, one of the two local papers. Ironically, Carpenter had been the court-appointed referee in the Montauk partition suit and had recommended the sale in bulk of the Montauk proprietors' shares. Now he was on the other side and obviously knew the risks involved if a similar suit got underway over the bays; risks, that is, to Esterbrook's oyster company. In any show of competitive bidding with Whitaker the price might escalate beyond reach, or Esterbrook might get more than he bargained for—not just Mecox Bay but all of the bays. Carpenter also may have been aware of Henry Maxwell's interest in Shinnecock Bay, in fact it is very likely that he was, and that would have made for an added complication. Whitaker later claimed that he had been willing to bid $8,000 for Mecox Bay alone. It was therefore in everyone's interest, including that of the proprietors, to ward off the potential threat of Whitaker's partition suit. There were risks besides for the trustees of the proprietors. They were unsure of their right to sell lands under water, had retained an attorney, and were aware of the partially adverse, if mixed, reports submitted to the town trustees earlier in the year. And they were aware of growing public sentiment. Any court proceeding of any sort, and most especially a partition suit covering all the bays, creeks, and ponds, could all too easily open up to challenge their claim that the lands under all these waters—one-fifth of the total area of the town—were common land.

Whitaker, like Grinnell before him at Montauk (and it is quite likely that he knew Grinnell) purchased a fifty right of commonage in 1881 thus allowing him as a proprietor to bring such a partition suit. He did so in June 1882, represented by two Southampton attorneys, Thomas F. Bisgood and George W. Whitaker. George Whitaker was Edward

Whitaker's father, a very significant element in this strange and convoluted story. But an even stranger feature of this remarkable sequence of events, which were constantly threatening to spin out of control, was that George Whitaker had been elected to the board of the proprietor trustees only the previous year and was now representing a client—his son—whose interests were entirely opposed to those of the proprietors. Moreover, there is every reason to think that George Whitaker arranged the purchase of Whitaker's commonage right as an essential precondition for embarking on a partition suit, a suit it transpired that the trustees were adamantly opposed to. The suit did not materialize, at least at this juncture, quite possibly because the president of the trustees, David R. Rose, and Whitaker's fellow trustees either attempted to talk him out of it or persuaded a delay.

Nevertheless, Whitaker and Bisgood filed a complaint in State Supreme Court naming both bodies of trustees (town and proprietor) in just such a partition suit. The suit encompassed "all lands above and beneath waters of all proprietor lands . . . the location of all of which lands the plaintiff (Edward Whitaker) is unable to describe" except for Mecox Bay, the other bays, Long and Short Beaches, and Fresh Pond (a large body of water west of North Sea that the proprietor trustees had included in their package). The suit languished and was still pending a year later but, undeterred, Whitaker's attorneys in September or early October obtained a preliminary or temporary restraining injunction in Supreme Court in Brooklyn halting the auction sale. J. Lawrence Smith, attorney to the proprietor trustees, then succeeded in having the injunction dissolved by Judge J. R. Barnard in Supreme Court in Riverhead on October 23. Smith argued that the trustees were "clothed with the power of sale by the legislature," referring to the 1818 legislation, and that the preliminary injunction "fail(ed) to show any breach of duty by the trustees." For good measure, Smith noted that "there is an inconsiderable amount of property remaining and it is now a wise exercise of their trust power to make the sale." He asked that the plaintiff's motion to make the preliminary injunction a permanent one be denied. Judge Barnard agreed. Understandably, neither attorney—whether for Whitaker or the proprietors—sought to raise the contentious issue of the lands under water that obviously constituted far more than "an inconsiderable amount of property." It was in neither of their interests to do so. Had they done so, Barnard might have balked and asked uncomfortable questions about the legal status of these particular lands scheduled to be sold. As it transpired, Barnard was to be the presiding judge in Esterbrook's appeal in 1887 against the original ruling of the court in 1885 that the lands under water belonged to the town and not to the proprietors. Judge Barnard concurred with that ruling.

After Barnard lifted the injunction on October 23, 1882, the trustees of the proprietors proceeded expeditiously to the sale but did not follow through on the rescheduled auction that had been announced for November 16. Instead they sold all the lands and bays privately on November 10 to a predetermined group of buyers, the most important of whom were Henry Maxwell and representatives of Richard Esterbrook. Possibly, given the volatile state of public opinion, they were concerned to eliminate the chance of a confrontation with other townspeople in the public confines of a post office auction on Main Street. So, in a considerable departure from tradition—all previous sales of lands and privileges in the nineteenth century had always been public—the sale went unannounced.

Henry Maxwell, representing the interests of the LIRR and the LIIC (the interests of both of which were identical), purchased a quitclaim deed to the lands under the waters of all the bays west of Canoe Place and at the same time gained title to much else besides that had an indirect bearing on the Mecox issue. All the conveyances—Esterbrook's, Maxwell's, as well as those of others—had been disposed of on the same day and were, at least in the minds of the proprietor trustees as well probably in those of many others, interconnected. The trustees had in fact given Maxwell two deeds, both of which specified lands under water and any common lands that might not have been laid out or, if they had, had not been taken up by their original allottees. Both were blanket conveyances. The first conveyed any common land, "known or unknown," in the Town Purchase west of a line drawn from Holmes's Hill on Peconic Bay southward to Halsey Neck and south of the North Sea Line. It included all the lands under Shinnecock Bay and all creeks leading into it as far west as Ponquogue Point, as well as lands under Old Fort Pond, Middle Pond, Cold Spring Bay, Bulls Head Bay, and the east part of Canoe Place Pond (later incorporated as part of the Shinnecock Canal). The second deed included all the lands under water west of Ponquogue Point as far as the Brookhaven town line, the west part of Canoe Place Pond, beach and shore in the Canoe Place Division as far as Red Creek Pond (which had been quitclaimed to William Pelletreau on the same day as the Maxwell purchase), and any other undivided lands in the Quogue and Topping's Purchases. These latter consisted of lands in the two Last Divisions (laid out in 1782) in the Quogue Plains. Henry Maxwell paid the trustees $500 for each of the two deeds.[44]

By 1882, despite some efforts at identification, the proprietors were forced to admit that they did not know where precisely the alleged common land was but hazarded a guess that there was not much of it. Hence, it has to be supposed, the blanket quitclaim deeds. It would be up to any prospective purchaser to identify the location of any lands he acquired, no small task unless it happened to be shore land, and then trace any outstanding title claims to them. Possibly this was of little importance to Henry Maxwell in 1882 for the lands he was concerned with—the beaches and the lands under the bays—had never been privately owned in the first place. Besides, his total investment had been a mere thousand dollars. Later, however, a portion of the Maxwell claim in the Quogue Plains was challenged in the courts, but long after his death.[45]

The circumstances and nuances of Whitaker's case are freighted with irony, even pathos, something that could not be said of the Maxwell claim and its later trans-substantiation. Here was a member of the proprietor's board, a well-known attorney, pleading in court the interests of an individual—his own son—whose interests were wholly opposed to those of his fellow trustees. Back in the spring, he had voted along with them to sell the bay bottoms, and purchased a right for his son, only to discover belatedly that the other trustees had very different ideas in respect to who might be the prospective purchasers. Edward Whitaker was not to be one of them. One can only imagine that George Whitaker would have encountered some difficult moments with his colleagues at board meetings that must have tried his composure. Yet this was a small town and ties of class and kinship in most instances ultimately outweigh temporary differences of opinion and interest. A year or two later after matters had to some extent calmed down, and the proprietors were about to become in a sense spectators at their own trial, Edward Whitaker gave a reception at his father's house in Long Springs. Among the guests were David R. Rose, David H. Rose (his brother and proprietor of a popular North Sea watering spot, Rose's Grove), Captain Jetur Rose, James E. Jennings (another trustee and North Sea neighbor), all their wives, and Thomas Bisgood, George Whitaker's law partner. The two lawyers, like White, were founding members of Southampton's Democratic Association.

However, Judge Barnard's decision to lift the injunction against the proprietors had not been the end of it. Edward Whitaker continued to pursue his partition suit the following spring, again represented by his father. Although that failed also—the trustees had empowered their attorney to "take all suitable action"—Whitaker still persisted. As late as 1890, he brought another suit against both proprietor and town trustees. It was dismissed without costs. But possibly it was all too much for the proprietors. Their trustees, and themselves, had been under fire for most of the decade. A month after Whitaker had filed his last suit in Supreme Court, the trustees distributed the remaining monies to themselves and their fellow proprietors, leaving nothing in reserve for potential legal expenses, and over the summer decided to get out of the land business and resigned en masse.

It is difficult to say with any certainty what the attitude of the town was to this body of proprietor trustees. They had been in power since before the Civil War with few changes in personnel and had operated largely out of the public eye. They kept their own counsel, rarely opened their books (the last disclosure of income was in 1868), and were re-elected with routine regularity year after year. They handled the business of the proprietors with extreme efficiency, always with an eye to maximizing revenue from the remaining common lands, and were extraordinarily astute in pulling off profitable land deals. All twelve of them were well known, prosperous, for the most part major landowners, and individually highly regarded. Yet they were also widely perceived as a hidden government, manipulating town affairs exclusively for the benefit of the proprietors, and still exercising substantial powers within the town despite the limitations placed on them by the 1818 legislation. None of them had served in any significant capacity in town government, except for Pelletreau, since the end of the Civil War seventeen years previously. As a corporate body, it appeared that these trustees entered 1882 with a reputation for sharp dealings and were much distrusted as a result.

Many thought, White most outspokenly, that they had not only become far too influential in matters affecting the town's lands—as though the town had relinquished (despite 1818) all vestige of legal claim to them—but had become particularly active in affecting the decisions or lack of them of the town trustees. This latter body had largely pursued what could best be described as a quietist strategy since 1865 and could only be pushed reluctantly into action by an aroused public opinion. The proprietor trustees, in contrast, had shown no hesitancy in testing the limits of their authority over the lands they claimed legal title to under the legislation. They were just as serious in staking out control over some of the contested products of those lands, seaweed in particular. In fact the struggle over who owned the seaweed in the mid-1860s was the last time the town trustees had taken them on over a significant issue. They lost the ensuing litigation. When, in 1859, the proprietor trustees had successfully gained the legislative partition of the Shinnecock Hills over the generally muted objections of most in the town—again excepting White—the town trustees remained inexplicably silent.[46] And now, in 1882, the proprietors were poised to sell off lands under water to which at best they had only a tenuous claim. Again the town trustees seemed paralyzed, even in the face of a public outcry, and refused to act. The proprietors were also held responsible for the loss of the Shinnecock Hills to Austin Corbin's development interests a year earlier, a move accomplished by key proprietors of the Hills who were also either members of the proprietor trustee board or closely connected to it. This did not arouse the town trustees either. Overall, they seemed overmatched or lost in a deep slumber while the townspeople, who were under no illusion that the proprietors had the public interest at heart, were left with little choice but to throw out the town trustees and elect new ones.

There had been little turnover among the proprietor trustees in the previous decade. White thought they had been a cohesive and single-minded group since 1859, but the truth is that they had been that way since the 1820s if not the 1800s and had been dominated by the same families throughout the century. For reasons that cannot be readily explained, they were predominantly North Sea men. Roses, Jennings, Bishops, Scotts, Harris, all were from that enclave above what was still called the North Sea Line, that original 324 acres at Cow Neck first purchased by John Ogden and his associates in 1651 that resulted in the establishment of a small community with its own trading port and inn at North Sea Harbor. North Sea from its very beginnings seemed to cultivate the entrepreneurial instinct—Ogden had been the first to speculate in the lands west of Canoe Place (the eventual Quogue Purchase) and had been active in whaling—so perhaps that helps to explain the trustees' acquisitive interest in land and drew their ancestors to the area in the first place. By the 1870s, North Sea was a part of School District 15 and covered a much larger area, much of it owned by the men in question.

They were all neighbors, traced through generations of families that reached back to the seventeenth century. George Whitaker, although his tenure as a proprietor trustee was short for understandable reasons (he resigned in 1883 after only two years), had his farm in Long Springs just to the south. There were exceptions to this North Sea pedigree. Pelletreau was one, more than likely recruited for his knowledge of the early divisions of the common lands and the general history of the town, really a quite unsurpassed knowledge. Like his fellow trustees, he was deeply interested in land and its profitable acquisition or disposal. He also was a master of the title search, an indispensable skill for the trustees though not apparently put to use in the identification of common lands for sale in 1882, and advertised his services in the paper "accuracy guaranteed." But Pelletreau was the odd man out among these heavy landowning interests and eventually resigned from the trustees in 1884.

Much of the real power lay with the Rose family and with Lewis Scott. Between 1861 and 1890, there were never less than three Roses, and commonly four, on the twelve-member board. It also had become a virtual tradition since 1818 that a Rose should serve as president of the proprietor trustees. Only once, between 1843 and 1853, did the board elect anyone who was not a Rose. In the period in question—the 1880s—the presiding patriarch of the family, Colonel David Rogers Rose, was the president. He served until his death at the age of ninety-two in 1889. It was a dynasty. But Scott was an equally formidable figure. Although he had fallen afoul of the trustees in the late 1850s over a claimed tract of proprietor land in Sebonac, he had no difficulty managing his election to the board in 1861. He was to be a key player in the 1859 partition of the Shinnecock Hills and in the subsequent purchase of the Hills at auction from the proprietor trustees. He owned three hundred acres of prime land in North Sea, as well as lands elsewhere, with an assessed value in 1882 of $5,000 and a personal estate of $17,000. The *Seaside Times* dubbed him "the millionaire of Southampton" a sobriquet he might reasonably have thought was well earned. He had been assiduously accumulating land and wealth since the 1820s. He was one of the three largest tax payers in the town in 1882, almost equal to Wyllys Betts. Similarly, David Rose owned a great deal of land—350 acres—and the Rose family as a whole collectively owned one thousand acres.

There were two other families not of North Sea with a major stake in land who established a fairly continuous presence on the board in the nineteenth century. These were the Posts and the Fosters. The Posts had always been an influential factor and the proprietor trustees had never been without one since the early 1800s. James Post, who had been town supervisor in the aftermath of the 1818 compromise from 1822 to 1828, became clerk to the trustees in 1826 and served until 1854. After a ten-year hiatus he was replaced by his son, Edwin, already a major landowner by that time. He remained until the end in 1890 and retired a wealthy man. He lived off South Main Street on ancient family farm property hard by the South End Burying Ground. As described in an earlier chapter, Post was the defendant in a celebrated lawsuit brought by the town concerning his alleged desecration of Southampton's first burial ground. Preceding him on the proprietors' board were two other Posts who similarly did very well, amassing much of their wealth in the western part of the town. These were Oliver Post and then his son George O. Post. The latter was not far behind Scott in the assessment of his property in 1882.

The Fosters had been a leading family in Southampton since the 1640s. They were less omnipresent on the trustees' board than the Posts but were firmly established by 1875. The two families had been inextricably connected by marriages since the eighteenth century, particularly in their Quogue branches. George Post married a sister of Erastus Foster, a major landowner, and Albert J. Foster married a Post. Over the years there were other key alliances besides. After 1875, there were never less than two Posts on the board (in 1878 there were three) and if one went off, he was replaced by another. Thus, Isaac Post Foster was replaced in 1886 by his son Edward, the town clerk at the time, although not for very long. He lost a close election for the clerkship in the same year. In like fashion, James H. Foster had replaced Albert Foster a few years before. In 1882, James Foster was vice president of the summer colony's Southampton Village Improvement Association, an organization with concerns as far removed from those of the proprietor trustees as could be imagined. Later, he became president, the only local citizen ever to be elected by that association before 1920. The Fosters were more directly engaged in town and village affairs

(James Foster also was a justice of the peace) than any of the other proprietor trustees. Most of them, apart perhaps from Edwin Post, had little interest in village matters and the doings of the summer colony and chose to remain undisturbed in their North Sea fastness to concentrate on the larger issues of land sales.

But the Fosters, like the Roses and the Posts, assumed a permanent presence on the board as a matter of right. They were rich in land, having accumulated property in both the eastern and western sections of the town, and were bound to other leading proprietor families by ties of kinship, class, and mutual interest. In 1862, several Fosters between them owned almost fifteen hundred acres in various parts of the town, although much of it in Quogue, while the Posts could claim ownership of about one thousand acres, again west of Canoe Place. Edward Foster followed the family tradition. Beginning as a school teacher he entered politics. When that ended in an upset election he went into real estate.

It is hardly surprising that these trustees, given their proven ability to amass valuable property, should also have been able to accumulate individually a very large number of commonage rights or fifty-pound rights. True, they were a declining currency the value of which had greatly diminished as much of the remaining common land had been sold off through the nineteenth century but they were not nonetheless unimportant. Pelletreau himself had written before the 1882 final sales of undivided lands "there are now only a few insignificant pieces, and a 'proprietor right,' once so important, is (now) little more than a name."[47] He observed a year later that in the 1680s when three-fourths of the town was undivided the three full rights in commonage bequeathed by Edward Howell represented the equivalent of one thousand acres.[48] This was undoubtedly the case, as true as his earlier remark, but in both instances he seems to have been motivated by an understandable wish to defuse the controversy provoked by the sales of the bottoms of the bays and various ponds. In fact, the value of commonage rights would be substantially enhanced if the lands under water were included as common and undivided lands. For the proprietor trustees this may have been one of two principal motives, the other obviously being the desire to capitalize on the emerging pattern of outside investment. It was obviously not simply a matter of ridding themselves of a few half-forgotten or economically marginal parcels lying fallow in remote corners of the town. These were indeed, as Pelletreau said, largely insignificant. Their counsel, J. Lawrence Smith, had said much the same in his brief to Judge Barnard. So if the trustees had anything else in mind besides an opportunity for a quick profit, it was to pull off a last coup and increase the value of their own not inconsiderable rights.

Most of the trustees were very well endowed with them. In the Town Purchase there were 155 fifty-pound rights in commonage distributed among approximately one hundred persons in varying proportions. In 1882, the date of the last dividend issued after 1868, almost half of those rights—seventy-four—were in the hands of the twelve members of the proprietors' board. This had been the case at least as far back as 1861 when more than sixty rights in commonage were owned by board members. Two men particularly, Lewis Scott with twenty rights and Edwin Post (who acquired a good part of his from George O. Post) with twenty-two, owned the lion's share. Scott had accumulated his through various astute trades by 1861 suggesting that commonage rights still maintained their value up to that time. His possession of so many probably persuaded the board, the differences over Sebonac conveniently forgotten, that he should be elected to it that same year. The Rose clan collectively had accumulated twenty-four commonage rights by 1861. Proprietor capital in common land therefore, ostensibly spread among large numbers of proprietors, was in fact concentrated in a very few hands.[49]

Although a dividend in the Town Purchase had been declared in 1868, there had been no distribution of revenues to the proprietors accruing from the Quogue and Topping's Purchases between 1863 and the "final dividend" declared in 1890, a lengthy span of twenty-seven years. In 1863, the value of the dividend was relatively small—$758.74—and allocated at $5.80 a share in Quogue and only 61 cents in Topping's. It indicates that the value of resources and especially timber in the largest part of the town were declining after mid-century. This is corroborated in the town's assessment rolls. Upland in both purchases, primarily woodland, had an average assessed value of $1 an acre in 1887. In the Aquebogue Division in Flanders nine hundred acres were assessed at $1,000. However, not all land was considered to be of so little value. Meadowland on the shores of the bays was still thought of as an important resource. Three hundred and seventy acres owned by George Post, originally purchased from the proprietors by Oliver Post in 1846, were assessed at $33 an acre. Yet this was low in comparison to the average assessment on farmland in the Town Purchase. In the same period of the 1880s, this was assessed at between $100 and $200 an acre. But that the western lands were no longer a lucrative source of income also suggests, as Pelletreau said, that there was very little undivided land remaining to be leased out for one purpose or another. There were 118 rights in commonage in the Quogue Purchase and 135 in Topping's Purchase. Of these the proprietor trustees individually owned only a modest number, eighteen and twenty-five respectively, with most in the possession of Fosters and Posts. But again, it generally confirms the view that the motivation for the land sales lay in the prospective value of the undivided lands under water.

CHAPTER 5

MECOX REDUX

I: THE BLANKET SALES AND THEIR CONSEQUENCES

Judge Barnard had dissolved the restraining injunction on the auction sale at the end of October 1882, allowing the proprietor trustees to proceed with it on November 16, the date to which they had adjourned it while still under injunction. But instead they chose to abandon the auction altogether and authorized the committee on lands, which consisted of David R. Rose, James H. Foster (who had replaced Albert Foster on the board earlier in the year), and Edwin Post, to arrange a private sale. It was not announced until later but took place in an afternoon at the beginning of November. It was obviously very well prepared for at their November 2 meeting within a few days of Barnard's decision the committee was instructed to sell all remaining undivided lands to Henry W. Maxwell, William S. Pelletreau, Richard Esterbrook, William H. H. Rogers, Theron O. Worth, Rufus Sayre, and Orlando Hand "as described in their respective deeds." Rogers and Worth were the original purchasers of Mecox Bay with Esterbrook and later conveyed their titles to Esterbrook and his real partners. They simply may have been front men. The buyers were notified in advance, advised of the time and place of the sale, and the deeds drawn up: "the said deeds to cover all the lands and premises of said Proprietors remaining in said town in which they have any title." The deeds were to be delivered to the respective parties by the president of the trustees, David Rose, and the sales ratified a few days later. All the deeds were recorded by November 13 at the county clerk's office in Riverhead, a full three days before the rescheduled auction that was, for all anybody knew, still to be on November 16 but instead had been quietly cancelled.

It had all taken place in such a hurried if well-organized fashion for two reasons. First, Edward Whitaker had threatened to appeal Barnard's decision to lift the injunction and, secondly, there were rumblings from the riparian property owners around Mecox Bay. One of those owners, Henry P. Hedges, had begun to organize his fellow proprietors along the banks of the bay and its creeks on the grounds that they, not the proprietors of the undivided lands (nor the town for that matter), owned the bottom of the bay. Hedges threatened an action of trespass if any new company, claiming ownership, actually planted oysters in the bay. He was an esteemed figure in the community whose ancestors were among the first inhabitants of Easthampton in the late 1640s. A Yale graduate, a Sag Harbor lawyer, district attorney for Suffolk County, and later surrogate and county judge, he was a man to be reckoned with. Among his accomplishments was a history of Easthampton.[1] He was wealthy and owned some two hundred acres in the vicinity of Bridgehampton, some of it bordering on Mecox Bay. Besides this, he had been a principal stockholder in the Montauk lands and had profited considerably from the auction sale of Montauk in 1879. It might be thought curious, given Hedges's own stand on the bay question, that he should in fact come (with Everett Carpenter) to represent Richard Esterbrook in the first Mecox Bay trial in 1885. However, Hedges had obtained a prior agreement from Esterbrook, whose neighbor he was on Ocean Road in Bridgehampton, that the riparian owners would be recompensed for any rights they might claim or possess and could retain the use of a certain amount of bottom adjacent to their properties. Ultimately then, Hedges threw in his lot with Esterbrook.

Henry Hedges was too important to ignore, and at least partly for this reason it may explain why the trustees of the proprietors moved quickly to a private sale, and why Esterbrook was the chosen buyer, though Esterbrook, through his marriage to David Rose's niece, obviously had the inside track to begin with. It may also explain why the bay bottom was sold in several sections to three different individuals, two of whom—Worth and Rogers—were local residents and both, like Hedges, Ocean Road neighbors, but neither were principals in Esterbrook's venture. Possibly factored into the trustees' approach to the sale—dividing the bay up and putting it in several private hands—was the desire to forestall or preempt Edward Whitaker's threatened partition suit, a suit that would demand that the bay be sold in bulk rather than in sections. As it was, Theron Worth, a riparian owner, bought one-third of the bay and William Rogers another third while Esterbrook took the remainder. Both Rogers and Worth did well for their trouble when they sold out their interests the following spring to Esterbrook and Stephen French. French, like Everett Carpenter, had remained in the background up to this point.

Edward Whitaker had kept his own counsel through fall and winter 1882 but, incensed by the secrecy of the sale and exasperated by the hostile tenor of the letters in the newspaper, he fired off a diatribe of his own to the *Seaside Times* in March 1883. It was approximately one week before his father either resigned or was eased off the proprietors' board and one week before the commonalty voted overwhelmingly in the annual town meeting to appropriate $500 to retain counsel for advice on the town's rights to the waters and the lands under them. Whether the moment was propitious or not, Whitaker had a number of things to get off his chest. In the process he shed some light on why the trustees let the bays go so cheaply. He began by saying that the trustees had sold the common lands "for a mere song to preferred vendees" noting, in a clear reference to William Pelletreau, that a part of them had gone to "one of their own number . . . becoming seller and buyer at the same time, a position forbidden by law." He then went on to say that it had been his intention to purchase both bays through a corporation issuing enough stock to cover the price. The stock would have been available for purchase by townspeople.

He claimed that two partners of his, who were unnamed, were willing to advance up to $25,000 toward the purchase price "and other little expenses" likewise not enumerated.

He said he would have bid $8,000 for Mecox Bay alone, but in fact his first offer was for only $800—"it was not to be supposed that we were going to offer eight million first pop"—and then said, in apparent contradiction, that he had in fact offered $8,000. The proprietor trustees, however, had refused to fix a price, at which point Whitaker and his associates decided to embark on a partition suit. It was intended as a friendly suit, not an attempt to engage in litigation, but a suit to obtain "a quick judicial determination upon the rights of the parties" insuring that each owner "gets his just share . . . when an actual division cannot be made." Then a public sale is ordered and the proceeds divided, all of this under the supervision of a court-appointed referee whose role it is to protect the rights of individual owners. But what did the trustees do, he asked? They retained counsel and resolved to fight it, thereby insuring a lengthy and expensive court case. Whitaker suggested that at this point the trustees panicked and under "the flimsy pretext of fear of a law suit" sold "privately and secretly" before the rescheduled auction. He also alleged that they voted to sell at anywhere between $1 and $2,000 or at an artificially low price.[2] There is nothing in the proprietors' records to indicate that they were willing to entertain such a spread, but it might be assumed that it was indeed discussed and that the information came to Whitaker from his father.

George Whitaker, for his part, while "anxious to buy cheap" on behalf of his son, had felt constrained to suggest the high price of $50,000. This, Edward Whitaker rather loftily declared and quite ignoring the conflict of interest his father had got himself into, as well as the preemptive nature of the price named that was obviously designed to shut out Esterbrook, was "a very honorable and praiseworthy act." The trustees on their side, he alleged, had hunkered down and settled on a self-defeating course of action even while anxious for "a big price . . . for the benefit of us poor owners (the proprietors in general), who happened to be too low in the scale of humanity to be elected to the exalted position of trustee." His father may have understandably blanched a little at this small display of petulance, but now off the board, he was free to pursue the fight unfettered by any possible qualms of conscience. He left the board that same April after the proprietor and town trustee elections (held separately) but the Mecox trial was still a long way off.

It is difficult to credit Whitaker's allegation that the proprietor trustees were so intimidated by the threat of legal action that they let everything go for next to nothing yet, notwithstanding, that is exactly what they did. They may have feared that a partition suit—or any suit—would expose their proprietary interest in the bays as factitious despite the legal assurances of their counsel who, for all anyone knew, might have harbored doubts of his own. There also may have been some dissension on the board in respect to this. A few months after the sale, George White reported that none other than Lewis Scott, a man "known for his shrewdness all over the county," had expressed his own reservations. According to White, Scott had bluntly stated that "they (the proprietor trustees) have no more right to sell the bottom of these bays than they have to sell the Presbyterian Church."[3] Later in the year, White quoted him again: "One of the largest holders of rights (he could only have meant Scott) says Post, Foster and Co. had no right to sell the waters of the town."[4] Perhaps Scott had second thoughts. There is no way of knowing, but all the 1882 meetings at which the trustees resolved to sell the bays show unanimous votes. Scott attended them all. If he had doubts, they were—in the nature of action minutes—unrecorded. White later claimed that another (this time unnamed) trustee said that he would not take any money from the sale, that it was "blood money squeezed from the poor of the town." But the use of quitclaim deeds, rather than any pretence of seeking fair market value as in any conventional real estate transaction, does seem to indicate that the proprietor trustees were unsure whether they possessed a good or clean title to the bays or not, whether the bay bottoms really were common or undivided lands. This was White's explanation of what to him was a panicky fire sale. It was also Edward Foster's view. Foster was of the opinion that the trustees wanted above all else to avoid a potentially expensive partition suit that would have eaten up the proceeds of the sale. Foster was still town clerk and not yet on the proprietors' board when he wrote this. Later, after 1886 when he joined the board and when the trial was over, he was not to be heard from again on the issue.

There were two blanket conveyances to Henry Maxwell, the details of which were reported earlier, each of them at the remarkably low price of $500. He acquired all of what was left of the common and undivided lands west of Halsey Neck, all the ponds, creeks, and lands under the waters of the western bays as far as Brookhaven with the single exception of Red Creek Pond. which had gone to Pelletreau. The one puzzling aspect of the two deeds is why the proprietors failed to separate the sale of common lands above water from those beneath or, rather, what were claimed to be common lands under the bays, ponds, and creeks. Their title to the lands above water was undisputed—as we saw they had sold them off piece by piece privately or at auction throughout the nineteenth century—and their right to do so as the equitable owners had never been challenged. The only reasonable answer is that what little remained of these lands was not worth much except for the shores of the bays and the ocean beach (their title to which, they must have known, was potentially subject to challenge) and that they did not know precisely where they lay. It must have seemed easiest and simplest to throw everything together and quitclaim it all in one simple package.

One question that might be asked is whether Maxwell and the LIRR and its spin-off, the LIIC, knew what they were getting or whether they even cared. Their interests were in the Shinnecock Hills and the potential for resort development the Hills represented. Through the efforts of John Bowman, the Hills were already in their control. As for Maxwell, he was a banker and a broker as well as a vice president of the railroad, a young man of thirty-two, and was probably under straightforward orders from Austin Corbin to get the most he could for the least amount of money. He was simply a front man in dealing with the Southampton proprietors just as was Bowman in negotiating the purchase of the Hills from their proprietors (essentially the same group of men in overlapping directorships). The railroad had been silent during the whole emerging controversy of 1882 and 1883, waiting perhaps to see how it played out. Corbin's sole interest in the bays was in the ownership and development of the shoreline and beaches the two deeds appeared to give him. But whether he cared or not he now had, or the LIIC was now about to have, a titled interest in the bottoms of the bays as well as the surrounding shores. Several miles of shoreline fronting the Atlantic beach along Shinnecock Bay were acquired a little later in a separate transaction arranged by John Bowman. This time, the proprietor trustees were not involved. Bowman purchased meadow lots along the beach from their owners in fee. Between Maxwell's purchase and Bowman's, Corbin had within the space of little more than a year pulled off a real estate coup that was to have a major impact on the town for a long time to come.

The second major conveyance of undivided lands by the proprietors was to Rufus Sayre, a well-established and prosperous farmer with an ancestry that reached back to the founding of Southampton in 1640. The two Sayre brothers, Job and Thomas, had contributed to the purchase of Daniel Howe's vessel in 1639 and Job Sayre had had the unfortunate experience of being arrested by the Dutch in the abortive attempt to settle Schout's Bay on the north shore of Long Island several months later. The Sayres were an old family, part of the elite, and had always been significant owners of land and commonage rights. A contemporary Thomas Sayre, a cousin to Rufus Sayre, had served on the proprietors' board until 1880. Rufus Sayre was thus well connected.

Sayre's deed, quitclaiming lands to him in the eastern part of the town for $550, specified all undivided lands, meadows, and marshes east of the line between Halsey Neck Lane and Holmes's Hill excepting lands above the North Sea Line, the bottom of Mecox Bay, and a strip of beach land known as Foot of the Beach at Hog Neck east of Noyack. This last had been sold to Orlando Hand for $25. But it did include beach land either side of that—Long and Short Beach or Hog Neck Beach. Burial grounds were specifically excluded from the sale. Maxwell's deeds had said nothing of this, but it must be presumed. Richard Esterbrook and his associates obtained Mecox Bay for $2,000. Added to Maxwell's, Sayre's, and the other small purchases the proprietor trustees showed a small profit of about $3,600, a sum far beneath what many believed was the true market value of the lands and especially the lands under the bays. It was not much but in the end and after the conclusion of the Mecox Bay case, which disputed the proprietors' right to sell, there is no evidence that any money was ever refunded to the purchasers.

Rufus Sayre, nevertheless, did not hold on to his newly acquired interests for very long. Two years later he sold them at no gain to himself to two members of the proprietor trustees' land committee, the same committee responsible for arranging the 1882 sale in the first place. These were none other than Edwin Post and James H. Foster. It smacked of a prearranged deal with Sayre cast in the role of a go-between to avoid any appearance of a conflict of interest. Once the dust had settled over the secretive loss by private sale of the common lands and shores, and the town's attention was focused on the impending Mecox trial, Sayre quietly signed over his own purchase in 1885. At some point Foster relinquished his interest and Edwin Post became the sole possessor of the various quitclaims. None of this might have mattered very much had not an astute Southampton lawyer and later county justice, Harri Micah Howell, stepped into the picture much later in 1896 and purchased at least some, perhaps all, of Post's interests. The price was not disclosed. For years afterward, Howell slowly but profitably divested himself of these interests quitclaiming them on a first-come first-serve basis to all who needed them.

After years of success in this small side business, however, one particular stretch of land came to be contested and Howell found himself in court as a defendant. The lands in question were the meadows and beach banks from Wickapogue Pond to a point just east of Mecox. On the basis of his deed, Howell claimed an interest short of outright ownership in the beach lands and other lands elsewhere in the town quitclaimed to him by Post via the Sayre deed originating with the trustees of the proprietors. He began selling quitclaim deeds to prospective buyers of beach front and other property. As Harry Sleight put it in one of his many diverting and invaluable commentaries on town affairs, "(t)itle companies declined to insure certain titles without the interest of Mr. Howell being wiped out, and the only way to do this was to buy a quit claim from him. This has been done it was asserted (in court), in hundreds of parcels."[5] With a quitclaim deed in hand new owners had no difficulty in insuring title for Howell's right was the only outstanding right. For well over twenty years after 1896, Harri Howell had been conducting a brisk business, a lucrative sideline to his law practice on Main Street, assuaging the concerns of new summer homeowners. And of these there were many, this being a period of rapid expansion in the summer colony. East of Halsey Neck almost everybody had to come to Howell. They were probably not unhappy to dig into their pockets for $100 or $200 to extinguish Howell's claim and buy peace of mind.

But unfortunately for Howell, the proprietor trustees had sold lands to Rufus Sayre that were not theirs to sell. It was exactly the same problem that was to plague the new owners of lands in the 1920s that had come to them through the Maxwell deed in the Quogue Purchase when a later claim was contested. Inadvertently or not, the proprietors had sold private lots in the great divisions there as well as remnants of common land. With the Sayre interests Howell had had a long and profitable innings—he never had to refund any money and most of his quitclaims were genuine—but found himself a defendant in a case against him in 1928. His long string of luck ran out when he pressed a quitclaim deed on the purchaser of a beach lot on the ocean at Mecox Bay. The land had been sold by Baldwin Cook, now ninety-four in 1928, who had inherited it from his father, Harvey Cook. The latter had bought it at auction from the proprietor trustees in 1846, an auction attended by a ten-year-old Baldwin Cook and even dimly remembered by him. The new buyers of Cook's land refused to pay the quitclaim price to Howell, and Cook, anxious to complete his sale, decided to test Howell's claim in court. There was a record of the trustees' original auction sale in their journal and the lot in question had been surveyed and monumented. It was legally much more clear-cut than the Quogue case and the Supreme Court judge had no difficulty in rendering a decision in favor of Cook and against Howell. It was a suit to quiet title and it effectively put a stop to any further sales of quitclaim deeds by Howell.

As a footnote to this story of minor but perfectly legal gouging, Howell had had the proprietor trustees' land records in his possession from the early 1890s until 1912 when, for a brief moment, a new trustee board was elected. He must have spent many a profitable hour studying those records. The 1912 board was brought into committee to examine a number of unspecified title questions that had been raised. Howell was elected clerk to the committee and Pelletreau assumed the chairmanship. They were natural choices as both had spent many years searching title claims and were acknowledged experts. They knew each other well and had corresponded regarding these matters in the past. A revealing exchange of letters between them in 1899 illustrates the occasional precariousness of the ground on which Howell stood and the anxiety it provoked in him. At this early date, a good thirty years before he found himself in court, Howell was not sure whether the title to some of the land he claimed an interest in was really common land or previously owned. He wrote to Pelletreau as follows and evidently in reply to a previous letter that has not survived:

> I note that you call the title I bought of Edwin Post a "shadow"—now please don't advise Dr. Thomas to chase it (the land referred to is at the beach in Old Town and belonged to Gaillard Thomas). Is there any record of the original allotment of his Old Town property? If I begin to convey strips of beach I will look to Olyphant and others (summer owners) as if they must buy peace or prepare for a fight. I don't care to put myself before the community in that light.

He ended with a small protest that Pelletreau had "erred in supposing that I bought the lands, highways, beachbanks and beaches as a speculation." It would be uncharitable to ask for what other purpose he acquired them but Pelletreau's reply was reassuring. At the same time it went some way toward clarifying the occasionally tenuous nature of the quitclaims business.

> I am sorry that you persist in misunderstanding my motives in writing to you in regard to the claims in question. I think I can truly say that there is not a single item of lands covered by your claims that I do not most fully understand. You must not think that I consider the rights sold to you by Mr. Post "shadows." Some of them are very substantial rights and you ought to get something for them. I simply said to Dr. Thomas, "it would be a prudent thing to get a quit claim from Mr. Howell and his fellow owners." Your claim to anything south of Mr. Gulliver (another summer owner) is simply a shadow, but if they are willing to pay you anything for a quit claim why not do it? Your right to the fee of the land on the east side of Old Town Pond is not a shadow but a fact, and I think that the Doctor would be willing to pay for it. These people and others come to me as a disinterested authority and I give them the best advice I can. The idea that you wish to "blackmail" them or anyone else is what I do not believe and I have no reason to think that anyone does.[6]

He added somewhat plaintively that "I wish that you could understand me better." This must have gone some way toward reassuring Howell regarding the propriety of certain aspects of his business for he showed no signs of abandoning it, pursuing it in fact for many years to come.

Yet this exchange reveals the imprecision or ambiguity contained in the original deeds of the proprietor trustees in conveying lands to various purchasers, Sayre and Maxwell in particular. The deeds did not convey the lands outright (some part of which were indeed common lands), the absolute fee in them, but only a quitclaimed interest that amounted to a declaration that their own title to some of the lands was uncertain. Quitclaim deeds merely extinguished whatever interest the proprietors themselves may have had or, for that matter, may not have had. It was simply prudent to obtain one. But it did not resolve questions of ownership. Such deeds merely said that their conveyors disclaimed any equitable interest in the property in question and had in essence conveyed it away. In the case of Mecox Bay the proprietors had sold such an interest, but this was as much determined by the politics of the Bay question as by any doubts about prior private ownership. Obviously there was no such private ownership or so it must have seemed at the time. They neglected to consider that in the past—before 1818—the town trustees, acting in their capacity as representatives of the proprietors of the common and undivided lands, had sold landlocked ponds or parts of them to various individuals. But this was not the paramount issue at the time. The real question was whether the bottom of Mecox Bay was town rather than proprietor land, that is, whether it was public land.

With a suit pending and an injunction just lifted, it is not difficult to see why Richard Esterbrook, his fortuitous marriage apart, had the edge over Edward Whitaker in the Mecox Bay stakes, even if his bid was considerably lower. In the first place he had the support of Henry Hedges. But not only Hedges. Two other extremely important figures in the community were also backing Esterbrook—Everett Carpenter and Stephen B. French—and this had to weigh strongly with the proprietor trustees. Moreover, Pelletreau, a good friend to Hedges and close to Carpenter and French, had thrown his support to Esterbrook. Pelletreau was in favor of developing the bays, having long thought them to be moribund and in need of economic rejuvenation. Like the others he was progressive, a Republican—Hedges had helped establish the county Republican Party in 1856—and welcomed the introduction of modern capitalism in Southampton. He may have thought, as he once put it, that the railroad came in "like a serpent into paradise" but he understood that it would inevitably create economic opportunities that otherwise would not exist. Whether it was to be resort development on the Hills, beach companies and hotels, factories at Sag Harbor or, for that matter, an oyster company at Mecox, Pelletreau saw that this was Southampton's future. He may have had some conservative and possibly nostalgic regrets—the exodus of young people from the farms into service on the emerging summer estates and the general decline in traditional ways of life it denoted pained him—but, on the whole, he supported these modernizing trends. And besides, he was himself doing quite well out of them.

So also were Stephen French and Everett Carpenter. French, like Pelletreau, was of Huguenot extraction. He was born in Riverhead in 1829 but his parents soon removed to Sag Harbor, which at that time was in its heyday as a whaling port. Almost inevitably he went to sea, signing on to a whaling ship at the age of seventeen for one voyage to the South Pacific before heading for the California gold fields in 1849. The whale fishery was entering its steep decline at the end of the 1840s, and French was one of many in the whaling ports of the East Coast who took sail for San Francisco. After an adventurous few years—he dug for gold, kept a hotel, a store, and was involved in a scheme in the Sandwich Islands (Hawaii)—he returned to Sag Harbor somewhat richer than when he had left and went into partnership with his brother in forming a trading company. In the 1860s, he entered politics as a Republican and was elected county treasurer in 1869. He ran for Congress in 1874 but lost. According to Henry Hedges, who compiled a brief and laudatory biography of French, President Ulysses Grant appointed him an appraiser at the Port of New York in 1876, a position from which he later moved to the honorific title of commissioner in the city's police department.[7] There is no record of this particular appointment and in 1881 he was back in Sag Harbor running his business. Earlier he had bought an interest in the *Sag Harbor Express*, the community's Republican newspaper.

As noted in the first chapter, Everett Carpenter like Stephen French was similarly an eminent citizen of Sag Harbor. A few years younger than French and originally from Massachusetts, Carpenter came to Long Island in the late 1850s to pursue a law practice and a political career. He was extremely successful at both. He had been a Brown University graduate. In Republican politics he was widely respected, becoming chairman of the Republican Committee of Suffolk County about 1873. In 1879, he was elected to the state assembly but remained for only one term, returning to his law practice in 1881. His prowess in assembly debate and in committee was apparently only matched by his ability in the courtroom. Pelletreau wrote a small appreciative sketch of him and thought that as a legal scholar at the Suffolk bar he was without peer.

These then were Richard Esterbrook's friends and supporters. He had come to Bridgehampton only in 1879, or 1878 at the earliest, and enlisted some of the key men of the town for advice and eventual collaboration. And he had married a Rose, a daughter of one of the most prominent citizens of the nineteenth century in Southampton. Before putting together a scheme for planting oysters in the bay, one of the first things Esterbrook did in Bridgehampton, following a practice that was becoming increasingly common, was to buy ocean-front land. In 1881, he purchased twenty-five acres at the foot of Mecox on the Bridgehampton side for $3,000, suggesting that money was no obstacle in the future purchase of the bay and the development of a business enterprise. Three years later, he doubled his investment by selling the lot to a local man, M. H. Woodhull, for $6,000. Woodhull was reported as planning to build a hotel on the property with accommodations for three hundred guests. He eventually abandoned the project, but the Mecox area clearly was becoming very desirable. A steamship service from Water Mill to the bathing houses at the beach had just begun plying the waters twice a day. Leon de Bost and Pelletreau had hoped to establish a beach club in the vicinity while Gaillard Thomas, who already owned land at Old Town, had begun speculating in beach property farther east toward Flying Point. He also, like Woodhull, thought to build a hotel and casino, but ultimately shelved the idea in favor of putting up cottages for summer rental.

Real estate development, or sheer speculation in real estate, was proceeding at an accelerated pace along the ocean front from Quogue to Wainscott in the early 1880s. Even the sleepy villages of the North Fork were not immune. Little Hog Neck in Cutchogue (now attractively rendered as Nassau Point)—five hundred acres of level land with unrivalled views up and down the bays—had been sold in 1884 to a New York syndicate with plans for establishing a resort on it. A similar syndicate from Brooklyn had its eyes on Robins Island, buying it outright in 1881 for a gun club. The boom in land in 1884 was at least partially triggered by the financial panic that swept through Wall Street in the spring. Rail and iron stocks retreated, banks that had borrowed heavily to speculate in rail stocks during a period of massive and largely uncontrolled railroad expansion saw their explosive growth evaporate. Banks and brokerage houses failed, stocks fell across the board, European capital withdrew, and stockholders in general got out as fast as they could and put their money into safer havens. And generally that meant land. It had been an article of faith since the late seventeenth century that real estate never loses its value. This was certainly the case in the increasingly feverish conditions of the Southampton real estate market (see Chapter 2). Esterbrook, like so many others who had descended on the area in the previous five years, merely took advantage of it. It was an extraordinary decade for real estate investment and rising property values. Business may have been bad around the country but the growth of American wealth had been so great since the mid-1870s that the impact of the recession was barely felt in Southampton. Real estate ventures and new capital projects continued unabated.

Despite the fact that Esterbrook was under the threat of an ejectment suit from Southampton's town trustees, he and his associates went ahead with plans for Mecox Bay. In spring 1883, he took delivery of a three-ton steamboat at Sag Harbor, carted it to Water Mill, and built a sixty-foot dock out into the bay to moor it. In August, the Mecox Bay Oyster Company was finally incorporated with a capital stock of $500,000, an astoundingly high figure for what seemed to be a fairly modest enterprise. In comparison, Joseph Fahys' far larger watch-case company in Sag Harbor had been capitalized the year before for no more than $100,000. The directors of the new company were Stephen French, Esterbrook, Everett Carpenter, and several others from New York. French was president, Esterbrook treasurer, and Carpenter secretary and attorney. In November, Esterbrook brought out a party of fifty from New York to observe his oyster operations, a sure indication that the company was up and running. There was much talk of a canning factory—canning shucked oysters had been routine for decades—while the *Seaside Times* marveled that one apparently natural as opposed to a cultivated oyster measured out at eleven inches.

But the incorporation provoked a sharp reaction in the community. One letter to the Southampton paper complained that "a cloud rests upon the title to this property which will only be raised by a long and expensive law suit." The new investors, it continued, are more likely to be assessed for legal fees than to receive dividends, and why, the pseudonymous writer wanted to know, was the *Sag Harbor Express* pushing this investment so vigorously. The reason for this was self-evidently apparent. French was part owner of the paper. Esterbrook and Carpenter protested immediately, objecting to the "insinuation" that French was "roping in" investors. As to the projected litigation from the town trustees: "we have waited in vain" since April for an opportunity to contest the town's "invalid claim" but were prepared to fight all efforts "to prevent the progress of a great public industry"[8] But the court case was still a year and a half away and, as it turned out, if anyone was guilty of delay it was Carpenter.

Not everybody was unhappy with the new company. In Bridgehampton and Water Mill, there was considerable support as it was expected to provide some additional employment in these communities. Yet even those who thought that Bridgehampton would suffer if the courts ultimately closed down Esterbrook's operation had reservations about the size of the stock issue and the efforts underway to market it. One supporter who commented that "many may not take a fancy to the methods of Steve French, and may consider the capitalizing of the bottom of Mecox Bay at $500,000 as one of the hugest watering operations of this watery age" [sic] still thought the project should be allowed to continue.[9]

George White disagreed. Some months later in April 1884, he and the town trustee board were returned to office by an overwhelming margin. With almost one thousand people voting, it was the largest turnout in the history of Southampton's elections. It was at that meeting that an appropriation of $5,000 for legal expenses was approved. Judges Carter and Young had made their report to the town and the trustees were now authorized to proceed with legal action. In July, they asked the two judges, retained as attorneys, to prepare the case. Six months passed and nothing happened. Then in March 1885, White revealed that probably late in the previous year an attempt to serve a summons on the purchasers of Mecox Bay had failed. The trustees, he mystifyingly claimed, "could not find any owners." This was at the very least peculiar and there is no ready explanation for it unless Everett Carpenter was already employing delaying tactics (which seems quite likely given what was to come), but in the event the trustees' attorneys were able to serve papers on the oyster company itself if not on any particular individuals. White anticipated that the case would be tried in April 1885 but this turned out to be a forlorn hope. The annual town meeting came and went at the beginning of that month without any hint of progress. Lawyers for both sides began taking pretrial testimony from various witnesses in Southampton. What did come to light was that Carpenter was indeed, for whatever reason, delaying the process. It was feared that he "will ask for another postponement." He did. It was then reported that the case was to be carried over to the following term "the defendants not being ready."

II: THE TRIAL

William Pelletreau had been away in White Plains preparing a history of Rockland County. But before he left, he had been concerned by the lack of progress in the Mecox Bay case and had written in May 1885 expressing his frustration at the delay. He laid the blame squarely at the door of the defense, in effect, Carpenter. Unusually blunt, he remarked that "(t)he public has just cause for indignation that the suit against the Mecox Bay Oyster Company has been postponed. For this there is no excuse. It is pitiful to see the 'learned counsel' for the defense engaged at this late date in collecting evidence which he ought to have had, and might have had, more than a year ago, thus causing a needless and vexatious delay."[10] He then took himself to White Plains to write his new history. Startled perhaps by this public denunciation from an old friend, Carpenter nonetheless went about his business of collecting testimony from various witnesses and prepared himself for the case to come. At the end of the summer he was ready. The case came before Judge Edgar M. Cullen in the fall term of the Supreme Court at Riverhead at the end of October. The testimony was voluminous—it came to almost six hundred printed pages—the examinations and cross-examinations of witnesses many, and Carpenter, although he ultimately lost, acquitted himself with his reputation for eloquence and erudition intact. Here is what happened and what Judge Cullen thought of the matter.

In the Trustees of the Freeholders of the Town of Southampton versus the Mecox Bay Oyster Company Limited, an action of ejectment,[11] it was plain from the outset that the attorneys for both sides planned to base their arguments on interpretation of the powers granted the town by the original patents in the matter of the management of the lands and the waters and the disposal of land, and their subsequent modification and supposed amplification by the 1818 and 1831 legislation. It raised, however, a deeper issue. Did the original Farrett grant conferring the right to purchase lands from the Indians and the ensuing deed from them in late 1640 convey the land to the settlers and their successors as members of a company rather than as a political body—a town—that is, simply as tenants in common? And if so, did this remain in force after Southampton was erected into a legal entity through the incorporation of town trustees, first in 1676 (as merely patentees) and then again in 1686 under the terms of the Dongan patent? Another way of putting it is to ask if the company continued in existence, its shareholders and their heirs and assigns endowed with original corporate rights, after the town was created a body politic under external administrative authority, coexisting in presumed harmony with this new political association (the town). Did the successors to the original purchasers, their heirs, and others who had bought shares in the enterprise, continue on as tenants in common after the town was granted corporate power or were they absorbed into the town possessing in consequence no more than equitable rights to the lands they had divided and allotted and only vestigial rights in the remaining common lands? Did they retain any legal title to these remaining common lands?

Because of the complexity of this issue—it raised questions not anticipated in medieval law regarding the formation of townships surrounded by broad lands—a great part of the record of the trial was taken up with a recitation of the principal historical documents that had outlined for the original and later inhabitants the nature and limits of their jurisdiction or authority. Of those documents placed in evidence the patents of 1676 and 1686, granted by Governors Andros and Dongan at the direction of James, Duke of York (and since 1685 James II), were obviously of the greatest significance since they had established the town as a corporate body under provincial rule with the power to elect trustees. The Dongan patent, particularly, spelled out the nature of this body politic consisting of freeholders and commonalty and specified the rights and responsibility of its trustees as well as those of other offices it created.

Similarly, the state legislation of the early nineteenth century separating the interests of the proprietors in common from those of the freeholders and commonalty and their trustees was exhibited and used by both sides in the case. The act of 1818, an act relative to the common and undivided lands and marshes of Southampton, restricted the authority of the proprietors to the management of such lands and excluded them from any regulation of the waters and their products. This latter function was vested in the town trustees to the exclusion of the proprietors. The act further permitted the proprietors to form themselves into a corporation and elect their own trustees for the purpose of managing and regulating the common lands. These trustees also were empowered to dispose of these lands by sale or lease as they saw fit. In 1831, for reasons discussed earlier, the town trustees sought legislative confirmation of their legal status as an incorporated body, that is, as the trustees of the freeholders and commonalty. This did not represent any legal change, but simply legislative recognition of their continued existence as a corporation with certain defined powers. In effect, the act of 1831 confirmed the role of the town trustees as described in the provisions of the Dongan patent but with one obvious exception. The town could no longer possess an equitable interest in the common and undivided lands, indeed, if it ever had one. It may, however, have always held the legal title to such lands, a condition that the earlier 1818 legislation had appeared to recognize in its last clause.[12]

The central question of the trial inevitably came down to the following: Did the definition of the common and undivided lands of the town, as thought of in the patents and the legislation, extend to include the lands under water? This was by no means as easy a question as might at first sight appear because the court had to consider two separate sets of issues. First, how had the town trustees before 1818 customarily exercised their powers of jurisdiction over the common lands and waters they were charged with managing by the Dongan patent? And second, how had two separate bodies of trustees after 1818 exercised their new and restricted responsibilities in respect to these same lands and waters? For example, it emerged at the trial that from time to time in the early nineteenth century the town trustees had leased out portions of the bottom of Mecox Bay to small local companies for oystering. David Burnett testified that his father had formed just such a company to lease oyster lots from the town in the early 1800s and again in the 1830s. This followed a practice that had been well established in the eighteenth century. Thus in 1767 and 1769, one-acre water lots had been leased at Mecox to three companies to plant and harvest oysters.

The revenue from such leasing had accrued to the proprietors, and not the town, as was the case with all other fees from leases of common lands for various purposes. But it raised a difficult question. If the land under Mecox Bay was common land held by the proprietors, and the proprietors had profited from it, how after 1818 could the town trustees legally lease it to Burnett and others; that is, lease land that was possibly not theirs to lease? At the same time, the trustees clearly assumed their right to control oystering. In 1833, for example, they prohibited the use of dredges and rakes in the bay, an evident if unintended reference to the bay bottom. Again, in 1842, the trustees approved the sale or lease of water lots in Sag Harbor for the construction of Long Wharf. These underwater lots were obviously understood as town lands as opposed to lands owned by the proprietors. The trustees of the proprietors laid no claim to them and never contested the town's grant to the wharf company.

There was one subsidiary issue brought up by the defense though it had no material impact on the outcome of the trial. In examination of several witnesses, owners of land at Mecox including his own associate for the defense, Henry Hedges, Everett Carpenter tried to determine whether Mecox Bay might be considered a fresh water pond or, if not quite fresh water, simply a pond. It was fed by a number of streams, cattle were occasionally observed to drink from its banks or from those of its creeks, and the outlet to the ocean was generally artificially opened. David Burnett, in his testimony, acknowledged that the bay seldom went out on its own and only when the water level was particularly high. Similarly, ocean storms breaking over the narrow strand of beach rarely created an inlet. If enough seawater broke into the bay, the action of it going back out with the tide might build enough pressure to force a cut in the beach but this was an unlikely event. The logic behind Carpenter's strategy was clear. Several land-locked ponds had been sold by the proprietors in the past and sold as undivided land. Otter Pond near Sag Harbor and Poxabogue Pond east of Bridgehampton were notable instances, just as were the wholesale quitclaiming of ponds to Pelletreau, Maxwell, and others in the 1882 sales. Poxabogue Pond had been sold in 1793 to David Howell and Company for thirty-five pounds. Otter Pond was sold in 1782 and resold to John Jermain in 1793.

Mecox Bay was not an arm of the sea and was only irregularly tidal. Carpenter wanted to know why it was not then a pond. This argument formed no part of Judge Cullen's eventual decision in the case, though he recognized that Mecox was not an arm of the sea, but it did serve White with an opportunity after the trial was over for a few choice comments. "The company which is trying to rob the town of Mecox Bay," he said, "says it is a fresh water pond. . . . The title not being perfect the company undertook to put it into Wall Street by that name (Bay not Pond) as a blind pool, at five hundred thousand dollars, and now calls it a worthless fresh water pond."[13] White, as usual, could not pass this one up. If Carpenter's argument had prevailed, and Mecox was deemed a land-locked pond, the existence of any oysters on its bottom would have been a minor miracle.

Yet generally the trial unfolded less on testimony on issues such as this than with the presentation of a large array of historical documents besides the patents and extensive quotation from the town records. Apart from the Andros and Dongan patents, and the acts of 1818 and 1831, other documents were put in evidence essentially in an effort to provide the legal historical background to the question of the ownership of the lands and the waters. For the most part they were introduced without comment or discussion and not employed by either attorney. The court declared that they were on offer from both parties and that either might make use of them as they desired, the judge reserving the right to exclude them if he thought them irrelevant or superfluous. They included the Farrett grant to the original patentees of 1639/1640 and the Earl of Stirling's confirmation of the grant; Charles II's grant of a proprietary to his brother James, Duke of York; the commission of Thomas Dongan as governor of New York; James II's commission to Thomas Dongan; the Indian deeds of 1640 and 1703; the Indian deed to Lion Gardiner in 1658 and its assignment to John Cooper; the Indian deed to Thomas Topping in 1662, and a number of other lesser deeds, receipts, memoranda, and determinations. Included among them were the land records and commonage books of the trustees of the proprietors.[14]

Except for the patents—particularly the Dongan patent—few had any direct bearing on the case, but they were available to Judge Cullen as evidence to assist him in forming an opinion or for him to throw out if they did not. The same may be said of a lengthy and exhaustive recitation of the original divisions of land in the seventeenth and eighteenth centuries. This eloquent and informative presentation was made by Pelletreau as a witness for the defense. It took up fully one-fourth of the complete testimony and remains invaluable for the historian—it is a pity Pelletreau never thought to include these descriptions of the divisions in his many writings—but beyond showing the town's or, more precisely, its proprietors' historic responsibilities for managing and dividing the common lands, its utility for the court is open to question except to portray the continuing responsibilities of the proprietors as a body of tenants in common. Of much greater relevance was the use of the town records. In particular, those that related to the management of the fishery in Mecox Bay as well as throughout the town were very much germane to the case. How the regulation of the products of the waters and the revenues accruing from the sale of privileges giving access to these products—from seaweed to shellfish and the general fishery—passed from the proprietor trustees to the town trustees in 1818, and continued in the same fashion thereafter, was carefully exhumed from the records. Edward Foster, as town clerk, presented them. They did show that the town trustees, before and after 1818, controlled the fishery irrespective of who stood to gain from the sale of privileges, whether the proprietors before 1818 or the town afterward.

There were in all this some light as well as illuminating moments in the course of the trial. One in particular was provided by Edwin Post, the long-time clerk to the proprietor trustees who had been called as a witness for the defense. At the time, Post was embroiled in a dispute with the town over an ancient right-of-way he claimed off his South Main Street property that ran through a portion of the South End Burying Ground, the town's original cemetery. White had joined the fray in this particular matter and Post was soon to find himself in court over it. Possibly this had affected his mood for, under cross-examination by the counsel for the town trustees regarding the relationship between that body and that of the proprietor trustees, Post provided only grudgingly the most elliptical of information and only after James Carter had made the most strenuous efforts to draw it from him. The exchange between them was quite surreal but it displayed for all to see the extent to which the proprietors had become alienated from some of the central interests of the town and had fallen back on a defensive strategy, the cemetery issue—a private one between Post and the town—apart. The salient elements of Post's testimony are as follows:

Q. What is the full name of the body of which you are clerk?

A. The proprietors of the common and undivided lands of the town of Southampton, is, I think, the wording.

Q. What do they call themselves?

A. They call themselves the proprietors.

Q. They are not proprietors—they are trustees of the proprietors, are not they—the body of which you are clerk?

A. I am clerk of the trustees; yes.

Q. Trustees of what?

A. Trustees of the proprietors.

Q. Of the proprietors of what?

A. Of the common and undivided lands of the town.

Q. That is to say, the name of the body of which you are clerk is the trustees of the proprietors of the common and undivided lands of Southampton?

A. Yes; lands and meadows.

Q. Is that the corporate name or as near as you recollect, if it has any corporate name?

A. That is the name; the meetings are headed under that.

Q. Is it a body of trustees?

A. Yes, sir.

Q. How are they chosen?

A. Chosen by the body of our proprietors—by the owners of this land that is named there in that book; they meet in the town of Southampton on town meeting day and elect their trustees for the year.

Q. And only those persons who are known to be and who are the proprietors of common and undivided lands in Southampton participate in the choice of those trustees?

A. No others.

Q. And you are the clerk of that body?

A. Yes, sir.

Q. How long has that body had an existence?

A. In that shape since 1818.

Q. Is there another corporate body known to you by the name of the trustees of the freeholders and commonalty of the town of Southampton?

A. I am not able to say.

Q. Do you know of any such body?

A. I do not know of any body, except this new body of trustees that were made trustees under the act here from 1818.

Q. Do you not know of any other body of trustees in the town of Southampton?

A. The trustees that are elected town meeting day from 1818, I know—before those trustees were . . .

Q. Since 1818, has not there been chosen by the electors generally of the town of Southampton a body of trustees?

A. Oh, certainly.

Q. You know those?

A. Yes.

Q. Is not that name of that body the trustees of the freeholders and commonalty of the town of Southampton?

A. I do not know what it may be.

Q. Is not that your understanding about it?

A. I have not thought anything about it.

Q. Has not there always been chosen such a body on town meeting day?

A. There has always been trustees chosen town meeting day.

Q. Has not there been such a body as that chosen by all the electors?

A. Up to 1818 none was allowed to be town trustee but such as were proprietors; in 1815, I believe, one or two were elected, but up to 1818 every man who was eligible to be a trustee was a proprietor.

Q. There have been a body of trustees called the trustees of the freeholders and commonalty of the town of Southampton?

A. Since 1818.

Q. Was not there such a body before that?

A. I do not know what you would call them.

Q. Do not you know that there was such a body?

A. I know that there was a body of twelve trustees that managed the town business, and this trustee business—one body.

Q. Now since 1818, there has continued to be such a body?

A. Yes, since 1818, there has.

Q. And they are plaintiffs in this suit?

A. I suppose they are, yes.

Q. There was such a body before 1818, was not there?

A. Not that was not proprietors.

Q. There was such a body?

A. There was a body of that kind, I suppose you would term them so.

Q. And by the same name were not they?

A. Yes, they were the trustees of the town of Southampton.

Q. And chosen under the town charter?

A. Yes, sir.

Q. And they are chosen now under the town charter?

A. Yes, I suppose they are.

Post's feigned ignorance of the patent arrangements served only to underscore the gulf that had developed between the town and the proprietors. If his testimony revealed anything at all, it was a refusal to accept the newly emerged preeminence of the town trustees in town affairs and nostalgia for the old regime prior to 1818 when the proprietors were in more or less undisputed control. At that time, the leading men of the proprietors monopolized the town trustees' board and used it to further their own interests and those of the proprietors in general. Before 1815, no townsman who was not a proprietor was electable. It was partly that which had precipitated the crisis and led to the petition to Albany for a change in political arrangements to reduce the power of the proprietors. Post made it perfectly clear what he thought of the ensuing legislation—he rejected it—and just as clear what he thought of the post-1818 trustees.

But his testimony may not have worked well for Carpenter's case for the oyster company. Earlier in the trial, Carpenter had been anxious to present the proprietors in as favorable a light as possible. He had used Pelletreau's evidence on the divisions of the common land to good effect and before James Carter's damaging cross-examination had managed to elicit useful and cooperative responses from Post himself. Now, late in the trial, this may have all come undone. Post's testimony potentially undermined Carpenter's careful portrayal of the proprietors as responsible and benign caretakers as well as owners in fee of the town's undivided lands above and below water.

Judge Cullen took some time delivering a judgment. The trial had taken place at the end of October but it was not until January 1886 that he released it. Cullen argued that the case turned on the interpretation of the colonial patents of 1676 and 1686 that had created the town as a corporate entity and confirmed the grant of its lands within its territorial limits.[15] The lands had been purchased from the Indians by the first settlers under the original Stirling patent of 1640, confirmed by both Governors Nicholls and Andros in 1665 and 1676, and granted again to them under the authority of Governor Dongan. Those named in the patent (there were twelve) were made "one body corporate and politic to be called by the name of the Trustees of the freeholders and commonalty of

Southampton and their successors." These trustees were, Dongan said, "(t)o have and to hold the same (lands) unto the said freeholders and commonalty . . . and their successors, forever, to and for the several respective uses following, and to no other use intent and purpose whatever." Cullen understood this to mean that the town, through its representative trustees, took legal title to all the lands and waters within its limits. The defense had taken the opposite position that no legal title resided in the town but passed "at once" to the individual purchasers construed to be the proprietors, namely, those who had bought the Indian titles to the lands in the first place, their successors and those who later purchased proprietary shares. Cullen did not accept this at all, taking the view that the Farrett grant of 1640, the Indian deed of the same year, and the later Indian deed of 1662 were without force after 1686. In other words, Cullen wished to date tenure or proprietorship in the lands as beginning with the Dongan patent and not before. This was a strange position in law to take for it was commonly believed in the northern colonies in the seventeenth and eighteenth centuries that, following English common law, for every parcel of land there had to be some form of tenure. Each parcel thus had to have a tenant or proprietor. Before the arrival of the settlers, therefore, the proprietors of the lands in question were the Indians. They subsequently transferred their title, knowingly or not, to the settlers.[16] The manner in which the settlers understood and implemented or organized that title among themselves was a crucial element in Carpenter's case. Cullen's position severely undermined it and essentially preordained the course that future appeals were to take.

Nevertheless, Cullen, ignoring the chain of title and its particular nature before Dongan, argued that from 1686 to 1818 the town was in "undisputed possession and control of all the common lands" and that it was understood by all that the town held legal title to them. It was the town trustees who from time to time divided and allotted lands to those with proprietary rights and also to those who did not—ministers and artisans—as inducements to settle. No one took title to lands directly but only mediately through the town, the rights of individual purchasers being regarded as "solely equitable" and in relation to their proportionate share. The town then was the only source of private title and it was also the town, through its trustees, that had unrestricted authority over the management of its undivided lands and waters. The latter, Cullen pointed out, were never divided and no private interest in the waters was ever recognized. In the earliest recorded agreement among the undertakers, the Disposall of the Vessell, it was forthrightly stated that "no person shall challenge or claim any proper interest in seas, rivers, creeks or brooks howsoever bounding or passing through his grounds, but freedom of fishing and navigation shall be common to all within the banks of said waters whatsoever." And lastly, the statute of 1818 incorporating the trustees of the proprietors assigned the waters and their products to the jurisdiction of the town and expressly excluded the proprietors from any authority over them. Thus, lacking any legal or equitable right in the waters and by extension the lands under them, the proprietors could in no circumstance sell such lands. Judge Cullen found for the town trustees and awarded them costs of $719. The case had so far cost the town $2,200.

The *Seaside Times* claimed the decision was a victory for the town although there was no great outpouring of celebratory correspondence in its pages. White "with an unusually pleasant countenance" visited the Main Street office of the paper with a telegram announcing the decision but had little to say. The *Times*, nonetheless, thought that "the people owe [White] a debt of gratitude for his untiring exertions on their behalf." But it was not the end of it. Everybody expected an appeal and notice of it was not long in coming. Carpenter requested a new trial a month after the decision but Cullen denied it. Then in March he appealed Cullen's denial before the general term of the second judicial department of the Supreme Court. Then, for unaccountable reasons, there was a lengthy postponement and little was said of the Mecox Bay case for nearly a year. In June 1886, Carpenter had filed appeal papers but nothing more was heard from him until December. At that time the case was to be heard before the appellate division of the Supreme Court in Brooklyn, yet Carpenter requested a postponement until February 1887 on the grounds that it was proving difficult to read and transcribe what he called "the ancient records."[17] The court granted the request but in February the appeal had still not been heard.

Finally in September, the case was argued before three justices of the court, Judges J. F. Barnard (presiding), J. O. Dykman, and C. E. Pratt. Their majority decision was published in December, rejecting the oyster company's appeal, and a judgment issued in January 1888 a full two years after Judge Cullen had found for the town trustees. Judge Pratt dissented from the majority view as presented by Barnard and wrote a lengthy rebuttal of the trustees' claim to the lands under water. This opinion is of particular interest, for it presents an entirely different perspective on the relations between town and proprietors and a different interpretation of what the statutes of 1818 and 1831 had or had not accomplished. Pratt's views were a sophisticated combination of legal and historical reasoning and are worth considering in detail. They stood in radical contrast to those of Barnard and Dykman, which, although no less well thought out, represented a more conventional and traditionalist position. They were very much in accord with those of Judge Cullen.

Barnard began with his understanding of the Stirling patent as a grant of land to a civil community "in church order and civil government" and noted that the first inhabitants of Southampton had "all title to civil government, whether in church or commonwealth." Thus the town was not simply a collection of individuals, and nor were the lands granted to individuals as tenants in common. For example, no individual purchases of land from the Indians were permitted and (it might be added) the town, in town meeting, clearly objected to the individual acquisition of lands west of Canoe Place from the Indians in 1658 and 1662. To put a stop to this freelance speculation by Thomas Topping, John Cooper, John Ogden and also the ever-present John Scott—one of the arch real estate speculators of the seventeenth century—the town had to rely on the intervention of Governor Richard Nicolls. Barnard agreed with Cullen that the Farrett grant and the Stirling confirmation of it were probably no longer in force having been first superseded by the Andros patent of 1676 and then by that of Governor Dongan a decade later. The kernel of the Andros patent was that while it granted lands to "named individuals" (the patentees) in free and common socage, though importantly on behalf of all, all lands in the town were to have a relation to the town in general "for the well government thereof." In this Andros was consistent with Farrett. Again, Andros did not consider the settlers as merely tenants in common, purchasers of a tract of land and dividing it among themselves as they thought necessary. The Andros patent was also, it is perhaps needless to say, consistent with the understanding of English law in the seventeenth century. Legal geography entailed that all lands were cut up into towns. The town was the "house-covered space" surrounded by broad lands the totality of which was the borough understood as an agrarian commonwealth. The term *borough* did not enter into the language of the colonial patents but the meaning—through the use of the terms town or township—was the same.

Under the Dongan patent all rights to land, once the Indian rights were extinguished, were "invested into the freeholders of the town" and the lands assigned to the management of trustees. These trustees, Barnard argued, were "clothed with the power to possess all the lands unappropriated to individuals before (the patent) was granted." He did not address the fact, and perhaps did not feel it was necessary to address it, that probably well over three-fourths of the inhabitants in 1686 were heirs to the original purchasers or those who came shortly thereafter and were in possession of commonage rights. Had he done so, that is, recognize that the large majority were first and foremost proprietors he would have had to deal with the question of whether these inhabitants simply constituted a body of tenants in common of certain lands and that "the town" was a later construction based on that fact. This was to become Judge Pratt's point of entry. As to the 1818 legislation, Barnard recognized that it had created a dual form of government. The act had erected a corporation "to manage the lands held in the proprietors as tenants in common" and at the same time had assigned the right and responsibility to control the waters of the town to the trustees of the freeholders and commonalty. However, he went on to say, the legislature intended no change of title: "(i)f the lands belonged to the town, the legislature could not change the title . . . (l)and and waters are acquired by the same title, and the legislature did not change the title to either." Like Cullen before him, Barnard thought that the town held the legal title while that of the proprietors was solely equitable.[18]

Judge Pratt did not agree with this conclusion at all and took the position of the defendant that title to all the lands had always been vested in the proprietors. Carpenter had pursued this argument throughout. His contention was that under the Dongan patent the title to the undivided land was in the purchasers as tenants in common as outlined in the Farrett and Indian deeds. Pratt clothed this interpretation with a persuasively detailed historical analysis. Essentially, he said, Southampton was from the very beginning, and regardless of what came afterward, a capitalist enterprise.[19] The Farrett deed first of all "plainly attests a sale of lands as distinguished from a voluntary grant" and the Indian deed that provided for "all the lands, woods, waters, water courses . . ." was acquired in pursuance of this patent. Moreover, these deeds always ran to named individuals and their "associates" or "co-partners." This was true of the original undertakers' agreements, although the names were not always the same, and later remained true of the Andros and Dongan patents. Always there were named parties. The title to the lands was then vested in individuals and vested in them before the land was divided.

The word "town" or "body politic" occurs nowhere in these early documents prior to settlement, or in the Indian deed, and Pratt thought that what references there were to "civil government" were of little import. Any group settling in the wilderness might wish to live in civil harmony and erect laws for their mutual benefit, but this did not endow them with "corporate power" or establish them as a corporate municipal body. Pratt did not raise the question, but he also might have noted that they were under no external jurisdiction, not even affiliated with the Massachusetts Bay Colony of which they were merely a distant offshoot. They were limited only by the conditions of the Farrett grant as derived from the Stirling patent for Long Island. Even after 1645 when, for security reasons, they submitted to the general court of the Connecticut Colony in Hartford they did not become a recognized political body except in an informal and quasi-legal sense. At that time, in fact, Connecticut had no patent of its own. It was a squatter colony and not therefore, strictly speaking, a colony or town either though it possessed legitimacy as an approved extension of the Bay.[20]

So what was Southampton? It was what it called itself, a company, a private business association with a subscribed capital in different and not necessarily equal shares. And the agreements entered into with other parties, for instance the Indian deed, were in the nature of private transactions. The company had declared in advance that the lands of their future "plantation" would be divided in house lots, planting lots, and commons: so much for each stockholder according to their share in the company. Future allocations of land through the laying out of divisions were to be at the pleasure of the undertakers or shareholders and their heirs and assigns. The town as such existed in nominal terms only, a collection of dwellings, house lots, gathered around a meetinghouse. Newcomers or "incomers" might be admitted as undertakers, that is, as purchasers of shares in the company and so could participate in the tenancy of the lands or they might not. They might simply be offered land on a conditional basis for the skills they brought with them—smiths, millwrights, weavers, cordwainers, and the like—and not admitted to proprietary status. This being the case, they would not possess shareholder voting rights in the company's affairs.

Judge Pratt, then, presented early Southampton as "a purely business situation," as he put it, ultimately a company based solely on financial contributions.[21] This was reaffirmed in 1648 when the settlers or planters relocated from Old Town to what became Main Street. They agreed to divide the town into forty house lots allocated among them according to the proportionate share of each in the valuation they put on the town. The town remained in the company, and the company also was the source of all legitimate authority. In respect to the purchase of the Indian lands—the approximate "eight miles square" between Canoe Place and Hog Neck—the company had first purchased the right to buy such lands from Farrett and in the subsequent transfer obtained a legal title to them in the form of the Indian deed. Equitable title or ownership in fee to particular tracts of land among the company's shareholders, whose successors were later called proprietors, must be presumed to have been established later when the lands were incrementally laid out and allotted. Pratt looked at this somewhat differently. He argued that equity in the company had already been established in the Disposall of the Vessell (the company's charter) prior to the purchase of the patent and the land, but once the lands were acquired the equitable title was "merged . . . into a purely legal (one)." Still, that same equity in the company was the basis on which individuals could subsequently acquire land of their own.

He then turned his attention to the Andros patent. This grant of 1676, although essentially coerced as Governor Edmund Andros had demanded that Southampton (and Southold) bring in their former grants and exchange them for new ones, left everything as it was in respect to the lands. It recognized the validity of the Indian purchases and confirmed old grants. It granted no new land but confirmed the rights of freeholders both in severalty as private owners and as tenants of previously granted lands that had remained in common possession. It did not disturb or prejudice the terms of the Farrett grant and ratified the status of real property as vested in the proprietors or freeholders as an association of individuals. But what it did do was grant corporate powers to this association, now to be called the "freeholders and inhabitants of Southampton." Andros's purpose here, it must be noted, was not to enhance the status of Southampton by incorporating it, but to provide a political mechanism to subordinate the town to the administration and jurisdiction of the province of New York.

Both Southampton and Southold had resisted this since the governorship of Richard Nicolls and that of his successor, Francis Lovelace. In 1670, they had energetically if in the end unsuccessfully repudiated the laws of the province—the Duke's Laws—as inapplicable to their circumstances as plantations. And when in 1675 the Dutch briefly retook New York and expelled the English, both towns sought protection from the Connecticut Colony to which jurisdiction they wished to return. Even after the English were safely back in New York and the Dutch gone for good, they continued to cast longing eyes toward Hartford. But to no avail. After the Dutch were forced out, Andros was appointed governor in place of Lovelace. In short order, by threatening them with the loss of their existing patents, he brought the eastern towns into line. Southampton's freeholders, whether they liked it or not, had corporate power of a sort thrust on them. Unwillingly they became a body politic firmly integrated into the new order. But the Andros patent did not, Judge Pratt contended, change the title to the lands.

Ten years later, this new corporate status was clarified by the Dongan patent. Thomas Dongan had been asked by the Shinnecock to settle a dispute between the Shinnecock Indians and Southampton over the location of the eastern bound of the town.[22] In doing so, he updated and elaborated the Andros patent; in effect producing a new one. Dongan recited the Andros grant word for word thus reconfirming that title to the lands lay in the association of freeholders. The mere erection of the town into a political body, Pratt argued, had not implied that legal title was displaced from individuals and reposited in the town. But then he admitted that the issue became confused. In formalizing the legal status of Southampton, Governor Dongan had specified not only the creation of a town but that it was to be managed by regularly elected trustees who were to be the incorporated representatives of the town at large. There were to be twelve of them corresponding to the number named in the grant as patentees. These trustees were to be known as the trustees of the freeholders and commonalty of the town of Southampton. This was Dongan's corporate term for the association, distinguishing it from that of Andros that contained no reference to trustees but only to certain officials charged by the patent with responsibilities to the provincial government.

But it was the reference to "the commonalty" that was confusing. It replaced "inhabitants" in the Andros patent. In the seventeenth century, the term *commonalty* had several distinct meanings. It could mean simply a community, a commonwealth, a town, and usually a self-governing one. Or it could mean a body corporate, a corporation, and here it could be used in reference to a private corporation such as a guild or university or to a municipality as a chartered public body. Or, it could refer to the general membership of a community, the common people as distinct from those with rank, title or privilege, gentleman as opposed to the "vulgare inhabitants" who lacked position, wealth, or status. It is this last sense of the term that seems to have been intended in the patent.[23] There are several reasons for thinking this.

First, Dongan deliberately separates "freeholders" from "commonalty" just as Andros had separated them from "inhabitants"; second, while freeholders by far outnumbered other inhabitants at the time, there was an increasing number of the latter who were clearly not considered as tenants in common with corresponding commonage rights; and third, later in the document, the annual election of trustees, constables, and assessors was to be by "the Majority of voices of the freeholders and freemen of the towne." This seems to exclude other inhabitants, although it did not necessarily preclude them from voting on other issues. The town records bear this out. However, this last matter did not concern Judge Pratt. What bothered him was the inclusion in the patent of the reference to "the commonalty." It suggested to him that the implication or even intention of the patent was to run title to the undivided lands, most of which were not taken up in 1686, directly to the town through its elected trustees. If "commonalty" meant anything it meant all the inhabitants regardless of freehold status, and if so, did this mean that the habendum clause of the patent—who or what had legal title to the lands—must then necessarily run to the very body created to represent the interest of all the inhabitants, freeholders, or proprietors and commonalty alike?

Judge Pratt did not think this was the case, but to sustain his argument had to rely on a clause in the patent that was in seeming contradiction to what followed it. In resolving the issues in dispute with the Shinnecock, Dongan found that "the ffreeholders . . . have lawfully purchased the lands within the Limitts and bounds aforesaid of the Indyans and have payd them therefore according to agreement so that all the Indyan right by virtue of said purchase is invested into the ffreeholders of the Towne of Southampton." It seemed perfectly clear from this that the freeholders held the legal title to the lands not yet taken up, lands that included "Rivers Rivolets waters lakes ponds Brookes streames" or, in sum, all, and that they had done so as tenants in common. But then a few lines later the habendum clause appears to run everything to the town now defined as the freeholders and commonalty. Unfortunately, there are occasional inconsistent elements in the Dongan patent and it is frequently repetitious, verbose, and obfuscatory even if not by design. Frederic Maitland once remarked of English medieval municipal charters that over time they had become "shrouded in misty complexity," a gradual movement, he thought, from "curtness to verbosity."[24] Governor Dongan or, rather, Mathias Nicolls, the provincial government's attorney who had drafted all official documents since 1665, must have absorbed and nurtured this distinctive legal trait. It can be imagined, however, that Southampton's patentees and other freeholders who took the trouble to pore through the patent's dense thickets of prose must have concluded that it both resolved their problems with the Indians and posed no threat to their interests. Read one way, it left everything as it was—in their hands. Read another, it put the lands not yet taken up squarely in the town. But who was the town? In fact, if not exactly in the patent, it was them, the original proprietors and their heirs and assigns. So, at any rate, they must have thought.

Undeterred by these confusions Judge Pratt pressed on. He pointed that the term *proprietor*, one replete with definite meaning and replacing that of freeman and freeholder, "seems gradually to have crept into use" in the late seventeenth century and became the accepted term in the eighteenth century. Even in 1687, it was "the proprietors" who were to pay for the charges of the Dongan patent rather than the town. Conceivably, the new trustees might have chosen to raise the money from town rates or impose a tax on all the inhabitants but they did not. Instead they offered new shares in the Town Purchase east of Canoe Place to select individuals with all privileges in any future divisions of land. It can be concluded from this that controlling the size of the stock issue and thus the number of stockholders was much more important to the proprietors than the cost of the patent. Opening up the purchase of the patent to the general run of taxpayers would inevitably raise questions about ownership. Naturally, the proprietors would want to avoid this as far as they could. They must have been aware that elsewhere in New England, if not in New York, local proprietary control of town lands by original purchasers was already subject to challenge by the growing numbers of inhabitants who lacked any rights in land and constituted a "shareless population."[25] By offering new shares to a lucky few who could afford them the proprietors avoided any immediate challenge to their control and maintained intact their monopoly of the revenues generated by the sale of privileges in town lands. From their point of view, to have included the full commonalty in the purchase of the patent by imposing a tax would have been folly.

The cost of the patent was forty shillings in annual quitrent and the trustees offered to sell fifty-pound commonage rights for three pounds each if the buyers would undertake to pay a proportionate share of that cost. There were fifteen such subscribers increasing then the number of full shares by five.[26] This was the only occasion after the issue of an additional share in the Town Purchase for the use of the minister in 1649 that the proprietors increased the stock. In fact, in the latter half of the eighteenth century it was common practice for the proprietors to advance the town money from their own revenues for specific purposes when it was short of funds, always in the expectation that it would be reimbursed out of future taxes. It was a significant example of the financial power they were still able to exert by their control of the stock and the land. This became one factor among several that led to the revolt of the inhabitants against the monopolistic rule of the proprietors in the early 1800s. But the decision of the trustees to restrict the financing of the patent to the body of stockholders underscored the division in the town between freeholders and commonalty that had been first spelled out by Governor Andros and then enshrined in the Dongan patent.

Finally, Pratt turned his attention to the outcome of the revolt of the 1800s in the compromise legislation of 1818. He did not think that the statute incorporating the proprietor trustees and transferring the control of the productions of the waters to the town in any way changed the title to the lands and the lands under water. That remained with the proprietors. The best that could be said of both the acts of 1818 and 1831 was that they were "noncommittal" in respect to the question of title, leaving it alone and possibly anticipating that the "waters" in some fashion might become the subject of some future litigation although not necessarily the lands under them. The so-called "saving clause" at the end of the 1818 statute seemed to suggest that the legislature was unprepared to countenance an alteration in title. It had stated simply, as we saw, that "nothing herein contained shall in any manner affect or alter the right, title or interest of any person, or the inhabitants of said town to any of the before mentioned premises." It was sufficiently vague to be interpreted in different ways but Judge Pratt thought that if the act had all along recognized the proprietors as the owners of the undivided lands as tenants in common, then that title should extend to include the lands under water, lands that also lay within the limits of the original purchase. There was nothing in the act to gainsay this. At the same time it is quite likely that the legislature gave no thought to a distinction between lands above water and lands below because it was nowhere addressed in the act, the sole concern of the act being to distinguish the land and the waters. It had only spoken of the right of the town trustees to manage the waters and their products and had been silent in respect to the land under them. The proprietor trustees, in selling the bays, had gambled on this interpretation and Pratt himself evidently considered it unassailable—the legislation left the status of the land beneath the waters undetermined or simply assumed. Still, the legislature must have been aware that bay bottoms had been leased by the town trustees for planting and harvesting oysters on numerous occasions. If the trustees could lease them, they must have been in possession of a title to them, either by long-standing and customary use or by the assumption that they lay within the patent limits of the town. But then at that time the trustees were all proprietors and the income from the sale of leases appeared in their accounts and not in those of the town. If nothing else, the pre-1818 trustees, managing the lands and waters for the proprietors, must have made the assumption that lands under water were like any other common lands and were therefore owned by the proprietors.

But Pratt's opinion was in the minority and, however, clearly and logically argued, the other two judges chose not to debate it in their own published views. Neither did the *Seaside Times* acknowledge its contents. Yet it must have encouraged Everett Carpenter to continue the fight for in February 1888 he filed a second appeal. This was a year in the making. Not until summer 1889 was the suit argued in appellate court and it was October before the presiding justice issued a judgment and his opinion. This was Judge Brown. Like Cullen and Barnard before him he found for the respondent in the appeal, the town trustees.

It was clear to Brown from the outset that both the Andros and Dongan patents vested title to the undivided lands in the town erected by both as a body corporate, but that in no way did this interfere with the equitable rights of individual proprietors. Several recent cases of trespass or ejectment in Long Island towns that had very similar patents to Southampton's had resulted in court decisions that recognized and affirmed the legal title to the common lands as resting in the towns in question. In one such suit, the town trustees of Brookhaven had successfully established their rights to lands under water in Great South Bay, a part of which had been sold to private parties. Brown did not see why these cases were not directly applicable to the Mecox Bay question. But he went further. In neither the Andros nor the Dongan grants did he see any other purpose than to establish title to the lands in a corporate community, the freeholders and inhabitants or commonalty of Southampton, a body now recognized through the incorporation of its trustees under the laws of the province of New York. There was nothing to suggest that it was vested in individuals as tenants in common despite what he referred to as "the peculiar phraseology of the habendum clause." If indeed the Farrett and Indian deeds had initially granted the lands to the original purchasers as tenants in common, Brown argued that this was clearly no longer in force after 1686.

Both before and after 1686 in fact, individuals took private title to lands and exercised commonage rights, where there were any, through the town and invariably did so in town meetings. The voluminous records of the divisions of lands and their allotment showed that this was a town function and understood by all to be within its jurisdiction. But Brown had some difficulty in reconciling the legislation of 1818 with this preexisting state of affairs. His opinion was that if the act recognized the legal title to the lands as in the proprietors as tenants in common then "it could not be sustained as an exercise of legislative power." But there was ambiguity here. On the one hand the act empowered the new proprietor trustees "to sell, lease or partition the same" (the undivided lands) while, on the other, it was silent as to where the legal title lay. Brown felt it must continue to lie with the town trustees. But if that was the case, were the various sales the proprietor trustees made through the nineteenth century up to 1882, almost all at public auction, themselves legal sales? He did not address this issue but based his view of the validity of the legislation on the fact that it resolved issues facing the town as a whole and was acquiesced in by both parties to the dispute, the committee of inhabitants and that of proprietors.

In respect to the sale of the bottom of Mecox Bay, and by implication the bottoms of other bays, he was unequivocal that the proprietor trustees had sold them illegally. The town trustees had sole rights to the waters and their products, the lands under them had never been privately owned, and the title to them lay as it always had in the town. Since the days of the original settlers the waters had always been inviolate. Whatever the 1818 act had or had not said about title—it spoke only of control or management as did the reaffirming legislation of 1831—the "original consecration" must still be presumed to be in effect, reinforced by "long user and occupancy." Judge Brown said of the bays that there had been a "distinct recognition by the Legislature of the State on two occasions that the title thereto was in the town" but then overlooked the fact that it actually did not. The weakness of both pieces of legislation was that they failed to recite the history of all the ancient rights and titles, examine their implications, and show what if anything had been changed and what had not. This failure had led to all the skirmishes of the nineteenth century and to this final denouement in the Mecox trial and the two ensuing appeals.[27]

With the appeals process concluded, the trustees of the proprietors wound up their business. They had no lands left to sell and no lands under water. A year after Judge Brown's decision, they called a last meeting of the proprietors and offered their resignations. Their president, David R. Rose, had died in 1889 at the age of ninety-two and had been succeeded by his son, Jetur Rose, then sixty-six. Rose had been abroad for a year. He was invited to captain a new steam whaler, built in New Bedford, on its inaugural voyage to the Pacific. He left in September 1888 bound for Honolulu. From there he took ship for the North Pacific as first mate on a whaler. Returning overland to San Francisco from Alaska, and thence by packet to New York, he arrived home just in time to deal with his father's death and the news of what was in many ways the proprietors' defeat in the courts. It was his last voyage. Jetur Rose died three years later. Another member of the old guard, Lewis Scott, had passed away the year before the last Mecox appeal. He died at his North Sea farm in August 1888 aged eighty-seven. White followed him at the end of 1892. These four men, and one should include among them Edwin Post (who was to die in 1901 at the age of eighty-five), had dominated the struggle over the town's lands and waters and issues of public and proprietor rights for most of the previous three decades. Their passing in many ways symbolized both the demise of the old order of land and class and Southampton's attempts to come to terms with the new realities of wealth and external interest and influence.

In March 1890, several months after Judge Brown's decision, Edward Whitaker, the same Whitaker who had played a significant role in shepherding the Shinnecock Canal project through the legislature some years earlier, filed his partition suit in Supreme Court in Riverhead naming both the town trustees and the proprietor trustees as respondents. At this late stage in the Mecox Bay stakes it was something of a quixotic gesture. The proprietor trustees had nothing left to partition and it was hardly likely that any court would rule against the town trustees. The proprietors were not now legally, if they ever had been, tenants in common of the lands under the bays, and they could not, if they ever could, dispose of them in bulk (the point of a partition suit) or in parcels. Three courts, in finding against Richard Esterbrook Jr. and his associates in the oyster company, had also effectively found against the proprietors. Jetur Rose filed a stipulation in Supreme Court asking that Whitaker's suit be dismissed without costs. The court agreed. A few weeks later the trustees of the proprietors decided to pay out "all the money on hand" from Edwin Post's efficiently administered treasury. Having done so, they collectively resigned in October, not to meet as a corporate body for twenty two years and then with a different and smaller membership led by William Pelletreau and the lawyer Harri Howell. This formidable bastion of landowning right and privilege had been finally broken 250 years after its original ascendance. All things considered, the summer colony and its preoccupations apart, the 1880s had been a very turbulent decade and 1890 an historic year in ways that could not have been anticipated in 1882. The 250th anniversary of the founding of the Town of Southampton was much celebrated in pageant, song, speech-making and tableaux-vivant of all descriptions. The ancestors—the founding proprietors—were much mentioned but the modern proprietary regime (the heirs and assigns of those same founders) so recently defunct though still vivid in everybody's memory was not.

Richard Esterbrook, his quiver empty and with four years of court decisions against him, had no choice but to close down his oyster farming operation. There is no existing record of how well it had developed between its beginning in 1882 and 1890 but, given the market for oysters in New York and the freight service over the Sag Harbor branch line from Bridgehampton to Long Island City, there is no reason to think that it had not been a lucrative business. Esterbrook retired to Tremedden on Ocean Road wondering perhaps at the obstinacy of George White and the town trustees and the town in general, his "great public industry" at an end. He died two years later at the age of fifty-six but with little to show for it—his principal asset was stock held in his father's New Jersey company and his debts several—and was buried in Bridgehampton cemetery. Antoinette Rose Esterbrook lived on for many years; but after her death and some ensuing conflicts over property among the grandchildren, Tremedden was torn down.

III: AFTERMATH

Trouble in connection with the waters had been brewing on another front. Men from Riverhead were caught poaching in Shinnecock Bay in summer 1892. The trustees immediately cited the ban on nonresident fishing and clamming in town waters. The acts of 1818 and 1831, White said, gave the town trustees sole authority over the products of the waters, and since at least 1686—it was actually much later—nonresidents had been prohibited from taking fish.[28] If Riverhead thought this ban was draconian, as they did, he suggested they try fishing in Southold where men were permanently posted to arrest "foreign" fishermen. Better still, he said, why not buy part of Great South Bay which Brookhaven was advertising for sale and fish without trespassing. It was a popular campaign in Southampton if not in Riverhead. "Our waters," he wrote, "are what is building this town up" and produce $75,000 a year in income, income which in part contributed to taxes. Beginning in 1893 the nonresident fishing regulations were drafted by the trustees with particular thoroughness.[29] White's was an old-fashioned view, perhaps out of step with the changing times, but it played well with the baymen. They, after all, had been the political force that had brought him into office in the first place.

But White and the trustees stumbled a little in 1891. Having reaffirmed the town's title to the waters and the lands under them in the Mecox trial, the trustees voted to lease them out on application for the purpose of oyster planting. This was a surprising and politically ill-judged move. These trustees had come into office in 1883 on a Free Bay platform riding a wave of popular support, appropriated town funds to fight what everyone thought was an historic legal battle, won, and claimed back what was widely regarded as a key part of the town's heritage. The backbone of that support had been the baymen. Now, Shinnecock

Bay particularly—their bay—was to be taken away again. The bay now was healthier, a result of continuing efforts by White to open and maintain an inlet for extended periods. Moreover, the Shinnecock Canal was a bare year away from completion raising hopes that circulation in the bay would be permanently stabilized and the fishery revived. In the event, the trustees must have heard the voters for a few months later they rescinded the decision. Nonetheless, it was on the agenda two years later for the town meeting of April 1893 but then tabled until the following year. It was then voted down. White was dead by this time, having passed away the previous December. But before his death, he had begun to experience some slippage at the polls. In the 1893 election he managed only 644 votes to continue on the board, down from almost 900 in 1892. Perhaps the baymen felt betrayed but George White, for his part, may well have thought the town should make money from what it now indisputably owned. Leasing out a few small sections of the bay would hardly be such as to threaten their livelihood. The controversy lingered on long after his death.

Ultimately, the attempted capitalization of Mecox Bay came to nothing, driven back by old forces of tradition and assumed patent right in Southampton as well as by the vociferous protests of baymen whose livelihood on the western bays was apparently threatened. Whether it was actually threatened by the Maxwell purchase of an interest in the bay bottom is open to question, but it was the perception of the threat that counted in the western communities. Similarly, Esterbrook's venture at Mecox if properly managed—perhaps a big if—might have resulted in the long-run stabilization of that bay's resources and benefited the surrounding community by increasing income from local employment. But these possible impacts—no effect on Shinnecock Bay and potential improvements at Mecox—counted for little in the overheated political atmosphere generated by the proprietors' 1882 sales. The frenzy of indignation that followed, as much directed at the proprietors as at the putative buyers, precluded any possibility of a rational assessment of the situation. So inexorably the town trustees, born along by an aroused populace, took the matter to court. There appeared no other option. The proprietors, it seemed at the time, had sold out the town and the townspeople, through their trustees (now anointed as the saviors of the town's rights), wanted back whatever it appeared they had lost. It occurred to no one that a deal might have been struck with the new owners of the bays—John Bowman earlier on had hinted as much—and that both the town and they might have benefited from some form of compromise.

But compromise was impossible from the beginning. Free Bay forces had immediately politicized (and monopolized) the issue and demanded that it be fought out on the terrain of the old patents; that if the patents had not explicitly allocated the lands under the waters of the town to the proprietors, then ipso facto they must be public lands to be managed by the town for the benefit of all of its inhabitants. So as much as the ensuing legal fight reflected an antipathy to outside capital encroaching on the economic life of the town, its main thrust was to challenge the remaining although decreasing power of the proprietors and their trustees. It was the latter's claimed rights under the Dongan patent that were put to the test and in the end rejected in court. It brought to a conclusion a struggle for control of land between town and proprietors that had begun seventy years previously. But it was a struggle that had been foreordained very much earlier in the seventeenth century by the ambiguities contained in the Dongan patent. On the one hand, the patent seemed to put the lands squarely in the town, but on the other it seemed to put them permanently in the hands of the heirs and assigns of the first purchasers. It was exactly this fatal ambiguity that set the stage for an inevitable confrontation, first in 1818 and then in the 1880s.

The patent had never envisaged that a demographic imbalance might emerge between the proprietors of the undivided lands and the commonalty who were eventually to outnumber them many times over and yet remain economically and politically subservient. Nor was there any reason why it should have anticipated it. The Mecox Bay case dramatized that political and economic fact just as the compromise or, perhaps better to say, stand-off in 1818 between proprietors and inhabitants had previously dramatized it. The 1818 legislation, and the subsequent act of 1831 reaffirming both it and the status of the town trustees, had resolved nothing for the town beyond giving its trustees control of the waters and their productions. It had not, and could not address the status of the proprietors, for long an economic elite monopolizing the lands of the town. That question could only surface when the proprietors, running out of lands to dispose of as the nineteenth century unfolded, began to lay claims to lands in which it had no clear or immediately obvious rights: first, rights in the Shinnecock Hills; then the shores of the bays surrounding the Hills (proprietor rights to which were reaffirmed in the 1860s); and lastly to the lands under water. The proprietors' claim to the ocean beach should be added to this list, a claim rejected by the town trustees after the proprietor trustees' sale of beach land at Agawam to Wyllys Betts in 1881. But that claim was upheld in court in 1892 and in subsequent appeals, although with an important proviso in respect to public access, sometime after the proprietor trustees closed their books.[30]

In all these cases the proprietors had gambled and overreached themselves in most, aggravated their relations with the rest of the town, and set the stage for an inevitable and, as it turned out, final confrontation. It is surprising perhaps that it did not come earlier, particularly when they arranged with the legislature for the partition of the Shinnecock Hills in 1859 and then sold them off in 1861 in a prearranged deal with some of their fellow proprietors, but it did not. The town in general and the town trustees in particular were either unready, uninterested, or caught off guard by this sequence of events where the proprietors obtained legislative approval in very questionable circumstances to terminate an ancient lease of the Hills to the Shinnecocks that was not theirs to terminate. We turn to this issue in the next chapter.

So the eclipse of the proprietors did not come until the end of the 1880s brought about by an ill-judged and secretive attempt to sell off the bays. The collapse of the proprietor trustees, through their collective resignation, also spelled the end of the 1818 legislation with its artificial construction of two bodies of trustees with separate jurisdictions over the lands and waters in the same town. It had obviously never been a successful arrangement to begin with. One crucial result of the legislation had been to remove the proprietors even further from public scrutiny than had hitherto been the case, although there had been little if anything in the way of public oversight and accountability before

1818. But at least the act of 1831 had reaffirmed what had been left implicit in 1818, and that was the continuing existence of a corporate body of town trustees to be elected by the inhabitants from among themselves and to be directly accountable to them. This was perhaps the one notable achievement of those years. These trustees may not have always functioned particularly well through the nineteenth century—there were long periods of slack administration—and they were often loathe to confront the proprietors, still the seat of real economic power, but in the 1880s they achieved a remarkable political and legal victory that ultimately brought down the proprietors. The Mecox affair might have remained a small matter, land grabs being hardly uncommon in the late nineteenth century, but the town chose otherwise. The result was a substantial increase in its autonomy and the reinvigoration of its trustees, now a body enjoying greater support and legitimacy since the 1840s, one that, even if only temporarily, had loosened its ties to the elite and was willing to risk the possibilities and dangers of mass support.

Main Street c. 1900 from the Presbyterian Church steeple.
Collection of the Southampton Historical Museum

Looking west across Lake Agawam to new summer cottages on First Neck.
Older home lots are in the foreground.
Collection of the Southampton Historical Museum

Windmill Lane and Job's Lane.
Collection of the Southampton Historical Museum

The Rogers Memorial Library.

Collection of the Southampton Historical Museum

The Parrish Art Museum.

Collection of the Southampton Historical Museum

Flooding from Town Pond at Job's Lane.

Collection of the Southampton Historical Museum

The 1707 Presbyterian Church in its final incarnation in the early 1900s.

Collection of the Southampton Historical Museum

Captain George G. White c. 1885.

Collection of the Southampton Historical Museum

Dr. T. Gaillard Thomas in the 1890s.

Collection of the Southampton Historical Museum

The Hoyt house on the Shinnecock Hills and the village's former windmill.
Collection of the Southampton Historical Museum

The Shinnecock Hills Golf Club, early 1900s.
Collection of the Southampton Historical Museum

Tournament Day at the Meadow Club, 1902.

Collection of the Southampton Historical Museum

Dune Church in "its sandy sanctuarial cradle."

Collection of the Southampton Historical Museum

Shinnecock Canal at an early stage of development.

Collection of the Southampton Historical Museum

Cat Boats on Mecox Bay.

Collection of the Southampton Historical Museum

Southampton Inn and Cottages on Shinnecock Bay in the 1880s.

Collection of the Southampton Historical Museum

Southampton Beach.

Collection of the Southampton Historical Museum

Bathing Pavilion and St. Andrew's Dune Church.

Collection of the Southampton Historical Museum

Southampton Bathing Pavilion c. 1895.

Collection of the Southampton Historical Museum

Docks in front of Dune Church. The Betts colony opposite.

Collection of the Southampton Historical Museum

Lake Agawam's south end and summer cottages on First Neck Lane.

Collection of the Southampton Historical Museum

CHAPTER 6

EARLY HISTORY OF THE SHINNECOCK HILLS

I: MONTAUK AND THE SHINNECOCK HILLS

Mecox Bay was a case of small-scale capitalism up against traditional small-town interests and a contested system of land ownership. The sale of Montauk in the town of Easthampton in 1879 and the Shinnecock Hills in Southampton two years later raised other issues. Montauk initially went to one man, Arthur W. Benson of Brooklyn, but eventually fell to a conglomerate of development interests beginning with Austin Corbin and the Long Island Railroad in the 1890s and concluding with Carl Fisher, the Miami-based resort tycoon, in 1925. After a brief but hectic few years of glamour and excitement, Montauk died as a development zone until the 1960s and even later, its revival becoming partially dependent on the integration of almost half of its land into the New York State parks system. The Shinnecock Hills were acquired by Corbin's agents in 1881—John Bowman and others—and were never again owned by local interests. They were the object of one failed development scheme after another between then and 1925 when the remainder of the unsold Hills went on the auctioneer's block. Like Montauk, the Hills languished between the Depression and the war until as late as the 1960s. After that they became gradually suburbanized, almost the last cheap oasis of middle-class real estate left to local Southampton. What, besides this, is the connection between Montauk and the Shinnecock Hills? Both were the last undivided and undeveloped tracts of land in either town, and both were sold to resort interests by groups of proprietors in each for major gains. Underlying these sales was the considerable fact that they were also the ancestral lands of two of the principal indigenous communities remaining on eastern Long Island, the Montaukett and the Shinnecock Indians.

Both groups had been identified with them for millennia. The Sugar Loaf Hill burial site in Shinnecock, for example, dates back to about 1,000 B.C.[1] They had lived on Montauk and the Hills in distinctive villages, farmed the land, hunted and fished, buried their dead, and in general maintained a common culture and language. They also were interrelated by marriage as they were to other Algonquian groups in the area—notably the Corchaugs on the North Fork, the Unkechaugs to the west, and the Manhanset Indians of Shelter Island—as well as to larger and more powerful tribes across Long Island Sound in

Connecticut. Exogamous marriage practices helped sustain and stabilize informal systems of alliance between these communities over long periods of time though, in the case of the Pequots in Connecticut, the relationship was asymmetric. Traditionally, the eastern Long Island tribes had been in a tributary relation with the Pequots, exchanging tribute—especially wampum—for protection. But the disintegration of the latter after the disastrous Pequot War of 1637 had a significant impact on Long Island.

It was a leading factor in the Montaukett sachem Wyandanch's decision to encourage English settlement. This was primarily to ward off a threat by the Niantic chief, Ninigret, to step into the power vacuum left by the Pequots and impose a new tributary status on the Montaukett, the Shinnecock, and others. The Niantics were a southern branch of the Narragansetts of Rhode Island. Wyandanch was to have continuing problems with the expansionist Narragansetts throughout the 1640s and 1650s. The Montaukett sachem's new guarantor of security was Lyon Gardiner whom he persuaded in 1639 to settle on what was to become Gardiner's Island.[2] The Shinnecock quickly followed Wyandanch's lead a year later and for much the same reasons. In exchange for military security, sixty bushels of corn, and some trade goods, Mandush and other Shinnecock leaders signed away all their lands to the Southampton settlers from Canoe Place on the west to an indeterminate eastern boundary in Wainscott. These lands included the Shinnecock Hills. Some years later in 1645, Governors Theophilus Eaton of New Haven and Edward Hopkins of Connecticut, having obtained the residue of the Stirling patent on Long Island lands from James Farrett in 1641, purchased what is now Easthampton from Wyandanch. This did not, however, include Montauk. The purchase extended eastward only as far as Napeague Harbor, ending at a point short of the Hither Woods and the Indian fort overlooking the harbor. At that time Easthampton covered about 31,000 acres. A small settlement was established there three years later by nine families from Southampton, weary of the lengthy controversy over the allocation of town lands, the relocation of the town plot from Old Town to Main Street, and of disagreements in regard to the laying out of the Great Plain for new immigrants. It is possible that there were religious disagreements as well.[3] But they were primarily looking east to the broad attractive expanse of fertile plain, grazing lands, and deep woodland beyond Sagaponack that stretched as far as Amagansett. Beyond Amagansett lay Montauk. Governor Eaton had paid Wyandanch and other sachems thirty pounds in trade goods for Easthampton, a better deal by far than the Shinnecock had obtained for Southampton. Wyandanch was happy for other reasons besides. The new settlement furthered his goal of developing adequate security arrangements for the Montaukett.

But the Shinnecock Hills and Montauk shared other significant characteristics in common that ultimately were to give them a similar ecology and hence value to both Indians and colonists alike. Both formations were products of the ice sheet when it finally began its retreat some twelve thousand years ago. It left a mass of debris strung out in a ridged moraine along the northern shore of Long Island from Brooklyn to Montauk. Much of this moraine land is quite narrow—a good example are the wooded hills from North Sea to Noyac—but at Shinnecock and Montauk the moraine extends to the south as if the glacier at these points had shoved material below it before beginning its final retreat. The result of this glacial action was the creation of a succession of low hills and valleys before the moraine land fell abruptly into outwash plain. This was the case at Shinnecock where Shinnecock Bay was once a flat expanse of swampland or, more dramatically, at Montauk where the ice sheet left enormous deposits of rock and other material to be pounded and ground up by the ocean. The jagged appearance that these hills would have early presented—a tumbling mass of boulders and mud brought from far to the north—was slowly softened by the action of drifting sand driven by wind until they achieved the gentle contours familiar today. Eventually, they became heavily wooded providing natural cover for game and ideal hunting grounds for the Indian bands that later settled there and found winter shelter in south-facing valleys. The Indians also found security from attack in these valleys and constructed forts in strategic locations. Montauk, in particular, was virtually invulnerable to attack. Surrounded by water on three sides, the only approach to it by land was over the long narrow stretch of Napeague Beach. Prudently, the Montauketts had raised a fort overlooking, it and for good measure had built another in the highlands further to the east. Shinnecock was less protected but its bluffs to the north overlooking Peconic Bay and its wooded valleys provided some necessary defense.

To what extent the Shinnecock Hills were as wooded in the seventeenth century as they once were is not fully clear. The Hills lie three miles to the west of the village of Southampton, and from the description of the earliest division of land in the Great Plain situated between them, the evidence suggests that woodland extended much farther south than it did later. The same was true east of the village in Scuttle Hole, even in the eighteenth century, as descriptions of divisions there similarly indicate. Yet the Hills must have already contained extensive grasslands since by the latter part of the seventeenth century the settlers were routinely pasturing their cattle and sheep on them. However, a century and a half later they appeared virtually empty of any sort of timber, much of it probably cut or burned. Writing in 1845, Nathaniel Prime noted that the Hills were "now perfectly naked, except extensive patches of whortle-berry (or) bay-berry, and other small shrubs, not more than two or three feet high; with here and there an aged thorn-bush, which has acquired the form and stature of a tree."[4] How much of the loss of woodland was due to natural processes and how much to felling trees for fencing and firewood cannot be known, although Prime notwithstanding, there was enough timber for both in Shinnecock Neck and Sebonac throughout the nineteenth century. But 150 years of fencing the Hills for pasturage and the fuel needs of the settlers and of those of the Shinnecock residing there must have contributed to denuding them. In 1861, for example, the new Southampton proprietors of the Hills purchased 2,000 chestnut rails, 150 chestnut posts, and 1,400 locust posts, all for fencing.

Much of Montauk, in comparison, was covered in dense woods in the seventeenth century. Cornelius van Tienhoven, secretary to the Dutch West India Company in New Amsterdam, reported in 1650 that it "is entirely covered with trees, without any flats."[5] This must, however, have been an exaggeration since the inhabitants of Easthampton were already running their livestock on Montauk in large numbers by 1655. Easthampton was fast becoming a cattle town at that time, and the main focus of its development interests between 1660 and 1687 was the acquisition of all of Montauk for its vast tracts of rich pastureland. Still, despite the long-term effects of deforestation through the mid-1800s, Montauk still contained much woodland and abounded in game of every description. Writing about 1808, Timothy Dwight noted that Montauk was "nowhere in the proper sense forested, but ornamented in several places by groves and scattered trees."[6] After 1840, it gained a reputation as a sportsman's paradise and hunters descended on it from all over. Ironically, it was precisely this that ultimately led to the loss of Montauk to resort interests at the end of the century. At the insistence of its new owners, the last cattle, sheep, and horses were driven off Montauk in 1895; effectively putting an end to more than two hundred years of annual cattle drives. The same fate had met the sheep and their Southampton owners on the Hills a few years before.

The Shinnecock Hills and Montauk then shared much in common. They were both rolling upland, shaped by the same glacial forces, and covered with similar vegetation from grassland to low shrubs and woods. And historically each was colonized three times. First by the Indians millennia ago who found in them secure and sheltered habitation and all their possible needs for subsistence, whether in the ponds, bays, and woodland where fish and wildlife were in abundance or in the fields they cultivated in open areas. But their claim to the lands was much diminished and later dissolved by the coming of the English settlers in the 1640s. In a succession of expropriatory deeds and legislative acts, the settlers slowly supplanted their indigenous neighbors confining them to ever narrower tracts of land. Montauk and the Hills were simply too valuable as pasturage to leave them in the hands of their original owners. Coexistence was possible but on English and later American legal terms only. Then finally, unable to resist the inviting prospect of a major sale, the Easthampton and Southampton proprietors sold out their respective shares in the lands they had acquired by one means or another from the Indians for in both cases a quite handsome sum. It was not perhaps such a large amount when divided among numerous individual shareholders but nor was it inconsiderable. Montauk, at almost twelve thousand acres and three times the size of the Hills, fetched $151,000 at auction in 1879, whereas the Hills were sold privately and not a little secretively for nearly $50,000 in 1881. There then began a third wave of colonization, local ownership although not local jurisdiction having been decisively though lucratively given up to distinctly un-local interests without much of a hue and cry. In Southampton, only George White complained. These outside interests, as is seen here, became intricately intertwined with one another even if they were not so at the outset.

The question remains: What was so attractive about the Hills and Montauk to outside investors? They were remote, desolate, and windswept places, removed even from local civilization given the limited transportation of the time. The middle of Montauk was fully twenty miles from Easthampton, a distance to be traversed over a sandy track and across the mosquito-infested wastes of Napeague. The Shinnecock Hills, as the highest point on the south shore of Long Island before Montauk, were four miles in extent and divided the two parts of Southampton from one another: the small settlements to the west of Canoe Place, which had only begun to develop as distinct communities after the beginning of the nineteenth century, and Southampton village itself beginning a little east of the Hills. Communication between the two before the arrival of the railroad in 1870 was slow and arduous. A poor winding road guaranteed an hour's journey at best to Canoe Place, and in the depth of winter few would have ventured it. Writing in 1873, Richard Bayles thought that these "huge piles of sand . . . formed an almost impassible barrier, which divided the intercourse of civilization upon one side from that upon the other." Much earlier, Timothy Dwight had described them as "a succession of disagreeable sand hills [which] exhibit a desolate and melancholy aspect."[7] Like Dwight before him, Bayles painted a dark and brooding picture of the Hills, bestowing a romantic gloom on them fairly typical of travel writers of the time, which contrasted sharply with the sunny advertisements for "charming villas" that were to come a decade later. Even the railroad, that emblem of modernity and progress, was not to be exempt from this romantic vision. The Hills, he wrote, are "now pierced by the iron band over which the locomotive trundles . . . shrieking and panting like a frightened living thing, straining every nerve in its frantic haste to evade the ghosts of dusky savages whose soil it has desecrated and whose peaceful slumber its unearthly yells have disturbed."[8] But Bayles spoke truer than perhaps he knew. The Shinnecock had never been reimbursed by the Long Island Railroad in its purchase of a right-of-way through the Hills in 1869 and never would be. One cannot leave Richard Bayles without his recital of a legend of the Shinnecock Hills that, although obviously well known in the nineteenth century, has long been lost. To say the least, it has a chilling air about it—almost Transylvanian—and would not have made good advertising copy.

> Here we are told that the dare-devil traveler who challenged all the grim spirits of the infernal regions to deter him from crossing these hills on a dark and stormy night, many years ago, was soon after found lying dead by the roadside, without a mark of violence upon him except that his tongue was drawn out "by the roots" and hung on a neighboring bush. As his money was found untouched in his pockets, it was evident the mysterious deed had not been perpetrated for plunder, and as the peculiar nature of the wound seemed to forbid the supposition that human hands were responsible for the deed, its commission was ascribed directly to the fiends of darkness whose vengeance the hapless traveler had defied.[9]

Bayles went on to Montauk where, like Prime before him, he found less the terrifying aspect of barren hills he had encountered at Shinnecock than luxuriant grasslands fed by innumerable streams, springs, and ponds. Both remarked on the general absence of timber in the area, but what struck them particularly was the abundance of fresh water. To Prime, Montauk was "one of the last spots on the earth where we should look for extensive swamps, copious springs, and large ponds of fresh water."[10] But here he found them "in the greatest profusion." He described them in some detail, noting that Great Pond (now Lake Montauk and not then opened to the sea) was the largest body of fresh water on Long Island covering some six hundred acres. Bayles was similarly impressed but reserved his best writing for a romantic reflection on the wild beauty of the place and its "unfathomed past." Other writers before Bayles, contemporaries of Prime, had been equally struck. When two early tourists visited Montauk in 1840, they recorded that there was "a sublimity and wildness, as well as solitariness here, which leave a powerful impression on the heart."[11] For his part, Bayles had this to say:

> Wrapt in a halo of solitude, Montauk sleeps peacefully amid its wild surroundings and dreams of its un-written tragedies, its un-told legends, its forgotten history of unknown ages past. A little more than two hundred years ago it was part and parcel of the common wilderness, and in common with the whole land was the home of the American savage. . . . But, like a magnificent dissolving view, as the traces of savage life disappeared from the scene, the outlines of civilized life were developed and intensified. Wigwams gave place to cottages, farm-houses, and mansions . . . and as if by magic the few and simple accessories of the native dispensation vanished before the hand of the white man.[12]

They did indeed, although Montauk was never settled by its white proprietors in the seventeenth and eighteenth centuries. They left the Montaukett on their land, if in ever more circumscribed portions of it, satisfied for the most part to cut timber and pasture their cattle there. When Bayles wrote these words, not a half dozen years before Arthur Benson purchased Montauk from its Easthampton proprietors, there were little more than a handful of Indians left on the peninsula. Bayles thought there were only eight adults and an equal number of children. To him this was "the remnant of the tribe." In all likelihood he was unaware that the large majority had migrated to other parts throughout the nineteenth century, unable any longer to find a living without leaving it. This may well have added to the attraction of Montauk for Benson. He might reasonably have thought that if there was to be an Indian problem, he could surely handle any difficulties that a few impoverished families might throw in his way. Unlike Bayles, this hard-headed business man from Brooklyn was not romantically inclined beyond the dream of a proprietorship of extraordinary proportions and a lifetime of fishing (he was in fact to die with rod and line in his hand). Bayles looked nostalgically to the past and a pre-settler past at that. Despite an incipient and sentimental racism characteristic of the period in general, he betrayed a degree of ambivalence toward the advances of civilization and exalted what he took to be the primitive. In a curious passage in the last pages of his book he seemed to reject the long process of settlement since the seventeenth century in favor of a precolonial innocence:

> The history of this romantic spot since it passed under the control of the white settlers is but little more than a monotonous blank. Across this void we naturally look with curious eye to inquire into the history of that period of aboriginal occupancy which immediately preceded it.[13]

It is an odd remark to make in light of the fact that he had previously outlined the circumstances under which Montauk had been purchased from the Indians and the form of proprietary organization that the settlers had adopted and that had persisted with little change for two centuries. It had hardly been a "monotonous blank." But unknown to Bayles in 1873, all was to change, and in a very short time at that. The institutional fabric of collective ownership, which had supplanted and ultimately driven off the Indians, was extinguished and new forms of proprietorship installed in its place.

In the last analysis, what attracted outside investors to the Shinnecock Hills and Montauk was their unspoiled beauty; they had never been extensively cultivated or divided. Apart from the inevitable loss of woodland, they were hardly changed since the early days of settlement in the seventeenth century. And no one could help but notice that they were refreshingly free of people. Nobody lived there except a few Indian families on Montauk and a small reservation community numbering about 170 that had been effectively removed from the Hills proper in 1859 and confined to Shinnecock Neck. And both were owned by bodies of proprietors who, as tenants in common, could dispose of their lands as they pleased free of interference from towns and town trustees or even the state. As undivided lands held in common there were no private owners to deal with or buy out. Instead, prospective purchasers had the advantage in both cases of negotiating directly with trustees of a land corporation composed of its leading proprietors. In neither case were they particularly difficult to persuade. By the late 1870s, both trustee groups, with the willing support of their stockholders, were ready to sell if they could get a good price. To Austin Corbin and his railroad associates the two areas were ideal for resort development in both hotels and summer homes. He had additional plans for a deep-water port and a transatlantic steamship service based at Montauk, but these plans never materialized. In fact, Corbin encountered serious difficulties in even gaining a foothold on Montauk well into the 1890s. He was successful in gaining control of the Shinnecock Hills in 1881, but development there proceeded rather slowly over the course of the decade. On Montauk, Arthur Benson had beaten him to it and had become its sole proprietor the year before Corbin took over the LIRR in late 1880 and began considering the possibilities presented by the east end of Long Island. Benson initially was not interested in development except in an entirely modest way. He wanted a small community of like-minded friends, a little cottage colony and a club house overlooking the ocean, from where they could fish and shoot wildfowl to their heart's content. He also planned to build and stock a farm—primarily a sheep farm—for his son, Frank Sherman Benson, and actually took steps in that direction. But Benson or not, Corbin wanted at least some part of Montauk for his own purposes and worked on him throughout the 1880s to let him in. He eventually succeeded but not in any real substantial sense until after Benson's death in 1890. His son proved much more amenable to a deal and sold out a good portion of the family inheritance—about half of Montauk—at a very handsome profit.

II: THE 1703 LEASE OF THE HILLS

Any consideration of the later disposition of the Shinnecock Hills must begin with the 1703 Indian deeds briefly alluded to in the first chapter and the almost simultaneous lease agreement the Southampton settlers entered into with the Shinnecock. This agreement provided for a 999-year lease to the Indians of all the 4,200 acres of the Hills and Sebonac and Shinnecock Necks for a nominal quitrent of one ear of corn a year.[14] It was executed reluctantly by the settlers. In a series of negotiations lasting almost a week in August the Shinnecock were induced to sign no fewer than five documents, almost as many as they had signed in the previous sixty years.[15] The key document was a deed granting all the Shinnecock land to the Trustees of the Commonalty of the Town of Southampton from Seatuck on the west (the town line with Brookhaven) to the Easthampton town line. For this the Indians received a sum of twenty pounds. On the same day, they endorsed the 1640 deed to the Town Purchase and the 1666 deed to the Quogue lands west of Canoe Place. The circumstances of the Quogue purchase had been settled by Governor Richard Nicolls at the time, under the terms of the Duke's Laws relating to land purchases from the Indians, and was also then confirmed by the Shinnecock. A second confirmation was given by the Indians in 1686 a few weeks before Governor Thomas Dongan signed the town's second patent. Apparently this had been requested by the town in order to buttress its legal claim to the lands should any question arise in New York. And now in 1703 a third confirmation was demanded, this time in the shape of an entirely new deed.

What led to this sudden and unanticipated flurry of negotiations, through which Southampton intended to establish once and for all its title to the Indian lands it claimed to have purchased, had its origin in the governor's office. The royal governor at that time was Edward Hyde, Lord Cornbury, a cousin to Queen Anne and a well-known Tory and Anglican. In taking office in 1702 as the replacement for Lord Bellomont who had died suddenly, Cornbury resumed the practice of Bellomont's predecessor, Benjamin Fletcher, in handing out land and privileges to supporters and favorites. Before him, Thomas Dongan had bestowed similar favors on selected members of New York's upper class, Dutch and otherwise. Several of the large tracts he distributed among wealthy individuals in the 1680s, as well as to himself, were erected into manors as, for example, Lloyd's Neck in Huntington. In the early 1690s, Fletcher also had given his blessing to the business of piracy that had developed in the context of the Anglo-French war—King William's War—to the considerable profit of his many merchant friends in New York and, no doubt, to himself as well. He had also granted enormous tracts of crown land to particular favorites. Stephanus Van Cortlandt, for instance, had received 86,000 acres in Cortlandt Manor in Westchester and Sagtikos Manor on the south shore of Long Island, while Frederick Philipse assumed his lordship of 92,000 acres in Westchester, Philipsburgh Manor. Not all were so lucky to receive quasi-feudal lordships as were both Van Cortlandt and Philipse, but other successful New York merchants fell into hundreds of thousands of acres scattered around the province. In his four years in office, Lord Bellomont, a redoubtable member of the Whig ascendancy under William of Orange, made considerable efforts to clean up the corruption, land-grabbing, and piracy that had become routinized during the Fletcher regime but death and an unfortunate involvement with Captain Kidd interrupted him.[16]

With the arrival of Cornbury, however, life in New York returned more or less to normal. Cornbury was not one of those governors who nineteenth-century American historians were fond of describing as "men of broken fortunes, dissolute and ignorant, too vile to be employed near home"—after all, he was the Queen's cousin—but he was as unprincipled as any man to fill the office in all matters save religion.[17] He also was known for his quite bizarre personal behavior. One eccentricity was a developed taste for cross-dressing and from time to time, so it was claimed, addressed the assembly decked out in female finery. He left unpaid bills all over town and his wife, Lady Cornbury, was said to shake down the most fashionable wives of the elite for their jewels and clothes. An exasperated New York finally saw the back of him in 1708, when the Whigs won a majority in Parliament and the new government recalled him, although not before a group of irate merchants had him thrown into debtor's prison for all those uncollected bills.

But at the beginning of his term in office, Cornbury found little difficulty in satisfying the needs and interests of those leading citizens who had done so well under Fletcher. In doing so he gained their support, however tenuous and brief it turned out to be. Their interest was in grants of land and his in maximizing the amount of land available to him for allocation to favored supporters. In 1702, having been in office only a few months, he or his advisors came up with a scheme to identify and grant Indian lands in the province to which towns had no obvious and unambiguous title. This entailed both a search of all Indian deeds describing lands sold to settlers and their conditions of sale and an examination of town patents for any discrepancies, omissions, or irregularities that might be inconsistent with the deeds themselves.

This practice was not new. In 1685, when Governor Dongan called in all the existing municipal charters for review and confirmation, largely to increase royal revenues from quitrents, he threatened reluctant towns with the possibility of locating unpurchased Indian lands within their charter limits and disposing of them as he saw fit. Alarmed, Easthampton and Southampton quickly capitulated and sent in their Andros patents of 1676. This must explain the sudden dispatch of Major John Howell from Southampton to New York in November 1686 a few weeks before Dongan signed the new patent. He was to consult "about the present affaire of making good our title to our land called in to question at Shinecock."[18] Title to the Indian lands would seem to have been legally established by the Andros patent, which confirmed Governor Nicholls's award of lands to the town, but the threat of potential seizure by Dongan may have impelled Southampton to seek further confirmation prior to the issue of a new charter. Related to this was an unusual indenture agreement drawn up between the town and the Shinnecock a few months later. It was a lease, guaranteeing the Shinnecock occupancy and planting rights in Shinnecock and Sebonac in perpetuity, and was signed in April 1687 four months after Governor Dongan's patent had been received. It seems to have been an insurance policy. It would show the colonial authority as well that Southampton's Indians were securely settled in one place and not running all over the countryside. This had been an issue which preoccupied all colonial governors since 1665. If all Indian lands were to be systematically alienated, where were they to live? The lease was Southampton's answer to this. At the same time it consolidated or further validated their legal title to the Indian lands. However, the arrangement lasted only sixteen years. But its existence had serious implications for the negotiations that were to take place between the town and the Shinnecock in 1703.

In September 1702, Governor Cornbury gave two New York merchants license to purchase any vacant or unappropriated land in Suffolk County. The two were Rip Van Dam and Jonathan Bridges. Not much is known about Bridges but both were well connected. Van Dam had influence in trading circles in London and the West Indies and later pursued a political career. He became president of the city council in the late 1720s and was briefly acting governor in the months following Governor John Montgomerie's death in 1731. Bridges and Van Dam took themselves to eastern Long Island within a week or so of Cornbury's carte blanche offer. It appears that they went immediately to Easthampton. Rumors must have reached them in New York that the Montaukett Indians had become thoroughly dissatisfied with the failure of the Easthampton trustees to honor the terms of the third and last deed to the lands on Montauk. Three indentures had been agreed to between 1660–1661 and 1687 in which the Montaukett gave up virtually all their rights to their own lands. They retained residence and some cultivation rights, rights to hunting, fishing, and limited access to timber; but after 1687, Easthampton men had gained almost complete control of the peninsula. The Indians accepted a purchase price of one hundred pounds sterling and had elected to be paid at the rate of two pounds a year. Evidently there had been arrears in these payments for in early 1702 the Montaukett complained, probably not for the first time, that they had not been paid the previous year. There were other sources of tension. There were angry complaints, for example, that sheep grazing was destructive of their fields. The trustees agreed to pay something in the way of damages but reported in their own records that they found the Montaukett generally "obstinate and averse to agreement."[19] It was obviously an unhappy situation filled with distrust and tension on all sides. On hearing of it, Van Dam and Bridges stepped in with alacrity.

The two of them persuaded the Indians to set aside the 1687 deed giving Easthampton the land east of Fort Pond to Montauk Point and sign a new one at what must have appeared to them as the attractive price of two hundred pounds. Later accounts suggest that the negotiations were well lubricated. "Trickery and strong waters" were said to have been used, but by far the larger factor must have been the Montaukett's own general dissatisfaction. Van Dam and Bridges had moved fast and caught Easthampton off balance. The deed was signed on October 14, barely a month after Cornbury had approved what was after all really a fishing expedition. It took years to undo and a good deal of Easthampton's money. The circumstances under which the Montaukett were essentially brought to heel, and the conditions that were imposed on them for their seeming folly, are discussed elsewhere, but new and more rigorous deeds were drawn up in March 1703 covering the land in question. Thirty-two Indians were persuaded to sign them.

As for Van Dam and Bridges, they were eventually bought off by Easthampton, although the matter was not fully settled and their claim extinguished until 1712. The affair cost the town upward of three hundred pounds and led to a further deterioration in relations between the two communities. But the 1703 deeds were intended to confirm the town's rights to acquire all lands by lawful purchase from the Indians within the bounds of the town. These bounds had been determined in Governor Dongan's patent of 1686, and earlier by Richard Nicolls in 1666. Both patents specifically included the right to purchase

Montauk. It was also an exclusive right and gave Easthampton the means to keep out interlopers and fight Van Dam successfully in the courts. Lord Cornbury, and Van Dam as well, had completely ignored these patent rights. Yet the latter's claim to posterity is not inconsiderable. He was among the very first in a long line of real estate speculators who turned their attention to the opportunities to be found in land in the eastern section of the island. Only Richard Smith in Huntington and the chimerical John Scott in Brookhaven and Southampton preceded and perhaps overshadowed him. Their land deals in the seventeenth century were possessed of a swagger and panache that was breathtaking.[20]

When news of Van Dam's bargain with the Montaukett reached Southampton, the trustees realized immediately that they might have a similar problem on their hands and potentially a more serious one at that. It did not concern the Shinnecock Hills and the Quogue lands to the west, the title to which, as far as anyone was concerned, had been confirmed in the Dongan charter of 1686. What was at issue was the eastern boundary of the town with Easthampton. Both the Farrett grant from the Earl of Stirling in 1640 and the Indian deed later that year had been vague in regard to the eastern limit of Southampton. James Farrett had merely referred to it as lying over against Hog Neck and "Mr. ffaret's Island" or Shelter Island, while the Shinnecock deed spoke only of "all the old ground formerly planted lying eastward." At the time, none of this mattered much and the settlers slowly extended their fields and activities east into the areas of Sagaponack and Wainscott in the next decade or so. Governor Eaton of New Haven and his Connecticut associates, who had purchased the residue of the Stirling grant from Farrett in 1641 covering the lands east of Wainscott, presented no objection and very likely knew nothing of this eastward drift anyway. Nor did the Shinnecock, and more especially the Montaukett, voice any complaint. Only after Easthampton purchased its lands from Eaton in 1648 did the question of Southampton's easternmost boundary arise. It remained controversial between the two towns for almost half a century.[21]

At a Southampton town meeting in 1657, two representatives of the Shinnecock sachem, Mandush, were called on to testify as to the eastern limit but were able to say only that "it went to george cake (Georgica) or wainscot at the least, or there abouts," an explanation that surely satisfied noone.[22] Governor Nicolls, in settling the dispute over the purchase of the Quogue lands in 1666 and awarding Topping's purchase to the town, said nothing of the boundary with Easthampton, but a decade later the Andros patent for Southampton explicitly affirmed it as lying at Wainscott "where the bounds are settled betwixt their Neighbours of the Towne of East Hampton, and them." Governor Dongan's patent ten years later in 1686 simply repeated Andros' wording, and since his patent for Easthampton in the same year contained much the same language, it might be inferred that the issue was now settled. However this was not the case. Despite the patents, the boundary was still vague. Over the following decade there were continuing disagreements over who was settling where in the Wainscott plain. This particularly affected those inhabitants who preferred to look to the east for their lands in the seventeenth century, these being the most accessible and open to cultivation, than to those lands far to the west of Canoe Place in Quogue.

Finally in 1695, the differences between the two towns were resolved. Thomas Chatfield of Easthampton wrote to a committee of Southampton men that "whereas you pretended to us that ye Lyne between your and our Towneshipps Lyes Imperffect and have desired that our Towne by a committee would Give you a meeting ffor ye settleing of said Line" and suggested that the two committees meet and mark out a town line agreeable to both sides.²³ This they did and there the matter might have rested had it not been for the activities of Van Dam several years later. Neither town had thought to inform the governor's office in New York of this settlement, thereby still leaving it open to question. It could be construed as an unauthorized interpretation of the patents and of the Indian deeds to both towns, possibly even as an illegal alteration of the conveyances. In either case, it had been done without any consultation with the Shinnecock and Montaukett as interested parties and might then also be seen as in violation of the Duke's Laws of 1664 governing relations with the Indians. These had promised "speedy redress gratis" in any court for "(a)ll Injuryes done to the Indians of what nature whatsoever." This alone might not have alarmed the settlers unduly but, town line or no town line, it remained the case that all the pre-existing documents described the lands between the towns in far too nebulous a fashion. Nebulous enough to encourage any intelligent businessman like Van Dam, armed with a real estate license from the governor, to lay a claim to them.

During the ensuing year of 1703 nothing as calamitous as this happened. Perhaps Van Dam had realized in March when the Montaukett were persuaded by Easthampton to repudiate their agreement with him that, however empty and undeveloped those lands might have seemed, they were not just there for the taking. Evidently he wasted no time in Wainscott and there is no record of any further trips to the eastern part of the island. Nonetheless, Southampton took no chances and in August went to work on the Shinnecock. To give full legal weight to the document they wanted, the architects of a new Indian deed—Howells, Halseys, Fordhams, Piersons, Scotts, Toppings, all leading men of the community at the time and for years to come—described it as granting all the Shinnecock land to the trustees of the commonalty. And these men were all trustees. Following the custom of the time, which was to affix as many Indian signatures as possible to any agreement, they had sixteen of the Shinnecock sign it. Additionally, three of their sachems agreed to put their marks to an endorsement of the 1640 and 1666 deeds. Legality was everything and it was clear that Southampton wanted nothing less than a complete acknowledgment that title to all Shinnecock lands lay fully with Southampton. The deed settled the eastern bound of the town by explicitly referring to the Easthampton town line. None of this was accomplished without a great deal of cajoling, bribing, and a liberal application of alcohol. The Indians quitclaimed their land from Seatuck to Wainscott plain, south by the ocean and north by Peconic River and the bay, for twenty pounds sterling, but it was apparent that there was deep unease about it and probably considerable opposition.

They had now more than half a century of experience of land transactions with the town and realized that this deed, which they had not understood of earlier ones, gave the whites outright possession. Land was property, simply a commodity to be bought and sold. The deed was perfectly explicit. The Indians could not "by any way or meanes hereafter Claime Chaleng or Demand any Estate Right title or intrist In or to ye premises or any part or parcel thereof . . . and every of them shall be utterly Bared forever (from doing so) by these presents." There was not even a clause covering usufruct and residence rights, although these would have been assumed from previous deeds and the 1687 lease and was contained in the subsequent lease signed concurrently. But the negotiations took close to a week and almost broke down. They were adjourned over a weekend during which the Shinnecock delegation, home in their villages, encountered strenuous objections to what was about to be transacted. The sachems involved in the negotiations had been individually bribed, offered twenty pounds to distribute among their people, and heavily plied with rum (several gallons worth).

On the Monday, they apparently came back with a counter proposal. They would sign the deed confirming the alienation of their lands but in exchange for a deed of some description giving them the Shinnecock Hills and Sebonac where almost all of them lived. Thus was born the thousand-year lease. The idea for a lease almost certainly originated with the town trustees. The precedent for it had already been established in 1687 when a lease in perpetuity had been signed. Why the trustees had not raised this matter the previous week is unclear. Did they assume that the old lease was still in force and that the rights of the Shinnecock would continue to be protected by it? Perhaps, but that would not have been clear to the Shinnecock. The terms of the deed presented to them must have appeared to them as so severe, denying any and all claims to their land, that it constituted an abrogation of the 1687 agreement. So they came back demanding some guarantee of occupancy and other rights that the 1687 lease had provided. It is questionable whether the Shinnecock would distinguish at that time between a deed and a lease. Much later in the nineteenth century many of them (for specific and obvious reasons) refused to do so. But that the lease was for one thousand years must in 1703 have convinced them that it was essentially a deed in perpetuity. The quitrent of an ear of corn would have been understood as a courtesy, a mere acknowledgment of the agreement, and not as a leasehold rent. It also replaced the astonishingly high quitrent of forty shillings a year (now quietly dropped) in the 1687 agreement. But for the trustees, the Shinnecock demand for a new agreement gave them an opportunity to rewrite 1687 in far more restrictive terms. It was as much an instrument of control as a guarantee of rights, few as these were.[24]

It is also important to realize that the lease was the first step toward the eventual adoption of a reservation policy, toward confining an Indian community to a specific territory where it could be managed and generally disregarded. Southampton's trustees may not have understood it at the time, but the Shinnecock had done them a favor by demanding a guarantee. The trustees' only possible misgiving was that their hand had been forced as the Hills were extremely valuable to them, but the terms of the new lease largely took care of that. Yet this was not the first time that consideration had been given to reserving land on which to settle the Indians. In 1664, shortly before English forces took New Amsterdam and Southampton was severed from Connecticut, a committee of the Connecticut general assembly met in Southampton with representatives of the three eastern towns under its jurisdiction. Among the matters discussed were the difficult relations between Southampton and the Shinnecock. On petition from several inhabitants, the committee directed that "a better settlement of their Indians . . . (on) a suitable parcel of land" be found and fenced for "their security." It was to be done by April 1, 1665.[25] Nothing came of this, possibly because Southampton was preoccupied with a change of jurisdiction it did not want, but the seeds of a later reservation policy were certainly there. Similarly, the colonial government after 1665 was itself increasingly preoccupied with the settlement of the Indians. The 1703 lease was fully in accordance with that long-term concern.

The lease was drawn up and executed in two copies on the same day as the indenture to all the Shinnecock land. Both deeds were in the name of the trustees of the commonalty of the town, which—in the case of the lease—while giving it maximum legality, was to raise serious concerns a century and a half later when it was abrogated. The lease agreement was signed on behalf of the Shinnecock by three sachems, Pomguamo, Chice, and Manamam, each of whom, it has to be said, had been well rewarded for their part in gaining acceptance of the confirmation deed to the Indian land. The bounds of the Hills the Shinnecock were henceforth to inhabit were spelled out clearly as beginning at Canoe Place on the west as far as a line to the east beginning at a place "called the weare house by the North bay" (Barker's Island) and extending south to Heady Creek. This line was known almost to the end of the nineteenth century as the Indian Line. It divided North Sea from Sebonac and the Hills. The northern and southern boundaries were the bays. Apart from the nominal rent of "one ear of Indian corn" every year, the terms of the lease were not generous. It gave the privileges and advantages of "plowing and planting and timber for fireing & fencing and all other conveniencies and benefits" but specifically excepted "meadows, marshes, grass, herbage, feeding and pasturage, timber, stone and convenient highways." The meadows and marshes referred to were the Shinnecock Meadows, a small strip of salt marsh in Shinnecock Neck not occupied by the Indians that had been divided in 1648, and the Sebonac sedges on Cold Spring Bay that had been lotted out in 1653. They were of greater value to the town than to the Indians, who then had few, if any, cattle; but the lease excluded a lot that the Indians might reasonably be thought to have benefited from. The three sachems did succeed in attaching a rider to the lease to the effect that the Shinnecocks would be free to cut "flaggy bulrushes and . . . grass as they usually make their matts and houses of" and to dig groundnuts, but this was a small concession only that they were able to extract from the trustees.

The last clause proved to be the most contentious of all and was to become a source of growing friction between the two communities in the second half of the eighteenth century. It provided that the Indians were not to keep any of the land "within fence or inclosed from the last of October to the first of April," that is, at any time outside the growing season when the settlers let their livestock to pasture in all parts of the Hills including in and around Indian settlements. In fact, the Hills had been fenced since the early 1650s and there were several disputes in subsequent years. In 1673, several sachems were summoned before the court "for the settling (of) some matters of Difference" and told firmly that they must maintain their half of the fence at Shinnecock Neck. They were also to provide a gin keeper and construct a water fence at the bay.[26] In 1679, land was to be fenced at Sebonac "provided it intrench not upon the interest of the Indian" who were encamped in a small settlement at Millstone Brook.[27] There were, however, instances of cooperation or attempts at cooperation. Earlier, in 1663, the court ordered that a three-rail fence be erected "between the Indians and us." Any cattle, sheep, goats, or hogs "found within said fence after the 8th of this present month (May)" were to be impounded.[28] Still, later town records are replete with references to damaged crops, failures to fence, and injuries to cattle. It was this problem, or succession and accumulation of problems, which had led the proprietors of the undivided lands (rather than the trustees of the town) to approach the Shinnecock in the first decades of the nineteenth century with a view to partitioning the Hills with the Indians on one side and the proprietors on the other. By the 1780s, the Hills had become the only land left in the town that was not divided. The proprietors eyed it while the Indians were tenants on it, but they were tenants of the town rather than the proprietors, a fact that the proprietors had either forgotten or chose to ignore.

There were a few puzzling questions associated with the signing of the deed and the lease that have never been satisfactorily cleared up. Matters appeared to have been settled with the agreement to both documents to the satisfaction of both parties when, a few days later, the trustees procured twenty-one new signatures to a confirmation of the deed. Now thirty-seven Shinnecocks had signed. Despite having disbursed a considerable amount of money to be distributed among the members of the tribe, the trustees must have thought that it was better to err on the side of safety in case the deed was ever challenged in the English courts. Effectively, they collected the signatures of well over half of the Shinnecock males, the Shinnecock then numbering about 150 men, women, and children. According to Strong, however, only half of those who had signed both documents were listed in the 1698 census of Southampton.[29] It is difficult to know what to make of this but, as Strong points out, the census may not have been complete. There were numerous "scattered heathens," or newcomers unaccounted for, who did not make it into the census.[30] Or there was fraud.

There were other difficulties. Two copies of the one thousand-year lease were signed, one for the Shinnecock and one for the trustees, but it was not until ninety years later that the Shinnecock received their copy. In 1791, the town trustees had petitioned the New York State legislature to establish a regular system of elected leadership among the Shinnecock to replace the traditional forms of sachem authority. The objective was to provide a stable mechanism for handling the increasing number of disputes between townspeople and Indians over fencing, pasturing livestock, and even ploughing and cultivation on the Hills by Southampton farmers.[31] The subsequent legislation, an act passed in February 1792 "for the benefit of the Shinecock Tribe of Indians," provided for the annual election of three trustees who were authorized to lease out land to farmers at their discretion and appropriate plots or parcels for the use of their own tribal members.[32] It was clearly an effort to control a growing practice in the late eighteenth century where individual Shinnecocks had become accustomed to making private deals with farmers for the lease of Hills land for cultivation. The last part of the act precisely covered this practice. Although the legislation called for the supervision of the trustee elections by the town clerk and three justices, which latter were required to approve the results, this rationalization of tribal authority—in effect making it consistent with the forms of municipal organization—gave the Shinnecock better control over their own affairs and in their dealings with the town. At any rate they accepted it without protest, although it must have appeared to many of them at the time that here was yet another instance of the imposition of indirect rule.

The following year, 1793, the Shinnecock trustees received their copy of the lease from the clerk to the town trustees, Caleb Cooper. Why had it taken so long? The best guess is that in the first years of the eighteenth century the town trustees deemed it prudent not to hand over the lease fearing some possible challenge, or fearing that what was to them the unreliable leadership of the Shinnecock might deny it and with it the all-important deed to their Southampton lands. A simpler explanation is that the trustees assumed that none of the Shinnecock would be able to read it. In later years it may well have been forgotten, one paper among many left to languish in the town's offices. But once the trusteeship act was in force someone, probably Caleb Cooper, evidently reached the conclusion that if there were now Shinnecock trustees, approved by the legislature, they should certainly be given their copy of the lease. The establishment of the trusteeship system—its formalization by the state—may also have reflected emerging trends in federal regulation of Indian affairs in the late 1780s.

In 1789, President Washington had recommended and the Senate had approved a policy of negotiating treaties with Indians in the same way as was done with foreign powers. This was to insure uniformity in all treaties. The next year, the Trade and Intercourse Act was passed establishing federal authority over Indian relations with whites. The law regulated all trade with Indians, required that all traders be licensed, and that they follow prescribed rules of conduct. It also prohibited states and potential others from acquiring Indian land without congressional approval. There seems to be no connection between this legislation and the petition for a trusteeship system, but evidently the town trustees thought it a wise course of action to approach the state legislature for help in introducing some order into the rather ad hoc nature of their arrangements with the Shinnecock. The town's ability to control its own citizens in striking private bargains with individual Shinnecocks for the sublease of Hills land had clearly been weakened. Besides this, there is some reason for thinking that by the 1780s the town trustees—all of whom were still proprietors—had come to regard the whole of Shinnecock as simply too important a resource to be left to a set of customary arrangements governing the annual pasturing of livestock, fencing, and the use of fields and woodlands. That had been the situation, with growing difficulty, for much of the century and it appeared to many townspeople to be time for a change. This quickened interest in the Hills also coincided with the division of the last of the town's common lands at the beginning of the 1780s. The Hills were the sole tract of undivided commons remaining.

There was one further complication, or at least potential complication, resulting from the signing of the 1703 deed and its various endorsements. In every way the town trustees had sought to clothe the agreement with all the legality they could muster. They had garnered a large number of signatures, elicited (and paid for) confirmations of the 1640 and 1666 deeds, clearly established the eastern boundary of the town at Wainscott and, grudgingly or not, settled the Shinnecock on the Hills under the terms of a lease. All this, except the last, had been accomplished with the clear purpose of circumventing any designs Rip Van Dam or potentially others may have had on town land. However, what was entirely new to this deed was the precise determination of the town line with Easthampton. It had only recently been agreed to by the two towns in 1695 and was obviously not to be found in previous deeds or in the two patents (Andros and Dongan), which confirmed the extent of Southampton's lands and hence the original purchases from the Indians. But for unknown reasons, except possible hostility to the colonial authority, the trustees apparently never submitted the deed to Lord Cornbury's administration for ratification as they were required to under the Duke's Laws. Narrowly defined, the deed contained new land lying to the east that could be interpreted as newly purchased from the Shinnecock. Without crown approval, and there is no indication that it was ever subsequently approved, some doubt might be cast on its legal validity.[33] After spending so much energy and some small amount of the town's treasure on gaining a final agreement with the Shinnecock, it can only be judged that this was an extraordinary oversight. It can hardly be said that it haunts the present but it did raise questions much later when a new agreement abrogating the lease covering the Hills was reached in 1859. We return to this shortly.

III: THE HILLS IN THE EIGHTEENTH CENTURY: CONTESTED GROUND

The question of fencing the Hills since the middle of the seventeenth century goes to the heart of the issue of their eventual partition in 1859. Today, the evidence of fencing can be seen in the names of roads off Montauk Highway leading into the Shinnecock Reservation—Middle Gate Road, West Gate Road—each referring to the old cattle gates which stood in the fence running the length of Shinnecock Great Neck from Heady Creek to Old Fort Pond.[34] Cattle went onto the Neck in October, after the Indians had gathered their corn and vegetables, and pastured there through the winter. They were driven off in April. In the first years of settlement, livestock were not numerous—there were only forty or so families in Southampton in the mid-1640s—and what few of them there were found plentiful grazing land in the Great Plain just east of the Hills. But as numbers grew, more of them strayed into the Indian planting fields on Shinnecock Neck. Predictably, complaints of damage to their crops began to be heard from the Shinnecock. In December 1649, the town called several of them in, led by their sachem Mandush and apparently in the presence of Wyandanch, the Montauk sachem, and in essence demanded that the Indians protect their own crops. Having first pointed out in an unveiled reference to the 1640 deed that they were planting on ground "that belonged not to them But to the said Towne," the townspeople forced through an agreement which stipulated that the Indians should "make a sufficient fence against all sorts of cattle . . . thereby to secure their corn." If they did not, then any subsequent damage was their responsibility.

The fencing was to be done at Heady Creek, dividing the Great Plain from the lower portion of the Hills and Shinnecock Neck, and apparently at Sebonac Creek to the north of the Hills, that is, on a north to south line.[35] There was an Indian field at Sebonac which was to be separately fenced. This arrangement was fairly soon abandoned, at least in the Great Plain, as the town realized the advantage of open access to the pasturelands of the Neck. Cattle herds were increasing, and grazing on the Great Plain alone was probably insufficient to support them. In fact, the town wrote access to the Indian lands "without molestation" into the agreement. It was to take place in the fall "at the expiration of ten days after their Indian corn shall bee gathered." Only hogs, the most destructive and least controllable of all domestic animals, were excluded from the Indian lands. Ultimately, only a fairly short section of fence was then required—between the two creeks bounding Shinnecock Neck—but it was to be the cause of endless trouble and controversy. One other demand was made: the Shinnecocks were to fill in their corn barns or storage pits for "the safety of the said English theire cattle." The thoughtlessness of this must have been galling to Mandush and his associates for by what other means were they expected to store their crops over the winter.

Fencing and livestock were as natural and necessary to the English settlers as they were alien to the Indians. Coming from an agricultural tradition of mixed husbandry in England, raising crops was always strictly segregated from pasturing animals to protect the fields. Fences were the only answer to this problem. They were also, as William Cronon points out, visible symbols of an improved landscape.[36] To the colonists, enclosing the land as much as tending crops and livestock or building permanent dwellings and shelters was a conspicuous element of such improvement. It also enhanced their sense of rightful title to the land they had acquired from the Indians. Possession alone, simply sitting down, was never conceived to be enough. That ran counter to the activism of Puritan ethics. Such deep-seated beliefs imbued them with a sense of innate superiority to the Indians, a people who, as far as anyone could see, had made no effort in their countless generations to improve the land they inhabited. They had no fences, no livestock, no permanent dwellings. In contrast, the colonists set about domesticating the landscape to suit their purposes wherever they settled.

In Southampton in the 1640s, the settlers wasted no time in enclosing their fields and home lots. Each inhabitant was required to maintain a fence at his home lot and raise sufficient fencing at his planting lots in the first divisions of land. Fence viewers were appointed to insure the work was kept up and fines levied where it was not. Fines were also levied against those who allowed their livestock to stray and pounders appointed to locate them, identify them by their earmarks or other mark, and herd them in a common pound. In fencing the common fields, every inhabitant with proprietor rights (which in the early years included almost all of them) was expected to contribute his share of the work according to the amount of his right. Thus in 1643, "the little Common" or the Little Plain was to be fenced according to "each man's proportion." On the other hand, water fences and town gates in the Little Plain were said to be the responsibility of the town and the work hired out accordingly. Building and maintaining fences must have consumed a great deal of the town's energy, as well as timber, and they had to be up to code. This usually meant a four- or five-rail fence with particular attention paid to the lowest rails where free-ranging hogs—the bane of all farmers—were wont to squeeze through. Hogs could destroy anything from a corn barn to a clam bed, and they multiplied faster than any other livestock. Fences were to be "horse high, bull strong, and pig tight." As more common land was divided and lotted out in the seventeenth and eighteenth centuries, at distances increasingly far from the original settlement, the demand for fencing grew almost exponentially. Certainly in the seventeenth century no single issue occupies as much attention in the town records as does the issue of fencing. It attests to the singular importance of cattle and other domestic animals in the local economy, and their ever-increasing numbers throughout the town.

This would be of no comfort to the Shinnecock. Faced with the prospect of marauding cattle trampling through their crops in the growing season, they had little choice but to acquiesce in the agreement with the settlers and develop the unfamiliar skill of fencing their fields. When the fences came down in the fall under the provision that "(t)he said English shall have free liberty without molestation to put (their) cattle (hoggs only excepted) within the said Indians their said boundaries," they might awake on winter mornings to the lowing of cattle in their backyards. If this new experience did anything, it was to drive home to them that the land was no longer "theirs" in any recognizable and customary sense. Yet the town did attempt to honor its side of the agreement. The settlers trained the Indians in the art of fence building and agreed to share the labor of fencing every spring; by 1653 the Shinnecock were to provide "their share of fencing betweene them and us with 5 railes." Frequently they raised fences of brush that may have been as effective as a rail fence. The settlers were also strict enough in controlling incursions from hogs: there were to be none "within the libertae of the Indians, mentioned in the covenant between the towne and them."[37] In 1658, for instance, they reimbursed the Indians for damage done to their land by a stray hog. The offending creature was sold at "outcry" for seventeen shillings and the proceeds duly presented. But overall it was an extremely unsatisfactory set of arrangements for the Shinnecock.

Both before and after 1703, they found themselves treated or reluctantly tolerated as guests in their own lands. The 1703 lease agreement did nothing to change this; in fact it simply reaffirmed the town's rights to do what it always had done on the Hills since the beginning. Throughout the eighteenth century, the town trustees minutely regulated what could and could not be done at Shinnecock and Sebonac, and not simply by its leasehold occupants who enjoyed none of the proprietary rights available to the townsmen. The trustees stinted cattle and other livestock according to the commonage rights of inhabitants; determined when cattle could go into the Neck after the Indian fields had been "laid common"; limited how much timber could be cut or upland grass mown and carted away; how much stone or seaweed taken from the shores; generally prohibited the removal of husks and cornstalks from the Indian fields; imposed fines for stray animals; decided on watering places for cattle (generally known as "the tubs"); hired out the mowing and sale of the sedges at Sebonac; determined the location of convenient highways and laid them out; and controlled the numbers of sheep going on "Shenecock Plain" (the upland above the necks).

It bears repeating that after 1738 the Shinnecock Hills was one of the last great tracts of undivided land remaining to the town and one that was within easy reach, two miles or so west of the settlement. To the east the Great North and South Divisions had just been laid out that year, taking up fully half of all the land toward Easthampton and leaving only a small stretch of unallotted land due north of Southampton's town plot. This later was divided in 1763 and came to be called the Little South Division. To the west of the Hills and Canoe Place four large divisions had been surveyed and lotted out among the proprietors in the Quogue and Topping's Purchases, again in 1738. All that remained in these two purchases that was not in private hands were the several miles of woodland that lay between Brookhaven and the Peconic River estuary and the North or Peconic Bay beyond. These fell to the layers out or surveyors in 1763 and 1782. So the Hills perhaps assumed even greater importance in the eyes of the proprietors—their interests still represented by the town trustees who were still exclusively elected from among the leading proprietors—than they had hitherto. Other than the bay fisheries and the annual sales of common grasses and sedges, the Hills were a major source of revenues accruing to the proprietors' accounts. Fifty years after the 1738 divisions, the proprietors began to explore ways in which they could exert better control over the whole of Shinnecock and potentially extract more income. They were not especially successful in the latter, although they could continue to sell the common grass, sedge, timber, and seaweed privileges to the general run of inhabitants, but they could attempt better dealings with the Shinnecock. The establishment of the Shinnecock trustee system, to some extent rationalizing the relationship between the two communities, went some way toward achieving that end. But after 1790, it is not clear what the proprietors of the common lands working through the town trustees wanted to do with the Hills, beyond the customary use they had made of them for generations. If they wanted to divide them, the one thousand-year lease stood in their way. If they wanted to sell them outright, and there is no indication that they did at this early date, the same problem obtained. But what they did want was first an end to the bickering and occasional confrontation over fencing, cattle, damage, and injuries that had plagued their relations with the Shinnecock since the beginning of the lease and before, and second, better access to the rich pastures and cultivable fields of Shinnecock Neck and the adjacent Little Neck.

In the late 1760s, the town trustees had prohibited the townsmen from sowing flax (an important crop), oats, or corn in the Indian fields on penalty of forty shillings per acre. This order was repeated periodically over the next twenty years or more without any explanation, but it seems to reflect a growing practice where the Shinnecock had begun renting out fields in Shinnecock Great Neck to individual farmers. They also may have done so at Sebonac and Cold Spring, both of which contained areas of suitable planting land. Deals were undoubtedly made between individual Shinnecocks and farmers with their own lands nearby the Hills, but in either case there was no town regulation. At the same time, it became clear that the town, which is to say the proprietors and the trustees, were taking over much of the responsibility for fencing the necks at Shinnecock and Sebonac against the trespass of cattle. In May 1769, as an instance of this, the trustees appointed a committee to employ men to fence Shinnecock Neck "at the proprietors cost."[38] Later in the year they met with the Indians to discuss improvements to the fence at Sebonac. In spring 1771, in an evident attempt to control the use of Indian lands, the trustees voted that the Shinnecock "shall have the benefit" of the fence across Shinnecock Great Neck in exchange for "the privilidg of the Indians fence at Sebonack this year."[39] It was then agreed that Sebonac Neck should be hired out for pasture or mowing. This was the first time on record where cattle were to go on Indian lands on the basis of bids received rather than by proprietary rights in commonage. In the past livestock had gone on the plains in the spring usually at the rate of two grown cattle or four yearlings or one horse to a fifty right. This was to continue, but renting out land already leased to the Indians, land that was enclosed and presumably ready for spring planting, set something of a precedent. It was hardly in the interest of the Shinnecock, whether they planned to cultivate their fields at Sebonac that year or not. Yet the following year we find that Sebonac Neck has again been hired out "for the benefit of the Proprietors . . . until next Town meeting day (1773)."[40] The precedent appeared to be becoming a habit.

What we begin to see in the last third of the eighteenth century, just prior to the development of the Indian trusteeship system, is a series of incremental shifts in the usage of the Hills that departed from the traditional practices of the previous one hundred years. The trustees, on behalf of the proprietors, hired out parts of the land on a routine seasonal basis. The Sebonac sedges at Sebonac Creek, located around Bullhead Bay and much of it inside the Indian Line (not to be confused with the meadows at Cold Spring Bay that had been divided in 1653 and excepted from the Indian lease), had come to be thought of as particularly valuable. In 1776, they were sold at auction for mowing and pasture for the season for forty-five pounds. The following year, for mowing alone, they were sold for twenty-two pounds and thirteen shillings. In 1780, Elias Foster paid forty pounds for the privilege, while in 1782 four men separately bid a total of more than sixty pounds for the privilege of both cutting sedge and pasturing cattle on the common grass. This small area had become the single most important source of proprietor revenue in the space of a few years. At the same time, increasing numbers of cattle and other livestock were put on the Hills at any and all times of the year. The trustees no longer relied on the Shinnecock to maintain their half of the fence, assuming responsibility for it themselves. Besides which, fencing was seen as something less and less for the benefit of the Indians and more as a convenience for the owners of livestock. Fencing was used to protect areas of meadow, enclose pasture for a season for its improvement, or to separate livestock. A cryptic notice in May 1779 informed the Indians that if they planned to plant corn in Shinnecock Neck that year, they should fence it themselves "and not depend upon the fence that belongs to the white people which may be taken up at any time as the Trustees shall order."[41] Then in 1784, the town trustees sent a delegation to the new state assembly with a petition to "make a general field at the Towns cost" of the whole of Shinnecock. It was to be shut up at either end with fencing at both Canoe Place and Shinnecock and Sebonac.[42] The reasons for such a petition are not obvious unless there was concern in the town that such an enclosure might generate a protest among the Shinnecock. It evidently had no implications for the terms of the 1703 lease, which had given the trustees virtually free rein over the Hills.

It seems clear that whatever limited protections the 1703 lease afforded the Shinnecock, they were honored in only a rather haphazard way by the town trustees. Yet there were at least three instances in the 1780s when the trustees assisted them. It has to be remembered that the Shinnecock were few in number at this time and had been since the beginning of the century. From the scant census data available between 1698 and 1790—the only two censuses that listed Indians separately—the Shinnecock population never numbered more than approximately 150 men, women, and children. Furthermore, many of the men were away at sea for extended periods in the whale fishery. They also were scattered in different village locations in the Hills. An initial interpretation of the scant facts available is that there may have been four settlements in the late eighteenth century, all of them small, seasonal, and easily movable. Wigwams were easy to pick up and transport from place to place. There were apparently settlements at Shinnecock and Sebonac Necks, a smaller village near Cold Spring Bay, and a more permanent settlement across Canoe Place and technically outside the area of the Hills lease. The Canoe Place settlement was probably located on land laid out in 1738 in the Lower Division, Quogue Purchase, or at least on the edge of it, just south of the present Montauk Highway and on an arm of Shinnecock Bay.[43] Perhaps this scattering made the Shinnecock easier to ignore. There would have been no more than a handful of dwellings at each location (as late as 1838 the U.S. Coast and Geodetic Survey showed only fifteen houses in Shinnecock Neck) and apparently no church or meetinghouse anywhere before 1745. This is a speculative and unconfirmed date—the first Shinnecock church is thought to date from much later in 1792—but the existence and location of meetinghouses does provide a clue to the location of villages.

The nature of the Shinnecock leadership at the time was similarly unclear. There are no references to sachems or leadership groups in either the town records or town trustee records of the period, perhaps reflecting the fact that there had been no record of serious trouble or difficult relations with the Shinnecock for much of the century; really since the fateful signing of the deed and the one thousand-year lease in 1703. To what extent they cultivated their lands beyond small plantings of corn and vegetables is unknown, or whether they maintained common fields or small garden plots. But they had become accustomed to entering into private agreements with farmers to let unused lands and to lease rights to cut wood. These were in no sense privately owned plots but belonged to the common stock of land under the terms of the lease. This had been the cause of problems as far back as the 1760s. At that time a delegation of Shinnecock women had complained to the trustees that some of their men had sublet land to farmers and often the same piece several times over. To put some order into this state of affairs, an agreement was worked out, but the practice continued and in later years the agreement was widely ignored. In 1782, a delegation again petitioned the trustees for help in enforcing the agreement concerning wood lots. The trustees obliged and ordered an end to wood cutting on penalty of twenty shillings for every load carted off. They also revived the ban on planting Indian land and with it a penalty of forty shillings an acre for violations, later raised to sixty shillings.[44] The proceeds of the fines were to be shared among the Shinnecock. It was a rare instance of support but a significant one.

Then in 1790 there appeared to be something of a breakthrough in relations between the town and the Shinnecock, possibly shifting them away from their previous moribund and unproductive state. It is difficult to determine exactly what was occurring between 1790 and 1794—apart from the town's successful petition to the legislature to establish

Shinnecock trustees—for the town trustee records give only the briefest of descriptions, and naturally enough do not waste time with explanations. But change was definitely in the air. In April 1790, the records report that cattle and horses were to go on the Hills at the end of the month in the usual way, and then announce an Indian Agreement. Ten members of the Shinnecock apparently approached the trustees with a proposal to develop fields in the vicinity of Cold Spring and run fences southward toward Shinnecock Bay both there and at Canoe Place "for the purpose of plowing & planting." In return the "Proprietors" were to "have the privilige of pasturing Shinecock Neck and Sebonak Neck three years from this date without molestation."[45]

Having said that the Indians themselves petitioned the town, it is just as possible and perhaps more likely that the trustees in there capacity as proprietors were responsible for the plan, offering a large tract for planting in exchange for unencumbered control of the two Necks, or what was evidently the land then most valuable to them. Second, in respect to fencing Cold Spring, the trustees required that it be built under the supervision of three townsmen, one of whom was to be chosen by the trustees. This committee was also to lay out the field in lots and allocate them to the ten Shinnecocks and their families named in the agreement. If the Indians desired more of their people to plant "in their inclosed field," then, the trustees said, the committee would be willing to lay out more lots. Although the agreement was overwhelmingly favorable to the proprietors, whose paramount interests, again, were in the Necks, it did represent some gain to the Shinnecock. They would at least control fields in which fencing was not dismantled in the fall, thus resolving the question of damage by cattle on the loose. Neither is it unlikely that the location of the field in the western part of the Hills beginning at Cold Spring was selected because a significant number of Shinnecocks were already there or had moved there from the Necks; in effect, had moved further away from the townsmen to land which was in no great demand. If that was the case, then it was not perhaps such a breakthrough after all even if the agreement provided for a settled area for raising crops—a sort of noninterference zone—that had not existed before. Overall, with the proprietors now in effective control of Shinnecock and Sebonac Necks and the Indians cultivating less valued ground to the west, it very much looked as if it was the proprietors who had gained the real advantage.

That they had done so, and wanted to consolidate it, is suggested by an offer to the Shinnecock they made later in the year. Although the trustees appeared to have made a firm deal with the Shinnecock that they not plant in Shinnecock and Sebonac Necks for three years, the agreement may not have been accepted by all. In November, the trustees voted to give the Indians twenty pounds toward the cost of finishing their meetinghouse if they agreed not to farm Shinnecock Neck in 1791. The offer was repeated the following September and eight pounds toward the cost of the meetinghouse deposited in an account a month or so earlier. The full amount was to be paid over in October 1792 providing that "the Proprietors in Commonage shall have the grazing of Shinecok Neck during the whole of the year 1792 without molestation." If not, there was to be "no such present."[46] An agreement must have been reached for eight pounds was reported as paid in late 1791, perhaps as an evidence of good faith, and the full amount in August 1792.

Still, there were probably some holdouts among the Shinnecock, otherwise the trustees would have been unlikely to put themselves to all this trouble and expense. That they were a minority, however, can be inferred from the records of the Shinnecock trustees. They had met for the first time in April 1792 and two of the first trustees elected—Samuel Waukus and Abraham Jacob—had been signatories to the Indian Agreement of 1790 establishing the Shinnecock fields at Cold Spring. The records note that the trustees were elected for "regulating Division & improvement of their lands" and are clear that these—"the Indian Land"—are located at Cold Spring. The trustees voted that "the Land to the westward of Cold-Spring Creek over to the field by the South Bay . . . shall be improved by the owners of Shinnecock for Corn & Beans & Potatoes this Season and none to the Eastward." Besides these crops, rye, flax, oats, and summer wheat were also to be raised.[47] There seems to be no mention of the situation at Shinnecock Neck, nor is there any reference to the building of a meetinghouse, but for the previous year (1791) there is an allusion to a crop lost "for want of Sufficient fence" on ground that in 1792 is not to be improved for planting. This may have referred to Shinnecock Neck "to the Eastward." However, what is quite clear is that these new Indian trustees were fully in charge; and that the major, if not exclusive focus, of economic activity was now to be at Cold Spring. What is not clear is how long this arrangement lasted.

The development of a Shinnecock church is important here because its first location provides us with an idea of the establishment of some considerable part or even all of the Indian community across Canoe Place or off the Hills proper. When this first occurred is unknown but that it did is indisputable. This settlement to the west lasted into the late 1830s or 1840s at which time the Shinnecock began moving or moving back to Shinnecock Neck. The generally accepted view is that the first Shinnecock church was built in 1791 or 1792, toward the erection of which the proprietors had contributed twenty pounds, at a place half way between Good Ground and Canoe Place. Its location is still marked by the grave of its first minister, the Reverend Paul Cuffee.[48] Cuffee died in 1812 and a few years later the church fell into disrepair. A part of it was then said to have been moved about 1820 near to its present location on Canoe Place Road and south of Montauk Highway. A small cemetery was attached to it, remnants of which could still be seen in the 1950s a few hundred feet to the west. The church appeared to serve a considerable community of Shinnecock for a number of years. A map made in 1836 by J. Calvin Smith shows the area as the sole location of wigwams. Yet in 1838 the U.S. coastal survey indicates Shinnecock Neck as the only location of wigwams, a discrepancy that might simply be due to the neglect or inattention of the surveyors. The other part of the "Cuffee" church, as it was called, was thought to have been moved to Shinnecock Neck sometime in the 1840s, drawn across the ice of a land-locked Shinnecock Bay, and consecrated in 1847.[49]

There is a potential difficulty with this story, and a mystery concealed within it. Two maps made thirty years apart reveal the location of the first Shinnecock church as at Cold Spring Bay, not west of Canoe Place but east of it and just off what later came to be known as the old North Highway. Both the map of 1797 and the Burr map of 1829 put it in exactly the same place.[50] There are no wigwams near it, but there are no wigwams shown anywhere else either, yet this is unquestionably the area where the Indians had begun to plant their fields in 1791 and 1792. It does suggest, then, that if there was a church, a settlement had developed there or close to it and probably well before it was built. The rest of the story is not inconsistent with this, although it does seem odd that according to the Burr map there was no church at Canoe Place before 1829. The Canoe Place village grew, the church was removed to it, and then later some part of it was brought across the ice to Shinnecock Neck as that settlement established or reestablished itself and wanted for a meeting house. Gaynell Stone, in her analysis of Shinnecock maps through time, generally follows this interpretation though does not pursue the question of why Cold Spring was chosen, if indeed it was chosen, as the original site for a church.[51]

If all this is true, and the sole evidence essentially seems to lie in two maps, a small mystery surrounds the question of why Paul Cuffee was buried where he was, put to rest in what then in 1812 appeared to be as yet unconsecrated ground. This hardly seems likely or even remotely possible. The only plausible conclusion can be that the maps were wrong. Some hint of this is to be found in a document written years later. In 1868, the Reverend James G. Downs was appointed pastor to the church at Shinnecock Neck. Sometime in the 1870s he wrote a brief history of the Shinnecock church, much of it based on the 1845 account of Nathaniel Prime. But buried within it is the claim that Azariah Horton established the first Shinnecock church in the early 1740s. Horton was a missionary appointed by a New York society in 1741 to instruct the Long Island Indians in Christian ways.[52] Downs, although not Prime, says that the Shinnecock church was the first Indian church on the east end of the island and that it was "located near the east end of the Shinnecock Hills on the north bay."[53] This certainly puts it at Cold Spring. If Downs was correct, then the meetinghouse toward which the town trustees subscribed twenty pounds in 1791 was constructed west of Canoe Place after all, the previous Cold Spring church—Horton's church—having fallen into disuse or disrepair sometime earlier. The main body of the Shinnecock community must then have been located there at least as far back as the 1770s or before, but some may have remained at Cold Spring, the site, so the Reverend Downs thought, of the first church.[54] But if one issue is clearer from the preceding discussion it is that the Shinnecock, whether by choice or necessity or earlier rather than later, established communities much more in the western part of the Hills than in the east.

Leaving the question of the church aside, there are yet other difficulties in understanding the nature of the interactions between the Shinnecock and the trustees or proprietors in the early 1790s. In December 1791, despite the September agreement that the proprietors should have the Necks for grazing for three years, the trustees appointed Obadiah Rogers and Caleb Cooper a committee "to confer with the natives . . . about purchasing the Shinecok Neck as now inclosed."[55] But no report followed and it was business as usual the following spring, the cattle going on the Neck under the usual regulations. The Indian records are also silent in the matter. Instead, in April 1792, and in the presence of the two townsmen instructed to confer with them, the Shinnecock trustees set out the ground rules for allocating land to individual Shinnecocks and their families and then appointed themselves a committee to lay out that land for planting. It is clear that this land was in

Shinnecock Neck and not at Cold Spring—there is no further mention of Cold Spring at all—for the next several entries are taken up with hiring out individual lots to Southampton men in Shinnecock Neck. This can be the only interpretation of the word "purchase" in the town trustee records; the lots were of one acre and were to be hired out for planting. In fact, virtually all the entries in the Shinnecock records from their inception in 1792 until 1799 are taken up with recording these individual leasing arrangements. But they reveal several important developments.

First, the Shinnecock trustees had taken on the responsibility of laying out quite extensive fields in the form of divisions in both Shinnecock Neck and Little Neck and had lotted them out in one acre parcels to members of the community. There may have been as many as six divisions in the two necks. There are references to the "3rd Division in Shinnecock Neck" or the "2nd Division in Shinnecock Great Neck" as well as the laying out of Little Neck, but perhaps most interesting of all, there were two women's divisions. The divisions also contained many numbered lots—the highest recorded was No. 131—suggesting that several hundred acres were laid out and apportioned among the inhabitants. The drawings of the lots took place annually, always under the supervision of town justices, and with so many to distribute most Shinnecocks would draw several lots. Second, these divided lands were exclusively for hire and not for cultivation by the Shinnecock themselves. It has to be inferred from this that they had their fields elsewhere, that is, at Cold Spring two miles or so to the north. There are one or two indirect references to this. In 1794, a blank lot was to be laid out somewhere to the west "for the Benefit of the Tribe," and the following year a field "for improvement for corn" was to be laid "somewhere on the Commons" providing it was not in Sebonac Neck. But in 1796, the Indian trustees voted, in the notable absence of town justices at the meeting, that their planting field not be "apportioned out (somewhere) on the Commons" but in Sebonac, that is, in land the proprietors thought was covered by previous agreement. It was agreed that Caleb Cooper and William Herrick should lay out between 150 and 190 acres and "make report to the trustees at their next meeting." The two justices must have acceded to this for they later signed the minutes.[56] Additionally, each "house or Wigwam that is inhabited for the summer" was to have a half-acre garden plot. So Sebonac was not laid out for hire while Shinnecock was, and it was Sebonac that appeared to be the summer home of most members of the community. Mark Harrington's excavations at Sebonac Creek in 1902 attest to a long-standing and substantial community there.[57]

Thirdly, the whole system of land tenure and subleasing had been rationalized and brought under control. This was as much beneficial to the Shinnecock as it was to the proprietors. There were agreed on rates for subleasing land—generally twenty shillings an acre, formal methods for allocating lots, and controls over the leasing process. Principally, it gave the proprietors what they most wanted and put some money into the pockets of the Shinnecock. It was, if nothing else, an effective mechanism for getting them out of Shinnecock Neck, the area at that time most valuable to the proprietors. A last thing to note as the eighteenth century was drawing to a close is where most of the Shinnecocks were residing in the Hills. One clue is to be found in the reference in their own records to their summer habitation at Sebonac Neck where, in 1796, they wanted to have their fields again. Previously they had agreed to move them and presumably themselves to the area of Cold Spring and Canoe Place. So it seems most likely that they had developed, renewed, or long held a winter settlement at Canoe Place, where they had built a meetinghouse and laid out nearby fields in Cold Spring, and returned to Sebonac in the summer. Since, after 1792, much of Shinnecock Neck was laid out for hire in the spring and turned over for pasture in the fall and winter, it is doubtful if any of them lived there in this period. As for the Canoe Place settlement, it is apparent that it was well established before the new church was built. That there was also a Cold Spring settlement in the late eighteenth century seems to be attested by a line in the March 1793 town trustee records: Caleb Cooper, the clerk, was to go there to invite the Indians to attend the next meeting of the trustees.[58] But it disappeared sometime early in the nineteenth century as its residents, and those at Canoe Place, began to migrate back to Shinnecock Neck. Why they did so has never been clear, but it is beyond doubt that the main body of the population had established itself in the Neck by the 1840s. If it was not, the erection of a second (or third) meetinghouse there cannot be plausibly explained.

IV: THE PROPRIETORS' ASSAULT ON THE HILLS 1804–1858

So that is how the eighteenth century ended. Possibly under pressure the Shinnecocks had moved to the west, with the larger part of them settled beyond Canoe Place and well away from their traditional fields in the necks. They had not exactly relinquished the Hills but moved back to them only in the summer, to a summer encampment at Sebonac where they were not particularly welcome. The provisions of the 1703 lease guaranteeing them "the privileges and advantages of plowing and planting . . . and all other conveniences and benefits whatsoever," although not ignored, had been interpreted in a way that turned them into lessors of their own most fertile lands. In acquiescing in their division into lots and seasonal rental, the Shinnecock had unwittingly become integrated into the town's market economy. It was certainly advantageous to them because the rental fees were fairly generous, but it nonetheless represented an effective mechanism of economic and social control. In part they came to subsist on rentier income and eventually, were to become habituated to it, exhibiting in consequence an emerging pattern of dependency. The position of the town's proprietors was doubtless that here was valuable land that would otherwise go to waste for want of proper cultivation. If then there were specific economic constraints, political integration was effected through the Indian trusteeship system. This was administered through close supervision by the town's representatives. There is every indication in the records of meetings between 1792 and 1835 that the trustees elected raised few if any objections to the way in which Indian lands were subject to division and use by the town. Probably they had little choice, and if they complained they did so in private. The appearance of an independent elected leadership and communal autonomy would have left few doubts in anyone's mind about the real status of the Shinnecock and their governing body. In fact, it transpired in the 1820s that the town's three mandated justices heavily influenced the annual election of trustees in advance of the elections each April. The same family names recur with reasonable frequency through the first forty years of the trusteeship system.

The beginning of the 1800s saw increasingly tighter regulation of the Hills by the proprietors. This squeezed the Shinnecock and their activities into ever narrower areas, while the proprietors gained complete control of the use of the Hills on a year round basis. In an "Act respecting Shinecok Great Field" in April 1804 and renewed annually, it was ordered that "the whole of the Indian Land shall be shut up for the use or grazing of the Proprietors of Commonage with good fence and easy Gates and Bars acrost the highways."[59] The Hills were then enclosed at both ends. Sheep were to winter over in Sebonac and then go on the Hills in the spring after shearing, while cattle and horses would go on in May. These were, of course, the livestock belonging to the proprietors and not those of the general run of inhabitants, though as earlier noted the trustees would quite routinely hire out pasturage rights to non-proprietors. In 1806, for example, the Overseers of the Indian Field (there had been a standing committee for some time now) were instructed to lease twelve fifties of commonage in order to raise money for the repair of a sheep pen. The fields under the control of the Shinnecock trustees also were open to bid by all townspeople, although few outside the proprietors could probably afford to avail themselves of the opportunity. If the townsmen found their access to the Hills severely restricted or only available for a seasonal rent, the Shinnecock labored under a similar burden. In 1805, at the end of June, they were told that if they wanted to pasture cattle and horses in Shinnecock Neck they would pay a fee: three dollars for each cow and six dollars and a half for a horse. It was to be paid to the overseers within two weeks.

In winter 1805, a delegation of Shinnecocks—probably consisting of Absalom Cuffee, James Bunn, and David Waucus, the three trustees at the time—presented a list of complaints to the state legislature. Various matters must have come to a head that year for them to have undertaken such a course of action, but the sudden imposition of fees for pasturing their own cattle on what to them was their own land was very likely a major cause. There was another controversy brewing that summer that threatened their relations with the town and was probably a factor leading to the petition as well. It did not boil over until the following spring, but the town trustees were in the process of taking steps to exclude a number of Shinnecocks from drawing lots in their own fields. In April 1806, eight Shinnecocks and their families were to be debarred from the drawings that year unless they could prove their title to the land, or "the Indian land" as it was described. The Cuffees were the prime targets of this directive, including Absalom Cuffee, but James Bunn was also named. It is impossible to know what led to this, or precisely what it meant. Leasehold title was guaranteed by the 1703 lease and the Cuffees and others were covered by it as much as were other Shinnecocks. There was no other source of title. It looked as if it was an attempt to lock out anyone associated with the petition. Later in the year Nathan Sanford, on behalf of the town trustees and proprietors, delivered an opinion (subsequently forwarded to the Shinnecock) to the effect that the 1703 lease provided that only Indians "properly so-called" had any right or interest in the lands under lease and excluded "Negroes,

Mulattoes (and) Whites." It was evidently an attack on the Cuffees and the Bunns and an attempt to exclude them on the grounds of mixed blood. In a second clause, Sanford argued that the lease squarely laid the responsibility for preventing any damage to crops for want of adequate fencing on the Shinnecock alone.[60]

Immediately following this in October, William Herrick, newly appointed as clerk to the town trustees that year, was instructed to inform the Shinnecock of the trustees' distress at their action. For moral support or intimidation he took along with him Reverend David Bogart, the Presbyterian minister. The matter did not end there. In the following spring of 1807 the Indian trustees themselves voted against excluding Cuffee, Bunn, and the other families from the drawings. Herrick, Caleb Cooper, and Obadiah Rogers, the three justices, voted to bar them, the town trustees having already taken the precaution of indemnifying them in the event of any future suit.[61] There the matter apparently ended for it is not mentioned again in any record, but it was probably resolved at that Shinnecock trustee meeting when the vote went against the town justices. It was an instance of the extent to which the Shinnecock felt increasingly constrained by the town and chafed under the often arbitrary regulations and demands imposed on them. It settled into a pattern of control and intimidation that was to last another fifty years until they finally gave up, or were pressured into giving up, and surrendered the Hills to the proprietors.

How it came about that the Shinnecock were so emboldened as to take their grievances to the legislature is unclear, but their neighbors, the Montaukett, may have influenced them. A few years before, in 1800, the Montaukett also had addressed a petition to the state recounting their difficulties with the Easthampton trustees respecting the lands at Montauk. The charges were serious enough to merit an eventual visit in 1807 by a committee of the state senate. On hearing the report of the committee, the senate did recommend that the Montaukett be provided a permanent area of settlement on Montauk but did not conclude that state intervention was necessary to establish it. In good part this was because the Easthampton proprietors of Montauk resisted the idea and the senate, perhaps not wishing to interfere unduly in local matters, did not pursue it. But it did agree that the Montaukett, and other Indian communities within the state, were entitled to state protection. For the Montauk Indians it was a disappointment, but it was something.[62] It may have encouraged the Shinnecock to take their complaints outside Southampton and to the state authorities. Had they persisted with the petition, it might have resulted in at least some legislative interest in the situation on the Hills—very little different as it was from that at Montauk—but there is no evidence that they did.

It still is widely believed in Southampton that the proprietors began to bring pressure to bear on the Shinnecocks to divide the Hills with them because they anticipated that the LIRR would eventually build a spur off its main line to Riverhead and Greenport (which had been opened in 1844) to connect with the South Shore towns to the east. Any such line would cut south and east from Riverhead and run through the Shinnecock Hills to Southampton and points beyond. The argument of many was that this would increase the value of the lands along the projected line of the road, both for individual farmers who owned lots in various adjacent divisions and for the proprietors who held rights in the common lands of the Hills. All would cash in by selling their respective rights-of-way to the railroad. This was in the mid-1850s and a little before the legislature approved the partition of the Hills in 1859. It was not an unreasonable argument to make because the railroad's future plans were known at the time and the projected South Shore line had been included in the most recent map of Long Island published in 1858.[63] One interesting feature of the map is that it shows the railroad running much farther north of its future path through the Hills and considerably north of Southampton village. A second reason for thinking that the rush to divide the Hills was impelled by the railroad's prospective planning relates to the Shinnecock. The state laws of 1836 governing the relationships between railroad companies and Indians provides that railroads must "contract with the chiefs of a nation of Indians, over whose land it may be necessary to construct such railroad, for the right to make such road upon such lands" including a right of occupancy and maintenance.[64] Possibly this is why the company projected its route well to the north and away from Shinnecock Neck where, by the 1850s, a majority of the Shinnecock had now settled or resettled (the new church there had been built in 1847). In routing it this way, railroad officials may have thought it less likely that they would have to deal with the Indians under the terms of the law. Besides which, the land in question was certainly thought of as town or proprietor land (the question of which body had the legal title to it probably did not arise at the time) under the 1703 Indian deed to all of Southampton's lands. All of this must have been known to the railroad, the town, and the proprietors when the route was originally surveyed. However, Gaynell Stone thought, in an article on the reservation lands, that the proprietors pushed for the division of the Hills precisely to prevent the Indians collecting "a rental or sale fee for their land the railroad was to traverse," a fee which they presumably wanted.[65]

Much later in 1900, in Congressional hearings in New York on Indian complaints, Nathan Cuffee did testify that the Shinnecock received nothing for the railroad's right-of-way when the decision to build the line was finally made in 1868, but it is fairly evident that the railroad felt it was under no state obligation to deal with the Indians in the first place because they merely leased the property.[66] Town officials and the proprietors' own trustees would have assured them of that. Finally, the relatively small payments Southampton farmers received for conveying land rights along the twenty-nine-mile route in Southampton town from Eastport to Sag Harbor, only four miles of which were through the Hills, were hardly such as to justify the trouble and expense of petitioning the legislature to abrogate the Indian lease and divide the Hills. In 1868, nearly eighty landowners along the right-of-way received payments from the town commissioners appointed for the purpose totaling just over $4,900 for an average of about $60 each.[67] Although it was true that twelve owners received three-fourths of this amount, with one—Mary Huntting, one of the largest taxpayers in town—earning $1,199, none were proprietors or among those who purchased the Shinnecock Hills at auction in 1861.[68] Of course, it could not have been known in 1859 that what most farmers were to get for a right-of-way through their fields was relatively little, but the townspeople in general and the proprietors in particular, realistic as they were, were unlikely to delude themselves into thinking that railroads would drive anything less than a hard bargain. In any case, right-of-way costs were to be born by the town and would be absorbed by the bond issue required by the railroad to underwrite construction. It was in the town's interest to hold down such costs.

Nor did the LIRR have any current plans in the 1850s to extend its line farther to the east beyond surveying a potential route. There was no public discussion of the issue and no campaign mounted in the towns affected to lobby for it.[69] A decade later, when the advantages of a railroad were fully understood in Southampton (and also in Easthampton), major efforts were made to persuade another railroad company in competition with the LIRR to construct a line. Southampton also agreed to finance a bond issue to underwrite the construction and provide the land. Had it not been for this threatened competition the LIRR might well have put off indefinitely any implementation of plans it had tentatively developed in the past (and which were probably gathering dust in its New York offices) to extend its operations farther east. The threat to its monopoly of eastern Long Island came from the South Side Railroad (SSRR), a company that was not formed until 1860, and which then immediately put itself into competition with the LIRR. It was in fact formed for that very purpose. The SSRR did not begin construction of a South Shore line from Brooklyn to Babylon until April 1866 (after the Civil War had ended) reaching Babylon a year later and then pushed on to Islip and Patchogue. The line to Patchogue was open for service by spring 1869. A year earlier, Southampton together with Brookhaven began negotiating with the SSRR to bring the line farther east.

Thoroughly alarmed at this development, the LIRR stepped into the picture and offered to build its projected branch line from Manorville to Eastport and then on to Southampton, Bridgehampton, and Sag Harbor. At that point, the SSRR abandoned its plans to build east of Patchogue and Southampton agreed to help finance the LIRR's branch line, much of which ran through the town. The loser in this sudden turn of events was Brookhaven whose villages between Patchogue and Eastport were abandoned. The line reached Southampton in April 1870. It was a result, if anything, of the cutthroat competition for control of Long Island's railroads rather than of any process of rational planning by Southampton or anyone else.

One further point might be added. By the late 1860s, Long Island towns and villages were falling over themselves to attract a railroad through or near their communities, the long-term benefits of which were apparent to all. The least of their concerns was any marginal private profit that might be made from the sale of lands for a right-of-way. Some may have anticipated a windfall gain—Easthampton landowners were particularly hopeful in the 1880s when the LIRR's Montauk extension was surveyed—but most were simply happy to have a line planned for their neighborhood. The historian par excellence of the Long Island Railroad, Vincent Seyfried, notes that in Brookhaven Town such was the "popular enthusiasm" that the inhabitants actually donated rights-of-way and even depot buildings.[70] Promotional campaigns by townsmen and merchants were mounted in all the South Shore villages from Moriches to Sag Harbor as well as in Easthampton. Again, none of this had been seriously anticipated in the 1850s. In any case, the Southampton proprietors were by that time quite secure in the knowledge that they, and not the Shinnecock, had ultimate control over the Hills. Any benefit from a projected railroad would accrue to them, whether the Hills were formally divided or not. The 1703 lease could not protect the Shinnecock from that undeniable fact. The relevant document was the 1703 deed, not the lease. The reasons underlying the request for a legislative partition of the Hills must then be looked for elsewhere. The LIRR, of course, could have insisted on negotiating with the Shinnecock in order to comply with state law, but it did not or chose not to.

As far back as 1824, the proprietors had begun to explore the possibility of dividing the Hills with the Shinnecock. The proprietors were now a distinct body with their own incorporated trustees under an act of the legislature as discussed previously, a result of the agreement with representatives of the town in 1818 to retain their interests in the common lands while giving in exchange full control and management of the waters and their products to the town trustees. This had followed several years of acrimonious dispute in which a growing number of townsmen who were not proprietors had maintained that the town trustees, all of whom had always been proprietors, had established a complete monopoly of the annual revenues from the common lands and the waters entirely for their own benefit. After this historic split, the proprietors, or rather what were now the trustees of the proprietors, did not withdraw from town affairs but, for the first time, were free to pursue their collective interests without thought to the constraints of public opinion. One of their first priorities was dealing with the Shinnecock Hills and Shinnecock Neck. Tensions with the Indians had not relaxed since the early 1800s. There had been complaints, suits, petty aggravations, and heavy-handed efforts by the proprietors to charge the Shinnecock for the use of the land they were already paying a quitrent on. James Bunn, for instance, was charged six dollars in 1822 for the privilege of pasturing his cows in the Neck and required to post security for the payment. He evidently failed to provide either and the following year Abraham Rose, as a committee to prosecute, was authorized to bring charges against Bunn and one other. It seemed to have become an annual round of small and needless harassments. The Shinnecock themselves were no doubt perfectly capable of provoking the proprietors when it suited them (Bunn in their experience was perhaps no easy man to deal with), but they were in a permanently weak position and vulnerable to any action the proprietors might choose to take.

Yet evidently precipitated by this action of the proprietors, James Bunn and others filed a complaint with the state legislature. In it they claimed the Shinnecock to be the "right and lawful owners" of the Shinnecock Hills and then proceeded to enumerate several grievances. First, that voting in the annual Shinnecock trustee elections was controlled by the town with the effect of excluding "almost the whole of us" from exercising the rights guaranteed by the 1793 trusteeship act. Second, that the Shinnecock have "allowed" the townspeople to enclose meadowland "for their convenience," land that "they now pretend to claim as theirs by possession" but that also was land cultivated by the Shinnecock. Third, the petition complained of illegal impounding of Shinnecock cattle, trespassing on Indian fields, and raised the issue of their right to gather seaweed on the shores of the bays. Finally, the petitioners asked that the trusteeship law be amended to provide for the appointment of a clerk to manage their own trustee affairs "without being under the control of the justices."[71] Of most interest here is that as early as 1822, before any attempts were made by the Southampton proprietors to gain unencumbered possession of the Hills, at least some of the Shinnecock were prepared to argue that the 1703 lease was no lease at all but in effect a deed and that they, the Indians, were the "right and lawful owners" of this land.

Nothing seemed to come of this petition (legislators did not descend on the Hills) but matters again came to a head in 1824, and the subject of dividing the Hills was for the first time presented to the Shinnecock. General Abraham Rose, a former town trustee and president of the new proprietor trustees between 1818 and 1821, David Rose, his cousin and the town supervisor during those key years as well as the president of the proprietor trustees (1822–1827), and James Post, then the town supervisor (1822–1828) and a powerful force among the proprietors (he was clerk to the proprietor trustees 1824–1854), were appointed a committee in October to meet with the Shinnecock "& agree, if they can, to divide the Indian Land with them."[72] How it was to be divided, or on what terms, was not recorded. The Shinnecock, presumably through their trustees, must not have reacted favorably for the following June the committee paid them another visit but only to report, "they did no business." As is evident, the committee was a powerful one consisting of well-known and highly respected men both in the town and among the proprietors. Abraham Rose had been one of the principal architects of the compromise of 1818 and had led the committee of proprietors that reached a final agreement with a town committee to separate their interests from those of the town trustees. Having become the first president of the new corporation of proprietor trustees after 1818 he resumed that position in 1828 and served in that capacity until 1842. David Rose was also on that 1818 proprietor committee (opposing the town's committee) even though he was town supervisor at the time.

This was, if anything was, an indication of the separation of the two governmental functions in Southampton: that of town administration headed by the supervisor and of the town trustees controlled by the proprietors. In consequence, there was no perceived conflict of interest between Rose's role as supervisor and his membership on a committee of what was then still a board of trustees under proprietor control. This separation of powers became even more marked after 1818 when the proprietors no longer controlled the election of town trustees and withdrew as candidates. Nor was he the last Rose to be a key member of the proprietors also to serve as supervisor. His son, David Rogers Rose, was elected in the late 1830s and 1840s, as similarly was Abraham Rose's son, Maltbie Gelston Rose. After him, Edwin Rose, a cousin to Maltbie, was elected on no fewer than five occasions between 1841 and 1861. And James Post, town clerk between 1812 and 1821, succeeded David Rose as town supervisor in 1822 until 1827, and also became clerk to the proprietor trustees in 1824. He remained in that capacity for the next thirty years until, after a brief interlude, he was followed by his son, Edwin Post.[73] Abraham Rose, David Rose, and James Post: It was, it is hard not to conclude, a committee of big men that met with the Indians.

Unwilling to accept the apparent prevarication of the Shinnecock, the committee approached them again in 1826 but before doing so consulted an attorney. Between February and April the proprietor trustees met on several occasions to determine what they should do. They carried the 1703 lease and other papers to Hull Osborn, the attorney for the proprietors at the time and subsequently, and requested that he give an opinion of them in writing at the next meeting. His opinion was not recorded; but at the next meeting in March, they asked for his advice on the legality of fencing Shinnecock Neck along "the Old Ditch" while at the same time continuing with its usual spring construction. James Post, in charge of fencing, was to stop if Osborn's opinion was negative. Then in April, buried among some routine matters regarding the viewing and sale of some land and the leasing of meadow lots, the trustees reached a consensus on the Shinnecock issue. Evidently, Osborn had said that there was nothing in the lease to prevent the proprietors approaching the Shinnecock with a view to partitioning, or anything illegal in the event of such a partition, for the trustees voted to go ahead. Abraham Rose was in the chair. It was agreed that it was "the sense of this Meeting . . . that if the Indians will take Shinecock from the Tubs at Heady Creek, west to Box Cove all the land to the southward & give up to the Proprietors the other Indian land to the use of the said Proprietors if the Proprietors shall agree to it & approve of it at a Proprietor's meeting." Later in the meeting, the trustees voted that "if the Indians will agree we will give them all Shinecock Neck as it is now fenced."[74]

So they had fenced it in anyway perhaps anticipating objections to partition from the Shinnecock leadership. And it is obvious there were objections. Negotiations must have collapsed, for two weeks later cattle were to go on the Neck at the usual rate. James Post was to take them in and Thomas Reeves hired as overseer. But it looked very much like a provocation. Normally, cattle were put on the Neck at the beginning of November after the growing season, and that had been the case until 1824, but at the end of 1825, the trustees decided to take them on in the spring. The views of the Shinnecock at the time cannot be known—their records contain nothing except annual election results after 1822 and are missing after 1835 until 1880—but there can be little doubt that the proprietors' proposal and subsequent action met with consternation.[75]

There is nothing in the proprietor trustees' own records to indicate that they approached the Shinnecock again for many years after this failure. Given how detailed and meticulous these records were, it would be surprising if the trustees had in fact raised the issue and not reported it. But after 1826 and throughout the 1830s, the only references to the Hills are quite ordinary and relate to pasturing, fencing, the hiring out of fifties and the like. But in 1843, the trustees renewed their efforts to persuade the Indians to give up the Hills in exchange for the Neck. Abraham Rose had stepped down as president the year before, after fifteen years, and took no part in the negotiations. He died a year later, over a decade before the final pressure for a deal was applied to the Shinnecock. Abraham Rose, more than any other proprietor trustee, had born the main responsibility since the 1820s for the attempt to restructure relationships with the Shinnecock over the question of the Hills. John P. Osborn was the new president while James Post continued as clerk. In one of his first acts, Osborn appointed a committee of himself, Selden Foster, another former and future town supervisor, and David Rogers Rose, the nephew of Abraham Rose, to confer with the Shinnecock "to see if they can agree on the division of the Hills and the Neck and have it confirmed by the next Legislature."[76] This was the first mention of possible legislative action. At the same proprietor meeting, Osborn apparently obtained an interim agreement with the Indian trustees that for a term of six years some division should be made on the existing fence line whereby the Shinnecocks would "improve the south half" and the proprietors the north. Where earlier the proprietors had put most of their emphasis on the value of Shinnecock Neck (and had done so since the seventeenth century), now and since the 1820s they turned their attention to the rest of the Hills. With the Shinnecock increasingly in residence south of the fence they very likely concluded that the Neck, apart from its fringe of divided meadow, was lost. Besides, the Hills and Sebonac contained 3,200 acres and a variety of terrain and vegetation and perhaps had become a larger prize. Shinnecock Neck contained roughly eight hundred acres.

But then again the issue dropped from sight and did not resurface until December 1848. If the interim agreement remained in force, it was set to expire the following spring. Osborn, Post, and another of the many Roses earlier referred to, Maltbie G. Rose, who was to become president of the trustees a few years later, were to be a committee "to get all the information they can respecting our rights in the Indian land, and to get counsel on the same and to try to find out how we can improve our rights."[77] This fleeting and altogether tantalizing reference is nowhere followed up in the proprietor trustees' book, but it seems to raise two questions: What were they to do after the agreement expired? Did they have any legal rights in the Indian land other than the proprietary rights they had always legitimately exercised under the terms of the 1703 lease agreement? In the 1820s, Hull Osborn evidently had counseled that they did, but if the Hills were ever to become a subject for legislation, the trustees needed to be certain that they and not the town trustees were the legal body to bring the matter before the legislature. Unfortunately, they left no record of what if anything they learned of their rights in the Hills, but it can be assumed they concluded that they could legally proceed according to plan. After this, the proprietors began to exert steady pressure on the Shinnecock to divide the Neck and the Hills. In each year after 1849 they sent out committees to confer with them on the issue. But there were obvious, although unreported, problems with the negotiations that lasted seven or eight years; each spring the committee of the trustees returned from Shinnecock Neck empty handed.

Grazing livestock and fencing the Neck meanwhile continued unabated and with it the associated grievances and complaints which had become habitual. The trustees had begun to hire out a larger number of pasturage rights in the Neck—as many as thirty fifties each year—substantially increasing the number of cattle on Indian lands. They also leased grazing rights for cash in separate transactions. In 1853, Austin Rose, a trustee himself, paid $30 for the right to pasture his sheep throughout the Hills even though the Shinnecock had allotted "part of said land for planting without fencing." Several Shinnecock men seized the sheep and held them in a standoff with Rose. Rose filed a complaint through his cousin, Abraham T. Rose, the well-known county judge and Bridgehampton attorney, and took the Shinnecocks to court. The proprietor trustees for their part resolved to defend Rose against any litigation over trespass or damage resulting from the suit.[78] Ultimately, as might be expected, the Indians lost the case, were denied a motion for a new trial and lost a subsequent appeal. The legal process dragged on for several years at considerable expense to the Shinnecock defendants and was not brought to a conclusion until a year after the Hills were partitioned. The circumstances of the case, however, as well as the various hearings, are instructive both for what they reveal of the quite tense relations between the Shinnecock and the proprietors and the legal approach the proprietors were beginning to employ over the question of the Hills. In general, they indicate that the Shinnecock felt themselves to be under growing pressure and found the overall situation difficult to bear. The impact on the proprietors, on the other hand, appears to have led them to intensify their efforts to gain possession of the Hills and employ increasingly coercive means to achieve that.

In spring 1853, Luther Bunn, James Bunn, Francis Willis and several other Shinnecock men had found 320 sheep and lambs belonging to Austin Rose in a "close" they claimed possession of in unfenced planting fields at Cold Spring. The men rounded them up and held them until Rose was informed of the matter and came in with the county sheriff and had him release the sheep—"wrongfully" as the Bunns later claimed.

The sheep were alleged to have been eating and destroying corn. In his complaint, Rose asked for $5 in damages and $89.75 in costs, noting that the sheep were worth $320. For their part, the defendants demanded the return of the sheep with unspecified damages and costs. The attorney for the Shinnecock was George Miller of Riverhead, a man with long experience of them both in and out of court. He had defended Vincent Cuffee in 1838 in a suit brought by the proprietor trustees against Cuffee for pasturing his cattle and horses on the Hills. That case turned on whether the 1703 lease excepted from its terms the "grass herbage and pasturage" and thus excluded the Shinnecocks from the right to pasture. The court determined that it did and Miller lost the case. The attorneys for the proprietors had been Abraham Rose and S. B. Strong. Strong was then at the bar, but now in 1853 he was a county circuit judge and found the Austin Rose suit on his docket. That certainly did not augur well for the Indians concerned.[79]

This case also turned on the construction of the 1703 lease but, as it turned out, in a much more far-reaching way. It came to trial in August 1854 before a jury although Judge Strong subsequently dismissed the jury and rendered his own verdict without benefit of its opinion. It had been agreed between the attorneys of both parties that only two issues should be considered in the trial. First, whether the lease gave the defendants—the Shinnecock—the right to plough and plant in the Hills. And second, given that the lease gave the proprietors the right to pasture throughout the Hills, including in the ploughed fields of the Indians, whether the right to plough and plant carried with it an obligation of the Shinnecock to fence their fields. This question—the obligations of the respective parties to fence the leased premises—was to be settled at the trial. It was, but the ensuing judgment went against the Indians. Judge Strong said that in general anyone claiming a right in the land of another must adopt any requisite measures of protection "as it respects the general owner." In this particular case he argued that it could be inferred from both the 1687 and 1703 leases that the burden of fencing was expected to devolve on the Shinnecock. In 1687, the lease provided that they shall "get make and maintain a good five rail fence." The 1703 lease granted to the Shinnecock timber for fencing, implying, Strong said, that "they were to make some fences, and those would not be a security for any other than the fence around the lands under cultivation." For good measure, he continued, the lease stipulated that the Shinnecock could not keep any part of the land within fence between the end of October and the first of April. If the proprietors were to be responsible for building and maintaining fences, this restriction on the Shinnecock would not have been necessary. In finding for Austin Rose, Strong concluded that in failing to fence their crops at Cold Spring the Shinnecock defendants were negligent. "(W)hatever damage was caused wholly or partly by such negligence," he thought, "it gave them no right to distrain the plaintiff's cattle."

However, perhaps to give the appearance of greater legal weight to his conclusion, Strong embarked on a line of reasoning that went considerably beyond the arguments and testimony as they had been presented in court. It so incensed George Miller that he demanded a new trial. Strong began by saying that whatever rights were conveyed to the Shinnecock by the lease were inconsiderable. It did not convey the entire or even the principal use of the property, reserving its primary use to the proprietors. And in no sense did it convey any title to it. The fee of the land rested fully with the proprietors. What remained to the Shinnecock was what he described as in the nature of "incorporeal hereditaments," marginal rights to raise summer crops and cut timber. But on the question of title, Strong went far further than the case technically permitted him and raised issues that Miller clearly thought were gratuitous. He cast doubt on the validity of the 1703 lease on the grounds that it was merely a grant to several sachems "and their people belonging to Shinnecock." The grantees were not incorporated "nor were they as a body capable of taking the fee to lands." He chose not to question whether in these circumstances the lands could descend to the heirs of the original grantees, but his purpose was quite clear. It was an effort to define the lease as an essentially ephemeral instrument that provided only the most marginal of rights to the lessees.

George Miller called for a new trial in November 1854 shortly after Judge Strong released his opinion. In his affidavit rejecting Strong's opinion, Miller pointed out that neither he nor Abraham Rose had raised or contended the arguments that Strong had latterly introduced. In fact, he said, he had been "taken utterly and entirely by surprise" and had no indication until the close of the trial that they might be an issue. In rebuttal he referred to a recent case which he had had the satisfaction of winning on behalf of the Shinnecock. In 1850, two suits were brought by Shinnecock men against several townsmen—one of them by Luther Bunn—for removing seaweed heaped up on the shores of Shinnecock Bay.[80] The counsel for the defense, Abraham Rose, argued that the seaweed was rightfully the property of his clients and that the beach in question belonged to the freeholders and commonalty of the town. (He did not mention that the shores belonged to the proprietors). Additionally, the town trustees from time to time routinely regulated the heaping up and removal of seaweed as a function of their authority over the products of the waters. Judge McCoun, the presiding justice in the case, rejected this argument and turned to the 1703 lease for support. His decision affirmed the Shinnecock leasehold title to the shores on Shinnecock and Peconic Bays as within the boundaries of the lease, thus giving them the right to remove seaweed and other "drift stuff." The judge ruled that the Shinnecock were "the absolute owners for the term of the lease of the whole territory within its bounds from high water mark" on the bays, except for tracts of salt meadow, and subject to the rights of the proprietors to pasture. The Shinnecock as "owners of the soil" retained "the right of accretion." This interpretation and ruling was in marked contrast to the opinion handed down by Judge Strong four years later. But McCoun's decision and interpretation of the lease was widely ignored. When the seaweed question came up in the 1860s as a dispute between the town trustees and the proprietor trustees, no reference at all was made to the Shinnecock right of accretion as established by McCoun. The Shinnecocks did attempt to bring it up themselves much later in the 1880s but with no success. By that time—after the 1859 partition of the Hills—the only shoreline they possessed was on Shinnecock Neck and much of that was salt meadow in private hands.

But George Miller's spirited application for a new trial was denied and his only recourse proved to be an appeal against the judgment of damages and costs amounting to $94.75. Several appeals were filed in Supreme Court between 1857 and 1860, none of them successful, while the costs kept rising. Ultimately, when the original judgment was affirmed in April 1860, the defendants had been cumulatively assessed $254.51 in costs, damages, and interest. Luther Bunn was required to swear out an affidavit to the effect that his assets were worth $500. But the real damage to the Shinnecock lay in the nature of Judge Strong's assertions in respect to the 1703 lease, that it afforded only marginal or insignificant rights and protections and that in no sense did the Shinnecock have any sustainable fee to the lands on the Hills. It left them in a thoroughly weakened position, one appeal after another denied and each affirming Strong's position. If anything encouraged the proprietors to push for a final resolution of the status of the Hills, it was this. At a moment when the Shinnecock were enmeshed in what must have appeared as a failing appeals process, the proprietors moved in with a new proposal to divide the Hills. Nor were they particularly fastidious about it. In late 1858, a committee of the proprietor trustees came on the Neck armed with a petition and looking for signatures. For the Shinnecock it could not have come at a worse time.

CHAPTER 7

PARTITION AND SALE OF THE HILLS

I: 1859–1861

The new president of the proprietor trustees in 1858 was Edwin Rose. He had just replaced his cousin, Maltbie Rose, and had plenty of experience in town government. His first act was to appoint a committee of himself, Austin Rose, and Jonathan Fithian "to treat with the Indians upon the subject of a Division of interest and if no agreement is made before the 1st day of November next then to remove the fence from the Neck."[1] This was also a prestigious committee, like its predecessors since the 1820s, and perhaps one calculated to put the maximum pressure on the Shinnecock. Jonathan Fithian had been town supervisor since 1856 and was also a justice of the peace, as was Rose. At this time, Fithian was clerk to the proprietor trustees. Rose himself had briefly served out a term as supervisor some years earlier, had been re-elected twice, and was elected again in 1859 and also in 1861. Although Austin Rose was, if nothing else—he held no town office—a member of a powerful family and a farmer of considerable means. He also had soundly beaten the Shinnecock in court. These were the men who made the final approach to the Indians, negotiated with them through the year, and presented a final report to the trustees in December. According to much later testimony given by other Shinnecocks, the negotiations were not pretty.

At a special meeting just before Christmas, the committee reported that "they had made a bargain" by which the proprietors would convey the Neck in fee simple and the Shinnecock would "release to the Proprietors the residue of the Indian lands."[2] The line of division was to be along the fence line or the Indian ditch extending from Heady Creek to Old Fort Pond. There was no mention at all of a petition to the state legislature to have this agreement formally approved, but in fact two copies of such a petition had already been signed by both parties and forwarded to Albany. It was a petition "praying for the passage confirming an exchange of lands" and was in a committee of the assembly by January 7, 1859. The twelve proprietor trustees signed one copy; while the other was signed by twenty-two members of the Shinnecock. The rationale for dividing the lands was that it would put an end to the long-standing differences between the two groups. The petition recognized that the agreement could not be consummated without the consent of the legislature, as it required the Shinnecock to surrender the one thousand-year lease in return for the reconveyance of a certain portion of the lands covered by it. The trustees of the proprietors, and not any other corporate body, were explicitly to effect this re-conveyance. Under these terms it was passed into law.

The full title of the legislation was "An Act to enable the Shinecock tribe of Indians to exchange certain rights in land with the trustees of the proprietors of the common and undivided lands and marshes in the town of Southampton" and was passed on March 16, 1859. It was to take effect immediately. The preamble to the act was more explicit than the petition had been in explaining the reasons behind the proposed separation of interests. In part, it said:

> (T)he rights of said tribe of Indians and said trustees of said proprietors are of such a nature as to be conflicting, and have become the cause of frequent and expensive litigation, and render the improvement of the land far less valuable than the same would be if equitably divided and improved in severalty; and whereas, a verbal agreement and arrangement has been entered into . . . for the full and clear release each to the other, of all their rights on either side of an established and well defined line, to the end that each may improve and own in severalty all the land on their side of said line."[3]

The legislation also expressly stated that, although the Indians occupied Shinnecock Neck "and are living therein as a tribe, subject to certain rights of pasturage," the true owners were the trustees of the proprietors. "The fee of the land," it said, "is in said trustees" as were other lands "held in the same manner." The legislators evidently had not recognized that this assertion could be construed as in conflict with the terms of the town's patent of 1686 that had assigned the administration of all the lands of the town to its trustees. The proprietors held equitable rights in the land in question, and individual rights of commonage, but the town in this case possessed a prior right inasmuch as its corporate trustees had entered into a lease agreement with its occupants. Moreover, the legal rights of the town to all town lands, descending first from the crown and later affirmed by the state, raises the question of whether any other groups or individuals within or outside the town could enter into land agreements with the Indians. It was certainly in conflict with the Duke's Laws, laws that had never been essentially discarded.[4]

Scarcely a month after the act had passed, the trustees of the proprietors drew up an indenture agreement with the Shinnecock trustees—Stephen Walker, David Bunn, and Wickham Cuffee, all of whom had apparently signed the original petition to Albany—finalizing the separation of their respective interests.[5] The Shinnecock were to have the Neck, as agreed to, and the proprietors would take possession of the Shinnecock Hills, Sebonac Neck, and also Ram Island in Bull Head Bay. Several years earlier there had been some discussion of whether Ram Island was "inside" the Indian Line or to the east of it. If it was to the east, the sedges on its shores were then to be advertised for sale. Whether the proprietors hired them out or not is uncertain, but by including them in the indenture the trustees probably wanted to establish decisively the island's status as proprietor land to avoid any possible future controversy. Given such a meticulous interest in the details of the lands they were to obtain, it is a little surprising that they paid no attention to the Shinnecock Meadows, the narrow fringe of salt grass bordering Shinnecock Neck. This had been divided in the seventeenth century and the lots had been privately owned since then. But they are not mentioned. They had been reserved from the 1703 lease, protecting the interests of individual allottees, but were not mentioned in the 1859 legislation or in the ensuing indenture agreement. The issue was not resolved until the middle of the twentieth century when the need for salt hay had largely disappeared.

Years later, probably in 1885 in preparation for a suit challenging the right of the proprietors to sell the Hills, an affidavit was signed by twelve Shinnecocks alleging that the signatures to the petition were forged. Some names were signed by others unknown to the tribe, some were already dead, some minors, and others who were alive at the time later denied signing it at all. It was included in testimony relating to the Shinnecock at hearings held in 1900 at New York by the subcommittee of the Senate Committee on Indian Affairs. Three of the signatories to the affidavit also testified at the hearings. One of them, David Killes, a young man in 1858 and later a Shinnecock trustee, was asked directly if the signatures were forged. Killes responded that he "remember(ed) the day when Capt. Lewis Scott, Austin Rose, and Capt. Jetur Rose drove on the reservation. They said the petition is going down to Albany tomorrow, and he said to my father, 'Are you going to sign it?' He said 'I told you I would never sign it.' He said 'Luther' (my uncle), 'are you going to sign it?' He said, 'I never will sign it;' but they forged the names and put them on."[6] James L. Cuffee, a Shinnecock trustee at the time, testified that Austin Rose asked him to sign the petition but that he had refused. His name nonetheless appeared on it along with those of seven other Cuffees, including that of his uncle. Other testimony supported these allegations. The most revealing aspect of it is simply that possibly a majority of the Shinnecock (it cannot be documented), for all the peace outright ownership of the Neck might give them and despite the outcome of the Austin Rose trial, did not want to give up the Hills. Partition would cut them off from access to needed resources from timber to seaweed, sharply curtail hunting, and mean the final end to any settlement at Sebonac. The only gain would seem to be freedom from the annual depredations of loose cattle, yet now they would need to maintain year-round fencing without any help from the proprietors. It was not a good deal for them, and it is perhaps astonishing that the legislature never took the trouble to enquire further if their petition fully reflected their wishes and needs, or if, indeed, it was a genuine petition in the first place.[7] As for those signatures on the petition, if Killes and others are to be believed, 1859 looked like a reprise of 1703.

The proprietors had now finally got their hands on something they had coveted for thirty-five years, and in the process succeeded in confining the Shinnecock to a small preserve of land. Valuable although it had been to them, they could well afford to cede the Neck. There was no apparent outcry in the town. George White's may have been the lone voice of protest. In fact, it is quite likely that the legislative triumph of the proprietor trustees was popularly accepted. For one thing it solved the problem of the Shinnecock. They were now conveniently confined to a smaller area of land in which few besides a limited number of farmers had any interest. And the general view of the Shinnecock in the town was one of indifference even contempt. William Pelletreau, who was shortly to become town clerk in 1862, later wrote that "nobility of character" was a virtue that novelists attributed to "the aborigines on our soil" [sic]. He himself thought, "if anything of this has descended to their posterity the writer during a long and intimate acquaintance has wholly failed to perceive it."[8] In more polished phrases than were usually heard it summed up the opinion of the time.[9] Second, the status of the Hills was hardly a matter to incite much concern. It had been a proprietor domain since the seventeenth century and the majority of inhabitants had never had anything more than limited and sharply restricted access to it. The legislation and subsequent agreement with the Indians was therefore a proprietor matter, and most casual readings of the earlier 1818 legislation assigning rights in the common lands to the proprietors would have confirmed that. If anything suggests that the town received the news of legislative partition with less than equanimity, it might be found in the fact that Edwin Rose, president of the proprietor trustees and a principal architect of the solution to the Hills problem, was elected town supervisor two weeks after the legislation was enacted. He also was elected justice of the peace.

The issue of whether the proprietors had any legal right to petition the legislature for the abrogation of the lease as a means to partition the Hills then never surfaced in the immediate aftermath, and perhaps there was little or any understanding of it at the time.[10] The standard histories of Southampton, written much later and after the Hills had passed through the hands of a succession of private owners, make not the slightest reference to its questionable legality.[11] George Rogers Howell, however, much later wrote a thoughtful analysis of the issues for the local paper in 1886 shortly after the Hills were sold to the Long Island Improvement Company, Austin Corbin's development vehicle. Howell questioned the right of the proprietor trustees to enter into an agreement with the Shinnecock to cancel a lease they were not even a party to. In 1703, he said, the parties to the lease as well as to the quitclaim deed to all the town's lands including the Shinnecock Hills were the Indians and the trustees of the commonalty. The commonalty, under the town's 1686 patent, included all the inhabitants and not just those with proprietary rights even if the latter at the time were still the clear majority of inhabitants. Howell did not mention that in 1703 a body such as the proprietor trustees did not exist but had been created by state legislation in 1818 as the trustees of the proprietors of the common and undivided lands and marshes, but he certainly would have assumed it and had pronounced on the implications of 1818 before. The relevant legal body in 1703 was that of the town trustees and Howell's point was that it was still so in 1859. The rights of the proprietors in the Shinnecock lands were solely equitable rights, expressed as commonage rights, although the town through its trustees retained the legal right via its quitclaim deed from the Shinnecock and the accompanying lease agreement as well as in virtue of its legal sovereignty over town lands. But the enabling legislation made no reference to the town at all or to the nonproprietors who were now, rather than the proprietors, a majority of the inhabitants.

Howell did point out that there was some vagueness in the wording of the 1703 deed, though not in the lease, regarding for whose "proper use" and "benefit" the town trustees were to hold the land quitclaimed to them by the Indians. They were "each particular Inhabitant of said township according to their Respective appropriated Rights, and ye undivided Land to ye proprietors according to their severall Rights and proportions." Possibly, this was the opening the counsel to the proprietors had seized on to claim legitimacy for the proprietors' actions and the subsequent legislation. Shinnecock was, and always had been undivided land and nobody had previously disputed their rights in it. Nonetheless, Howell concluded that it was "a question for the courts to determine if the agreement of 1859 was not vitiated by this change of name in the parties to the deed, and therefore also whether the sale of 1861 of the hills is not void."[12] At the time of writing, however, Howell ignored one potentially crucial issue, namely that the legislation of 1818 had in effect transferred legal title to all the remaining undivided lands from an existing corporation (the town trustees) to a new one and with it, it has to be inferred, all authority to dispose over them as it wished. This could be held to include the abrogation of any lease entered into by a previous authority. Two weeks later, Howell came around to something like this interpretation.[13] But regardless of interpretation, the division of the Hills never was effectively challenged in the courts, either by the Shinnecock, the town trustees, or any other party who might conceivably gain some benefit from doing so.[14]

However, three members of the Shinnecock did at least attempt to mount a court challenge to the legislation in July three months after it was signed into law. Through George Miller, the Riverhead attorney who was still embroiled in the Austin Rose case, Luther Bunn, James Bunn, and David Bunn filed a complaint in State Supreme Court against both the trustees of the proprietors and the Shinnecock trustees on behalf of themselves and the tribe as a whole. Luther and James Bunn were two of the defendants in the Rose suit.[15] In it the plaintiffs demanded that the court first restrain the trustees of the proprietors from making any attempt to sell or convey any part of the Hills, and second that the legislature be enjoined to repeal the act just passed and immediately cancel the conveyances exchanging the Hills for Shinnecock Neck. Although there is no record that the complaint was ever heard in court, the arguments it presented went well beyond the question Howell later raised in 1886 as to whether the town or the proprietors had the legal authority to petition for the abrogation of the lease, or for that matter, whether the Shinnecock trustees themselves could do so. Essentially, the complaint said that the 1703 lease was not a lease at all but a conveyance in fee simple of the Shinnecock Hills to the Indians in exchange for a confirmation deed to the settlers quitclaiming all the lands of the town, containing, it said, more than 100,000 acres. The "deed or lease" was executed at the same time and was "part of the same transaction." In other words, the commonalty had simply quitclaimed the Hills back to the Shinnecock for a nominal quitrent, excepting from the deed only the tracts of salt meadow that were in private hands.

This, the complaint continued, was "equivalent in its legal effect to a conveyance" in virtue of which the Shinnecock became "the absolute owners" of the premises in question. George Miller did not bring up Judge McCoun's 1850 opinion in respect to this and in support of it but in effect went well beyond it. The deed or lease was subject to the rights of the lessors to remove stone or timber and pasture cattle on areas of the Hills not under cultivation, but these rights were interpreted as "mere easements" and subject to cancellation.

In particular, the right to pasture could be extinguished at any time by simply bringing the whole of the Hills under cultivation. The complaint then turned to the consequences of the 1818 legislation which had created the trustees of the proprietors as a corporate body and conferred on them the right to manage the undivided lands (including the Shinnecock Hills) and the alleged right to dispose of them as property held in common without any consideration of the 1703 agreements. But the plaintiffs charged that, at least in respect to the Shinnecock lands, the legislature in 1859 had completely misunderstood the situation and had inadvisedly passed the act under "an entire misapprehension" that the fee of the land lay with the proprietors. To the contrary, the proprietors "have no valuable interest whatever" in the Hills except for the rights enumerated above which were, again, simply easements.

Yet the complaint ultimately seemed to back away from the direct implication of its principal argument, namely, that the proprietors had no valuable interest and that the true owners were the Shinnecock under a so-called lease that was in reality a conveyance of the lands in fee simple. In a subsidiary argument Miller raised the issue of whether the partition of the land had been equitable and just, as the preamble to the legislation had required, and concluded that it was not. The proprietors had got by far the best of the deal—more than three thousand acres as against six hundred for the Shinnecock—and also had gained three miles of shoreline on the bays where seaweed and other "drift stuff" washed up. Seaweed and other products of the waters, it was expressly claimed, had always been recognized under the 1703 lease as the property of the Indians. This issue was to come up again in 1885 when another suit was contemplated, and was discussed at the time by Howell in his 1886 letter. It played no part, however, in the "seaweed trial" of 1866, which pitted the town trustees against the proprietors over which had the right to the seaweed privilege. But the seaweed question was incidental to the argument, the main thrust of which was that the plaintiffs wanted the legislature, after repealing the act, to authorize a division of the land "that will be commensurate in some degree to the extent of the interests of the respective parties in the said lands." It looked very much like a retreat, for having said that the proprietors had no valuable interest at all, the plaintiffs were now prepared to acknowledge that they did, or at least some partial interest. Perhaps it was George Miller's fallback position, reflecting a realistic assessment that the main argument—powerful and compelling as it was—was unlikely to persuade the legislature or the court. Unfortunately for the Shinnecock it was never put to the test.[16]

But the threat of litigation may have deterred Rose and the proprietors from moving immediately toward advertising a sale. They began a survey of the Hills in mid-1859 in preparation for one at the same time the Shinnecocks were preparing their suit, and probably for that reason postponed going ahead. But a year went by and nothing happened. Finally, in late 1860, judging that no legal threat would materialize or that the courts and the legislature would simply dismiss it, the trustees put the Hills up for sale. This they did in February 1861.

It is difficult not to believe that this had long been the whole purpose behind the effort to get control of the Hills. It is doubtful that the trustees had this in mind in 1824 or 1826 when the question of dividing the Hills was first put on the table. Then the motivation focused entirely on the perennial difficulties they encountered with the Shinnecock. The best solution to that was obviously separation. This continued to be the case up until the 1850s when the pressure to separate began to be increased. But there are several reasons for thinking that the trustees began to shift their views in the late 1850s and to contemplate a sale. First, the value of the land would be bound to increase if the 1703 lease was abrogated and the Shinnecock, as an encumbrance, removed from it once and for all. Second, very little of the Hills was susceptible to division and allotment along the lines of previous practice. It was primarily and always had been common grazing land and there was little else that could be done with it. Whether it was sold or not, commonage rights and their sale would continue to be the principal criterion for access to pasture. In fact, when the Hills were sold—and they were sold to farmers—this practice was continued for another twenty years. The trustees gave absolutely no thought to some possible new use of the land. And, as we saw, the question of the railroad coming through the Hills was still well over the horizon. So division or some projected new activity on the Hills was not in anybody's mind. Thirdly, the trustees had one major buyer in mind or one who would at least put up 20 percent of any future purchase price.

This was Lewis Scott, one of the Rose's North Sea neighbors, and a man of many parts as we saw earlier in the last chapter. Scott was on his way to becoming one of the largest, if not the largest landowner in Southampton, and by 1860 had accumulated twenty fifties in proprietor or commonage rights in the Town Purchase as well (all of that lying east of Canoe Place). This made him a major stockholder in the proprietors' company, there being a total of 155 such rights in that purchase alone. Surprisingly perhaps, Scott had never been elected to the proprietor trustees' board, although he was to be in 1862 and remained a member until his death in 1888. He was part of that same board that sold Mecox Bay and other lands under water in 1882. But Scott in the 1850s had been in bad odor with the trustees for some time. In 1853, he was to be prosecuted for occupying land at Sebonac that the proprietors claimed to be common land, that is, their own land. Even in 1859, after the legislative triumph of the trustees in which Scott himself played no small a part, he was to be sued for trespass on common lands. A committee was appointed to view common lands across from Scott's own North Sea lot and prosecute him for trespass if he refused to pay "a reasonable price" for them. He was not an easy man to deal with, as the Shinnecock had found out for themselves in the course of the negotiations over the petition to separate their interest in the Hills in 1858. Lewis Scott was one of the three men later identified as coming on Shinnecock Neck to force the issue through. Scott's involvement, the only non-trustee named, suggests that there was a good deal more to the petition than the simple division of the Hills and the Neck to relieve the accumulated tensions between the parties concerned.

Some weeks after the indenture with the Shinnecock was recorded the proprietor trustees charged a committee with making a complete survey of the whole property now indisputably in their hands. This appeared to be leading to an imminent sale and certainly would have had to be undertaken if the Hills were to be sold. But no such sale took place for well over a year very probably as a result of the threatened suit by the Bunns. In the interim there was much discussion among the trustees of who were to be the prospective purchasers. Besides Scott, one-third of their own number had committed, or were in the process of committing themselves, to buying out the proprietors. Ultimately, of the twenty-two members of the new company that purchased the Shinnecock Hills in 1861 four of them were proprietor trustees: Austin and David R. Rose, Edward White, and George O. Post. This is not a particularly striking proportion, but even a superficial look at the other eighteen names reveals many family connections. There was another Post, two members of the Foster family related by marriage to the Posts, of whom one of them, Isaac Post Foster, was later elected to the proprietor trustees. Jetur Rose, David R. Rose's son, who had gone with Austin Rose and Scott petition in hand to Shinnecock Neck, also bought in. The Whites of Sebonac were also well represented by Edward and Peter White—Edward White was David Rose's brother-in-law—while two prominent North Sea families, the Jennings and the Harris families, accounted for four of the twenty-two eventual purchasers. Both later were also represented on the proprietor trustees' board. Besides these, there were Sayres, Jaggers, Bishops, and Burnetts. It was a cohesive group, all of them successful farmers and proprietors, but clearly dominated by North Sea men, especially the Roses, Scotts, Harris's, Whites, and Jennings, the same North Sea interests that had controlled the proprietors since early in the century.

This group was evidently firmly in place by late 1860. In January 1861, the trustees, probably convinced by then that the Indian complaint would come to nothing, resolved to advertise for sale at public auction the Shinnecock Hills, Sebonac Neck, Ram Island, the common sedges at Sebonac, as well as the South Beach meadows.[17] The last two had never been part of the Indian land but were proprietor lands and were simply thrown into the sale. They excluded from the sale the allotted meadows and marshes at Shinnecock Neck, an item that had been oddly missing as excepted from the 1859 indenture agreement with the Shinnecock, as well as those bordering Cold Spring Bay. Both were in private hands. The auction notice, published in the *Sag Harbor Corrector*—the only local paper of the time—a scant three days before the sale itself, was careful to state that title to the property was "now undisputed and indisputable"; that the claims and interests of the Indians had been extinguished by mutual agreement and that this had all been ratified by the legislature. It also noted that a good part of the land was "ready for the plough and susceptible of being converted into fine farms" while the remainder was well adapted to sheep and cattle grazing. Those persons, it went on, "desirous of establishing themselves in the sheep-growing business would do well to examine this property." The terms of purchase were to be liberal and would be made known on the day of the sale.[18]

It was scheduled for February 19 (a bare three days after the auction notice) at the house of Captain Charles Howell where the trustees always met. Rose and Fithian were "to carry the sale into effect," neither of whom were to be principals or participants in it. At the same January meeting, the trustees agreed on minimum prices for the various properties: the Hills and Sebonac Neck were to be bid in at no less than $4,500; Ram Island and Sebonac sedges at not less than $400; and the meadows at South Beach for at least $500. As it turned out, they were to be pleasantly surprised, unless, as is probable, they knew the outcome in advance. How this auction was conducted will remain forever unclear, or how public it was. It was not reported. But the *Corrector*, in its February 23 issue, did report that the property was bought by "L. Scott and a company" thus dispelling any notion that the sale was anything less than prearranged. Perhaps only Scott and a few interested bystanders attended, the business concluded in a few minutes amid mutual congratulations. The Hills came in at $6,250, nearly $2,000 more than the agreed on minimum; Ram Island and its neighboring sedges sold for $476; and South Beach for $535. A month later, a warranty deed for $6,726 was signed (it did not include the South Beach purchase) and the trustees declared a dividend for all proprietors holding rights in the Town Purchase amounting to $5,011.42 or $32 a share or fifty right.

So it was all fixed. But a more important question is why the proprietor trustees, having gained the Hills after so many years of effort, went to the considerable trouble and expense of essentially selling them back to a group consisting largely of themselves and their close associates. One reasonable explanation is that they were unsure of title and feared that the Shinnecocks might some day again threaten to sue them over the issue of the abrogation of the lease and the legislative loss of the Hills. By selling the Hills (at a public auction) to what could be claimed to be an independent group of new proprietors, they may have hoped to forestall any future legal challenge, their claim of title—"undisputed and indisputable"—now buttressed by a warranty deed that was duly recorded at the county seat.

There also may have been a further and more immediate factor involved. There had been a developing dispute with the town since the late 1850s over the proprietors' annual sale of the seaweed privilege on the shores of both sides of the Hills. Seaweed was particularly abundant on the bays and was a valuable commodity the harvesting of which always had been closely regulated. The town alleged that these were products of the waters and were therefore to be managed by the town trustees under the terms of the 1818 legislation relating to the waters of the town and the common lands. For some reason this issue had been neglected after the 1820s, and the proprietor trustees had either continued or resumed the practice of hiring out the seaweed much as they annually sold the common grass. In 1860, the town trustees took the proprietors to court. In 1861, after the conclusion of the annual town elections and little more than a month after the Hills sale, the town voted $500 for the legal defense of its interests in the waters adjoining the Hills and the right of the inhabitants to go freely on those shores to collect seaweed.[19] Edwin Rose, who had so recently presided over the auction sale and at this same town meeting had just been elected supervisor, and—in that new capacity—had entertained the resolution to protect the town's interests, may have experienced some slight twinge of embarrassment at this turn of events.

Yet it had all been predicted in advance, and Rose might have taken some comfort in the knowledge that the Hills, now no longer under the jurisdiction of the proprietor trustees, were at last in private hands and thus presumably beyond the legal reach of the town and its trustees. In this he was only partly correct for the town, new ownership of the Hills aside, went after the proprietors rather than Scott and his company. Nevertheless, in 1860 the proprietor trustees had already girded themselves for a suit and this was a probable additional motivation to conclude a sale. That April, they had hired out the shore on both sides of the Hills "for the purpose of getting seaweed" and decided that if the suit went against them, they were prepared "to defend the privilege of the several purchasers." That they would not give up without a fight is indicated by a reference in the auction notice the following year to the five or six miles of waterfront the property on both bays possessed and the ensuing value of its fishing and seaweed privileges. New ownership, however, did not deter the town. Scott et al continued to hire out the seaweed for a purely nominal fee (a precaution perhaps) after taking over, but were confronted by the town in 1862 with new efforts to wrest control of the products of the waters around the Hills. Another $500 was appropriated for the town trustees to defend the rights the town "may have in and to the waters, fisheries and seaweed, and productions of the waters, adjoining the land on Shinnecock Hills lately sold by the Proprietors . . ."[20] Meanwhile, the town trustees themselves began leasing the seaweed privilege. In 1862, they collected $80.66 in fees, continuing the practice for several years while at the same time pursuing their suit. Yet in the end, the strategy of the proprietor trustees appeared to succeed but for unanticipated reasons. New ownership did not remove the Hills from the jurisdiction of the town in respect to the waters but still, in 1866, the town trustees lost its suit against the proprietors and the right to recover its products anyway.

There were complexities in the case that need not be examined in detail here, but the key question related to the ownership of the shores. It was over this issue that the town trustees lost the case as the court did not take up the town's rights to the waters under the 1818 legislation. The proprietors had sold the Hills from "water bound to water bound" but whether or not the shores or beaches of the town were proprietor land was open to challenge. Previously, in 1850, they had been declared Shinnecock land but that was before the abrogation of the 1703 lease. The town claimed they were public or town land and constituted a public highway with free access to all inhabitants. If they were a public highway, then all that was cast up on them—gravel, seaweed and the like—belonged to the town and was under the management of the town trustees. The court, however, found for the proprietors. The shores were common and not public land and products found on them belonged to the proprietors. This went well beyond the 1818 legislation dividing the interests of the town and proprietors, but was not conclusively settled until 1892.

At that time, the town trustees sued Frederic Betts over his claim of ownership of the beach at Agawam, which his brother had purchased from the proprietor trustees in 1881. Although Betts partially won that case—his property was to extend as far as the mean high tide mark—the town trustees, on appeal, were able to establish that land at the beach was nonetheless a public highway. A year later the town trustees reached an agreement with the Long Island Improvement Company, the then owners of the Shinnecock Hills after Scott and his associates had sold out in 1881, in which they reserved rights to "all necessary highways" above high water mark on the shores of Shinnecock Bay and Peconic Bay. But thirty years had passed, through many of which the seaweed privilege had been routinely farmed out by Scott and his fellow Shinnecock proprietors. At the conclusion of the 1866 litigation, they lotted off both bays for the purpose. And in 1868, they retained counsel to recover the revenues the town had collected from the sale of seaweed between 1862 and 1866. Scott was nothing if not a good businessman. He recovered $200 from the town trustees in back payments. It certainly appears as if the proprietors had less to worry about in 1861 than they had originally thought.

Immediately after the sale in 1861 the trustees lost no time in declaring a dividend. It was executed on the same day in March as the deed of sale. The new proprietors—a group of tenants in common merely and not yet for some years an incorporated body—could not expect to extract any more revenue from the Hills, or any additional use of them, than could the old proprietors. This was still 1861. The railroad was as yet undreamed of, let alone any new or different development of the Hills, and all that Scott and his associates could look forward to was the continuation of a regimen of pasturing sheep and cattle that had been in existence since the late 1600s. These proprietors, now owning the fee of the land, went about business in much the same customary way as had their predecessors. They were much more concerned, however, to put it on a paying basis and operate it as an efficient capitalist enterprise. Selling the sedges and leasing out the seaweed privilege was much the most lucrative of the new organization's activities. By the late 1860s, the profit from these natural and renewable resources never totaled less than $200 a year.

The group was organized as the Proprietors of Shinnecock Hills and Sebonack Sedges, a company that issued fifty shares of stock (or, following past practice, fifties) divided among 22 subscribers. Lewis Scott purchased nine shares, the largest number, while most of the other members of the company purchased no more than one or two. The three Roses—David, Austin, and Jetur—between them held ten shares, ensuring that they and Scott effectively held a majority interest with 40 percent of the stock. These four men dominated the five-member board of trustees throughout the 1860s and 1870s, all of them serving as president at one time or another, and were ultimately responsible for engineering the 1881 sale of the Hills to development interests from New York. Another key figure on the board was Albert Jagger who served as clerk and treasurer until his death in 1886. He was later described as a man "of rare judgment, extreme caution, severe economy, scrupulous honesty, untiring industry, and great modesty," qualities which were undoubtedly much appreciated by his colleagues.[21]

The twenty years following the 1861 purchase can best be described as relatively prosperous and routine ones for the new Shinnecock Hills proprietors. Their year-end accounts showed healthy balances, thanks largely to the annual sales of seaweed and sedges. With the seaweed case behind them, and decided in their favor, they had no trouble finding customers. They had few difficulties with the Shinnecock, at last safely fenced out of the Hills, beyond cases of trespass or wood cutting on what was legally now thoroughly private property. In one case, according to David Killes in his 1900 testimony, a rancorous Lewis Scott sent a bill for $114 "against the tribe" after arresting several men for cutting firewood. "We are cramped in every direction," Killes said. It was not until the late 1870s that the Shinnecock began to mount a new legal challenge to the 1859 legislation and subsequent sale of the Hills. However, the suit died in 1885 for want of money. At that time, the Shinnecock's own trustees sold some woodland at Canoe Place in the Westwoods to raise money for the suit but the sale was later declared illegal.[22] The court ruled that the trustees were not authorized to dispose of tribal lands without an enabling act of the legislature. The last time that had been done was in 1859, the irony of which would have been lost on no one. It was the last time the Shinnecock sought to challenge the act.

No such restrictions applied to the Shinnecock proprietors. On several occasions they bought or sold land though mostly in insignificant amounts. They purchased meadow lots from private owners at Cold Spring and Sebonac to enhance income from the sale of sedges, and made one and possibly two real estate sales. One such sale in 1873, described in the proprietors' journal as encompassing three hundred to four hundred acres along Shinnecock Bay, may not in the end have been made at all since it is not listed in a later exhaustive title search. The prospective purchaser was Naturin Delafield, a New Yorker of an old merchant family, apparently interested in raising cattle.[23] A price was set at $15 an acre and the agreement signed by the trustees in 1874. Yet the accounts show no trace of this sizable sum—between $5,000 and $6,000—that should have appeared in them. Nor do the assessor or tax rolls of the time reflect such a transaction. The 1882 rolls show the acreage of the lands owned by the Shinnecock proprietors as virtually intact at 3,150 acres, further suggesting that the Delafield purchase fell through. The other sale was to Uriel A. Murdoch in 1876 and this is recorded in the abstract of title.[24] It was for four acres in Little Neck, again at $15 an acre. Murdoch was one of the first summer residents in Southampton and the first to buy on the Shinnecock Hills, predating later purchasers by ten years.

Possibly in anticipation of the Delafield purchase, earlier in 1872 the Shinnecock proprietors had retained two Sag Harbor lawyers well known to us from the previous chapter, Thomas Bisgood and George Whitaker, to petition for incorporation. This was obviously to clear up or close off any lingering title questions. In April that year, the proprietors had voiced concern that their rights were "now called in question at Albany" and were if necessary to be defended. They need not have worried. In June, the legislature ratified the petition and erected the grantees of the 1861 deed into a corporation under the title of the Trustees of the Shinnecock Hills.[25] They were now no longer simply tenants in common but a legal corporation. The act of incorporation gave the proprietors the right to draw up bylaws and elect trustees, gave them the power to buy meadow and marsh land up to fifty acres, and the power to sell land under their corporate seal. It was yet another step toward affirming the claim of "undisputed and indisputable" title to the Hills that had been boldly proclaimed in the auction notice of 1861. A few years later it would ease the transition when the Hills company passed into the hands of a new group of investors. One section of the legislation, however, did seem to leave the door open to a potential future challenge. It said that "(t)his act shall not affect the Tribe of Shinnecock Indians nor their right, title, or interest if any to said Shinnecock Hills and lands." Shoe-horned in at the end, it may have reflected a few misgivings on the part of some in the legislature. It might also have given some hope to the Shinnecock, enough anyway to contemplate renewed litigation.

II: ADVENTURES IN EXPANSION: THE LONG ISLAND RAILROAD

The major event of the first twenty years in which the Hills were under private and apparently unencumbered ownership was the coming of the railroad. This occurred in 1870 and had profound consequences for the future of the area. Before his death in 1875, Oliver

Charlick, then president of the LIRR, had predicted on a trip to Southampton that the Shinnecock Hills would one day make a fine summer resort.[26] Six years later, the new president of the railroad, Austin Corbin, quickly realized their development potential and moved immediately to acquire them. He had become president only in late 1880. Within eight months, his agent, John A. Bowman, had bought out the Shinnecock proprietors on Corbin's behalf and two years afterwards delivered the Hills to the LIIC (a creation of the railroad) of which Corbin himself was president. By 1886, a hotel, a depot, and several handsome summer cottages had been erected on the Hills. A golf course, a yacht club, a second depot, an Episcopal church, and other accoutrements of summer living quickly followed. It was all effected with dizzying speed. But in 1870, no one among the Shinnecock proprietors—not even Scott of whom it was later said that he was blessed with "a keen eye for speculation"—had the first idea of what the railroad might bring. In 1868, the trustees had readily provided the town with a four-rod right-of-way through the Hills as negotiations with the LIRR were finalized, but by 1871 they were already complaining to the railroad that cattle were often killed or maimed by passing trains. Brush fires were another hazard. Demands for reimbursement were routinely made and just as routinely ignored by railroad officials. Oliver Charlick was anything but sympathetic to the problems encountered by the villages and towns along the line of the road. Yet there is no hint that the line was little more than an irritant to the Shinnecock proprietors in the 1870s, an occasional menace to livestock, but its potentially fiery impact on pasturage may have been a factor influencing the decision to sell.

On the other hand, John Bowman made them an offer that was impossible to resist. For $45,000 he would take over the company, buy out all the shares, appoint new trustees, and operate, as he disingenuously told the *Sag Harbor Corrector*, a sheep farm. This was in August 1881 three weeks before the deal was finally consummated and all the shares had been transferred. Bowman was a banker and developer from Detroit, Minnesota and had met Austin Corbin out west in the 1870s when both were engaged in the business of foreclosing on farm properties they had previously refinanced before quitclaiming them back to their owners. Corbin was operating out of Davenport, Iowa at the time. Yet in the *Corrector*, Bowman acknowledged barely a passing acquaintance with him. He had this to say:

> I am the man who is buying the land, and Mr. Corbin has nothing to do with it. I suppose the rumor got started because I always do my writing in Mr. Corbin's office when I am in the city. I began negotiating for the lands in April. I have bought a great deal of Long Island—Manhattan Beach for instance—and about three weeks ago I secured seven shares (of the Shinnecock company) and contracted for more. The land consists of fifty shares, owned by twenty two persons. There are 3,300 acres in all. The owners are old men and trade slowly. The land is eighty miles from New York, and is not available as a summer resort. I intend making a sheep ranch of it such as we have out west. People from Montana will go in with me and form a stock company.[27]

The paper duly reported that Bowman "further said that the land cost very little. Montana stock farmers thought that the comparatively short distance from the New York market would enable them to deliver the mutton at less expense and in better condition than is now the case in transporting the carcasses from the West." It was a remarkable series of statements, designed he must have thought for an audience of innocent rustics. The "people from Montana" were all railroad men, Corbin's men, and all were installed on the Shinnecock board of trustees within weeks of the article appearing. None of them would have come closer to a sheep than through a passing train window. But Bowman kept up the pretence for two more years before he and Corbin put the property of the company up for auction. It was knocked down for $101,000 in October 1883 by Elizur Hinsdale, counsel to the LIRR, and the shares of the company transferred to the LIIC.

Still, the Hills did remain open for pasturing sheep for several years after 1881, but they were sheep belonging to the old Shinnecock proprietors not to John Bowman. They produced a minor return on his investment of between $150 and $200 a year resulting from the fees the new trustees decided on charging: 25 cents a head, later raised to 30 cents. There is no reason to think that Scott, the Roses, and others objected to this or found anything to concern them in the story put out for local consumption about stock farmers from Montana. They had pulled off a remarkable coup, selling off land that apparently had no other use apart from grazing, or land that "cost very little," for in most cases $1,000 a share. Scott and his son made $11,000 on the deal, the Roses $8,000, and Albert Jagger $2,000. All of this was accomplished on an initial total investment of $6,000 twenty years before. If John Bowman felt the need to conceal his intentions from the general public, then that was his affair. Besides which, it may have been imprudent to draw too much attention to the real dimensions of the purchase (the selling price was never published) or its ultimate purpose. Even a Southampton that was quickly and for the most part happily adjusting to the expansion of the village real estate market, resulting from the growing summer trade, might have reacted in a negative way. And then there was the title question; and, of course, the Shinnecock Indians. The last thing the Shinnecock proprietors needed was publicity and any attendant threat of legal action.

John Bowman remained in Southampton for several years to come. He was elected president of the new Shinnecock Hills trustees until 1883 and was actively involved in finalizing the transfer of the Hills to the improvement company. Scott helped him find a small farm on Noyac Road in North Sea a few dozen yards from Jetur Rose's house, the last president of the old trustee board. He became a well-known citizen, his doings reported and his letters published in the *Seaside Times*. Eventually he returned to Minnesota. But he was in every way Austin Corbin's stalking horse in 1881. It is to Corbin, his railroad, and his plans that we now turn.

The sale of the Shinnecock Hills was nothing less than a seismic shift in the history of Southampton. No alienation of lands to outsiders on this scale had ever taken place, and they were lands that obviously had meant much in the town's history. Its long-term effect was to turn the Hills into a private enclave from which the public (let alone the Shinnecock) was largely excluded, and to which access by road was to be severely restricted. In all respects, it mirrored what had taken place at Montauk after its purchase by Arthur Benson in 1879. Progressively through the 1880s and 1890s, Easthampton residents found their traditional hunting and fishing rights on the peninsula curtailed and their livestock ultimately turned off. The town essentially lost Montauk, except for its road and real estate taxes, just as the Montaukett Indians had lost it two centuries before to a group of Easthampton proprietors. Precisely the same thing had now happened in Southampton. First the Shinnecock were dispossessed of the Hills and then the town's proprietors sold out to a group of private farmers, themselves proprietors, who in turn found it absurd to continue pasturing sheep and cattle on land that represented such an extraordinary potential for development. It also is possible they were influenced by the experience of the Montauk proprietors, which was fresh in everybody's minds. Acre for acre, both tracts sold for about the same price.

But what was happening in eastern Long Island was certainly not unique to the area. Across the country, wherever railroads had penetrated land booms followed. Railroads were the engine of economic growth after the Civil War and responsible for a large part of the country's new wealth and the success of its industries. Railroads were in the process of tying the country together and opening up new and often vast tracts for development, whether it was farmland in the west or suburbs close to the major cities. The scramble for railroads on Long Island and the cutthroat competition to build them by different companies was a case in point. Austin Corbin had himself said that the development of LIRR and the development of Long Island were "exactly parallel" and predicted in 1882 that one million people would live on the island before long. He had in mind the growth of the eastern suburbs of New York City, in what was then still Queens County, and the commuter lines to serve them—passenger and freight charges on these profitable routes were where the real money lay—but he was just as interested in niche markets for the new rich who were the primary beneficiaries of post–Civil War expansion: hotels, resort developments, first-class steamship lines.

He was not alone in thinking this by any means. Railroads were opening up desirable resort locations for luxury purposes in many parts of the country at the same time he began to consider the prospects eastern Long Island might offer. Newport, Bar Harbor, Jekyll Island, Georgia, and the Carolinas in general, the Monterey Peninsula, Pasadena and Santa Fe, South Florida and Key West, were all enticing destinations and wholly dependent on railroads for transportation. Henry Flagler, for example, linked Miami to Key West with a single track in the 1900s long before the highway was built through the keys. Corbin had the same visionary ideas for Long Island. Writing later in 1903, Peter Ross said that the island had become "a paradise for the land boomers." With his "glowing descriptions and confidently expressed hopes . . . (the boomer) turned strips of sand into foundations of wealth," while the railroad "will open up the entire island to business and pleasure to an extent now little dreamed of and make it become a veritable fairyland of homes and resorts."[28] Corbin was in at the beginning of this and became the most influential boomer of all.

He was fairly typical of a breed of self-motivated mid-nineteenth-century entrepreneurs, innovative, ruthlessly competitive, constantly in search of new investment opportunities, and an experienced financial and real estate manipulator. In 1880, he was fifty-three and president of the Corbin Banking Company in New York with offices in the Boreel Building at 115 Broadway. He had formed it in partnership with others in 1874. He lived in Brooklyn Heights where he had bought a house on First Place after coming to New York in 1865. There in Brooklyn he got to know a number of men who later became associates in his eastern Long Island projects. Notable among them were Arthur Benson, an oil and gas entrepreneur and self-styled proprietor of Montauk, and his son, Frank Sherman Benson; Henry Maxwell, a neighbor on First Place, vice president of the LIRR after 1880 and the investment banker who bought the land under the waters of Shinnecock Bay in 1882; Charles Pratt, the owner of most of Brooklyn's oil refineries under his Astral Oil Works which was later merged with John D. Rockefeller's Standard Oil Company in 1874; his son, Charles Millard Pratt, a Standard Oil Executive and president of his father's company after the latter's death in 1891. He went in with Corbin on a major Montauk purchase in 1895; Henry Huttleston Rogers, Charles Pratt's partner at Astral Oil (later Pratt & Co.) and a director of Standard Oil, estimated to be worth $100 million at his death in 1909. Henry Rogers' son bought three hundred acres at Cow Neck, adjacent to the Shinnecock Hills, in the early 1890s and a beach cottage at Old Town in Southampton. There were others besides in what was then the flourishing city of Brooklyn, but it was among these men particularly that Corbin found similar interests in developing Long Island.

Corbin came from relatively humble origins in New Hampshire, the son of a farmer and sometime politician and lawyer. He studied law locally then was fortunate enough to be admitted to Harvard Law School, graduating in 1849. After a desultory year or so of practice back in New Hampshire, he went west looking for greener pastures. In Davenport, Iowa, where he settled for fourteen years, he found his true métier in finance and went into banking. He was invited into a partnership by a wealthy Davenport banker, becoming immensely successful and especially in the area of farm loans. He loaned cash on farm properties all over Iowa and in surrounding states, including Minnesota where John Bowman was in the same business. But then he branched out into foreclosures and not only on loans, his or anybody else's. The 1850s were tough times for small western farmers, and most of them were very small. Taxes also were as much a problem to them as loans. Corbin found a profitable business in buying up county and town tax lists of those far behind in their tax payments. He got the certificates, waited three years for the deeds, and quitclaimed back his interest to the owners on his own terms. One by one, they trooped into his bank hat in hand. It was not illegal, but Corbin devised a questionable method of his own for maximizing and perpetuating his profits. He added expiration dates to the quitclaim deeds so that in some reasonably distant future, when the land was sold and the cloud on the title was discovered, they reverted to him. He collected again, and sometimes again. Seyfried notes that "(e)ven into the 20th century throughout Iowa and adjoining states, Corbin appeared as purchaser on thousands of pieces of unredeemed land, and the estate reaped an income for years on quit-claim deeds to these parcels."[29] When he tired of these easy pickings, as they must have seemed after years of the same routine, he sold his shares in the bank for three times what he had paid for them and came to New York in search of larger challenges. He was a wealthy man and not yet forty years old.

He opened a small banking firm in downtown Manhattan and slowly built up a reputation among other investment bankers including J. Pierpont Morgan and his father Junius for his hard-headed views of western development. The bank became the Corbin Banking Company specializing in western lands and railroads. His interest in Long Island began with a chance visit to Coney Island in 1873 when his son fell ill and the family doctor recommended the recuperative powers of sea air. The western end of Coney Island at that time was already developed as a day-tripper resort for working-class Brooklynites escaping the heat and humidity of the city at week's end. The beaches were served by a small independent railroad running a dummy train through Brooklyn's streets—the Prospect Park and Coney Island Railroad—that brought thousands to the amusement area developed after 1865.[30] But to the east lay two miles of empty, pristine beach, a wilderness begging for development. Corbin promptly put together a syndicate, bought six hundred acres of beach front (or Bowman, as he had also claimed to the *Corrector*, bought it for him), put two luxurious hotels on it with close to one thousand rooms between them—the Manhattan Beach Hotel and the Oriental—and purchased a Brooklyn railroad, reorganized as the New York and Manhattan Beach Railway with himself as president. The Manhattan Beach opened in 1877. It was lavish and decidedly upscale. Its clientele was drawn from downtown Brooklyn and an emerging midtown Manhattan, and definitely not from the masses who thronged western Coney Island every summer weekend. The Oriental was opened in 1880. They were both extremely popular but ultimately failed. They were too large and the season was too short. The Manhattan Beach went bankrupt in 1906 and was demolished in 1911. The Oriental was razed in 1916. The land was sold off for building lots. The other end of Coney Island suffered no such fate but went from strength to strength into the last decades of the twentieth century.

At the end of 1880, Corbin made what was probably the biggest move of his career. Forming a syndicate consisting largely of railroad men, he purchased a controlling interest in the LIRR. The LIRR had been ailing since the early 1870s along with the other railroads on the island with which it was in deathly competition. All were casualties of overexpansion. By 1874, there were three separately owned railroads on Long Island, each with their various branches, for example, the LIRR's Sag Harbor branch line off its central or main line that had preempted the South Side's bid to open up the east end of the island. The other two systems were the Central Railroad of Long Island, which controlled the lines on the north side of the island, and the South Side Railroad, which had built out from Brooklyn to Patchogue by 1868 and dominated the south shore communities. The lines of these three companies crossed and intersected each other, or ran closely parallel, so much so that in one or two communities there were three depots within walking distance of one another. As one historian of the LIRR pointed out, the island "was flooded with more railroad facilities than it could use or profit by."[31] The three companies also were engaged in an enervating but inevitable war of rates. The first to go under was the SSRR. Overwhelmed by debt, it defaulted on its bonds. After foreclosure in 1874, the SSRR was bought out by Conrad Poppenhusen and his son, owners of the Central Railroad, and renamed it the Southern Railroad Company. But this was a temporary and unsuccessful solution. All three companies continued to lose money. In 1875, the LIRR earned well under $1 million, and the other two less than half that. Much to the rejoicing of his long-suffering customers, long the victims of capricious and vindictive abuse (the saga of the Quogue depot is worth recalling), Oliver Charlick was pushed out and replaced by Henry Havemeyer.[32] This lasted but a year. Poppenhusen seized the opportunity to buy up a majority of the LIRR's stock, assumed the presidency of the company, and consolidated the three lines in one. Finally, there was a common system for Long Island.

Poppenhusen selected the LIRR to manage overall operations of the group, leased out the Southern and Central railroads, and established common passenger and freight rates. But only the LIRR made money. The earnings of the other two were well below their operating expenses and the cost of the leases. Despite the fact that the Poppenhusens were able to obtain $1.2 million in credits from Drexel, Morgan and Company, putting up 35,000 shares and $900,000 in bonds as collateral, within a year they defaulted on the interest on the bonds and were forced into bankruptcy. In 1877 Drexel, Morgan, left holding the stock and with large outstanding loans on its hands, petitioned the State Supreme Court to put the system into receivership. At the request of J. P. Morgan an old friend from the Baltimore and Ohio Railroad, Colonel Thomas Sharp, was appointed receiver. Sharp terminated the leases of the Central and Southern, depriving them of the LIRR's financial support and sending them into immediate bankruptcy. The Southern Railroad, with its principal line to Patchogue, was reorganized in 1879 as the Brooklyn and Montauk Railroad Company and operated by the LIRR under lease. The next year it ceased to exist as a separate entity and came simply to be known as the Montauk Division of the LIRR as it still is today. Sharp cut costs dramatically in the three years he was receiver, stabilizing the system's financial structure and demonstrating that it could possibly be run profitably. Given the chaos of the previous few years it was an extraordinary achievement. In 1880, he and Drexel, Morgan began looking for a buyer.[33]

Colonel Sharp knew Austin Corbin socially and persuaded him that the railroad was a good investment. Corbin put together his syndicate—it included Henry Maxwell as well as his brother, John R. Maxwell, president of the Central Railroad of New Jersey—and together they purchased the 35,000 shares held by Drexel, Morgan. They also bought up some $200,000 of liabilities and judgments against the railroad for a total outlay of about $800,000. The new company was incorporated in December 1880 with an authorized capital stock of $1 million and Corbin appointed as the new receiver. He assumed control at the beginning of 1881 and immediately began to put into effect even more drastic economies than Sharp had imposed. He fired more than one hundred employees, cut service on the Greenport or main line, and raised fares. There were protests all over the island, but it revived the railroad.[34] Its share price improved and in June the stockholders authorized the directors to increase the capital stock to $10 million. In September, Corbin applied to be discharged as receiver, a request that the court quickly granted. He was now the president in fact and in law. Earlier in the summer, he announced plans to extend the south shore line from Patchogue to Eastport, finally making it possible to run trains from Jamaica right through to the east end of the island through Southampton and Bridgehampton to

Sag Harbor. This line, the original brainchild of the defunct SSRR, was to become one of Corbin's most profitable routes. It took in farming communities and summer resorts all along the south shore, the latter already a growth industry. At the same time, he began exploring the feasibility of constructing track from Bridgehampton to Easthampton and Montauk. Shortly after he took over the railroad, he moved its headquarters to offices at 115 Broadway where his own Corbin Banking Company was located.[35]

It was clear from the moment he assumed control of the LIRR that Corbin had a particular interest in eastern Long Island and was well on the way to producing plans for its development. In spring 1881 he already had John Bowman in place in Southampton negotiating with the proprietors of the Shinnecock Hills. A year later, Bowman was out in Easthampton dealing with what was a colorful and bizarrely corrupt board of town trustees for the purchase of quitclaim deeds to Easthampton's beaches. Bowman was certainly not acting alone or freelancing in this venture. He was at the time president of the Trustees of the Shinnecock Hills and in that capacity acting on Corbin's behalf. In late 1881, Corbin began devising plans with Jacob Lorillard, head of the American Express Line, for a luxury steamship service from Fort Pond Bay on Montauk to Milford Haven in Wales. In January 1882, he and Lorillard incorporated a new steamship company, reputedly capitalized it at $10 million, and announced plans to construct three ocean liners capable of making the Atlantic crossing in six days. In the same month he alerted the press to the proposed extension of the south shore line from Bridgehampton to Montauk and claimed that the 120-mile trip from a projected passenger terminal at Fort Pond to Long Island City on the East River would be made in just two hours. He also reported that he had met with Arthur Benson to discuss a railroad right-of-way on Montauk and said that the latter "was naturally anxious to facilitate the new scheme."[36] Benson was not initially happy with the idea, preferring the lonely wilderness of his proprietary, but eventually came around. Corbin had perhaps won him over earlier by involving him with Bowman in the Shinnecock purchase in 1881, an involvement that earned Benson a substantial windfall gain. In January 1882, Corbin had also unfolded his plans for the formation of the LIIC, to be capitalized at $1 million (later reported in 1886 as $475,000) and backed by British real estate money. It was scheduled to be the parent organization for several of his land development projects. And finally, his new vice president of the railroad, Henry W. Maxwell, as we saw in a previous chapter, was about to appear in Southampton to negotiate with the proprietors of the common and undivided lands for the purchase of the lands under the waters of the western bays.

Given the extraordinary difficulties facing him in reorganizing an island-wide railroad system, it might be thought that Corbin would have delayed jumping into these new, although related, projects with such alacrity; at least until the company had settled down. But these were the projects that were nearest to him, and once general policies were in place regarding fares, freight charges, outstanding debt, leases, and the varying efficiencies of different lines, he left the day-to-day running of the railroad to others. In this he was excellently served by the new management team and particularly by the new superintendent of the railroad, Isaac Barton, whom he had brought over from Corbin's own New York and Manhattan Beach Railway. In fact, J. Pierpont Morgan was so impressed with the way in which Corbin untangled the mess at the LIRR (pace Colonel Sharp) that in 1886 he brought him in to revive the bankrupt Philadelphia and Reading Railroad, a mammoth coal and anthracite line. Drexel, Morgan had reluctantly bailed the company out two years earlier but had failed to get it to reorganize effectively. Morgan installed Corbin as president of the Reading and was later to congratulate him for turning it around and accomplishing "the end we both had so much at heart."[37] Corbin also involved himself with other railroads in the 1880s, in one instance mounting a salvage operation for a faltering New England line that served his own state. He was a consummate and persuasive fixer. Nonetheless, it is possible to conclude that in the case of Long Island he was less interested in the LIRR itself than in the glamorous possibilities it offered for pursuing bold schemes of upscale development.

The instant success of the Manhattan Beach Hotel may have had something to do with it. It led him to build the Oriental in 1880 and then a year later plunge into a new project for a hotel in Babylon. In October 1881, just as John Bowman had finalized the acquisition of the Shinnecock Hills, Corbin paid $65,000 for fifteen acres of land south of the railroad and immediately west of Babylon. It had belonged to Electus B. Litchfield, a fellow Brooklyn railroad magnate, and was his country estate. Almost immediately, he transferred title to the property to his newly formed LIIC and began formulating plans for the construction of a 350-room hotel based on the model of the Oriental. It was completed in March 1882 and opened at the beginning of the summer. At the same time, Corbin sold his house in Brooklyn Heights and moved to Babylon where he occupied the old Litchfield mansion. However, the hotel never did very well. No more than one-third of its rooms were ever occupied and Corbin sold it ten years later at a considerable loss. It closed its doors in 1897—Corbin had died the year before—and was subsequently dismantled, its wood recycled for cottages on the property. He had named it the Argyle Hotel in honor of the Duke of Argyle (today it is the site of Argyle Park) whose son, Lord Campbell, he had visited in England earlier in 1881. Campbell was the president of the London Land Improvement Company Ltd. The purpose of the trip was to obtain capital for luxury development on Long Island. It was this visit that led to the formation of the LIIC later in the year, "backed," it was said at the time, by "limitless foreign capital." His English investors later became heavily involved in his Montauk project for a fast transatlantic passenger service. It was a successful trip, unlocking the bounty of the aristocracy, so much so that he invited his new English friends to the Argyle when it opened the following summer.

While there, he took them by special train to the Shinnecock Hills to look over his other development property. Here too Corbin planned another hotel—as well as summer cottages—which the *Seaside Times* described as "large or larger" than the Argyle. The party disembarked in the middle of the Hills at a high point overlooking Shinnecock Bay, probably Sugar Loaf, and here Corbin entertained them to a lavish picnic while the train continued on to Sag Harbor where it was repositioned on the turntable for the return trip to Babylon. Southampton dignitaries and summer residents were in attendance and, for local color, a number of the Shinnecock were invited. It must not have escaped their attention that the luncheon was held on a site that was close to, if not on, sacred ground. For at least one thousand years, if not much longer, it had been a burial place. The *Seaside Times* did not report this but did note that Corbin and his investors planned on spending $3.5 million on the Hills. Possibly this was an exaggeration, but besides the projected hotel a five hundred-acre residential park was planned on a "cruciform" design with appropriately luxurious villas. The *Times* said that Corbin "believed in the seashore from Coney Island to Montauk." This was certainly not an exaggeration. Last but not least, Bowman must surely have been invited to this gathering of investors. It was less than a year after his statement to the *Corrector* disavowing his connection to Corbin and proclaiming his hopes for a Montana-style sheep station, but nobody apparently asked him about it or, if they did, it went unreported. At the time, Bowman was engaged in another speculative deal in Medford—also for Corbin.[38]

III: THE FORTUNES OF THE LONG ISLAND IMPROVEMENT COMPANY

Exactly one year before this celebratory excursion to the Hills, both a celebration and a sales pitch, Bowman had approached the trustees of the Shinnecock Hills with an offer of $25,000 for the shares of the company. It was summarily rejected. Of the twenty-three shares present, twenty voted against and the trustees reported in their journal that "under existing circumstances we consider it best not to sell." A week later this body of "old men slow to trade," as Bowman was to put it, began transferring a majority of the fifty shares to him. Between July and September 1881, Bowman purchased thirty-six shares and Arthur Benson the remainder. What had happened? Quite simply he had doubled the price so that most shares sold for $1,000 each instead of the $500 originally offered. Curiously, however, ten shares were sold by individual proprietors for $500 each in the same period. There is no ready explanation for this, but it did mean that the total purchase price of the company's assets was $45,000 rather than the $50,000 that is usually reported. In September, the existing trustees, except for Lewis Scott, resigned and were replaced by Bowman's, or rather Corbin's men. Bowman became president, replacing Jetur Rose, while the three other vacancies were filled by James K. O. Sherwood, Henry A. Wheeler, and Frederick W. Dunton. Albert Jagger was retained as clerk and secretary at a small annual salary but was no longer a board member. The following spring, Scott stepped down and was replaced by Wallace Kirby. Bowman transferred one share to each of the new trustees. All four of them were Corbin men. Sherwood became president of the trustees after the company's shares had been transferred to the LICC in 1883 and continued as president through 1889 when Dunton was elected for one year.[39] Frederick Dunton was Corbin's nephew and was associated with others of his enterprises. Kirby was a senior partner at Long Island and Western Lands headquartered at 115 Broadway. Significantly, one of the first acts of the new trustees in early 1882 was to hold sheep owners responsible for all injuries to their livestock. The company was to be held "harmless for loss or damage" as was the LIRR. So much for the sheep station.

In November 1882, the trustees of the proprietors of the common and undivided lands had conducted their hurried sale of what few remnants of common lands that remained in the town and the lands under the waters of the bays. They had conveyed by quitclaim deed property in the Quogue and Topping's purchases as well as the western bays, particularly Shinnecock Bay, to Henry Maxwell. Maxwell had acquired them on behalf of Corbin and the LIIC and, in January 1883, he transferred his interest to that company. Perhaps this partly explains the delay between the purchase of the Shinnecock Hills and their subsequent sale and transfer to the LIIC in late 1883. Realizing the public outrage the sale of the bays had provoked in Southampton throughout 1883, Corbin must have decided to postpone the transfer of the Hills as long as possible in order to avoid any complications it might create for Maxwell. The town trustees were already threatening a suit against Richard Esterbrook Jr. and his oyster company for the purchase of Mecox Bay and the entire town was itself girding for a fight. Although Maxwell appeared safely in the background, the situation had become volatile enough that he, and now the LIIC, might easily have been drawn into it. This may also account for the ludicrous story Bowman concocted about the alleged interests of sheep ranchers in Montana. Although this was in summer 1881, it already was public knowledge and had been so for a year that the bays might be put up for auction. In early 1883, and just after Maxwell's interest in the western bays had been conveyed to the LIIC, Bowman wrote another letter, this time to the *Seaside Times*, reassuring the public that "the new company" claimed only the bay bottoms and not the waters or the fishery. Burnishing his image as a man of simple farming pursuits, he noted that the company might erect fish pens in small areas but nothing more. William Pelletreau, as we saw earlier, gave his unequivocal support to this pretension.[40] Corbin was too shrewd a businessman to announce his intentions in advance, but it was perfectly clear that he wanted not only the Hills but the shores and waters around them and was not about to jeopardize either.

Finally in September 1883, Bowman and his fellow trustees of the Hills company moved to put the Hills, Sebonac Neck, Ram Island "together with meadows and lands under water" up for sale at auction, if sale it can be called, "for cash to the highest bidder." The Mecox Bay litigation was still well off in the future and there was no particular reason to delay any further. The auction notice was published in the *Seaside Times* on September 13 and the auction itself was scheduled for September 22 at the newly opened Real Estate Exchange at 111 Broadway, that is, at a prudent remove from Southampton. The tract was said to contain four thousand acres or about eight hundred more than the assessed acreage the proprietors of the Shinnecock Hills were liable for. In that year, incidentally, the assessed value of the Hills was recorded in the rolls at $12,000, well below market value.[41] The additional acreage can be understood to include in part at least some of the lands under water that Henry Maxwell had picked up the year before that may not have been conveyed to the LIIC. They were said to contain "several large ponds" including especially Canoe Place Pond.[42]

But the greater part of the additional land advertised for sale lay in the beach meadows along the West Beach in Quogue. This was a tract of salt marshes west of Tiana that had been sold for $535 at the 1861 auction of the Hills to Scott and his associates by the trustees of the proprietors of the common and undivided lands. It had been routinely hired out for its sedges in the intervening years, and had been included in the sale of stock to

Bowman and Benson as among the assets of the Proprietors of the Shinnecock Hills. It therefore became part of the 1883 auction sale. The land to the east of Tiana consisting of the Pine Division of Meadows, which had been lotted out in 1687, was not part of the sale but had been picked up separately by the LIIC the previous year. This was a ribbon of beach front and salt meadow running the length of the shore from Cooper's Neck to a point due south of Tiana, that is, directly across Shinnecock Bay from the Hills. It was still in the hands of the heirs and assigns of the original seventeenth-century owners as late as 1882. In June 1882, Bowman or some other Corbin associate, but probably Bowman, managed to get control of the entire tract. There were forty-one lots in the division and the purchasers, described by the newspaper as "parties from abroad," apparently approached each owner in turn with an uncharacteristic offer to name their own price. It was a successful strategy for all of them sold out. Together with the beach west of Tiana, it gave the LIIC four to five miles of pristine Atlantic shoreline containing possibly as much as five hundred acres. It potentially represented an extraordinary opportunity for development but nothing at all was done with it until long after Corbin had departed the scene and the LIIC had become a distant memory.[43]

The *New York Herald*, in reporting the upcoming auction, noted without any obvious irony that it was thought "advisable that the property shall be all under one ownership, and the sale which is to take place is arranged with a view to bring about that result," as if it was not in fact technically already under one ownership. There was no outcry in Southampton. Only George White, president of the town trustees, raised objections. On the same date as the auction notice he protested the sale and brought up the very issue that could conceivably cast doubt on it. This was, of course, the 1703 lease of the Hills to the Shinnecock. "The title," he said, "has not been acted on since by the town." It should have been a bombshell but it was not. The town was preoccupied with the Mecox Bay affair, and it had been clear since 1861 that the town was not especially concerned with the Shinnecock Hills or with the fate of its inhabitants, the Shinnecock, who were its rightful occupants under the lease if not ultimately its rightful owners. White simply had pointed out that the town had never abrogated the lease. The *Seaside Times*, to its credit, reprinted the lease in its entirety in its next issue two days before the auction, but it was insufficient to galvanize public opinion. The town seemed not to recognize the connection between the sale of the lands under water and the sale of the Hills and that essentially the same outside interests had a stake in both. By the time it did, two or three years later, it was too late. The town may have won back the waters as a result of the trustees' successful suit against the Mecox Bay Oyster Company, but the LIIC had an equitable title to the Hills, the shores surrounding them, and much of the ocean beach.

Yet White's solitary protest did have the effect of delaying the auction. It was postponed one month until October 20 while, presumably, the LIIC's lawyers evaluated the situation. They evidently concluded that there was no reason not to go ahead. There were only three bidders—Elizur Hinsdale, the LIRR and also LIIC attorney, Arthur Benson, and Jerome Kelly, a Corbin associate and railroad man and not a spoiler. Hinsdale opened the bidding at $25,000 and the three of them smoothly and rapidly drove up the price until Kelly bid

$100,000. Benson followed with $100,500 and then Hinsdale knocked down the property for the LIIC for $101,000.[44] It looked very much like the auction of Montauk at Sag Harbor in 1879. At the last moment, at the conclusion of a run-up to an agreed on price, Arthur Benson stepped in and coolly withdrew $151,000 in bills from his breast pocket, or so it was later reported. This was not the case here, but there were at least two good reasons for holding this auction. One might have been that the two principals—Bowman and Benson—responsible for securing the Hills to begin with should be handsomely recompensed for their trouble and, moreover, paid out of the proceeds of a legal sale. But second and far more significantly, there was the question of title, the question White had brought up at the last minute. *The New York Times* erroneously reported that the LIIC owned only thirty-six of the fifty shares in the company—Bowman's shares—but that the sale was made to enable the LIIC "to obtain a clear title." Although obviously the LIIC had put up the money in 1881 for Bowman to purchase those shares, he remained the majority legal owner up to the time of the auction. In the sequence of events after the auction, Bowman first purchased Benson's shares in November 1883, a month later, and then in January 1884 turned over all the Shinnecock property—its fifty shares—to the LIIC.

But it was the fact of holding the auction itself, legally announced by the trustees of the Shinnecock Hills or the rightful owners, which must have persuaded Elizur Hinsdale as counsel that this was the one way by which any question of title could ultimately be quieted. It lent a semblance of legitimacy to the transfer. Otherwise, why not just pay off Bowman and Benson, privately buy their shares, and take over the property? One other fact tends to support this view. In 1884, the LIIC did not dissolve the trustees of the Shinnecock Hills as it might have done quite legally. Instead it continued the five trustees in office, each with one share, with the LIIC represented on the board with forty-five shares as proxy for the company. In part, this may have been simply to assuage local opinion should it turn negative, but it seems more likely a cautionary move to retain at least the fiction if not the fact of the trustees of the Shinnecock Hills in the event of any future challenge. This fiction was maintained through 1895 when the LIIC sold out its remaining property on the Shinnecock Hills to the Shinnecock Land Company (SLC). This company in turn continued the tradition. As for Bowman and Benson: having reported the sale of the Hills to the LIIC on November 13 at the company's Broadway offices, Bowman officially was paid $2,500 for his services and later in 1884 left Southampton. He was last heard of in St. Paul, Minnesota in 1890 where he was called on to swear an affidavit that he had delivered the deed conveying the Shinnecock Hills in January 1884. Benson, for his part, doubled his money. Having bought fourteen shares for $1,000 apiece, he received $28,280 for his pains from the proceeds of the auction sale. It appeared to endear him further to Corbin as a sound and reliable businessman. Within the year, Benson softened his views of the latter's plan to insert the railroad into his own private fiefdom on Montauk: like, as William Pelletreau might have said, "a serpent into paradise."

Then, unaccountably, there was almost no movement in the development of the Hills for over two years after Bowman handed over his shares to the LIIC. Nor was there much local comment or controversy in the wake of the sale and transfer of stock. Reports and sightings of Corbin were similarly few and far between. He appears to have visited Southampton on no more than a handful of occasions between 1884 and 1886. He brought a party of investors to the Hills in spring 1884 to survey a site for what was described to be "a mammoth hotel." The *Seaside Times* reported that he and the LIIC were prepared to spend "vast amounts" in laying out building lots and that the new resort was to be "a select and quiet place," but a year later complained that there was "not the slightest apparent movement" on work on the Hills. Not long after that, the editor impatiently inquired what if anything was being done: "When will the long talked of improvement on the Hills be commenced?" he asked. It was a good question. The efforts to acquire the title to the Hills between 1881 and 1883 had been thoroughly planned and just as carefully carried out. The LIIC was well organized, solidly subscribed with a large capital stock, and had complete control of its local subsidiary. No one, after White, had raised any further title questions. George Rogers Howell did not publish his concerns about title until September 1886, and then retracted them, but by then the question of title was hardly such as to disturb Corbin and his lawyers unduly.

At the beginning of 1885, several Indians threatened a suit against Scott and the old trustees of the Hills alleging that they did not "obtain the consent of the tribe and had no right to transfer the life interests of the Indians." Two Shinnecock trustees had sold woodland in the Westwoods at Canoe Place for $700—to Miles B. Carpenter, the owner of the Canoe Place Inn—to finance the suit. But then nothing came of it and there is no record that it ever came to trial. Additionally, in a later action in 1890 a court declared that the sale of Indian lands was invalid except by an enabling act from the legislature. This suit originated in an action of trespass brought by other and later Shinnecock trustees against an employee of Carpenter's for cutting wood on Indian land, that is, the land Carpenter thought he had bought in the Westwoods. The court, in ruling the sale to be invalid, upheld Shinnecock possession. But already in 1885 it was clear that Corbin had little to fear from the Shinnecock.[45]

From 1882 to 1884 Corbin was absorbed in a good many other matters. Possibly a higher priority than the development of the Hills was Montauk. He had managed to gain the consent of Benson for a right-of-way on Montauk as far as Fort Pond Bay, the projected locus of his steamship terminal, and had had the plannned rail route surveyed east of Bridgehampton. He traveled to England at least twice to consolidate the backing of his investors there for the passenger service between Montauk and Milford Haven on the Welsh coast, and began planning the design and construction of a fleet of fast ships. As early as 1882, a model was developed in Greenport "embracing the principles on which a fish is built," especially, so it was said at the time, those of the salmon. He also plunged into a lobbying campaign with Congress to obtain federal recognition for Montauk as a port of entry. This, as well as the financing of the steamship line, and the extension of the south shore line to Montauk, dragged on for years without much apparent progress. The line was not constructed until 1895, British interest in the transatlantic venture began to falter as did the financing, and Congress ultimately failed to approve the scheme. While in London on one of his trips, Corbin floated an idea for a grand hotel there—to be called

The United States—but nothing came of that either. With his other involvements in hotels and railroads—salvaging the Reading in 1886 was a major investment of his time—Corbin had little time for the Shinnecock Hills.[46]

He did, however, become embroiled with the state over the question of the height of the railroad bridge that was to cross the proposed Shinnecock Canal at Canoe Place. At the beginning of 1884 he had thrown the support of the LIIC behind this newly revived project because it was designed to improve circulation in Shinnecock Bay and thereby eliminate its stagnant and unhealthy condition. Having acquired the shores of the bay, as well as the South Beach, to have left the bay in its existing state almost certainly would have discouraged prospective buyers of property on the Hills. Yet what he had not bargained for was a successful effort by the supporters of an inland water route from the Peconic bays to New York harbor at lobbying the state for a sufficiently high railroad bridge over the canal, high enough to accommodate vessels carrying freight. Corbin had already bought out the Sag Harbor Wharf Company in an effort to control the New York traffic in Long Island Sound, in particular the New York and Sag Harbor Steamship Company, and had installed Elizur Hinsdale as its chairman, and was not about to be blindsided by yet another competitive freight route. The state engineers had initially called for a canal bridge level with the canal banks and without a draw. This would have suited Corbin perfectly—nothing but a rowboat could have passed beneath the tracks—but the inland waterway lobby held out for a twenty-four-foot high span and got it. Corbin took the state to court in late 1885 and lost. Other than this, Corbin was not to be heard from in Southampton until much later in 1886.

The Shinnecock Hills were nonetheless well in hand. Under the new trustees, with James Sherwood succeeding Bowman as president, it was very much business as usual. The new regime continued in the old ways of the old. The seaweed privilege and the South Beach sedges continued to be advertised for sale in the *Seaside Times* each spring between 1884 and 1887. Sheep peacefully grazed the Hills over the same period. Albert Jagger, who was now paid $25 per year, kept the books and was able to report a modest profit of $200 to $300 a year. Perhaps the only noteworthy achievement of these trustees during a quite tranquil two years was the lease of twenty acres of woodland on Peconic Bay to a group from Sag Harbor desiring to erect cottages and a club house. The lease was for ten years at $10 an acre. But the rest of the Hills remained untouched. The most desirable section, constituting about fifteen hundred acres, lay on a gentle escarpment overlooking Shinnecock Bay and running from Sugar Loaf to Fort Pond. It was all south of the railroad. To the north lay swamp and brush fronting parts of Peconic Bay, particularly in Sebonac, none of it regarded as suitable for residential development. It also was without roads. In between, lay the desolate and windswept heights lacking in all but the poorest vegetation, which early observers had been so fond of describing. The valued land was all to the south and east and commanded spectacular views across the bay and out to the ocean. It was here finally, in 1886, that the LIIC (not, obviously, the trustees of the Shinnecock Hills) began to sell lots and planned the construction of the long-awaited hotel.

In company with Henry Maxwell, vice president of the railroad, Corbin descended on the Hills in April by special train and immediately began formulating plans for the construction of both the hotel and a Hills station to serve it, though both were still a year away. Corbin was still president of the LIIC, but there was one interesting addition to the list of principal incorporators. This was Samuel L. Parrish, who was to become an important figure in the LIIC and in its successor, the Shinnecock Land Company, which he founded in 1895. He was even more important for the development and modernization of the village of Southampton between the 1890s and late 1920s. For this latter reason we defer full discussion of him until later, but in the context of the Hills he had as much to do as Corbin with their development. He was a real estate and railroad lawyer in downtown Manhattan sharing offices with his partner, Francis K. Pendleton, at 44-46 Broadway, a few steps from Corbin's own offices. He first came to Southampton in this same year, 1886, probably at the suggestion of another railroad lawyer, Charles L. Atterbury, who had purchased property on Agawam in the early 1880s and worked on Broadway out of an office close to Parrish's and next door to Corbin's. Atterbury was to buy thirty-six acres at Sugar Loaf from the LIIC a few months later, while Parrish spent his first summer in Southampton at a boarding house popular with summer residents. Like Corbin, he had a sharp eye for speculative investments.

Some months after Corbin's visit, the first building lots on the Hills were sold, all of them overlooking Shinnecock Bay. They did not sell particularly rapidly or, for that matter, for very much. By the end of the year, no more than five or six lots had been picked up and work begun on only one cottage. Up island newspapers claimed they were going for as much as $3,000 an acre but this was either a confused report or a vast exaggeration. Most were selling at between $200 and $300 an acre. Charles Atterbury, for example, paid just under $7,000 for his thirty-six acres at Sugar Loaf, perhaps the most prime location of all. Two years later, three tracts totaling fifty-one acres were sold for $7,750 to Corbin's daughter, at as little as $152 an acre, yet this was undoubtedly an insider price.[47] Compared with real estate prices in the village, which had shot up between 1880 and 1886, this was almost ridiculously low. There, the average price for an acre of land around Lake Agawam was already $4,000 and showed no signs of stabilizing. Even to the west of the village, where land was gobbled up as fast as it went on the market, prices were as much as ten times higher than on the Hills. In 1888, four acres on Captain's Neck went for $16,000. This was something of an exception, but a mile to the west of Captain's Neck $16,000 might have purchased between seventy and eighty acres of waterfront on Shinnecock Bay. Oliver Charlick's 1870s prophecy that the Hills would become "the great watering place of the future" must have seemed to some observers more than a little optimistic. But at the time anyone else might easily have said that these were early days.

Yet this rather modest beginning did not seem to deter Corbin. He was back in October 1886 to announce the construction of the Hills depot and a hotel and cottages. At the same time, the president of the Shinnecock Hills trustees, James Sherwood, announced that because improvements on the Hills were about to be undertaken, all pasturing of sheep would be terminated. Perhaps surprisingly, this drew no reaction. There would, Corbin said, be eleven cottages on the Hills by 1887 as well as the planned hotel, but the following January only two were reported as under construction. Still, the depot was built in the spring and a resident agent put in charge of it in the summer.[48] A temporary track was laid off the main line angling down to the bay to transport construction materials for the hotel and cottages. Nor was Corbin deterred by slow sales from going ahead with the hotel, but it was to be a quite simple affair, far in conception from the palatial models in Babylon and Coney Island that had preceded it. It was to be erected west of Little Neck overlooking Far Pond. At the end of 1886, the Shinnecock Inn and Cottage Company was formed and incorporated with an extremely modest capital stock of $25,000. The offices were in New York and the directors of the company—Corbin, Parrish, and Henry Maxwell among them—took the majority of the stock. Others involved were Francis Pendleton, John R. Weeks, who later became president of the Shinnecock Hills trustees, William S. Hoyt, a friend of Corbin's and the first to build a cottage on the Hills in the spring of 1887, and Wager Swayne, a Unionist general in the Civil War and an early member of the Southampton summer colony. Swayne had a cottage built near Sugar Loaf, also in 1887. The Hoyts' own cottage, of a charming low-slung arts and crafts design, sported a windmill. It was the last grist mill in the village of Southampton and Hoyt arranged to have it trucked to the Hills from Windmill Lane. Like Atterbury, Hoyt was one of the early settlers on the western shore of Agawam and had been enticed to the Hills by their rustic charm and cheap real estate, as well as by what he could get for his Agawam property. His wife, Janet Ralston Hoyt of earlier mention, with the help of Samuel Parrish later founded the Summer School of Art on the eastern edge of the Hills and brought in an already famous William Merritt Chase to run it.

The first act of the cottage company was to purchase ten acres of land at Far Pond from the LIIC, the president of which was now no longer Corbin but J. Rogers Maxwell, Henry Maxwell's brother, and a fellow director of the LIRR. The price for the land was $2,000. The Shinnecock Inn was constructed in the spring of 1887 under the supervision of William Hoyt. At the same time, Hoyt had been given the contract to arrange for the construction of the Hills station, and assumed overall managerial responsibilities for the LIIC's property on the Hills a little later. He and his family moved into their new cottage that spring, while the inn was formally opened in August. It too was of great charm, unpretentious and set on a pleasant hillside sloping down to the water. A few small cottages were dispersed about it. The rather humble character of the inn, however, did not appeal to everyone. A *New York Times* reporter sniffed that it was "a rather diminutive affair which discourages chance custom," so it was obviously no Manhattan Beach. Whether from a change of heart about luxury accommodations, or for want of investment, Corbin had apparently settled on a resort of rustic simplicity. Perhaps, who knows, he had been influenced by Arthur Benson whose unpretentious tastes on Montauk were already well advertised. A small church was also planned, to be within easy distance of the inn and at the center of this southeastern section of the Hills. This was St. Michael's and All Angels Episcopal Church. It was erected in 1889 and resembled, although constructed of wood, an English country church with some whimsical beaux-arts flourishes added in the style of the time. But so few houses were built in the 1890s that its congregation was condemned to be small and its visiting ministers put up in the homes of the faithful. Its designer might plausibly have been Stanford White (he was at work on at least two houses on the Hills during this period), but Grosvenor Atterbury also was thought to later have had a hand in it. It burned down in 1905 in a brush fire and was re-erected.

But these small beginnings in 1887 did not lead to a building boom. By 1890, there were less than a dozen cottages on the Shinnecock Hills, all in the same area overlooking the bay, and the LIIC was beginning to reassess its investment. All in all, over these first three years, it never sold more than 340 acres, the majority of them to men connected to the LIIC itself. Parrish and Pendleton bought several separate parcels between them. James Parrish, Samuel's older brother, purchased land just south of the railroad, much too close to it as it turned out, and erected an enormous cottage (if cottage it could be called), a vast chateau-like edifice fully three hundred feet long. But it met the same fate as the church, a casualty of the frequent brush fires that in a good wind could sweep through twenty acres in a few minutes. Corbin also purchased property for his daughter, Annie (later Annie Borrowe). By the beginning of the 1900s, she had accumulated five sizable parcels. But these insider purchases did little to enhance the value of surrounding property, or encourage sales, and not much for the LIIC's profit margin. Prices remained stubbornly low at under $300 an acre, but so did demand. In contrast, new summer housing construction was booming in the village in the late 1880s, as was speculation in real estate in the extensive tract of farmland from Cooper's Neck to Heady Creek. But west of Heady Creek was almost no-man's land. In good part this resulted from a problem of access. There was only one passable road through the Hills, a broad sandy track through the center, and none within worth calling by that name. This quickly became an issue.

In 1888, William Hoyt went to A. H. Penney, Southampton's highway commissioner, offering LIIC land for the construction of a well-maintained four-rod road north of the railroad if the town would in turn reduce and harden the existing road—the South Highway—to a width that could be more easily maintained. The road to the north would follow an old cattle track, eventually becoming the North Highway. At the same time, the LIIC was attempting to upgrade some small existing roads and build a new one from the inn at Far Pond to Peconic Bay (later Tuckahoe Road), all at a cost to the company of $15,000. But Hoyt's proposal, although it met with Penney's approval, encountered stormy resistance in Southampton. The question of local access to the Hills had already become controversial. In 1886, the first year sheep were banned from the Hills, James Sherwood posted warnings offering $50 rewards for the arrest or conviction of anyone found gunning. If anything, this was as extreme as the old system of imposing fines on the Shinnecock for cutting wood or grazing an occasional cow. The boot now seemed to have shifted firmly to the other foot. George White, among others, was swift to react: "I suspect we should have to send to England," he said, "for a permit to cross Shinnecock Bay (and) their improvements on the Shinnecock Hills are a shingle at every cross-road offering a $50 reward for the conviction of anyone shooting a gun."[49] A year later, just as the Shinnecock Inn was about to open, the *Seaside Times* vigorously complained that driving to Shinnecock Bay now meant trespassing. The old highway was no longer public (this was not in fact true) but now ran through private land. Similarly, it continued, the shore was privately owned and there was no public access to the bay.

Other voices swelled the chorus of indignation. Benjamin Squires, no stranger to protest as his involvement in the Mecox Bay affair showed, weighed in on Hoyt's proposal and accused Penney of being in his pocket. Squires had conjured up a vision of "a broad eight rod wide boulevard across the hills, lined with trees and carpeted with green grass" to take people to picnics from "far and wide," the very road that Hoyt wanted to reduce by half.[50] But Penney and the road commissioners would have none of it. He blasted Squires' view as "sentimental bosh."[51] William Hoyt and the LIIC got their two four-rod roads, although it was to be many years before an elaborate system of intersecting roads connecting the north and south sections of the Hills was developed. The issue of public access to the shores of the bays was not settled until 1892. This had been in dispute between the town trustees and the LIIC since 1887 when the Shinnecock Hills trustees ceased farming out the seaweed privilege. The question came down to whether the shore could be considered a highway. The LIIC had claimed ownership of the shore as part of its purchase of the Hills, as had the Shinnecock Hills proprietors before it and the proprietor trustees before them. But the decision in the Betts case in 1892 respecting ownership of the beach at Agawam came down firmly on the side of the town. Frederic Betts may own the beach in front of his property up to the mean high-water mark, but the beach as a whole along the line of the dunes was a public highway. This settled the dispute on the Hills. The town trustees gave the LIIC a quitclaim deed to the Hills—a new development, incidentally, in the overall title question—reserving both all highways on the Hills and fifty feet of shoreline above high water on Shinnecock Bay, and seventy-five feet on Peconic Bay.[52] In return, the LIIC relinquished its claim to the lands under water that Henry Maxwell had acquired by quitclaim from the proprietors ten years earlier. This was evidently in consequence of the final decision on Richard Esterbrook's failed appeal in the Mecox Bay case in 1889.

The LIIC could easily afford these concessions as the real issue to them was not some local inhabitant occasionally collecting seaweed on the shores of the bays but whether they could sell real estate. Nor were better roads enough. Samuel Parrish knew this when he replaced J. Rogers Maxwell as president of the LIIC in 1890. A year later, John R. Weeks became president of the Shinnecock Hills trustees and held the LIIC's proxy vote of forty-five shares in the company. Weeks had his office in the same building on Broadway as Parrish and Pendleton. Beginning in 1890, the annual meetings of the Hills trustees—now simply routine re-elections of the board—were held in Parrish's offices. All decision making regarding the Hills had essentially become Parrish's responsibility. Then, in his second year as LIIC president, Samuel Parrish had an exceptional stroke of good fortune that promised an end to the company's lackluster progress on the Hills. A few members of the summer colony had discovered the game of golf while wintering in Europe at Biarritz. Returning to Southampton, one of the new converts—Edward Mead—approached Parrish to help them locate a suitable site for a golf course. Where else but the Hills? Casting about for some help in an unfamiliar matter, he had Charles Atterbury bring an obscure Scottish professional down from Montreal to look over the land. Atterbury had railroad connections in Montreal and at the Montreal Golf Club, generally regarded as the oldest golf club in North America. A site for a golf course was quickly settled on, although Parrish at first thought to suggest an area near where the Art Village was established later that year, perhaps with an eye to its easy proximity to Southampton. But the golf expert, Willie Davis, muttered something about the need for turf grass and Parrish took him farther into the Hills. The site the two of them chose, and which Davis pronounced as fit for golf, was a tract of seventy-five acres on both sides of the railroad and less than a mile north of the Shinnecock Inn. Davis laid out a small nine-hole course in summer 1891 (expanded to twelve the following spring) crossing the tracks at several points, while Mead, Parrish, and forty-two other summer residents formed and incorporated the golf club.

It was immediately popular among the summer colony and by the following year the new club—the Shinnecock Hills Golf Club—had signed up seventy-five members. To Parrish and the LIIC, it was a gift from heaven in an otherwise moribund real estate market. Perhaps in recognition of this Parrish arranged a knock-down price to the club of $33 an acre. But more than that there is much to indicate that Parrish thought the instant popularity of the game and the new club could help anchor real estate development on the Hills and encourage more summer residents to move there. Both the central location of the course and its proximity to the railroad and the inn suggest this. In a calculated move designed to showcase both the Hills and the club, Parrish arranged for McKim, Mead, and White, the fashionable architectural firm, to design a shingle-style club house set on the highest elevation east of Sugar Loaf.[53] It overlooked both bays and the railroad, and the golf course flowed down the hill beneath it. It was the first thing anyone would notice from a train as it came through the cutting from Canoe Place. The club house, much expanded from its early cottage appearance, still sits on the same hilltop today. In 1893, the LIRR added a second depot on the Hills, at Tuckahoe Road, convenient to both the inn and the club. Such was the enthusiasm for the new game that it was called Golf Grounds Station. The interests of both the new club and the real estate company were well served by this inspired choice.

Yet the golf club had no discernible effect on the growth of real estate on the Hills. A few members bought property and built cottages, but the membership as a whole continued to reside in the village. Samuel Parrish's second attempt to awaken interest in the Hills came in the same year. Janet Hoyt approached him with an idea for an art village—essentially a summer school for art students from New York and elsewhere—under the direction of a distinguished artist. Hoyt was an amateur landscape painter herself. Before moving to the Hills, she had been captivated by the views of Lake Agawam from the grounds of her cottage and apparently painted many scenes of it. She is said to have been responsible for introducing a new name—Silver Lake—for this venerable body of water that for more than two centuries had simply been known as Town Pond. But apart from her love of painting, Hoyt most wanted to put Southampton on the map as a center for art at least as important as the artists' community in Easthampton. The summer colony in Southampton, she felt, was far too philistine in comparison, single-mindedly devoted as it was to sporting and recreational pursuits.

Parrish was enthusiastic about the idea, helped form the Art Village as a corporation (he became its counsel), and donated twenty-five acres of LIIC land on the edge of the Hills at the end of the Shinnecock Road as Hill Street was called in the nineteenth century.[54] A small-scale village was laid out on the site complete with streets and a cluster of attractive modestly sized cottages. It was perfectly adapted to its function as a summer school of art. At the same time, Parrish provided three acres for William Merritt Chase near the Hills station and asked Stanford White to design a cottage for him. These moves may not have spurred real estate sales, but like the inn, the golf club, the Episcopal church, and the yacht club, the Art Village provided another important link attaching the Hills to the village of Southampton. Yet its most significant and lasting contribution lay in the art produced by Merritt Chase, the artist in residence for the next ten years, and his students, most of whom were young women. For more than a decade, he and they carried their easels all over the Shinnecock Hills (and Shinnecock Neck, where the Indian trustees welcomed them to paint for a small annual fee) and produced some of the most sparkling plein-air landscapes yet to be seen in American art up to that date. Parrish unfortunately never bought any of them for his collection housed in the new art museum in Southampton that he established for the purpose in 1898. His tastes ran more to the less well-known Italian painters of the fifteenth century he happened upon on visits to Europe, but later museum administrators did ultimately manage to acquire a substantial number of Chase's works.

IV: FAILED DEVELOPMENT

Despite all these notable innovations on the Hills between 1887 and the early 1890s, major development remained elusive. A corresponding willingness by the LIIC to invest sufficient funds to make the area more attractive for summer living was similarly lacking. In its ten years of outright ownership before selling out to a consortium led by Samuel Parrish, the LIIC invested no more than $50,000 in improvements and made very little more than that in land sales. Estimates vary as to how much land was in fact sold but it was probably about seven hundred acres.[55] The first sales in 1886 and 1887 comprised 340 acres, but given that there were only a dozen cottages constructed by 1893, it is improbable that much more than three hundred additional acres were sold in the intervening six years. This does not include the seventy-five acres for the golf club and some other property it acquired in 1892. Nothing, of course, had been sold on the South Beach. By the following year, the LIIC began to look for a way out and it was apparent that Corbin was losing interest.

Corbin at this time was preoccupied with other problems. After 1887, and notwithstanding some earlier doubts by his English investment partners, he became increasingly absorbed in his Montauk project for a transatlantic passenger service with a terminus at Fort Pond Bay. He managed to have a government survey of the proposed harbor inserted into a Congressional bill. But there were two problems with Fort Pond Bay. Sea conditions in winter dictated that ocean vessels would be at severe risk in riding out storms in harbor without a breakwater. The government, after seeing the report in 1889, effectively vetoed the breakwater by refusing to build it at public expense. Its cost would have run into several millions. Second, the Engineers Corps (which was to become the Army Corps of Engineers) cited the dangers of the approaches into Fort Pond Bay in thick weather and recommended against improving the anchorage. Undeterred, Corbin went to England again in 1890—interest had been revived in the Fort Pond/Milford Haven scheme and new partners secured—and he was instrumental in forming the Milford Dock Company. In 1892, he lobbied for Congressional legislation to confer American registry on any passenger vessels to be constructed. And in 1894, a Senate bill was introduced for the establishment of a free port at Montauk. This would have been a major development for Corbin, provided he could get support and funding for the harbor, for it would have given him duty-free warehousing, transshipment, and export manufacturing privileges. Clearly, he was thinking beyond first-class passenger service and saw the possibility of extensive freight operations. American merchants, especially in New York, were completely opposed to the prospect of this competition and lobbied against the bill. Arthur Benson had died in 1889 but his son and heir to the Montauk estate, Frank Sherman Benson, was at least initially also opposed. The last thing he and his father had anticipated was an industrial port in the heart of their unspoiled wilderness.

Beginning in 1890, Corbin encountered other difficulties that may have contributed to his inattention to what was happening, or not happening, on the Shinnecock Hills. His nephew, Frederick Dunton, and one of his closest allies in his business dealings, had taken it into his head to invest heavily in a bicycle railroad project in Patchogue. Corbin reacted immediately and rather irrationally to this as a potential threat to the LIRR. Dunton had been president of the Corbin Banking Company at one time and had just retired from it as cashier and vice president. He had also been much involved with the LIIC and had served as a Shinnecock Hills trustee since 1884. In 1890, he was made president of the trustees, the same year Parrish became president of the LIIC, and quite possibly to keep an eye on Parrish. But he was out of the picture the following year, replaced by John R. Weeks, probably as a result of the developing conflict with his uncle over the new railroad. It escalated into a railroad war of old, like the Oliver Charlick days, with each buying land and laying track in the area of Rocky Point and Wading River where Corbin wanted to extend the Port Jefferson branch. For his part, Dunton was endeavoring to build nothing more threatening than a cross-island bicycle road.[56] Dunton's venture eventually failed but it led to a permanent estrangement between the two men. It remained unresolved at Corbin's death in 1896.

A much more serious rift developed between Corbin and two of his most trusted business partners and directors of the LIRR, the Maxwell brothers. They had been associated with Corbin since he took over the railroad in 1880 and had been essential to the success of many of his projects—including the takeover of the Shinnecock Hills. Like Dunton, the Maxwells were part of the inner circle, a small body of men Corbin had implicit trust in and relied on heavily. In April 1891, J. Rogers Maxwell, Henry Maxwell, and Henry W. Graves (also a director of the railroad and an investment banking partner of Henry Maxwell) withdrew from the board of directors and put their stock up for sale. It was valued at $3 million and represented a quarter of the total capital stock. The ostensible reason for this sudden move was a desire to devote their energies to the Central Railroad of

New Jersey, which they owned, but it was widely thought at the time that there were deep disagreements with Corbin over policy.[57] Set alongside the feud with Frederick Dunton, the loss of these two loyal officials and presumably long-time friends and advisors, must have come as a major shock to Corbin. Additionally, in order to retain control of the railroad he was obliged to turn to Charles M. Pratt of Standard Oil for financial help in purchasing the Maxwell stock. Pratt also was a director of the railroad and later went in with Corbin in his purchase of a large slice of Montauk from Frank Benson.

So these were a complex and difficult few years for Corbin, which perhaps explains both why he paid less attention to his Shinnecock Hills interests than he otherwise might and why in 1893 he was ready to turn them over to other interested parties. Whether he approached Parrish, or Parrish him, is unknown, but it was Parrish who organized a small company of Southampton summer residents and relieved the LIIC of its property on the Hills. This was the Shinnecock Land Company. Its principal incorporators were Parrish, his older brother James, Charles Atterbury, William Hoyt, Francis Pendleton, and James P. Lee, a nephew of Parrish's. All of them, except Lee, owned land on the Hills and had a direct interest in the success of the company.[58] The new company bought out the LIIC's extensive remaining property on the Hills and the South Beach for $220,000 or a little under $100 an acre. It should have been a bargain. At an approximate selling price of $200 an acre, the value of the property might well have been as much as $500,000. In fact, one of the conditions of the $200,000 mortgage taken out by Parrish and his friends was that land free of the mortgage could not be sold for less than $200 an acre. But success remained just as elusive as it had for its predecessor. The SLC had more than 2,500 acres to sell, much of it in the central and northern sections of the Hills. Most of the prime locations overlooking Shinnecock Bay and south of the railroad were already in private hands, whereas the land to the north was still relatively inaccessible and not nearly as desirable unless it fronted Peconic Bay. In its ten years of operations after taking over from the LIIC, Parrish's company managed to sell no more than five hundred acres. Little of it was sold on Peconic Bay and none at all in Sebonac Neck, much of which was covered with swamp and brush. Sebonac Neck remained empty of development until 1906 when 205 acres were sold for the construction of another golf course. This was to be the National Golf Links of America. But by then the SLC was out of business and was unable to reap any benefit from it.

Early on in 1894 Parrish did make a considerable effort to interest the Shinnecock Hills Golf Club (he was the club's secretary) in the acquisition of additional land for the expansion of its golf course but met with limited success. Golf had taken off in Southampton after 1892 and by the end of its third season some members of the club began to formulate plans for further growth. A proposal circulated through the club recommending increasing the membership limit to one hundred, floating a bond issue of $20,000, and building a second golf course. At the time, there were still only twelve holes of golf on its original property of seventy-five acres. The plan called for purchasing another seventy-five acres or so south of the railroad down to Old Fort Pond and adding six new holes to make a full course. Second, it recommended buying one hundred acres to the west on which was to be laid out a second eighteen-hole course and a little links for juniors (actually two such links; one for boys and one for girls). It is hard not to see the hand of Samuel Parrish and his fellow stockholders in the SLC in all of this. All but William Hoyt were members of the club and James Lee was about to publish a book about it.[59] Nothing, however, came of this ambitious plan. Instead, the club scaled it back drastically and settled for buying sixty acres to the west and expanding the existing golf course to eighteen holes. It was not a complete failure but much more had obviously been hoped for.[60]

The Shinnecock Land Company folded in 1905. It sold its remaining property of about two thousand acres for close to $250,000 dollars to the Shinnecock Hills and Peconic Bay (SH & PB) Realty Company, a corporation with headquarters in Brooklyn and a capital stock of $300,000. It too came on to the Hills with grandiose plans for development. As luck would have it, it was blessed with an immediate sale. An obsessive golfer and wealthy investor from Chicago, Charles Blair Macdonald, together with seventy other members of America's business elite, put up $40,000 to purchase upland and swamp at Sebonac Neck for a golf course. The National Golf Links was opened in 1910 to international acclaim and for many years was thought to represent a revolutionary development in golf course architecture. It was superseded by the architecture of the 1920s but remained a monument to Charles Macdonald, its designer. It put the Shinnecock club very much in the shade, as if a great cathedral had been erected next to a homely little country church.[61] For many years until Macdonald's death, and perhaps partly for this reason, relations between the two clubs were often less than cordial. The cultures of the two clubs also were distinctly different. Shinnecock was very much a family club where women played a prominent role, whereas the National pursued its golf in a spartan atmosphere of manly sports; an "eveless eden" it was once called. The president of the realty company, William C. Redfield, a former secretary of commerce, was quite ecstatic at this instant pay-off on investment. In his first report to the stockholders at the end of 1906, he gloated that Macdonald and his co-religionists "intend to make this golf course famous both here and abroad, desiring that it shall be so well known that visiting foreigners and golfers from all over America shall make it a center for this sport. The advantage to your property of having located there two of the oldest and certainly the best of golf courses is obvious."

Redfield threw himself into the development of the Hills with a zeal and energy that had been apparently lacking among Parrish and his friends. He engaged Olmsted and Vaux, the best-known landscape firm in New York, to survey and subdivide a good part of the Hills that had not already been sold. This was an ambitious undertaking and covered 1,320 acres in the central and northern sections. The subdivision was mapped out in eighty blocks that were further subdivided into 352 smaller lots varying in size from three to five acres. These were to be building lots. Withheld from the subdivision were the remaining parts of Sebonac Neck and meadowland at Cold Spring Bay. These latter were the Sebonac Meadows, which had been divided in 1653 and were still in the hands of the heirs or assigns of the first owners. Redfield took the view that the various titles to these meadow lots were not sound, and that the only clear title rested with the realty company. In 1907, he took two of the owners to court—the Aldrich brothers—for trespassing and for removing sand, gravel, sedge, and seaweed at the borders of Cold Spring Bay. The company lost the case in State Supreme Court, much of which rested on the fact that meadow lots had been specifically reserved from the 1861 auction sale of the Hills by the trustees of the proprietors and had been reserved in every subsequent transfer of ownership.[62] Redfield valued the meadows as a promising site for future waterfront lots. They were eventually sold for that purpose, but not by Redfield.

The new company did much in its first year to improve the roads on the Hills. A priority was the North Highway, which, despite William Hoyt's earlier efforts, had never been sufficiently hardened. It was finally made usable, which is to say passable by automobiles, at a considerable cost of $11,000 and then turned over to the town in a public relations gesture aimed at securing the town's good will. At the same time, Redfield made efforts to upgrade several roads crossing the Hills from north to south. This was essential if the northern section was to be developed. By and large these efforts were well received in Southampton. By now, twenty-five years after the Hills had been auctioned off in New York, opposition to development in the town—whether on the Shinnecock Hills or anywhere else—had virtually disappeared, a result of the general real estate boom. A new generation of town leaders had emerged at the turn of the century that was generally favorable toward development. It was also doing very well out of it, as was the town's tax base. If the SH & PB Realty Company could turn the Hills around, there would be no objections in the political and real estate communities. The days of sheep and railroad tycoons were as good as forgotten.

Not content with merely upgrading the roads, Redfield obtained the consent of the state railroad commissioners to build three undergrade crossings beneath the tracks of the Long Island Railroad in order to expedite automobile travel from north to south. Not content with this either, he contracted with the railroad to build a depot in the western part of the Hills at Peconic Road, to be called the Suffolk Downs Station, and to rebuild the rather poor little station at the golf club, known to all as the Golf Grounds Station. There were now to be three depots within three miles, barely enough time to get out of one before arriving at another. But Redfield's principal achievement in his first year as president was the construction of a new hotel. The Shinnecock Inn and its cottages had gone the way of many wooden structures on the Hills in previous years, succumbing to a brush fire, and needed to be replaced. A new site for the hotel was selected a little to the east of the Hills depot and at the southern tip of the projected National Golf Links. This was no doubt deliberate. In 1907, Charles Macdonald had no immediate plans for a club house, and it would have made eminent sense to Redfield that the many well-heeled golfers expected to descend on the National would need a place to stay.

As it turned out, he and the railroad also thought to move the Golf Grounds Station farther to the west and closer to the hotel (and thus to the National) but was stopped by the Shinnecock Hills Golf Club or, rather, by its combustible president, Judge Horace Russell. Russell, a self-described old railroad man himself who knew what it meant "to submit to the whimsical caprices of residents along the line of the road," wrote to the LIRR's president that "it would not serve anybody's convenience, so far as the golf club is concerned, if it were to be moved to the west end of the golf club property; the Railroad Company might just as well discontinue the station altogether."[63] That ended that, but one might well wonder if Redfield threw in the removal of the depot to sweeten the deal with Macdonald. We will never know. But the hotel went up in 1907 and was open for business that summer. It was also called the Shinnecock Inn. It cost $60,000 and was wholly owned by the SH & PB Realty Company. It and its contents were valued at $75,000. But it was insured for only $51,000 when it unfortunately burned to its concrete foundations a year later. Like the earlier inn, it was never rebuilt and the golfers had to look for alternative accommodations. The foundations are still there, slightly overgrown, behind the ninth green and the half-way house.

Redfield made other improvements on the Hills. He took over the bath houses on Peconic Bay just west of Cold Spring Bay, expanded them and put them on a paying basis, reporting that they had been "overwhelmed with business" during the summer of 1906. He proposed to have the inlet to Cold Spring dredged, and construct a small protective breakwater, in order to build a marina for yachts and motor boats in the bay. And he promised to do something about "the mosquito problem," an unwanted adjunct to country living, by filling in many of the more insalubrious swamps in the northern sections. Finally, the company, in agreement with the railroad, offered to bear some of the expense of rebuilding St. Michael's Church which had burned the year before. Each would contribute $800. Overall, Redfield estimated that the company would spend $80,000 on improvements in 1907, much of it, of course, on the construction of the Shinnecock Inn. All of these changes, beginning with the imaginative plan to subdivide well over one thousand acres of the Hills, were a major departure from the relatively modest efforts to improve the Hills by the two previous companies. But the changes did not produce the expected growth in sales that they were designed to attract. There was a severe banking crisis in 1907—a full-scale panic on Wall Street—and this may have slowed the real estate market in Southampton to some degree, yet sales did not pick up thereafter. They did in the village, but the village had always had a competitive edge over the Shinnecock Hills and this continued to be the case throughout the teens and into the 1920s.

Arguably, although exact figures are hard to come by, the LIIC and the SLC sold more land between them from 1886 to 1906 than did the SH & PB Realty Company in its seventeen years of existence to 1924. Its two predecessors, for all their ultimate failure, managed to dispose of fifty-one parcels of land, almost half of them between twenty and fifty acres each. True, five individuals purchased 40 percent of those parcels, and there were only twenty-nine separate owners, but it amounted to a fair record of long-term progress. The SH & PB Realty Company could not boast anything like this success. Even the automobile, now the preferred mode of private transportation and one that vastly improved access to the Hills, seemed to have no effect on the real estate market. A comparison of the Olmsted and Vaux survey map of 1906 with a similar map put out for auction purposes in 1925 is instructive in this respect. This map was prepared for a firm of Brooklyn auctioneers, Jere Johnson Jr. and Company, and was based on the 1906 survey. It shows virtually no land sales. The eighty blocks covering thirteen hundred acres in the middle of the Hills were almost completely or more than 90 percent unsold. Similarly, and rather surprisingly, the lots around Far Pond and Middle Pond were also unsold. These were in good locations on Shinnecock Bay and within easy reach of Southampton. Where the company had some success was on Peconic Bay west of Cold Spring, but this was a comparatively small acreage. Its one big sale was in Sebonac Neck adjacent to the National Golf Links. There, in 1917, a friend of Charles Macdonald's bought 309 acres on the bluffs overlooking Peconic Bay. Charles Sabin, a wealthy New York banker, was the purchaser. He called it Bayberry Land and built a sprawling mansion in the middle of it. Macdonald himself acquired more than one hundred acres on the east side of Bull Head Bay and erected a massive brick house of Georgian design from which he could survey much of his golf course. Ram Island in Bull Head Bay was also sold—to another banker, George C. Clark. Additionally, the Shinnecock Hills Golf Club more than doubled its holdings to two hundred acres in various small purchases in the 'teens.

But this was all. From its spectacular beginnings in 1907, the SH & PB Realty Company vanished into bankruptcy in the early 1920s. The Title Guarantee and Trust Company held a mortgage of $150,000 on the unsold property until 1925 when it was purchased by the Environs Realty Company, again of Brooklyn. Environs Realty was represented by Jere Johnson, the Brooklyn auctioneers, who put the remaining fourteen hundred to fifteen hundred acres up for auction in Southampton in July of that year. Of the original 352 building lots subdivided by Olmsted and Vaux, 339 went on the block. A further 350 acres in several parcels to the north of the Art Village and toward Sebonac Neck also were put up for sale. In its promotional literature, Jere Johnson noted that the company anticipated two classes of buyers. There would be those who buy for their own use and there would be those "who, cognizant of the great purchases that are being made of the most available acreage in the vicinity of Southampton by some of the shrewdest real estate developers in America, will buy for profit." It was clear which class of buyer the auctioneers were after. In a line impossible to resist in the general hubris of the 1920s, Jere Johnson added that "today the unit of value at Shinnecock Hills is the acre. Before long it will be the square foot."[64] A mirthless chuckle might have escaped the lips of Austin Corbin, Samuel Parrish, William Redfield, and others associated with all the attempts to sell the Hills in the past forty years, had they happened to read this last effort to whet the appetite of the speculators it was aimed at. Corbin was, of course, long since dead, but Parrish was tempted to attend the auction sale and did so. He might have told Environs Realty, had he been asked, that the auction was unlikely to be a great success, but as it turned out it went rather well and Parrish himself picked up one or two choice parcels.

Jere Johnson did everything in its power to attract as large a number of prospective buyers to the auction as it could. It was held in Southampton on a Saturday in late September at a site north of the Art Village. Special trains were put on to bring people out from Brooklyn and New York's Pennsylvania Station, while the fields round the auctioneer's tent were turned into a parking lot for several hundred cars. The *Southampton Press* reported that more than twelve hundred attended, lending the proceedings something of a festive atmosphere, but probably not many of them could be said to be serious buyers. Many were local residents, some of whom did buy, but most were on a day out curious to see if the Hills were at last to be sold off. The Shinnecock would also have been interested spectators—their eight hundred acres on the Neck lay immediately to the south of the site of the auction—but what they thought of this final phase of dispossession in the hands of a barker from Brooklyn went unrecorded. A number of summer residents participated as well, among them Arthur Claflin who had bought James Parrish's land south of the golf club and put up his own manor house on it, Samuel Parrish, and James Parrish's son. The three were all successful purchasers. James Parrish Jr. bought thirty-six acres on Tuckahoe Lane at the very edge of the Hills for the rather reasonable price of $375 an acre. But the biggest buyers represented Brooklyn real estate interests, buying, as Jere Johnson had said, for profit.

The auction was still at best a mixed success. Of the 339 building lots ranging from one to six acres, only 130 were disposed of. However, they sold at remarkably high prices and in locations that had not previously generated much interest. Cold Spring bay front lots fetched as much as $1,000 an acre. But it was land at Canoe Place bordering the Shinnecock Canal that produced the largest surprises. This had been originally laid out in 1906 as small plots for business and residential use, few of which had ever sold. These were picked up by two Brooklyn investors for approximately $40,000. Similar-sized lots to the south on Old Fort Pond also sold for $1,000 an acre. Yet the land in the middle of the Hills, more than one thousand acres blocked out by Olmsted and Vaux, found few bidders. This was land that the SH & PB Realty Company had staked its future on, but it was just as resistant to the market in 1925 as it had been in the years after 1906. Nobody wanted it. Large acreages to the east and close to the Southampton village line—the old Indian line—fared better. Of the 350 acres separately advertised as "suitable for subdivision, private estates, golf links and the like," all north of the Art Village and in the vicinity of Tuckahoe, half were sold even if at rather modest prices. The Southampton Golf Club, just formed that year and with only a nine-hole course on flat farmland, purchased eighty-seven acres next door to the Shinnecock Hills Golf Club for a second nine holes. The price was $200 an acre, a price that the old LIIC might have been happy with in the 1880s but was now one that was about rock bottom. The same held true for other sales in Tuckahoe. Two years later, the president of the Shinnecock club, Lucien Tyng, purchased one hundred acres on behalf of the club for the same price, much of it from Environs Realty and all of it in Tuckahoe.

Jere Johnson claimed that the auction brought in a total of $351,000, which, if true, spelled an extraordinary turn around for the Shinnecock Hills and an excellent return on investment for Environs Realty. But was it true? Given how much of the Hills still remained unsold, and despite the rather striking prices paid for some comparatively small but desirable sections, this seems to be a rather optimistic figure. This was the view of others at the time and later. A small incorporated body of property owners on the Hills, known as the Shinnecock Hills Association, formed to protect their interests and further the "proper development" of the Hills (a sort of successor to the old defunct Trustees of the Shinnecock Hills), thought that as a result of the auction much of what was sold "passed into the hands of a great number of small and in many cases weak owners." In its 1941 yearbook, the association noted that "in fact today it appears impossible to determine what proportion of these sales were genuine and how many parcels reverted to the Environs Realty Co. and it is said that the existing tax list by no means covers the entire acreage of the Hills."[65] Press reports of the auction at the time suggest that no more than three hundred or four hundred acres of lots were sold—to which must be added 175 acres in Tuckahoe—and that Environs was still left holding upward of one thousand acres that no bidder would apparently take under any circumstance.

The Hills thereafter languished through the 1930s and 1940s and prices fell back to almost nineteenth-century levels. A handful of owners controlled the largest properties. The three golf clubs, possessing between them fifty-four holes of golf and arranged in such a way that it would be possible to play a good part of all three courses with barely a road to cross, alone contained six hundred acres. Adding Bayberry Land, adjacent to the National, brought the total up to nearly one thousand acres. These large accumulations of land dominated the northern section of Tuckahoe and Sebonac Neck as far west as Cold Spring Bay, all of it old Indian land. To the west of Cold Spring and in the area of Canoe Place lay small housing developments on the shores of Peconic Bay and Shinnecock Bay similar to those springing up around Old Fort Pond. The middle remained as empty as it was in the 1900s resisting any form of development. While south and east of Sugar Loaf large owners dating in many cases back to the nineteenth century predominated. But over a period of fifty years all attempts by successive real estate companies to transform the Hills into a fashionable resort with a mixture of hotels and villas had met with failure. The only notable exceptions to this were the golf clubs. Southampton Golf Club thrived on its local membership, consisting of small entrepreneurs and farmers, while the National Golf Links and Shinnecock Hills lived up to the reputation William Redfield had predicted for them in 1907. But in all other respects the pattern of future growth had been set by the outcome of the 1925 auction. This had been either a last-gasp effort to revive the promise of the Hills as a developer's paradise or, depending on the viewpoint, a fire sale—notwithstanding the gaudy prices of some few properties. In reality it was neither of these, whatever speculative buyers had thought at the time. The character of the sales indicated that the only possible future lay in reasonably priced middle-class housing, whether for summer or local residents. The depression and war years interfered with this form of development, but by 1960 that pattern of growth had been quite clearly established. At the same time, prices finally began to rise from their historic low levels.

The first intimation of this came in 1959 when a subdivision was laid out northeast of the Shinnecock golf course. This went by the bland suburban name of Country Club Knolls, a spacious one hundred-acre countrified estate of split-level ranch-style housing for the middle class, a typical design of the time. Lots were sold for between $3,000 and $6,000 an acre, depending on location. This was not lost on the Shinnecock Hills Golf Club, which had surplus land to dispose of itself. Of its three hundred acres, the club used only about two hundred for golf. Lawrence Condon, counsel to the club and one of the principal architects of its revival after the war (it had narrowly averted collapse in 1943 for want of money and members), checked with local real estate brokers and found that its land was now worth $3,500 an acre. Through the 1950s, the club had valued its assets at no more than $100,000, the amount of the mortgage taken out during its postwar reorganization in 1949. Now, Condon said in 1961, "we are actually looking at a cool million." Several efforts were made to sell unused land in the 1960s, even to consider a small housing estate on part of an earlier golf course that had been abandoned, but very little came of it. However, the club did manage in 1963 to sell about eleven acres south of the railroad to a local real estate speculator, Henry Simonson, for $13,000. Simonson had already acquired a good part of the old Claflin estate (which had formerly belonged to James Parrish) in anticipation of a major land deal with Long Island University.

The university, with its main campus in Brooklyn (representing, if only symbolically, yet again old Brooklyn interests in the Shinnecock Hills dating back to the nineteenth century) was well into the process of planning a Southampton campus for the Hills. Adding Claflin's land to what he had purchased from the golf club, Simonson apparently sold the committee that arranged the real estate financing of the university more than thirty acres for $6,250 an acre or nearly six times what he had paid the club for its eleven acres. He was said to have walked away with $200,000. It was perhaps the single most significant land sale in the history of the Hills and must have been particularly galling to the Shinnecock golf club's board of governors. They had labored for so many years under the assumption that their three hundred acres were worth only $300 an acre. Now they were valued at $3,000, yet they had sold them for $1,000, while a speculator had turned them over for $6,000. It was an old story. In a century of deals, beginning with Lewis Scott in 1861, if not with the trustees of the proprietors of the common lands who had sold to Scott, Simonson's was probably the best deal of all. As for the Shinnecock Hills as a whole, beginning with Country Club Knolls they became gradually suburbanized and were graced with a college that took in the children of middle-class suburbanites, mostly from elsewhere. It was an apotheosis of sorts but one that did not quite match the dreams of the earlier visionaries.

Remarkably, there was little clash between the town and the succession of would-be developers over the fifty years beginning in 1882 leading into the Environs sale by Jere Johnson, and there was none thereafter. There was no public debate except on the question of the fate of the bays and local access to the beaches, and that was largely confined to the late 1880s and 1890s when it was fueled by the controversy generated by the Mecox Bay and Betts cases. The town appeared simply to accept, and in some instances embrace, the ambitious plans of development companies and voiced little concern that the Shinnecock Hills had become wholly owned and operated by outside forces. When the Shinnecock Hills and Peconic Bay Realty Company unveiled its far-reaching plans on 1907 to cover the Hills with roads and housing lots, public reaction was generally positive. The issue of how the Hills had fallen into their hands in the first place, and those of their predecessors in the Long Island Improvement Company and the Shinnecock Land Company, had by this time been generally forgotten.

The murkiness of the process by which the Indian lease was cancelled, casting a shadow on the title of future generations of owners, was similarly thrust into the past. The Shinnecock were, as we have seen, unsuccessful in forcing a review of the 1859 act in the legislature. Nor was the title, as far as the record shows, ever tested in court. It was an issue in 1885 when several members of the tribe attempted to bring it to court, but locally, only George Rogers Howell and George White questioned the legitimacy of the title.

One of the first to buy property on the Hills, General Wager Swayne, did learn in 1887 that his own land title could well be worthless but neither he nor others were deterred by this.[66] Very probably the idea was simply dismissed that a small and marginalized group of impoverished Indians, lacking sufficient resources and any political support at all, could mount any realistic challenge to what was in effect a fait accompli. Besides which, current owners of Hills property could not help but be aware that the courts were almost totally unsympathetic to Indian problems, while public interest in them was nonexistent. The experience of the Montaukett Indians also would have been well known at the time. Their attempts at legal action against both Arthur Benson and Austin Corbin respecting their lands on Montauk met with one defeat after another. If the Shinnecock resisted, they could expect the same fate.

By 1907, it could safely be said that Southampton had made its peace with development and welcomed what it took to be manifestations of progress in an era that loudly proclaimed progress. After all, the Shinnecock Hills were still there whoever now owned them. And the succession of new owners seemed to have nothing but the best of intentions, adding one amenity after another and apparently respectful of the beauty of the area. If there were to be three railroad stations, hotels, churches, good roads, golf courses, and fine houses, it was surely an improvement over sheep and fish factories. The loss of the land, and from the town's point of view it was never anything less than proprietor land, was hardly a matter to lose any sleep over. Once the town had got over the initial shock of the 1881 sale and subsequent auction in New York, it settled into the role of what can best be described as that of interested observer. The early years of controversy were quickly forgotten, just as were the objections of the Shinnecock. The latter never doubted, naturally and with much justice on their side, that they were still the original and rightful owners. That they had been unable to bring the issue into the courts for want of resources in the 1860s or 1880s was perhaps both tragic and unavoidable. But even had they done so, their chances of success in reversing the 1859 legislation and gaining a more equitable distribution of the lands on the Hills, let alone the legal recovery of the Hills intact, must be judged as very low indeed. In 2005, the Shinnecock did make an attempt comparable to that they had made in the 1860s to regain the Hills but the suit subsequently languished as the tribal leadership turned its attention to the suddenly more real possibility of gaining federal recognition. This had long been the goal since the 1970s and the possibility of it finally being granted by the Bureau of Indian Affairs in 2010, as indeed it was, could conceivably lead to the dropping of the suit demanding the return of the Hills or some genuine compensation for their loss.[67]

CHAPTER 8

THE SUMMER COLONY CONSOLIDATED 1888–1900

I: SUMMER LIFE

Several chapters ago we found Southampton's summer colony leadership in 1886 embroiled in various village issues of greater or lesser significance. The Moore family had been safely removed to Sebonac from the marshy ground at the head of Lake Agawam where their presence, in sight of the cottage estates carved out down the shores of the lake, had been found to be both offensive and unhygienic. Gaillard Thomas and Salem Wales had not handled this situation with the sort of tact it might be thought was necessary and had found themselves, despite the support of the business community, defending their actions as not simply a matter of civic duty but also on the less disinterested grounds of the heavy investment—$500,000—their fellow colonists had made in lakefront real estate (and none more so, it might be added, than Wales, the Moore family's closest summer neighbor).

The obduracy of Edwin Post had ensured that the case involving the desecration of the South End cemetery bordering his property would drag on until spring 1888. The judge in the case found for the town arguing that Post's "wilful invasion" of the property of another constituted an actionable trespass. The summer leadership had largely stayed in the background during the dispute, leaving it to George White to marshal the anti-Post forces, but by bringing it to the town's attention in the first place with various expressions of outrage the leadership had only succeeded in placing it in an embarrassing position it would have preferred to avoid. Other matters that had preoccupied the Village Improvement Association, and would do so for years to come, were street watering, the failure of the railroad to do anything about its unprepossessing little depot and the unkempt state of the grounds surrounding it, the condition of the lake and the choking weed that infested it and resisted all efforts at removal, and the relaxed attitude of shopkeepers toward maintaining high standards of neatness outside and around their establishments.

To take street watering alone, it was expensive, largely ineffective in quieting the dust, and had involved the construction of an unsightly water tank over the village pump at the corner of Main Street and the Bridgehampton Road. James Foster, once it was clear that the tank was not an aesthetic success, had suggested in 1886 that it be left there for a year in the hope that its presence would eventually be accepted as simply part of the habitual landscape. In 1888 it was still there, now abandoned and unused and just as disliked. Unsuccessful efforts were made to sell it, auction it off, or give it away. Despite remonstrations from the *Seaside Times* that summer, the association did nothing to have it removed. One resident wrote that the tank was "a great blemish on our former handsome street." It had also, incidentally, occurred to many local inhabitants that a good part of the dust problem was attributable to the large and expensive carriages that the ladies of the colony insisted on using in their excursions into the village. Adelaide Douglas, for example, one of the sportiest women in the colony and later the mistress of J. Pierpont Morgan, took to driving a spider-phaeton with a matched team of calico ponies on her rounds.[1] Already faint whiffs of Newport were in the air along with the dust.

Interest and involvement in the activities of the SVIA declined in the late 1880s and continued to do so until 1892. Attendance at annual meetings was sparse and those who did attend were more likely to be from the local business community whose interests were more directly affected. In this group, the work of the association was seen as potentially beneficial for economic growth in general and real estate expansion in particular. From the beginning, businessmen had been quick to understand that a growing summer resort would in the long run improve economic opportunities for most sectors of local society but especially perhaps for them. Summer residents looked at matters differently. They appreciated what their leaders were doing—the lake, the streets, the depot, or whatever it was that enhanced their quality of life—but were broadly content to leave matters in the hands of those who had seized the reins. By 1887, there were estimated to be about one thousand visitors residing in the village in the summer. Most were boarders, perhaps as many as 80 percent, but among those who owned or rented cottages for the season only about twenty men and some wives took an active role in the operations of the SVIA. Of those who did not who were members, or were informed that they were members whether they wanted to be or not, a large number in most years failed to pay annual dues. In 1895, for example, Thomas reported that as of August, 130 cottage residents had not paid dues. Dues were then $10 a year while Thomas reported that no more than $400 had been collected, including $100 from local members. Based on these figures, total membership that year appears to have been 170. In the early 1890s, dues income was similarly low and the activities of the association correspondingly limited.

But where were they all on an August Saturday afternoon when annual meetings were typically held if they were not in the Village Hall? There were a variety of summer pursuits that the colony enjoyed and threw themselves into with the kind of zest and energy characteristic of the American ideal of bourgeois life in the gilded age. While the women of the colony and their children settled in for the summer in their cottages and sank into a placid routine of lunches, teas, dips in the ocean (never before noon and only after summer boarders had returned to their lodgings for their lunches) and games of tennis or croquet, the men—after a sweaty week in their downtown Broadway offices—disgorged from the Friday afternoon train hungry for other forms of competitive action than the city provided. Tennis rapidly became the principal sport of the 1880s but sailboat racing on

Lake Agawam (when the weed permitted it), as well as polo and other equestrian activities were close seconds. Golf came a few years later, as discussed in the last chapter, when the Shinnecock Hills Golf Club was formed in 1891. For a few years in the 1890s, golf replaced tennis as the premier sport; but tennis reclaimed its preeminent position by 1900, a younger second generation of summer residents having taken the place of their parents on the grass courts of the Meadow Club at the foot of First Neck Lane. And there was always the beach. Battling the surf was highly popular, affording the young men of the colony a chance to show off their skill and daring while the ladies sunbathed (heavily covered though they were) in front of Mrs. Howell's bathing station. For the more sedentary there were walks in the neighborhood, sometimes rambles or carriage rides toward Long Springs or Barrel Hill on Peconic Bay. There certainly was plenty to do for the athletically inclined as well as for those whose athletic abilities had diminished with advancing age. Decidedly, for almost everyone there was every excuse for not attending a meeting of the SVIA in the Village Hall where it was more than probable that Thomas or Wales would expatiate at considerable length on the condition of the streets, the lake, or the association's finances or even render a learned paper on a life-threatening disease or the hygienic advantages of cremation as opposed to burial.

Lawn tennis was a relative newcomer to the American sporting scene in the 1870s and appealed immediately to the rich, whose exclusive domain it became, for its grace and skill and individual competitiveness. It also was admired for its English roots and popularity among their upper-class cousins in Europe. Team sports such as baseball and football, although engaged in at elite colleges and enthusiastically followed by alumnae out of institutional loyalty, were not favored by the upper classes. Cricket was an exception, as was polo, perhaps again because of their essential and much esteemed Englishness; but in general, athletic teams were associated with professional leagues and clubs where players were recruited from lower social classes. Baseball was fast becoming a mass spectator sport in the late nineteenth century while all high schools, rural communities and urban neighborhoods had their own teams and entered into fierce local rivalries with each other. They also provided the pool of talent necessary to fill out the rosters of established or new clubs and promote the professional or semiprofessional leagues from which they were constituted. Southampton played baseball and fielded teams against their archrivals in Westhampton, Quogue, and Easthampton (the scores were always reported in the *Seaside Times*), but the summer colony did not. If there were matches with other summer communities as there were with Easthampton and Quogue, they were tennis and later golf matches. These too were reported in the paper but the audience for the results was not the same. There were class differences in sport just as there were in religion.

Tennis in Southampton originated in summer 1879 when the wives of Frederic Betts and Dr. Albert Buck began to invite their friends in the colony to join them on Saturday afternoons for informal games in the meadow between their properties on First Neck Lane. Rackets were provided and tea was served. The game quickly caught on, and within a year, the one court in the meadow being found inadequate to accommodate all those wishing to play, operations were removed to the more spacious grounds of Thomas's estate between

Gin Lane and the ocean and several courts there were laid out. In August 1881 the first of what became annual matches with the Easthampton Lawn Tennis Club was held. Tennis had also captured the fancy of Easthampton summer residents and their club had been formed in the same year Mrs. Betts and Mrs. Buck began playing. The club had two or three courts at The Circle off Main Street and remained there for a decade until the Maidstone Club was incorporated in 1891. At that time tennis, for want of enough courts and other facilities, was removed to a site overlooking Hook Pond (there was no golf at Maidstone until 1894) and twelve courts and a clubhouse constructed. In August 1882 the matches with Easthampton held on Thomas's courts were extraordinarily well attended indicative of the growing popularity of the game. Lunch was served to one hundred guests and a regatta was held on the lake just across the road.

The following year, the Agawam Tennis Club was organized under the leadership of J. Metcalf Thomas, Gaillard's son, but shortly renamed itself the Meadow Club in recollection of its modest beginnings on the other side of the lake. Officers were elected, a schedule of dues established, and a membership committee formed while Metcalf Thomas became president. Some investment was made in the grounds to improve the surface of the courts, provide some means of irrigation, and construct a small club house. The club also joined the National Lawn Tennis Association, the forerunner of the USTA, and under its auspices was designated the site of the Long Island Championship, which recently had been introduced. It quickly became apparent, however, that the club was to be and would remain extremely exclusive. This, of course, is hardly a surprise. Membership policies of private clubs then as later always confined their admission of new members to "people like us." In this case, people like us were fellow cottagers, those who owned or rented cottages for the season and could be regarded as full-time summer residents, people who would be elected to the SVIA. The Meadow, like other clubs after it, imposed just such a residence restriction. It excluded two important categories of people: local inhabitants who, although year-round residents, would never be considered for membership and were only selectively admitted to the SVIA for reasons of political necessity; and second, summer boarders.

That there was a boarder dispute in the making in Southampton would have caused no raised eyebrows. By 1885, boarders far outnumbered cottagers by as much as five to one. It was no matter that many boarders—Samuel Parrish was to be one for a brief year before putting down his markers and buying property—were eventually integrated into the cottager elite, becoming property owners in their own right. There were simply too many who did not, milling around at the beaches, clogging the lanes and byways of the village, gawking at the carriages and their finely dressed occupants or enthusiastically applauding the sailboat races on Lake Agawam. Perhaps they could not afford to buy into the cottage colony as prices began to escalate in the mid-1880s. But they were relatively well-off, middle class but perhaps aspiring to greater heights, hoping to enjoy their summers in what were becoming known as the Hamptons; yet, still, not quite making it. In 1885, there were several hundred such boarders, each of them paying on average $10 a week for room and board. Their story, the story of the hangers-on, deserves a telling beyond the pages of Edith Wharton, but for lack of data is unlikely ever to be told. An incident, nonetheless, does stand out and is emblematic of the status distinction that had quickly developed between the permanent and transient summer populations in Southampton. It concerned the policy of the Meadow Club toward admitting spectators to its grounds.

In July 1885, the local paper noted with approval the increasing numbers of summer visitors putting up in boarding houses for part of the season. It signified a substantial growth in trade and reflected the visible transformation of the village into a summer resort, a change that the *Seaside Times* heartily approved. At the same time, it issued a veiled warning. There were to be "no dudes here" such as might be found in other upscale watering places, an allusion perhaps to a socially indeterminate element that had surfaced in Saratoga and Newport and were seen as insidiously undermining their respectability—social climbers, bachelors of uncertain background, demimonde types, gamblers; in short people not "like us." For various reasons, including this one, Southampton was considered to be the anti-Newport, a place of rustic charm, healthful relaxation and, above all, a simple social life. It was no more to be filled with men (and women) of dubious pedigree or certain forms of new wealth than it was to be overrun by a middle class hovering at the edges of society and aspiring to membership. But "dudes" was about as far as the newspaper was prepared to go.[2]

A few weeks later, nonetheless, the true dimensions of the problem began to reveal themselves. A self-described "summer boarder" wrote to the paper that he or she (it is not clear which) had been ushered off the premises of the Meadow Club when all the writer had wished to do was to watch tennis and engage (in a disarming phrase) in a modicum of "social intercourse." Were boarders not allowed on club grounds for this purpose, he or she wished to know? A reply by Metcalf Thomas appeared two weeks later. He wanted to make it clear, he said, that the club did have membership policies and rules, that anyone seeking to join would require the support of two members and the endorsement of the membership committee, and that indeed suitable candidates for admission should by all means apply. "Otherwise," he concluded, "outsiders are not expected on the grounds." It was a small thing and in its way entirely to be expected. The president of what was fast becoming the center of the colony's social universe, and would do so when the club moved into its elegant new quarters in spring 1888, had announced to all who might be interested that there were to be well-defined limits to social intercourse in the new Southampton. The fences had well and truly gone up and notice served on the legion of summer boarders that they could expect no more than to look in from the outside. When the Meadow Club did move two or three years later—back to First Neck Lane—a writer for the *New York Telegram* remarked that the "far-famed" club was "fenced in by barbed wire and red tape" and that the "Pond" people or "Ponders," as they were now called in an unfortunate new sobriquet, "pride themselves on their exclusiveness." "Summer Boarder," if that distressed individual was still around in 1888, might have been less than enchanted to hear this. Barbed wire replaced old-fashioned wooden fencing in the 1880s and predated privet hedges whose potential had yet to be fully explored. They were perfectly effective, good enough for the Meadow while farmers liked them but they were unaesthetic and hell on horses. They also kept out boarders.[3]

J. Bowers Lee, a banker and later treasurer to both the Meadow Club and the Shinnecock Hills Golf Club, bought five acres on the west side of First Neck Lane steps from the beach in 1885 and built a cottage. He moved in the following year. Shortly after that he acquired another five acres adjoining his property. In 1887, tiring of life at Agawam, he put the land and the house up for sale and moved to the western extremity of the village where, as we saw, he established a small plantation of his own on Lee Avenue at Captain's Neck. The Meadow Club promptly bought his land and house for $30,000. The club had recently incorporated for this purpose and raised the money to finance a mortgage through its members, who were stockholders, by subscription without any difficulty. Given that the SVIA had to subsist that season on a little under $600 in membership dues, it was apparent where the priorities of most summer residents lay. Nor was the purchase price entirely without precedent, astronomically high though it first appears. A month or so earlier Leon de Bost had sold his house and land on South Main Street, nine acres in all including two acres of lake frontage, to John Kilbreth for $21,500. Twenty years previously, it had belonged to William Pelletreau and probably cost de Bost well under $1,000. Real estate prices continued to climb in the favored part of the village and to most summer residents, perhaps especially to those who were fortunate enough to be elected to the Meadow Club, money was no obstacle to their advance. The club, well in funds, planned to build a large hall adjacent to its new club house for dancing and other indoor amusements as well as construct twelve to fifteen grass courts, a baseball field for juniors, and space for the occasional cricket match.

All of it and more remains today more than a century later but now is enclosed by tall privet hedges instead of barbed wire. The new club house and grounds were an immediate hit in that first summer of 1888 and absorbed all the attention and interest of the majority of summer colony members. The Meadow, as it was always called, took its place alongside Dune Church as a central institution of summer life. It was not only the tennis and the enjoyable frequency of tournaments that attracted people, but the fact that for the first time summer residents had their own place to go to; a club where there would be teas, dances, dinners and parties to organize and attend. Something had been missing in Southampton's social life and suddenly the Meadow Club, reincarnated in its new premises on what quickly came to be called Meadow Lane and no longer dependent on the generosity of Gaillard Thomas for a place to play, filled that empty social space. Even the club house, Bowers Lee's former cottage, was usable year-round and contained rooms where members and their guests could put up on overnight visits. The club, far more than the SVIA (despite its useful works), came to define the essential nature of the summer colony and gave meaning to a style of life that hitherto lacked a cohesive and collective focus. It also was centrally located in the heart of the colony that was now clustered thickly and permanently around the lake and near the beach. In the Meadow Club we can see the true birth of "the Hamptons," an expression that was to enter the lexicon of terms and phrases metaphorically used to describe American resort life. A year or so later, the Maidstone Club, in a very similar metamorphosis, came to play the same role in Easthampton in unifying summer life and focusing its activities in one symbolic location.

In the same year Maidstone was formed, the Shinnecock Hills Golf Club opened its small course and the Stanford White designed club house on the Hills three miles distant from the village. It was destined to become one of the three clubs that defined the arc of summer life in Southampton. The third was the Bathing Corporation but that did not materialize until the first part of the twentieth century. The beach pavilion, such as it was before 1900 when a more durable structure was built, could never be described as a club—it had no facilities to speak of—but functioned as a "place" where sand, surf, and sun could be enjoyed by all (including local inhabitants). In this last respect, it was almost democratic, although one wonders if the two communities mingled quite so freely with one another. According to George White, testifying at the Betts trial in 1892, "the city people . . . didn't think it suitable to bathe with the country people." The Betts case—the issue concerned ownership of the beach—was shortly to go to court and feelings ran high in the village over what was seen as an attempt at control over a public space by one or two summer owners of adjacent property. Moreover, it would not have been forgotten that George Schieffelin and Wales had toured the beach not many years before and pronounced the rustic bowers—simple shelters covered with oak branches—erected on it "a disgrace" and ordered their removal and the beach cleaned up. Or, as White put it, they "cleaned out" the "little shanties" that locals put up for their pleasure and convenience.[4] The village had retaliated and White's town trustees had sat on a proposal by Betts and Thomas for a palatial beach casino on land donated by Betts just to the east of Dune Church, imposing impossible leasing conditions, and ultimately forced their withdrawal.

Tennis was not, obviously, the only game in town. From the early 1880s, Lake Agawam, its ancient shores increasingly surrounded by summer property and the condition of its waters a focus of minute attention, had become the perfect venue for sailboat racing. Regattas were held on what was called "our lake" as early as 1882 and two years later the Agawam Yacht Club was formed. The most popular vessel was an early version of the catboat, a fourteen-foot skiff with one sail and a mast forward, and later perfected in the 1890s by a Hampton Bays boat-builder, Gilbert Smith.[5] On any given Saturday from June to September as many as thirty of these small boats might be observed sailing a marked course up and down the lake. Shallow as it was in places and often shoaled at its southern end, it was small wonder that the SVIA did everything in its power to eliminate the weed that infested it and fouled the steering gear. The lake now boasted three bays, actually shallow indentations in the shoreline at its southern end and not markedly noticeable as "bays," all of them named for summer residents with adjacent property: they were Schieffelin's Bay, Murdoch's Bay, and Betts's Bay. Naming continued to be a folk activity of the colony and gave their members an enhanced sense of ownership of place. Races followed a course inside a series of buoys strategically placed in each of these bays. "Ponders"—one cannot avoid inverted commas—viewed the proceedings from spacious lawns abutting the lakefront.

In 1888, a second yacht club was formed calling itself the Shinnecock Yacht Club with a small dock on Shinnecock Bay near the recently opened Shinnecock Inn and Cottages at Fort Pond. The bay was far larger than Agawam and although equally shallow in places subject to much fiercer winds off the ocean and called for considerably more skill in sailing small boats. The catboats, some built larger and with centerboards, fully came into their own. The existence of the inn and now a new sailing club encouraged Thomas to begin pushing for an extension of Gin Lane, which began at Old Town Road at the edge of Wickapogue, past the Meadow Club (where it became Dune Road), past Cooper's Neck Pond and Halsey's Neck Pond to a dead end on Shinnecock Bay and at a little dock on what later became Meadowmere Lane. It was to be called Seaside Boulevard.

Thomas wrote to the paper explaining his plan, which was to cost $1,500, and revealed that the Long Island Improvement Company was willing to provide a matching grant of $750 if the balance were to be raised by subscription in the summer colony. But it was clear that he had something more ambitious in mind. He and Wales had long thought that opening new roads was a necessity for developing summer resorts, both for improving access within the village and opening up the surrounding countryside. They had campaigned for a road to the beach from the station, for the eastward extension of Gin Lane to Wickapogue Pond, and were in the midst of persuading the road commissioners "to do their plain duty" and upgrade the narrow lane around the head of the lake that, Thomas averred, was "a menace to travelers." This was Pond Lane that later, if briefly, was renamed Park Avenue. But Seaside Boulevard turned out to be a much larger project and ultimately was to run parallel to the beach as far as Tiana for a distance of six miles.[6] It was clearly this that caught the attention of Corbin and the LIIC.

The beach front between Shinnecock Bay and the ocean was the company's property, much of it picked up by John Bowman in 1881 from the owners of lots in the Pine Division of Beach Meadows (first divided in 1687) and none of it developed. For Thomas and his friends the new road, properly loamed, would provide enjoyable rides along the shore. For the LIIC it was an opportunity to integrate its interests in both the beach and the Shinnecock Hills more firmly with those of the summer colony. The Hills continued to exist in relative isolation from Southampton, despite the company's much-advertised plans for their development, and seemed impervious to the real estate boom occurring in preferred sections of the village. Possibly Corbin thought that building lots could be sold all the way down the beach. They never were at least before the 1920s and then only as far west as Halsey Neck. Seaside Boulevard was eventually built—under the name of Dune Road—but the property along it remained undeveloped for another century until as late as the 1980s. At that point new summer residents, sitting on million-dollar one- or two-acre parcels, managed to persuade the village highway authorities to do their plain duty and macadamize the road as far as Shinnecock Inlet. It was done with a degree of reluctance reminiscent of local sentiments the century before.[7]

Thomas's interest in opening up a seaside road along the barrier beach between Shinnecock Bay and the ocean may have had as much to do with horseback riding as with the simple pleasures of afternoon drives and picnics. He was himself a fairly accomplished horseman and was given to hosting informal races on his other property near the dunes in Wickapogue as well as an annual September event open to all in Southampton. The races in September were a benefit sponsored by the SVIA from which its treasury did handsomely from a paying public. They included sweepstake pony races, farmers' races for draught animals, and, most especially and popularly, a menagerie race that was open to all fowls and animals except horses and dogs, each for generous purses. The 1887 account of the latter is worth repeating: "Kid led in a canter to the returning post when she stopped. The goat then took the lead, but the Shanghai rooster coming with a big rush at the finish beat the goat by a short head on the post. The pig has not yet arrived."[8]

But these were not quite the equestrian sports that were introduced in the first years of the summer colony. Riding, even more than lawn tennis, was very much a mark of high social status in late nineteenth-century New York as, in diluted form, it still is today. Its expense, the traditions associated with it inherited from the English upper classes, its elaborate codes of dress and behavior—not to mention the necessity of early training—ensured that it was available only to the privileged few. Polo—a form of uninhibited aggression in the saddle—was intermittently played but may have been too strenuous for most, the skill and daring required in nonstop action placing more of a premium on youth and strength. Much more to the taste of the colony was fox hunting.

In 1883, the Hampton Hunt Club was formed by Thomas, Frederic Betts, Schieffelin, Wager Swayne, and others with its headquarters in Tuckahoe. It rented an old farmhouse from George Whitaker in Long Springs and used it as a club house. Whitaker, as discussed earlier, was the father of Edward Whitaker who was to make an unsuccessful and much-publicized bid on the bay bottoms in the proprietors' sale the year before. He was to become the master of hounds, a natural role for him perhaps because he also served the county as its game warden. Fox hunts on the Shinnecock Hills beginning at Tuckahoe Gate on the old Indian Line[9] with ceremonial toasts, the participants outfitted in scarlet coats, became highly popular and were held at regular intervals. Occasionally in the 1890s, a fox shot across the new golf links on the Hills, the hounds in pursuit, disturbing the golfers in their leisurely rounds who were similarly and confusingly attired in formal red coats as well. One imagines the horror of the fox running full-tilt through a red-suited foursome seeking to escape those identically clad tooting their horns and thundering after him. Wager Swayne, the ex-general with property on the Hills, became secretary of the club.

Later, in 1901, the Southampton Horse Association came into being and purchased forty acres in Tuckahoe where it laid out a racetrack, a hurdle course, polo field, horse sheds, and a grandstand. It complemented the Hampton Hounds perfectly (they later merged) and equally suited the summer colony's perception of itself as devoted to healthful outdoor recreation. Yet subtle changes were occurring affecting that self-image. Until the 1890s—the gay 90s—there was little in the way of nightlife to interfere with the summer round of strenuous daytime activity and peaceful contemplation—a book here, an easel there, a quiet hour at the beach. But inevitably it came as the children of the founders grew up. Dances—hops—in the capacious new premises of the Meadow Club or, for that matter, in the Maidstone's new club house or new village hall, soaked up the unexpended energy of the young and satisfied their desires for excitement. Sensual summer nights no doubt did the rest. In a lament to the Easthampton paper Dr. Everett Herrick, the abstemious president of the Maidstone, summed it up for his generation:

> This year, tennis is not the chief end of man. Perhaps the new village hall is responsible for the inauguration of something heretofore unheard-of in East

Hampton—i.e. "late hours." One cannot battle the surf in the morning, play tennis all the afternoon and dance all night, and live. Tennis has suffered. The long and short of it is, that East Hampton isn't what it used to be. Late hours and ultra-fashionable tastes are out of place here. Let us all come here another summer to have a good time, but a restful one.[10]

But nightlife was in its infant stages and would not even begin to approach Newport levels of extravagance for another thirty years, well beyond the timeframe of this history. Summer life in Southampton (and Easthampton) continued to meander on its pleasant and rather placid way mostly unaffected by the social excess found elsewhere. Dr. Herrick actually had little to lose any sleep over.

II: THE VILLAGE

Between 1888 and 1894 the Improvement Association undertook little in the way of new efforts to upgrade the village. It had not run out of ideas but falling revenues and flagging membership interest appeared to hamper its activity. It continued to search for a satisfactory method of watering the streets and was able to let out a contract to a local company willing to do it. It ruminated ceaselessly about the proper naming of streets and lanes. Having settled on Dune Road as the replacement for the much misunderstood Gin Lane in 1888 it reversed itself in 1890, under pressure from adjacent property owners, and reinstated the original name. Unsure whether Dune Road would be continued westward under the guise of Seaside Boulevard, as Thomas had projected in 1888, the executive committee the following year directed that the extension west of First Neck Lane to Shinnecock Bay be named Agawam Road. It was all a little confusing. A year or so later it became Meadow Lane in recognition of the Meadow Club. But even today confusion abounds as to where Meadow Lane ends and Dune Road begins, a confusion compounded by the desire of status-conscious homeowners west of the Meadow to have a Meadow Lane address. Its soft English inflection, calling up old country lanes in Kent or Sussex, perhaps had something to do with it as well. In the same spirit and in homage to the venerable tract of land leading west from the village, always known as the Great Plain and first divided in 1648 (if not in fact in 1643 when lots in "the new ground" were initially allocated), Great Plains Road was formally received into the pantheon of newly created ancient names.[11]

There were new issues to be brought up however, several of them constructive and important for the future of the village and its modernization. As early as 1888, the SVIA began to investigate the feasibility of developing a central water supply system in the village. This would eventually replace dependence on private wells and, in doing so, reduce the risk for disease. It was a project well beyond the limited resources of the association but within the reach of the town and private investment. In 1894, the Southampton Water Works Company was organized as a joint venture with some representation from the summer community. James Pierson was elected president and Edward Foster secretary. Samuel Parrish and two other summer residents became directors. The company acquired forty acres north of the village, drove wells and built a plant and pumping station. It laid six miles of mains in the village, extending them to sixteen miles in the early 1900s, and eventually reached more than five hundred households. Ultimately, it provided a solution to the dust problem by installing hydrants and sprinklers on the principal streets. But that lay in the future. The association continued to wrestle with the best way to deal with the dust and concluded that contracting it out to a private company was unsatisfactory. In 1895, it resolved to buy and operate its own watering carts "in order that it may in future control the sprinkling of the streets and have it conducted in accordance with its views," a clear indication that, despite the expense entailed, the job had not been done very well in the past. It was to cost $850 but, as Thomas reported at the annual meeting, the association had finally turned a corner and was in funds for the first time in years.[12]

Other suggestions for physical improvements contributing to the modernization of the village in these years included a public drainage system discharging surface water into the ocean and street lighting. Windmill Lane and the foot of Job's Lane were especially susceptible to flooding in heavy rains as early photographs of ferrying inhabitants across the street attest. Street lighting began in a small and quite voluntary way with the suggestion in 1889 that each cottage owner place a lantern at the entrance to his residence. Charming though the suggestion was, it was clear that the association had more in mind. Some larger scheme of village lighting was attempted in the next several years but it evidently strained what limited resources were available. Reporting for the executive committee in 1892, Thomas felt that this task should be taken off the shoulders of the association and the responsibility assumed by the town. "Our taxes (of late)," he said, "have greatly increased and in return the town should surely light our streets" adding, "and repair our sidewalks and keep our roads in order." The early 1890s were lean years for the association's finances and Thomas found himself caught in this and other matters between a desire to control the provision of desirable amenities in the village and the recognition that only the town, not the association, was in a position to undertake large-scale municipal projects.

This was a new and perhaps unanticipated development. The more ambitious the association's plans became, the more dependent it was on outside agreement and support for carrying them out. In some matters the summer colony could turn to private capital to develop particular projects. A case in point was the Southampton Company formed some years earlier by Wyllys and Frederic Betts with local as well as summer capital to fund the renovation of the old Methodist church for a new village hall. The Southampton Bank, which opened on Main Street in 1888, was formed in much the same way. It had been the brainchild of Wales in 1886, a modernization project as much to help the summer colony as the local business community. Wales had rounded up the usual business and political leaders—James Pierson, Edward Foster, Edgar A. Hildreth, L. Emory Terry, Erastus Post—and between them raised sufficient capital to start operations. New York or summer interests on the board of directors were represented by Wales and James Townsend, Adelaide Douglas's brother and the owner of considerable beach property. The bank's initial capital offering was $50,000 which was quickly subscribed. Deposits by the end of 1888 stood at

$57,000, more than justifying the investment, and quadrupled a decade later. It was the first new bank on the East End since the Sag Harbor Savings Bank had been formed in 1859.

The SVIA may have found its own resources inadequate for some tasks but its moral will remained intact. It could still play the role of village scold. Thomas and Wales continued to complain that local merchants, in their desire for trade and profit, could not resist defacing the fences with business signs. They risked, said Thomas, losing the patronage of those customers they had come to count on most. Then Wales, after a tour of the Academy School on Job's Lane, called for its removal to a more healthful location on the grounds that it lacked the necessary air, light, and space for exercise that were required for the welfare of children.[13] It was a laudable sentiment, delivered with all the sincerity that might be expected from him, but in this as in many other matters Wales never stopped to think that he might be treading on local toes and in particular on those of the parents and teachers. It was a question in his mind, rather, of his civic duty to inform the authorities of anything that he thought was amiss in his adopted community. So, for example, having stocked Lake Agawam with young bass in an earlier gesture of generosity, he was appalled to find that the youth of the village had almost immediately fished them out. He wrote immediately to the paper. He and Thomas were by upbringing thoroughly patrician in temperament, a trait that came naturally to men of their class, and for all their good intentions and sentimental attachment to the village it was inevitable that their manner should inspire a certain amount of local resentment. Criticism was seldom publicly expressed, but it is hard to imagine that local leaders and the general run of inhabitants remained mute among themselves.

Both men, for instance, had advocated cultivating grass plots parallel to the sidewalks on the village's principal streets. It was a nice decorative touch and, together with the extensive planting of shade trees (of which there were several hundred by 1900), part of the association's general plan for village beautification. Wales, however, discovered to his horror and chagrin that these "green swards" were routinely plowed up by town highway labor to provide dirt for loaming the adjacent roadway. He realized that under present practice it was a necessary act of vandalism but beseeched all who would listen, hands upraised to the heavens, "must this thing continue for all time? Is there no remedy?" Yes, he thought, there was. If only "the people of the town would wake up to the fact that Southampton is growing" they would realize that earth from nearby sites could be had for the taking. The town should condemn these sites for public use "at little cost" and spread earth on its streets accordingly. If we cannot find the requisite earth now, he said, "what, I ask, is to be done five or ten years hence?"[14] Frederic Betts did have an answer to that question ten years later. The automobile age was then for all practical purposes on Southampton even if only affecting the privileged sector of the community. Betts offered that the time had come (this was 1898) to construct "permanent hard roads" to accommodate this new mode of transportation. But in Wales's day the roads were dirt and motor traffic a distant dream. His concern was the protection and maintenance of grass verges. It perhaps did not occur to him that a source of earth for road maintenance might be on someone's land or farm near the village. Well, it could always be condemned in the public interest provided that the town's road commissioners agreed. There was not as yet, and would not be for several years, a village highway authority to which Wales could take his suggestions and complaints. It was, nevertheless, to come.

Southampton village was incorporated in September 1894 under a recent state law authorizing the incorporation of population centers of a minimum size as villages within existing townships.[15] In 1890, the town's population was approximately eight thousand of whom a little over one thousand were permanent residents of the village. A further two thousand lived in Sag Harbor, incorporated much earlier in 1818 primarily to designate it as a separate fire district following a series of disastrous fires. By the early 1900s, the two villages accounted for half of the town's population and more than half of its taxes. Incorporation would mean many things to Southampton. It could hold its own village elections for mayor (then called president) and trustees, raise its own taxes, appoint its own fire and police departments, maintain its roads and sidewalks, sprinkle its own streets, enact its own ordinances. It would give the village considerable independence from the town. Not everyone, however, was in favor of incorporation when it was brought before the voters. In May 1894 some preliminary steps were taken toward incorporation with the state. In July, a referendum was held on whether to incorporate. Whether the result was surprising or not, the vote was close. Of 199 votes cast, 113 were in favor and 86 against. Possibly there was concern about the prospect of additional taxation—village residents already paid a disproportionate share of town taxes—but in the absence of a newspaper record for the time there is no way of knowing if that or other reasons were the case.[16] A month later, incorporation was approved by the state and on September 4, after an apparently abortive election two weeks before, the new Village of Southampton elected its first president and board of trustees.

Fairly clearly a number of the principal business leaders and politicians in the town who resided in the village were behind this move, particularly Pierson the town supervisor, Bowden, Henry Fordham, the two Fosters, Albert Post (who was to be the village's first president) and White. For some of them, perhaps most, it may have been regarded as a necessary defensive reaction to counter the widening influence of the SVIA and its ability to control the direction of change within the village (although not outside it). Although most of these men were members of the association, took part in its affairs, and were elected to its offices and its executive committee (the policymaking arm), the real power remained with a nucleus of key summer leaders (Thomas, Wales, Betts, Schieffelin, and several others). There could be and frequently was agreement between these two groups but the lives and interests of each ran on different and certainly not parallel tracks. Yet what is surprising—at least on the surface—is that the impetus behind village incorporation may have originated in the association itself.

At the July 1890 annual meeting a resolution was introduced calling for the appointment of a committee by the chair of the meeting (who, although not the association's president at the time, happened to be Thomas) "to consider the subject of the practicability and advisability or otherwise of incorporating the village of Southampton, with directions to report to the Executive Committee." The committee was to consist of three permanent residents (Pierson, Fordham, and White) and two members of the summer colony (Betts and Thomas). There is no surviving record of the deliberations of this committee or its report but it can be assumed that it duly recommended incorporation. The motivation behind the association's interest in the establishment of a purely village authority appears to have been twofold. First, it had become clear to the summer leadership that the financial burden of assuming responsibility for improvements in the village in the context of declining dues revenue had become difficult to bear. Thomas himself was later to state that he was tired of importuning fellow summer residents for contributions (who had a habit of disappearing around a corner at his approach) and vowed when he became president in 1895 that he would have nothing further to do with soliciting funds. Secondly, a small village leadership and only a local electorate to worry about might well prove to be a more manageable body to deal with than the larger and more far-flung bureaucracy of the town and its non-village power centers (for all supervisor James Pierson's careful consideration of the association's needs and desires). A village government, focused on village needs alone, might be more susceptible to direct influence and persuasion. Evidence for this is to found in the almost immediate effort after incorporation to recommend village ordinances to the new administration.

There was a discussion of this question of local regulations between the new village president and trustees at a meeting the following summer with a group of "cottage owners" (in reality the association's executive committee) called by Gaillard Thomas for the purpose. The village president was Albert J. Post, then seventy-three, and a man much respected in the community. He had served as town clerk from 1858 to 1861 and was elected to the town trustees during his last year as clerk. He was a member of that body for more than forty years, much of that time acting as its clerk, and was the only standing trustee to survive the blood-letting of 1882 in the aftermath of the scandal created by the proprietors' sale of the bay bottoms that had led to the Mecox Bay case. The entire board except for Post had been replaced at the annual election. He continued as clerk to the town trustees until 1903. In 1894, some months before assuming the village presidency, he was elected town assessor serving in that capacity until his death in 1907. It would be hard to find a man with such a wealth of political and administrative experience in Southampton and also Suffolk County affairs and the village was duly grateful to have him. He was village president until 1902 except for one year—1901—when Samuel Parrish replaced him. He was thus a good match for Thomas with whom he would have to deal continuously through the 1890s. Thomas had decided in 1895 that if the Improvement Association was to survive and flourish he alone had better take charge. He was reelected each subsequent year until 1902 when ill-health or general fatigue with the job forced him into retirement. Also in 1895 Albert Post was elevated to a vice-presidency in the association, a shrewd and practical move that it must have been hoped would ensure that the village and the association would after all run on parallel tracks.

At the late summer meeting with Post and his trustees, Frederic Betts offered a resolution "that this meeting request the Executive Committee of the Village Improvement Association to submit to the Board of Village Trustees such ordinances as they may deem desirable for the better government of the Village." It was accepted by all in attendance.

A few weeks after at the association's annual meeting, Betts moved the passage of certain ordinances by the village trustees in regard to "the establishment of a curb line; the driving of cattle in the street; the carting of garbage; the dumping of rubbish etc." It was to be printed and circulated in the general community. The following year a local farmer, Fletcher Howell, offered a lot on his property north of the village for use as a dump, concern having first been voiced that a "dumping ground" within the village was inappropriate and would cause a nuisance. Who was to pay for this is not clear. It shows up neither in the association's accounts nor in those of the village. The village was certainly in funds by 1896 and the association's finances had finally righted themselves under Thomas's supervision. The village's budget for 1895, its first full year, was $6,200 and steadily rose through the decade easily surpassing that of the association. By 1898, when village taxation yielded over $7,000 in revenues (a fair part of which was assessed against summer residents), the association began to feel that the village government was not pulling its weight in funding what the association regarded as necessary improvements in the village. We shall return to this question shortly.

Regarding the enactment of village ordinances, which had essentially not existed at all before 1894, it is fairly clear that the association played a fundamental role in drafting them. A village publication in 1908, a pamphlet designed to give residents a fuller picture of village affairs and government, lists eighteen separate ordinances.[17] Many of them reflect the preoccupations and concerns of the summer colony, some of them the particular *betes noires* of summer residents like Salem Wales. There was, for example, an ordinance relating to "peace and good order" reflecting perhaps growing concern in the 1890s about unruly behavior in the streets.

There had been some particularly disquieting instances of this even in the late 1880s at the time of the annual spring elections when anti-temperance forces had managed to get their men on the excise board. The "rum element," as it was disparagingly called at the time (there had been a strong and effective temperance movement in Southampton since the 1870s), had rampaged through the streets in triumph the night of the vote assisted not a little by watch-case workers from the Fahys factory in Sag Harbor (always a drinking town) who had been trucked in to cast their decisive votes.[18] The summer colony was not present for this display of popular feeling having been "on leave" (it being before the beginning of the season); but had prudently, if tardily, supported the temperance forces aware that, whatever the election results, they would have little effect on their own predilection for an afternoon cocktail at the Meadow or in the safety of their cottages well out of sight of the Methodists who largely controlled the temperance lobby. But in the 1890s there had been occasions when roistering in the streets and the odd assault on a summer renter had disturbed the pacific predispositions of the association. If it demanded action to preserve the harmonious character of this rural village, it took the form of an ordinance prohibiting "the gathering of unnecessary crowds upon the streets or in doorways and stairwells adjacent thereto, or loitering about such places, and all disorderly, noisy, riotous or tumultuous conduct" on penalty of $5 per offense. One startling ordinance promulgated in 1894 but dropped three years later took aim at "all common prostitutes, all keepers of houses for the resort of prostitutes, drunkards, tipplers, gamesters" and promised that they would be proceeded against to the full extent of the law. A brothel, it was later said, operated in the marshy hinterland south of Job's Lane.

There were various other ordinances promulgated against disorderly persons not a few of which betrayed the preoccupations of the association in its continuing desire to maintain and promote an image of bucolic tranquility. Ball playing and stone throwing on streets and other public places were prohibited. Those arrested for intoxication were liable to a $3 to $10 fine. "Vulgarity"—use of profane, vulgar or obscene language in public—carried a fine of up to $25, a larger penalty than for mere drunkenness. But where the hand of the association seemed most apparent was in ordinances relating to the protection of trees. Injury to shade trees planted along the sidewalks of the village, or their destruction, was an offense ($5–$25). Similarly, horses and other animals could not be hitched to trees within the precincts of the village on penalty of a $5 fine. Sidewalks and their ornamental grass plots were another focus of concern as were "encroachments" on village streets. Such encroachments were taken to include the attachment of sheds or other temporary structures outside places of business and especially the display of business signs advertising the wares within, long an issue with the summer colony who wanted no vulgar representations that might (indeed would) interfere with their vision of the appearance of an ancient village. Oddly, there was nothing in the ordinances prohibiting the disposal of rubbish in the streets. Frederic Betts had brought this up in 1895, and it was mentioned the following year at the association's annual meeting under the heading of "the suppression of nuisances" and the necessity of keeping the streets clean. A village dump had then been established and perhaps for a few years local shopkeepers had been superficially diligent in carting their refuse to it. But by 1899 their attention to this civic duty may have languished. In that year and the next the Village trustees issued a flurry of resolutions intended to control any possible backsliding by both retailers on the main streets and the general populace at large.

The issuance of these orders, at the same time, seemed to coincide with the expression of growing dissatisfaction by the SVIA with the willingness or commitment of the Village trustees to address conditions in their jurisdiction. This dissatisfaction erupted, in an uncommon display of frankness between representatives of the two groups, at the association's annual meeting in September 1900 and was spread for all to read on the pages of the *Seaside Times*.[19] The trustee resolutions, which probably came too late to appease Thomas and the association, in fact did confront what had always obsessed the summer leadership: neatness and order in the village. In June 1899, the trustees offered a $25 reward for information leading to the arrest of anyone seen discarding "cans, rubbish or other refuse upon the highways, beaches or other public places within the limits of the Village." Not content with this rather general edict, or perhaps pressured to add more detail, in May of the following year the trustees resolved that any person "throwing turf into any highway of the village, scattering or dropping any loose building material or rubbish on said highways" would be subject to a fine. One senses, in the reference to turf—the "grass plots" and their witless destruction—the influence of Wales. In August, a month before the SVIA's fateful and confrontational meeting, the village trustees trained their attention on the growing legion of shopkeepers with premises on the main streets. They resolved "that every person owning land fronting on a public street be required to gather up all rubbish and loose stones and cut the grass and weeds between such land and the center of the street between June 15th and July 1st, and between August 1st and August 15th, in each year." Finally, the summer leadership might have said to itself, they are doing what we have always wanted and pleaded for these last fifteen years. But it was all too late. Thomas and the SVIA, strong supporters of village government a decade earlier, were profoundly disillusioned with the small progress Albert Post and his trustees had apparently made in improving conditions within the village. But perhaps Thomas's conception of a self-governing village and Post's diverged.

When he had assumed the presidency of the association in 1895, Thomas was aware that the organization's finances were in parlous shape and that the physical improvements it had embarked on making—plank walks, docks and pavilions at the lake, effective street watering, and so on—had suffered in consequence. Much was in disrepair. He laid the blame squarely on those whose support for the association bordered on apathy. In his annual address, he observed that "every community like ours is always divided into two classes": There were those "generous in finance, reasonable in expectation, and reticent in criticism" and then there was a second class, thankfully (he hoped) becoming smaller, that manifested just the opposite traits. The following year there was some improvement. Dues collection was up—more than $2,000 had been subscribed by the end of August—but it was still barely sufficient to keep pace with annual maintenance needs. The approximate annual budget of the association for maintenance and repairs was $2,500 in these years, almost half of it spent on sprinkling the streets, leaving nothing for new capital projects. These, if any, were funded out of annual benefits put on by members of the colony—equestrian events, tournaments, dances, bicycle races—or through the generosity of individual members. The association could boast nearly $3,000 worth of physical assets of the sort enumerated above but they all required upkeep. It had no debt to speak of, but when heavy bills were due it often fell to one or other of the summer leaders to reach into their pockets to cover the expense.

The following year, Thomas came up with the suggestion that each cottage owner give $6 a month for four months between June and September. If there were one hundred cottagers, he said, the association would benefit by $2,400. This strategy appeared to pay off in 1897 for $2,530 was collected by the beginning of September. Added to a surplus of $923 carried over from 1896, the association was for once well in funds. There was a similar surplus in the years 1897 to 1900 when income exceeded disbursements by several hundred dollars. However, the carryover of funds from one year to the next masked the fact that income from dues never rose above $2,800 in any one year while disbursements to meet outstanding bills were roughly equal to the amount collected from the membership.[20]. Essentially, the budget available to the association for these years was stabilized by the new schedule of dues at about $3,000 annually. It was adequate to cover annual maintenance charges, which were rising through the second half of the decade, but little else besides.

When, for instance, a committee was formed in 1896 to establish ways in which the station grounds at the LIRR depot might be improved, it recommended the purchase of additional land at a cost of $2,500. At a special meeting called to hear the report the committee was instructed to raise the required sum by private subscription. The association had thus become much more dependent than it had in the past on the willingness of some of its members to engage in direct fundraising activities. In the 1880s, the cost of a capital project whether it was shade trees, a dock, a water cart, a section of plank walk, and so on, could largely be underwritten by the operating budget augmented by the proceeds of an occasional benefit event. This was no longer the case.

It was not lost on Thomas, Betts, and others in the SVIA that although *they* were actively engaged in promoting what they saw as positive changes in the physical conditions of the village, the new village corporation appeared to be doing very little in this direction. Moreover, since the beginning the village budget had been twice the size of the association's. In 1898 it stood at $7,070; in 1899 $8,474; in 1900 it was $10,000; a year later $15,640. Where was all this money going? Unfortunately, Albert Post and his treasurer and trustees provided few details beyond the expense of maintaining more than twenty miles of village highways (not a small matter), police and fire protection, fees due the water company and street lighting that the village had finally agreed to undertake. But it did not seem to the association that the village had fully taken its priorities to heart. After 1897, a steady stream of demands flowed from the association requiring the attention of what seemed to be an increasingly beleaguered village government.

As briefly noted previously, Frederic Betts had begun to lobby for the construction of permanently hard road surfaces on the main streets of the village. It would eliminate much of the dust and reduce the expense of watering as well as provide a better surface for automobiles that were beginning to make an appearance in Southampton. In 1898, he offered a resolution to this effect urging that the "prosperity and advancement of the village" required modern roads and that the appropriate authorities (i.e., the village) being in funds could well afford it; an oblique reference to the healthy state of the village's tax revenues to which summer residents contributed a not insignificant amount. Betts may have been far too optimistic in respect to the village's ability to pay for such a major undertaking and in fact nothing was done for several years. The matter came up again for the association's review at its annual meeting the following year but this time there was some recognition of the potentially enormous capital costs involved. Again there was a resolution, this time introduced by Samuel Parrish. Having asserted that the condition of village roads had become "intolerable," he moved that "it is the sense of the meeting that the village should be bonded for $40,000 to build first class roads of such character as may later be determined upon."[21]

A year earlier the Town of Southampton (not the Village) had begun to investigate the feasibility of building a "stone" (i.e., macadam) road from the Easthampton town line to as far west as Brookhaven. A committee reported back in June 1899 that after visiting various counties in New York and New Jersey it was apparent that the cost per mile of constructing a macadam road would range from $7,000 to $15,000 depending on the thickness of the materials used and the width of the roadway. No state or county aid, it however noted, was likely to be available for a major project like this in Southampton in any foreseeable future. The committee, chaired by supervisor Pierson, was split on whether to go ahead. Pierson and two others argued that the benefit to the town was not sufficient to justify the expense. A minority asserted that such a highway could be constructed for $6,000 per mile and recommended that a bond issue of $200,000 be put before the voters. In the event the minority report was adopted but the question was not publicly debated until the 1903 elections.[22] The delay can be explained partially by the enactment of state legislation in 1898 shifting town elections to every other year beginning in 1899, a move that was sharply objected to in Southampton as a violation of the Dongan patent.[23] The first biennial election was thus in 1901 but the pressure of other business was so great that the highway question was deferred. At the next election in 1903 a more ambitious plan of road-building was presented. Macadam roads were to link not only Easthampton and Brookhaven but spurs were to be built connecting to Riverhead and Sag Harbor. The project was to be financed with a $250,000 bond issue. The vote was heavily negative: 291 were in favor and 618 against, a dramatic two-to-one margin.[24]

However, a few months after this major defeat for the highway lobby in the town the Village of Southampton did authorize a bond issue of $35,000 for paving Main Street. The vote was one hundred in favor to forty-four against. It was Christmas Eve but the voters were skeptical enough to delay the inclusion of the full amount in the upcoming year's tax levy. Nonetheless, work did get under way the following spring—on Job's Lane as well as Main Street—although it was not lost on the SVIA that almost five years had elapsed since it had first importuned the village authority to do what many considered was its plain duty. But the costs were large. It was not enough to pour tar whatever many may have thought in regard to the engineering involved. Road foundations had to be built, culverts, gutters, storm sewers, catch basins, curbstones, stone or brick sidewalks, all these had to be constructed. Between 1904 and 1908 approximately $70,000 was expended on what had turned out to be a massive project to modernize the village's streets. In addition to this, some $12,500 had been raised in private subscription for various related street modernization projects, some of it by local business and some by summer residents. Work on Dune Road and Meadow Lane, for instance, was underwritten by Frederic Betts, Henry Howland, and James C. Parrish at a cost to them of $4,100. Overall, it was a major investment in village infrastructure.

But in 1899, this was all well in the future. In the meantime, there was a growing sense of frustration and disappointment in the SVIA at the apparent inability or disinclination on the part of the village authorities to cope with what its leadership thought were other pressing problems. No sooner had Parrish introduced his own motion on village roads than Wales weighed in on an issue dear to his heart. It was again conditions in the marsh at the head of the lake. It had been twelve years since the Moore family had been unceremoniously dispatched to the outer reaches of the village and since the town board of health had reluctantly agreed to condemn the marsh as unfit for habitation. The board had somewhat skirted the question of outright condemnation but had agreed to discourage any further settlement in or near it. But now small businesses and shanties had crept back into its confines or set up on its indeterminate and shifting perimeter. Wales's parsonage lot on Pond Lane, his fine cottage and that of his son-in-law, Elihu Root, overlooked, it will be recalled, this unwanted scene of local life. Wales wanted an end to it and urged "the authorities to use all lawful means to stop any further encroachment of this character which, if allowed to continue, will cast a reproach upon the good name of this Village as a health resort and put in peril its sanitary condition."[25] Frederic Betts, the previous year, had unsuccessfully attempted to draw the village's attention to the problem and requested that "precautions be taken against water contamination." Wales obviously wanted to go further and get any unlawful tenants out once and for all.

The minutes of the 1900 meeting of the association, handwritten by Henry Fordham now its long-time secretary and treasurer and also clerk to the village board, do not betray the extent of the anger felt by many at the various perceived failings of the village government but do show that its leaders intended to keep pushing for what they considered as necessary and desirable improvements. The first matter to come up was police protection. Southampton had enjoyed the services of a constable or (later) constables since the seventeenth century and indeed had built it own lock-up for the temporary confinement of unruly inhabitants in the earliest years of settlement. In the nineteenth century, the town as a whole never had anything less than five constables, three justices of the peace, and its own justice court. But as the villages of Southampton and Sag Harbor grew in population, separate village policing became more of a priority in the 1880s. A decade or so later the summer colony found that this provision of local police protection was not fully adequate. Thomas had had his house broken into twice during the off-season (his best wine liberally consumed) and other summer residents had suffered similar intrusions. Wales, for instance, had his gold studs and other items of value removed from his household. Fighting had occasionally broken out in the streets, drunkenness was a problem, and summer residents had once in a while been assaulted (or, perhaps, simply insulted). In a call to arms, Frederic Betts presented a resolution requesting the increase of the police force as necessary for preserving public order and, one suspects (although he, if not others in attendance, left it unsaid), for the protection of the property of fellow summer residents. There was no word as to the reaction to this by the village government but many in the village might well have thought that there was hardly a crime wave to justify such a reaction.

In a second effort to put pressure on Albert Post and the village trustees, Betts thought it was high time that "the expense of cleaning the streets and picking up paper and refuse . . . be assumed by the Corporation of the Village and that this subject be respectfully brought to the attention of the Village authorities and that an apportionment for that purpose be earnestly requested." Betts added, leaving nothing to chance, that any appropriation "be used under the supervision of the Association," a reminder to the village of who ultimately thought themselves to be in charge of the matter. In the past, the association had taken on this task itself and employed a street cleaner for the purpose at a cost of approximately $200 for four months of work; the streets being kept free of rubbish only in the summer months—refuse and paper allowed to fly freely in the other (and windier) months of the year when the principal disapproving witnesses were absent. Moral suasion of shopkeepers had also been employed but this had never been more than sporadically successful.

Undeniably the SVIA was unhappy with the pace of progress in the village, a village the summer community or at least its principal leaders had adopted more than twenty years before and had come inevitably to think of as their own. They had done, they surely thought, so much for it over those years but the effort (and the money) expended had been all too often one-sided. It was time that the village was made to realize this. In a most curious development the disaffection of the association with the village government's conduct of affairs and with the public at large was publicized in the *Seaside Times*. Unusually, it took the form of an almost verbatim report of what was said at the annual meeting rather than the publication of the president's generally measured synopsis of the association's achievements for the year, its financial balance sheet, a summation of its various resolutions, and the usual encomiums.

Evidently Charles Jaggar, the new publisher of the *Times* since 1896 and a Princeton PhD, was responsible for the article that appeared the week following the meeting. Whether he or one of his underlings wrote it is difficult to determine but in a strange admission the writer acknowledged that the text of Thomas's address had been delivered the week before to Jaggar with Thomas's instructions to publish it. It had also been delivered to George Burling, the publisher of the *Southampton Press* and the new rival paper to the *Seaside Times*, and he did publish it. Jaggar, however, had sat on it until after press time and had apparently told the printer "that he did not know when he should let us have it." Possibly the apparently inflammatory substance of the address caused him to wonder whether Thomas truly meant it to appear in print. At the same time, realizing that much damaging criticism of the village and its government had been included in the actual press reporting—which, because he was a journalist, one imagines it was difficult for him to suppress—Jaggar had had inserted in the article a statement of editorial support for the work of the Improvement Association. Endeavoring to find a natural way to show his loyalty, he slipped in a few comments to that effect following a discussion of Thomas's pained report of backsliding among the membership. Of 116 cottagers subscribing to the association, Thomas had said, thirty-six had failed to do so leaving the association with a deficit of $1,000 that "could only be made up by an appeal for more funds to those who have already generously subscribed." Again, apathy had reared its head and Thomas, typically, had pointed the finger at the guilty few and made it all but known who they were.

The tone of the publisher's comments was quite at odds with the straight reportage, eye-opening as that undoubtedly was, contained in the rest of the article. Having begun by saying that the SVIA "is too valuable an institution to suffer from lack of proper support and while we do not propose to appoint ourselves its official organ . . ." Jaggar continued in the next sentence to suggest that this was exactly the role he envisaged for the *Times* perhaps, at the same time, slightly fearful that the *Press* might insinuate itself into this role given Burling's long acquaintance with Thomas. If he or the paper were unable to contribute in cash to the reduction of the deficit, the "hearty support" of the *Times* for "this valuable promoter of the public health and happiness . . . can be worth $1,000 to the Association." "Who shall (then) say," he beseeched, "that the Times has not done its part."

But Jaggar's posturing was almost a sidebar to the main story. The substance of the address by Thomas reproduced "from memory and from the meager notes we took" (said Jaggar) was, intended or not, scathing in its effect. Noting that the growth of Southampton placed a great burden on the SVIA and its need for money, the president enumerated the principal sources of expense to the association, all of them well-known (including the cost of printing), and turned a cold eye on those who had failed to subscribe that year and support its work. But that was only the beginning. The real object of Thomas's animus, according to the newspaper, was the village itself. The text of the address, which was in fact printed a week later and distributed to the association members although too late to limit the damage done by the *Times* report of it, was couched in far more circumspect language than Jaggar's hasty effort to make up for his initial failure to print it. In fairness to Thomas, he devoted no more than two brief paragraphs of a three-page report to expressing his dissatisfaction with the village authorities and those unfortunately for posterity were garbled by printing errors. The most that can be gleaned from them is his opinion that the village authorities "absolutely refuse" to give any assistance in dealing with "unclean streets" and "the smothering dust" enveloping them that costs the "ladies of the community" far more in damage to their clothing than would the simple expedient of village watering of the streets. If any relief was to be afforded from these twin "evils," he said, the association would have to provide it, indeed as it always had, itself. The village should certainly assume these responsibilities "in view of our valuable patronage and heavy taxes" but years of experience had taught him that this was no more than a vain hope.

Still, Thomas's views of the village and its government were blunt and obviously long considered but not nearly as intemperate as Jaggar had reported. Moreover, Jaggar, anxious perhaps to compensate for his error or emotionally wrought from the experience, appeared to embellish his reporting with remarks and phrases that were nowhere to be found in the address by Thomas. A more charitable interpretation might be that he conflated the doctor's own measured observations with impulsive comments from an aroused and irate audience:

> The SVIA is the sole provider for the wants of the town. No one else ever does anything. The SVIA makes the walks, builds the docks, and has looked after the sanitation of this community till the diseases formerly endemic here have been stamped out and it has become perfectly healthy there having been no sickness here at all this season. The summer residents come here season after season for the purpose of enriching the natives and yet the natives are totally inappreciative of this benevolence and do nothing in return for its gratuitous bestowal. The village authorities do not rise to the occasion. They are thoroughly incompetent and do nothing; there is no hope for them and it is of no use to look to them for anything. The SVIA is the only organization that ever does anything for the public welfare here and it ought to be better supported.

The address, and the sentiments expressed in it, was apparently received with nodding approval by the small band of summer residents present. One wonders, nonetheless, what was the reaction of the few "natives" at the meeting. Albert Post was very likely in attendance as one of the vice presidents, as would be Henry Fordham (the long-suffering secretary), and one or two others. Post was re-elected for the following year but his name disappears from the list of officers thereafter suggesting that he may have resigned in protest at the characterization of village government by Thomas as uncooperative or incompetent. Henry Fordham was re-elected as treasurer and secretary and did remain with the association one more year until his death in 1902. Of the dozen or so in attendance at the meeting, there may have been one or two other local residents. What they heard, and not only from Thomas, must have been a shock. It was as if, in the ensuing discussion, a dam had burst at the conclusion of his remarks; a break that neither side seemed willing to prevent occurring.

This discussion, the paper reported in its September 6 issue, "seemed to indicate a very unfortunate lack of sympathy between the summer residents and the home people." The "home people," inhabitants of long-standing and in possession of long memories, counter-attacked immediately:

> The wealthy cottagers, who have the means to spend the whole summer and some of them the whole year in pure pleasure seeking and recreation, seem totally incapacitated for understanding the sentiment of our hardworking, poor but honest, Puritan population engaged in a fierce struggle for existence every day in the year except Fourth of July and Sundays.

More may well have been said that was left unreported, and in more detail, difficult as it is to imagine that the attack by Thomas on the local authorities was accepted without an exquisite rebuttal of the pretensions and claims of the summer colony and its association. The floor, however, was open to summer residents—Frederic Betts, the author of all those resolutions, surely in the lead—to express their long-held and well-nurtured grievances:

> The Village Trustees were severely criticized for their "inactivity" and "incompetence" and it was demanded that these trustees be removed from office and others put in their place. Among the ways suggested for enforcing this demand were for all the summer resident property owners to register here and vote at village elections or else to induce some New York merchant to establish a store here, pledge him the trade of the entire summer colony and thus bring ruin on the home people if they refuse to submit to the authority of the SVIA.

With slightly less drama the meeting, or at least those remaining who had not left in protest, approved the resolutions by Betts that the village should pay for street cleaning and the augmentation of the police force. Of the latter, it was generally thought that a large enough police force should be employed "to guard the valuables of the summer residents against theft and their servants against drunkenness."[26] Actually, there was very little reported crime in Southampton at the time. The earliest figures from 1902 show twenty-six arrests for that year, five for intoxication. Whether this was from the inefficiency of the police or the general absence of crime it is impossible to say.

It cannot help but be remarked that Jaggar's newspaper, with the unexpected and ill-advised publication of this article, had for all its good intentions damaged whatever credibility the SVIA possessed in 1900. Perhaps over the years it had used up its goodwill with the local population in general—its principal local support deriving from the small and increasingly prosperous business community—but to have it exposed in the public prints for all to read, its querulous members venting their various outraged sentiments, was more than the association might want to bear. Perhaps it is too much to say that it undid years of work to cement ties with the village and its leadership but the impact of the article was that in the short term it lost the support of that leadership.

The *Southampton Press*, which came out two days after the *Times*, could not however quite contain its glee at the mess Jaggar had obviously made of the report on the meeting and, at the same time, take the high moral ground in a succinct and effective editorial. Burling, a veteran in reporting the doings of the SVIA when he managed the *Times*, also scooped Jaggar by publishing the address by Thomas in full and limited the paper's report on the proceedings to "the failure of the townsfolk to subscribe to the expense column of the association and kindred topics." Delicately, the paper avoided detail. Instead, and soothingly but quite obviously with Jaggar in mind, Burling airily concluded his own editorial comment by noting that "(t)here is no chance of a rupture as indicated by a few wild rumors in the metropolitan press [*sic*]. The matter will be amicably adjusted, satisfactory to everybody, and, understanding the true situation, there seems to be no legitimate cause for further friction."[27] Perhaps the *Press* inadvertently neutralized the impact of the *Times* expose and, in so doing, reassured Thomas that whatever damage had been done might swiftly be repaired. It must have been an arduous week for Jaggar.

Possibly Thomas and Betts (Betts especially) did not care all that much (never mind Jaggar) about how the confrontation had played out in the press. Weary exasperation with what was very likely a slow and unresponsive village administration might easily have suggested to them that such a confrontation was necessary and inevitable. Better then to clear the air with a speech, however inadequately or distortedly reported, and deal with the consequences. That they were eminently prepared to do this is suggested by the fact that they were at this point quite ready to attempt a takeover of village government itself. A few months after the August meeting they put up one of their own, Parrish, to run against Post for village president. The result surprised everyone. Parrish won. He lasted but a year in the position—Post was elected for the last time in March 1902—yet it was a victory for the SVIA. A fair number of summer residents did register in the village—twenty-six by October and more may have registered later—and their votes were probably significant in defeating Post. Fortunately, the threat to import a New York retailer in order to shut down and "bring ruin" to local shopkeepers never materialized. It would have meant open warfare and undercut two decades of effort by Thomas to place relations with the village on a stable and reciprocally civil footing. But Thomas, his remarks spilling into the public domain, had himself done more than a little to loosen the spirit of cooperation he had long attempted to foster.

In fairness, however, Post and his trustees had handled village affairs quite effectively in the first six years of incorporation. It was true the beginning had been rocky. The village vote—a narrow majority in favor of incorporation—was not auspicious but the *Seaside Times* had rallied in support. It envisaged a body of wise men, conservative, careful with the taxpayers' money, untainted by politics. Above all "we don't want any 'rings' here or boss rule in Southampton," perhaps casting a nervous glance at the state of Democratic politics in New York City ninety miles to the west.[28] But almost immediately, as if in defiance of these high-minded sentiments, there was a nasty election contest. There were in fact two elections in 1894, the first in mid-August and the second two weeks later. What transpired at the first is not known nor is it clear who constituted the opposing slate of candidates, but at the September election Post and his slate of three trustees (all of whom had run in the first) prevailed. Of 165 votes cast, Post garnered 161 and the trustees all won with overwhelming majorities. As might be expected it was a Republican board, but Henry A. Fordham, a key leader of Southampton's Democratic Association for more than twenty years (along with White) was elected village clerk. Politics, after all, had managed to insert itself into the electoral process as if the *Seaside Times* had at the last moment been unable to ban it.

Village business, for all this, began almost immediately and seemed to proceed smoothly despite this brief upset in the transition to village democracy. Village taxes were held to a minimum while town taxes were reduced to local residents to offset them. Throughout the 1890s, the principal budget items, consuming half the village's tax revenues, consisted of highways (there were many petitions for new roads) and water supply. The Southampton Water Company, which was in the process of gradually extending its mains and hydrants, regularly charged more than $2,000 a year for its service or about the same amount expended on highways. Police and fire protection cost another $1,000, while later in the decade electric street lighting became a substantial expense.

Yet apparently not everybody—outside the SVIA, which became increasingly skeptical of the conduct of village government as the decade wore on—was happy with Post and his trustees. In January 1896, 103 residents petitioned the board "to call a meeting of the electors thereby to determine whether the same (the village) shall continue to be an incorporated village in accordance with the provisions of section 90 in chapter 426 of the General Statutes of the State of New York enacted in the year 1847 as amended . . ." etc.[29] The signers of the petition requested a special election to settle this question the following month. What had led to this, or whether the SVIA had a hand in the matter (as seems not unlikely) is far from clear. There was no particular crisis to advert to, as far as it is possible to tell, and taxes were low. However, the voters turned aside this threat to village autonomy. The vote was 209 for continuance and 107 against.[30] But in the September trustee elections of that year voter turnout was extremely low with less than one hundred casting votes. Something had happened but whatever it was had not been serious enough to dislodge Post from office.[31]

Matters appeared to have settled back into a routine in the years leading up to the fateful SVIA meeting in August 1900. Most business transacted concerned new roads, but a contract to lay telephone lines (primarily—naturally perhaps—to serve the summer enclave at Lake Agawam) was signed and automobile speed limits established (seven miles per hour). One other unexplained and potentially disquieting incident did occur in these years. In October 1899, the village trustee records report that Post was appointed to fill the office of president of the village, a post he had just resigned from for unknown reasons and was thus briefly vacant. Apparently, he was persuaded to accept and his administration accordingly returned to normalcy. He was re-elected the following year in March (the election date had been shifted from September to coincide with town elections) but then, in March 1901 and not eight months after the SVIA debacle, Parrish was elected as his replacement. The turnout was large, more than three hundred, and Parrish elected with 191 votes. How many votes were polled for Post was not recorded but he was returned in 1902, this time running against Jaggar, by a vote of ninety to three in another small electoral turnout. Poor Jaggar! Perhaps the memory of his reportage of the SVIA meeting two years before, and his slavish devotion to the SVIA, lingered on. Some consideration of Parrish's brief tenure as village president is given in the next section.

III: THE PARRISH YEARS

In the aftermath of the 1900 confrontation, Gaillard Thomas imperturbably continued on his chosen path, a shepherd and guide to his flock, a beacon in the darkness of village obduracy. He was re-elected to the presidency of the association for 1901 and then again for 1902 but in July of that year offered his resignation. He had, he said, "grown old in the work" and felt that someone younger and more active than he would be of greater benefit to the organization in which he had taken "so much pleasure and pride."[32]

He was replaced by Dr. Albert H. Ely, a prominent New York physician and an old friend of his. Ely had no previous experience as an officer of the SVIA but served it well as its president until 1918. In Southampton he was best known as one of the principal founders of the Southampton Hospital Association in 1909 and for his successful efforts in getting the village's first hospital built in 1912.[33] In 1918, Grosvenor Atterbury designed a thirty-room mansion for him on the Shinnecock Hills. It was reputed to be an occasional summer White House for Warren Harding in the 1920s where Ely was said to receive him in an exceptionally grand manner. He had earlier been appointed the president's personal physician. The enormous house, in its extravagance reminiscent of Newport (which by the teens, Southampton had increasingly come to resemble), eventually was sold and converted into a hotel—the Scotch Mist Inn—after World War II. It burned in the 1960s, a victim of perennial fires scorching the Hills.

The resignation of Thomas marked the end of an era for the summer colony and perhaps the beginning of a re-evaluation of the role of the SVIA in the affairs of the village. Under Ely, it drew in its horns to a considerable extent, preferring to operate quietly behind the scenes and in much more of an advisory capacity to village government. Possibly Ely realized that the confrontation between the village and summer residents in 1900, while long in the making, had severely damaged relations between the two and potentially undermined the long-term efforts of the association at promoting what it understood to be positive change. Whether Thomas understood this or not, it was evident to some that the well-publicized display of petulance and threats of reprisal against the village community were bound to provoke a backlash.

But both Thomas and Wales were dead before the next annual meeting in 1903. Wales died in December 1902 and Thomas three months later. At seventy-seven and seventy-three, respectively, they were the patriarchs of the association and its natural leaders. Both had a profound sense that it was their mission to transform Southampton, modernize it and enhance its attractive rural and historic qualities, and above all make it safe and hygienic for a growing summer population. It had come at some considerable cost however. The effort over twenty years to remake the village and have it conform to an imagined idea of rustic antiquity, as well as to introduce modern amenities to suit the requirements of a large and highly visible summer population, inevitably created resentment in many quarters. Thomas and Wales never really understood this. They had always thought that they had nothing less than the best interests of the total community at heart and felt injured and misunderstood when their efforts were rejected or ignored. What in addition was entirely natural to them, a patrician style—much on display in the insensitive handling of the Moore business—did little to aid them in attempts to gain the support of the village. Admonitory letters to the press, particularly from Wales whose condescending manner infuriated many, did not help. It ultimately came down to a question of class and class differences in comprehension. Thomas and Wales never fully understood local interests, or tried to understand them, and never realized that the summer colony's growing presence in Southampton was seen by many as akin to a foreign occupation. Their deaths left an ambiguous legacy yet no one could deny that they had both, Thomas more especially, essentially established the foundations of the summer colony and its institutional organization and direction.

It is of speculative interest that neither Parrish nor Betts were chosen to succeed Thomas in the presidency of the association. In the circumstances of the 1900 debacle, it must have been apparent that Betts carried too much baggage. Since the late 1890s it had been Betts who had drawn up the most contentious of the association's resolutions. It had been Betts who had allowed himself to be drawn into acrimonious disputes with White over the new village hall and the construction of a beach casino, and it was Betts who had fought White's town trustees to a standstill over the question of title to beach lands. Betts for these reasons, his legal acumen also unfortunately too often on display, would have been a poor choice. He was to follow Thomas to the grave two years later, perhaps affording Ely greater room for diplomacy and enabling him to avoid further unproductive clashes with the village. Parrish, on the other hand, came with a great deal to recommend him. He had been a vice president and a member of the finance committee and, most notably, the creator of the village art museum and donor of its collection not four years before. By all measures, as we shall see, he was the man to fill Thomas's shoes even if, as was evident, he lacked the hero-founder's charisma. He was perhaps simply too modest for the job and possibly also too much involved in his several other projects. In any event, speculation aside, the association endorsed Ely. Like most successful physicians of the time he was used to taking charge and for many years did so to good effect.

Parrish did not have an especially memorable year as president of the village but at least it was quiet and without much incident. Naturally, of course, he was caught between the demands of his elected office and the general constituency he represented and the expectations of the association (which had helped to elect him) that he would do wonders on its and the summer colony's behalf. Nonetheless, from the point of view of the village he was as good a choice as could be expected if a summer resident was to run for office. For one thing he lived in the heart of the village at the corner of Meeting House Lane and Main Street, having purchased the fine homestead of Captain Albert Rogers from his heirs in 1899. Thus he did not live in the colony's preferred precinct huddled at the south end of the lake and along the beach. He did build a house for his widowed mother on First Neck Lane in the late 1880s but lived there for a very short time until her death in 1895. It was one of a few Stanford White designs in the village and still stands. In Captain Rogers's house—it dated from 1840 but the property on which it stood had been in the Rogers family since 1645—Parrish could step from his door and chat with the neighboring shopkeepers and businessmen on Main Street, look in at his new art museum down the block on Job's Lane, or wander over to the village hall or the post office where the village trustee office was located. After Frederic Betts's death in 1905 he bought the first of these buildings from the Southampton Company that Betts and his brother had formed in order to purchase it from the Methodists in 1883 (they in turn had got it, as we saw, indirectly from the Presbyterians in 1843) and transformed it into a young men's association and gymnasium. Parrish was unusual among the summer colony in choosing to live in such close proximity to local residents (nobody else did), his doorway giving on to the dusty street, tin cans and old papers blowing up and down despite the remonstrations of the SVIA, but he was an unusual man to begin with.

Once in office he attempted, really quite successfully, to take charge. His first move was revealing. An indication that there may have been some discontent with the previous administration's exercise of authority is suggested by the new board's decision immediately after the election to hear citizen complaints. The village board was to meet every Monday morning in the courtroom above the post office to address "all complaints in regard to the conduct of the affairs of the Village coming within the jurisdiction of the President of the Board."[34] There is no record in the trustees' journal of just what complaints were brought to the attention of the board or who brought them, but evidently the policy was meant to inject some transparency into government activity that may have been previously lacking. Parrish was obviously responsible for this move toward greater accountability. It had been high on the list of the SVIA's concerns about village government. A further indication that Parrish was behind it occurred the following February just before the 1902 election when the board called for what was billed as a "mass meeting" of village voters at Agawam Hall to hear reports from Parrish, the trustees and the treasurer.

Other than this shift toward more open government, the year of Parrish's administration was no more eventful than those of the Post regime. There was a shortfall in the village budget (the budget was now more than $15,000), necessitating a loan from the Southampton Bank. The board had been billed by the LIRR for the village's share of the costs of constructing a railroad underpass at North Sea Road. This had not been anticipated perhaps because it had always been assumed that this was a matter between the SVIA, which had campaigned ceaselessly for roads under the tracks on safety grounds, and the railroad.

The LIRR, understandably, was more interested in profits rather than safety and had only reluctantly agreed after more than a decade to finance a part of the construction costs. The rest, it said, was up to the village. In an effort to save money—it seemed to be a year of austerity—the village board decided that street sprinkling should be handled directly by the road commissioner rather than contracted out. There were problems with the electric light company. The board decided not to pay its bill until the streets lights could be reliably expected to come on each and every night. The new administration's actions were all generally routine examples of what any village government might be expected to do.

What Parrish did appear to accomplish most in his year as president lay in the effort to open village government to more public scrutiny than hitherto. Yet Post before him had caused to have published the village budget, expenditures and broad decisions so it is not altogether obvious what was new in Parrish's own efforts at transparency. Perhaps the most that can be said is that Parrish more than satisfied the expectations of the SVIA leadership. Village government was now more open to it than before even though village residents might not have discerned much difference between the Parrish and Post years. But Parrish, for whatever reasons, chose not to run for a second term. His real estate interests in the village and on the Shinnecock Hills, and the further development of his art museum on Job's Lane, may have persuaded him against it. But he was to remain an important personage in the village for thirty more years until his death in 1932.

We have already had occasion to discuss something of Parrish's activities in Southampton in relation to his interests in the development of the Shinnecock Hills. He had not apparently arrived in the village before 1886, then a youngish man of thirty-seven, and probably brought there by Charles Atterbury or the Betts brothers (or both), lawyers like Parrish. Real estate drew him to the village, initially investment in the Hills, but later in the village itself. In April 1886, he is mentioned in the *Seaside Times* as one of five principal stockholders in the Long Island Improvement Company, Corbin's Long Island Railroad subsidiary, capitalized at $475,000. As discussed earlier, the LIIC had acquired the Hills from the Trustees of the Shinnecock Hills in 1881 through Bowman and Benson. The other four stockholders, apart from Corbin himself, were all Corbin's men. Parrish knew Corbin from his law practice in New York. They occupied adjacent offices on lower Broadway. In 1889, having partially relocated to Southampton, he became president of the LIIC, an on-site presence that Corbin probably thought was advantageous insofar as the Hills was one of his two major projects (the other being Montauk). In 1893, when Corbin lost interest in the Hills, Parrish formed the Shinnecock Land Company and bought the remaining unsold property for $200,000 allowing Corbin to get out without too much of a loss.[35]

Parrish was born in Philadelphia in 1849 into a Quaker family that came over with William Penn in 1682. Educated at Exeter and Harvard, he went to law school in Philadelphia where he briefly practiced law and then removed to New York City in the late 1870s. It was said that his education was financed by his older brother, James C. Parrish, who had done rather well out of Civil War contracts in the 1860s but the evidence for this is slight if certainly intriguing. James followed his brother to Southampton about 1890 and, taking advantage of Parrish's position at the LIIC, bought land just south of the Shinnecock Hills

Golf Club and erected a block-long extravaganza of a cottage on the property. It later burned, a victim of cinders thrown out by passing locomotives belonging to Corbin's railroad in one of the many similarly caused conflagrations that routinely engulfed parts of the Hills.

In New York, Parrish formed a law partnership with an old Harvard classmate, Francis Key Pendleton, and specialized in real estate and railroad law. The two set themselves up at 44-46 Broadway, a preferred address for anyone seeking access to the principal monopolies running these businesses. Pendleton also followed Parrish to Southampton and with him became a player in the local real estate market. Apart from his interest in the Shinnecock Hills, Parrish bought a fair amount of land in the village of Southampton itself. Without much ado in the mid-1890s he acquired most of the small properties on both sides of Meeting House Lane between Main Street and Old Town Road, much of it from the Rogers family. This included land at Old Town that he donated to Ely's hospital association in 1910 for the construction of a hospital. The building was completed in 1913. Adjacent to the hospital on Herrick Road, Parrish and his brother built a substantial and graceful hall after World War I to be used for meetings and other events. It was designed by Grosvenor Atterbury. After Parrish's death in 1932 it was named the Parrish Memorial Hall and today is used primarily for cultural events.

As a young man Parrish had cultivated a deep interest in the arts and in later years traveled to Europe in search of paintings, sculptures and other objects to build up a collection. This was not an uncommon ambition—quite obviously—for successful businessmen in the late nineteenth century. Most of the great collections in the United States today have their origins in the desire of worldly men to be remembered as much for their refinement of taste as for their talent for making money. Parrish, in a small and fairly modest way, seems to have been no exception to this. He was not an adventurous collector. His tastes ran to the lesser known artists of the Italian Renaissance, copies of classical paintings, busts, portraits, sculptures—even a copy of the Bayeux Tapestry—all of them, one has to assume, relatively affordable. He was conservative, not to say narrow, in his selections and, unfortunate though it may be to say this, for all the pride he took in his burgeoning collection it remains little more than a testimonial to the general aesthetic mediocrity of the bourgeois age in which he lived. One hastens to add that there were many exceptions to this—the collections of Pierpont Morgan and Henry Clay Frick come to mind—but exceptions take vast amounts of money and expert advice and Parrish had neither.

Still, on one of his collecting trips to Italy in 1896, Parrish conceived the idea of establishing an art museum in Southampton to house his collection. His mother had just died, he was about to retire from his law practice in New York, and he was investigating the likelihood of buying the Rogers homestead. He had already involved himself in the development of one arts project in Southampton in 1891—the Summer School of Art—and, as president of the LIIC, had provided land for the Art Village on Hill Street at the edge of the Shinnecock Hills and a plot on the Hills for its director, William Merritt Chase, where Stanford White at Parrish's request designed a house for him. Parrish was never a fan of Chase's plein air semi-impressionist landscape painting and included none of his paintings, or those of his students, in his founding collection for the museum he established a few years later. His conception, while stodgy even for that time and certainly in relation to the current impressionist revolution in art, was nonetheless very much heartfelt. The object of his museum was to afford "an opportunity for all, and especially the young, to enjoy artistic productions" from Greece, Italy, and England, as he put it in the preface to the catalogue of its contents in 1898.[36] The focus was to be educational and enlightening. Earlier he had explained to the newspaper that he was led to appreciate in Europe "how many things can be there obtained at a moderate cost that are of great educational value from an artistic and historical point of view."[37]

Possibly, Parrish was inspired and galvanized into action by the example of the construction of an imposing new library on Job's Lane at the corner of Main Street in 1896, what was to become the Rogers Memorial Library. It was designed by his friend and associate at the Shinnecock Hills Golf Club, Robert H. Robertson. Parrish had just become the president of the club and Robertson its secretary. Robertson—possibly the only man at the club who knew anything about golf having been educated in Scotland—was an extremely successful architect in New York, having designed downtown business buildings (including the offices of McKim, Mead, and White) as well as churches, college administration buildings and club houses such as the Saint Andrews Golf Club in Yonkers (of which he was a member and vice president). Robertson, like Atterbury, was a good man to have around in Southampton if interesting, indeed cutting-edge architectural design was to be considered important. On Job's Lane it was and Parrish surely took this to heart when Robertson's library was erected.

The library project had begun in 1893 with a bequest of $10,000 and a parcel of land from Harriet Rogers who had died the previous year. The origin of the ownership of this land is confusing. It was the lot on which the Southampton Academy had sat for more than sixty years. The academy had been shut and the building moved farther down the lane in 1891. At the time and before the school was closed, Edwin Post and William Pelletreau had bought up the shares in the Academy cornering the stock. Whether this included the land under the school is unclear but it was a prime corner lot and would have been of great interest to any investor. However, it had been in the Sayre family since the seventeenth century as had most of the north side of Job's Lane and appears to have come into the possession of Harriet Rogers only at the time the school was closed, perhaps then purchased from Post and Pelletreau or just possibly from the Sayres. She, in fact, had owned the adjacent lot on Main Street since 1872 (also at one time Sayre land) and may have wished to consolidate the two parcels with a bequest for a library in mind.

The idea for a library was not new in Southampton. Since at least the 1860s there had been a reading room and various literary societies in the village—the quiet perusal of reading material in suitable surroundings being thought essentially valuable for the young—but nothing on the scale of the Rogers Library had been previously contemplated. It would eventually contain several thousand volumes and include a collection donated by Pelletreau in memory of his mother. In January 1893 a library company was formed consisting of Edward Mead (of the publishers Dodd, Mead), Wales, Pierson, and L. Emory Terry (like Pierson a local citizen who was eventually to write a brief history of the settlement of Southampton) and formulated plans for the development of the property.[38] In 1895, Robertson submitted his architectural design that he had donated. It was to be an extraordinary building of two floors, low-slung and extending down the lane from the corner of Main Street. Constructed of red brick from local kilns, it was faintly reminiscent of a Swiss chalet incorporating, as it did, some occasional half-timbering and an elegant roofline. The interior was light and airy, graced with a gently curving staircase to the upper floor and large skylights. Once built in 1896 it looked, or—we should say—later came to look, as if it had always belonged on Job's Lane. Laudatory opening addresses were given by Wales, Thomas, Judge Howland, and local dignitaries including George Rogers Howell (still the assistant librarian at the State Library in Albany), Edward Foster, Henry Hedges, and Pelletreau.[39] Its construction cost $18,000 and was financed by private subscription. Parrish later contributed $5,000 to the endowment fund, sat on the board and became president of the library corporation in 1914 upon the death of Pierson its incumbent. The library was the first major piece of public architecture since the Methodist Church in 1883, the Southampton Bank just north on Main Street (another Robertson design), and before that the Presbyterian Church constructed across the intersection of Job's Lane with Main Street in 1843.

It initiated a slow process of rebuilding this central area that eventually included a classical village hall next to the bank building, a line of upscale stores on the opposite side of Job's Lane and across from the village hall on Main Street (built in the 1920s largely on Parrish's initiative and designed by Atterbury), and, of course, the art museum that quickly followed the library and had also been the work of Atterbury. These buildings anchored Southampton's downtown (an expression that would probably not have been understood in 1900) and continue to do so today. At the same time, this effort in urban renewal meant the destruction of many old buildings, some, like the old Sayre house on the corner, a relic of the seventeenth century. Yet who, it at least might have been asked by some and perhaps especially those in the business community, wanted Southampton to resemble Easthampton where weathered clapboard was at a premium and paint regarded an extravagance. Southampton was to be a modern village, a smooth blending of the old and the new, its history well on display and carefully preserved but not weighing too heavily on its bright new future. It was history lightly observed.

On returning from his collecting trip in Italy, Parrish formed and incorporated the Southampton Art Museum and purchased a two- to three-acre tract from the Sayre family immediately west of the Rogers Library. Grosvenor Atterbury's architectural conception was quite startling combining beaux-arts and neoclassical features. The building fronted on Job's Lane but was recessed sufficiently to allow for wide steps and a patio at the entrance. The façade was in red brick. The back of the building looked out on what Parrish described as "the nucleus of a small botanical garden," which eventually was to contain several species of non-native trees that he arranged to have imported, and was adorned with a large decorative fountain. The interior of the building, beyond a long entrance hall, was dominated by a vast oval-shaped exhibition space. Skylights partially covered the ceiling areas providing natural lighting for the exhibits. The building was later enlarged to its present size in 1902 and 1913 with the financial help of his brother. Parrish installed his collection in the museum immediately on its completion and wrote the lengthy and detailed catalogue of its contents cited above. Published in 1898 it went through two later editions. The volume was dedicated to Atterbury who also designed the later additions to the museum building. Besides early Italian paintings, the collection included reproductions of Roman, Greek, and Renaissance sculpture in marble, bronze, and plaster and copies of the effigies of all the Plantagenet and Tudor monarchs. Among several unique features of the collection were marble copies of the busts of the first eighteen Roman emperors. These were eventually placed outdoors where they stand on their pedestals today, a singular line of imperial sentinels. In 1902, a pipe organ was added to complement the autotype reproduction of the Bayeux tapestry.

The effect of it all was certainly splendid but one is forced to ask whether the museum was created entirely for the benefit of the community of Southampton or, as one might reasonably expect, to add to the legacy of Parrish as well. Perhaps we should say in fairness that it was probably both. But did Southampton really want this—there were, unlike the library, no local citizens on the original board of directors—or was it seen as a strange architectural insertion into the plain but wholesome and rather harmonious appearance that the village presented at the end of the nineteenth century. It is impossible to tell because no public record of dissent or criticism, if any was made, has survived. Down the street was the old barnlike structure of Agawam Hall where annual town meetings were held; almost across from the new museum was John Hen's saloon, its owner annually praying that the voters will approve a "license" excise board; next door to it a garage heralding the arrival of the automobile age; at its foot the marshy ground at the head of the lake though this was in process of being reclaimed. The Southampton Press, however, devoted a lengthy and laudatory article to the opening of the museum from which, it could be inferred, a positive reaction in the village had settled in. The *Press*, like its competitor the *Seaside Times*, was progressive and Republican. In the climate of the times neither paper was unlikely to regard any new development, particularly something as prestigious as a museum, as anything less than a sign of progress and modernity. And, indeed, it many respects it was.

Progress was also in evidence at the foot of Job's and Windmill Lanes. A Soldiers and Sailors Monument dedicated to the memory of those who served in the Revolutionary and Civil wars was in process of construction at the time the museum opened. It had been conceived in 1896 by General Thomas H. Barber, a summer resident since the late 1880s and the owner of an estate off Ox Pasture Road. He had been brought out of retirement by the War Department in 1898 to command American troops in Honolulu at the outbreak of the Spanish-American War and participated in the ceremonies attendant on the annexation of the Hawaiian Islands. The development of the war memorial continued in his absence, but he was much repaid by the War Department's contribution of guns, projectiles, and the heavy chain that marks the perimeter of the site. It was dedicated to the village in 1900 and completed in 1902. The memorial was a popular addition to the foot of Job's Lane for it commemorated the service of Southampton's citizens and was locally supported by subscriptions amounting to $2,000. Much of the work and material for the project was voluntarily contributed. Summer colony noblesse oblige was for once heartily endorsed. Village trustees resolved in 1897 that General Barber be tendered thanks "for his interest, activity and success in the enterprise and that the dedicatory exercises be at a date to be named later."[40] The library, the museum, the memorial—all constructed within seven years—redefined Job's Lane. Old Job Sayre, whose muddy well-trodden path down to Town Pond it once was, would have been mightily surprised.

It is difficult to assess comparatively the different impacts Samuel Parrish and Gaillard Thomas had on the development of the village. The two men were very different. Thomas led his cohorts into the promised land of summer bliss and crusaded indefatigably for more than twenty years to transform his chosen site into the seaside Eden he envisaged, to cajole the natives out of their backward ways and persuade them of his beneficent conception of their future. As we have seen, it was mostly an uphill battle and there were many missteps on the way. Parrish, on the other hand, represented a second generation of summer residents, more interested in real estate and development projects than Thomas and less interested in the issues that perennially haunted the Improvement Association. Ultimately, Parrish was the modernizer, for better or worse, whereas Thomas had contented himself with creating an increasingly hospitable environment for his fellow summer residents. Despite his own interests in beachfront real estate and the potential development of seashore amenities (the failed casino project and a hotel at Old Town particularly), it has to be said that he possessed a heartfelt desire to augment what he conceived to be the spirit and history of the place. That it was at variance with how Southampton viewed itself and its past, and what its inhabitants might want to do with their community in conformity with their own conception of that history, seemed not to have occurred to him. Neither man, in the last analysis, ever comprehended the wide gulf between the two communities or the extent of local suspicion that the summer colony's activities and motives always seemed to generate.

CHAPTER 9

THE BETTS CASE

I: A PUBLIC OR A PRIVATE BEACH

By 1892, the year of the Betts trial, all the beachfront land south of Gin Lane and Dune Road between Coopers Neck Lane on the west and Old Town Road at the edge of Wickapogue was in the hands of summer residents. This was a stretch of beach, dune, and upland about one and a half to two miles in extent and containing approximately 140 to 150 acres.[1] There were twenty private owners including St. Andrew's Dune Church and a sole local leaseholder, Ella Howell and her bath houses located on a small tract of common land leased from the trustees of the proprietors of the undivided lands.[2] Two miles of shorefront was of course as nothing in comparison to the thirty miles of Southampton beach between Brookhaven and Easthampton, but this section lay due south of the village and contained a small stretch of beach that had been long claimed as public land as distinct from common land owned by the proprietors.

Essentially, this was the issue that went to the heart of the Betts case. George White, as president of the town trustees, brought an action of ejectment against Frederic Betts in November 1891 on the grounds that the trustees on behalf of the town were the owners in fee of Betts's land and that they therefore demanded its recovery. The suit and the subsequent trial graphically symbolized all that had separated the two communities from each other and all that had gone wrong between them almost from the beginning. The action originally named Saint Andrew's Dune Church as a co-defendant with Betts but the church was dropped from the suit by mutual consent. The reasons were not specified but clear enough in outline. The church had received its land as a gift from Betts in 1887 under the terms of a bequest in his brother's will. The latter, C. Wyllys Betts, had been the original purchaser of the whole tract in 1881, having formerly leased it a year or so earlier, under two deeds given him by David R. Rose, president of the proprietor trustees, on the understanding that the land in question had always been a part of the undivided lands of the town or proprietor land. As one of the founders of the church, Betts had generously given it the use of a small section of it on the dunes in 1879. The land in dispute was not all the land that Betts owned, only that which ran south of Town Pond to the ocean, east to a line at Mrs. Howell's bath houses (later revised as at Dune Church when the church was withdrawn from the suit) and west to a line south of the government lifesaving station on the southwest corner of Town Pond. His property on First Neck Lane, north of the passing road at the foot of the pond and fronting its west bank (it had been named Betts's Bay it will be recalled) was not in question. Wyllys Betts had built several houses on this land but only one on the dunes in the area contested by the town trustees.

Named Sandymount, it sat directly above the beach overlooking the ocean. His First Neck property had at one time in the seventeenth century been John Cooper's land and his barn close in the Great Plain division and Betts's title to it was thus not in dispute. In this connection, none of the other summer owners with the exception of one had taken title to their beachfront property from the trustees of the proprietors. All of it had previously been in private hands. The exception was a "gore piece" at Old Town Pond that was common land and had been conveyed to Gaillard Thomas by the proprietors. However, it lay north of the beach on the landward side of the beach banks or dunes and out of the zone claimed as public land by the town trustees. Where summer owners did face potential problems was in the vagueness of their titles in describing the southerly limit of their respective properties at the beach, whether it was at the crest of the dune, the line of the surf, or simply "the ocean." The Betts trial went some way toward clarifying this issue but most owners, desiring to protect title, obtained quitclaim deeds.[3]

There were several events or episodes that led up to the Betts trial and made a legal confrontation with the town trustees more or less inevitable. Since the beginning of the 1880s, White was no friend to the Betts brothers. He had reacted sharply to their plan to renovate the old Methodist church on Main Street for a village hall. He was enraged when Wales and Schieffelin went on the beach and cleared out the "little shanties" put up by local people for protection against the sun. These were the rustic bowers, in the past known as wigwams, that lay below both the bathing station and on that part of the beach that Betts claimed as his property. Wigwams had a long history. They went back to the old inshore whaling days, although now in the 1880s these were more or less over, and had been constructed as shelters for whaling crews and other villagers associated with bringing whales ashore and cutting them up. Wales and Schieffelin had found these various makeshift structures a "disgrace" and had them removed. Then, as if this were not enough, Wyllys Betts had thought to fence off his property, what at least he took to be his property and perhaps rightly so, across the beach to the surf to high tide line or perhaps even low tide, at any event to a point well south of the dune. His deed from the proprietors did describe the southerly bound of his property as at "the ocean" but, as it later transpired at the trial, no local property owner of shorefront land in anyone's memory had ever fenced the beach beyond the landward or northern side of the dune or considered the beach a part of his property. That most obdurate of witnesses in the Mecox Bay trial, Edwin Post, attested to as much in the Betts trial and others concurred. The threat by Betts to fence off the beach was probably not carried out but it aroused White and others in the village to such an extent that some said that they would burn down such a fence were it to be constructed. The shores, they asserted, were free for the commonalty to cross over at will without let or hindrance from any interloper.

There were a number of issues in the affair that the court in Town Trustees versus Betts attempted to resolve. One concerned property lines at the beach. Just what did it mean if a deed described the southerly bound of a shorefront property as at "the ocean" or, as was also commonly put, "south by the beach"? Was it to high or low tide line? Did the title include the strand, the area between mean low and high tide, or simply to what was usually meant by "the beach," that is, the soft sand between the surf at high tide and the line of the dunes always bearing in mind that the line of the surf was variable? Extraordinary high tides, for instance, might wash away a dune and part of the upland property above it. Where then was the property line? Had it retreated from the waves or did it remain fixed at some previously determined point on the beach even though it was now under water? And what if the ocean receded and beach land accreted to the benefit of the property owner, adding to his property? These matters may be perfectly clear to us now but they were not so at the end of the nineteenth century. A good part of the problem lay in the indeterminacy of the old patents defining the limits of the lands of the town on which subsequent titles to private property were based. In the case of the Dongan patents for both Southampton and Easthampton, the southern bounds simply were described as "being the Sea." Later, in the case of Southampton, the northern and southern limits of the town were described as being "from water bound to water bound," but this did nothing to clarify the status of the shores and what could be held to be lands belonging to the town or, more accurately, belonging to the town proprietors. As to the latter, they claimed the shores were common land and theirs to dispose of. And, in fact, they did dispose of them, dividing beach meadows and lotting them out along the beaches and the shores of the bays beginning in the 1650s. For the most part, beach meadows were surveyed and marked out as ending at "the beach" but nowhere said where the beach began and ended. Similarly, in the nineteenth century the trustees of the proprietors sold off beach lots in 1846 in the Quogue flats (the Great Sedge Flat) to George O. Post and a consortium bounded as "southerly by the Beach" and then again to the same party in 1861 on the south side of Shinnecock Bay as "south by the Beach."[4] It should be noted here that the beach, that is, the seaward side of the dune was regarded as worthless because nothing of value grew on it. Sea grass grew on its south slope and had value because it protected the dune from erosion—cutting it was forbidden—but nothing grew on it that was harvestable. The meadow grass or sedges—the "common grasses"—that grew on the adjacent shores of the bays on the narrow strips of land between these inland waters and the beach were what was valuable and were what the proprietors had always divided and allotted, or sold. But because the beach was uninteresting as a source of valued products no steps were ever taken to define where it began and where it ended.

But the beach, such as it may be considered, was valuable in two other important ways. It was first of all and since the beginning of settlement in the seventeenth century used as a highway. There were few serviceable roads outside the village until well into the eighteenth century and the use of the beach as a highway was convenient for at least short distances. For example, churchgoers in the small settlement at Bridgehampton and Mecox used the beach to get to Sunday services before their own church was established in the

1690s. It was a circuitous route, but provided the beach was not breached by the ocean or overwashed in winter storms, it was the simplest way to reach Southampton.[5] The beach was also used to transport products such as meadow grass from the divisions of beach meadows lying to the west of the village and probably also to drive cattle and horses from one pasture to another. It had then an important commercial use. However, its importance was set to decline by the nineteenth century as highways were built and better maintained than in earlier days obviating for the most part the need to use the beach as a cart way.

Yet a beach highway it remained in the eyes of the inhabitants in the years leading up the Betts trial, a cherished part of their history whether it was only occasionally used or not really used at all. Whether the beach continued to be used as a highway as late as the 1880s did not figure as an issue in the trial for what mattered was that it had not been discontinued as one. As early as 1881 in fact, summer residents had objected to this use of the beach and claimed ownership to low water mark. George Rogers Howell, who delivered himself of several opinions relating to this question in the newspaper, argued that the trustees of the proprietors could not sell the beach banks (as they had sold them to Betts) because they in fact constituted such a highway and the proprietors cannot sell highways.[6] This was a canny argument but one hardly likely to engage the interest of the court. The argument ran as follows: the use of a road by the public for twenty years makes it a public highway but if it falls into public disuse it reverts to the adjacent property owner(s) through whose land it runs. This had certainly been established at an earlier trial when the proprietor trustees sold a part of a highway in Westhampton in 1795 to Timothy Halsey for the purpose of erecting a windmill. The proprietors claimed it as common land that they had a right to sell. The court, on the other hand, argued that the fee of the land to the middle of the road lay with the owners on either side and could not be sold, unless by the owners in fee, and only if the road had been abandoned. In this case it had not. The court found for the town on the grounds that the public had never ceased to pass over the road and that the windmill was consequently an illegal trespass on a public right.

Howell's argument could be applied to another road routed through property owned by Frederic Betts—there was a passing road rounding the foot of the lake used by the public that Betts wanted closed—but it could not be applied to a beach highway.[7] Several times, Howell asserted that the proprietors could no more sell beach banks than they could sell highways because (he claimed) *ipso facto* the beach banks were a highway. But were they? The most natural course for a beach highway to take for ease of travel would be along the strand at low tide. Here, the sand was relatively hard-packed and negotiable by wagon twice in twenty-four hours. Even above the high tide mark the beach could serve as a cart way though with more difficulty in the soft sand.[8] But Howell stuck to his idea that the sand dunes with their frequently steep slopes and severe undulations were also the highway, only adding by way of qualification that the dunes were used by people "when (they) were compelled to do so by high tides." "The road," he added to drive home the point, "works back as the sea works on," a fact that would have been of little comfort to a summer owner who might envisage a highway passing through his front yard. However, Howell had clearly not taken note of exceptions in Wyllys Betts's deed from the proprietor trustees that duly observed the right of the public to pass and repass along the shore, to bathe in the ocean, or to land and draw up boats on the seaward slope of the dunes.[9]. Yet Betts had threatened to fence the beach down to the surf, to the limit of his property, and Wales and Schieffelin, to make matters worse, had "thrown down" the little shelters the townspeople had erected for their convenience in front of the property owned by Betts. It was no wonder that White had raised the cry that this was "the people's beach" and had set the town trustees upon Betts, the latter now a symbol of all that was disliked in the summer colony.

It was in many ways, and as it transpired at the trial in 1892 although to no legal avail, very much the people's beach, a fact little understood and even less accepted by the summer colony whose idea of the beach was of a pristine place created and, if necessary, swept clean so that nothing should interfere with their pleasurable experience of it. It was almost a mythological encounter, and certainly understood as one by White, between the force of historical argument for the community's rightful possession of a ground sanctified by ancient usage and the upstart claims of wealthy interlopers whose connections to the beach were non-existent and whose interests in it were ephemeral and frivolous. The beach—the South Beach no more than a mile below the village—had been a site and a focal point of village activities since the middle years of the seventeenth century. It had been well adapted to the various purposes put to it. The upland above it and the town pond had been protected by beach banks or dunes—a "silly name" said White at the trial—and convenient lanes or sluiceways ran through the banks to the sea enabling the townspeople to "land property" on the beach and "cart or transport" it inland, all of which they had always been entitled to do both before and after 1818.

Above all, this particular stretch of beach at the foot of Town Pond and convenient to the village had been a work space for the townspeople since the 1640s. It was here where the first whale watches were instituted in 1644 when the inhabitants were divided into four squadrons each with specific rotating duties but all instrumental in getting a whale ashore once it had been spotted. It was cold, miserable, grueling and bloody work and always undertaken in the winter when right whales passed offshore on the way to their southern grounds. The wigwams, so-called for their resemblance to Indian dwellings, were first constructed here to provide shelter for the whale watchers and a warm fire for all those involved in the work of cutting up the whales once landed. There had been a wigwam, long vanished since occasional offshore whaling had come to an end by the 1880s, beneath Sandymount, Betts's house on the dunes. Its exact location was an issue for Betts's lawyers at the trial. Butchering the whales took place on the beach. The blubber was cut into strips and tried in iron pots under a strong fire, the oil skimmed off the bubbling surface of the water.

At the beginning, this was probably done at the beach but as off-shore whaling became an industry later in the seventeenth century try-works were established inland. One had existed for well over a century if not very much longer at the Point, a small headland on the west bank of Town Pond adjacent to property owned by Wales (previously dedicated to the minister in 1649 as parsonage land) and later sold to Wales by the proprietor trustees.[10]

Drift whales—with which the whole business providentially began—might, of course, beach anywhere along the thirty miles of the town's shores and many probably went unnoticed in the sparsely populated early years of the settlement. But if they came ashore somewhere between Mecox and Captain's Neck whaling crews would be off to seize them, cut them up and cart them inland. Whaling in Southampton in the seventeenth century became a most lucrative source of income as it did elsewhere in the New England colonies. In Plymouth Colony and Rhode Island, for instance, it was said that the oil from a right whale earned more than a family farm could hope to do from cultivating the land and the same may well have been true of Southampton.

So the South Beach, the village center for whaling activities and specifically that part of the beach comprising Frederic Betts's expansive property, was an old sacred ground of village work and economy and a source of wealth. If whaling had all but ceased at the end of the nineteenth century, fishing boat crews still put out from this beach, landed their catch, and carted it inland to market. The fishermen hauled up their boats to the safety of the beach banks and spread their nets to dry on the landward side. In the 1880s they were still precisely engaged in this old activity. With all this history, and the local sentiment associated with it, it is less than surprising that White—an old whaling captain with close to thirty years at sea behind him—would inevitably seize the opportunity to claim the beach for the town.

The suit—the Trustees of the Freeholders and Commonalty of the Town of Southampton against Frederic H. Betts—when it came before Judge Edgar Cullen in State Supreme Court in Riverhead in November 1892 was something of an anti-climax. The passions of the moment, the expectations of the populace who to a man expected a vindication of the town's claims and the boot given to Frederic Betts, were dissipated by Cullen's finding and decision. Here was a judge who had in the past sided with the people—the Mecox Bay decision was fresh in everybody's memory—but now Cullen, the people's judge as some must have felt, had found for a man they (and none more so than White) had found obnoxious, a foreign presence on native soil, an intruder sitting atop their beach, fencing it in, lording over it for all the world as if he owned the history of the town and the town itself. But the inhabitants and White were to be disappointed. There was much testimony (invaluable testimony for the historian, as some of it that we shall see, will attest) but the court held that for all the South Beach's historic associations it was and always had been common land owned by the proprietors and theirs to sell or lease as they might wish.

The town trustees appealed—twice—and on the first (which partly went against Betts and almost resulted in a new trial) it appeared to be the case that the several judges of the Supreme Court's appellate division (second department), while seemingly affirming Cullen's decision, had referred the case for re-argument to the first division of the appeals court. Ultimately, and after five years of legal back and forth and the death of White, the town trustees lost the case. They won only what they had always had, an easement on the beach for a public highway and the continued right to land boats, cart and transport property, and so on. Betts and his expensive though probably pro bono New York counsel—Elihu Root and Charles Atterbury—were left by the court with Betts's property intact, and Betts, well satisfied with the result, sitting atop his dune overlooking a largely empty beach but for a few fishing smacks drawn up beneath him and drawn up there, for all he knew, forever.

The case from the beginning, as both counsels and the several justices saw it as the case ascended through the various stages of appeal, hinged on the interpretation of the legislation of 1818 that had separated the interests of the town from those of the proprietors. But what had the act contained, what possibly may it have left out meaningfully if not intentionally, or for that matter deliberately, what may it have unwittingly written in that was to be actually or potentially mysterious for future generations to decipher? It was seemingly impossible to tell. There were as many points of view as there were stakes in the matter. Nobody could ever quite agree—whether lawyers, historians, or laymen—on what the legislature had meant in 1818 or could infer from its language when, on petition from the committee representing the inhabitants of the town and the committee representing the proprietors of the common and undivided lands, it had—apparently in a quite straightforward fashion—awarded the lands (above water only, or so to some it appeared) to the trustees of the proprietors (which body it had created to administer them) and the waters (except mill streams) and their products, including especially seaweed washed up on the shores, awarded to the town to be administered by its trustees. But, by the occasional opacity of the language it used, the legislature had raised too many confused and confusing questions.

Some, like White, saw in the act and particularly in its famously delphic "saving clause" (endlessly explored by many for its meaning) a plot—"that nothing herein contained (in the act) shall in any manner affect the right, title or interest of any person, or the inhabitants of said town to any of the above mentioned premises"—a plot by the proprietors to hold on to everything until some envisaged or hoped-for future test of it in the courts might somehow restore to them all their lands both under and above water, and of course the waters and their products themselves, and their uncontested authority over them. Others—George Rogers Howell notably—changed their minds (Howell at least once) on whether the act had properly and legally transferred authority over the undivided lands to the newly created proprietor trustees. This did not concern the foreshore, or the lands under the bays, but the status of the 1703 lease of the Shinnecock Hills to the Shinnecock Indians, an issue far removed from the Betts trial and the question of the ownership of property on the shores. Could the legislature, on petition from the proprietor trustees in 1859 (and from the Shinnecock also although under, it must again be said, murky circumstances) agree to these proprietors canceling a lease in their own name, a lease that had been drawn up and signed in 1703 by an altogether different body—the town trustees—long before the proprietor trustees even existed? Or, in the act of transferring authority to manage the undivided lands (of which the Hills were indisputably a part), did the legislation ipso facto transfer the leasehold rights of the town trustees to the new body? None of this concerned the shores directly, of course, but it was a good example of the ambiguity of the legislation in general.

In regard to the shores, however, a very relevant question here was who owned the products of the waters that washed up on them. In the famous seaweed trial of 1866, again concerning the Shinnecock Hills, it was clear that under the legislation the shores of the Hills were common and undivided land belonging to the proprietors but that the public had the right to freely go on them to collect seaweed (a valuable product), pass and re-pass over them, land property, cart goods, and the like. But the problem with the town's suit against the proprietors (who claimed the right to sell the seaweed privilege) was that the proprietor trustees had recently sold the Hills and their surrounding shores to a group of private investors in 1861 (led by Lewis Scott) that had begun to hire out the seaweed privilege for themselves, replacing the proprietor trustees who had routinely sold it at auction just as they sold the common grasses. By any interpretation of 1818, the proprietors had acted illegally in charging the inhabitants for the right to collect seaweed, but the town trustees had done nothing to prevent it in the forty years since the legislation. Yet had they acted illegally? Before the Hills were partitioned by the legislature in 1859, a partition that reduced the access of the Shinnecock to the shore to the immediate surrounds of Shinnecock Neck (what became their reservation), the Shinnecock had possessed the right under the 1703 lease to collect seaweed and "other debris" from the entire shores of the land under lease. Their "right of accretion" had been affirmed in their own seaweed trial of 1850 when townsmen had trespassed on the shores of the Hills and removed seaweed. The Shinnecock won this suit as we saw in an earlier chapter.

Then in 1859 the lease was abrogated, the undivided lands of the Shinnecock Hills and their shores (except for the Neck) reverted fully to the proprietor trustees, and the trustees began to restrict access to the shores and control what the inhabitants could take from them. In 1860, the town trustees brought suit against the proprietors. In 1861, the proprietor trustees sold the Hills (and their shores on Shinnecock and Peconic bays) to Scott et al., and Scott then commenced hiring out the seaweed privilege. Meanwhile, the town trustees, under the mantle of 1818, also began hiring out the seaweed privilege as they assumed was their right. In 1862, they collected $80.66 in fees but escrowed them as they did with the fees collected between 1864 and 1866. But when the whole matter finally came to trial in 1866, the court was uninterested in the town trustees' case. Confused perhaps by the 1859 legislation dividing the Hills and unsure as to how to connect it with the 1818 legislation in respect to the public's use of the shores and its access to them, the court found for the proprietors and declared the shores of Shinnecock Hills private land inviolable by the town.

Nonetheless, the town continued to claim the shores of the Hills but then and only after the conclusion of the Betts case in 1892, in which the court found for Betts, did the trustees announce at the annual town meeting that they had quitclaimed any and all interest in the Hills that they may have had to the LIIC, the new owners of the Hills. They reserved only "necessary highways" and fifty feet of the shore above high water mark on Shinnecock Bay and seventy-five feet on Peconic Bay presumably (it was left unsaid) for the right of the public to pass and repass along the shores. Nothing was said about the seaweed privilege. But the town got from the LIIC in return for this piece of largesse the lands under water in Shinnecock, Quantuck, Cold Spring, and Bulls Head bays—as if this had not already been settled several years before by the Mecox Bay trial when the bay bottoms were declared to be the property of the town and under the administration of its trustees. State Supreme Court, it will be recalled, had denied the claims of Richard

Esterbrook and his oyster company to the bottom of Mecox Bay, which had in 1882 been illegally quitclaimed to Esterbrook and his associates by the trustees of the proprietors at a nominal price, and the same court affirmed the town's ownership.[11]

Such then was the curious and not always or altogether fathomable background to Town Trustees versus Frederic Betts. The act of 1818, to which all sides in a legal dispute over land had willy-nilly to turn whether they liked it or not, seemed always to be fraught with peril for some and an apparent opportunity for others or perhaps, as sometimes happened, a nettle to be grasped in prayerful hope. The trustees of the proprietors had tested it in one way or another in and out of court throughout the nineteenth century and always with one thought in mind: What was their land and where did it end? Ultimately, was it at the bays or beneath them, on the shores but how far on the shores? For obscurity and difficulty of interpretation, the act was the equal of the Dongan patent of 1686 and its predecessor, the Andros patent, which it recapitulated and added to. Both were always recited in nineteenth-century court cases, but whether out of superstition or from the hope that they might cast light on the matter in hand or because they might throw dust in the face of opponents, was never clear. But, as might be expected, they were dutifully entered into the record in the Betts trial even though they could essentially help neither Frederic Betts nor the town trustees. In the Mecox Bay case, Judge Pratt, the dissenting justice in the decision affirming the town's rights in the bay bottoms, had forcefully argued that the rights to any land lay not with the town (a later legal construct erected by Thomas Dongan in 1686), but with the original proprietors, their heirs and assigns, who had settled Southampton in pre-provincial times under the terms of the Stirling grant to Long Island lands.[12]

This argument was not adduced in the Betts case for it was clear to both sides that the Dongan patent could not help in determining the precise location of the water bound on the shores of the town that could help establish what either the town or the proprietors could claim as their land. Unfortunately, the patent was silent on this question, it probably never having occurred to anyone in the governor's New York office that a precise (if possibly variable) line on the town's beaches describing the limits of the town's property might be a useful thing to include. All Dongan's lawyers could say—it was probably in the hand of Mathias Nicolls, the former governor's brother—was that the bounds of the town went from "sea to sea" or south by the ocean. All that then may be said was that the Dongan patent, while assigning all the inland waters to the "town" (whether the town as now erected in 1676 and 1686 or the body of preexisting proprietors), said nothing more than that the bounds of the town lay at some indeterminate point where the surf lapped the beach below the ebb of the tide. Beyond that shifting line the watered land, the ocean itself, belonged to the crown and, of course, much later and after Dongan, to the state. The patent then, beyond its ritual incantation for legal and public effect, could be of little help to Betts's lawyers or assist the town trustees and Thomas Young, their lawyer, in determining who owned the beach.

The case was in essentials open and shut. Betts's lawyers, Elihu Root and Charles Atterbury, had no difficulty in establishing that the proprietor trustees' sale of land to Betts down to the ocean was perfectly legal. There was no real question that this particular part of the beach was and always had been common and undivided land. The proprietors since the seventeenth century had made divisions of such land, whose southern bound was always described in surveys as at the beach, along the thirty miles of the town's shoreline, because the fringes of the bays and ponds north of and abutting the beaches contained valuable meadows of sedge grass. Those parts of the beach and adjacent sedge flats that had not been lotted off, or which had reverted to the proprietors for various reasons, had been sold at auction in the nineteenth century. As we saw, George O. Post had benefited from two such sales of meadows in Quogue in 1846 and 1861 as had Abraham T. Rose in a similar sale at Mecox also in 1846. True, they were insider sales to powerful proprietors but that was not the point. The proprietor trustees could fully claim that they had always divided or sold beach land from the beginning of settlement. If there were some sections that were not divided such as the land at the foot of Town Pond, a section one eighth of a mile in extent, it was because the meadow grasses bordering the pond were of no great value. These grasses were never sold by the proprietors because, as Edwin Post observed in his testimony at the trial, it was "poor meadow" constantly overblown by sand from the nearby dune.[13] Unlike most areas of the town's beaches, where a good two hundred to three hundred yards separated the bays from the dunes providing ample room and protection for the sedges, the foot of Town Pond was a scant fifty yards from the sand) This meadow-less land was what the proprietor trustees had sold to Betts. So Betts's land had never been divided and its impoverished growth of sedge had within living memory been deemed unworthy to be hired out and cut. It was a sort of no man's land, of no particular economic value from the standpoint of the proprietors until its fortuitous sale to Wyllys Betts, but it had been used by the public as a convenient landing place for its boats and for other purposes, all no doubt with the tacit acceptance of the proprietor trustees who had no particular reason to object and perhaps good political reasons not to, and who also, as individuals, could take advantage of this public space as much as anybody else never mind that it was proprietor land.

It seemed impossible to deny that the land sold to Betts had ever been anything else than the undivided land of the proprietors. Moreover, the town or at least its assessor had accepted this. Wyllys Betts, and after him his brother, had been assessed annual taxes on the property and had duly paid them (Wyllys Betts had headed the list of largest real estate tax payers in 1882), surely an admission by the town that this was private and therefore assessable land. As Betts's lawyer, Atterbury, put it in his answer to the suit, the town had "entered the same upon the assessment rolls and books of said Town, and have for many years past levied and collected taxes from this Defendant . . . and are now in possession of the money collected for said taxes and have not offered to return the same or any part thereof and are thereby estopped from asserting any right, title or interest in or to said property or any portion thereof, as against this defendant."[14]

Well they, that is, White and the town trustees, were by no means "estopped" from asserting their right, title or interest in the property though they had little to fall back on but tradition and its claims. It was evident from the outset of the trial, which was held over two days in Riverhead in late October, that there was to be no real argument regarding the legality of the proprietors' sale of land to Betts. Thomas Young admitted as much during the testimony of Edwin Post, the long-standing clerk to the proprietor trustees, acknowledging that the trustees had all the authority necessary to execute the deeds to Betts. The best he could do was to explore with several witnesses the extent to which the beach had been historically used as a public space.[15] Young sought to focus the attention of the court on this question while Atterbury, his opponent, quite naturally led his witnesses in the opposite direction in an effort to discredit this strategy or at least to minimize its effect. Atterbury clearly had the best of it and was able to show that there was nothing particularly sacrosanct about this part of the beach that could not be said of others in the immediate vicinity. He had Post describe how the lanes to the beaches had always been fenced each year by the proprietor trustees (and before them by the town trustees acting for the proprietors) in order to protect the common or meadow grass along the bays on the north side of the beach banks from the depredations of cattle. This was done, Post said, every year between May and September, that is, during the growing season and done at the proprietors' expense. In the fall, the fences were taken down and cattle (the proprietors' cattle) were allowed to graze on the stubble left at the conclusion of the mowing season. This was as true of the area of Town Pond as it was of any other part of the beach adjacent to the bays. There was a gate and fencing at the corner of Gin Lane and the road to the beach by the property owned by Thomas, all maintained by the proprietors just as these same proprietors sold the common grasses (if there were any) at auction in June. It was testimony that gratifyingly supported the defense's contention that this part of the beach had always been common and undivided land belonging to the proprietors.

In a vain hope to right his ship, Young cross-examined William Pelletreau, a defense witness and long a supporter of the rights of the proprietors. He had him recite the eighteenth-century town trustee records on fencing the beaches evidently to show, by taking the opposite tack to the defense, that the proprietors respected the rights of the public by never fencing across the beach to the ocean as Betts either had or had threatened to. Pelletreau quoted the record for May 22, 1720 in which the trustees ordered that "the beach shall be fenced":

Q. The beach shall be fenced?

A. Yes sir.

Q. What does that mean?

A. That means that in the Spring of the year these lanes were to be fenced.

Q. It does not mean that any fences were put on the beach?

A. No sir.

Q. Not across to the ocean?

A. No sir.

Q. But the lanes that led on to the beach were fenced?

> A. Yes sir.
>
> Q. (by defendant's counsel) So that cattle could not get on to the beach?
>
> A. Yes sir. There was a gate (the Little Plains Gate) . . . at the corner of Dr. Thomas's lot within my remembrance.[16]

There was no help for it. A little further in Pelletreau's testimony, Atterbury nailed down the extent of the proprietors' land west of the Little Plains Gate.

> Q. You know the land of John Cooper?
>
> A. Not positively. The tract on the west side of the land I spoke of has always been called Cooper's Neck from the earliest times.
>
> Q. The land from within the Little Plain Gate round to the south end of John Cooper, his land which lieth against the pond called the Captain's Pond?
>
> A. That includes all the shore of the Town Pond and round as far as Captain's Pond was.[17]

Captain's Pond, which had been recently filled in, lay west of Town Pond at some point toward Cooper's Pond and appears to have been situated in the middle of Betts's property, that is, on what was formerly the undivided land of the proprietors. A few moments later, Atterbury, quoting from the trustee records of 1726, noted that an inhabitant, John Jessup, "shall have the use of the common land from within the Little Plain Gate round to the south end of John Cooper his land which lieth against the pond, commonly called the Captain's Pond" and asked Pelletreau if that included "the premises in controversy here" to which Pelletreau replied unhesitatingly that it was. The trial was as good as over.

But there were boats drawn up on the beach banks, nets spread and left to dry, wigwams once upon a time constructed—all mute testimony to the public character of this particular part of the beach. Young did his best to make the most of these incontestable facts and put White on the stand. Calling his attention to the age-old activity of fishing in the sea and along the beach with seines and nets and boats, he asked White where these various implements were kept. Atterbury objected to this on the grounds that it was immaterial and irrelevant but in doing so gave Young the useful opportunity to lay out his case before the court before getting to White and the details he would provide.

> (T)he place in question (Young said) was appropriated by the town and by the joint consent of the trustees and the people of the town, for the purpose of a public place upon which boats, nets and other apparatus connected with fishing could conveniently be kept, repaired, mended and in condition for ready use, and also for the purpose of hauling up from the sea and from the shore, swept by the tides, boats, nets and other implements connected with fishing; and for the purpose of carrying fish, the blubber of whales and other product of fishing from the water and from the shore to the town.

(F)rom time immemorial (he then went on to say) the premises in question had been used by the inhabitants of the town for such purposes; and that the use of the premises for these particular purposes constituted substantially the only use to which the place in question was put from time immemorial down to a time within the period of twenty years, and that such use by the inhabitants of the town was never in any manner obstructed by any claim of adverse right on the part of any individuals or proprietors or either, or by trustees for proprietors; and that such use was never in any manner prohibited or restrained by the Board of Trustees of the Freeholders and Commonalty of Southampton, or by the people in town meeting or by any other body.[18]

Atterbury's objection was overruled and Young, no doubt thankful for the forbearance of the court, had White affirm that fishing boats were indeed drawn up to the dune and, where possible, on its landward side. But White's testimony concerning communal activities at this particular section of beach seemed more to refer to recollections of his boyhood past in the 1830s, vibrant in his memory as it was, than to any workaday question of how the beach was used now in the 1880s and 1890s. Young drew from White that the work life of inhabitants in the past had always revolved around farming, fishing and whaling. In the inland bays eeling, clamming, and oystering had always been staples that paid good wages and supplemented the income of small hard-scrabble farmers, while fishing off the beach had been pursued the length of Southampton's shores. Fishing boats, as many as half a dozen at any one time, were always drawn up on the beach banks closest to Town Pond and pulled through the sluiceways to the landward side for protection. These sluiceways or openings in the banks also served as cart-ways to haul fish into the village or whale blubber to be tried out at try-works on the west side of the lake. Whale boats, little different from fishing boats and about the same size, were also drawn up on this section of the beach and usually put on crutches. There were, White thought, six or seven of them in the days when as a boy he worked in a crew. If boats needed repair they were mended on the spot just as fishing nets were left to dry on the banks and stretched and bent there. This part of the beach was in every respect a whaling station, he said, and had been so since 1665. Young took this opportunity to remind the court that as far back as 1653 the town court had ordered that any who bring a whale ashore "shall lay it (quoting the town records) above high water mark and not meddle by dividing or diminishing it or any part thereof until it be brought to town at the town's charge and laid in or about the Town Pond . . ." This was as good a testimony as any that historically this part of the beach had been dedicated to a communal use.[19]

There had also, for instance, always been wigwams there—one had been constructed next to the dune below what was to become Sandymount—but probably did not survive beyond the 1860s (actually, White could not remember one being on the beach beyond 1844). These were rudimentary shelters made of branch poles about thirty feet in circumference and twelve feet high with a hole at the top to let out smoke. In the whaling season a crew of three or four was stationed in each to keep watch. It was cold, wet work and they kept a fire going. If a whale was sighted offshore a signal was given from a stage pole and the whole village, sometimes as many as 150 people, he said, would come down to the beach to watch or take part in the whale hunt. It appears to have been the case that there were several such wigwams at intervals along the beach on both sides of Town Pond but probably no farther than Old Town on the east and Cooper's Neck on the west, that is, within signaling distance of the village. If the weather was bad during a whale hunt, the townspeople took shelter in one or other of them.

The difficulty with White's testimony, graphic though it was in describing the long relationship the inhabitants had always had with the beach and the sea, was that in respect to whaling at least it portrayed a part of Southampton's history that was already far in the past. Until the 1840s, it was not uncommon in a good year for six whales to be taken and two or three in other years. White recalled that about twenty whales were tried out at the Point during this period, adjacent to what became Salem Wales's land not six feet from what he could not again resist referring to as Wales's "fancy fence."[20] But by the 1870s whales were seldom seen. White had to admit that no whale had been taken for more than a dozen years.[21] For the purposes of the trial, any admission that offshore whaling had effectively disappeared unfortunately took something of the bite and relevance out of his account.

The case for the trustees however, that this narrow stretch of beach was "given, dedicated or appropriated" for public use, was not yet fully lost. White endured some particularly aggressive questioning from Atterbury who began by casting doubt on his motives for bringing the suit. An excerpt or two from the record will serve to indicate the tenor of Atterbury's cross-examination:

Q. You have been a leading promoter of this litigation, have you not?

A. I can't say. I have been elected nine years by a near unanimous vote of the town as a trustee, and nine years (as president) by the Board.

Q. Have you not been the man who has been the greatest promoter in this lawsuit?

A. I can't tell, more than the rest of the inhabitants of the town.

Q. Do you mean you have not had more to do than the rest of the inhabitants of the town in getting up and furthering this lawsuit?

A. I can't say. I think the inhabitants authorized me to do it, and I expect to do my duty. When I am doing anything I expect to do it.

Q. Can you say really whether you had more to do than the other inhabitants with this litigation?

A. As president of the Board I have, but as an individual I don't think I have.

Q. You have taken a very deep interest in it, have you not?

A. When I see my property robbed from me of course I made the fight.

Q. You have taken a very deep interest in it, have not you?

A. No more than a great many of the inhabitants do.

Q. (Question repeated).

A. No deeper than the rest. I have taken a great interest in it.

Q. You have strong feeling upon the subject, have not you?

A. I can't say. No more than the rest.[22]

In such fashion did a smart railroad lawyer take on a country whaling captain of advancing years. It was without doubt a surprisingly hostile beginning given that Atterbury was a summer resident and White a leading political figure in the town. But perhaps we should see the exchange as a reflection of the widening gulf between the two communities. After all, this was precisely what the trial as a whole represented, the beach being merely the stage—and ultimately the most important stage given the history of the beach—on which the bitter feelings of both communities were expressed. Atterbury's serpentine attack on White was an attack on his probity, dourly resisted by White, but when it came to matters of substance where Atterbury had limited knowledge, White had the best of it.

The first matter to come up was the seemingly innocuous matter of "wreckage" and other debris washed up on the beach. Ships foundered quite frequently along the coast of Long Island in the nineteenth century, particularly vessels under sail that were driven on the beach by storms or otherwise stranded offshore on shoals or bars where they were in danger of breaking up. Under common law any such wreckage became the property of whoever found it. When asked about what was done with it, White responded that wreckage was carried through the sluiceways up on the beach banks "out of the way of the tide" and left there until its owner got around to carting it away. Sometimes it was left there four or five years: White had brought up the keel of a vessel a while back and had rediscovered it buried in the dune when the sand blew off the top in high winds.[23] But Atterbury wanted to nail down the one question uppermost in his mind of whether this was the only section of beach where wreckage was brought up from the surf. Of course it was, as White pointed out. There were sluiceways, four of them, and a hard or traversable road to the village; it was in every way convenient. On farther points on the beach well away from the village there was almost no possibility of carting heavy material in the absence of roads. The idea of a Dune Road or Seaside Boulevard extending westward on the length of the beach had only recently been raised by Thomas and it had obviously not been suggested to address the needs of fisherman or others wanting to transport loads of various kinds to the village. This was not Atterbury's concern but he got White to admit that it would be "foolish work" for inhabitants to lay claim to salvage far down the beach and then be unable to transport it.[24]

It was not quite clear who won this round but, on balance, it would seem to go in White's favor: The beach at the foot of Town Pond was and had been for long years a public venue for salvagers as much as for fisherman just as it had been earlier for whaling crews. It also was a public bathing place, as White innocently pointed out, before it had been as good as taken over by summer residents. They had made little pretence that they enjoyed the proximity of "country people" as fellow bathers and, as he bluntly put it to Atterbury with unconcealed relish, had effectively "cleaned them out."[25] Atterbury, not wishing to dwell on this unfortunate lack of comity between the communities, turned his attention next to the sluiceways all four of which were so convenient to Town Pond and the village.

Were there not other sluices in the immediate neighborhood, he wanted to know, were there not lower and more surmountable dunes along other parts of the beach? As it happened there were cuts in the beach banks at irregular intervals extending within a mile or two on either side of Town Pond. To the west there were sluiceways serving as roads to draw up boats at Cooper's Neck and Halsey Neck. Just to the east Frog Pond Lane constituted a road down through the beach banks and was used to pull fishing boats away from the surf. There were similar roads at Old Town and Mecox, the latter used by fishermen in Watermill. This transpired in later testimony given by Charles White, a cousin of George White and once the keeper of the life saving station at Town Pond, but it was hardly enough to put a dent in the latter's position that the beach at Town Pond was a privileged public space. Wearily (he had been on the stand over an hour) White informed Atterbury and the court that the beach banks everywhere along the beach were twenty feet or more in height, that there were few adequate places to land boats, and that the sluices at Town Pond were perfect in every way for bringing up boats, fish, wreckage, blubber, and the like being next to a good road to the village a mile away and therefore close to the village itself. In every way, he concluded, the precincts in question—a narrow tract of beach a few rods in extent—belonged, and had belonged since time immemorial, to the inhabitants of the town who, as he had previously pointed out, he represented.

II: THE BEACH LOST

Powerful as the argument was, however, it was not enough to convince the court. Judge Cullen delivered a judgment in favor of the defendant, dismissing the complaint, and ordered the town to pay $241.44 in costs. In April 1893, the inhabitants at the annual town meeting voted $500 for the trustees to pursue the lawsuit further and Young filed an appeal.[26] Yet it was three years before it appeared on the calendar of the appellate division of State Supreme Court, second department. The result was a surprise, not exactly a reversal of Cullen's decision, but the justices were divided and could make no decision. The case was then referred to the first department for re-argument. At the initial appeal two justices, Hatch and Bradley, argued forcefully that the act of 1818 dividing the interests of the town from those of the proprietors made an important distinction between two types of common land. There were first the common and undivided lands, meadows, and mill streams of the proprietors to be solely managed by their owners as tenants in common through a body of trustees incorporated by the legislature. And then there were other common lands referred to in the act that were in the public domain and were to be managed by the town trustees. These included lands under water (an issue already settled by the

Mecox Bay decision regarding the bay bottoms) and other lands, more especially, the lands constituting the foreshores of the town.

Judge Hatch wrote fifteen closely reasoned pages in support of the argument that the legislation included a specific reference to the common lands of the town that continued to be administered by the town trustees as they had been before 1818.[27] For this reason he found the facts out of which the plaintiffs' case had arisen to be "peculiar, novel and interesting." They were certainly that but Hatch's elaborations on them were ultimately unconvincing. He built his case on a number of lines in the fourth section of the legislation. This section outlined the rights of the trustees of the proprietors to recover penalties for any breaches of their regulations respecting their lands and to maintain suits for any trespasses on them but added an important limiting condition:

> Provided, nevertheless, that nothing in the aforesaid recited Act shall be construed to give the proprietors or their trustees any power to make any laws concerning the waters (other then mill streams), the fisheries, the sea weed, or any other productions of the waters of said town, or in any manner or way to debar the inhabitants of said town from the privilege of taking sea weed from the shores of any of *the common lands of said town*, or carting or transporting to or from, or landing property on said shores, in the manner heretofore practiced; which waters, fisheries, sea weed and productions of the waters shall be managed by the Trustees of the Freeholders and Commonalty of the Town of Southampton, for the benefit of said town, as they had the power to do before the passing of this Act.[28]

Hatch himself had italicized the "common lands of said town," a talisman for his whole argument, to suggest that there were in fact two types of common land. To justify this further he then invoked the famous "saving clause" in the act that had troubled many in the past, including White, Scott and especially George Rogers Howell. This clause had provided that "nothing herein contained shall in any manner affect or alter the right, title or interest of any person, or the inhabitants of said town to any of the before mentioned premises." Scott, for example and as noted before, believed that it had been inserted in the act at the suggestion of a shrewd proprietor (possibly Abraham Rose) as a potential cover for any future claims the proprietors might bring against the town for the recovery of lands or interests (seaweed for instance) that the act had seemingly removed from their jurisdiction. The clause was in fact sufficiently vague to admit of all sorts of interpretations as Howell (and perhaps Pelletreau also) seemed to recognize.

But Hatch was untroubled by it. To him it was crystal clear that "the before mentioned premises" referred to nothing else than "the common lands of said town" and the shores thereof, that is, lands belonging to the town as distinct from the private lands of the proprietors. He then claimed that the act expressly declared that nothing in it "shall alter or affect the title of the town." It is not splitting hairs to note that the act said nothing of the sort. Its final clause was framed to include the protection of the right, title, or interest "of any person, or the inhabitants of said town"—individuals—but did not contain any reference to the protection of any such separate right of the town itself, a corporate entity, other than those trustee managerial rights and responsibilities in the waters and their products that had been previously enumerated in the act. Similarly, the rights of inhabitants in the use of the shores were recognized in the act as in the nature of various easements that the proprietors were required to grant. Why would the legislation be explicit in this last matter—that the inhabitants were not to be debarred from "taking sea weed from the shores . . . or carting or transporting to or from, or landing property on said shores, in the manner heretofore practiced"—if it had not already earlier recognized that the shores were an integral part of the common and undivided lands of the proprietors? If the shores were, as Hatch put it, part of the common lands of the town, why would the legislature build in an elaborate series of protections of the usage rights of the town's inhabitants who, one would think, would have no need of such protection? The only body that might deny such access and refuse to grant necessary easements surely would be the owners in fee, the proprietors.

Judge Hatch, however, persisted throughout his argument in referring to the shores, all the shores along the ocean and around the bays and not just the narrow section of beach at the foot of Town Pond, as common lands belonging to the town. But his position seemed to shift in a subtle but unmistakable fashion as he went deeper into the subject. He fell back on the facts of long and customary usage just as had Young, the attorney for the town trustees. The "common lands" of the town, the shores in dispute, were not so directly claimed to be "owned" by the town—a circumstance in which the town might possess both the legal and equitable title—but had been "appropriated for the general and common use of the inhabitants." These were Young's words as approvingly quoted by Hatch. Young was less concerned with the language of 1818, which perhaps he realized was not unambiguously supportive of the town's case, than with persuading the court of the deep historical connection of the inhabitants to a very particular part of the beach and that this alone conferred on the town a genuine right of ownership that could not be gainsaid by proprietor claims. As Young had put it to the court:

> (T)he inhabitants insist that the beaches generally, but more particularly the place in question was land which had been devoted from the beginning to the use of the people of the town generally, and that by reason of such constant devotion for a period of two hundred years and upwards, the land has become impressed with a common right in all the inhabitants of the town, of which they cannot be deprived, and that the security of this common right demands that the title should continue to be held by the trustees of the town; and that it was as much the purpose of the act of 1818 to preserve for the benefit of the people of the town whatever interests in the undivided lands were common to all the inhabitants, as to secure to the proprietors their private interests.[29]

It was a worthy argument and no one would deny that, in Hatch's words, the shores had in some sense been "appropriated and devoted by universal usage and custom to the benefit and advantage of the community." But this was not enough to confer equitable rights of ownership in fee of the shores on the town, such that the town trustees might have the power to "sell, lease, or partition" them, or be charged with their perpetual management on behalf of the town's inhabitants. Young was much nearer the truth, and nearer to admitting this, when he acknowledged that the 1818 legislation was concerned to protect whatever interests the inhabitants might hold in common in the undivided lands belonging to the proprietors. He was far from saying that the title to the shores lay with the town, that they were community property.

Not to be deterred Hatch invoked the Andros and Dongan patents, then as now a crowd-pleasing tactic never failing to draw an audience when it came to a consideration of the town's historic rights and claims. Hatch thought that both patents addressed the issue at hand, that issue essentially being the public interest, and that it was amply clear that each tended to "promote the conveniences, needs and necessities of the civil and political community, in whom the title (to the town) was vested, primarily for the benefit of the inhabitants . . ." The earlier 1676 patent of Governor Edmund Andros was the most explicit. Andros said, and Hatch quoted him, that "all the lands and plantations within the said limits or bounds, shall have relation to the Towne in general for the well government thereof."[30] Ten years later Dongan recapitulated Andros at the beginning of his patent and then held, after enumerating all the lands in the town and their descriptions, that in addition the twelve grantees named in the patent shall be the first of annually elected trustees of the "freeholders and commonalty of the towne of Southampton and their Successors forever" and shall have and hold "all the aforecited tract and parcel of land and premises . . . for the severall and Respective uses following and to no other use intent and purpose whatsoever."[31] Hatch chose to advertise the passage beginning "(the) uses following" but did not go into what these uses might be or for whom they were intended. Governor Dongan however did. Dongan made it clear that the grant of land to the town was for the "only use benefite and behoofe of the said respective present ffreeholders and Inhabitants and to their severall and respective heires and Assignes forever."[32] By "only use" Dongan clearly meant "exclusive use" and by "ffreeholders and Inhabitants" and their heirs and assigns he was just as clearly referring to the original purchasers of the town and those who had later acquired shares in the enterprise. The freeholders and inhabitants were not two different groups but one corresponding to what began to be called at the time of the patent the "proprietors." The vast majority of inhabitants in 1686 were proprietors, there being only a small class of town citizens that possessed no shares or rights in the town purchase or, to say the same thing, rights in the town's common and undivided lands. Dongan made room for this small class or category by acknowledging their right to vote in some town matters but made it plain that this did not extend to town elections. Only "freeholders and freemen" were to be eligible to vote for town trustees and other office-holders, that is, only proprietors.

Where does this lead us? Dongan gave title to the lands of the town to its proprietors for their exclusive use and disposal, lands that were to be managed by town trustees (until 1818) whom the proprietors elected. But now the nineteenth-century descendants of the original proprietors—both their heirs and assigns—found their sale to Wyllys Betts of common and undivided lands on the shores, land as much common as any other, challenged as illegal and challenged specifically as land really belonging to the town as far back, according to some, as the 1650s. It is not material to debate Dongan's use of terms, that freeholder, inhabitant, freeman seemed to be used indiscriminately or loosely without regard to their actual referents. It must have been clear in Dongan's own mind, or in those of his lawyers, that the one category of persons the patent was concerned with was that of proprietors or owners, that is, the leaders of the town in accordance with the terms of the original Stirling grant of 1640. There was no other category to which the patent might be addressed. Who else was there? It was no matter that there were a few individuals overlooked—an occasional blacksmith or cordwainer with no more than a small plot of land—the fact was, as Dongan well knew, that the town was the proprietors howsoever he might have referred to them. Moreover, it was not in Dongan's interest to alter unduly Southampton's political and social structure by enfranchising some small number of men without town rights. His administration had inherited towns like Southampton all across the colony of New York and his interest in all of them was to tie them more completely to the colonial government, control them effectively by doing so, and improve their ability to pay taxes (a primary objective of both Andros and Dongan). No thought of "democratizing" land-owning patterns, or opening town meetings to all and sundry, would have crossed his mind any more than such a move would have occurred to Southampton's proprietors.

All, of course, had changed between 1686 and 1818 as the town had grown and the proportion of shareholders—holders of rights in the common and undivided lands—to the general run of inhabitants had shrunk (in the eyes of some) quite alarmingly. It was this last demographic fact after all that had led to 1818 and the stand-off between inhabitants and proprietors. Judge Hatch had signally failed to see this and had argued that the general run of inhabitants were essentially the town and always had been, that the town was an entity distinct from the proprietors and that therefore, necessarily, there were "the common lands of the town." These lands were held by Hatch to be distinct from those recognized by the act of 1818 as the private lands belonging to the proprietors in common—lands, it needs emphasizing, that were by 1892 residual and entirely insignificant if not now nonexistent. The proprietors had, as will be recalled, gone out of business in 1890 two years before the trial having no more common land left to sell, lease or partition.

Judge Bradley lent his support to Hatch's extended argument in a brief review of the issues in the case. He did raise one important question that had escaped Hatch's attention, namely that the fences enclosing the divided meadowlands along the shores between the bays and the ocean, fences to keep cattle out during the growing season and until the sedges were mown, were located on the north side of the line of the dunes. The beach land between this line and the ocean had, he said, no value for agricultural purposes and, therefore, "its divisibility, demise or sale may not have been in contemplation."[33] This land, worthless for any other purpose than landing fish, drawing up boats, and so on, must then have been what the act had referred to as "the common lands of the town," that is, "the before mentioned premises" to which the inhabitants of the town could claim some "right, title or interest" that the act sought to protect. Perhaps so but this did not render the town the owner of the beach. All the legislation had made sure of was that the inhabitants should have continued unimpeded access to the beach to land boats, dry and mend nets, claim wreckage, cut up whales, and cart fish and blubber to town through conveniently placed sluices or lanes. Moreover, the legislation had not singled out this particular section of the beach for its protection but had intended that all the shores of the town be so considered. Bradley's argument, any more than Hatch's, did not amount to saying that the shores were not the common and undivided lands of the proprietors but only that they were the common (or public) lands of the town, quite ignoring the fact that the legislature had built into the act some protection of the rights of inhabitants to go on and off the shores as they chose.

Moreover, it is an interesting fact that until members of the summer colony purchased land up and down the beach no one had thought to challenge the proprietors' right to sell, lease or partition sections of it. As Pelletreau noted in his testimony, and in his recitation of all the divisions of meadowlands along the shores beginning in the late 1640s, the proprietors' allotments of meadows all ran to the beach or the ocean as did their deeds in the early nineteenth century to particular individuals and groups (Post et al. in 1846 and 1861, Rose in 1846, Rufus Sayre in 1882). None of these allotments and transactions had ever been questioned in the town, largely, one suspects, because they were internal matters involving only townspeople. Quite clearly also, for well more than two hundred years no proprietor had ever kicked any townsman off the beach on the grounds that it was the collective property of the proprietors as tenants in common. Yet their property it was and theirs it was to sell, lease or partition. It was, in this particular case, the identity of the current owner—Frederic Betts, a summer resident—that was at the heart of the matter.

A year later the town trustees and the inhabitants in general, having been much encouraged by the view of the court that the case should be re-argued, agreed that the appeal should be renewed. The case was heard in June 1897, almost six years after the initial trial, before five justices in New York it having been transferred to the first department of the appellate division. All five sustained Judge Edgar Cullen's original 1892 decision in favor of Frederic Betts. Judge Pardon C. Williams (surely a heartening first name to any defendant in trouble) presented the opinion of the court.

In the face of Hatch's and Bradley's misgivings the town trustees' appeal stayed alive but not for long. Judge Williams began by noting that the act of 1818 did not reserve or except the beach or seashore from the common lands that the newly created trustees of the proprietors were empowered to manage and sell. The most that could be said was that the act conferred certain usage rights on the general inhabitants, a right to use the beach for some purposes, but such rights constituted no more than an easement and were not inconsistent with the equitable title of the proprietors.[34] In respect to the undivided property in the town, including the beaches, Williams made it clear that prior to the act the town trustees had held the title to it in trust for the proprietors, whose property it was, and not for the general body of the inhabitants. There were not then two types of common land, one owned by the town—the beaches—and another—the upland—owned by the proprietors in common. Williams thought that this was a misconception (willed or not) on the part of the town trustees, that is, that there were "the common lands of the town" and the undivided lands of the proprietors. But obviously this was not the case. The "common lands of the town"—the beaches—had not been managed or leased or sold by the town trustees after 1818 but in fact had been managed by the trustees of the proprietors as the act had indicated. No objection to this had been raised in the town until 1885 when Betts and others in the summer colony attempted to impose restrictions on the use of the stretch of beach in question. Previous to that it had been the proprietors who shut up the beach, regulated the seaweed, leased sections of it for particular purposes, and occasionally sold lots adjacent to it down to the ocean. No one in the town, for instance, had complained about the lease of a few rods in the 1870s to Ella Howell and her husband for the purpose of providing a bathing place or, for that matter, had objected to the sale of a small plot to Pelletreau next to it.

In summary, there were no common lands belonging to the town—including lands dedicated for public purposes such as cemeteries, parade grounds, schools, and so on—only the undivided common lands, marshes, meadows and mill streams belonging to the proprietors as tenants in common and as such recognized by the legislation.[35] The proviso or "saving clause" of the legislation, which Judge Williams next addressed and made quite short work of, sharply clarified this particular issue that had so vexed others before him. That proviso, referring to the "before mentioned premises," was simply included to protect any rights or interests that inhabitants may have acquired in any of the lands covered by the act. It was, Williams said, "an express declaration that there was no intent to interfere with any vested rights of persons or inhabitants of the town" and added, in order to explain its generality, that "(t)he Legislature did not pretend to know or to determine what such rights might be, if any."[36] It was a plain and persuasive interpretation and one that was, we might be inclined to add, a far cry from the paranoiac suggestion of some that this last clause had been inserted at the behest of the proprietors in order to protect any putative future interests.

Williams had effectively dismantled Judge Hatch's earlier argument, exhibiting it as a strained and ultimately fallacious interpretation of the 1818 legislation on which the case turned. The power to sell the beach or shore, as apparent from the legislation, lay with the trustees of the proprietors and with them alone. The transfer of their title to Wyllys Betts and later after his death to the defendant, his brother, had been legally made while the town trustees had no claim to the property on which they could base their suit. The complaint and appeal was dismissed with costs reaffirmed. All that the town trustees could show for their efforts was the uninterrupted continuation of customary rights to the use of the beaches that the inhabitants had always enjoyed and which, ironically, had always been protected by the very act that the case had turned on.

EPILOGUE

The reaction in the town to the decision in the Betts appeal was muted. For many, especially in the business community for whom the issue of the undivided lands was already a thing of the past after the proprietor trustees disbanded in 1890, it was much ado about nothing. The beach was still there and the traditional uses to which it had always been put since "time immemorial" were now doubly protected by the action of the court in affirming and explaining the intent of 1818. As for the town trustees, with the death of George White several years earlier, they lacked a real leader. White had fought tooth and nail for the rights of the inhabitants since he became president of the trustees in 1882, but fifteen years later the ground had shifted. Mecox Bay had been a decisive victory for White and his trustees—the land under all the bays belonged to the town—but, like the status of the shores, the bays reflected a set of traditional rural interests that the summer modernization of Southampton was rapidly surpassing. Moreover, those interests that White so dearly held were those of the poorer classes in the town. Yet clearly those who depended on the fisheries to augment their small incomes, whether off the beach or harvesting shellfish in the bays, were by the 1890s of declining significance. There was too much new money about and interest in the issues of the two trials among the general inhabitants—but especially among the dominant and forward-looking Republican majority in town affairs—was correspondingly low. Nonetheless, there was no question that the controversies over who owned the lands under water and who owned the beaches were far more than a matter of town trustees versus proprietors. Underlying both was the power of outside economic interests to influence the future in Southampton.

At the same time that the decision of the appeals court was handed down, however, the town trustees were embroiled in an even more contentious issue and, this time, one that was almost entirely local in scope. After White's death in 1893, the trustees, following the Mecox Bay decision, had decided to lease out lands under the waters of the bays to various individuals and companies for the purpose of gathering shellfish. Before 1818, as we earlier saw, the town trustees, acting on behalf of the proprietors, had always done this. Through much of the nineteenth century, few leases were issued by the proprietor trustees for the simple reason that oystering had declined and Mecox Bay had become unproductive. The Mecox Bay imbroglio changed all that. The proprietors, in quitclaiming the bay bottoms to outside interests, had intentionally or inadvertently opened up the question of who owned these lands. After much public furor, the courts decided that the town possessed the title to all the lands under water, a signal victory for the town and the baymen. But now, hardly was the ink dry on the appellate court's decision on the bays, than the newly emboldened town trustees took it on themselves to offer shellfish leases for limited sections of Mecox and Shinnecock bays. The inhabitants reacted and separated themselves into Free Bay and Leased Bay factions. This issue consumed town trustee politics in the mid-1890s and partly upstaged the trustees' failure to convince the court that the shores—the beaches—belonged to the town. But the controversy over the use of the bays did serve notice that the baymen and other fishermen were fully resolved that their voices would continue to be heard. Summer interests, and the triumph of Betts, may have been much in the news (especially in the ever-submissive *Seaside Times*) but it was still evident—whether they were declining in significance or not—that the older staple interests of the town still commanded attention.[1]

But the newspaper was little interested in this intramural dispute. It was of minor import to the *Times* (or the newly established *Press*) who was permitted to harvest the bays—whether the inhabitants at large with their meager apparatus for harvesting clams or oysters or those with the wherewithal to lease sections of the bays and close them off to others. On balance, both papers favored a leased bay on the usual Republican grounds that it constituted economic progress. But, as might be expected, the *Times* was deeply relieved at the appellate court's decision to affirm Frederic Betts's ownership of his lands extending to the beach at the foot of Lake Agawam. Its October 28, 1897 edition gave over the entire front page to the outcome of the appeal, reprinting Judge Williams' opinion in full and endorsed it in a fulsome editorial. An excerpt bears reproducing:

> A contrary decision would have tended to unsettle a large number of titles, and would have been most disadvantageous to the growth of the town as a place of Summer residence. The Dune property has year by year, increased in its attractions to those seeking to escape from the heat of the cities and the very fact that the title of that property has been in controversy has greatly hindered development. It was doubtful policy on the part of the Town trustees to raise the question, and the decision of the Supreme Court is most positive that they had no valid claim to the premises in question.[2]

The decision, it went on to say, affirmed the validity of all beach titles given by the proprietor trustees since 1818 and was to have no effect on those transferred previously. The paper, it should be added, was not without concern for the historical users of the beach. Throwing a bone to the fishermen—their nets, wigwams, their boats—it noted that the decision "carefully refrains from nullifying any secondary rights or easements that may have been acquired . . . (that) may doubtless be exercised there hereafter as heretofore." The "may," used twice in the same sentence and indicating a somewhat conditional probability, may have grated on some in the village.

The Betts trial was important because it essentially gave the beach down to high tide, subject to the aforementioned easements, in perpetuity to the residents of the summer colony.

Just as they had come to control the shores of Lake Agawam now there could be no question that the beach was theirs to develop. The only minor obstacle to obtaining an insurable title to beachfront property that summer owners faced was the necessity of purchasing a quitclaim deed. These could be readily had, as we have seen, from Harri Howell the astute lawyer who had bought up the outstanding interest in much formerly proprietor land east of Halsey Neck from the assigns of Rufus Sayre (Edwin Post and James H. Foster) for $550 in 1885. Sayre had acquired his interest in various parcels from the proprietors via quitclaim for the same price in 1882, at the exact moment when the proprietor trustees had divested themselves of all their remaining interests, real or imagined, in the lands of the town. All a summer owner now need do to quiet title and sleep undisturbed at night was enter Harri Howell's Main Street office with $50 in hand and emerge with the appropriate document. Howell pursued this small but steady business with the summer colony for thirty years before he made one minor miscalculation over a beach lot in Mecox that had been sold by the proprietors to a local party in 1846 and in which, therefore, Howell and before him Sayre (and Post and Foster after Sayre) had no interest to sell. In 1928 his string of good fortune ran out in a Riverhead courtroom when a judge determined that he had wrongfully claimed an interest in the Mecox land in question.[3]

But buying quitclaims from a small town lawyer in the 1890s and thereafter was a minor inconvenience to summer residents desirous of beach property. In almost exactly twenty years since Gaillard Thomas had purchased his beach land from a perspicacious farmer in 1877, the growing summer colony had taken possession of nearly three miles of beach and, thanks to the outcome of the Betts trial, was assured that there would be no future questions raised about its dominance of this interstitial part of the town—the indeterminate boundary of the ocean to the south and the limit of arable land on the north.

The summer colony had begun with the beach when Thomas, with equal perspicacity, had staked his claim to a stretch of unwanted land "outside the fence" and too close to the ocean for the comfort of most sanguine Southampton inhabitants. The earliest summer residents however, perhaps equally cautious of the waves, had eschewed building as close to the ocean as the doctor and had taken possession of the lands around Town Pond. In doing so, they perhaps wished to assure themselves of some protection, but it was much more likely in those early days that they found the beach an unappealing environment next which to live. All changed in the next few years as sea bathing became an enjoyable pastime and the ocean lost its terrors. Perhaps the existence of St. Andrew's Church perched behind its dune had something to do with it. At any event, after Wyllys Betts purchased his land, it was not long before the summer community began to take command of beachfront property in the late 1880s and began moving there in increasing numbers. The circumstances and outcome of the subsequent Betts trial then were doubly important. It rallied the summer colony against a doubtful claim of town ownership and convinced it that the beach was effectively theirs regardless of traditional claims. Thereafter, there was never any question that summer owners controlled the beach in the immediate vicinity of the village and did so by the simple act of buying dune property and building on it. In so doing, but in full accord with public easements, they would find themselves able to constrain local access to it just as they had earlier limited the access of inhabitants to boating, bathing, skating and fishing in and on the village pond. Whether in fact or in intent, the Betts trial had given the summer colony the opportunity to extend its dominion—easements or not—over a crucial section of town lands. It was a hard thing for the town to swallow but swallow it eventually it did. Apart from access roads—the few remaining sluices—and various easements to go on the beaches, the town never did regain its time-honored if limited control. The Betts trial had made sure of that whatever future town trustees might have to say about the management of the shores once the proprietors were out of the way. Simply put, the beach was now open for development.

And developed it was. As far as the summer colony was concerned, that meant no more than the construction of palatial estates up and down the dunes and inland in the Great Plain. This began in earnest in the 1900s and did so without reference to or interference from the village authorities. Zoning and any restriction on building was, of course, a thing of the far future. Over the years the summer colony made its own rules but did limit itself to banning the construction of commercial establishments. There were to be no hotels—or, later, motels—sullying the beach. Neither village nor town government had any say in this matter but much later absorbed almost by osmosis the central message that the beach was forever to remain a private summer sphere. The inhabitants would continue to have access to it—as the Betts decision affirmed—but it would be a contained access via the little lanes, the former sluiceways, that poked through the dunes here and there between the mansions that increasingly flanked them. Eventually, these lanes—they were to become town trustee roads—were given names. Not the sort of names perhaps that the summer colony might have attached to them but bureaucratic appellations. Thus there would be Roads A, B, C, and so on. They still exist.

The ban on commercial enterprises, once laid down and later enshrined in village law as though the village itself had first thought of it, was never breached. A stylish and exclusive beach club, eventually built in the 1920s on what had been Mrs. Howell's humble little property, was another matter. The Bathing Corporation, as it was officially named, was never meant to be anything other than a dues-paying concern and the exclusive domain of the summer colony. On the east side of the church in the dunes it was little more than a stone's throw from the Meadow. An early morning set, followed by a brief hour of devotions, would naturally culminate in a leisurely lunch at the beach club. The local population found itself slowly pushed off this small but now highly privatized and exclusive section of beach. Eventually they drifted a mile to the west in the as yet unbuilt area of Cooper's Neck. There they established their own beach club. All thoughts of the harmonious intermingling of the two communities in a common pleasurable activity—an afternoon at the beach—thus inevitably vanished, a casualty, as everyone knew, of the social inequality that colored all relations between them and accounted for the mistrust that had grown up on both sides.

In some important respects little has changed since. In 1941 Archibald Manning Brown, a well-known architect and designer of low-income housing in New York and the president of the Shinnecock Hills Golf Club, wrote rousingly to what was left of his members (the Depression had taken its toll on the summer colony, its real estate and its club memberships) that "Shinnecock MUST not die." The club at that time had been reduced to not much more than thirty members and could barely pay its taxes let alone maintain a golf course, but undeterred Brown went on that "having millions of dollars invested in houses, in clubs, in all kinds of services for our enjoyment and convenience . . . under well-nigh perfect conditions" this was no time to be faint of heart. Conditions would inevitably improve. They always did. True, the banks had foreclosed on some summer property in the late 1930s but this was not destined to last. Brown sounded much like Thomas in the 1880s, less defensive perhaps, but equally assured of the summer colony's privileges as rightly guaranteed by its investments in the community.[4]

What was different in Southampton after the nineteenth century—the formative or incubatory period of the summer colony we have been dealing with—was the slow change in the attitude of the local community to what had become by 1930 an entrenched upper-status group with second-generation roots and an abiding sense of entitlement to its own privileged place in the village. There was nothing any longer tentative about the claims of ownership to Southampton by this group as there had been in the 1880s when the founding summer leadership sought to mold the community in the romantic rural image it had bestowed on it. During and after the presidency of Dr. Ely, the Village Improvement Association purred along largely avoiding controversy while tending to its fetes and small beautification projects. Its members, particularly the wives, took a deep and innocent interest in the welfare of the community and its poor and indigent members. Relations with the natives and their representatives in village and town officialdom took on a new and stable harmony as the years of hot reaction and confrontation receded into the past. All passion seemed to have been spent with the Betts affair and, in any case, there were no more charismatic leaders on either side to stir the imaginations of their supporters or constituents. Dr. Thomas and Captain White had exited the scene and nobody had replaced them.

The common ground, if there ever was a common ground, uniting the two communities was now money, how much were the summer people prepared to spend to satisfy their wants and how much profit could enterprising locals reasonably expect to turn on a variety of transactions between them. By 1930, so much money had passed through so many hands, fuelled by an unending real estate boom, that the small business elite of the 1890s had been transformed into a large and prosperous bourgeois class, exuding success, that had fully repressed in its collective consciousness the heady days of moral principle that had once fired up the village under White's impassioned leadership. By and large, there were few moments after 1930 when the political imaginations of the public were united and crystallized on an issue relating to the doings of the summer colony. Money had miraculously and harmoniously integrated the two cultures for close to a quarter of a century and there was nothing to be gained by hewing to matters of principle that might divide them. A long period then ensued from 1933—the year when the summer clubs began firing the help out of economic necessity and the colony began retreating to the city—to let us say for convenience 1963 during which Southampton went into hibernation. This was Southampton's long twentieth century, forty years when there was no money to speak of and the town relapsed into a sort of peaceful and thankful silence between booms. There was only one restaurant of any merit—Herb McCarthy's, although the rich of that time were not known for their refined culinary taste—and of the fashionable stores of the 1920s almost all but Saks Fifth Avenue had left town.

The recovery of the 1960s and 1970s was, however, anemic at best. Real estate was slow to move and business on Main Street plodded along—wending, one might say, its somnolent and weary way to meager yet, in the circumstances, acceptable profits. New shops and restaurants were slow to emerge. There were no brokerage houses. Club memberships were down and most of the summer clubs resorted to recruiting locals, itinerant Southerners and media types—not "our sort," it was true (though they were quickly to become our sort), but they corresponded to an unquestioned economic necessity as clubs sought to pull themselves up by their bootstraps. It was a slow-moving and tranquil time. There may have been a little glamour here and there—Hedy Lamarr, Rita Hayworth and Gary Cooper were occasionally to be seen at Herb's—but overall the impression of the period is one of a lingering and exhausted but rather pleasant dowdiness. Wet bathing suits and old Brooks Brothers shirts seemed to sum it up quite fittingly. There were the usual summer parties and fundraisers but the glitz of the 1920s was gone and it was not soon to be recreated. Sadly, the period since the end of the war had certainly failed to live up to the expectations of the esteemed manager of the Bathing Corporation, William Dunwell, who had predicted in a 1944 letter to the president of the golf club that everybody would come home from the war and that "with all the immense amount of money floating around there will be a grand and glorious fling." But this was not to be the case or, if it was, it was not happening in Southampton.

The 1980s ushered in a new era of brashness and money riding a speculative Wall Street boom that rivaled the run-up to 1929 in its extravagance. New money fell voraciously on Southampton swallowing up the flat, windswept and treeless expanses of farmland where potatoes and corn had formerly been raised. Enormous and tasteless designs in faux Queen Anne style, vague and formless imitations of McKim, Mead and White, sprang up in place of the crops to satisfy the pretensions of this latest wave of nouveaux riches. The traffic became unbearable as once again Southampton became the summer haven of legions of Manhattanites who descended weekly on the area and points farther east. The old rich from Park Avenue and the estate section in the old Ox Pasture and Great Plains divisions wrung their hands about the vulgarity of it all but nonetheless admitted many of the newcomers to their clubs after only a perfunctory vetting. It was all too much. Polo, of all imaginable sports, once again became popular after over half a century of neglect. Attending polo matches, merely to be seen as in attendance, became the ultimate symbol of the new refinement of a class with nothing but money to burn and a desperate yearning for social recognition. Mrs. Van Rensselaer would have recognized the type as indeed would Nathaniel West. Local business, beginning with real estate and housing construction, perked up of course. New restaurants, hopeful little boutiques, gourmet delicatessens, services of all sorts emerged to cater to the needs and desires of the new clientele. Landscape gardeners became overnight millionaires.

Many features of the boom, briefly interrupted though it was by the 1987 stock market crash, were not dissimilar to the feverish speculation that gripped Southampton in the 1880s almost exactly a century before. Money poured in, real estate shot through the roof, farmers sold out and enterprising locals and a few carpetbaggers did very well. As in the 1880s the politicians, ever appreciative of the effect on their constituents (and on themselves) of prosperity, calmly watched as Southampton's land base shrank as more and more farmland, woodland and coveted waterfront property was given up and turned into rich enclaves of summer residence. As George White would have noted, and written about apoplectically to the paper, there were again signs prohibiting or limiting access everywhere you looked. Dune Road, running the length of the South Beach from Halsey's Neck to the Shinnecock Inlet and within the village, is a flagrant case in point. Once a dirt road, and subject to periodic flooding, it became a raised two-lane macadam highway. This was done at the behest of summer residents after the beach was subdivided into small and exclusively priced lots in 1981and after considerable haggling over whether they or the village was to pay for it. The village lost. Prior to that date, the beach was accessible to anyone at any point along its three-mile length who wanted to park and tramp across the dunes and had been so since time immemorial. One day, almost immediately after the road was hardened to provide safe and reliable access to its new wealthy homeowners (there were no more than six at the time), No Parking signs were erected by the village authorities along its length. Access to the beach except at two small parking areas effectively vanished. Thus have matters remained ever since.

But there are no more George Whites to bring this or like matters to our attention. He was perhaps Southampton's last true hero since the days of settlement in the 1640s when his own ancestors arrived. His legacy for Southampton to me was to lay out in the starkest terms the choices facing the community as it made the uncertain transition to modernity. In the very long run Southampton has benefited in important ways from the presence of the summer colony. Its hospital, art museum, and library attest to the well-intentioned generosity of summer residents while the village and its environs in general have the look of a prosperous and successful community, one that on the surface seems to have preserved the spirit of its past. But modern Southampton came at a cost. From the beginning it lacked the economic and political resources to withstand the sudden and inexorable invasion of wealth in the 1880s. It was too much to expect that the inhabitants, including even the proprietary elite, could have anticipated an ever-rising real estate market that would prove irresistibly attractive to farmers, an emerging class of brokers and outside speculators. A real estate system resulted that guaranteed a permanently rising property market that would last (with a few adjustments for economic downturns) into the present. Real estate became a machine for printing money in land sales, new construction, and the revaluation of existing residential and commercial property. Even the smallest dwelling in almost the humblest part of the village could command the attention of the real estate broker and continues to do so today. Neither White nor his frequent but ultimately admiring opponent, Gaillard Thomas, could have foreseen what kind of community Southampton was eventually to become and how, all blandishments to the contrary aside, it had lost touch with its past. Its past now had become the introduction and history of the summer colony to which the real past of the village and town had become a mere adjunct and ornament, a facsimile of the past to both inhabitants and colonists.

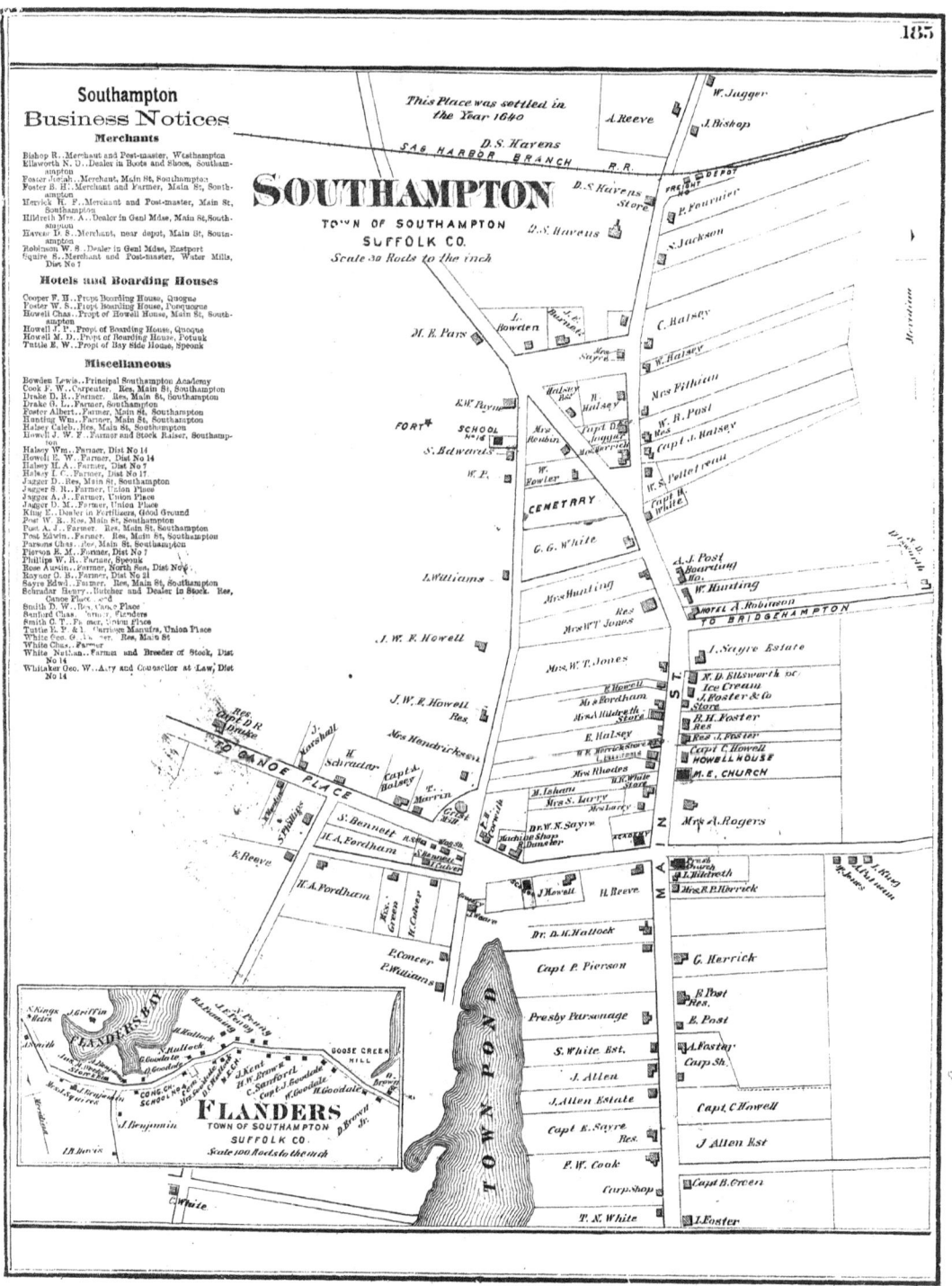

Village of Southampton 1873—Main Street (Beers, Comstock & Cline Atlas, New York 1873)

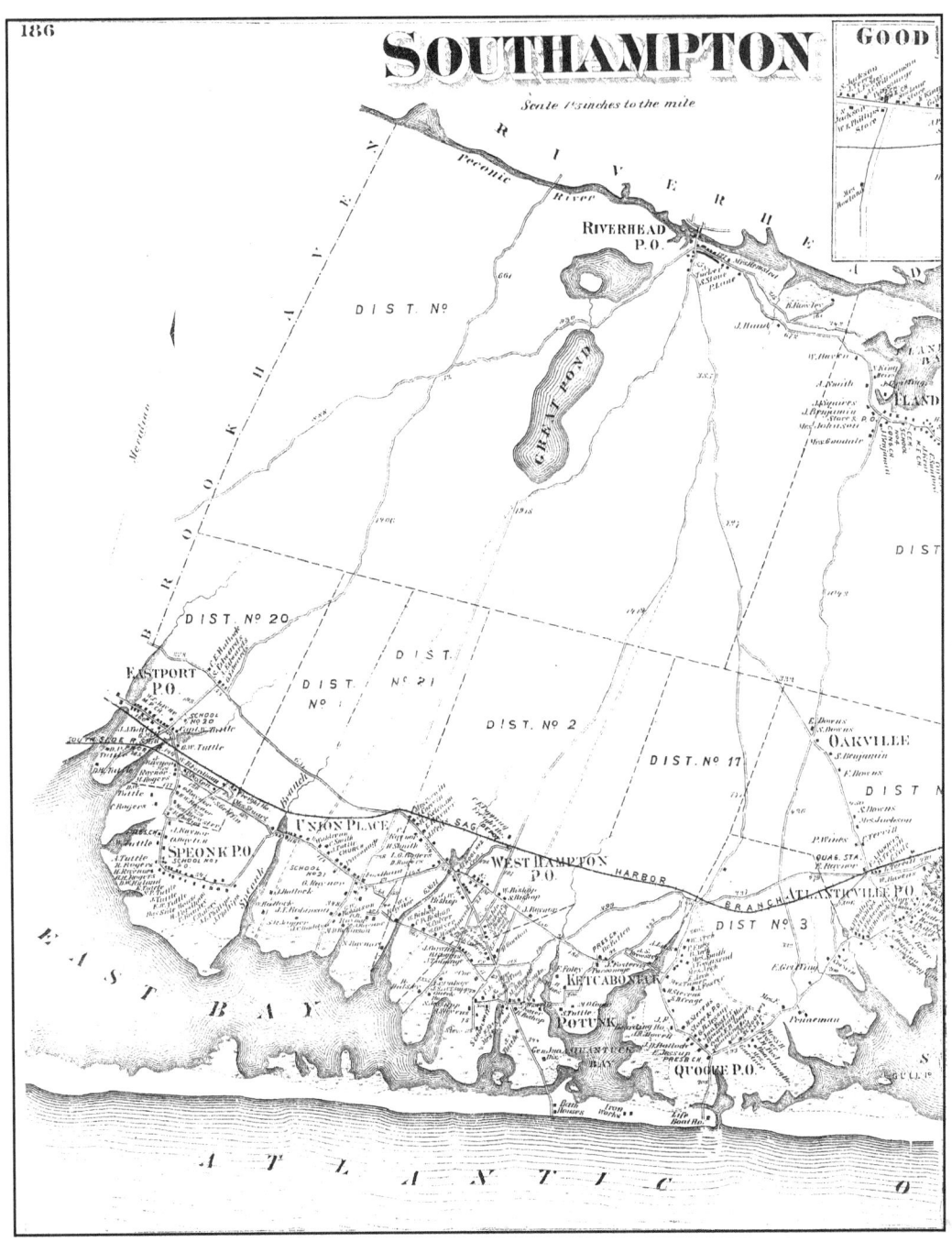

Town of Southampton 1873—Western Section from Quogue to Eastport and the Brookhaven town line 1873 (Beers, Comstock & Cline)

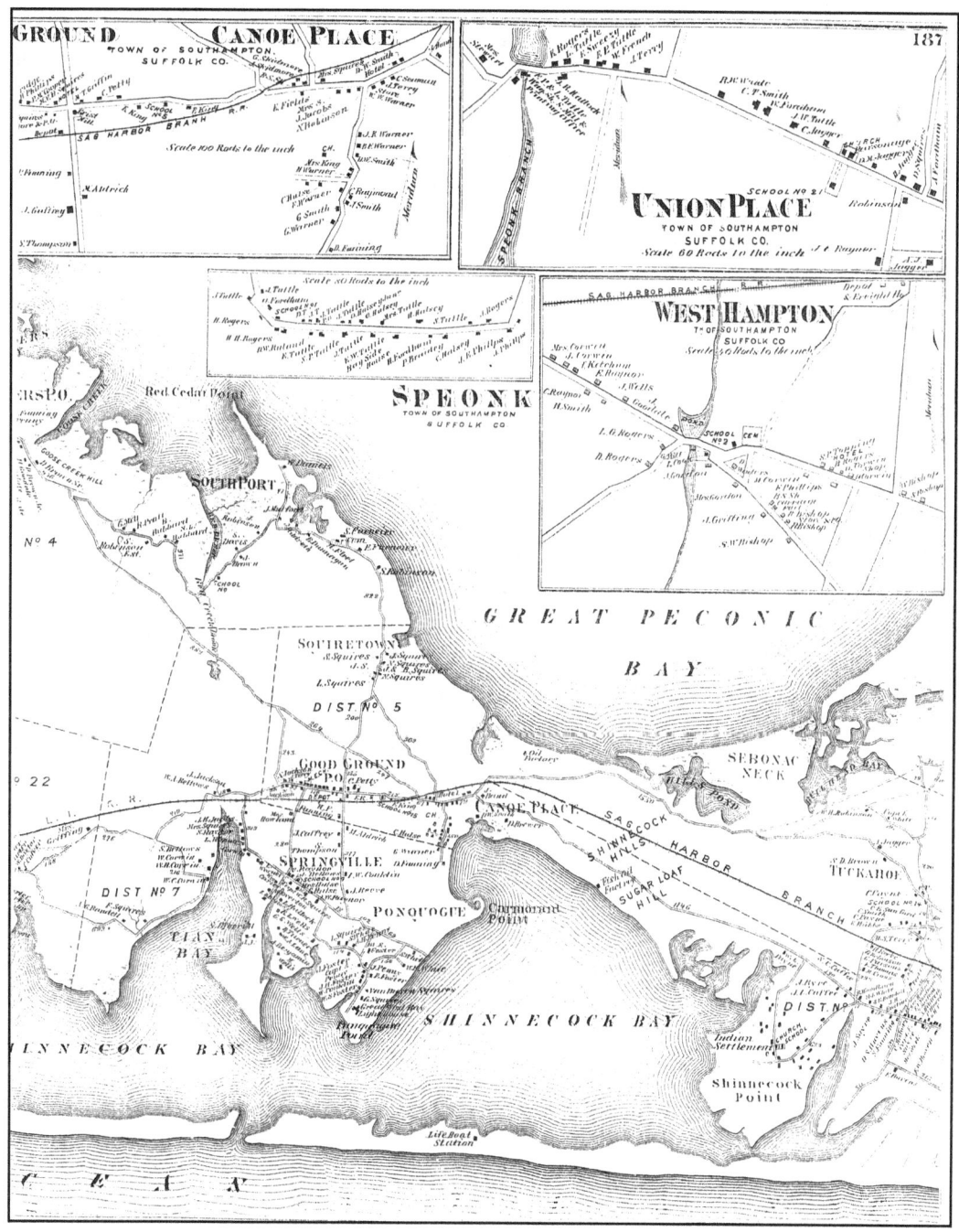

Town of Southampton 1873—Western Section including the Shinnecock Hills, Canoe Place and Good Ground to Tiana 1873 (Beers, Comstock & Cline)

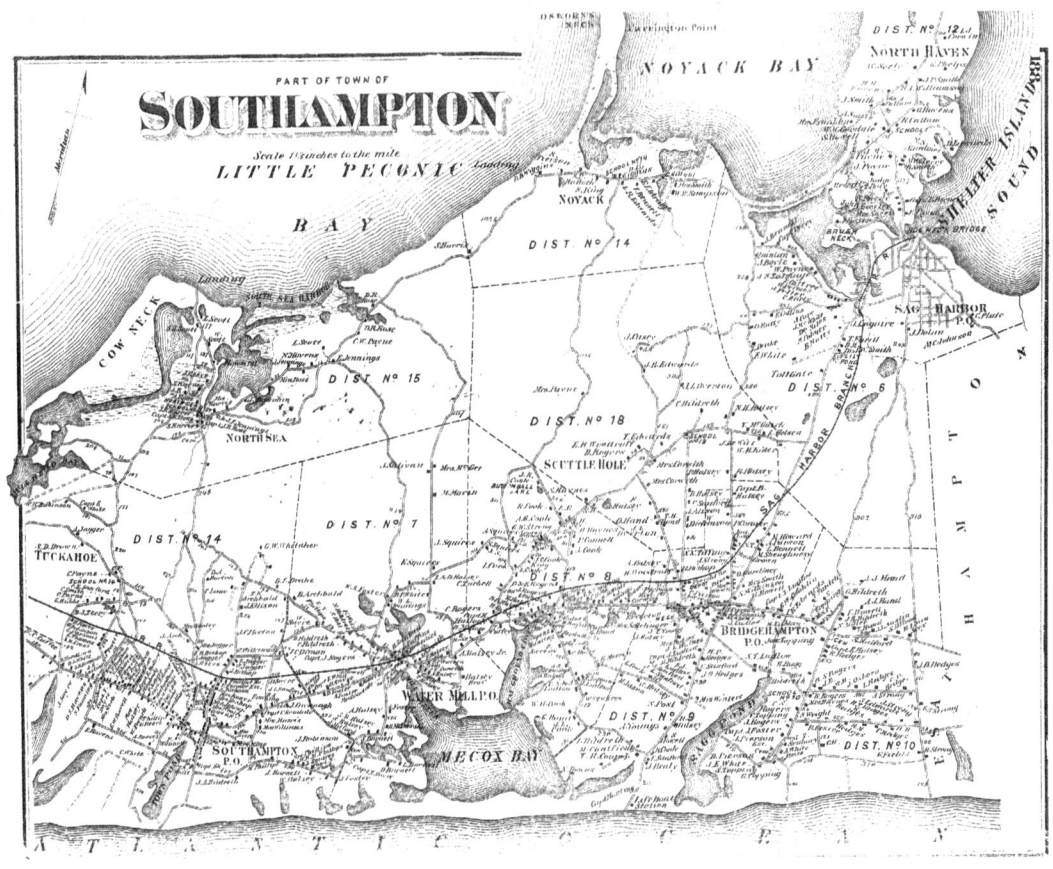

Town of Southampton—Eastern Section to Bridgehampton, Sag Harbor, North Haven and the East Hampton town line 1873 (Beers, Comstock & Cline)

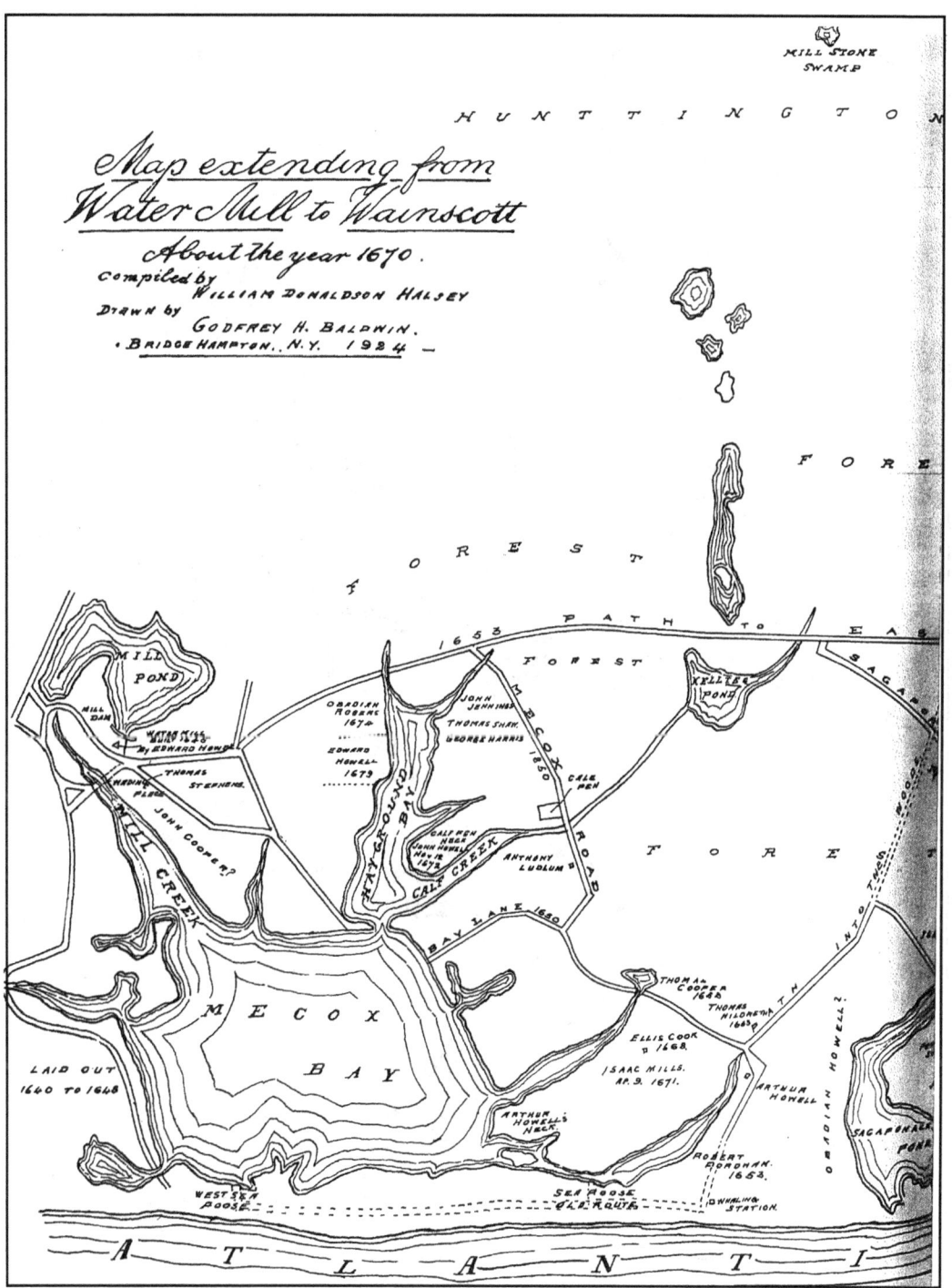

Mill Pond, Mill Creek, Mecox Bay and Location of the Sea Pooses 1670. (Compiled by W. D. Halsey 1924)

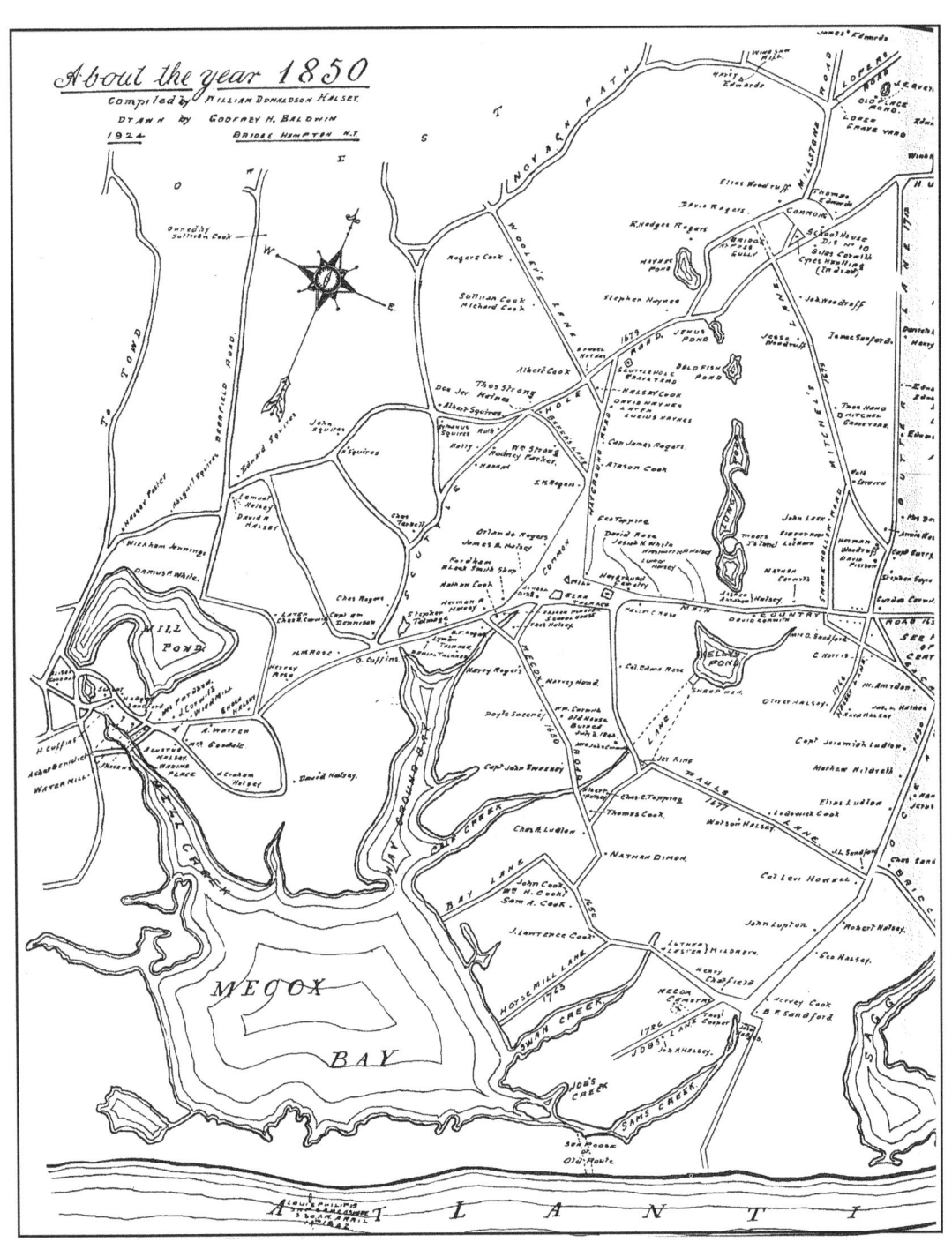

Watermill and Mecox to Sagg Pond circa 1850. (Compiled by W. D. Halsey 1924)

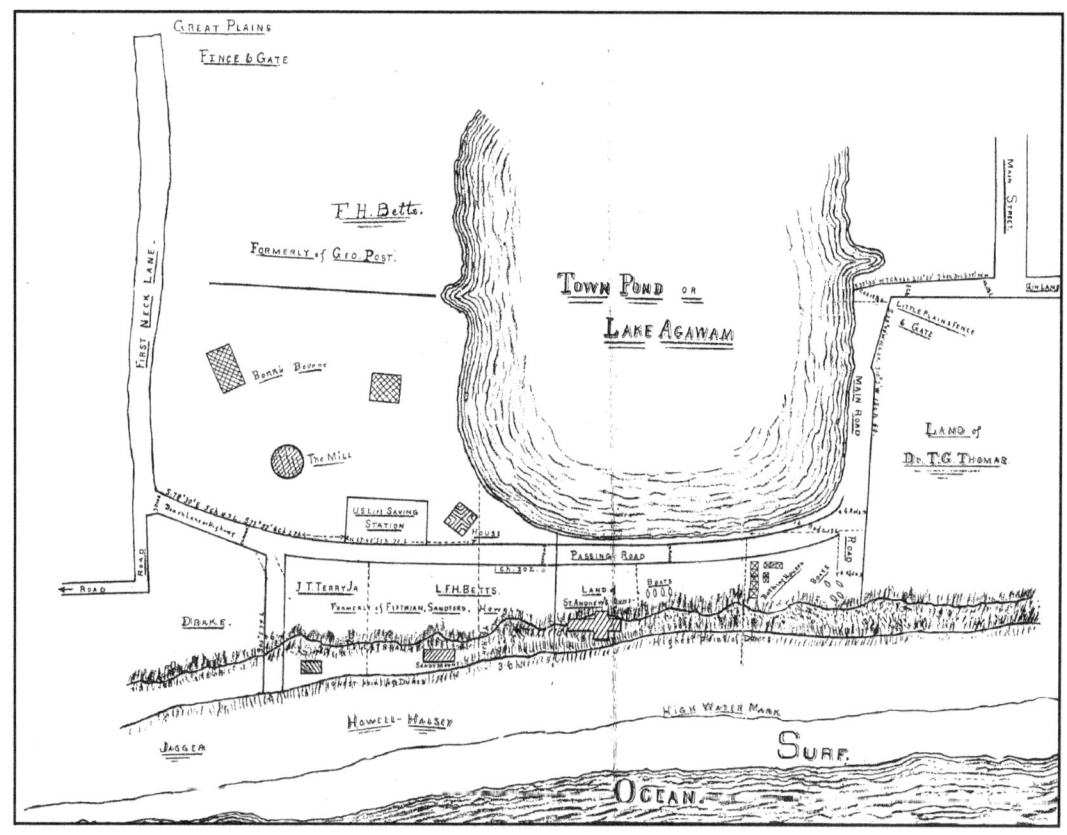

Map used in Litigation: F. H. Betts vs. Southampton Town Trustees 1891–2. (Drawn by W. S. Pelletreau 1891)

NOTES

ABBREVIATIONS FOR NOTES

JTPSH: Journal of the Trustees of the Proprietors of the Common and Undivided Lands of Southampton

JTTEH: Journal of the Town Trustees of East Hampton

LRTPSH: Land Records of the Trustees of the Proprietors of the Common and Undivided Lands of Southampton

LSNY: Laws of the State of New York

RSI: Records of the Shinnecock Indians

RSVIA: Records of the Southampton Village Improvement Association

RTEH: Records of the Town of East Hampton

RTSH: Records of the Town of Southampton

RTTSH: Records of the Town Trustees of Southampton

RTVSH: Records of the Trustees of the Village of Southampton

ST: *Seaside Times*

NOTES TO INTRODUCTION

1. See William S. Pelletreau, "Southampton" in *History of Suffolk County, New York* (New York 1882) 28. Also Richard Post, *Notes on Quogue 1659–1959* (East Hampton 1959) 63.

2. Reprinted in Peter Ross and William S. Pelletreau, *History of Long Island Vol. II* (New York and Chicago 1903) 310–311.

3. Alice Garner, *A Shifting Shore: Locals, Outsiders, and the Transformation of a French Fishing Town 1823–2000* (Ithaca 2005) 119.

4. George Rogers Howell, *History of Southampton, Long Island* (Bridgehampton NY 1866, 2nd edition Albany 1887).

5. In the late nineteenth century there was some confusion either at the post office or in the Long Island Railroad schedule as to the spelling of Easthampton. It had become East Hampton and has remained so ever since. In opting for Easthampton I was looking for consistency with both an older

spelling and how the other Hamptons—Southampton, Westhampton, Bridgehampton, and so on—are still presented.

6. Published in the *Sag Harbor Corrector* March 10, 1838.

7. Henry P. Hedges, *History of the Town of East-Hampton, New York* (Sag Harbor 1879)

8. Fenimore Cooper, like Payne before him and others later in the nineteenth century such as Timothy Dwight or Richard Bayles who are cited afterward, had no difficulty embracing the romantic version of rural American life prevalent at the time and clung to even today by those mourning the passing of a simpler and apparently truer form of society.

9. From an editorial comment in the *Seaside Times* (*ST*), Southampton's weekly newspaper, January 25, 1883.

10. Within a few months of their arrival, the first settlers negotiated a land agreement with the Shinnecock Indians, an agreement that gave them title to the lands east of Canoe Place (the location of the Shinnecock Canal) to roughly Wainscott at what is now the Easthampton town line. Subsequent Indian deeds put all the land west of Canoe Place as far as Brookhaven in their hands. The Shinnecock, whose conception of land ownership was entirely different, were probably unaware that they had "sold" their land. Rather, in return for gifts and some guarantees of security, they understood that the deeds gave the settlers merely certain occupancy and use rights in the land in question. Of course, Gaillard Thomas's situation and that of those who came shortly afterward was quite different. He and others bought land in fee simple from private owners. But the permanence of the invasion of the New Yorkers, as that became obvious to local opinion in the 1880s, must have been as much a surprise to Southampton as had the arrival and permanent settlement of their ancestors to the Shinnecock two centuries before. Relations between the Southampton settlers and the Shinnecock Indians are examined in Chapters 6 and 7.

11. The transformation of Montauk between the 1660s and the early twentieth century, and its fatal impact on the Montaukett Indians, is discussed in my article "On Montauk" in an anthology devoted to Wyandanch, the seventeenth century Montaukett sachem (forthcoming, East Hampton 2011).

12. *ST* September 16, 1886.

13. See Jerry E. Patterson, *The First Four Hundred: Mrs. Astor's New York in the Gilded Age* (New York 2000) 207–235 for "the list" and for a complete and entertaining exposé of New York society at the end of the century.

14. May King Rensselaer (with Frederic Van de Water), *The Social Ladder* (London 1925) 243. The Bradley Martin's fancy dress ball at the Waldorf Hotel cost more than $100,000 and was held in the depths of the 1890s depression. Fearful of riotous protest by New York's legion of unemployed the first-floor windows of the hotel were nailed shut by an apprehensive management. Of the twelve hundred guests, Cornelia Martin had invited, only six hundred showed up—stricken, so it would appear, less by conscience than by the fear of assault.

15. Sven Beckert, *The Monied Metropolis: New York City and the Consolidation of the American Bourgeoisie 1850–1896* (Cambridge 1993) 272.

16. Van Rensselaer op. cit. 154.

17. Edward H. Moeran, "Southampton's First Vacationers," *Long Island Forum* (Vol. VI No. 3, April 1943) 71–73.

18. In 1878, William Pelletreau compiled a map of Main Street that traced the ownership of each property or house lot back to the middle of the seventeenth century. The first thing to be noticed is that there is no Mrs. Brown anywhere on this map, which suggests that she leased rather than owned her house. If this were the case, she probably leased from Pelletreau. Second, the map shows that three properties close to each other had been bought by three of the de Bosts in 1869 and 1870. On the west or Town Pond side of the street A. D. de Bost had purchased from the Cook family in 1870. Directly opposite on the east side Louise de Bost, Leon de Bost's wife, had purchased from Pelletreau in 1869.

Next door Mary L. de Bost also had purchased from Pelletreau in the same year. Pelletreau had originally bought both properties in 1863 and could hardly have overlooked his own real estate transactions in the exquisitely detailed map he drew. Cleveland Amory, who knew Moeran in the 1940s, concurred with him that de Bost arrived before Gaillard Thomas and built the first cottage (or renovated an existing homestead) in 1875. He added that Thomas was de Bost's family physician and merely followed him to Southampton. The doctor kept his own counsel on this aspect of the story. Cf. Cleveland Amory, *Last Resorts* (New York 1948) 21.

19. See William S. Pelletreau, "The New Southampton," *Long Island Magazine* (Vol. I No. 3 October 1893) 87–88. See also his address at the 275th anniversary of the founding of Southampton (Sag Harbor NY 1915) 86. According to Pelletreau, de Bost always insisted that he brought Thomas to Southampton but that if de Bost was the "discoverer," Thomas was certainly the originator of the resort. See further Lizbeth Halsey White, "Southampton Records and Landmarks," *New York History* (Vol. XIV No. 4 1933) 379.

20. Given the stubbornly Protestant morality of the vast majority of Southampton's citizenry it is not likely that their beach attire and behavior would have been such as to give offense to Thomas. This was not always the case elsewhere. Alice Garner reports that in Arcachon in the 1840s the town council passed ordinances requiring that "bathers conduct themselves with decency on the shore and in the water." Dress regulations were strict and bathers "of both sexes (were) prohibited from speaking to each other or making indecent gestures while bathing or on the beach." It seems clear that the people of Arcachon, or its poorer classes, had taken a relaxed view of what should be worn at the beach and how they should comport themselves. Victor Hugo was apparently horrified in Biarritz in 1843 that young local women swam in chemises "full of holes, without worrying what they showed," while in Blackpool on the northwest coast of England working class day trippers bathed naked provoking a "regulatory crisis" for the Victorian bourgeoisie of that seaside resort. Cf. Garner op. cit. 109–110.

21. Pelletreau 1903 op. cit. 311.

NOTES TO CHAPTER 1

1. These were Nathaniel S. Prime's *History of Long Island from its First Settlement by Europeans to the Year 1845 with Special Reference to Ecclesiastical Concerns* (New York 1845) and Benjamin F. Thompson's two-volume *History of Long Island from its Discovery and Settlement to the Present Time* (New York 1843).

2. Richard M. Bayles, *Historical and Descriptive Sketches of Suffolk County* (Port Washington NY 1873).

3. For details of the controversy see Rev. Epher Whitaker, *Southold: Being a Substantial Reproduction of the History of Southold, Long Island* (Southold 1881; 2nd edition edited by Charles E. Craven, Princeton 1931) and George Rogers Howell's address at the 250th anniversary of the founding of Southampton (Southampton 1890).

4. Bayles op. cit. 327.

5. For this see Joseph S. Wood, *The New England Village* (Baltimore 1997) 52–71.

6. Timothy H. Breen, *Imagining the Past: East Hampton Histories* (New York 1989) 137–139.

7. Virginia DeJohn Anderson, *New England's Generation: The Great Migration and the Formation of Society and Culture in the Seventeenth Century* (Cambridge 1991) 32–33.

8. Sumner Chilton Powell, *Puritan Village: The Formation of a New England Town* (Middletown, CT 1963) 3–21.

9. Frederic W. Maitland, *Township and Borough* (Cambridge 1898) 2–10.

10. For these and other documents relating to Southampton's settlement see *Records of the Town of Southampton* (RTSH) Vol. I (Sag Harbor 1877). Also reprinted in the appendices to James Truslow Adams, *History of the Town of Southampton: East of Canoe Place* (Bridgehampton, NY 1918) 257–259 and following.

11. See particularly Patricia Seed, *Ceremonies of Possession in Europe's Conquest of the New World 1492–1640* (Cambridge 1995) 20 ff. Seed introduced the phrase "peopling and planting" to define the behavior of New England settlers, contrasting it with the Dutch West India Company's strategy of "touching and trading" in New Netherland.

12. John Frederick Martin, *Profits in the Wilderness: Entrepreneurship and the Founding of New England Towns in the Seventeenth Century* (Chapel Hill 1991) 133, 138.

13. Max Weber, *The Protestant Ethic and the Spirit of Capitalism* (translated by Talcott Parsons, New York 1930).

14. RTSH Vol. I op. cit. 24. Similarly, the officers of the Massachusetts Bay Company—"the assistants"—redefined themselves as administrative officials of the new colony once they and its charter were transplanted to New England.

15. See Howell 1887 op. cit.; Pelletreau 1882, 1883 op. cit.; Adams 1918 op. cit.

16. There is some controversy still over the year of Southampton's settlement—whether it was in 1639 or 1640—partly resulting from how old-style dating was interpreted. The most serious problem is the dating of the Earl of Stirling's written confirmation of Farrett's deed to the settlers as being August 20, 1639. Historians of Southampton are unanimous that this was a mistake and that the date should read August 20, 1640. However, the earl died in February 1640 and was interred in Scotland in April. Scotland had adopted new-style dating in 1600 abandoning the calendar that ended one year in March and then beginning a new one. The documents concerning Stirling's death all bear 1640 dates. The best explanation of this puzzle is that Farrett gave the settlers at least one deed in spring 1639 (o–s) and that Stirling sent his confirmation of it from Scotland that same 1639 summer (n–s). A thorough treatment of the issues surrounding the actual date of settlement is to be found in Isabel Macbeath Calder's "The Earl of Stirling and the Colonization of Long Island" in *Essays Presented to Charles McLean Andrews by his Students* (New Haven 1930) 74–95.

17. The Pequot War of 1637 had ended barely two years earlier and was fresh in the minds of Long Island Indians. The virtual annihilation of the Pequot by Massachusetts Bay forces had left a political vacuum among Indian tribes in Rhode Island and Connecticut and set the stage for ambitious sachems to expand their influence in areas like Long Island. The Shinnecock and Montaukett particularly were preoccupied with the prospect of such a threat. It led Wyandanch, the Montaukett sachem, to encourage Lyon Gardiner, a military participant in the conflict, to settle an island in 1639 in what became Gardiner's Bay, that is, in Montaukett territory. Similarly, the Shinnecock welcomed the Southampton settlers as prospective protectors. On the Pequot War see Alfred A. Cave, *The Pequot War* (Amherst 1996).

18. See Belle Barstow, *Setaukett—Alias Brookhaven: Birth of a Long Island Town, with Chronological Records 1655–1679* (Bloomington IN 2004) 36.

19. John A. Strong, *The Algonquian Peoples from Earliest Times to 1700* (Interlaken NY 1997) 243–244.

20. For consideration of political shifts in Southampton see Chapter 4.

21. See Anderson op. cit. 65.

22. For a life of the third earl see G.P.V. Akrigg, *Shakespeare and the Earl of Southampton* (Cambridge 1968).

23. Akrigg op. cit. 110.

24. A small caveat should here be inserted to give heart to the royalist interpretation. In 1890, George Rogers Howell published, perhaps mischievously, an excerpt from what he thought "might" have

been his ancestor Edward Howell's journal describing the seagoing progress of the settlers from New Haven to North Sea Harbor in June 1640, a journal that he claimed to have discovered in "an old desk." Rounding Orient Point and heading toward the Peconics—and perhaps into the outgoing tide and the prevailing southerly wind—Edward Howell and his associates spied Lyon Gardiner on his island fastness and hove to perhaps with the idea in mind of waiting out the ferocious tide pouring out of the bays and gaining some advice from the new owner (Gardiner had settled the island, known then by the English as the Isle of Wight, the year before). Now it is quite possible that Gardiner crossed paths with the Earl of Southampton in Holland in the early 1620s. Gardiner went there in 1623, aged twenty-two, as an army corporal and remained there until 1635 when he was engaged by Lord Saye and Sele and Lord Brooke to build a fort at the mouth of the Connecticut River in support of a projected colony planned by Puritan grandees in London. Henry Wriothesly, the earl, was in command of a regiment supporting the Dutch in 1622 and, since the English presence in Holland was quite small, it is reasonable to think that he and the young Gardiner became acquainted. Perhaps Gardiner was sufficiently impressed with the earl to suggest to Edward Howell that since his island was named for the Isle of Wight off the Channel coast of southern England, and because that island happened to be under the loving jurisdiction of the Earl of Southampton, what could be more appropriate than to name the new settlement for him. But this tenuous series of historical "facts," based entirely on claims derived from a journal that may never have existed and was very likely dreamt up by George Rogers Howell in order to perpetrate some obscure practical joke at the expense of the Rev. Epher Whitaker of Southold—his old rival in historical interpretation who adamantly claimed that Southold was established before Southampton in the 1640 settlement of eastern Long Island—is surely insufficient to anoint Henry Wriothesly as the patron saint of the town of Southampton.

25. Wood op. cit. 25.

26. George R. Stewart, *American Place Names* (New York 1970) 333.

27. See Howell op. cit. 42 43; Decennial Census of the United States for 1790, 1860, 1870, 1880 (Washington DC).

28. RTSH Vol. IV (Sag Harbor NY 1893) 336 ff.

29. Overall tonnage registered in the Sag Harbor customs district fell from 23,721 tons in 1860 to 8,168 in 1870, much of it locally built. Similarly, tonnage engaged in the whale fishery declined from a peak of 12,552 tons in 1840 to 476 tons in 1870. See H. A. Reeves, "Commerce, Navigation and Fisheries of Suffolk County," appendix to *Bicentennial History of Suffolk County* (Babylon NY 1885).

30. Dorothy I. Zaykowski, *Sag Harbor: Story of an American Beauty* (Sag Harbor NY 1991) 105.

31. For a lively and penetrating analysis of homesteading, politics and capitalism see Jack Beatty, *Age of Betrayal: The Triumph of Money in America 1865–1900* (New York 2007). See especially 105 ff. on homesteading and population loss in the Northeast.

32. Recent figures are taken from the Village of Southampton Master Plan: Summary (Southampton 1970).

33. For details of the controversy over ownership of the bottoms of the bays see Chapters 4 and 5.

34. Reeves op. cit. 99.

35. Minutes of the Board of Health of the Town of Southampton for May 4, 1874 (Town of Southampton Archives).

36. Montauk, its celebrated cattle drive, its fishing and its salty characters are rhapsodically portrayed in Jeannette Edwards Rattray, *Montauk: Three Centuries of Romance, Sport and Adventure* (East Hampton 1938).

37. As noted by Adams op. cit. 142.

38. Pelletreau 1893 op. cit. 95.

39. See Anderson op. cit. 30.

40. RTSH Vols. V and VI (Sag Harbor NY 1910 and 1915).

41. Assessment Records are sporadic for much of the nineteenth century but continuous after 1870. Available records are in the Town of Southampton Archives.

42. Laws of the State of New York (LSNY) 1818 Chapter 155.

43. Journal of the Trustees of the Proprietors of the Common and Undivided Lands, Marshes and Mill Streams of Southampton (JTPSH), (Town of Southampton Archives). The first five years of these records (1819–1824) are included in the Records of the Town Trustees of Southampton (RTTSH) Part II 1741–1826 (Sag Harbor 1931). After 1824 the proprietor trustees maintained separate records that were continuous until 1890 when they voted to resign as a body. The events in the 1880s leading up to this decision are discussed in Chapters 4 and 5. The proprietors' records were never published as neither were their land records (LRTPSH). These are to be found in a separate volume (Town of Southampton Archives).

44. The legislation is reprinted in RTTSH Part II op. cit. 395–397.

45. John Scott's life and exploits have been the subject of several biographies, all but one treating him as an out-and-out scallywag. Elisabeth Mowrer provides a more detailed and sympathetic portrait in *The Indomitable John Scott* (New York 1960). Scott spent little time in Southampton, less than ten years after the late 1650s, but enough to upset the town fathers on more than one occasion. He settled for a while in North Sea before moving to Setaukett, married a Raynor and fathered two children before disappearing in the West Indies. On Long Island he is best remembered for a number of shady real estate deals and a failed attempt to persuade the authorities in London to appoint him as "president" of Long Island while the Dutch were still in power in New Netherland and had long claimed the island for themselves.

46. The formation and development of the Southampton Village Improvement Association is the subject of much of the following chapter.

47. According to Jerry Patterson op. cit. 171, Dr. Charles H. Parkhurst, the minister at the Madison Square Presbyterian Church and a long-time scourge of Tammany Hall, was responsible for this remark. In the 1884 presidential election another New York minister supporting the Republican candidate, James Blaine, referred to Democrats as the party of "Rum, Romanism, and Rebellion." Unfortunately the remark was made at a campaign event in the city attended by Blaine who made the mistake of not repudiating it. This lapse was widely held to have contributed to Blaine's narrow loss to Grover Cleveland. For the full story see H. Wayne Morgan, *From Hayes to McKinley: National Party Politics 1877–1896* (Syracuse 1969) 228.

48. There had been an unsuccessful attempt in 1848 to persuade the state government in Albany to finance the construction of a canal connecting Peconic Bay with Shinnecock Bay at Canoe Place in order to improve freight transportation to New York. For various reasons it failed. Riverhead and Greenport were already served by the newly formed Long Island Railroad after 1844 and seagoing passage from Greenport, Sag Harbor and Northwest Harbor in Easthampton had long been a freight route up Long Island Sound to the East River.

49. Morgan op. cit. 40.

50. This curious and (to many observers at the time and later) disturbing episode in Southampton's history is discussed in a later chapter.

51. Philip C. Weigand argues that the population decline of Long Island Indians began well before Dutch and English settlement between the 1620s and 1640s. He suggests that the decline in numbers may have begun in the sixteenth century after Giovanni Verrazano's visits to New York and Rhode Island in 1523, a decline triggered by the transmission of European diseases for which Indian populations had no resistance. See "How Advanced were Long Island's Native Americans?," *Long Island Historical Journal* (Vol. 17 Nos. 1 and 2, 2005) 101–118.

52. The incident is well-treated in Edward H. Moeran, *"The Circassian Tragedy, Long Island Forum* (Vol. V No. 9 September 1942).

53. See Adams op. cit. 118–120.

54. Linda R. Day, *Making a Way to Freedom: A History of African Americans on Long Island* (Hempstead, NY 1997) 74.

55. RTSH Vol. IV op. cit. 2–53.

56. Day op. cit. 91.

57. The case of Pyrrhus Concer, a well-known figure in Southampton, is instructive. A former whaler and ferryboat operator on Lake Agawam in the 1880s, he had the distinction of being the only non-white taxpayer in the Town of Southampton. He appeared in the 1881 tax rolls as owning three acres assessed at $300 and was identified next to his name as "(colored)."

NOTES TO CHAPTER 2

1. For the Crusoean interpretation of early explorations of the beach see Jean-Didier Urbain, *At the Beach* (translated Catherine Porter, Minneapolis 2003) 116–18.

2. Van Rensselaer op. cit. 219. Other accounts of the Gilded Age that refer to Newport are Amory op. cit. 167–260; Eric Homberger, *Mrs. Astor's New York: Money and Social Power in a Gilded Age* (New Haven 2002) 167–172; Patterson op. cit. 181–189. Patterson drolly describes Newport as "Venusberg."

3. Van Rensselaer op. cit. 237.

4. Ibid. 242, 246.

5. Ibid. 277–278.

6. The *Seaside Times* began publishing in December 1881. Every spring it printed lists of summer residents who occupied their own cottages or boarded elsewhere. By 1883 there were at least nine commodious boarding houses sufficient to accommodate 350 guests. See the issue of June 14, 1883.

7. RTSH Vol. VI op. cit. 270.

8. Pelletreau 1893 op. cit. 88–89.

9. Beckert op. cit. 253–254. On the "competitive individualism" of New York's elite and those aspiring to membership see Homberger op. cit. 26–27.

10. *ST* December 29, 1881. A similar case occurred in Newport in the 1870s in connection with its well known Cliff Walk on the seaward side of the great mansions erected above it and along its length. Cf. Amory op. cit. 183–184.

11. The Betts trial and the generally contentious issue of beach lands is addressed in the final chapter.

12. *ST* June 4, 1885.

13. Assessment Rolls, Town of Southampton 1885 (Town of Southampton Archives).

14. Pelletreau 1893 op. cit. 95.

15. I am assuming that at that time tax assessments followed price movements in real estate fairly closely. This was not true then in New York where notoriously property was assessed for less than 60 percent of its market value. In the city, unlike Southampton, bourgeois property owners and realtors had a major influence in controlling property taxes.

16. *ST* February 16, 1882. A year or so later George Rogers Howell announced from his aerie in the state library in Albany that "the New York Annex has made a moral revolution in this village. The dollar is worshipped as it never was before by its native inhabitants." *ST* October 9, 1884.

17. *ST* March 2, 1882.

18. The pursuit of low-key projects, modest and relatively unassuming, was to be the mantra of the summer colony. It remains so almost to this day among the old guard or what is left of it. Understatement was a value occasionally bordering on shabbiness. There was to be no glitz. In this respect it was quite unlike Newport, Saratoga or, later, Palm Beach. All boasted large luxury hotels capable of accommodating hundreds of guests. This was not to be in Southampton (or Easthampton) and still isn't. For European seaside resorts of the period see Garner op. cit. 163.

19. *ST* March 9, 1882.

20. Beckert op. cit. 207–208.

21. David M. Scobey, *Empire City* (New York 2002) 84–85.

22. Cf. Edwin G. Burrows and Mike Wallace, *Gotham: A History of New York City to 1898* (New York 1999) 1045. These words were reminiscent of John D. Rockefeller's justification of his efforts to control the developing oil industry through the expansion of Standard Oil into its every corner. Cf. Ida M. Tarbell, *The History of the Standard Oil Company* (briefer version ed. David M. Chalmers, New York 1966).

23. Two examples of a Newport style were the Russell and Boardman houses on Oxpasture Road. The latter was sold to Morgan O'Brien, one time state attorney-general for New York and president of the Shinnecock Hills Golf Club in the 1920s. It was described as resembling a "canary yellow pagoda."

24. Now in the possession of the Southampton Historical Museum.

25. Cf. Burrows and Wallace op. cit. 577.

26. See John Cory, *The Golden Clan: The Murrays, the McDonnells and the Irish American Aristocracy* (Boston 1977). Nonetheless the clan sought to blend in and by the 1920s had adopted the dressed-down style of their Wasp neighbors.

27. Gaillard Thomas, growing up in South Carolina, would have known something of the impact of hurricanes and tropical storms while Southamptoners could have apprised him of the frequently devastating effects of winter storms in damaging the foreshore and much inland. But such local knowledge, assuming he had it, was no deterrent to erecting a church (or his own house) a few yards from the surf. Between 1886 and 1976, twenty-two tropical storms and hurricanes passed within fifty nautical miles of Long Island with impacts on the shoreline. In 1984 a study commissioned by the Long Island Regional Planning Board estimated that for every one hundred years, thirty-one tropical storms, of which sixteen would be hurricanes, could be expected to affect eastern Long Island. Winter northeasters are much more frequent and were estimated as having an 80 percent chance of occurring in any given year. Cf. *Hurricane Damage Mitigation Plan for the South Shore*, Nassau and Suffolk Counties, NY (Hauppauge NY 1984). Between 1886 and 1894, six tropical storms or hurricanes affected Long Island including three between August and October 1888.

28. Pelletreau 1893 op. cit. 91.

29. Moeran op. cit. 74.

30. Beckert op. cit. 189, 218–220.

31. Original records of the Southampton Village Improvement Association (RSVIA) from 1881 to 1919 are in the Village of Southampton Archives.

32. LSNY 1867 Chapter 790.

33. Minutes of the Town of Southampton Board of Health 1874–1892 (Town of Southampton Archives).

34. Burrows and Wallace op. cit. 1182.

35. P. Brynberg Porter, "Dysentery on Long Island" (Southampton 1880). (Town of Southampton Archives).

36. *ST* October 2, 1884.

37. Pelletreau 1893 op. cit. 94–95.
38. *ST* December 22, 1881.
39. Cf. Amory op. cit. 54.

NOTES TO CHAPTER 3

1. RSVIA July 7, 1883.
2. For consideration of the LIRR and particularly the activities of Austin Corbin, its president in these years, see the chapters on the Shinnecock Hills.
3. RSVIA July 7, 1883.
4. Small boat sailing on Agawam was already highly popular among summer residents. The first annual July 4 regatta was held in 1882 with large numbers of contestants.
5. Salem Wales wrote two articles for the *Seaside Times* in 1883 on the subject of cemeteries. In one he asked rhetorically, "how many feet of cubic gas per acre were exhaled from London cemeteries" and made a plea for cremation, an argument not uncommon at the time. The practice of cremating bodies was, he acknowledged, once thought "heathenish" but Wales did not think it would "interfere with (their) promised resurrection on the last day." He was not, as he proved on many an occasion, without humor. *ST* May 3, 1883.
6. *ST* June 4, 1885. White claimed to have spent ten hours a day for three weeks upgrading this road.
7. The Disposall of the Vessell is reprinted as an appendix in Adams op. cit. 256–259.
8. For the text of the Andros and Dongan patents, see Adams op. cit. 279–287.
9. See Frank W. Burnett's two-part article about Lake Agawam, *Southampton Press* May 6 and 13, 1954.
10. *ST* April 16 and May 7, 1885.
11. *ST* June 21, 1883.
12. *ST* May 7, 1885.
13. *ST* May 21, 1885.
14. Pelletreaus were latecomers to Southampton in the eighteenth century while the Whites were early arrivals in the late 1640s. But Pelletreau, although having few commonage rights and not much land, was a proprietor and a member of the landed elite. He was, besides, not a farmer but an intellectual and writer and much involved in local politics since the 1860s when he was elected town clerk. Much respected though White was in the community, there were obvious differences with the upper-class Huguenot, Pelletreau, and his proprietor connections. From his writings on Southampton, Pelletreau often seems to present himself as all things to all men. George White was too single-minded to tolerate that for very long. This may partly account for their frequently acerbic exchanges.
15. *ST* June 4, 1885.
16. Town Trustees versus Frederic W. Betts is reviewed in greater detail together with the general issue of the status of beach or shore lands in Chapter 9.
17. Cf. Pelletreau 1882 op. cit. 13 and *ST* April 12, 1883.
18. *ST* February 15, 1883; March 13, 1884.
19. *ST* August 16, 1883.
20. *ST* August 23, 1883.
21. *ST* August 30, 1883. The last divisions of land were in fact made in 1782 and were called Last Division, Quogue Purchase and Last Division, Topping's Purchase respectively.

22. RTSH Vol. I op. cit. 153.

23. *ST* July 29, 1886.

24. *Brooklyn Daily Eagle* July 31, 1886. In the same article the *Eagle* took a shot at Post noting that Southampton's cemetery was now "covered with earth and shrubs."

25. Town of Southampton versus Edwin Post, State Supreme Court, Special Term (Riverhead December 1887) 7.

26. Town versus Post ibid. 64.

27. Ibid. 72.

28. *ST* August 5, 1886.

29. *ST* April 10, 1884.

30. *ST* August 26, 1886.

31. RSVIA August 7, 1886.

32. *ST* August 26, 1886.

33. *ST* September 9, 1886.

34. A talk given by Edward H. Foster to the Southampton Literary Society about 1890 (Edward H. Foster Papers, Southampton Historical Museum Archives).

35. RSVIA August 7, 1886.

36. Frank W. Burnett, *Southampton Press* May 6 and 13, 1954 op. cit.

37. RSVIA August 4, 1887.

38. The Southampton Historical Museum has in its archival collection many such account books from local businesses including those of E. A. & H. Hildreth.

39. George White died in 1893 at the age of seventy-seven. Gaillard Thomas's tribute to him is to be found in *Portrait and Biographical Record of Suffolk County* (New York 1896) 929–930.

40. This charming comment, made sometime in the 1920s by Mrs. Goodhue Livingston, was thankfully preserved by Cleveland Amory op. cit. 52.

NOTES TO CHAPTER 4

1. A small company of local farmers, closely connected to the trustees of the proprietors, had been formed in 1861 and purchased the Hills from the latter at auction. The circumstances and the subsequent fate of the Hills are addressed later.

2. In 1861, George White was virtually alone in objecting to the 1859 partition of the Shinnecock Hills through an enabling act of the state legislature (LSNY 1859 Chapter 46 101–103) and their subsequent sale two years later. From the beginning, White questioned the legality of the abrogation of the 1703 Indian lease by the proprietors and took the position few others did that since the town trustees had signed the lease in the first place only they could petition the legislature for permission to break it.

3. Moriches Bay at that time was considered a part of the Great South Bay and began west of Potunk Point in Westhampton. Potunk was once a significant port connecting the western part of Southampton with New York via an inside passage. Further east, the ditch connecting Quantuck with Shinnecock Bay was not navigable until 1895 when it was finally dug out and locks installed.

4. See Chapter 1 for a discussion of this division of interests, what had led up to it, and the ensuing enabling legislation removing the control of the waters and their products from the proprietors and assigning it to the town trustees (LSNY 1818 Chapter 155 op. cit.).

5. See particularly W. Keith Kavanagh, *Town Lands and the Trust Doctrine: Huntington, New York as a Case Study 1653–1972* (Huntington NY 1972) 103–107.

6. Live oysters if packed carefully could survive for lengthy periods and shipped long distances without spoilage. It required that they be packed in their natural liquid with the curved side of the shell down to prevent the liquor seeping out. By the early years of the nineteenth century the oyster trade in New York City expanded rapidly. After the opening of the Erie Canal in 1825 oyster sloops regularly unloaded in Albany for shipment further upstate and as far west as Buffalo. Freight service by rail after 1830 further opened western markets in Cincinnati, Cleveland, St. Louis, and Chicago. See Kurlansky, cited in note 8.

7. LSNY 1879 Chapter 251 328–329.

8. Mark Kurlansky, *The Big Oyster, New York in the World: A Molluscullar History* (New York 2006).

9. Kurlansky op. cit. 82.

10. Ibid. 243.

11. Ibid. 179.

12. Ibid. 130.

13. Ibid. 249.

14. It was named "Tremedden" in commemoration of his tin-mining ancestors in seventeenth-century Cornwall.

15. Austin Corbin's rise to power and acquisition of the railroad and after that in short order the Shinnecock Hills and other development properties including much of Montauk is covered later.

16. *ST* March 24, 1887.

17. *ST* March 8, 1883.

18. *ST* February 15, 1883.

19. *ST* March 15, 1883.

20. Nonetheless he had friends among the summer colony, most notably Gaillard Thomas, its leader. The two of them did occasionally clash, particularly on the question of the takeover of the ocean beach, but that did not stop Thomas from writing a moving and eloquent tribute to him at his death.

21. Trustees of the Freeholders and Commonalty of the Town of Southampton against Frederic H. Betts, NY State Supreme Court, Court of Appeals 1898 (21 App. Division, 435). The suit was tried at Riverhead in October 1892 and concluded after a second appeal filed by the trustees in 1898.

22. *ST* February 22, 1883.

23. Howell published a second edition of his history of Southampton in 1887, but in it barely mentioned the controversies besetting the town resulting from the 1818 legislation separating the interests of the proprietors from those of the town trustees.

24. *ST* February 22, 1883.

25. *ST* March 1, 1883.

26. *ST* February 22, 1883.

27. For a discussion of the canal see George Holzman, *History of the Shinnecock Canal* (New York 1925) and Mary Tarduro and David Havemeyer, *History of the Shinnecock Canal* (unpublished, Rogers Memorial Library, Southampton 1975).

28. *ST* January 25, 1883.

29. The village of Southampton did not become a self-governing entity until its incorporation in 1894. Up to that time all authority over the land area of what became the Village of Southampton rested with the town.

30. The secret ballot was introduced into American politics in 1890, but it was not until the end of the century that ballots were publicly printed. This replaced their distribution to voters by political parties that had to this time maintained tight control over the voting process. In the 1880s, Southampton's elections had been conducted by voice vote or a show of hands. Beginning in the early 1890s, votes based on paper ballots were tabulated and published in the newspaper.

338 / Notes to Chapter 5

31. RTSH Vol. VII (Sag Harbor 1928) 150.

32. RTSH Vol. I op. cit. 1–4.

33. RTTSH Part III (Sag Harbor 1927) 49–52.

34. RTSH Vol. VII op. cit. 168–169.

35. The trustees of the proprietors voted to resign in October 1890 having no more lands to dispose of or draw revenue from. See JTPSH October 3, 1890. For the distribution of dividends and lists of holders of commonage rights see the proprietors' land records (LRTPSH). Dividends were paid out at irregular intervals and were based on revenues collected from fees, leases, sales of common lands and fines.

36. *ST* April 12, April 19 and May 3, 1884 for these various exchanges and George White's rejoinder.

37. The attorney general then was Morgan J. O'Brien, later to become a distinguished jurist and a significant member of Southampton's summer colony.

38. RTSH Vol. I op. cit. 40–41.

39. RTTSH Part I (Sag Harbor 1931) 299–300.

40. Ibid. 168.

41. Ibid. 421–422.

42. Ibid. 234.

43. JTPSH June 6, 1882.

44. Liber 269 of Recorded Deeds 161, 164 November 13, 1882 Suffolk County Clerk's Office, Riverhead NY.

45. See Beers-Campbell decision State Supreme Court, Appellate Division 1928. Reprinted in RTTSH Part II Addendum (Sag Harbor 1931) 403–425. This matter concerned competing land claims over property that eventually became the Westhampton Airport. The case illustrates the murkiness of some of the 1882 land transfers.

46. The town trustees could easily have adopted the position that they alone, not the proprietor trustees, could legally petition the legislature to abrogate the 1703 lease of the Hills to the Shinnecock Indians. They did not, whether out of fear of the proprietors, ignorance or indifference, but they might well have reflected that they and not the proprietor trustees had made the lease with the Shinnecock and that a legally incorporated body called the trustees of the proprietors did not yet exist in 1703 and would not for another century.

47. Pelletreau 1882 op. cit. 11.

48. *ST* March 1, 1883.

49. See especially the land records (LRTPSH) for evidence of this monopolization of commonage rights.

NOTES TO CHAPTER 5

1. Henry P. Hedges, *History of the Town of East-Hampton, New York* op. cit.

2. *ST* March 29, 1883.

3. *ST* May 3, 1883.

4. *ST* December 20, 1883.

5. RTSH Vol. VIII Part II (Sag Harbor 1928) 453. Edwin Post may have held on to some part of the Sayre (later Howell) interests.

6. This exchange of letters came to light slipped into the proprietors' land records and evidently placed there by Harri Howell while the records were in his custody. They appear to have lain there unnoticed and undisturbed until 2001.

7. Pelletreau 1882 op. cit. 53–54.

8. *ST* December 6 and 13, 1883.

9. *ST* January 17, 1884.

10. *ST* May 14, 1885.

11. The full testimony of the trial (116 NY) together with all motions, decisions and opinions at both the trial and subsequent appeal in 1887 was published at Sag Harbor in 1889. Justice Brown's decision and opinion were published separately. Interestingly, Everett Carpenter's copy of the proceedings is to be found in the Rogers Memorial Library in Southampton, a gift of Elihu Root, Frederic Betts's attorney in Town Trustees versus Betts. Carpenter had evidently given it to Root perhaps to help him prepare for that case and Root eventually gave it to the Library.

12. This clause, as previously noted, provided that "nothing herein contained shall in any manner alter and affect the right, title or interest of any person, or the inhabitants of said town to any of the before mentioned premises" (LSNY 1818 Chapter 155 op. cit.). The clause, replete with suggestion, has always been the subject of a wide variety of interpretations. It was, as they say, "built to suit" whomsoever may wish to build.

13. *ST* February 18, 1886.

14. The texts of the Andros and Dongan patents are reprinted in the town trustee records RTTSH Part II op. cit. 379–381 and 385–394. See also the documentary appendix to Adams op. cit. 279–287.

15. For the text of Judge Cullen's opinion see 572 ff. of the trial record.

16. Cf. Kavanagh op. cit. 142.

17. William Pelletreau could have helped him here. The first three volumes of the town records, which he had transcribed, had been in print since 1877 and 1878. The fourth volume, covering the years 1809 to 1870, appeared in 1893—too late for Carpenter. Years later in a letter to Edward Foster regarding the original hand-written records Pelletreau remarked that "Thomas Sayre . . . used to say that 'Fithian can't read them and the Devil can't read them, but I can read them.' So my uncle told me. This shows, by the way, that yours truly can beat the Devil in one respect at least." Jonathan Fithian was town clerk in the 1850s. (See Edward H. Foster Papers op. cit. Southampton Historical Museum Archives.)

18. For Judge Barnard's opinion see the trial record 591–593. Judge Pratt's dissenting view follows it, 594–635.

19. In this interpretation Judge Pratt was a century ahead of his time. The dominant view of the New England town then and late into the twentieth century emphasized the communalism and Puritan basis of town life, seldom considering that commercial enterprise and land development were central to town founding. Cf. Martin op. cit. 1–3.

20. It was, as was the adjacent New Haven community and its sister towns, recognized as a de facto colony by Massachusetts Bay authorities after both joined the New England Confederation (the United Colonies) in 1643. This was a security alliance formed to counter potential Dutch and Indian threats to Bay interests. Cf. especially Herbert L. Osgood, *The American Colonies in the Seventeenth Century Vol. I* Chapter VII (New York 1904).

21. In this respect, it was analogous to the first year of the Bay Colony before it reinterpreted its charter and transformed itself from a trading company into a colony.

22. At the same time and a month before the patent was issued in December 1686, Major John Howell (Edward Howell's son) was dispatched to New York "by major voate of the towne" to clarify for

the governor "our title to our land called in to question at Shinecock." It suggests that land claims, at least in the eyes of the colonial government, were by no means fully secure even half a century after settlement. Cf. RTSH Vol. II op. cit. 287.

23. For discussion of the difficulties in interpreting seventeenth-century terminologies referring to different classes or categories of town residents see Martin op. cit. Ch. VII. Adams, for example, identifies commoners with proprietors, that is, those possessing rights in common, and inhabitants (the remainder of recognized residents) as "Non-Commoners." For this interpretation see Adams op. cit. 97, note. On the other hand, Sleight calls attention to a distinction between proprietors and freeholders that was already current in 1816 when the town began to square off against the proprietors' claim to a monopoly of the undivided lands and the waters (RTSH Vol. VII op. cit. 432). Perhaps the most that can be said is that the meaning of these terms had changed substantially since the seventeenth century. Freeholders—once identified exclusively as the proprietors—later came to mean by the end of the eighteenth century anyone possessing an equitable interest in property in the town even if they lacked commonage rights. It follows then that the commonalty in the Dongan formula of "freeholders and commonalty" was simply a rubric that originally covered non-proprietor freeholders, but later became redundant as all the commonalty were in fact freeholders.

24. Maitland op. cit. 18.

25. Martin op. cit. 193.

26. Cf. RTSH Vol. II op. cit. 295–296.

27. Decision, NY State Supreme Court, Court of Appeals, Second Division, October 8, 1889 (Town of Southampton Archives).

28. The 1831 act (LSNY 1831 Chapter 283) reaffirmed the power of the trustees to make laws regulating the fisheries and impose penalties for violations. Previously in 1829, the trustees had passed a law regulating fishing in Shinnecock Bay and authorized the president of the trustees, then Abraham Rose, to prosecute violators. George White held that these laws were still in force. Cf. RTTSH Part III op. cit. 19–24.

29. Ibid. 105–108.

30. Although the town trustees lost the Betts case in respect to ownership of beach land, they did establish that the beaches were used for a variety of public purposes, including that of highways, and won an easement reflecting this. Similarly, in 1893 the trustees exchanged with the Long Island Improvement Company via quitclaim deed any rights they may have had in the Shinnecock Hills for authority over the shores of the surrounding bays for purposes of maintaining a highway. Cf. RTTSH Part III op. cit. 40, 83. See also 139–140 for a later 1899 quitclaim to Frederic Betts of dune fronting his Agawam property to "their southerly slope."

NOTES TO CHAPTER 6

1. See William A. Ritchie, "The Stony Brook site and its relation to Archaic and Transitional Cultures on Long Island," *New York State Museum and Science Service Bulletin* 1959 No. 372, 75.

2. For a discussion of the relationships between the southern New England tribes in the seventeenth century, see particularly John A. Strong, *The Algonquian Peoples of Long Island from Earliest Times to 1700* (Interlaken, NY 1997); Alfred Cave, *The Pequot War* (Amherst 1996); Kathleen Bragdon, *Native Peoples of Southern New England* (Norman, Okla. 1996). For the Montaukett see John A. Strong, *The Montaukett Indians of Eastern Long Island* (Syracuse NY, 2001) and for a general history of Montauk see Jeannette Edwards Rattray, *Montauk: Three Centuries of Romance, Sport and Adventure* (East Hampton 1938).

3. Abraham Pierson, Southampton's first minister until his departure in 1647, may have had something to do with the exodus. As we saw, he was a man of high theological principle and held to the belief that only members of the church could become freemen. He had also not approved the town's decision in 1644 to unite with Hartford in the New England Confederation. It is possible that among the more secular minded in Southampton were those who removed to Easthampton. Support for this view is suggested by the fact that the new Easthampton settlers were in little rush to take on a minister. When they did, in 1650, they chose one who was very much a man of the world. This was the Reverend Thomas James. His entrepreneurial instincts were said to have been fully equal to his spiritual dedication.

4. Prime op. cit. 16.

5. Adams op. cit. 12.

6. Timothy Dwight, *Travels in New England and New York 1796–1815 Vol. III* (New Haven 1823) 217.

7. Dwight op. cit. 223.

8. Bayles op. cit. 325.

9. Ibid. 324.

10. Prime op. cit. 33.

11. John W. Barber and G.H. Howe, *Historical Collections of the State of New York* (Albany, NY 1842) 68.

12. Bayles op. cit. 421.

13. Ibid. 422.

14. It should be born in mind that the Shinnecock Hills encompasses several distinct areas, all of which were of greater or lesser interest to both Indians and settlers. Shinnecock Neck, south of the present Montauk Highway, was not on the Hills properly speaking but consisted of rich grassland and occasional planting fields stretching southward to Shinnecock Bay. It was highly valued land and also contained salt meadows fronting the bay. The upland above it in the southeastern section of the Hills was similarly good grazing land and was sometimes referred to as "Shenecock Plain." Beyond that lay the Hills themselves, more sparsely covered with grass but good for sheep pasture. Directly to the north was a good stretch of fertile land and salt meadow at Sebonac Neck, the latter surrounding Bull Head Bay. Sebonac Neck was traditionally a summer encampment for the Shinnecock Indians and at one time held a fort. To the west lay Cold Spring Bay and more valuable meadowland on its edges. Here, the Shinnecock established some planting fields for a brief period in the 1790s. Further to the west at Canoe Place, and on the periphery of what was defined as the Hills in the early records, was a Shinnecock settlement of long standing in which the Indians resided in the eighteenth century.

15. Other documents signed were a deed of release to the Quogue lands by the Unkachaug sachem and his sister, and a confirmation of the 1703 deed itself a week after it had been signed.

16. In 1695, William Kidd was approached by Whigs in London, Bellomont among them, to hunt pirates for profit in the Indian Ocean. He had spent several years since 1688 chasing French privateers for the colonial authorities in the Caribbean, but had lost his ship to his crew. They had comprehended the advantages of privateering for themselves even if Kidd had not. Financed by Bellomont and other Whigs, Kidd set sail for Madagascar in 1696, but somewhere in mid-voyage experienced a change of heart and took to piracy himself. When he returned to New York in 1699 laden, it was thought, with a large treasure worth half a million pounds, Bellomont (now the governor) was faced with a most awkward situation—Kidd had completely reneged on his original agreement—and felt, since London and especially the Tories were outraged, that he had no choice but to arrest him. Kidd was eventually hanged at Newgate prison in London, but the matter tarnished Bellomont's otherwise blameless reputation as governor for his remaining few years. Kidd reputedly had gone to ground in Gardiner's Island and buried his treasure before his arrest. This last aspect of the story refuses to die. The most recent telling comes from Robert

Gardiner who related it to Steven Gaines the author of *Philistines at the Hedgerow: Passion and Property in the Hamptons* (New York 1998). Others have it buried at Livingston Manor, a 160,000-acre tract above Kingston on the Hudson River then owned by Robert Livingston cf. Tom Lewis, *The Hudson, A History* (New Haven 2005) 104.

17. Cornbury was a staunch Anglican and did not endear himself to the Presbyterian faction in the city. For good measure, he also attacked the Dutch Reformed Church and appointed Anglicans to its ministry. He reinforced this by having the *Book of Common Prayer* translated into Dutch.

18. See RTSH Vol. II op. cit. 287.

19. See Records of the Town of East Hampton (RTEH) Vol. III op. cit. 7; Strong 2001 op. cit. 56; Marion F. Ales, "History of the Indians on Montauk, Long Island" in *The History and Archaeology of the Montauk Indians* ed. Gaynell Stone (Stony Brook 1993) 51.

20. See Mowrer op. cit.; also Wilbur C. Abbott, *Colonel John Scott of Long Island* (New York 1918).

21. Boundary disputes between towns were extremely common in the seventeenth and eighteenth centuries and frequently lasted for decades. Besides Easthampton, Southampton found itself in lengthy disagreements with its neighbors to the west and north—Brookhaven and Southold. The Brookhaven line was not settled until the 1780s, while Southold claimed Southampton land south of the Peconic River and, much later, the waters of Peconic Bay to its south and almost up to Southampton's shoreline.

22. RTSH Vol. I op. cit. 114.

23. RTSH Vol. II op. cit. 134–135.

24. Strong views the matter slightly differently and credits the trustees with offering the lease both as a palliative measure to appease the Shinnecock and as a means to confine them to a particular tract of land. Strong 1997 op. cit. 264.

25. RTSH Vol. II op. cit. 230.

26. Ibid. 202.

27. Ibid. 75.

28. Ibid. 222.

29. John A. Strong, "A Documentary History of the Shinnecock Peoples: How the Land was Lost" in *The Shinnecock Indians: A Culture History*, Gaynell Stone ed. (Stony Brook, NY 1983) 62.

30. Cf. Howell 1887 op. cit. 43.

31. Lisa M. Strong and Frank F. Holmberg II, "The Shinnecock Trustee System, 1792–1983 in Gaynell Stone ed. 1983 op. cit. 226.

32. LSNY 1792 Chapter 15 280.

33. Cf. Strong 1983 op. cit. 62.

34. There are two necks of land running to Shinnecock Bay—Shinnecock Great Neck and Little Neck. The latter does not appear to have been fenced against livestock until the end of the eighteenth century when the Shinnecocks laid it out for cultivation. Unless otherwise stated, Shinnecock Neck refers here to Great Neck.

35. Edward H. Foster, the town clerk in the 1880s, suggested a different interpretation of land use agreements at this time and later up until the 1830s. He thought that Shinnecock planting fields alternated between Sebonac Neck and Shinnecock Neck by common agreement. In some years, Sebonac Neck would be fenced eastward from Cold Spring Bay to Bull Head Bay, leaving all the Hills and Shinnecock Neck to the south available for pasturing. In others, the pattern was reversed and Shinnecock Neck fenced against cattle and used for Indian cultivation. (*ST* September 20, 1883) If true, this arrangement must have been abandoned after the 1840s when the Neck became the principal village of the Shinnecocks.

36. William Cronon, *Changes in the Land: Indians, Colonists, and the Ecology of New England* (New York 1983) 130.

37. RTSH Vol. I op. cit. 77.

38. RTTSH Part I op. cit. 255

39. This suggests that Edward Foster's view that Shinnecock planting fields were regularly rotated between the two necks was accurate.

40. RTTSH Part I op. cit. 295.

41. Ibid. 353.

42. Ibid. 417.

43. Although no deeds have been found, two explanations of a Shinnecock presence there are plausible. One is that Shinnecocks lived there prior to the 1703 lease and that the reference to the western boundary of the Hills as at Canoe Place was taken to include a settlement. "Canoe Place" is a sufficiently vague reference that it could be taken to include land across what was then Canoe Pond (later incorporated into the Shinnecock Canal). The second is that the Shinnecock purchased lots in the Lower Division from the proprietors or others sometime after 1738 when the division was laid out. Support for this view may lie in the evidence of a later Indian purchase to the north of Canoe Place in the Westwoods in the Canoe Place Division, Quogue Purchase, also laid out in 1738. This was a tract of eighty acres and was probably bought for its timber. No artifacts have been found there, suggesting that it was not inhabited. Besides which, there is no source of fresh water. Ownership of the land to the south of Westwoods, on which the Canoe Place church and cemetery stands today (formerly the Shinnecock church), became the subject of litigation in 1950. For this case see Henry S. Manley's analysis. Manley was the assistant attorney general who represented a Shinnecock family in the case. Cf. Henry S. Manley, "No Man's Land, Southampton," *Long Island Forum* (October 1953). This second explanation is the more likely of the two as the Canoe Place settlement and the Westwoods are never mentioned in later state legislation in respect to the Hills or in any subsequent deed of sale.

44. RTTSH Part I op. cit. 384–385.

45. Ibid. 488.

46. Ibid. 514.

47. Records of the Shinnecock Indians (RSI) (also known as the Indian Record Book) Vol. I 1, 2. The Shinnecock Trustee records for the years 1792–1835 and 1880–1908 are reprinted in Gaynell Stone ed. 1983 op. cit. 142–161. The original books are held in the Town of Southampton Archives.

48. See Abigail Fithian Halsey, *In Old Southampton* (New York 1940); Manley 1953 op. cit.

49. Halsey op. cit. 132.

50. The Burr map, and other maps referred to below, are reproduced in Gaynell Stone "Material and Visual Expression of the Shinnecock: Maps and Landscapes of the Shinnecock through Time" in Gaynell Stone ed. 1983 op. cit.

51. Gaynell Stone op. cit. 265.

52. Attempts at conversion of the Shinnecock, and Long Island Indians in general, were apparently not undertaken in earnest until the 1740s. Before then, according to Nathaniel Prime, they "exhibited no inclination to receive the blessed gospel" and languished in their own opinions and "the senseless rites of their ancestors." That is, until the arrival of Azariah Horton, a missionary appointed from New York, who traced and retraced his footsteps up and down the island for eleven years bringing the gospel to scattered groups of Indians from Rockaway to Montauk. Here is what he had to say of the Shinnecocks in his carefully kept diary of 1743 as quoted by Prime: "A beautiful sight to behold, those gathered together to worship and behold God, who before gospel light shone upon them, were wont to meet to sing and dance, carouse and give loose to vain mirth and jollity." Prime op. cit. 104, 107.

After Horton, Samson Occum, a Christian Mohegan, was sent to the island, first as a teacher and then after 1759 as an ordained Presbyterian minister. He labored six years, much of the time at Montauk, before going on to other pursuits. He was followed by the Reverend Peter John, a Shinnecock born in Bridgehampton, who had been ordained in Connecticut and was probably converted during the Great Awakening of 1741–1744. His grandson was Paul Cuffee. Cuffee as a young man was said to be "much addicted to the pleasures of the revel and the midnight dance" but surrendered to Christianity in another awakening in 1778. He began preaching at Wading River and Moriches and was admitted by the Long Island Congregationalist Convention in 1792. Commissioned by a missionary society in 1798, he concentrated his activities at Canoe Place and Montauk. He was an eloquent preacher, much loved and respected, and drew "a numerous and attentive" congregation. He had nothing to do with the founding of the Canoe Place Church, but was its pastor for thirteen years. The New York Missionary Society, which had employed him, erected the headstone at his grave. The Long Island Convention continued to provide religious instruction for the Shinnecock after Cuffee's death in 1812. In 1827, William Benjamin was appointed pastor at Canoe Place. He continued there until his death in 1860.

53. Reverend James G. Downs, History of the Shinnecock Church. Unpublished manuscript c. 1875 (Southampton Historical Museum Archives).

54. John Morice also thought Azariah Horton established a Shinnecock church, and a school as well, in the 1740s. Horton, however, makes no mention of it in his journal. Unpublished manuscript 1945 (Town of Southampton Archives) 267.

55. RTTSH Part I op. cit. 517.

56. RSI II op. cit. 31.

57. Mark Harrington, "An Ancient Village Site of the Shinnecock Indians" (1924) in Gaynell S. Levine, *Early Papers in Long Island Archaeology* (Stony Brook 1977).

58. RTTSH Part I op. cit. 541.

59. RTTSH Part II op. cit. 108, 127.

60. In respect to the Montaukett Indians the Easthampton town trustees adopted the same view of mixed ancestry in an effort to limit access to occupancy rights on Montauk.

61. RSI II op. cit. 36.

62. Strong 2001 op. cit. 84–85.

63. The Chace map of Long Island is partially reproduced in Gaynell Stone 1983 op. cit. 272.

64. LSNY 1836 Chapter 315: 461.

65. Gaynell Stone 1983 op. cit. 136.

66. United States Senate, Hearings of the Subcommittee of the Committee on Indian Affairs in relation to Certain Claims of the Montauk, Shinnecock, Narragansett, and Mohegan Indians (Washington D.C. 1900) 97.

67. Vincent Seyfried thought that many owners demanded "absurd sums" for their property. "One individual" apparently wanted $2,000 for the right-of-way through the Shinnecock Hills but was awarded only $200. Who this was is unknown. It may have been Lewis Scott. See Vincent Seyfried, *History of the Long Island Railroad Vol. III* (Port Washington 1966) 37.

68. Receipts for payments are in the archives of the Southampton Historical Museum.

69. In any case the Civil War had intervened and most, if not all, railroads put aside major plans for capital expansion until after the conclusion of hostilities.

70. Vincent Seyfried, *History of the Long Island Railroad Vol. I* (Port Washington 1961) 20.

71. New York State Assembly Papers Vol. 41 1809–1831 (New York State Archives).

72. RTTSH Part II op. cit. 296.

73. It was this Post, we saw earlier, who pronounced himself ignorant at the Mecox trial of any corporate body calling itself the town trustees.

74. RTTSH Part II op. cit. 305–309. Five meetings were held between February 21 and April 25, 1826 in which the Shinnecock issue, as well as other more routine matters, were raised.

75. The Indian Trustee record books (RSI) were, and still are, maintained in the Town Clerk's office. The missing years are believed to have disappeared in 1955 during or after the Cove Realty case. This had involved litigation over a strip of land on the northern edge of the Shinnecock Reservation. However, the records for 1880 to 1926 were published in the town records in 1927. Cf. RTSH Vol. VIII Part II (Sag Harbor 1928) 359–417. It suggests that some of the earlier records were already missing by that date. Their loss is unfortunate as they might have shed some light on the Shinnecocks' reactions to later efforts by the proprietors in the 1840s and 1850s to divide the Hills from Shinnecock Neck. At the same time, it must be admitted that the Shinnecock trustees might not have gone on the record over such a contentious issue.

76. JTPSH op. cit. April 11, 1843.

77. Ibid. December 12, 1848.

78. Ibid. April 26, 1853.

79. Austin Rose against Luther Bunn, James Bunn and Francis Willis. State Supreme Court, Riverhead August 1854 and Appeal 1860 (Southampton Historical Museum Archives).

80. Luther Bunn against Philetus Pierson and others. State Supreme Court, Riverhead March 1850 (Southampton Historical Museum Archives).

NOTES TO CHAPTER 7

1. JTPSH op. cit. April 13, 1858.

2. Ibid. December 23, 1858.

3. LSNY 1859 Chapter 46, 101–103.

4. It was also in conflict with Governor Richard Nicolls's 1666 determination in respect to who was to take title from the Indians of the Quogue and Topping's purchases. Then, the governor had said, that the lands in question "mentioned in their said deeds is belonging, doth and shall belong unto the towne of Southampton (viz.) that (hath and doe pay purchase) and their successors forever." See RTTSH Part III op. cit. 83.

5. The full text of the petition, legislation, and ensuing indenture agreement are reprinted in Gaynell Stone ed. 1983 op. cit. pp. 106, 115, 116–117. The legislation is also reprinted in RTTSH Part II op. cit. 395–397.

6. Senate Sub-Committee of the Committee on Indian Affairs 1900 op. cit. 91.

7. The committee testimony of Eugene A. Johnson, a Montaukett Presbyterian minister, suggests that the legislature did take a deeper interest in the matter than at first sight appears. It requested that the representative of the proprietors go back to Southampton "and bring us the names of twelve reputable citizens who will attest that it (division) is for the best good of the Indians, and we will legalize it." According to Johnson, George White did dissent and predicted that it would only bring trouble. Whatever other views of citizens were transmitted, the legislature went ahead anyway. So far as is known it did not consult the Shinnecock. See Senate Hearings op. cit. 89.

8. Pelletreau 1882 op. cit. 7.

9. For example, in 1888 a New York State Assembly Special Committee to Investigate the Indian Problem of the State of New York said in its report that the Shinnecock were "indolent and shiftless, living from hand to mouth" and had "entirely lost their native language." There was so much intermarriage that "they may fairly be considered one family." Its view of other Indian groups was even less flattering. The committee quite ignored the substantial anthropological record of the time, and in particular failed

to recognize that the Shinnecock, like other Algonquian bands, were kinship-based communities where marriage alliance was one of the principal keys to the continuity and solidarity of the group. See *Assembly Report* (Albany 1889) 55. New York State Archives.

10. A good question here is how well understood in 1860 were the legal intricacies of the town's internal relations and relations with the Shinnecock. William Pelletreau had not yet begun to transcribe the key documents of the patents, deeds, and leases that punctuated the town's history since the seventeenth century. Nor had he begun the transcription of the town records. By his own account, given their condition, very few were able to read them and none except the Dongan patent and the 1818 legislation were in print. Nearly a century later knowledge of agreements with the Shinnecock, and what they meant, had deteriorated to such an extent that even their own attorneys could become disoriented. See, for example, David Gilmartin's testimony in 1943 before a legislative committee on Indian affairs. He confused town trustees with the trustees of the proprietors and seemed to believe at one point that the 1859 Shinnecock deed to the Neck was in the form of a lease, perhaps confusing that with the lease of 1703. See Joint Legislative Committee on Indian Affairs, Public Hearing, Shinnecock Reservation, October 14, 1943. (Leg 216.0-2, 1943 New York State Archives).

11. Pelletreau 1882 op. cit.; Howell 1887 op. cit.; Adams 1918 op. cit.

12. *ST* September 2, 1886.

13. He had overlooked, he said, "the legal change of proprietorship between 1703 and 1859." The legislation of 1818 "transferred the whole title of the Shinnecock Hills, from any possible claim of the Commonalty of the Town, to the Proprietors." *ST* September 16, 1886.

14. In addition to Howell's criticism, John Strong has raised the question of whether the 1859 agreement might be in violation of a 1790 law (the Trade and Intercourse Act) "which stipulated that all alienation of Indian land be approved by the U.S. government. The federal government never approved the 1859 land transaction, which clearly alienated a considerable amount of land from the Shinnecock. The courts will have to decide whether or not, under the terms of the 1790 law, the loss of leased lands is equivalent to the loss of land through sale" Strong, 1983 op. cit. 63.

15. The David Bunn in the complaint was not the David L. Bunn who earlier signed the petition to the legislature. The latter was also a Shinnecock trustee.

16. The plaintiffs were also well aware that the 1858 petition to separate the interests of the Shinnecock and proprietors had been obtained under duress. The complaint noted that signatures to the petition were "procured by undue influence and unjust and oppressive conduct and threatenings toward the Indians on the part of the said proprietors and their trustees." A hand-written copy of the court proceedings is in the Southampton Historical Museum Archives.

17. JTPSH op. cit. January 8, 1861.

18. *Sag Harbor Corrector* February 16, 1861.

19. The Shinnecock also claimed the seaweed right under the terms of the 1703 lease but this was ignored and played no role in the subsequent trial. Although they had won the 1850 seaweed suit against several townsmen, reaffirming their "rights of accretion," it is questionable whether they could bring a valid case again having recently lost the Hills and with them the shorelines.

20. RTSH Vol. IV op. cit. 267.

21. Albert Jagger kept the journal and accounts of the trustees and it is due to him that we have a clear picture of the activities of the Proprietors of the Shinnecock Hills up to the 1881 sale and the circumstances of the sale itself. This journal is in the archives of the Southampton Historical Museum and was presented to the Southampton Colonial Society (the Museum) by Samuel L. Parrish in 1926. Parrish had found the journal in the papers of his older brother, James C. Parrish, after his death. It had come to the latter from Francis K. Pendleton, Samuel Parrish's law partner. Pendleton had obtained it from Wallace Kirby, an associate of Austin Corbin, and the representative of the Long Island

Improvement Company's interests on the board of the Shinnecock Hills proprietors in the 1880s. Parrish and Pendleton were both to become principals in the LIIC during the same period of time, eventually buying it out and forming their own development company, the Shinnecock Land Company.

22. Henry S. Manley, assistant state attorney general, briefly alludes to this case in a comment concerning land in dispute at Canoe Place in 1950 (King v. Warner et al). See his Office Memorandum, unpublished 1951 (Southampton Historical Museum Archives) 22. See also his article, "No Man's Land" 1951 op. cit.

23. Naturin Delafield did buy property in the town in 1876 but in Westhampton along Quantuck Bay rather than on the Hills. By 1883 he had acquired forty-nine acres, some of which was in Quogue. He also bought shares in Montauk in the 1870s, one of a small number of outsiders who did so.

24. In a departure from the real estate ventures of other members of the summer colony at the time Murdoch was principally interested in developing a farm. For the full record of all sales of lands on the Hills see Abstract of Title of the LIIC Ltd to Lands Known as "The Shinnecock Hills" and "Sebonac Neck" (Treasurer of Suffolk County, Riverhead NY, 1888).

25. LSNY 1872 Chapter 869.

26. *ST* November 18, 1886.

27. *Sag Harbor Corrector* August 27, 1881.

28. Peter Ross Vol. I 1903 op. cit. 584–585.

29. Seyfried 1975 Vol. VI op. cit. 107.

30. Mildred Smith, *History of the Long Island Railroad* (New York 1958) 39.

31. Ibid. 35.

32. In a similarly petulant act in 1869, Charlick, finding no great interest among Riverhead citizens in the proposed Sag Harbor Branch, moved the junction with the main line several miles west of Riverhead to Manorville both changing the surveyed route and angering the inhabitants. As noted earlier, the railroad moved the Quogue depot in the dead of night to a location in the woods remote from the village.

33. Seyfried 1961 Vol. I op. cit. 68–70; Vol. VI op. cit. 26; Smith op. cit. 34–38.

34. The *Seaside Times* was probably typical of local Long Island papers in its evaluation of Corbin's impact. "His year of management," it said, "has filled the land with lamentation. High freight rates, few trains, slow time, no better roads or cars and bungling management" appeared no better than "the Charlick reign." For a blistering attack on both Corbin and Southampton's board of assessors by an irate citizen accusing the board of "sycophancy" in failing to assess the railroad sufficient taxes see the March 16, 1882 issue of the *Seaside Times*.

35. This brief account of the history of the LIRR in the 1870s, leading up to Austin Corbin's assumption of control, indicates how much the development of Long Island was inextricably tied to the fortunes and policies of the railroad, its presidents and directors. The impact was felt all over but no more so than in the remote farming communities of the East End where their lands during the Corbin years became the object of intense speculation. The definitive account of the LIRR is to be found in Vincent Seyfried's seven-volume study (1961–1975) but Mildred Smith's earlier history, while less detailed, is still useful. Elizur Hinsdale, the company's counsel after 1881, also published a very readable if rather biased account in 1898. This appeared just after Corbin's death and shortly before the LIRR was taken over by the Pennsylvania Railroad.

36. *ST* January 26, 1882.

37. See Jean Strouse, *Morgan: American Financier* (New York 1999) 251–253.

38. Bowman purchased four thousand acres in Medford, a farming area north of Patchogue, subsequently transferring title to the LIIC. In 1886, it was laid out in farming lots of twenty to fifty acres. Tenant houses were built on each with the intention of renting them out to farmers, and an overseer's

house constructed for the use of a project manager, a slightly feudal touch. At the same time (1883), Bowman bought land for the company in Jamaica for suburban development, a tract originally named Hollis and the precursor of Jamaica Estates. In yet another real estate deal in 1886, one in which Bowman was apparently not involved, Austin Corbin bought at auction a failing hotel development at Long Beach for $375,000. The Long Beach Railroad, serving the development from Jamaica, was under lease to the LIRR at the time.

39. James Sherwood was also one of the incorporators of the West Jamaica Land Improvement Company in 1883, the Queens subdivision for which Bowman had bought land.

40. Pelletreau thought that the new ownership would transform the bottom of Shinnecock Bay "from its present unprofitable condition to one of usefulness and advantage." *ST* March 15, 1883.

41. In 1876, the Hills had been assessed at $7,000 and in 1886, after they had passed into the hands of the LIIC, at $20,000 or about one-fifth of their then-current market value based on the 1883 auction price of $101,000.

42. *ST* September 27, 1883.

43. Beach-front summer cottages were slowly extended west from First Neck Lane to Halsey Neck between 1890 and the 1920s, but the beach to the west of that as far as Shinnecock Inlet, permanently opened by the hurricane of 1938, remained almost empty of housing until the 1980s. The same was the case beyond the inlet as far as the village of Quogue. The LIIC's beach land passed from one real estate corporation to another for very nearly a century without any of them contemplating an attempt to develop it.

44. *New York Times* October 21, 1883.

45. A story circulated at the time, and was published in the *Brooklyn Eagle*, to the effect that Austin Corbin paid off "the chief of the Indian tribe" with $20,000 to drop the suit. The unnamed "chief" was said to have then absconded to Canada. This seems to be entirely false and cannot be corroborated. At the same time, Miles Carpenter said he bought the woodland at Canoe Place because he wanted to help the Shinnecock, the land itself being more or less worthless. Carpenter was also reported as restoring the Reverend Paul Cuffee's grave at the site of the original Shinnecock church, perhaps attesting further to his concern for the tribe. Notwithstanding this thoughtful act, Carpenter still found himself in court in 1890. What became of his $700 is far from clear.

46. He was reported as attempting to buy Robin's Island for $100,000, access to which was to be provided by a spur of the Greenport line to New Suffolk. He was also thought to be interested in Plum Island, as indeed was said of Arthur Benson, but there is no evidence of purchase by either.

47. Parrish bought twenty acres north of Fort Pond from the LIIC in 1887, reportedly for $2,185. It was the first of several parcels he purchased on the Hills.

48. The *Patchogue Advance* complained that Austin Corbin spent $10,000 for a station "on the bald hills of Shinnecock" while Patchogue had to make do with a barn or "a ropewalk," a fair comment probably on Corbin's ability to ignore those already in his pocket.

49. *ST* April 15, 1886.

50. *ST* September 27, 1888.

51. Benjamin Squires had entertained development plans of his own three years earlier. He advocated establishment of a gun club in a vast tract of uninhabited woodland running south from Flanders to East Quogue. It could, he thought, be "the best shooting ground in the State" and an excellent "deer range." All that was needed was the consent of the owners and some "cheap wire fence" to enclose it. In an enthusiastic presentation to the *Seaside Times*, he noted that "parties from abroad are prospecting for locations here." *ST* January 29, 1885.

52. At issue is whether the town trustees possessed any jurisdictional power under the 1818 legislation to issue quitclaim deeds to upland or lands above water. This in turn leads back to the question of whether the proprietors could abrogate the lease in 1859, a lease that had been drawn up in 1703 by the town trustees.

53. Stanford White was the architect. A water color of the club house as it appeared in 1892 is also attributed to him and is on display there.

54. One former art student later recalled that the existence of the art village on that site "was primarily due to the fact that some rich people owned some poor land." This was, of course, partly true. Its nearest neighbor was also the Shinnecock Reservation across the road on Shinnecock Great Neck.

55. Helen Wettereau, in her book *Shinnecock Hills Long Ago* (East Patchogue, NY 1991) arrived at a precise but unattributed figure of 810 acres.

56. Seyfried 1975 Vol. VI op. cit. 21.

57. Ibid. 22.

58. There were some replacements on the board of the Shinnecock Hills trustees following the Shinnecock Land Company's purchase (James Lee in particular was added), but after 1896 records of meetings—if there were any—were not maintained. It probably lapsed as a corporate body even if not legally dissolved.

59. Janet Hoyt, however, was a member and a powerful one. She had been instrumental at the very beginning in establishing a small course for women to the north of the club house. It was here where the Hoyt's daughter, Beatrix, cut her teeth and went on to win three women's national championships, the first at the age of sixteen. James P. Lee wrote what appears to have been the first book by an American on golf: *Golf in America* (New York 1895; reprinted Far Hills, NJ 1986).

60. Two years later, an opportunity for showcasing the charms of the Hills presented itself when the second U.S. Open and Amateur championships were held at the club. A large audience was in attendance but whether this had any effect on real estate sales is not known. Samuel Parrish became president of the club shortly after the tournament.

61. This was before Shinnecock Hills opened its new course—the current one—in 1931. The National did not go into decline after that but it had clearly been dramatically upstaged as continues to be the case today.

62. Shinnecock Hills and Peconic Bay Realty Co. vs. Frank E. Aldrich and William Aldrich, State Supreme Court, Riverhead 1907. The court awarded $172.39 in costs to the Aldrich brothers.

63. Correspondence 1907 (Shinnecock Hills Golf Club Archives).

64. Jere Johnson and Co., promotional literature (Southampton Historical Museum Archives).

65. Shinnecock Hills Association, *1941 Yearbook* (Southampton Historical Museum Archives).

66. In his Senate testimony in 1900, Eugene Johnson reported that "Col. Wager Swayne took his papers to real estate attorneys and they told him they were not worth the paper they were written on." Cf. Senate Sub-Committee Hearings op. cit. 89.

67. A suit to reclaim the Hills was filed in U.S. District Court by the Shinnecock Indians in July 2005 naming the State, County, the Town of Southampton, the Trustees of the Proprietors of the Common and Undivided Lands and private associations including the various golf clubs, Long Island University, the Long Island Railroad and others as respondents. In 2009, the Bureau of Indian Affairs agreed to "fast track" the process of federal recognition of the Shinnecock, a process that had languished since at least the early 1980s. If successful this would probably render the suit irrelevant and also open the doors to new economic opportunities for the Shinnecock in negotiation with New York State that would include especially casino development. The tribe finally gained federal recognition in fall 2010.

NOTES TO CHAPTER 8

1. See Jean Strouse op. cit. 328–330.
2. *ST* July 25, 1885; August 13, 1885; August 27, 1885.
3. *ST* August 23, 1888 (reprinted from the *New York Telegram*).
4. Town Trustees versus Betts op. cit. 213.
5. Helen Wettereau 1983 op. cit. 171.
6. *ST* August 30, 1888.
7. In the late 1990s, several summer owners with beach houses near the county park at Shinnecock Inlet mounted a suit against local residents who were accustomed for many years before houses were built on the dunes to drive vehicles on the beach for weekend picnics. On any given Saturday, there might be forty to fifty trucks parked above high tide in serried ranks facing the ocean with families enjoying a relaxing afternoon at the beach. This tradition began sometime after World War II, but to the beleaguered summer residents it was a tasteless intrusion into the tranquility of their seaside world. The suit aroused the village, petitions were circulated and a committee established to represent the interests of what turned out to be a tightly knit group of local families. They successfully defended against the suit.
8. *ST* September 8, 1887.
9. The Indian Line marked the boundary between Southampton Village and the Shinnecock Hills. West of it were the four thousand acres of the Hills leased to the Shinnecock Indians in 1703, a lease that was abrogated by the trustees of the proprietors in 1859. See Chapters 6 and 7.
10. *East Hampton Star* September 11, 1887.
11. On laying out the Great Plain see RTSH Vol. I op. cit. 33, 36, 54.
12. RSVIA op. cit. July 1895.
13. *ST* July 19, 1888.
14. *ST* August 16, 1888.
15. LSNY 1847 Chapter 426 and as amended in 1880 Chapter 172.
16. The *Seaside Times* was not preserved in any form except in scattered copies between 1890 and 1898. See note 31.
17. See Village of Southampton, Ordinances Pamphlet No. 2 (Southampton 1908).
18. In the 1886 town elections, the usually strong temperance movement was forced on the offensive. The newspaper report indicated that the liquor dealers were "thoroughly organized" and that their supporters turned out in force. It noted that "the factory at Sag Harbor was closed at noon, and free excursion tickets having been given the employees, they came up in a body in the afternoon train and voted solid (depositing nearly 200 votes) for license." *ST* April 8, 1886.
19. *ST* September 6, 1900.
20. See the annual financial reports of the SVIA 1897–1900 published in the records of the association.
21. RSVIA op. cit. August 1899.
22. RTSH Vol. VII op. cit. 319.
23. Governor Dongan's 1686 colonial patent, recognized by the State of New York in 1790, had stipulated that town elections be held annually and that the number of trustees of the freeholders and commonalty be fixed at twelve. In an effort at streamlining town elections in the state (including those of the handful of so-called "Dongan towns"), the legislature decided in 1897 to require biennial elections for all town officials (LSNY 1897 Chapter 497) and five years later in LSNY 1902 Chapter 133 that where town trustee boards existed their membership should be limited to five. This led to bitter

dissension in Southampton between 1899 and 1904, the legislation being interpreted as an assault on the town's sacred charter. For a time there were two rival boards of trustees elected—one annually of twelve and the other biennially of five—each issuing its various regulations governing the waters of the town and each, together with their partisans, rejecting the decisions and ordinances of the other. For a discussion of the issues by Harry D. Sleight and William Pelletreau, as well as the opinion of Justice Gaynor in a court case arising from the confused legal situation provoked by the dispute see RTTSH Part III op. cit. 151–172.

24. See RTSH Vol. VII op. cit. 336.
25. RSVIA op. cit. August 1899.
26. *ST* September 6, 1900.
27. *Southampton Press* September 8, 1900.
28. *ST* July 26, 1894.
29. Records of the Trustees of the Village of Southampton (RTVSH) January 1896.
30. Ibid. February 15, 1896.
31. Again, these events occurred in the period 1890–1897 when the *Seaside Times* was unfortunately not preserved and before the *Southampton Press* began publishing. The *Press* is on microfilm continuously after 1897 and several years of the *Seaside Times* are similarly available after 1898. Both are available in the Rogers Memorial Library in Southampton. The library does possess four volumes of a scrapbook of press cuttings compiled by George Rogers Howell between 1880 and 1900 but it is unsystematic and not continuous. It is not at all comparable to Edward H. Foster's scrupulously kept *Seaside Times* scrapbook that he maintained for every issue since its beginning in 1881 until 1889.
32. RSVIA op. cit. July 5, 1902.
33. Dr. Ely had suggested a hospital at the SVIA annual meeting in August 1908. The hospital, designed by Robert H. Robertson and his son T. Markoe Robertson, opened in February 1913. See John E. Heart, *Southampton Hospital: Its Inception, Growth and Future* (*ST* Pamphlet February 27, 1913). See also Mary Cummings, *One Hundred Years of Healing: Southampton Hospital 1909–2009* (Southampton 2009).
34. RTVSH op. cit. March 1901.
35. See Chapter 7.
36. Samuel L. Parrish, *Historical, Biographical and Descriptive Catalogue of the Objects Exhibited at the Southampton Art Museum* (New York 1898).
37. *ST* February 11, 1897.
38. L. Emory Terry, *New York's First English Settlement* (Southampton 1934).
39. *ST* September 26, 1895.
40. RTVSH op. cit. November 1897.

NOTES TO CHAPTER 9

1. See the Beers map of the Town of Southampton (New York 1894).
2. William Pelletreau also purchased a few adjacent rods of land in 1881, but then sold them when the beach casino project fell through. For the details of the deed see RTSH Vol. VII op. cit. 262.
3. In 1885, Harri Howell, a local attorney, had gained control of any and all residual interests in the remaining common land including beach lands in the eastern part of the town that had been

disposed of in the proprietor trustees' blanket sales in 1882. He was the source of most quitclaim deeds to summer owners.

    4. RTSH Vol. VII op. cit. 443.

    5. Pelletreau 1882 op. cit. 29–30.

    6. *ST* August 31, 1882; February 22, 1883. See also "The Old Beach Road" *ST* December 29, 1881.

    7. This was the subject of a separate suit that Frederic Betts lost. The grounds were that it had never ceased to be a highway along which the public continuously passed and repassed.

    8. Wide-wheeled wagons were introduced in the eighteenth century to ease this condition and were in general use to cart fish and other products well into the 1880s. See JTTEH 1870–1897 op. cit. 46.

    9. The trustees of the proprietors had included these provisions, as they did with other beachfront deeds, in order to comply with the 1818 legislation covering public rights in the use of the shores. The legislation had said nothing about passing highways but had stated that the proprietors could in no way "debar" the inhabitants from the shores "of the common lands of the town" or prevent them from taking seaweed, "carting or transporting" such products of the waters or "landing property on said shores in the manner heretofore practiced." See LSNY 1818 Chapter 155 op. cit. section 4. The first of Betts's two deeds to his property was recorded with the Suffolk County Clerk's office on March 4, 1880; the second on September 21, 1881 (Liber 247 and 258).

    10. The proprietors claimed the Point as common land and thus their right to sell it. George White, as one might expect, strenuously objected to the sale on the grounds that the Point was community property or public land and always or "from time immemorial" used for the purpose of trying out whale oil. The likelihood is, however, that the town trustees on behalf of the proprietors leased the Point to a try-works since the off-shore whaling industry began to be capitalized by private companies at the end of the 1640s. Parsonage land adjacent to it had reverted to the proprietors in the eighteenth century when the ministerial privilege had been abandoned. It had been owned privately before coming into the hands of Salem Wales. The proprietors' deed for the Point to Wales (they had sold it to him for $250) contained the provision that the public were entitled to harvest ice, fish, and land boats "and use the water as they have been wont to do."

    11. RTTSH Part III op. cit. 39–40.

    12. The Stirling grant and the Dongan patent are discussed in the first chapter.

    13. Town Trustees versus Betts op. cit. 90–91.

    14. Ibid. 8.

    15. Ibid. 85.

    16. Ibid. 147.

    17. Ibid. 156–157.

    18. Ibid. 205–206.

    19. Ibid. 214–215 and RTSH Vol. I op. cit. 91–92. This order, however, predated the Dongan patent by thirty years. The patent squarely put the ownership of the common and undivided lands, including the foreshores, in the hands of the proprietors. The role of the town, through the town trustees, was solely to administer them. In 1653, the matter was much more fluid, there being at that time only a town court.

    20. Wales had acquired the Point from the proprietors in the mid 1880s. See note 10.

    21. George White, in company with Jetur Rose, had in fact brought in one of the last right whales in 1882. *ST* February 16, 1882.

    22. Town Trustees versus Betts op. cit. 216–217.

23. Ibid. 214.
24. Ibid. 222.
25. Ibid. 213.
26. RTSH Vol. VII op. cit. 282.
27. Town Trustees versus Betts op. cit. 267–283.
28. Ibid. 268–269.
29. Ibid. 272.
30. Ibid. 279 (quoted). See Adams op. cit. 279–280 for the text of the Andros patent.
31. Quoted in Town Trustees versus Betts op. cit. 279. For full text of the patent see Adams op. cit. 281–287.
32. Ibid. 284.
33. Town Trustees versus Betts op. cit. 285.
34. Ibid. 292.
35. The act did not explicitly cover the lands under water (i.e., the many bays and ponds in the town). In 1882, the proprietors claimed at a minimum an interest in these lands and quitclaimed that interest to two purchasers, Richard Esterbrook Jr. and Henry Maxwell. The town trustees' suit against Esterbrook and his Mecox Bay Oyster Company resulted. The subsequent trial established that lands under the waters of the town were town lands. See Chapters 4 and 5.
36. Town Trustees versus Betts op. cit. 294.

NOTES TO EPILOGUE

1. Following the decision in the Mecox Bay trial, Southampton was overwhelmingly in support of a free bay, that is, bays open to the public under town trustee management to dredge for oysters and other shellfish wherever they were to be found. Yet with a free bay no one could cultivate oysters since none of the bays would be seeded by oyster planters leasing sections of the bottom. By 1895 it was realized that this policy would represent an economic loss to the town as stocks would be rapidly depleted and not replaced. It was agreed at a town meeting that about one thousand acres of bay bottom should be leased by the trustees to oyster companies for oyster cultivation. The rental fees, however, were never collected. Why the trustees themselves should not seed the bays periodically out of their own fees and fines was never addressed. The Free and Leased Bay question continued to simmer in town politics for another dozen years. See RTTSH Part III op. cit. 110.
2. ST October 28, 1897.
3. See RTSH Vol. VIII Part II op. cit. 453–455.
4. Shinnecock Hills Golf Club Archives. Three years later the club was sold for taxes on the steps of the Riverhead court house. Fortunately the buyer was the club's manager who transferred the lien back to the club when it was once again in funds.

REFERENCES

Abbott, Wilbur C., *Colonel John Scott of Long Island* (New York 1918).

Adams, James Truslow, *History of the Town of Southampton: East of Canoe Place* (Bridgehampton, NY 1918).

Akrigg, G. P. V., *Shakespeare and the Earl of Southampton* (Cambridge 1968).

Ales, Marion F., "History of the Indians on Montauk, Long Island" in *History and Archaeology of the Montauk Indians* ed. Gaynell Stone (Stony Brook, NY 1993).

Amory, Cleveland, *Last Resorts* (New York 1948).

Anderson, Virginia DeJohn, *New England's Generation: The Great Migration and the Formation of Society and Culture in the Seventeenth Century* (Cambridge 1991).

Barber, John W. and Howe G. H., *Historical Collections of the State of New York* (Albany, NY 1842).

Barstow, Belle, *Setuuket—Alias Brookhaven: Birth of a Long Island Town, with Chronological Records 1655–1679* (Bloomington, IN 2004).

Bayles, Richard M., *Historical and Descriptive Sketches of Suffolk County, New York* (Port Washington, NY 1873).

Beatty, Jack, *Age of Betrayal: The Triumph of Money in America 1865–1900* (New York 2007).

Beckert, Sven, *Monied Metropolis: New York City and the Consolidation of the American Bourgeoisie* (Cambridge 1993).

Bragdon, Kathleen, *Native Peoples of Southern New England* (Norman, OK 1996).

Breen, Timothy H, *Imagining the Past: East Hampton Histories* (New York 1989).

Burrows, Edwin G. and Wallace, Mike, *Gotham: A History of New York City to 1898* (New York 1999).

Calder, Isobel MacBeath, "The Earl of Stirling and the Colonization of Long Island" in *Essays Presented to Charles McLean Andrews by his Students* (New Haven, CT 1930).

Cave, Alfred A., *The Pequot War* (Amherst, MA 1996).

Cory, John, *The Golden Clan: The Murrays, McDonnells and the Irish American Aristocracy* (Boston, MA 1977).

Cronon, William, *Changes in the Land: Indians, Colonists, and the Ecology of New England* (New York 1983).

Cummings, Mary, *One Hundred Years of Healing: Southampton Hospital 1909–2009* (Southampton, NY 2009).

Day, Linda R, *Making a Way to Freedom: A History of African Americans on Long Island* (Hempstead, NY 1997).

Downs, Rev. James C., *History of the Shinnecock Church* (1875 unpublished, Southampton Historical Museum Archives).

Dwight, Rev. Timothy, *Travels in New England and New York 1796–1815 Vol. III* (New Haven, CT 1823).
Gaines, Steven, *Philistines at the Hedgerow: Passion and Property in the Hamptons* (New York 1998).
Garner, Alice, *A Shifting Shore: Locals, Outsiders, and the Transformation of a French Fishing Town 1823–2000* (Ithaca, NY 2005).
Halsey, Abigail Fithian, *In Old Southampton* (New York 1940).
Harrington, Mark, "An Ancient Village Site of the Shinnecock Indians" (published 1924) in Gaynell S. Levine, *Early Papers in Long Island Archaeology* (Stony Brook, NY 1977).
Heart, John E., *Southampton Hospital: Its Inception, Growth and Future* (Southampton, NY 1913).
Hedges, Henry P., *History of the Town of East-Hampton, New York* (Sag Harbor, NY 1879).
Holzman, George, *History of the Shinnecock Canal* (New York 1925).
Homberger, Eric, *Mrs. Astor's New York: Money and Social Power in the Gilded Age* (New Haven, CT 2002).
Howell, George Rogers, *History of Southampton, Long Island* (Bridgehampton, NY 1866; 2nd edition Albany, NY 1887).
Kavanagh, W. Keith, *Town Lands and the Trust Doctrine: Huntington, New York as a case study 1653–1972* (Huntington, NY 1972).
Kurlansky, Mark, *The Big Oyster, New York in the World: A Molluscular History* (New York 2006).
Lee, James P., *Golf in America* (New York 1895; reprinted Far Hills, NJ 1986).
Lewis, Tom, *The Hudson, A History* (New Haven, CT 2005).
Maitland, Frederic W., *Township and Borough* (Cambridge 1898).
Manley, Henry S., "No Man's Land, Southampton," *Long Island Forum* (October 1953).
Martin, John Frederick, *Profits in the Wilderness: Entrepreneurship and the Founding of New England Towns in the Seventeenth Century* (Chapel Hill, NC 1991).
Moeran, Edward H., "The Circassian Tragedy," *Long Island Forum* (Vol. V No. 9 September 1942).
Moeran, Edward H., "Southampton's First Vacationers," *Long Island Forum* (Vol. VI No. 3 April 1943).
Morgan, H. Wayne, *From Hayes to McKinley: National Party Politics 1877–1896* (Syracuse, NY 1969).
Mowrer, Elisabeth, *The Indomitable John Scott* (New York 1960).
Osgood, Herbert L., *The American Colonies in the Seventeenth Century*, 3 vols. (New York 1904).
Parrish, Samuel L., *Historical, Biographical and Descriptive Catalogue of the Objects Exhibited at the Southampton Art Museum* (New York 1898).
Patterson, Jerry E., *The First Four Hundred: Mrs. Astor's New York in the Gilded Age* (New York 2000).
Pelletreau, William S., "Southampton" in *History of Suffolk County, New York* (New York 1882).
Pelletreau, William S., "The New Southampton," *Long Island Magazine* (Vol. I No. 3 1893).
Pelletreau, William S. and Ross, Peter, *History of Long Island Vol. II* (New York and Chicago 1903).
Post, Richard, *Notes on Quogue 1659–1959* (East Hampton, NY 1959).
Powell, Sumner Chilton, *Puritan Village: The Formation of a New England Town* (Middleton, CT 1963).
Prime, Nathaniel S., *History of Long Island from its First Settlement by Europeans to the Year 1845 with Special Reference to Ecclesiastical Concerns* (New York 1845).
Rattray, Jeannette Edwards, *Montauk: Three Centuries of Romance, Sport and Adventure* (East Hampton, NY 1938).
Reeves, H. A., "Commerce, Navigation, and Fisheries of Suffolk County" in *Bicentennial History of Suffolk County* (Babylon, NY 1885).
Rensselaer, May King (with Frederic Van de Water), *The Social Ladder* (London 1925).
Ritchie, William A., "The Stony Brook Site and its relation to Archaic and Transitional Cultures on Long Island," *New York State Museum and Science Service Bulletin* (Albany, NY No. 372, 1959).

Scobey, David M., *Empire City* (New York 2002).
Seed, Patricia, *Ceremonies of Possession in Europe's Conquest of the New World 1492–1640* (Cambridge 1995).
Seyfried, Vincent, *History of the Long Island Railroad*, 6 vols. (Port Washington, NY 1961–1975).
Smith, Mildred, *History of the Long Island Railroad* (New York 1958).
Stewart, George R., *American Place Names* (New York 1970).
Strong, Lisa M. and Holmberg F. F., "The Shinnecock Trustee System 1792–1938" in *The Shinnecock Indians: A Culture History* edited by Gaynell Stone (Stony Brook, NY 1983).
Strong, John A., "A Documentary History of the Shinnecock Peoples: How the Land was Lost" in *The Shinnecock Indians: A Culture History* edited by Gaynell Stone (Stony Brook, NY 1983).
Strong, John A., *The Algonquian Peoples from Earliest Times to 1700* (Interlaken, NY 1997).
Strong, John A., *The Montaukett Indians of Eastern Long Island* (Syracuse, NY 2001).
Strouse, Jean, *Morgan: American Financier* (New York 1999).
Tarbell, Ida M., *The History of the Standard Oil Company* (briefer version edited by David M. Chalmers, New York 1966).
Tarduro, Mary and Havemeyer, David, *History of the Shinnecock Canal* (unpublished, Rogers Memorial Library, Souhampton 1975).
Terry, L. Emory, *New York's First English Settlement* (Southampton, NY 1934).
Thomas, T. Gaillard, *"George Gilbert White," Portrait and Biographical Record of Suffolk County* (New York 1896).
United States Senate, Hearings of the Sub-Committee of the Committee on Indian Affairs in relation to Certain Claims of the Montauk, Shinnecock, Narragansett, and Mohegan Indians (Washington DC 1900).
Urbain, Jean-Didier, *At the Beach* (translated by Catherine Porter, Minneapolis, MN 2003).
Weber, Max, *The Protestant Ethic and the Spirit of Capitalism* (translated by Talcott Parsons, New York 1930).
Wettereau, Helen, *Shinnecock Hills Long Ago* (East Patchogue, NY 1991).
Weygand, Philip C., "How Advanced were Long Island's Native Americans?" *Long Island Historical Journal* (Vol. 17 Nos. 1 and 2, 2005).
Whitaker, Rev. Epher, *Southold: Being a Substantial Reproduction of the History of Southold, Long Island* (Southold, NY 1881; 2nd edition edited by Rev. Charles E. Craven, Princeton, NJ 1930).
White, Lizbeth Halsey, "Southampton Records and Landmarks," *New York History* (Vol. XIV No. 4, 1933).
Wood, Joseph S., *New England Village* (Baltimore, MD 1997).
Zaykowski, Dorothy I., *Sag Harbor: Story of an American Beauty* (Sag Harbor, NY 1991).

INDEX

Academy Lane, 10, 14
Academy School, 266
"Act respecting Shinecok Great Field" (1804), 202
African Americans, 77; farm labor by, 49; lack of employment for, 48; relations with Shinnecock Indians, 47, 48, 49; socioeconomic marginalization of, 46, 48; in whaling industry, 47
Agawam Hall, 59, 93, 94, 287
Agawam Road, 264
Agawam Tennis Club, 258
Agawam Yacht Club, 261
Agriculture: confinement of small farmers to marginal land, 28; decline in prices after Civil War, 26; depression in, 28; diversification of production and, 27; fencing of land for, 34, 192, 193, 195; independent farm ownership and, 27; local economy and, 31; markets for, 31; pressure from Western farmers, 26; remaining farmland, 68; subsistence, 47; truck farming, 27
Aldrich, Frank, 349*n62*
Aldrich, William, 349*n62*
Alexander, William, 65
Amagansett, 5, 176; fishing industry and, 29
Andros Patent, 18, 37, 87, 156, 160, 162, 163, 165, 169, 185, 297, 307
Anglo-French War (1689), 182
Aquebogue Division, 142
Architecture styles: arts and crafts, 55; Beaux-Arts, 65; cottage, 64, 65; materials, 64; New England, 65; Queen Anne, 64, 65; shingle-style, 65; vernacular design, 65
Argyle Hotel, 232
Art Village, 56, 243, 250. *See also* Summer School of Art
Astor, Caroline, 7, 8, 9, 65
Atlantic Avenue, 80
Atterbury, Charles L., 65, 66, 239, 242, 246, 283, 294, 297, 298, 299, 300, 301, 304
Atterbury, Grosvenor, 56, 241, 280, 284, 286, 287

Babylon, 1, 205
Barber, General Thomas H., 287, 567
Barker's Island, 188
Barnard, Judge J.R., 136, 141, 143, 162
Barney, A.H., 66
Barney, Charles T., 66
Barrel Hill, 257
Barton, Isaac, 231
Barton, Ralph, 82
Bathing Corporation, 89, 261, 314
Bayberry Land, 250, 252
Bay bottoms: conflict over which proprietors entitled to ownership of, 143, 144; importance for supplemental incomes of town inhabitants, 123; Long Island Improvement Company and, 125; objections to sale of by town trustees, 112, 117; partition suit and, 134, 135, 136, 138; sale of by proprietors, 39, 112, 117; townwide issue of, 123
Bayles, Richard, 13, 14, 179, 180, 181

Bay Question, 116
Beach banks, 59
Beach Meadows, 262
Beach rights, vii
Beckert, Sven, 10, 56
Beers, F.W., 68
Bellomont, Lord, 182
Benjamin, William, 343*n52*
Benson, Arthur W., 134, 175, 179, 227, 228, 231, 233, 235, 236, 237, 240, 245, 254, 348*n46*
Benson, Frank Sherman, 228, 245, 246
Betts, C. Wyllys, 86, 173, 290, 298; abandons casino project, 89; claims beach as private property, 18, 59; early death, 56; establishing priorities for SVIA, 109; founding of Saint Andrews-by-the-Sea church and, 58; founding of Southampton Village Improvement Association and, 72; interest in beach hotel and casino, 89; Lake Agawam purchase, 118; proposal for new town hall by, 93, 94; purchase of beachfront property, 89; real estate holdings, 56; in SVIA, 78; threatens to fence in beach property, 89, 92, 290
Betts, Frederic H., vii, 82, 257; action of ejectment against, 289; claims beach as private property, 59, 86; concern for water contamination, 274; death of, 282; donation of land for church by, 69; establishing priorities for SVIA, 109; founding of Saint Andrews-by-the-Sea church and, 58; founding of Southampton Village Improvement Association and, 72; interest in beach hotel and casino, 89; interest in highway construction, 272, 273; involvement in dust problem, 107; president of SVIA, 78; proposal for new town hall by, 93, 94; real estate holdings, 56, 67; resolution on cemetery memorial by, 96; in SVIA, 268, 269; town suit against over beach ownership claim, 58; wins beach suit, 294, 304–310
Betts's Bay, 261
Betts case, 289–310. *See also* Ocean beach; advantage to summer residents in, 314; effect of indeterminacy of old patents, 291; importance of, 312, 313; issue of southerly limit of property, 290; lack of agreement on original legislation, 295; legal confrontation with village in, 290; trial in Riverhead, 294; village loss, 294, 304–310, 340*n30*
Bisgood, Thomas F., 41, 135, 136, 138, 224; in First Democratic Association of Southampton, 44
Bishop family, 103, 220
Block Island Sound, 22
Boarding houses, 1, 2, 3, 14, 72, 73
Bogart, Reverend David Schuyler, 10, 203
Borrowe, Annie, 241
Bowden, Lewis, 77, 81, 84, 94, 109; in marsh drainage issue, 106; secretary of SVIA, 83; town clerk, 106
Bowden family, 103
Bowman, John A., 116, 117, 118, 119, 127, 146, 147, 172, 225, 226, 228, 231, 233, 234, 262, 347*n38*
Box Cove, 208
Boyeson, Professor H.H., 67
Breen, Timothy, 15
Bridgehampton, 3, 14, 17, 40, 115, 116, 144, 151, 152, 205; African Americans in, 49; livestock raising, 31; Long Island Railroad to, 4
Bridgehampton Road, 14, 80, 93, 107, 255
Bridges, Jonathan, 184
Brookhaven, 21, 28, 194; fishing industry in, 113; livestock raising, 30, 31
Brooklyn and Montauk Railroad Company, 230
Brown, Archibald Manning, 314
Brown family, 10
Bryan, William Jennings, 43
Buck, Dr. Albert, 63, 72, 257; founding of Saint Andrews-by-the-Sea church and, 58
Bull Head Bay, 28, 112, 137, 195, 214, 250
Bunn, David, 214, 217
Bunn, James, 202, 203, 206, 210, 217, 345*n79*
Bunn, Luther, 210, 211, 212, 217, 345*n79*, 345*n80*
Bureau of Indian Affairs, 254
Burling, George H., 42, 275, 278
Burling, Walter R., 41, 42, 104, 105, 109; honorary member of SVIA, 79
Burnett, David, 134, 155, 156

Burnett, Frank W., 88, 108
Burnett family, 103, 220

Canoe Place, 17, 20, 21, 22, 30, 47, 136, 139, 179, 182, 194, 196, 197, 199, 201, 251, 252, 328*n10*, 332*n48*
Canoe Place Division, 91, 137
Canoe Place Inn, 237
Canoe Place Pond, 112, 124, 137, 234
Capitalism: rational bourgeois, 18; Republican fear of hostility to, 27
Captain's Neck, 67, 68, 239, 260
Captain's Pond, 300
Carpenter, Everett A., 41, 122, 135, 144, 150, 151, 152, 153, 155, 156, 160, 163, 339*n11*, 339*n17*; defense of oyster company by, 45; files appeal on Mecox Bay trial finding, 162; files second appeal in Mecox Bay case, 168–170
Carpenter, Miles B., 237, 348*n45*
Carter, James, 127, 153, 157, 160
Carter, Tuthill, 123, 127
Carter family, 44
Cemeteries, 95–101, 335*n5*, 336*n24*
Central Railroad of Long Island, 229
Central Railroad of New Jersey, 245, 246
Chandler, Charles F., 104
Charles II (King of England), 16, 21, 156
Charlick, Oliver, 82, 225, 230, 239, 245, 347*n32*
Chase, Janet Ralston, 55. *See also* Hoyt, Janet Ralston
Chase, Justice Salmon, 55
Chase, William Merritt, 55, 56, 240, 244, 284
Chatfield, Thomas, 185
Chice (sachem), 188
Circassian (ship), 47
Civil War: contribution to population decline, 26; decline in agricultural prices after, 26; political parties after, 42
Claflin, Arthur, 251, 253
Clark, George C., 250
Cleveland, Grover, 43
Cloth weaving, 32
Cold Spring, 200; Shinnecock Indians at, 47
Cold Spring Bay, 112, 137, 188, 195, 196, 198, 220, 247, 249, 250, 252
Cold Spring Pond, 28
Committee for Connecticut, 21
Commonage rights, 33, 36
Concer, Pyrrhus, 77, 78, 333*n57*
Condon, Lawrence, 251
Cook, Baldwin, 148
Cook, Harvey, 148
Cook family, 35
Cooper, Ananias, 132
Cooper, Caleb, 190, 199, 200, 201, 203
Cooper, James Fenimore, 4
Cooper, John, 156, 162, 290, 300
Cooper family, 35
Cooper's Neck, 61, 68, 88, 235, 241, 262, 304
Cooper's Neck Lane, 289
Cooper's Neck Pond, 65, 67
Corbin, Annie, 241
Corbin, Austin, 43, 82, 111, 116, 124, 139, 254, 283, 348*n46*; on board of Shinnecock Inn and Cottage Company, 240; failure hotel projects, 232; interest in Montauk, 175, 231; interest in shoreline development, 146; interest in steamship service, 237; lobbies Congress to make Montauk a port of entry, 237, 245; Long Island Improvement Company and, 225; loss of interest in Shinnecock Hills, 244; opposition to plans for ship service, 245; plans for construction of hotel and rail station in Hills, 238, 239; president of LIIC, 239; purchases controlling interest in Long Island Railroad, 229; real estate holdings, 147; seeks Hills for development, 225; withdraws from work on Hills development, 237; work on rail route on East End, 237
Corbin Banking Company, 228, 229, 245
Corchaug Indians, 175
Cornbury, Lord. *See* Hyde, Edward
Corwith, W.G., 81
Corwith family, 35, 41, 77, 103
Council for New England, 17
Cow Neck, 66, 139, 228
Cricket, 257, 260
Cronon, William, 192
Cuffee, Absalom, 202, 203
Cuffee, James L., 215

Cuffee, Nathan, 204
Cuffee, Paul, 198, 199, 343*n*52, 348*n*45
Cuffee, Vincent, 210
Cuffee, Wickham, 214
Cuffee church, 198, 199
Cullen, Judge Edgar M., 153, 156, 160, 294, 304, 309
Culver family, 103
Cutchogue, 151

Daughters of the American Revolution, 54
Davis, Willie, 243
de Bost, A.D., 328*n*18
de Bost, Leon dePeyre, 5, 10, 11, 54, 151, 260, 328*n*18; founding of Southampton Village Improvement Association and, 72
de Bost, Louise, 328*n*18
de Bost, Mary L., 328*n*18
Declaration of the Company, 18
Delafield, Naturin, 66, 224, 347*n*23
Democratic Association, 138, 279
Democratic Party, 41, 42, 43, 44, 45, 46, 119, 120
Dering family, 41
Development: capitalist, 18; economic, vii, 42; individualism and, 19; land, 18, 22; outside, 22; railroad, 62; transportation, 26
Disposall of the Vessell, 18, 87, 128, 161, 164
Dongan, Governor Thomas, 37
Dongan Patent, 127, 132, 154, 156, 160, 162, 163, 166, 169, 172, 173, 182, 183, 184, 185, 291, 297, 307, 350*n*23; confirmation on ownership of waters by, 18, 87; establishment of town trustee system and, 37; reference to beaches in, 88; waters as public trust in, 112
Douglas, Adelaide, 256
Downs, Reverend James G., 199
Drainage system, 265
Drexel, Morgan and Company, 56, 230, 232
Duer, William, 65
Duer family, 8, 65
Duke's Laws (1664), 182, 186
Dune Road, 67, 262, 264, 273, 289, 317
Dunton, Frederick W., 233, 245, 246
Dunwell, William, 316

Dupont family, 54
Dutch West India Company, 177
Dwight, Timothy, 178, 179
Dykman, Judge J.O., 162
Dysentery, 72, 73, 74, 75, 103, 105, 107

E.A. & H. Hildreth store, 94, 108, 336*n*38
Earl of Southampton, 23, 24, 330*n*24
Earl of Stirling, 17, 24, 65, 185, 330*n*16
Easthampton: early tourism in, 2, 3, 5; fishing industry and, 30; invasion of artists in, 4; lack of rail service, 4; livestock raising, 30, 31; purchase from Montaukett Indians, 176; social control of individual behavior in, 15; summer boarding houses in, 3
Easthampton Lawn Tennis Club, 258
East Hampton Star (newspaper), 42
East Marion: fishing industry and, 29
Eastport, 113, 205
East Quogue, 75, 116
East Riding Lane, 80
Eastville, 48
Eaton, Governor Theophilus, 176, 185
Eel grass, 134
Elm Street, 80, 83
Ely, Dr. Albert, 280, 281
Enstine family, 68
Environs Realty Company, 250, 252, 253
Episcopal church, 12, 58, 69–72; as symbolic meetinghouse for summer residents, 70; symbol of stratification of summer and town communities, 70; upper-class exclusivity of, 70
Equestrian activities, 263
Erie Canal, 26
Esterbrook, Richard Jr., 92, 114, 115, 116, 126, 129, 134, 135, 136, 143, 144, 145, 147, 150, 151, 152, 170, 171, 234

Fahys, Joseph, 41, 152; owner of Sag Harbor watch case company, 45
Far Pond, 240, 241
Farrett, James, 17, 18, 20, 154, 161, 176, 185, 330*n*16
Farrington's Pond, 14
Fencing, 192, 193, 195

Financial crisis of 1873, 62
First Democratic Association of Southampton, 44
First Neck Lane, 54, 56, 61, 63, 65, 66, 67, 80, 81, 86, 257, 259, 264, 282, 290, 348*n43*
Fisher, Carl, 175
Fishing industry, 29, 30, 113, 114, 337*n6*. *See also* Mecox Bay affair; Whaling; dredging for oysters, 114, 115; facilitation by rail routes, 113; pollution in NYC and, 115; shellfish, 29
Fithian, Jonathan, 3, 96, 339*n17*; justice of the peace, 213
Flagler, Henry, 227
Flanders, 142; African Americans in, 49
Fletcher, Benjamin, 182
Flying Point, 151
Fordham, Henry, 267, 274, 275, 276, 279
Fordham family, 186
Fort Pond, 66, 184, 238, 261
Fort Pond Bay, 231, 237, 244, 245
Foster, Albert, 140, 143
Foster, Edward, 54, 61, 97, 106, 141, 286, 339*n17*, 342*n35*, 351*n31*; on cemetery committee, 95, 97; cooperation with SVIA on some projects, 83, 84; interest in new town hall, 94; at Mecox Bay trial, 120; on proprietors board of trustees, 120; questioned right of proprietors to sell bays, 120; recognition of economic gain from summer residents, 60; Southampton Bank and, 265; Southampton Water Works Company and, 264, 265; suggests town buy beachfront property, 61, 62; town clerk, 44, 45, 60, 77, 84, 95, 120, 146, 157
Foster, Elias, 195
Foster, Erastus, 140
Foster, Isaac Post, 120, 140, 220; proprietor trustee, 85
Foster, James, 77, 106, 143, 255, 313; involvement in dust problem, 107; justice of the peace, 83, 141; president of SVIA, 109; real estate holdings, 147; vice-president of SVIA, 78, 140
Foster, Selden: town supervisor, 208

Foster family, 35, 40, 68, 103, 140, 220
Fourth Neck, 116
Free Bay Board, 126
Freetown, 48
French, Stephen B., 45, 135, 144, 150, 151, 152, 153
Fresh Pond, 112, 136
Frog Pond, 80, 304
Fugitive Slave Act (1850), 48

Gardiner, Lyon, 17, 156, 176, 330*n17*, 330*n24*
Gardiner's Bay, 6, 30, 124
Gardiner's Island, 17, 48, 176, 341*n16*
Garner, Alice, 2
Georgica, 185
Georgica Pond, 22, 130
Gin Lane, 11, 61, 63, 65, 67, 80, 258, 262, 264, 289, 299
Golf, 56, 242, 246, 257, 349*n59*, 349*n60*
Goodale, Captain Charles, 11
Good Ground, 17, 56, 198. *See also* Hampton Bays
Governance: administrative system, 37; separation of administration of lands and waters, 38, 39; two-tiered structure of, 37; village incorporation, 71, 72
Grant, Ulysses, 151
Graves, Henry W., 245
Great North/South Divisions, 34
Great Plains, 54, 61, 63, 67, 68, 191, 192
Great Plains Road, 264
Great Pond, 179
Great Quogue Land Grab, 21
Great Sedge Flat, 291
Great South Bay, 22, 28, 113, 114, 115, 169, 336*n3*
Greenport, 6, 230, 237; fishing industry and, 29; Long Island Railroad to, 1, 3, 4; shipbuilding in, 32
Griffing, James, 100
Grinnell, Robert H., 134, 135

Hallock, Dr. David H., 73, 77, 94, 106
Halsey, Abigail Fithian, 49
Halsey, Augustus, 54
Halsey, David, 132, 133

Halsey, Isaac, 56
Halsey, Silas, 132
Halsey, Thomas, 54
Halsey, Timothy, 292
Halsey, Zebulon, 132
Halsey family, 35, 126, 186
Halsey Neck, 67, 137, 146, 148, 304, 313, 348n43
Halsey Neck Lane, 67, 147
Halsey Neck Pond, 262
Hampton Bays, 56, 261
Hampton Hounds, 263
Hampton Hunt Club, 263
Hampton Road, 14, 80
Hand, Orlando, 143, 147
Harding, Warren, 280
Harriman, John, 64
Harrington, Mark, 200
Harris, Sidney, 63
Harris family, 220
Harsell, Blaize, 65
Havemeyer, Henry O., 64, 230
Havens, Walter, 68
Havens family, 68, 103
Heady Creek, 61, 67, 188, 191, 208, 213, 241
Health regulations, 72, 73, 74, 75
Hedges, Edwin, 122
Hedges, Henry P., 3, 41, 44, 135, 143, 150, 151, 155, 286
Hedges family, 35
Herrick, Dr. Everett, 263
Herrick, George, 101
Herrick, Henry, 104
Herrick, James, 97, 100, 101
Herrick, William, 200; trustee clerk, 203
Herrick family, 35, 77, 103
Highways: automobile age and, 266, 267; early routes, 5; macadam, 272, 273; reserved to proprietors, 36; town trustee, 36; travel rights to, 36
Hildreth, Edgar A.: interest in new town hall, 94; Southampton Bank and, 265
Hildreth family, 14, 41, 68, 77, 103
Hillcrest: African Americans in, 49
Hill Street, 14, 63, 67, 244, 284

Hinsdale, Elizur, 226, 235, 236, 238
Hither Woods, 176
Hog Neck, 21, 134, 147, 164, 185
Hog Neck Beach, 147
Holmes's Hill, 137, 147
Homestead Act (1863), 27
Hommedieu family, 41
Hook Pond, 258
Hopkins, Governer Edward, 176
Horton, Azariah, 199, 343n52, 344n54
Howe, Daniel, 147
Howell, Charles, 93, 94, 220
Howell, Edward, 121, 130, 141, 330n24, 339n22
Howell, Ella, 289, 310, 314
Howell, Fletcher, 269
Howell, George Rogers, 3, 56, 64, 237, 286, 292, 295, 305, 330n24, 333n16, 351n31; attempt to solve beachfront issue, 91; claims common law rights for lands under waters, 121; questions legitimacy of Shinnecock Hills title, 253; questions right of trustees to enter into agreements with Shinnecock Indians, 216
Howell, Harri Micah, 147, 148, 149, 170, 339n6, 351n3
Howell, Jedediah, 133
Howell, John, 2, 86, 89, 183, 339n22
Howell, Phillup, 132
Howell, Sylvanus, 11
Howell family, 35, 68, 103, 186
Howland, Judge Henry E., 65, 67, 82, 273; founding of Southampton Village Improvement Association and, 72; secretary of SVIA, 78
Howland family, 8, 66
Hoyt, Beatrix, 56, 349n59
Hoyt, Janet Ralston, 55, 240, 349n59; Art Village and, 56, 243
Hoyt, William, 240, 242, 246, 247, 248; founding of Saint Andrews-by-the-Sea church and, 58; installs gristmill on property, 55; management position in LIIC, 55
Hoyt family, 53, 54, 66, 87
Huguenots, 10, 41, 150, 335n14

Hunt, Howard W., 41
Hunt, John Howard, 41
Huntington, 182, 185; fishing industry in, 113; livestock raising, 30, 31
Huntting, Mary, 204
Hyde, Edward (Lord Cornbury), 182, 183, 184, 185, 342*n17*

Indian Agreement (1790), 197, 198
Indian Field, 6, 48
Islip, 205; fishing industry in, 113; livestock raising, 30

Jacob, Abraham, 198
Jaggar, Charles, 42, 275, 276, 277, 280
Jagger, Albert, 223, 226, 233, 238, 346*n21*
Jagger family, 220
James, Henry, 52
James, Reverend Thomas, 341*n3*
James (Duke of York), 21, 65, 156
James I (King of England), 17, 23, 24
Jennings, James E., 138
Jennings family, 220
Jere Johnson Jr. and Company, 249
Jessup, John, 300
Jessup family, 35
Jessup's Neck, 30
Job's Lane, 10, 12, 14, 56, 59, 79, 80, 82, 86, 93, 102, 265, 266, 282, 285, 286, 287, 288
John, Reverend Peter, 343*n52*
John Hen's bar, 14
Johnson, Eugene, 345*n7*, 349*n66*
Johnson, Jere, 249, 250, 251, 253
J.P. Morgan & Co., 56

Kelly, Jerome, 235
Kelly, John, 42
Kidd, William "Captain," 182, 341*n16*
Kilbreth, James, 53, 54; founding of Southampton Village Improvement Association and, 72; real estate holdings, 67
Kilbreth, John, 54, 260
Kilbreth, Judge: interest in beach hotel and casino, 89
Kilbreth family, 8, 53

Killes, David, 215, 223
King William's War (1689), 182
Kirby, Wallace, 233, 346*n21*

Lake Agawam, 11, 56, 61, 63, 84, 87, 102, 106, 118, 130, 173, 243, 255, 257, 258, 260, 261, 335*n4*; concern over purity of waters, 84; early settlers on, 240; effect of storms on, 85, 86; efforts to clean up, 85; issue of waste disposal in, 84; as preferred location of land purchase, 63; public access to, 87; sea grass in, 85, 86; viewed as private property by SVIA, 87, 88
Lake Montauk, 179
Last Division, 335*n21*
Lawn tennis, 257
Lee, J. Bowers, 67, 259
Lee, James, 246, 247, 349*n58*, 349*n59*
Lee Avenue, 68
Litchfield, Electus B., 232
Little Hog Neck, 151
Little Neck, 194, 240
Little Plain, 25, 89, 192
Little Plains Road, 80, 95
Little South Division, 194
Livestock: fencing for, 191, 192, 193, 195; grazing on Indian land, 191, 192; raising, 30, 31; regulation of, 38
Lloyd's Neck, 182
Long Island: agriculture in, 31; effect of decline in agricultural prices on, 26; ethnic immigration in, 25, 46; geography of, 21, 22; Long Island Railroad and, 1, 3, 224–233; loss of population, 26, 27, 28; need for rail service, 205; truck farming on, 27
Long Island Improvement Company (LIIC), 55, 116, 117, 124, 222, 225; bay bottom issue and, 125; claims ownership of shore of bay, 242; conceals intentions from proprietors, 225, 226; construction of hotel in Hills, 238; failed development at Shinnecock Hills, 244–254; formation of, 231, 232; interest in Shinnecock Hills, 146; obtains clear title to Hills property, 236; ownership of shoreline, 235; purchase of beach lots by,

Long Island Improvement Company (LIIC) *(continued)*
88; reassessment of investment by, 241; road upgrades by, 241; sells property on Hills to Shinnecock Land Company, 236; title to Shinnecock Bay transferred to, 129; works of, 233–244

Long Island Railroad (LIRR), 1, 43, 111; to Bridgehampton, 4; chooses not to negotiate with Shinnecock Indians, 205, 206; complaints about, 82; complaints of killed livestock to, 225; controlling interest purchased by Corbin, 229; dealings with SVIA, 79, 80, 82; demands for reimbursement ignored by, 225; depots at Shinnecock Hills, 243; development of, 347n35; to East End, 224–233; at Golf Grounds Station, 243, 248; to Greenport, 1, 3, 4; interest in Shinnecock Hills, 146; legal relationships with tribes, 204; to Montauk, 175, 230; non-payment for right-of-way through Shinnecock Hills, 179; to Patchogue, 113; plans for eastern extension, 205; profit from sale of rights-of-way to, 203, 204; removal of Quogue depot by, 82; to Riverhead, 1, 82; role in division of Shinnecock Hills, 203; safety issues, 283; to Sag Harbor, 4, 82, 113, 229, 232; to Southampton, 4, 14; South Shore line, 204; at Suffolk Downs Station, 248; transportation for farm products and, 113

Long Island University, 253
Long Springs, 12, 14, 257
Lorillard, Jacob, 231
Lovelace, Governor Francis, 165
Lupton, David, 132

Macdonald, Charles Blair, 247, 248, 250
Mackie family, 93
Maidstone Club, 258, 260
Maitland, Frederic W., 17, 166
Manamam (sachem), 188
Mandush (sachem), 176, 185, 191
Manhanset House (Shelter Island), 30
Manhansett Indians, 20, 21, 175
Manhattan Beach Hotel, 229, 232
Manorville, 82, 205

Martin, John Frederick, 18
Massachusetts Bay Colony, 17, 18
Maxwell, Henry W., 116, 125, 129, 135, 136, 137, 143, 228, 230, 231, 238, 245; acquires land on behalf of Corbin, 234; on board of Shinnecock Inn and Cottage Company, 240; real estate holdings, 146
Maxwell, J. Rogers, 230, 240, 242, 245
McAllister, Ward, 8, 9
McCarthy, Herb, 315, 316
McCoun, Judge, 211, 212, 217
McKeever, J. Lawrence: interest in beach hotel and casino, 89
McKeever family, 65
McKim, Charles, 65, 82, 94
McKim, Mead, and White, 65, 243, 285
McKinley, William, 43, 64
Mead, Edward, 67, 242, 243, 285
Meadow Club, 67, 257, 258, 259, 260, 262, 263, 264
Meadow Lane, 67, 260, 273
Meadowmere Lane, 262
Mecox Bay, 12, 22, 28; annual opening/closing, 130, 131; beach area of, 88; characteristics of, 130; considered public property of town, 133; economic importance of, 130, 131; farming rules for, 132; fishing industry and, 29; importance to town, 130; oyster beds, 29; poaching in, 132; private, unannounced selling of, 136, 137, 143–153; proprietor sale of, 29, 40, 143–153; question of ownership of bottom, 150; regulations against overfishing in, 132, 133, 134; sale as threat to local businesses, 116; salinity issue in, 130, 131; seapooses and, 130, 131; usefulness for watermill, 130
Mecox Bay affair, 92, 111–142, 143–174. *See also* Bay bottoms; extent to which trustees exercised continuous control as issue in, 133; importance of concept of generally accepted usage and custom in, 133; partition suit and, 134, 135, 138; previous leasing of bay bottom, 133; sale of bottom to Mecox Bay Oyster Company, 45, 46, 92; suit against Mecox Bay Oyster Company, 128–142; testimony at trial, 128

Mecox Bay Oyster Company, 92, 99, 117, 122, 126, 160, 234; closure of, 171; conveyance of deeds of sale to, 143; founding, 134; incorporation of, 152; partition suit competition for, 134, 135; suit against by town trustees, 127, 129–142, 153–171

Mecox Bay trial, 153–171; appeals to, 162–171; central issue of defining common and undivided lands extending to lands under water, 155–171; finding for town in, 161, 162; issue on right to purchase lands from Shinnecock Indians and ensuing deed for, 154; judgments in, 160–162; questions on original patents and legislation in, 154, 155, 163–171; reliance on historical documents, 156–160

Meeting House Lane, vii, 80, 93, 95, 282, 284

Menhaden, 29, 30

Methodist church, 59, 69, 93, 94

Methodist Episcopal Church, 93

Middle Pond, 137

Milford Dock Company, 245

Mill Creek, 130

Miller, George, 210, 211, 212, 217, 218

Millstone Brook, 188

Moeran, Edward, 10, 71; real estate holdings, 67

Montauk, 1, 144; characteristics shared with Shinnecock Hills, 175, 176, 177, 178; development zone failure, 175; early history, 175–181; early settlers to, 5, 6; hunting/fishing interests in, 6; land auction at, 134, 135; Long Island Railroad to, 175, 230; sale of, 175; state park system and, 175

Montaukett Indians, 5, 6, 17, 21, 175, 191, 254, 330*n17*; confined to Indian Field, 48; encouragement of English settlement, 176; give up rights to land, 184; interrelation with Shinnecocks, 175; lack of consultation with on boundary questions, 186; petition to state recounting difficulties with town, 203; restrictive covenants imposed on, 6; sale of land of, 6

Montauk Point, 5, 184

Montauk Proprietors, 5

Montgomerie, Governor John, 184

Moore, George, 108, 255; removal from property by town, 101–105

Morgan, H. Wayne, 44

Morgan, J. Pierpont, 229, 230, 231, 256

Morgan, Junius, 229

Moriches, 205

Moriches Bay, 112, 336*n3*

Murdoch, Uriel A., 224; real estate holdings, 66

Murdoch's Bay, 261

Napeague, 5, 178; fishing industry and, 29

Napeague Beach, 177

Napeague Harbor, 176

Narragansett Indians, 176

Nassau Point, 151

National Golf Links of America, 246, 247, 248, 250, 251

National Lawn Tennis Association, 258

Negro, Pieter, 47

New Netherland, 21

Newport (R.I.), 8, 52

New York and Manhattan Beach Railway, 229, 231

New York and Sag Harbor Steamship Company, 238

New York City: determinants of status in, 9; heterogeneity of upper classes in, 9; oyster market in, 113, 114; rapid growth of legal profession in, 9; social climbing in, 10; social elite in, 7, 8, 9; Social Register in, 9

Niantic Indians, 176

Nicolls, Governor Richard, 21, 160, 162, 165, 182, 184, 345*n4*

Nicolls, Mathias, 167, 297

Ninigret (sachem), 176

Noggenock, 21

North End Burying Ground, 95

North Haven, 21

North Main Street, 14, 79, 82, 95

North Sea, 40, 102, 136, 140, 176, 188, 220, 226

North Sea Harbor, 20, 25, 28, 66, 139, 330*n24*

North Sea Line, 137, 139, 147

North Sea Road, 95, 282

Noyack, 147, 176
Noyac Road, 226
Nugent, Dr. John, 73

Occum, Samson, 343*n52*
Ocean beach. *See also* Betts case: bathing stations on, 12, 290; claims of ownership, 58; contested uses of, 12; dress code on, 12, 329*n20*; early views on, 2; as highway, 58, 291, 292; historical usage of, 92; as local work space, 12, 293; meadowlands along, 88; private ownship issues, 88–95; public right to, 58, 88–95, 118; removal of wigwams from, 290; as restful zone for summer residents, 59; seen as common land, 89; seen as public land, 89, 90, 118; sluiceways on, 59, 301, 304; transport of products over, 292; vulnerability to storms, 11, 22, 334*n27*; whaling and, 12; as work space for local townspeople, 59
Ocean House (Southampton), 2
Ogden, John, 21, 139, 162
Old Beach Road, 58
Old Fort Pond, 137, 191, 213, 251, 252
Old Town, 15, 53, 62, 151
Old Town Pond, 14, 25, 88, 92, 130, 290
Old Town Road, 262, 284, 289
Olmsted and Vaux, 247, 249, 250, 251
Orient, 4
Oriental Hotel, 229, 232
Osborn, Hull, 207, 209
Osborn, John P., 208
Otter Pond, 156
Ox Pasture, 61, 63, 67, 68
Ox Pasture Road, 68, 287
Oyster Bay, 17
Oysters. *See* Fishing industry; Mecox Bay affair

Park Avenue, 63, 262
Parkhurst, Dr. Charles, 332*n47*
Parrish, James C., 241, 246, 251, 253, 273, 283, 346*n21*
Parrish, James Jr., 251
Parrish, Samuel L., 95, 268, 346*n21*; art collection, 284, 286, 287; attempts to make governance transparent, 283; on board of Shinnecock Inn and Cottage Company, 240; development of art museum, 283, 284; formation of golf club by, 243; in LIIC, 239, 242, 283; president of Shinnecock Hills Golf Club, 285, 349*n60*; purchase of village hall by, 95; real estate holdings, 250, 283, 284; relieves LIIC of property in Hills, 246; role in modernization of Southampton, 239; role in village governance, 280–288; Southampton Water Works Company and, 264, 265; Summer School of Art and, 240, 243, 244, 284; village president, 278, 280
Parrish Art Museum, 56
Parrish Memorial Hall, 284
Patchogue, 113, 205
Patchogue Argus (newspaper), 41
Patents, vii, 17, 20, 21. *See also* individual patents
Payne, John Howard, 3, 4
Peabody, A.J., 54
Peconic Bay, 1, 20, 22, 30, 88, 91, 124, 137, 177, 194, 211, 238, 241, 246, 249, 250, 252, 257, 332*n48*
Peconic River, 22, 186, 194
Pelletreau, William S., 1, 2, 45, 236, 286; attitude toward Shinnecock Indians, 49; on beachfront property claims, 91; in cemetery issue, 97; against common law rights for lands under waters, 121; disagreement with White on use of bays, 125, 126, 128, 129; expertise in title searches, 45, 76; in favor of bay development, 150; historical interest in Southampton, 76; on loss of young people from farms to domestic service, 31; negative relations with White, 91, 122; opinion on benefits of summer residents presence, 76; owner of shares in Southampton Academy, 285; part in Mecox Bay affair, 144; property ownership, 10; proprietor trustee, 91, 120, 122; quitclaim deed for Red Creek Pond to, 137, 146; recognition of economic gain from summer residents, 60; resigns from trustees, 139; sale of Mecox Bay and, 143; service to town trustees and proprietor trustees, 30, 39; on summer resident-local resident relations, 55; support for Esterbrook, 150; support for

proprietor rights, 40, 120, 121, 122, 234; support for Salem Wales, 63; testifies in Betts case, 299, 300; testimony at Mecox Bay trial, 157; town clerk, 2, 120, 216, 335n14; town trustee, 120; transcription of old town records to print, 2, 3; views on Gaillard Thomas, 7
Pendleton, Francis K., 239, 240, 241, 246, 284, 346n21
Penney, A.H., 241, 242
Penny family, 44
Pequot Indians, 176, 330n17
Pequot War (1637), 330n17
Philipse, Frederick, 182
Pierson, Abraham, 20, 341n3
Pierson, Henry, 119
Pierson, James, 75, 109, 120; interest in new town hall, 94; in New York Assembly, 119; president of board of health, 106; recognition of economic gain from summer residents, 60; resolution on cemetery memorial by, 96; Southampton Bank and, 265; Southampton Water Works Company and, 264, 265; town supervisor, 44, 60, 73, 77, 106, 119, 267; treasurer of SVIA, 78, 83
Pierson, Philetus, 345n80
Pierson family, 35, 186
Piracy, 182
Plum Island, 348n46
Poaching, 132, 171
The Point, 63, 64
Polo, 257
Polytheism, 48
Pomguamo (sachem), 188
Pond Lane, 54, 63, 87, 108, 262
Ponquogue Light, 117
Ponquogue Point, 137
Poospatuck Reservation, 48
Poppenhusen, Conrad, 229
Porter, Dr. P. Brynberg, 73, 75
Port Jefferson, 245
Post, Albert, 122, 126, 267, 268, 274, 275, 278, 279, 280
Post, Edward, 140
Post, Edwin, 77, 99, 140, 141, 143, 149, 157–160, 170, 255, 285, 299, 313; in cemetery issue, 96–101; clerk of proprieter trustees, 77, 96; real estate holdings, 147; town trustee suit against, 100
Post, Erastus: Southampton Bank and, 265
Post, George O., 56, 88, 140, 141, 220, 291, 298
Post, James, 96, 100, 140, 208; town clerk, 207, 208; town supervisor, 207
Post, Oliver, 140, 142
Post, William: town clerk, 77; vice-president of SVIA, 78
Post family, 35, 40, 96, 140
Post House (Southampton), 2
Potunk Point, 336n3
Pot works, 30
Poxabogue Pond, 156
Pratt, Charles Millard, 228, 246
Pratt, Judge C.E., 162, 163, 164, 165, 167, 168, 339n19
Presbyterian church, 12, 69, 93
Prime, Nathaniel, 13, 177, 179, 199, 343n52
Privies, cesspools, and wells, 73, 75, 84, 99, 105, 264, 265
Property ownership, vii; accumulation in hands of small number of owners, 28, 35, 36; by adverse possession, 100, 101; agricultural, 27; beachfront, 58, 88–95; collapse of commonage system of, 36; commonage rights and, 33; distribution of land among proprietors, 34; individualism in, 19, 34; initial divisions and, 32, 33; land improvement and, 18, 19; land prices, 11, 239; open field system, 33, 34; patterns of, 28; patterns of land distribution in, 34, 39; plantation companies and, 18, 19; private, 18; proprietary system of, 28; by proprietors, 33; purchases from Indians, 20, 21; Puritan concepts of, 18; speculative purchases, 21; volume of land sales/exchanges and, 33
Proprietors. *See also* Trustees of the Proprietors: accused of forging Shinnecock Indians names to agreement to sell Shinnecock Hills, 215; conflict with town inhabitants, 50; control of larger portion of real estate, 39; control over Shinnecock Hills in dealing with LIRR, 205, 206; distribution of monies to trustees,

Proprietors *(continued)*
134, 135, 138; domination of town trustees by, 38, 39; eclipse of, 173; efforts to close sluiceways, 85, 301, 304; exploration of division of Shinnecock Hills with Indians, 206; as first town trustees, 37; held responsible for loss of Shinnecock Hills, 139; highway system and, 36; loss of reputation by, 123; partition and sale of Hills by, 213–224; pressure on Indians to relinquish Shinnecock Hills, 201–212; property ownership by, 33; responsibilities and expenses of, 38; sale of lands of questionable ownership, 148, 149, 150; sale of lands under waters by, 39; sale of ocean beach property to, 88, 89; seek ways to control Shinnecock Indians, 194; seen as self-serving, 122; suit for rights to land in Hills, 210, 211; tax contributions of, 38, 60; tight regulation/control of Hills by, 202; Trustees of the Proprietors and, 35; trustee system for Shinnecock Indians by, 194, 195

Proprietors of the Shinnecock Hills and Sebonac Sedges, 223, 235

Prospect House (Shelter Island), 30

Puritanism, 18, 49; economic stratification and, 50

Quantuck Bay, 1, 112, 347*n23*

Quinn, John, 127

Quinn family, 44

Quitclaim deeds, 92, 112, 118, 136, 137, 148, 150, 156, 186, 217, 228, 234, 290

Quogue, 1, 17, 21, 141, 151, 182, 234, 298; beach land in, 88; removal of Long Island Railroad depot from, 82; summer boarding houses in, 2

Quogue flats, 291

Quogue Plains, 32, 137

Quogue Purchase, 21, 27, 35, 122, 123, 128, 137, 139, 142, 148, 194, 196, 234, 335*n21,* 343*n43,* 345*n4;* Last Division in, 32, 34

Railroads. *See also* Long Island Railroad (LIRR): failure of, 62; overexpansion in, 62, 152

Ram Island, 214, 220, 221, 234

Rattray, Jeannette Edwards, 31

Real estate, 60–69; agricultural, 54; assessment values, 61; beachfront, 52, 53; boom in due to financial panic, 151, 152; changing hands from locals to summer residents, 60, 61; competition in, 61; complaints from locals about boom in, 61; drift westward, 67; effect of financial crisis on, 62; exorbitant prices for, 61; impact of prices on townspeople, 68, 69; increasing prices, 260; new money and, 316, 317; nonresident, 60; private ownership of, 87; rapid growth in market, 60, 64; reluctance to sell on part of locals, 54; residential, 54; as safe investment, 62, 63; slowdown due to banking crisis, 249; speculative sales, 151; status of church property, 70; use value in, 63

Red Creek Pond, 91, 112, 122, 137, 146

Redfield, William C., 247, 248, 249, 251

Reeves, Henry, 54

Reeves, Thomas, 208

Republican Party, 41, 42, 43, 44, 45, 46, 119, 120, 150, 151

Rights-of-way, 18, 87

Riverhead, 22, 150, 153; fishing industry and, 29; livestock raising, 30; Long Island Railroad to, 1, 82

Robertson, Robert H., 71, 285, 286, 351*n31*

Robertson, T. Markoe, 351*n31*

Robins Island, 151, 348*n46*

Rocky Point, 245

Rogers, Captain Albert, 282

Rogers, Captain William, 132

Rogers, Harriet, 101, 285

Rogers, Henry Huttleston, 228

Rogers, Jonathan, 132

Rogers, Obadiah, 93, 100, 101, 199, 203

Rogers, William, 143, 144

Rogers family, 35, 81, 284

Rogers Memorial Library, 285, 286, 339*n11*

Ronkonkoma moraine, 22, 130

Roosevelt, Theodore, 64

Root, Elihu, 64, 273, 294, 297, 339*n11*

Rose, Abraham, 47, 115, 116, 206, 208, 211, 298; negotiation on separation of proprietor interest from town interest, 40; president of trustees, 207

Rose, Antoinette, 115, 116, 171

Rose, Austin, 209, 210, 211, 213, 215, 217, 220, 223; real estate holdings, 66
Rose, David H., 138
Rose, David Rogers, 116, 119, 138, 140, 143, 170, 207, 208, 220, 223; president of proprietor trustees, 289; town supervisor, 207
Rose, Edwin, 207; president of proprietor trustees, 213; as proprietor trustee, 41; town supervisor, 216, 221; as town supervisor, 41
Rose, Jetur, 138, 215, 220, 223, 226, 233; death of, 170; president of trustees, 119
Rose, Maltbie Gelston, 207, 209, 213
Rose family, 35, 40, 96, 140, 141
Rose's Grove, 138
Ross, Peter, 227
Ruggles, James, 65
Ruggles, Samuel B., 65
Ruggles family, 8
Russell, Judge Horace, 248

Sabin, Charles, 250
Sagaponack, 88, 176, 185
Sagaponack Division (1653), 130
Sagaponack Road, 116
Sagg Pond, 25, 85, 130
Sag Harbor, 119, 150, 152, 205, 350n18; African Americans in, 49; commercial activities in, 6, 41; construction of Long Wharf, 155; effect of decline in whaling on, 26; exodus to gold rush in California and, 26; fires in, 6, 7, 267; incorporation of, 6, 17; lease of water lots in, 155; Long Island Railroad to, 4, 82, 113, 229, 232; long wharf, 7; police protection in, 274; population, 267; as port of entry, 6; "rum element" in, 44; sailing service to, 3; shipbuilding in, 6, 32; underground railroad in, 48; whaling in, 6, 118, 331n29
Sag Harbor Corrector (newspaper), 41, 45, 220, 225, 229
Sag Harbor Express (newspaper), 41, 135, 151, 152
Sag Harbor Savings Bank, 44, 266
Sag Harbor Wharf Company, 238
Sailing, 256, 257, 258, 261, 335n4
St. Andrews Dune Church, 289

St. David's African Methodist Episcopal Church, 48
St. Michaels and All Angels Episcopal Church, 240, 249
Saint Andrews Dune Church (Saint Andrews-by-the-Sea), 58, 69–72, 118, 260
Salm, Peter, 66
Salt grass, 215
Sandford, Captain John, 132
Sandford, Joel, 133
Sandford family, 35
Sandymount, 92, 290
Sanford, Nathan, 202
Sanford family, 68
Sanger, Rufus: real estate holdings, 63
Sayre, Job, 12, 147, 288
Sayre, Rufus, 143, 148, 309, 313; real estate holdings, 147
Sayre, Thomas, 133, 147, 339n17
Sayre family, 11, 35, 220
Schermerhorn family, 8, 65, 66
Schieffelin, George R., 102, 261; clears wigwams from beachfront, 290; establishing priorities for SVIA, 109; founding of Southampton Village Improvement Association and, 72; interest in beach hotel and casino, 89; offer of town trustee lease to Betts, 90; real estate holdings, 63, 67; removal of beach huts by, 90; in SVIA, 63, 78, 84
Schieffelin, William: founding of Southampton Village Improvement Association and, 72; real estate holdings, 63
Schieffelin family, 8
Schieffelin's Bay, 261
Schout's Bay, 147
Scotch Mist Inn, 280
Scott, Colonel John, 40, 66, 185, 332n45
Scott, Lewis, 40, 139, 140, 141, 145, 215, 219, 220, 221, 222, 223, 234, 296, 344n67
Scott, Samuel, 66
Scott family, 40, 186
Scuttlehole, 130, 177
Sea grass, 85, 86, 291
Seapooses, 130, 131
Seaside Boulevard, 262
Seaside Times (newspaper), 41, 42, 56, 58, 161, 226, 232, 233, 234, 278, 350n16; ads for

sale of Mecox Bay in, 134; on beachfront property issue, 91; commentary on unsightly water tank, 256; complaints on Long Island Railroad in, 82; complaints on trespass rules at the Hills, 241; encourages townspeople to take part in SVIA, 77; lists of summer residents in, 333*n6*; in Moore controversy, 102, 103, 104; positive coverage of SVIA, 79; printing of Dongan Patent in, 117; publication of SVIA disaffection with village conduct of affairs, 275, 276; publishes auction notice for Shinnecock Hills, 234; on real estate, 61; report on health issues, 75; reports/letters on Mecox Bay affair, 144; reports on cemetery issue, 97; reports on SVIA, 79; reprints lease on Shinnecock Hills, 235; seaweed privilege advertisements, 238

Seatuck, 186

Seaweed, 120, 139, 206, 211, 218, 222, 242, 296; annual sale of privilege to, 221; disputes over, 40, 41, 212, 295, 296; privilege advertised for sale, 238; proprietor claim to, 39; rights to, 346*n19*; Shinnecock Indians suit over, 211, 212

Seaweed trial (1866), 218, 295

Sebonac, 103, 182, 183, 187, 188, 200, 238; Shinnecock Indians at, 47

Sebonac Creek, 191, 195, 200

Sebonack Sedges, 66

Sebonac Meadows, 247

Sebonac Neck, 195, 196, 201, 214, 220, 234, 246, 250

Senate Committee on Indian Affairs, 215

Settlers: artisans, 16; cooperative relations among, 15; in dispersed village arrangements, 14, 15; familiarity with urban market economy, 16; "hiving out" of, 18; individualism of, 15; organization of land tenures by, 16; "peopling and planting" by, 18; relations with colonial governors, 16; relations with local Indians, 15; tenant farmers, 16

Seyfried, Vincent, 205, 228

Sharp, Colonel Thomas, 230, 231

Shelter Island, 20, 21, 175, 185; fishing industry and, 29, 30; livestock raising, 31

Sherwood, James, 238, 239, 348*n39*

Shiland, Reverend Andrew, 77

Shinnecock Bay, 1, 22, 67, 112, 116, 196, 197, 239, 252, 261, 264; acquired by Henry Maxwell from proprietors, 116; fishing industry and, 29; health of, 124; income from, 123; water level in, 124, 125

Shinnecock Canal, 45, 124, 125, 129, 137, 172, 328*n10*, 332*n48*; issue over height of bridge on, 238; storms and, 125; transportation issues and, 124, 125

Shinnecock Hills, 187; areas of, 341*n14*; characteristics shared with Montauk, 175, 176, 177, 178; as contested ground, 191–201; Country Club Knolls, 251, 253; development of, 22; division never challenged effectively in court, 217; early history, 175–181; enclosured at both ends, 202; failed development of, 244–254; first subdivision, 251; fishing industry and, 30; golf course at, 242, 243; incremental shifts from traditional usage, 195; Indian deeds to, 181–191; under lease to Shinnecock Indians, 36; legislative partition of, 139; LIRR at, 243; old lands of the Indians, 22; partition and sale of, 140, 213–254; pressure on Indians to divide, 203; as private enclave, 226, 227; proprietors attempt to prevent Indians from collecting rentals from railroad, 204; real estate values in, 239; resort development of, 175, 225; romantic advertising vision of, 179, 181; sale of lots in, 140, 239, 240; sales difficulties, 252, 253; Shinnecock Indians at, 47; sold to developers, 50, 122; suburbanization of, 175, 253; temporary railroad track in, 239, 240; termination of sheep pasturage, 239; trustee board, 238; understood by town as private land, 50

Shinnecock Hills and Peconic Bay Realty Company, 247, 248, 249, 250, 251, 253, 349*n62*

Shinnecock Hills Association, 251

Shinnecock Hills Golf Club, 56, 243, 246, 248, 250, 251, 257, 259, 283, 284, 285, 314

Shinnecock Indians, 11, 175; abrogation of lease to Shinnecock Hills, 36; adoption of reservation policy for, 187, 188; attempt to establish system of elected leadership among, 189; attempts to regain Hills, 254; cede title to lands, 186; challenge rights of proprietors to sell Hills, 215–224; claim trustees forged Indian names to agreement to sell Shinnecock Hills, 215; complaint filed by to repeal act exchanging Hills for Shinnecock Neck, 217; conception of land ownership, 328*n10*; condescension towards, 49; confinement to small preserve of land, 215, 216; conversion attempts, 343*n52*; demands for lease to Shinnecock Hills/Sebonac, 187; development of church by, 198, 199; disagreements with town over planting/grazing, 191, 192, 193; encouragement of settlers by, 176; federal recognition of, 349*n67*; fencing obligations, 210, 211; file complaint against town with state legislature, 206, 207, 208; forced to provide fencing to prevent damage from town animals, 202, 203; guaranteed occupancy rights for Shinnecock, 183; harassment by town, 206; indenture agreement with town, 183; indenture to wealthy farmers, 47; interrelation with Montauketts, 175; lack of consultation with on boundary questions, 186; land agreements with first settlers, 328*n10*; leadership organization, 196; lease of land to local farmers by, 47, 199, 200, 201; lease of Shinnecock Hills by, 36, 181–191; legal defense of rights of, 211; loss of population by, 47; loss of title to Shinnecock Hills, 46; population, 25, 46, 196; practice of renting fields to town farmers, 194, 195; presentation of complaints to proprietors, 202; pressured by proprietors to relinquish Hills, 201–212; refuse to divide land with town, 208; regulations and demands by town on, 203; relations with African Americans, 47, 48, 49; rights to seaweed, 218; sale of land to settlers, 20, 21; settlement locations, 196; signing of one-thousand year lease by, 181–191; socioeconomic marginalization of, 46, 47, 48; subleasing of land by, 191–201; subsistence existence, 47; sue for return of lands, 46, 49; sue proprietors over seaweed removal, 211, 212; suits against farmers for trespass and damage, 210; surrender of thousand-year lease, 214; system of land tenure and, 200; tense relations with town, 15, 21, 187, 188, 206, 210; threaten suit against trustees for sale without tribal consent, 237; town demand that tribe protect their crops from town animals, 191; in town market economy, 201; trustee system for, 194, 195, 198, 201; unsatisfactory arrangements for town fencing demands, 192, 193; use of bribery on to sign away lands, 186, 187; use of Mecox Bay, 130, 131; in whaling industry, 47, 196

Shinnecock Inn, 240, 243, 248, 249

Shinnecock Inn and Cottage Company, 240, 261

Shinnecock Land Company (SLC), 236, 239, 283; buys out LIIC, 246; ceases business, 247; inability to sell properties, 246

Shinnecock Meadows, 215

Shinnecock Neck, 46, 181, 182, 188; fencing issue, 194, 209; proprietors allowed to use land for pasturing, 197; rental of fields to town farmers, 194; Shinnecock Indians at, 47, 191, 194, 196, 198, 199, 201, 208, 209; town attempts better access to, 194; town grazing on, 193

Shinnecock Reservation, 46, 191

Shinnecock Road, 14

Shinnecock Yacht Club, 261

Siebert, Louis, 66

Siebert family, 65

Silver Lake, 55, 56, 243

Simonson, Henry, 253

Slavery, 27, 42, 47, 48

Sleight, Brinley Dering, 41, 45

Sleight, Harry D., 148, 351*n23*

Sleight family, 41

Smith, Gilbert, 261

Smith, J. Calvin, 198

Smith, J. Lawrence, 134, 136, 141

374 / Index

Smith, Richard, 185
Smithtown: livestock raising, 30
Soldiers and Sailors Monument, 287
Southampton: adjustment to presence of summer residents by, 69; agricultural history, 13; agricultural population in, 32; ambivalence toward summer residents, 3; as anti-Newport, 52, 259; anxiety of quitclaim deeds to outsiders for bay bottoms; boarding houses in, 14; board of health in, 73, 74, 75; class stratification of, 50, 258, 259; common ground with summer colony, 315, 316; concern over unruly behavior in streets, 269, 270; decline in number of inhabitants, 26, 27, 28; department stores, 56; disagreement with Shinnecock Indians over planting/grazing, 191, 192, 193; disagreements with summer colony on health issues, 107; drainage system, 265; early history, 13–25; economic diversification of, 123; effect of decline in agricultural prices on, 26; emergence as political community, 16; ethnic immigration in, 25; family networks in, 35, 36; first settlers, 3, 5; fishing industry and, 29; geography of, 22, 28; growth of, 2–21; high degree of inequality in, 49; incorporation of, 267, 337*n29*; indenture agreement with Shinnecock Indians, 183; individualist impulses of settlers in, 15, 16; integration into emerging market economy, 15, 16; intent to establish title to Indian lands, 182–191; lack of integration in early years, 14, 15; land allotment in, 15; livestock raising, 30, 31; Long Island Railroad to, 4, 14; Methodist church in, 14; modernization of, 264–280; naming of, 22, 23; negotiation with South Side Railroad, 205; new money in, 316, 317; nineteenth century history, 25–39; objections to proprietors sale of lands under waters, 112; as original administrative center, 16, 19; patterns of land ownership in, 28; police protection in, 274, 279; political activity by founding families, 37; politics in, 39–50; population, 13, 25, 26, 27, 28, 267; populist politics in, 46; Presbyterian church, 13, 14; resentment over rich newcomers, 60; rusticity of, 2, 5, 13, 52; schools, 14; separation of governmental functions in, 207; settled by patent, 17; settlement arrangement in, 14, 15; social class and, 39–50; sources of wealth and influence in, 41; street lighting, 265, 279, 283; tax assessments, 34, 35, 53, 60; telephone service to, 279; temperance movement in, 14; tense relations with Shinnecock Indians, 187, 188, 206, 210; transformation into summer resort, 259; uneasy relations with proprietors, 120; water supply for, 264, 265; year of settlement, 330*n16*
Southampton Academy, 14, 285
Southampton Art Museum, 286
Southampton Bank, 265, 282, 286
Southampton Beach Association, 89, 90
Southampton Colonial Society, 54
Southampton Company, 94, 265
Southampton Historical Museum, 93
Southampton Horse Association, 263
Southampton Hospital Association, 280, 284
Southampton Press (newspaper), 42, 250, 275, 278, 287
Southampton Village Improvement Association (SVIA), 63, 72–78; activities related to condition of waters, 80; addresses purity issue in Lake Agawam, 84, 85; agenda of, 72; air of noblesse oblige by, 93; annual dues and system of premiums, 77, 256, 271; appropriations for projects, 79; beautification of village as priority issue, 75, 80, 81, 82; building of railroad station by, 83; business owners on, 108; calls for removal of school to healthful location, 266; concern for neatness and order, 269, 270; construction of embankment at Lake Agawam, 85, 86; damage to credibility through publication of Thomas' article, 277, 278; decline in power of, 88; declining interest in, 256; declining revenues of, 270, 271, 272; defeat on marsh drainage issue, 106; difficulty for local residents to find fault with goals of, 76; disappointment with village corporation sharing responsibilities, 272, 273; discontent with village "progress," 274, 275; drafting of village ordinances by, 269; drainage system project, 265, 266; early trials and successes, 79–88; election of town residents to, 78; falling revenues of, 264; fears

of taking over village by townspeople, 81; health committee, 103; health issues as impetus for formation, 75; inability to affect Long Island Railroad decisions, 82; investigation of provision of water supply, 264, 265; investment in beach access and pavilion, 90; lack of democratic participation on, 110; management of beach pavilion by, 12; membership, 77, 81; monopoly on decisionmaking on, 109; need for outside support for projects, 265, 266; presentation of projects to town as *fait accompli*, 95; preservation of rural charm of village and, 42; proprietary approach to issues of interest, 86, 87; purpose of, 71, 72; relations with town, 79–110; removal of Moore family and, 101–110; removal of offending properties and people, 81; requests depot work from LIRR, 79, 80, 82; requests to merchants to clean up property, 81; resolution to shopkeepers on street cleaning, 270, 271; South End Burying Ground and, 95–101; street sign erection by, 80; street watering issue, 255, 256; support for move to village government, 71, 72; support for *Seaside Times,* 42; tree planting by, 79, 80; underwrites ornamental plantings, 83; value of initiatives by, 93; village beautification projects, 266

Southampton Water Works Company, 264, 279
South Beach, 11, 36, 51, 67, 81, 124, 220, 221, 238, 244, 293, 294
South Country Road, 1
South End Burying Ground, 95–101, 140, 157, 255
South Field Town, 25
South Main Street, 10, 14, 54, 67, 93, 96, 140, 157, 260
Southold, 1, 13, 21, 22, 171; fishing industry and, 29; livestock raising, 30
South Side Railroad (SSRR), 205, 229
Speonk, 17, 88
Springs, 48
Squabble Lane, 68
Squire family, 44
Squires, Benjamin F., 116, 117, 126, 127, 242, 348*n51*
Steamship service, 151, 237

Steers, Susanna, 68; real estate holdings, 63, 67
Stewart, George, 25
Stirling Patent (1640), 20, 21, 153, 156, 160, 162, 185
Stone, Gaynell, 199, 204
Street lighting, 265
Strong, John, 21
Strong, Judge S.B., 210, 211, 212
Sugar Loaf, 232, 238, 239, 240
Sugar Loaf Hill burial site, 175
Summer colony/residents: activities, 255–264; adjustment of town residents to presence of, 69; belief in civilizing mission, 92, 93; class differences in interest in sports, 257; class stratification of, 258, 259; dealings with town trustees, 126; desire to emphasize separateness from village by, 70; disagreements with town on health issues, 107; early years, 51–69; establishment of church by, 69–72; exertion of influence on social organization and activities of town by, 69–78; founding of church to symbolize distinctiveness of community, 70; founding of Southampton Village Improvement Association, 71–78; growth of, 25, 26; imposition of tastes on town by, vii; issue with provision of public access and rights-of-way to villagers, 87, 88; lack of interest in extravagance, 52, 53; lack of sympathy with "home people," 277; low-key projects by, 334*n18*; major force in affairs of village, 50; need for police protection, 274; opinion that Lake Agawam belonged to them, 87, 88; patrician style of, 281; population, 256; in Quogue, 2; relations with townspeople, 60; renaming of streets, bodies of water, etc. by, 11; in second tier of influence in New York, 8; seen as interlopers, 92; sense of entitlement of, 315; sense of ownship by, 50; social class issues in, 70; treated as economic boon, 45; views on escaping diseases of the poor: 73, 74
Summer School of Art, 240, 243, 244, 284
Swayne, Wager, 240, 254, 263, 349*n66*
Sweeney, Doyle, 122; in First Democratic Association of Southampton, 44
Sylvester family, 41
Syncretism, 48

"Tammany braves," 42
Tammany Hall, 42, 72
Tax assessments, 34, 35, 38, 53, 60, 142
Taylor's Creek, 67
Temperance movement, 14, 44, 269, 350*n18*
Ten Acre Division (1651), 130
Tennis, 256, 257, 258, 263
Terry, L. Emory, 285; Southampton Bank and, 265
Terry family, 103
Third House (Montauk), 6
Thomas, Gaillard, 149, 255; beachfront purchased by, 88, 89; builds home on oceanfront beach, 51, 52; career, 7; community interests of, 6; concern with water purity, 12; death of, 83, 281; disaffection with village conduct of affairs, 275, 276; donation of ornamental well by, 107; "The Dunes" built by, 11, 52, 53; establishing priorities for SVIA, 109; establishment of recuperative home for women, 7; founding of Saint Andrews-by-the-Sea church and, 58; founding of Southampton Village Improvement Association and, 72; founding of summer colony by, 1–12; increase in beachfront holdings, 61, 62; interest in building beach hotel and casino, 1, 62, 89; involvement in dust problem, 107; in marsh drainage issue, 106; in Moore controversy, 103, 105; property ownership, 11; purchase of building for colony church, 71; real estate holdings, 67, 92; resignation from SVIA, 280; for seaside road, 262; spiritual leadership, 1; in SVIA, 78, 268; transformation of Southampton and, 2
Thomas, J. Metcalf, 258
Thompson, Benjamin F., 13
Tiana, 88, 234, 235, 262
Tilden, Samuel, 42, 72
Timber industry, 31, 32, 34
Timor (ship), 119
Topping, Thomas, 21, 156, 162
Topping family, 35, 186
Topping Purchase, 21, 27, 32, 35, 122, 123, 128, 137, 142, 194, 234, 335*n21*, 345*n4*

Town Pond, 10, 11, 12, 14, 50, 51, 54, 56, 59, 69, 88, 91, 243, 290. *See also* Lake Agawam
Town Purchase, 21, 128, 137, 142, 182, 219
Townsend, James, 265
Town Street, 14
Town trustees, 35; amicable existence with proprietors trustees, 123; antitrust feelings among, 126; attempts to intimidate Shinnecock Indians: 202, 203, 204; attempts to remove Betts from property, 90; authority over town waters, 115; in Betts case, 59; board ejected over Mecox Bay affair, 112, 122; claims on beach as "open road," 90; claim to jurisdiction over lands under waters, 112; conflict with proprietors over seaweed rights, 222; criticized for incompetence by summer residents, 275, 276, 277; dealings with summer colony, 126; decision to lease Mecox Bay after trial, 171; elected from local establishment, 123; establishment of, 36, 37; files suit against Mecox Bay Oyster Company, 153–171; Free Bay Board, 126; freed from control of proprietors, 39; grants for oystering from, 133; inability to find any owners of Mecox Bay to file suit on, 153; independent from proprietors, 133; initially chosen from proprietors, 37; jurisdiction of, 37; Lake Agawam issues and, 88; legal power over beach highway, 100; loss of authority to town, 99, 100; management of lands and waters by, 37, 38, 88; policy on leasing bay bottoms, 127; against proprietors in Mecox Bay affair, 111–142; quietist strategy of; reflection of small-town localism by, 126; regulation of fishing by, 115; reluctance to act against proprietors, 139; renewal of oyster act annually, 132; suit against Mecox Bay Oyster Company by, 117, 128–142
Toylesome Lane, 10, 54, 80
Trade and Intercourse Act (1790), 190
Trevor, Henry, 67
Trustees of the Freeholders and Commonalty of the Town of Southampton, vii. *See also* Town trustees

Trustees of the Proprietors, 35; amicable existence with town trustees, 123; claim of ownership of lands under waters, 112; collapse of legitimacy of, 123; disapproval of partition suit on Mecox Bay sale, 135; disposal of undivided common land by, 111; failure to separate sale of common lands above water from those under, 146; growing public sentiment against for sale of Mecox Bay, 135, 136; initial references to sale of Mecox Bay, 134; meet with Shinnecock Indians for land division purposes, 213, 214; partition and sale of Hills by, 213–224; perceived as manipulating town affairs, 138; reservations over legality of Mecox Bay sale, 145, 146; sale of bottom of Mecox Bay, 40, 45, 92; sale of lands under waters by, 112; sale of Shinnecock Hills by, 140; selling of rights in commonage seasonally, 36; take possession of Shinnecock Hills and other lands from Shinnecock Indians, 214–224; town dissatisfaction with, 122; try for control over products of lands and waters; try to divide Shinnecock Hills with Indians, 207, 208

Trustees of the Shinnecock Hills, 224, 231, 251
Tuckahoe Road, 241
Tuscany (ship), 118
Tweed, William, 42, 72

Underground railroad, 48
Unkechaug Indians, 48, 175

Vail, H.O., 81
VanBrunt, William, 77
Van Cortlandt, Stephanus, 182
Van Dam, Rip, 184, 185, 186, 191
Vanderbilt, William K., 9
Van de Water, Frederic, 52, 53
Van Rensselaer, May King, 8, 10, 52
Van Tienhoven, Cornelius, 177
Village Hall Company, 94

Wading River, 245
Wainscott, 3, 21, 22, 130, 151, 176, 185, 186, 328n10

Wales, Salem, 97, 99, 103, 255, 261; in cemetery issue, 97, 101; clears wigwams from beachfront, 290; death of, 281; establishing priorities for SVIA, 109; interest in health issues, 105; involvement in dust problem, 108; in marsh drainage issue, 106; in Moore controversy, 103; president of SVIA, 85; real estate holdings, 63, 64; Southampton Bank and, 265; work on Lake Agawam, 84, 103
Walker, Stephen, 214
Water Mill, 14, 111, 116, 130, 151, 152, 304
Waucus, David, 202
Waukus, Samuel, 198
Weber, Max, 18
Weeks, John R., 240, 242, 245
Wells. *See* Privies and wells
West Bay, 112
West Beach, 234
Whaling, 12, 47, 48, 89, 119, 290, 293, 294, 301, 302, 331n29; contribution to population decline, 26; decline in, 6, 7, 12, 26, 32, 118; deep water, 32; inshore, 12, 16; recognition of need for cooperative arrangements for, 15
Wheeler, Henry A., 233
Whitaker, Edward G., 170; interest in improvement of bays, 129, 130; part in Mecox Bay affair, 125, 129, 134, 135, 136, 137, 138, 143, 144, 145
Whitaker, George, 41, 135, 136, 224, 263; in First Democratic Association of Southampton, 44; role in Mecox Bay affair, 139, 145
White, Charles, 304
White, Edward, 220
White, Elizabeth Halsey, 10–11
White, George Gilbert, 64, 75, 255, 317, 345n7, 352n10; antipathy to Edwin Post, 99; anti-urban sentiment from, 92, 93; in Betts case, 290; brings action of ejectment against Frederic Betts, 289; challenge to Betts' title to beachfront, 89, 90; charge against town trustees in Mecox Bay scandal, 44; claims sale of Shinnecock Bay to Maxwell fraudulent, 128, 129; commentary on class differences, 261; complaints on trespass

White, George Gilbert *(continued)*
rules at the Hills, 241; cooperation with SVIA on some projects, 83, 84; death of, 127, 170, 172, 311, 336n39; delays auction of Hills, 235; disagreement with Pelletreau on use of bays, 125, 126, 128, 129; feelings on SVIA, 109; founding First Democratic Association of Southampton, 44; interest in new town hall, 94; as leader of town trustees, 44; leads fight for ownership of beachfront, 118; Mecox Bay trial and, 92, 99, 112; negative relations with Pelletreau, 91; objects to partition of Hills, 336n2; opinion that proprietors trustees were too influential in town affairs; opposition to Mecox Bay sale, 153, 156; on ownership of beach, 59, 60; president of town trustees, 59, 77, 109, 112, 289; protests sale of bay bottoms, 117; protests sale of Shinnecock Hills, 178, 215, 216, 235; questions legitimacy of Shinnecock Hills title, 253; supervision/maintenance of sidewalks by, 84; testifies in Betts case, 302, 303; town trustee, 123; work for rights of inhabitants, 117; work on Shinnecock Bay, 172

White, John, 118

White, Lizbeth Halsey, 49

White, Mary, 119

White, Peter, 220

White, Stanford, 65, 240, 241, 244, 260, 282, 284, 349n53

White family, 35, 68

Wickapogue, 53, 67, 68, 89, 130, 262, 289

Wickapogue Pond, 85, 148

William of Orange (King of England), 182

Williams, Judge Pardon, 309

Willis, Francis, 210, 345n79

Windmill Lane, 14, 55, 81, 86, 87, 101, 103, 265, 287

Winthrop, John, 17, 18

Wood, Joseph, 24

Woodhull, M.H., 151

Woodruff, John, 56

Woodruff family, 35

Worth, Theron, 143

Wriothesly, Henry (Earl of Southampton), 23, 24, 330n24

Wyandanch (sachem), 21, 176, 191, 330n17

Young, Thomas, 97, 100, 127, 153, 297, 298, 300, 301, 304, 306

www.ingramcontent.com/pod-product-compliance
Lightning Source LLC
Chambersburg PA
CBHW080437170426
43195CB00017B/2803